Also by Jon Savage

England's Dreaming
Time Travel
The Kinks

PIMLICO

811

TEENAGE

Jon Savage is a writer and broadcaster. After graduating from
Cambridge he published a fanzine called *London's Outrage*, and
worked for *Sounds, Melody Maker* and *The Face*. His first book,
The Kinks: The Official Biography was followed by *England's
Dreaming* (new edition 2005), the award-winning history of the
Sex Pistols, punk and Britain in the late seventies. He regularly
writes for the *Observer* and *Mojo*, and his television credits include
the BAFTA winning Arena documentary, *The Brian Epstein
Story*. His recent compilation CDs include *England's Dreaming,
Meridian 1970* and *The Shadows of Love*. He lives in Anglesey.

TEENAGE

The Creation of Youth Culture

———

JON SAVAGE

PIMLICO

Published by Pimlico 2008

2 4 6 8 10 9 7 5 3 1

Copyright © Jon Savage 2007

Jon Savage has asserted his right under the Copyright, Designs
and Patents Act 1988 to be identified as the author of this work

Grateful acknowledgement is made for permission to reprint excerpts from the following copyrighted works:
I Am the Most Interesting Book of All: The Diary of Marie Bashkirtseff, translated by Phyllis Howard Kernberger
with Katherine Kernberger. Translation © 1997 by Katherine Kernberger and the Estate of Phyllis Howard
Kernberger. Used by permission of Chronicle Books, LLC.
Materials from the Mass-Observation Archive, University of Sussex Library. Reprinted with permission of
Curtis Brown Group Ltd, London, on behalf of the Trustees of the Mass-Observation Archive. Copyright © The
Trustees of the Mass-Observation Archive.
The Diary of a Young Girl: The Definitive Edition by Anne Frank, edited by Otto H. Frank and Mirjam Pressler
and translated by Susan Massotty. Copyright © 1995 by Doubleday, a division of Random House, Inc. Used by
permission of Doubleday, a division of Random House, Inc.
"Generation without Farewell" from *The Man Outside* by Wolfgang Borchert, translated by David Porter.
Copyright © 1971 by New Directions Publishing Corp. Reprinted by permission of New Directions
Publishing Corp.

First published in Great Britain in 2007 by Chatto & Windus

Pimlico
Random House, 20 Vauxhall Bridge Road,
London SW1V 2SA

www.rbooks.co.uk

Addresses for companies within The Random House Group Limited can be found at:
www.randomhouse.co.uk/offices.htm

The Random House Group Limited Reg. No. 954009

A CIP catalogue record for this book
is available from the British Library

ISBN 9781845951467

The Random House Group Limited supports The Forest Stewardship
Council (FSC), the leading international forest certification organisation. All our titles that are printed on
Greenpeace approved FSC certified paper carry the FSC logo. Our paper procurement policy can be found at
www.rbooks.co.uk/environment

Printed and bound in Great Britain by
CPI Mackays, Chatham, ME5 8TD

TO JOSEPH LESLIE SAGE MC

AND

MARGARET DOROTHY SAGE

CONTENTS

COPYRIGHT.   YOUTH.

COMMERCIAL POSTCARD, EARLY 1900s

America used to be the big youth place in everybody's imagination. America had teenagers and everywhere else just had people.

—John Lennon, born 1940, interviewed 1966

THIS BOOK ENDS with a beginning.

During 1944, Americans began to use the word "teenager" to describe the category of young people from fourteen to eighteen. From the very start, it was a marketing term used by advertisers and manufacturers that reflected the newly visible spending power of adolescents. The fact that, for the first time, youth had become its own target market also meant that it had become a discrete age group with its own rituals, rights, and demands.

The invention of the Teenager coincided with America's victory in the Second World War, a decisive world-historical event which created the empire that still holds sway in the twenty-first century. Indeed, the definition of youth as a consumer offered a golden opportunity to a devastated Europe. For the last sixty years, this post-war teen image has dominated the way that the West sees the young, and has been successfully exported around the world. Like the new world order that it heralded, it is in need of redefinition.

But post-war youth culture is not as new as it might seem. From the last quarter of the nineteenth century, there were many conflicting attempts to envisage and define the status of youth—whether through concerted efforts to regiment adolescents using national policies, or through artistic, prophetic visions that reflected the wish of the young to live by their own rules. The narrative begins in 1875, with the autobiographical writings of Marie Bashkirtseff and Jesse Pomeroy, and ends in 1945; during that period every single theme now associated with the modern Teenager had a vivid, volatile precedent.

This, then, is the prehistory of the Teenager.

. . .

In January 1980, I became involved in a possible television series about the history of youth subcultures. At that time, I was a researcher at Granada Tele-

vision in Manchester, a company then well-known for its innovative and socially conscious programming. With the backing of my then producer, Geoff
Moore, we worked up a proposal that aimed to tell the story of all the "post-war
cults": "teds, beats, mods, rockers, hippies, skinheads, glitterboys, punks," as
well as "rude boys and rastas".

The impetus for the Granada idea came from Dick Hebdige's *Subculture: The
Meaning of Style*, which, published during 1979, had deservedly bridged the gap
between academia and a wider audience. *Subculture* was a product of the inter-
disciplinary approach pioneered by Birmingham University's Centre for Contemporary Cultural Studies. Fusing sociology with literary interpretation and
French theory, Hebdige's book offered a synoptic history of the many British
post-war youth cults, while not ignoring factors like class and race.

Hebdige's allusive approach chimed with my own observations of the London punk scene, where during 1976 the pioneers of this as yet barely named
movement threw together almost every single youth-cult style, stuck them together with safety pins, and then proudly paraded the results. A sixties mod
jacket might be worn with zoot-suit trousers and teddy boy "brothel-creepers":
huge, thick-soled shoes not unlike those worn by the Parisian *Zazous* during
the 1940s. The effect was at once striking, hallucinatory, and threatening.

This living bricolage, it transpired, had been suggested by the clothes sold
in the various incarnations of 430 Kings Road, the shop run by Malcolm
McLaren and Vivienne Westwood. Between 1971 and 1976 the shop's name
changed several times, from Let It Rock (Teddy Boy costume), to Too Fast To
Live, Too Young To Die (rocker and zootist gear), to Sex (fetish wear) and Se-
ditionaries (designer punk rock "clothes for heroes"). Each phase had been
marked by a rare degree of research and attention to detail.

But punk's historical collage also marked the moment when the linear forward motion of the sixties was replaced by the loop. Suddenly, all pop culture
time was accessible, on the same plane, available at once. In retrospect, this
process had begun during 1966—at the very height of pop modernism—
but it had taken ten years to become a living, working part of youth culture.
Taken even further in the early 1980s by the latest youth style, the New Romantics, this plundering of the past reaffirmed the fact that there was a long,
ill-documented youth history that went back beyond the Second World War.

During the course of the next eighteen months, the youth culture material
that my producer and I wrote for Granada Television became a pilot for a potential documentary series. Called *Teenage*, the first hour-long show covered
British youth culture in the years between 1945 and 1957: the transition between post-war austerity, the very first appearance of the Edwardians, later to

be called teddy boys, and the impact of rock 'n' roll during 1956 and 1957. For various reasons, however, the pilot was unfinished and the TV series cancelled.[1]

However, my interest in the topic held. During the next decade or so, I continued to collect any materials related to the topic of youth culture—particularly those marked by the buzzword "teenager". The more I read, the more I perceived that there was a whole back-history that pre-dated the Second World War. Reading about the *Wandervogel* or the American college market of the 1920s, I realized there was an untold story that did not chime with the generally accepted view that teenagers began in the mid-1950s.

My thinking was further crystallized when I found a copy of G. Stanley Hall's *Adolescence* in the early 1990s. Hall's preface contained a prophetic manifesto for the post-war youth culture that was still half a century away when he wrote. His view of adolescence as a separate stage of life subject to enormous stresses and strains—and therefore to be treated with special care and attention—was grounded, for the first time, in a very specific age definition. Within the two volumes of this mammoth book, it seemed, was one beginning of the story.

Adolescence also harmonized with two other founding twentieth-century documents: L. Frank Baum's *The Wonderful Wizard of Oz* and J. M. Barrie's *Peter Pan*. Both were highly romantic, uncannily predictive, and striving to define something that was in the air but which did not yet have a definitive name. At the turn of the century, the idea that youth would be defined as a separate stage of life was in its infancy, but these imaginative works explored the various possibilities of a sensibility, if not a whole society, based on the promise of youth, transitory or eternal.

This promise was embodied within America, the rising power of the new century. Hall explicitly linked his country—"a fiat nation"—with the life stage that he was attempting to define: "The very fact that we think we are young will make the faith in our future curative, and we shall one day not only attract the youth of the world by our unequaled liberty and opportunity, but develop a mental, moral, and emotional nurture that will be the best preparation for making the most and the best of them and for helping humanity on to a higher stage."

At the same time the European strain, epitomized by the Romantics and the revolutionary youth of the late eighteenth century, remained powerful. The Western empires of the late nineteenth century were undergoing similar developmental problems—urbanization, industrialization, and rearmament—

1. For some of the reasons for the cancellation of *Teenage*, see Mary Harron, "Teen Dream That Won't Fade Away", *Guardian*, July 13, 1982.

that resulted in a greater focus on the subject of youth. The dialogue between the United States, the United Kingdom, and northern Europe on juvenile delinquency had started during the mid-nineteenth century and formed a major part of G. Stanley Hall's copiously cited research data.

The prehistory of the teenager, therefore, could not be told simply through America, but had to include Britain, France, and Germany. I originally included material from Italy and Russia—including the fascinating story of the *bensprizorni,* the wandering youth of the 1930s—but it had to go for reasons of space. The same considerations initially informed my decision to stop the book in the mid-twentieth century. However, the more I went on I realized that the narrative had to end with the nearly simultaneous coinage of the word "teenager" and the explosion of the atom bombs that changed the notion of the future.

The book, therefore, tells the history of the quest, pursued over two different continents and over half a century, to conceptualize, define, and control adolescence. Apart from the dialogue between America, Britain, France, and Germany, it contains several different elements that encapsulate the tension between the fantasy and the reality of adolescence, and between the many varied attempts to exalt or to capture this fugitive and transitory state.

Personal testimony—in the shape of diaries written at the time by actual adolescents attempting to make sense of themselves and their world—is placed next to media reports and government policies. The ideal of youth as a separate, cohort-based class is contrasted to the realities of economic and social class. The many different attempts by sociologists, criminologists, and psychologists to normalize youth—as a stage of life that everybody has to go through—are counterpointed by stories of extraordinary adolescents, the ones who seem to embody an era or point forward to a future that has yet to occur.

Above all, the concentration brought by these societies to this topic reinforced youth's own conception of itself as important. It is fascinating to note, as the twentieth century gets into its stride, how the voices of youth become less corralled by adults and more frequently heard on their own terms. On another level, this book contains the story of how youth struggled to make itself heard, if not totally on its own terms, then on terms it could recognize and accommodate itself to. The eventual success of the teenager as a ruling concept owed much to this delicate balance.

. . .

Although this book covers a period of which I have no direct experience, it contains disguised autobiographical elements—if only in the selection of the material. I was born in September 1953, near the end of the first post-war baby boom. My father had served with distinction in the Second World War, about which he rarely talked, while my mother's early adolescence had been dominated by those six years. Her subsequent love of international travel was partly informed by her wish to break free after the years of rationing and restriction.

For the first thirteen years of my life, I was brought up in Ealing, a West London suburb: an environment almost designed to offer a tabula rasa after years of suffering and horror. My adolescent reaction against suburbia is now tempered by the understanding that this move was a natural, if not the only rational, reaction on the part of the wartime generation. The inner cities were still badly war-damaged—the bomb sites in central London lingered on until the mid-1980s—but the suburbs were safe, comforting, and in retrospect a great place to spend my first thirteen years.

Each generation has its own task. To try to abrogate another generation's experience is pointless, and potentially dangerous. Having experienced the storms and stresses of a 1960s and 1970s teenage, I came to realize that part of my cohort's task was to help to deal with our parents' war damage. The unresolved horror of that period, as well as the huge existential question posed by the fact of the H-bomb, informed the extreme manifestations of youth culture within which I thoroughly immersed myself.

Much later, I was able to talk to my father about his youth in the 1930s and 1940s, which helped me to understand what he went through. I was also fortunate enough to have a close relationship with my maternal grandfather, who was born in January 1904. His stories about life in the 1920s and 1930s fuelled my imagination, while his love of jazz and American popular music—he went to see the Original Dixieland Jazz Band in 1920—stimulated and legitimated my own musical obsessions.

The experiences of my family, therefore, have offered a way of orienting myself within the first half of the twentieth century. At the same time, I have attempted to be as thorough as possible with the material, and I hope to have left no major movement or manifestation totally unturned. If there are any sins of omission, they are purely my responsibility. However, it should be remembered that my brief and my inclination have been to produce a work of popular history rather than a multi-volume academic work.

There is one final point. It may be argued that I have concentrated too much on the extraordinary rather than the ordinary, the extreme at the expense of the routine. I would counter-argue that these particular youths are set against the attempts by academics, youth experts, and governments to standardize youth, and against the mainstream youth of the time. For instance, the small minority of German youth who resisted Hitler are contrasted with the millions of their contemporaries who joined the Nazi state organization, the Hitler Youth.

There is a dialectic within the book, therefore, between the extraordinary and the ordinary. However, if I have to make the choice, it would always be to find the extraordinary within the ordinary. This is informed both by my temperament and by the subject itself. It's an argument that goes back to the first publication of *Adolescence*. In an April 1905 review of the book, one J. M. Greenwood charged G. Stanley Hall with prioritizing "what one may call 'the freaks of the race', without giving sufficient weight to the average steady-goers who make up the great bulk of humanity".

This is a fair comment, but I think it misses the point. By its very nature, youth has long been charged with representing the future: the perennial mass-media typecasting of the adolescent as a genius or a monster continues to encode adult hopes and fears about what will happen. To ignore those who stand out as harbingers in favour of those who cleave to the status quo is to refuse engagement with the future if not to misunderstand the nature of youth itself. Like G. Stanley Hall, I am proud to be a romantic about the subject, if only because I hope for a better world.

TEENAGE

PART I

······························

1875–1904

CHAPTER 1

Heaven and Hell

Marie Bashkirtseff and Jesse Pomeroy

. . .

Man is not meant to remain a child. He leaves childhood behind him at the time ordained by nature; and this critical moment, short enough in itself, has far-reaching consequences. As the roaring of the waves precedes the tempest, so the murmur of rising passions; a suppressed excitement warns us of the approaching danger.

—Jean-Jacques Rousseau, *Emile*, book 4 (1762)

MARIE BASHKIRTSEFF, 1870s

JESSE POMEROY, 1874

"I WAS FLYING, very high above the earth, holding a lyre in my hand. The strings were constantly unstrung, and I could not produce a single sound from it. I continued rising, seeing immense horizons, clouds—blue, yellow, red, mixed, golden, and silver—torn, strange. Then everything grew grey and dazzlingly bright, and I was still rising until I reached a most frightening height, but I was not afraid. The clouds seemed wan, greying and shining—like lead. Then all grew dim. I continued holding my lyre with the loosened strings. And far below, under my feet, hung a reddish ball—the earth."

Marie Bashkirtseff awoke from this dream very early on the morning of Monday, December 27, 1875. The seventeen-year-old had drunk too much wine at supper and found further sleep impossible. She decided to unburden herself of her turbulent thoughts, and prepared to make ritual confession. "Now that it is 2.00 in the morning," she began, "and I am locked in my room, dressed in a long white peignoir, barefoot, and my hair loose like a virgin martyr, I can very well devote myself to better thoughts."

Marie's confession was made, however, not to the priests of her Catholic religion, but to the notebook that was her refuge: "This Journal contains all my life; my quietest moments are those when I am writing. They are probably the only calm ones that I have. To burn everything, to be in exasperation, to cry, to suffer everything and live, and live! Why do they let me live? Oh, I am impatient. My time will come. I certainly want to believe this. But something tells me that it will never come, that I will pass all my life waiting, waiting."

The journal was not just a safety valve but a bid for secular immortality. Marie wanted attention and fame. "If I should die young," she continued that night, "I shall burn this journal; but if I live to be old, people will read it. I believe, if I may say so, that there is no photograph as yet of a woman's existence, of all her thoughts. Yes, all, all. It will be interesting. If I should die young soon, and if by bad luck this Journal is not burnt, it will be said, 'Poor child, she was in love with Audiffret, and all her despair comes from that.'"

This impassioned outburst came at the end of a turbulent year. Returning to her family's adopted city of Nice that spring, Marie transferred her schoolgirl crush on the unattainable Duke of Hamilton onto the twenty-four-year-old Emile Audiffret. Over the next few months, she obsessively recorded the progress of her first real love affair. On December 26, Audiffret cancelled a date, a serious slight. Marie's mother had given the invitation, a piece of parental meddling that infuriated her fiery daughter.

In the autumn of 1875, Marie had turned seventeen. This prompted a major outburst. "I am tired of my obscurity," she wrote. "I mildew in the shadows. The sun, the sun, the sun! Let's go—have courage. This time is only a passage that will lead me to where I'll be all right. Am I mad? Or fated? Be it one way or another, I'm bored!" She was often bored: with the slowness of her mother, with the tedium of family holidays, with the inertia of the world. Life wasn't coming fast enough for a young woman who found herself in a race against time.

As the favoured daughter of wealthy Russian émigrés, Marie was impatient and spoiled. Her dresses were handmade in Paris to her own extravagant designs. She accompanied her family on their travels throughout Europe, revelling in their contacts with the beau monde. She had a whole suite of rooms in the Bashkirtseff house on the Promenade des Anglais in Nice, within which the inner sanctum was a bedroom that, covered with sky blue satin and topped with a Sèvres chandelier, resembled "the inside of a glove box".

Although highly indulged, Marie was charged with a special destiny. During her early childhood, her mother was informed by a fortune-teller that her daughter would be "a star". From that moment, Marie was brought up to be "the most beautiful, the most brilliant, and the most magnificent", and was encouraged in her whims. This feeling of being special gave her a confidence shared by few young women of her age and time. When she began recording her thoughts and her emotions in a journal, she had little doubt about its impact on posterity: it would be, of course, "the most interesting book of all".

Her early entries were much concerned with her looks: one day she would feel "quite beautiful", the next "a figure not even Satan would recognise". She felt like Frankenstein: "We know that I have a good posture, that I have broad shoulders, a high chest, hips and derriere well-rounded and prominent, and small feet. Within five minutes, I became a flat monster, emaciated, with sunken chest, and one shoulder higher than the other, which pushes everything else out of shape. My feet became flat and long, my eyes sunken and my teeth black."

Bodily self-consciousness was, however, the least of her problems. As she began to enter society, Marie realized that her family was shrouded in ill repute. Both Marie's uncle and younger brother Paul were in constant trouble with the law. Marie's mother had separated from her father, while her aunt Sophie was dogged by a long-running court case. Marie herself was suspect, thanks to her ebullience and her extraordinary fashion sense: a skating dress with trailing ostrich feathers was a little too fast for Nice's small-town mores.

The effect of these scandals was to bar the Bashkirtseffs from local society. Marie keenly felt the slights: "My name is tarnished, and that's killing me," she wrote after her family had been slandered by the Tolstoys, fellow Russian émigrés. "I cried like an animal, dismayed, humiliated." By the age of fourteen, Marie had added revenge to her already considerable drive: "I would be received in society because I'll not be a celebrity coming from a low class or a dirty street," she proclaimed in March 1873. "I dream of celebrity, of fame."

Propelled by the fortune-teller's prophecy and further fired by the snubs of provincial Nice, Marie poured all her resentments and frustrations into her notebooks. Almost every day, she wrote about herself and her family with an extreme candour, as if to purge herself of all the falsity that surrounded her. She saw no point in "lying or pretending". It was all out there on the page: her switchback changes of mood, her sibling rivalry with brother Paul, her first experiments with alcohol and tobacco, her rebellion against adults and their institutions, her obsession with her appearance.

This was not what was expected from young women in the 1870s. As Marie's biographer Dormer Creston later commented, this was the period when "large sections of the upper and middle classes, and in particular the women, were brought up with a deformed sense of piety". Marie consciously reacted against the contemporary feminine ideals of "self-repression, resignation, and intense domesticity". As she scornfully observed, "Well, they really have a good time—the men. The woman is always the victim. I would like to be a man. I would surpass every one of those gentlemen."

Already burning up with impatience and frustration, Marie received a mortal blow during the summer of 1875. "I have pain in the chest," she revealed that June. "It seems to me I have tuberculosis. But this chest pain worries me, and for the last five days I have spit blood. It's awful." This self-diagnosis would not be confirmed for a further seven years, but Marie was shocked to find that her more melodramatic rhetoric—"death for me is a close relative," she had stated that spring—had become likely fact. Time became ever more precious.

Marie's 1875 dream sourced an archetypal image of her faith and her name: the Assumption of the Blessed Virgin Mary. But it also evoked the same sense of boundless possibility that the Romantics had already attributed to pubertal youth. At sixteen Jean-Jacques Rousseau had believed that "I could do anything, attain to everything". As he remembered in his *Confessions,* "I had only to launch myself forth, to mount and fly through the air. I entered the vast world with a feeling of security; it was to be filled with the fame of my achievements."

However, Marie was too alert not to catch the threatening notes emanating from her subconscious: the unstrung lyre, the leaden clouds. She had all of her life in front of her, yet against this weightlessness were set severe constraints. Although she wanted to break the bounds of class, gender, family, and even her physical body, she knew that her time was flowing "very fast". The dream ended in queasy suspension: would she plunge earthwards, like Icarus, or continue to soar with her lyre magically restrung?

. . .

While Marie was grappling with her illness, another young person was engaged in autobiography. Like Marie, Jesse Pomeroy was facing a life-or-death struggle, but in his case it was of his own making. During the summer of 1875, he was incarcerated in Suffolk County Jail in the American state of Massachusetts, having been found guilty the previous December of first-degree murder. Although he was only fifteen—almost exactly one year younger than the Russian émigré—he faced the mandatory death penalty.

Pomeroy had already achieved fame, or, to be more accurate, its shadow: notoriety. Almost as soon as he had been arrested for the murder of Horace H. Millen in April 1874, his name had become a byword for a hitherto inconceivable depravity. His four-year-old victim had been found severely mutilated on the marshy South Boston coast: Pomeroy had stabbed him several times in the chest, punctured his eyeball, slashed his throat so deeply that the head was nearly severed, and finally indulged in an attempted castration. Not for nothing had he become known throughout America as the "boy fiend".

The hysteria mounted when Pomeroy's sadistic spate of abductions and mutilations was revealed. His ten victims had been, with one exception, boys aged between four and eight, and all had been subjected to a horrific catalogue of humiliations, beatings, and stabbings. In one instance, Joseph Kennedy had been slashed on the face, back, and thighs, and was then made to rub saltwater into his fresh wounds. When the body of Katie Curran, Pomeroy's first murder victim, was discovered in July 1874, the boy fiend would have been torn "limb from limb" if he had not already been imprisoned.

Although he had been sentenced in December 1874, Pomeroy had received a stay of execution while his fate was decided. His youth, coupled with the extreme atrocity of his crimes, had already prompted a fierce national debate about capital punishment.[1] Although the jury had recommended that his punishment be commuted to imprisonment for life, the majority view, expressed in newspaper editorials and hundreds of letters and petitions, was that Pomeroy should hang.

On July 2, 1875, Pomeroy's death sentence was confirmed by the state gov-

1. The youngest person previously executed in America had been an eighteen-year-old in the 1830s.

ernor's executive council: all that remained between him and the gallows was the governor's signature. While his life hung in the balance, Pomeroy was kept in solitary confinement. Instead of a Sèvres chandelier, sky blue satin walls, and a shell-shaped bed resting on carved lions' feet, he had an iron-framed cot, a wooden chair, and two slop buckets. The extreme isolation of his conditions, coupled with the prospect of imminent execution, exacerbated his desire to justify his actions.

He had two opportunities that summer. The first was provided by the *Boston Times*, which printed a two-part "autobiography" of the "moral monster". Instead of admitting his undeniable guilt, Pomeroy evaded the issue. "These are the reasons why I THINK THAT IF I DID THOSE THINGS I WAS INSANE or that I could not help doing it," he wrote, before concluding, "but notwithstanding all that, as I have said, I DO NOT THINK I DID THOSE THINGS." Elsewhere he insulted the trial witnesses and jurors, whom he called "twelve jackasses".

The real Jesse was revealed, however, in a series of letters he wrote in prison. During June 1875, a fourteen-year-old named Willie Baxter was arrested for theft and found himself in the next cell to the notorious killer. Although contact was strictly forbidden between prisoners, the two young men contrived to keep up a correspondence that lasted until Baxter was tried a few weeks later. Pomeroy was extremely glad of human contact: "Let us write good long letters to each other and so beguile our captivity but don't make too much noise."

Pomeroy was fascinated by his fame: "Tell me all you have heard of me, everything bad and don't think I will be angry." He also confessed to the murders that he had denied in court: "The girl came in the store one morn and asked for paper. I told her there is a store downstairs. She went down, and I killed her. Oh Willie you don't know how bad I feel for her and also the boy. What I said to the boy I have no reccollection [*sic*] but you know I killed him too. I feel very bad for him, and believe me I can't tell you the reason I did those things."

This was the extra element that fuelled Pomeroy's notoriety: the overwhelming urges for which there was no vocabulary in Gilded Age America. Compounding the cruelty of his crimes was the seeming impossibility of their explanation: not only did he refuse to take responsibility for them, but he could give no account beyond the barest language of compulsion: "Something made me." The best he could do was to describe a pain, almost like an electrical charge, that crossed from one side of his head to the other and triggered the attacks.

Pomeroy burst into the American consciousness as a horrific new type. There was nothing in the existing legislation to explain his affectless savagery, despite the fact that youth crime had been discussed and defined throughout the nineteenth century. The phrase "juvenile delinquent" had been coined in the 1810s, and in 1824, the first legislation defining "Juvenile Delinquents" had been passed in New York City. This held delinquents to be under twenty-one, the common-law division between children and adulthood.

With increasing urbanization, there had been a transatlantic pooling of youth crime data. In her influential 1853 book *Juvenile Delinquents: Their Condition and Treatment*, Mary Carpenter suggested that younger "children", as those in their second decade were still called, should be dealt with separately from adults in their early twenties, already hardened criminals. This taint of corruption, added to the diminished responsibility imputed to children, began to push the legal definition of juveniles lower, down to sixteen in some cases.

By the existing definitions, Pomeroy was still a child—fourteen when he committed his crimes—yet he was facing an adult's sentence. Despite the fact that his age would suggest diminished responsibility, the authorities and the public were faced with a youth who seemed very much in control of what he was doing and who was capable of distinguishing between right and wrong. Indeed, his demeanour throughout his interrogations by the police and cross-examinations in court offered nothing but an obdurate, precocious composure.

In the gap between the shocking reality of Pomeroy's crimes and the existing conceptions of juvenile delinquency, there was room for many different explanations. The most popular solution to the mystery of the young killer's motivation came from the then fashionable discipline of phrenology.[2] This claimed that criminals were throwbacks to a more primitive stage of human development, and that their physiological atavism was marked by irregularly shaped skulls, facial disfigurements, and other deformations.

Although Pomeroy was of average height, his head was markedly large for his body, and his right eye was covered with a milky film. For one journalist, "a single glance at the boy's countenance" was enough to "see how it was possible for him to perpetrate the outrages for which he was taken into custody". His eyes were "sullenly, brutishly wicked", with an "unsympathetic, merciless" gaze. With "the pallor of his complexion" and "the shuffling of one whose thoughts are of the lowest kind", he represented a textbook genetic throwback.

Another possible solution was found in Pomeroy's avid consumption of

2. The first definitive work on the subject, Cesare Lombroso's *L'uomo delinquente*, was published in 1876.

dime novels, the cheap paperbound adventure stories then popular among American youth. Titles like *Rangers of the Mohawk* and *Calamity Jane, the Heroine of Whoop-Up* described the battles between American Indians and red-blooded American frontiersmen in gory detail. Jesse was particularly taken with the activities of the Indians, identifying with the famous white turncoat Simon Girty, and revelling in the descriptions of torture and murder.

This line of inquiry led to a particularly obtuse exchange between the young prisoner and the famous publisher James T. Fields. When asked whether his homicidal passions had been excited by dime novels, Pomeroy mentioned with approval the "blood and thunder pictures, tomahawking and scalping". However, he shied away from admitting that they influenced his behaviour: "I have thought it all over and it seems to me now that they did. I can't say certainly, of course and perhaps if I should think it over again, I should say it was something else." "What else?" "Well, Sir I really can't say."

The puzzle represented by Pomeroy's actions dictated the terms of his murder trial. The only way to avoid the mandatory death sentence was to establish that he was of unsound mind. His attorney called in two "insane experts" as key witnesses. Dr John E. Tyler thought that the defendant was suffering from a compulsive "mental derangement" and was therefore "not responsible for his actions". Dr Clement Walker went further and blamed an obscure form of epilepsy for the murderer's "lack of control".

The pioneering testimony of the alienists cut no ice with the general public. As far as they were concerned, Jesse Pomeroy's crimes were the result of a "horrible monomania". For most people, he was just "a young demon" or a "mad dog" to be put down with dispatch. The *American Law Review* gave this theme a rhetorical gloss: "If the boy's impulse is under his control, there is surely no reason for sparing his life. If it is not, how does he differ from a wolf, except that he had the intelligence of a man, and is therefore more dangerous?"

It suited Americans to think of the young murderer as something subhuman. However, the one line of inquiry that was barely considered at the time would have shed a harsh light on the wider society. Pomeroy was a product of the continent's urban stews, the cities sprawling under the accelerating rate of immigration. Within this brutal environment, the young were often left to fend for themselves. There was very little schooling, endemic child labour, and puberty marked the moment when the fight for survival began in earnest.

In midcentury, the pioneering reformer Charles Loring Brace had commented on the "immense number of boys and girls floating and drifting about our streets with hardly any assignable home or occupation, who continually swelled the multitude of criminals, prostitutes and vagrants". Slum children were routinely demonized in press reports that highlighted the inexorable growth of organized gangs: the lawless youngsters that the *New York Times,* in 1873, called "half-drunken, lazy, worthless vagabonds".

Pomeroy was brought up in Chelsea, a poor district of Boston. His parents' marriage was marked by the drunken violence of his father, who was thrown out of the family house in 1872, around the time that the boy committed his first serious assault. While his mother worked to pay the bills, Jesse was left to roam the city. With his milky eye, he looked odd, and was a target for bullying. His insecurity about his appearance came up in one of his letters to Willie Baxter: "What do you think of me," he asked. "Do I look like a bad boy. Is my head large."

However, it was the furious beatings that he received from his father that left the deepest scar. His prison letters revealed an obsession with "floggings". "I will tell you about the hardest licking I got," he wrote to Baxter. "I played truant and stole some money from mother. My father took me into the woodshed and I had to strip off my jacket & vest and two shirt [*sic*] so as to leave my back naked. Father took a whip and gave me a very hard whipping. It hurt me very much and every time I think of it I seem to be undergoing the flogging again."

Undiscovered for over a century, these letters might have helped to solve the vexed question that Jesse Pomeroy posed for Gilded Age America. He had simply learned all too well from adult example. As it was, he was dehumanized and abstracted into a symbol of pure evil. In contrast to the naughty but lovable scamps to be found in contemporary "boy novels" like Horatio Alger's *Ragged Dick* or Thomas Bailey Aldrich's *The Story of a Bad Boy,* Pomeroy was a blast of chill horror: a Frankenstein's monster straight from the urban laboratory.

Like Mary Shelley's famous creation, Pomeroy was allowed no way back into society. He predicted his fate: "If they say I must die, I am dead. If they send me to prison for life, I am dead too." After his confidant Willie Baxter left Suffolk County Jail in the summer of 1875, the young murderer sweated for another year before his death sentence was commuted to life in permanent solitary confinement. Although he refused ever to accept his captivity, he would remain cut off from all human contact for the next forty-one years.

· · ·

During 1887, while Jesse Pomeroy was making his fifth, sixth, and seventh serious attempts to escape his cell, Marie Bashkirtseff's journal was published. The years after 1875 had seen some of her wishes fulfilled. At the age of eighteen, she threw off the provinciality of Nice and moved to Paris to study as an artist. Although she took constant cures, her tuberculosis advanced inexorably. In response, she painted as though her afterlife depended on it. Exhibiting at the Salon, she gained recognition for her portrait of slum children, *Un meeting*.

Marie finally succumbed at the age of twenty-five in April 1884. Earlier that year, she had written a preface to what she hoped would be her lasting testament: "I want my journal to be published. It cannot fail to be interesting. Does my anticipation of its being read spoil or destroy the merit of such a book? Not at all. I wrote for a long time without dreaming of being read. And now it is just because I hope that I will be read that I am absolutely sincere. If this book is not the exact, absolute, strict truth, it has no reason to be."

It was this candid quality that helped to make the journal a bestseller on its first French publication. In giving a frank and exhaustive picture of her youthful psyche, Marie Bashkirtseff exposed a kind of perception that was not recognized by the culture and the media of the day. Her book was compared to Rousseau's *Confessions*, but there were two crucial differences: Marie wrote from the female perspective, and she jotted down her feelings and experiences as they occurred rather than recalling them in late life.

Offering an unprecedented account of pubescent life from within, the journal's impact spread throughout Europe, America, and Great Britain. There were articles about her in magazines like the *Woman's World* and *The Nineteenth Century*, where the British prime minister, William Gladstone, called the author "a true genius, one of those abnormal beings who in this or that country seem to be born into the world once or twice in a generation". Marie had finally achieved the fame that she had so ardently sought, as a true "mind liberator".

However, as she had foreseen, this success was tinged with irony. The journal was a Faustian pact with her mortality: it was the knowledge of her telescoping life that had given her writing its force, but such intimate and iconoclastic material could only have been published after her demise. Her natural intensity had been ratcheted by her fatal diagnosis, but it was this very heightened atmosphere that made the book so attractive to the young. Marie embodied the Romantic vision of an accelerated life sealed by an early death.

• • •

Marie Bashkirtseff and Jesse Pomeroy shared more than their time. In their different ways, they forced their respective societies to recognize that the existing rituals between childhood and adulthood were obsolete. The physical stage of puberty, usually beginning around twelve or thirteen and ending at eighteen or nineteen, remained constant. However the "true genius" and the "boy fiend" showed that it was no longer adequate to think that adulthood immediately followed childhood: they were the harbingers of a new intermediate state that as yet had no name.

It wasn't as though they had arrived totally unannounced. There already existed a considerable body of work on this very topic. Indeed, Marie and Jesse both epitomized the "critical moment" of which Rousseau had warned over a hundred years earlier. In *Emile,* a tract so scandalous that it was burned upon its publication in 1762, Rousseau argued that puberty had such fundamental emotional and mental effects that it represented "a second birth". The symptoms were "a change of temper, frequent outbreaks of anger, a perpetual stirring of the mind".

Rousseau's ideas were developed a decade later by Goethe's classic Sturm und Drang novel *The Sorrows of Young Werther*, which mapped the emotional disintegration of a gifted but suicidal young man. Werther's fictional letters displayed much of the pubescent pathology that Marie would exhibit a hundred years later: the extreme mood swings, the sensitivity to social slights, and the self-pitying rhetoric—"I see no end to misery but my grave." Although Werther had the "sacred and inspiring ability to create new worlds" around himself, he was a man out of his time.

The international success of Goethe's 1774 novel sealed the Romantic view of youth as beset by storms and stresses, so much so that premature death— by suicide or accident—was symptomatic. This tendency reached its apogee in the work of the British Romantics, whose avatar was a young poet and forger named Thomas Chatterton. After he died from arsenic poisoning at the age of seventeen, he was commemorated by Shelley, Wordsworth, Coleridge, and Keats in a sequence of poems that celebrated him as a misunderstood genius whose youth, made permanent by death, would never fade.

The Western conception of youth was also altered by the economic and political turmoil of the late eighteenth century. The Industrial Revolution initiated huge migrations from the country to the city and inaugurated a new society based on materialism, consumerism, and mass production. In the anonymous, swarming cities, the traditional structures of work, neighbourhood, and family broke down. Youths and children bore the brunt of this revolution, working in dangerous and repetitive tasks, or roaming wild in the filth evoked by Henry Mayhew and Charles Dickens.

At the same time, there were new governments that proclaimed true democracy. Having forcibly thrown off the "despotism" of the British king, the thirteen united states of America made their Declaration of Independence on

July 4, 1776: "We hold these truths to be self-evident, that all men are created equal, that they are endowed by their Creator with certain unalienable Rights, that among these are Life, Liberty and the pursuit of Happiness." In comparison to the feudalism of old Europe, the young continent of America was open to everyone.

These democratic ideals were reaffirmed in the Declaration of the Rights of Man issued by the revolutionary National Assembly of France during August 1789. Explicitly based on the American model, it stated that "men are born and remain free and equal in rights". Four years later the National Council added another eighteen codicils. Article 28 stated that "one generation cannot subject to its law the future generations". Within a revolution dominated by youth, the meaning was clear: the idea of the generation gap started here.

The consequences of these events were played out throughout the nineteenth century. Tied into the new radical politics of equality, youth became on the one hand a source of hope and a symbol of the future, and on the other an unstable and dangerous cohort. At one extreme, its involvement in revolutionary movements like Chartism, socialism, and, after the Russian example, anarchism and Nihilism, showed that generational consciousness, converted into radical ideology, could be a threat to the social order.

At the same time, youth was associated with the drive towards mass inclusion, if not true democracy. The full inception of the mass age in the second half of the nineteenth century gave rise to the realization that no section of the population should be overlooked in the new social order. That resulted in fresh attention being paid to hitherto neglected classes like the urban working poor or youth itself. The growth of the mass media accelerated that process. By the 1870s, the young could read about themselves and buy products, like dime or boy novels, that were principally aimed at their age group.

The anonymity of the huge cities also offered its own opportunities. Within an age when life for most youths was severely constricted, the more determined could attempt the life first defined in Henri Murger's *Scènes de la vie de Bohème*. Focusing on a group of struggling artists and working girls in 1840s Paris, Murger's stories promoted the idea of an urban zone where prevailing moralities were relaxed, where dissident and artistic young individuals could pursue their visions and delay adulthood. Thirty years later, these bohemian enclaves had spread to Berlin, London, and New York.

These changes were not always regarded positively, as youth became a litmus test for adult fears. The Industrial Revolution and its contemporary political revolutions had set in motion forces that were barely within the control of men and their governments. The slum children, the boy murderers, the anarchists: they all represented a future that could be subject to savage, atavistic forces. Just as Frankenstein's creature turned against its creator, so could the young of the West turn against their parents and their institutions.

With his unusual empathy for the young, Rousseau had recognized the pubescent potential for extremes in *Emile,* and concluded that the interval between childhood and adulthood should be prolonged: "The period when education is usually finished is just the time to begin." By the 1870s, his recommendations were being taken seriously: after the shocking reality of wild children had been exposed by reporters, reformers, and novelists alike, the governments of America and Europe began to create the institutions of compulsory education.

But Rousseau was not just talking about an ideal school. He proposed a deeper kind of education that would recognize puberty as a separate life stage and offer it sympathetic guidance so that society would be spared its more virulent manifestations. In the mid-1870s, Marie Bashkirtseff and Jesse Pomeroy symbolized the twin poles of youth: genius or monster, creator or destroyer of worlds. The furious impulses exposed by the young diarist and the young murderer would lead enquiring minds to take up Rousseau's proposals. At stake was the future: would it be dream or nightmare, heaven or hell?

CHAPTER 2

Nationalists and Decadents

The European Counterrevolution

· · ·

I envisage a war, of justice or strength
of a logic beyond all imagining.
It is as simple as a musical phrase.
—Arthur Rimbaud, "Guerre" (1874)

CHURCH LADS' BRIGADE LEAFLET, 1890s

THE TRADITIONALISTS OF Europe knew what to do with all that excess pubescent energy. Never mind about allowing the young time to develop, what these savages needed was sports-based schooling, then regimentation into pre-military cadet organizations. During the 1870s, this impulse was given an extra impetus by the industrial ascendancy of Germany, an aggressive new nation-state that destabilized the old European order and began what would become a forty-year arms race.

At the same time, there was a strong reaction against the new militarism from the artists, writers, and thinkers who assumed the Romantic and bohemian view of youth as a separate stage of life. They sought both to escape from the materialistic demands of nineteenth-century mass society and to plumb the deepest regions of the youthful psyche. The so-called decadents, while they did not originate their name, nevertheless revelled in their moral and physical sickness as they simultaneously explored what it could be like to be forever young.

With the looming deadline of the new century, the decadents and the nationalists engaged in a struggle to imprint their visions of the future on European youth. The battle might have been as deadly as it was unequal, but both sides shared a romanticism that elevated youth by freezing it at its zenith. Whether it took the form of the hero, fallen in battle in his physical prime, or the shooting star represented by the pubescent prodigy, eternal youth was the Holy Grail: whether killed or self-immolated, it would never reach adulthood.

The clearest exposition of the militarist vision for youth was given by a forty-year-old German lieutenant-colonel, Baron Colmar von der Goltz. In his 1883 book, *The Nation in Arms,* von der Goltz accurately foresaw that, as one of the "revolutionary changes" in the science of war, the whole population would be involved in any national conflict. Having as its "aim the complete subjection of the enemy", the new condition of total war would demand complete commitment and major sacrifices from soldiers and non-combatants alike.

Von der Goltz observed that "the time from the eighteenth to the twenty-fourth year" was best suited to military service. He shrewdly suggested how to exploit the physical and psychological attributes of this age group: "The body is then quite vigorous enough to endure hardships, and the soldier is as yet free and unfettered. The grain of heedlessness, a quality peculiar to the freshness of youth, is an excellent incentive to martial achievement. A young field army, particularly one uniformly young, is greatly superior to any other."

His vision was both pragmatic and mystical: "It is only the young that depart from life without pangs. They are not as yet fettered to this earth by the thousand threads that civil life weaves round us. They have not as yet learnt to be sparing of the hours of life. The enigma which they are curious to solve still lies before them as a closed book. They mount the hill without perceiving the abruptness of the precipice on the other side. Their love of adventure rouses their eagerness for battle." As he concluded, *"the strength of a nation lies in its youth* [italics in original]."

Germany was well suited to militaristic nationalism. It was a newly unified country, an industrial powerhouse that was the wonder of Europe, yet it was still stuck in the dynastic system. In place of the bourgeois revolution that had transformed Britain, France, and the United States, there was an authoritarian social structure harnessed to medieval Prussian ideals, which insisted on "loyalty towards the Emperor, passionate love for the Fatherland, self-denial and cheerful sacrifice". During the 1860s, universal conscription spread through the country.

The German ideal of "ultimate victory" had already been justified by France's complete humiliation in the Franco-Prussian War of 1870–71. Although France had been the first country in the world to introduce conscription— during 1793, when the revolutionary government needed to defend itself against royalist troops—recruitment had taken place through an inefficient lottery. With the deficiencies in its military system so brutally exposed, the Third Republic brought in tougher rules during 1872 to cover the twenty- to forty-year-old age group.

The other major European imperial power, Britain, was protected by the sea and had no large standing army. Instead of universal conscription, Britain encouraged an aspirational ideal designed to prepare youth for armed service. The desired qualities were summarized in the 1888 *Book for Boys* by W. H. Davenport Adams as "enthusiasm, earnestness, indefatigable perseverance, purity of mind and body, discipline of thought, cautious judgement, elevated aspirations, prayerfulness, fixity of purpose".

During the last third of the nineteenth century, the British public schools— which, despite their name, were exclusive, fee-paying establishments—developed an educational ethos that merged religion, discipline, culture, athletics, and the spirit of service into a powerful, all-compassing system. The new educational ideology was initiated by Thomas Arnold at Rugby School during the 1830s, with its concentration on "first religious and moral principle; secondly gentlemanly conduct; and thirdly intellectual ability".

Acting to reform the bullying exposed by Thomas Hughes's mid-century novel *Tom Brown's Schooldays*, Arnold attempted "to form Christian men, for Christian boys I can scarcely make". In place of the old public school system, where in the lack of adult controls adolescents had been allowed to regulate much of their own time, Arnold's new regime successfully engendered a mutual respect between teachers and pupils that nevertheless placed ultimate power firmly in the teacher. This was not a Rousseauesque free-school idyll.

After the 1860s, this idealistic balance was subsumed within a cult of masculinity that emphasized physical prowess rather than intellectual development. This fitted Britain's strategy during the last third of the nineteenth century, when the principal necessity was the maintenance and extension of empire. Britain had not been involved in a major European conflict since the Napoleonic Wars, and within this Pax Britannica, the public school model was vital in the moulding of upper- and middle-class adolescents into the enforcers of the imperial order.

The buccaneering individuality of the early nineteenth century had become obsolete: it had fled across the Atlantic to the American frontier. In the place of the freebooting imperial conqueror came the ideal of the group player. Team games like soccer, cricket, and rugby football became the principal test of character, the new institutional rite of passage. For despite the social status of its pupils, the public school education involved a holistic, almost panoptic system that matched the severity, if not the brutality, of tribal rites.

Boys were taken away from their homes at the age of twelve and thirteen and placed into barracklike peer societies, usually called houses, largely administered through an efficient peer prefect system. At the same time, every minute of their day was accounted for through a meticulous timetabling that would enable a headmaster to find out where every youth was at any given time. This was deliberate: to quote Davenport Adams, "idleness" was the "sin of Sodom".

That this system was successful in imprinting its stamp was in no doubt. As an anonymous schoolboy wrote in the mid-1890s, "One athletic rage, / Has seized Marlburians of every age, / Now, filled with frenzy, cricket all will play, / Now, all-absorbing football rules the day, / Where'er you go, the topic is the same, / And all our talk at tables is 'the game'." Religious practice was factored into this obsession with athleticism and team sports: as one headmaster put it, "In every great public boarding-school the chapel is the centre of school life."

The ideal public school product was the muscular Christian, who combined self-discipline, physical prowess, religious observance, and the spirit of service into a new kind of moral manliness. In Davenport Adams's definition, self-improvement, diligence, and duty were the first steps on "a pure, and honourable, and industrious life". Loyalty to one's house was intertwined with loyalty to one's school, and then ultimately to one's country—a willing submission that lasted until death and beyond, to the eternal life endowed by dying *pro patria*.

However, the empire needed more bodies than the public school system could provide. The lack of universal conscription meant that there was little impetus for working-class youths to join the army, except as an escape from dire poverty or a quest for adventure. With plots that featured diligent boy heroes encountering famous historical figures like Moses, Hannibal, or Napoleon, the imperial novels of G. A. Henty might have promoted the idea that military service was exciting, but by the 1880s the demands of empire and the challenges of the new Europe prompted more concrete action.

With military enlistment becoming a pressing problem, reformers began to civilize the urban jungles. Following the example of Toynbee Hall, the scions of the public schools and universities moved into poor districts on a mission of social improvement. Setting up youth clubs and community centres, the settlement movement aimed to inculcate middle-class attitudes: as the founders of the Oxford Working Men's and Lads' Institute stated, "The more forward classes in society have the power to show those below them how to live."

At the same time, new voluntary organizations refined the regimented evangelism of the Young Men's Christian Association (established 1844) and General Booth's Salvation Army (established 1878) into a more specifically youth-directed programme. The pioneer was William Smith's Boys' Brigade, formed in Glasgow during 1883. Combining parade-ground discipline with Sunday school teachings, the Boys' Brigade had as its specific aim "the advancement of Christ's Kingdom among Boys, and the promotion of habits of Reverence, Discipline and Self-Respect, and all that tends towards a true Christian manliness".

Smith capitalized on the fact that a whole section of youth was not covered by the existing voluntary organizations. As an original Brigade member later recalled, "When we reached thirteen most of us felt we were too big for the Sunday School, and there was a gap of a few years until we were able to join the YMCA at seventeen." Military discipline was uppermost in the Brigade's activities. Each meeting began with a fall-in drill parade, with no excuse for latecomers, and a uniform of pillbox cap, belt, and haversack was issued to be worn over everyday clothes. The Brigade's motto was "Sure and Steadfast".

With its ethos of strict punctuality, discipline, and obedience to orders, the Boys' Brigade offered not only an ideal pre-military grounding but also a built-in good reference for any future employer. By the end of the 1880s, the Brigade had over ten thousand members and branches throughout Britain. Its success was copied by other organizations like the Jewish Lads' Brigade and the Catholic Boys' Brigade. The Church Lads' Brigade was an offshoot of the Band of Hope, the popular children's temperance group. All of these grafted "the religious shoot onto the military trunk".

At the same time, there was an increase in the number of cadet corps, an idea pioneered by public schools like Charterhouse and Dulwich College. In 1889, the Southwark Cadet Corps was founded in South London, and was merged with the Toynbee Hall corps into a full battalion two years later. Membership would help young working-class boys to avoid the temptations of "lawlessness" and the "low music halls". The visible growth of these groups, as they marched in uniform through the streets, led one newspaper to comment that in 1889 British society was "running pretty freely to militarism".

Bringing "civilization" to the "ill-educated, dirty, quarrelsome" savages of the urban working class was another expression of colonial values. All the imperial countries thought that their sovereignty was the inevitable product of racial superiority. By the time of the last great continental carve-up—of Africa in the 1880s—the yoking of nationalism to the genetic sciences had congealed into orthodoxies so powerful that they governed the policy of nations. As far as Africa was concerned, European superiority was predestined by blood.

. . .

Within this belief system, the aim of every nation was not just evolutionary progress, but the fulfilment of its own unique racial destiny. Von der Goltz's climactic formulation reverberated within Germany's allies and enemies alike. If the strength of the nation did in fact reside in its youth, then youth as a whole—not just those of service age but their younger cohort—was charged with a new importance. If the national destiny, as in Germany's case, was defined by military expansion, then there could be no counter-argument.

Any youth who did not measure up was not just weak or unpatriotic, but a threat to the future of the race. The effect was to reduce the opponents of militarism into subhuman savages. The name for these deviants was pioneered by the French psychiatrist B. A. Morel, who in 1857 coined the term "degeneration" to define defective humans living in degraded environments, and the term took root over the next few decades. Within the nationalist vision, anyone who refused or objected to military service was a degenerate, pure and simple.

However, there was a small section of the young who objected. Extrapolating from his brother's suicide, Frank Wedekind wrote *Spring Awakening* in 1891, an angry polemic against a German establishment that ruthlessly regimented its youth but failed to offer any real guide to life. The play touched a raw nerve with its depictions of youth sexuality and youth suicide. The latter was seen as a major social problem in 1890s Germany: according to contemporary books by the psychiatrist Emil Kraepelin and the sociologist Emile Durkheim, it was directly caused by the stresses and strains of industrial civilization.[1]

The fact that the young of the most advanced and most triumphal nation in the world were bent on killing themselves struck an ominous note in the midst of triumphant militarism. The young often reflect the dominant values of society back at adults, and these pubescent suicides revealed the presentiments of collapse that lay under the bullish surface of 1890s Europe. While their armies and navies spanned the globe, the great empires were beset by fears about the new mass age and the consequent devolution of human society.

In 1892's *The Crowd,* the French philosopher Gustave Le Bon delivered an influential polemic about the mass age. Within the new technological society, the "divine right of kings" had been replaced by the "divine right of the masses". By their very nature, crowds were atavistic: their "impulsiveness, irritability, incapacity to reason", and their "exaggeration of the sentiments" were exactly those qualities "observed in beings belonging to inferior forms of evolution—in women, savages, and children". The modern age was "a period of transition and anarchy", within which mass social control would be the key issue.

Within this dystopia, the position of youth would be of vital importance: not only because the children of today were the citizens of tomorrow, but also because degraded social condition had created a generation of degenerates. The future of the race was at stake. There was the pervasive fear that, if not purified, the race would die out and Europe itself would perish in a violent cataclysm. Because these fears were based on the likelihood of total war that underlay the remorseless logic of militarism, they began to generate their own momentum.

This longing for apocalypse was the central impulse behind both decadence and militarism. It had also, as Goethe and Wedekind had noted, long been a powerful manifestation of adolescent anger. But whose world would end? A

1. Emil Kraepelin: *Psychiatrie* (1893); Emile Durkheim: *Suicide* (1897). *Spring Awakening* was not performed until the twentieth century.

torrent of apocalyptic rhetoric streamed from nationalists and decadents alike in the 1890s, as they vied to define the new century. Coinciding with the accelerating arms race heralded by von der Goltz's influential book, this ideological conflict politicized the status of youth in northern Europe.

. . .

Civilizations do die. That was the message pumped out by the extreme racial theorists and the avant-gardists of the day. That was the message of the picture that caused a sensation in the 1891 Paris Salon, *Les derniers jours de Babylone* by Georges Antoine Rochegrosse. In *A rebours*, Joris-Karl Huysmans foresaw "the vast bagnio of America transported to the continent of Europe". Although he hated "the limitless, unfathomable, immeasurable scurviness of the financier and the self-made man", he brought down their materialism as a curse: "Well, crumble then, society! Perish old world!"

It was not surprising that the most extreme manifestations of this fin-de-siècle rhetoric should have originated in France, a country that in the last two decades of the nineteenth century was still racked by the political instability that had marked its history since 1789. Youth had played a major part in that revolution, and had remained prominent in the coups and rebellions of 1830, 1848, and 1871. Although the Third Republic had moved to extend conscription, a series of anarchist outrages in the 1890s meant that youth remained in a highly charged, politicized state.

The messiah of the new apocalyptic mood had been, in a very direct sense, the poet of his country's darkest days. During the winter of 1870–71, Arthur Rimbaud lived on the front line of the Franco-Prussian War, in the small town of Charleville near the Belgian border. On New Year's Eve, his family sheltered in their house while Prussian shells pounded the nearby medieval fortress of Mézières, just across the river Meuse from Charleville. At the age of sixteen, Rimbaud was surrounded by the detritus of war: maimed soldiers, smashed cities, disfigured landscapes.

He revelled in the destruction. "I saw a sea of flames and smoke rise to heaven," he later wrote, "and left and right all wealth exploded like a billion thunderbolts." As the second son of a French army colonel who had deserted the family ten years earlier, Rimbaud had more than enough reason not to love the military. When his older brother Frederick enthusiastically enlisted, he found it "contemptible"; after France had been defeated, he went around Charleville telling everyone how lucky his country was. It was as though the downfall of France had set him free.

ARTHUR RIMBAUD,
AGED SEVENTEEN,
BY ÉTIENNE CARJAT

At sixteen, Rimbaud was the archetypal provincial youth who had long out-grown his family and his home town. He couldn't wait to get away. The chaos created by the Franco-Prussian War externalized his internal fury and gave him an opportunity to test himself. That winter, he ran away from home and, somewhere amid the wasteland of the Prussian front line, he experienced a revelation: "Along the open road on winter nights, homeless, cold, and hun-gry, one voice gripped my frozen heart: 'Weakness or strength, you exist, that is strength.'"

Two months later, Rimbaud saw his fantasies become real, as the capital city's poor rose up with thousands of students and workers in the short-lived Paris Commune. For a brief period in April and May 1871, anarchists were in charge of the capital, and young poets ran the police force. Rimbaud was one of only thousands of young vagabonds who flocked to revolutionary Paris like moths to a flame: so many that the Commune formed two battalions from their numbers, the "Pupilles de la Commune" and the "Enfants perdus".

Although the Commune was smashed within weeks of Rimbaud's visit, the sixteen-year-old took away the sense of liberation that he had experienced and determined to apply it to his own work and life. The two would become indivisible. On May 13, 1871, he wrote to his friend Paul Demeny, "The problem is to attain the unknown by disorganizing all the senses. The suffering is immense, but you have to be strong, and to have been born a poet." He insisted that "je est un autre": his rhetoric would soon be translated into action.

For Rimbaud, poetry was a mystical calling. He followed the visionary dark line that began with the Romantics and passed through Edgar Allan Poe and Charles Baudelaire to its conclusion. After 1871, his poems were full of revolutionary turmoil, anti-bourgeois invective, pagan mysticism, and wild prophecies all melded together into a consistent cosmology. Above all, his visions were apocalyptic: "This is the time of the sweat bath, of oceans boiling over, of underground explosions, of the planet whirled away, of exterminations sure to follow."

It was as a presence that he made the strongest impact on his contemporaries. Invited to Paris that autumn by the poet Paul Verlaine, Rimbaud was touted around the capital's literary bohemia as the latest prodigy. Instead of the correct attitude of respect to his elders, the seventeen-year-old responded to what he saw as a patronizing attitude with a volley of scatological expletives and worse. He disrupted readings, terrorized his hosts, poured sulphuric acid in a friend's drink, and on one occasion wounded the photographer Étienne Carjat.

The two photos of Rimbaud by Carjat that still exist show a baby-faced young man with a clenched jaw, a thin, cruel mouth, exploding hair, and pale, adamantine eyes—the model of a young fanatic. Paul Verlaine called him "a kid Casanova" whose "handsome, rugged chin seems to say 'Bugger off' to any illusion that is not the result of the most irrevocable act of will". With his "superb mop of hair" and an "utterly virile disdain for clothes", the young man epitomized a "literally diabolical beauty".

For the next four years, Rimbaud pursued a folie à deux with Verlaine that passed through debauch, poverty, and ostracism to end in violence and exhaustion. "Boredom is no longer my love," he wrote in Une saison en enfer: "rage, perversion and madness, whose every impulse and disaster I know— my burden is set down entire." At the age of twenty-one, he stopped writing: when asked about his poetry by a friend, he replied, "Je ne pense plus à ça." Shortly afterwards, he emigrated to Africa and abandoned his former life.

The rocketlike trajectory of Rimbaud's career was fuelled by a forensic exploration of his explosive thoughts and feelings—a new sensibility symptomatic of what he called, in "Jeunesse", "the endless egoism of youth". When he was writing in the early 1870s, youth had no rights, an "extralegal position" of which he was acutely aware. His verse recast existing Romantic tropes through a massive dose of pubescent male pathology. Putting himself into the person of a Caligula-like prince in the poem "Conte", he asked, "Is ecstasy possible in destruction? Can one grow young in cruelty?"

Through his disappearance, he became a mythical creature, frozen at his youthful zenith as surely as Werther or Thomas Chatterton. Rimbaud had already foreseen his fate. In his May 1871 manifesto, he described what would happen once the seer had broken through: "He reaches the unknown and even if, maddened, he ends up by losing all understanding of his visions, he has seen them! If he dies after his leap into these heard-of, unnameable things, more workers in the horrible will come; they'll begin at the horizons where the other has collapsed!"

Rimbaud's status as the avatar of French decadence was sealed when during 1883—the same year as *The Nation in Arms*—Paul Verlaine published a selection of his poems in the anthology *Les poètes maudits*. With his "faith in poison" and ecstatic "insanities", Rimbaud set the template for a movement that linked sex and death in a new revelation, defined by Verlaine as "the collapse into the flames of races exhausted by sensation at the invading sound of the enemy trumpets". Deep within East Africa, the messiah was appalled at his unsought fame.

However, the style inexorably spread around Europe and across the Atlantic. As successive generations of decadents upped the ante in extremity, their ambition increased. By the 1890s, they had constructed a hermetic world that encompassed absinthe, morphine, bearded gurus, spiritualist seances, reviews that featured "hair-raising contributions from fake Rimbauds", and editorials that proclaimed a mission "to destroy the old order and prepare the embryonic elements of the great national literature of the twentieth century".

. . .

Thanks to its proximity to France, Britain was the most fertile European ground for the export of decadence, but there were other factors. By the last decade of the century, the certainties of high Victorianism had been undermined by the scientific critique of religion and the accelerating effects of the mass age. There was also an increase of extra-parliamentary political activity: the beginnings of mass socialism, the emergence of the New Woman and of women's suffrage, and the first discussions of homosexual rights. At the same time, urban outrages by working-class youths increased in visibility.

Within the public schools themselves, the crusading archetype was under attack. Classical studies had long been a staple of the public school system, and from the 1870s on, those sick of muscular Christianity reinterpreted the Latin and Greek syllabus into a new kind of aestheticism that represented a real alternative to God and sport. One of the most influential Hellenizers, Goldsworthy Lowes Dickinson, remembered that his schooldays had been "sunk in barbarism": "There is no doubt about the misery, the futility, the worse than waste of precious years."

In the early 1890s, the leading light of British aestheticism proposed another definition of youth. By the time his first novel was published, Oscar Wilde was already established as a provocateur and author. Although married with two sons, he had another life in the homosexual underworld. Part parable, part roman à clef about Wilde and his circle, *The Picture of Dorian Gray* recast the Faustian myth for the modern age: in this case, the deal was sealed on the promise of eternal youth.

The genesis of the novel went back to June 1884, when Wilde visited Paris on his honeymoon. He had already been introduced to the first full flush of Rimbaudian decadence, in the shape of Sarah Bernhardt's opium-addled protégé, the poet Maurice Rollinat, but the piece of writing that made the most impact on him was *A rebours*. Wilde identified so strongly with des Esseintes that Huysmans's hermetic aesthete "became to him a kind of pre-figuring type of himself. And indeed, the whole book seemed to him to contain the story of his own life, written before he had lived it."

Wilde oscillated uneasily between decadent debauch and socialist utopia, but he saw these tensions as a source of energy. In 1891, he published two major books that encoded the twin poles of his character: the philosophical essay "The Soul of Man Under Socialism" and the full-length novel *Dorian Gray*. If the former proclaimed that "it is through disobedience that progress has been made", then the latter enshrined youthful intensity: "Live! Live the wonderful life that is in you! Youth! Youth! There is nothing in the world but youth!"

The most shocking thing about Dorian Gray's tour through the demimonde of the day—the artists' studios, the music halls, the opium dens—was not the complete amorality with which he wrecked the lives of all with whom he came into contact. Rather, it was Wilde's depiction of his spoilt child's thorough dissolution within "dreams that would make the shadow of their evil real". This perverse glee was barely vitiated by the novel's moralistic conclusion, as the Faustian contract exacted its price. In place of youthful beauty lay an unrecognizable corpse, "withered, wrinkled, and loathsome of visage".

Wilde was far too canny to be proposing eternal youth as a serious supposition: Gray's descent into boredom and insanity made the dangers of that state quite obvious. However, his ambivalences caught him out. Although a critique of decadence, his hothouse novel helped further to popularize the style. Wilde tipped the balance further by adding a series of prefatory aphorisms—like "vice and virtue are to the artist materials for an art"—that were guaranteed to infuriate what Huysmans called England's "heavy guard room atmosphere".

If he had expressly planned it, Wilde could not have chosen a line of attack more unsettling to the imperial English. The values that he promoted—the twin sins of Sodom and socialism—were diametrically opposed to those of muscular Christianity. In place of team spirit, he suggested rampant individualism: "To realise one's nature perfectly—that is what each of us is here for." Instead of the rigid warrior, he defined man as "a complex multiform creature". Most of all, through his increasingly open homosexuality, he exposed the fault line that ran through the British single-sex educational system.

Wilde set out to influence the young. "It's absurd to talk about the ignorance of youth," he wrote. "The only people to whose opinions I listen to with any respect are people much younger than myself." As the high priest of aestheticism, Wilde was a magnet for young fans like the Oxford undergraduate Lord Alfred Douglas, who rushed to meet the author soon after the publication of *Dorian Gray*. Wilde had been pursuing a secret homosexual life for several years, but the relationship that the two openly pursued led to a head-on confrontation with the English establishment.

In an article called "Phrases and Philosophies for the Use of the Young", published in the December 1894 issue of a new Oxford magazine, the *Chameleon*, Wilde contradicted deeply held tenets about religion, time, art and history, and the relationship of generations. "The old believe everything," he wrote; "the middle aged suspect everything: the young know everything." Although Wilde did not write anything sexually explicit, other contributors did—most notably Lord Alfred, who celebrated "the love that dare not speak its name". When the scandal broke, Wilde was damned by association.

In the tortuous legal drama that unfolded at London's Central Criminal Court during April and May 1895, Wilde's influence over the young was a central issue. Stung by the harassment of Lord Alfred's father, the Marquess of Queensberry, he had sued for libel. His friends advised him not to, and their worst fears came true when the defendant entered a plea of justification that accused Wilde of sodomy with twelve youths. The prosecution held that these debauches had already been publicized in *The Picture of Dorian Gray*, a work "calculated to subvert morality and encourage unnatural vice".

The confusion of novel with author deepened during the three trials, with Wilde cast as Gray's corrupter, Lord Henry Wotton. The establishment's punitive determination resulted in a sentence of two years' hard labour for indecency and sodomy. In summing up, the judge told Wilde that he had been "the centre of a circle of extensive corruption of the most hideous kind among young men". This first successful conviction under the 1885 Criminal Law Amendment Act announced homosexuality to the public in the most negative terms: "a sore which cannot fail in time to corrupt and taint it all!"

The verdict was a personal disaster not just for Wilde, whose works were banned and who remained a figure of public vilification for decades beyond his death in 1900, but for the aesthetes and homosexuals whose fresh visibility his presence heralded. The medical metaphors used in the court and in the press to describe these diseased creatures accorded with the genetic theories popularized by Max Nordau's devastating critique of aestheticism, *Degeneration,* first published in Germany during 1892 but then enjoying a brief vogue in Britain.

Dedicated to Cesare Lombroso, Nordau's book identified the threat posed by artists who, like Baudelaire, Nietzsche, and Wilde, proclaimed the virtues of individualism against traditional moralities.[2] Nordau singled out Wilde as "the pathological aberration of a racial instinct". The treatment that he thought most "efficacious" to counter this *"fin de siècle* mood" was enacted in the spring 1895 trials: "characterization of the leading degenerates as mentally diseased: unmasking and stigmatizing of their imitators as enemies to society; cautioning the public against the lies of these parasites."

Wilde's cardinal offence was that he acted out in public what often occurred behind the ruling-class façade. As the journalist W. T. Stead observed after the verdict, "Meanwhile public school boys are allowed to indulge with impunity in practices which, when they leave school, would consign them to hard labour." The drama also distracted attention from a scandal involving the prime minister, Lord Rosebery, and another Queensberry scion, Viscount Drumlanrig—a relationship that ended with the younger man's suicide.

With these undercurrents, it's hardly surprising that the Wilde trial represented a determined attempt by the Victorian establishment to reject any examination of the cause and to blame the symptom instead. The children of the bourgeois, so vital to the country's future, had been seduced by this effete Pied Piper, and their very souls were at stake. One newspaper report made it clear that it was the "young men at universities, clever sixth form boys at public schools" who "should ponder within themselves the doctrines and the career of the man who has now to undergo the righteous sentence of the law".

2. Nordau singled out Marie Bashkirtseff for particular abuse: "a degenerate girl who died of phthisis, a victim to moral madness, with a touch of megalomania and the mania of persecution, as well as morbid erotic exaltation."

There was some basis to this charge. By the 1890s, there were already two class-defined groups of young people who refused to bow before Western imperial materialism: what, writing within an American context, Thorstein Veblen would later call the "hereditary leisure class" and "lower-class delinquents". Within Britain, they were joined by the middle- or upper-middle-class bohemian: thanks, in part, to Wilde's own efforts, the aesthetic lifestyle of romanticism had become entrenched within the British bourgeoisie as a third way between militarism and revolution.

The Wilde verdict halted British modernism in its tracks. Edward Carpenter's exploration on the relationship between feminism and homosexuality, *Love's Coming of Age*, was buried upon publication in 1896. Havelock Ellis's pioneering *Sexual Inversion*, offering case histories of pubescent sexual deviations, was banned a year later. Wilde's onetime collaborator Aubrey Beardsley observed the momentum of this "reaction": "Rabid puritanism comes in like a high wave and is immediately followed by a steady ebb-tide of brutal coarseness."

Throughout Europe, decadence receded before an aggressive new normality. In *Degeneration*, Nordau had equated physical fitness with mental and psychic health. He defined the qualities that were the polar opposite of decadence: strength of will, duty and work, submission before the immutable law of evolution. Near the book's end, he asked his readers to imagine a "competition" between the decadents, the sterile inhabitants of the "hospital, lunatic asylum and prison", and the "men who rise early, and are not weary before sunset, who have clear heads, solid stomachs and hard muscles".

In France, there was a concerted intellectual attack against the decadents. In a July 1899 speech, a radical young populist named Albert Mathiez attacked "these youths who live only for themselves" and "who perfume themselves and live like women". Their ultimate stupidity was the fact that they proclaimed themselves *"uprooted"*. This was the atomized individuality that the writer Maurice Barrès called "the immense I that hides them from the rest of the world". Although Barrès had drunk deep from the decadent well,[3] his 1897 trilogy *Les déracinés* (The Uprooted Ones) explored this disconnection.

Tracing the migration of seven provincial adolescents from Lorraine to Paris, the narrative of *Les déracinés* was bleak: "Isolated from their communities of birth, and trained only to compete among themselves, adolescents take the most lamentable view of life." In the lack of any adult provision or stable values, individualism led to murder. Barrès's critique of a moribund establish-

3. He had been an early supporter of the Bashkirtseff diaries.

ment slowly pushed him into active political agitation, as he sought to rally the generation that he had awakened, his "princes of youth", into a new mystical nationalism.

Recasting nationalism was also on the mind of an eminent English Victorian. Henry Newbolt was a lawyer, novelist, and editor who believed in "England as a world-wide and world-guiding power". He enthusiastically described an 1898 dinner at his alma mater, Clifton College: "At 3 in the morning I was still sitting on the bed of a man I'd never seen before, reading extracts from his diary of the Soudan. He is a captain of the R.A. and it was his howitzers that breached the walls of Omdurman. He came to Clifton the year after I left!"

Newbolt believed that "for shaping national character, and its component, individual character, war has at times been 'a most perfect instrument'". Later in 1898, he published a collection of poetry called *This Island Race*. In "Vitaï Lampada" (The Torch of Life), he enshrined the link between sports and chivalry that was at the heart of Britain's global dominance. Within pragmatic Albion, mysticism was measured out in overs, and Newbolt's ringing poem definitively stated the imperial vision for British youth:

There's a breathless hush in the Close to-night—
Ten to make and the match to win—
A bumping pitch and a blinding light,
An hour to play and the last man in.
And it's not for the sake of a ribboned coat,
Or the selfish hope of a season's fame,
But his Captain's hand on his shoulder smote—
"Play up! play up! and play the game!"

The sand of the desert is sodden red,—
Red with the wreck of a square that broke;—
The Gatling's jammed and the colonel dead,
And the regiment blind with dust and smoke.
The river of death has brimmed his banks,
And England's far, and Honour a name,
But the voice of a schoolboy rallies the ranks:
"Play up! play up! and play the game!"

This the word that year by year
While in her place the School is set
Every one of her sons must hear,
And none that hears it dare forget.

This they all with a joyful mind
Bear through life like a torch in flame,
And falling fling to the host behind—
"Play up! play up! and play the game!"

The echoes of this militaristic mantra were still reverberating two decades later, as the youth of Europe went to war. Like *Degeneration* and *Les déracinés,* "Vitai Lampada" was part of a very effective counter-revolution that appeared to banish forever the ghost of disease-ridden decadence. For all its vigour, however, Newbolt's poem was death-haunted;[5] for all their world-weary poses, the decadents celebrated a youthful lust for life that would reassert itself after the holocaust for which their "healthy" opponents had so enthusiastically prepared.

5. After the Great War, Newbolt blanched at its mention.

CHAPTER 3

Hooligans and Apaches

Juvenile Delinquency and the Mass Media

• • •

The best among the poor are never grateful. They are ungrateful, discontented, disobedient, and rebellious. They are quite right to be so.

—Oscar Wilde, "The Soul of Man Under Socialism" (1891)

"THE MONTGOMERY GUARDS: A GROWLER GANG IN SESSION",
c. 1890, BY JACOB RIIS

IN THE LATE-nineteenth-century metropolis, many children and adolescents were left to fend for themselves. In the lack of any adult-imposed structures, they organized themselves into barely controllable gangs. Jacob Riis found this out when, at the turn of the 1890s, he came across a group of young toughs in south Manhattan. Although he was used to dealing with homeless children, he found that he had to approach this older bunch of "rascals" with more caution. It was only by appealing to their vanity—he asked them to throw "cigarette-picture" poses in front of his camera—that he avoided getting beaten up.

The gang "accepted the offer with great readiness, dragging into their group a disreputable-looking sheep (the slaughterhouses were close at hand) as one of the band. The homeliest ruffian of the lot, who insisted on being taken with the growler[1] in his 'mug', took the opportunity to pour what was left in it down his throat and this caused a brief unpleasantness, but otherwise the performance was a success. While I was getting the camera ready, I threw out a vague suggestion of cigarette pictures, and it took root at once. Nothing would then do but that I must take the boldest spirits of the company 'in character'. "

They enacted their everyday crimes: "One of them tumbled over a shed, as if asleep, while two of the others bent over him, searching his pockets with a deftness that was highly suggestive. This, they explained for my benefit, was to show how they 'did the trick'. The rest of the band were so impressed with the importance of this exhibition that they insisted on crowding into the picture by climbing upon the shed, sitting on the roof with their feet dangling over the edge, and disposing themselves in every imaginable manner within view, as they thought."

The resulting picture, "A Growler Gang in Session", set a new standard in delinquent iconography. Within a low-density urban zone of sheds and yards, seven members of the Montgomery Guards announce their group mind with dress and gesture. Scowling against the washed-out sunlight, they all wear hats, dark clothes, and a defiant expression. Their insolence is embodied in the sneer on the face of the central juvenile and the determination of the younger drinker butting in to drain the jug to the brim. Confronted with this sight, you'd have run.

Manhattan's newspapers had long reported on the doings of the island's gangs. In the summer of 1857, the *New York Times* had publicly interceded in the fearsome conflict between the Bowery Boys and the Dead Rabbits. With their snappy group names and hair-raising exploits, young gangsters offered per-

1. A growler is a jug filled with stale or cheap beer.

fect subjects for the city's journalists. The former wanted the publicity, the latter got picturesque copy—living dime-novel plots—that nevertheless combined those two press ideals: titillation and censure.

By the last decade of the nineteenth century, the problem of juvenile delinquency had become more pressing. It wasn't, however, until the 1890 publication of the "Growler Gang" photo and others in Jacob Riis's *How the Other Half Lives* that Americans saw widely distributed documentary evidence of their urban young. A police reporter turned crusader, Riis found that the recently invented flash camera was the perfect instrument to record the lives of outcasts who were much discussed but rarely seen: in this case, he exposed a separate, if not autonomous, youth world.

Like the degeneration theorists, Riis aimed to show that degraded conditions resulted in degraded lives, and that youth were the most vulnerable: "Of the 82,200 persons arrested by the police in 1889," he wrote, "10,505 were under twenty years old." However, his purpose was not to consign the young Manhattan poor to the outer darkness, but to shed light on the problem. Integration rather than eugenics was Riis's way: the runaway success of *How the Other Half Lives* gave him the opportunity to influence national policy on the reform of housing conditions, public spaces, and public education.

Riis was only one of many writers to report on youth crime during the last decade of the nineteenth century. As their numbers grew apace with their assertion, slum children presented even more of a visible problem. If the mass technological and urban society was going to work, then everyone had to be brought into line in accordance with the bourgeois dictates of thrift, duty, and discipline. Urban chaos was no longer acceptable. The reform movement in America made delinquency one of their prime targets, at the same time as scandals in Britain and France made the topic national news.

These commentators did not take account of the impact that their sensationalist reportage would have on the cohort they objectified. Youth was a charged topic, and even more so when linked to crime and strange, barbaric customs. Being in print helped to confer status. Arriving in the public eye at the same time as the popular press first flexed its muscle, the slum savage offered a test case for the next century. Exhibiting an alarming, if not alien independence, the hooligan and the Apache heralded the symbiotic relationship between the mass media and youth.

This sudden flare of attention reflected the fact that, by the 1890s, many urban young were determined to live life their way. Never mind what reformers or journalists thought, they would get what they wanted by fair means or foul: intoxicants, weapons, clothes. Just as their extravagant dress brought them to public attention, new types like the hooligans and the Apaches used their startling appearance as a badge of honour. In doing so, they broadcast the very plumed defiance that their exposure was attempting to curtail.

.   .   .

It was in the New World that juvenile delinquency was at its most extreme. Between 1880 and 1910, the total urban population of America tripled, from 14 to 42 million. This huge increase came from two sources: from within the continent, as an estimated 11 million people left the country for the city, and from without, as immigration from Western and Eastern Europe reached its peak around the new century. This massive migration convulsed America in what the educationalist John Dewey called "a revolution as rapid, extensive, and complete as any in history".

Youth was at the sharp end of this revolution. Groups like the Montgomery Guards presented a visible reminder that the continent's institutions and infrastructure were failing to keep pace with the dazzling rate of change. In the lack of any state intervention, the social reportage of reformers like Riis and Jane Addams, together with the realist fiction of Theodore Dreiser and Stephen Crane, described with greater urgency than ever before the stark choices facing America's young. Nightmare visions they might have been, but with a practical aim: the improvement of everyday life for poor city dwellers.

The children of the urban stews made the running in this fresh focus on American social conditions. Because they did not appear to present a problem, and, indeed, because they embodied mainstream American values, middle- and upper-class adolescents were not so visible in the new mass media. The street arabs and the gangs of toughs were a living reminder that, for all America's wish to forge a new society independent of European traditions, and despite its rhetoric of freedom for all, inequity was embedded, if not actually promoted, in its economic and social systems.

Despite the aspirational propaganda, how you fared—apart from a few rare exceptions—depended on how you were born. If you were born into an apparently secure middle-class background, you were more likely to have traditional aspirations and ideals: if male, to enter the family business or a suitable job; if female, to make the best marriage possible or, failing that, entry into law or medicine. For young men in particular, there was a ready-made ladder of achievement to climb: primary and secondary education, then on to university and into business, industry, or the professions.

The beliefs instilled into middle-class American youth reflected their country's strategic position. Although the Civil War had eradicated the attractions of conflict for a generation, by the 1890s there was a new bellicosity, enshrined in the person of the civil service commissioner, Theodore Roosevelt, that accorded with the country's wish to become a player on the international stage. In his 1885 bestseller, *Manifest Destiny*, John Fiske had prophesied that within a century America would be "a political aggregation unmeasurably surpassing in power and in dimensions any empire that has yet existed".

The rulers of tomorrow were therefore to be inculcated in the skills and attitudes necessary to turn that vision into reality. Even before the Spanish-American War of 1898, militarism had become embedded within American life. What Roosevelt called the "iron qualities that must go with true manhood" were reinforced both by a spiritual ideal of "muscular Christianity" and a highly developed sports culture: baseball, football, and bodybuilding the main leisure activities of the country's middle-class males. In pre-imperial America, however, the ultimate aim of this training was not war but business.

In the same way that the public schools trained Britain's young to rule the British Empire, so sport both disciplined the young savage and prepared him for the "hard and dangerous endeavour" that Roosevelt held to be necessary for America to achieve its "true national greatness". This ideology did not offer any sense that middle-class youths formed a distinct cohort. Although there was the sense that "youth" was a period of flux, this was disappearing with the increasing stratification of education and leisure, which meant that young men were more under the supervision of their elders than ever before.

Although assertion on the part of privileged young men was thought to be in the natural order of things, it was not couched in any generational pleading. Adults ruled the roost. In Theodore Dreiser's 1893 state-of-the-nation epic, *Sister Carrie*, the mansion-dwelling George Hurstwood Jr might well have "manifested even greater touchiness and exaggeration in the matter of his individual rights, and attempted to make all feel that he was a man with man's privileges". But this was "an assumption which, of all things, is most groundless and pointless in a youth of nineteen".

By that age, many slum children were reaching the end of their lives. In the harsh environments of America's metropolitan laboratories, the struggle for survival used up bodies and souls with a particular intensity. Thanks to its very high levels of immigration and its peculiarly compressed environment, Manhattan was particularly tough on its young. Children were routinely abandoned on the streets: many died, while the luckier found sketchy employment as newsboys or flower sellers, joined a gang, or were recruited by the local Fagin. There was no welfare infrastructure, no safety net.

These youngsters' primary mode of social organization was local and territorial. It also reflected the city in which they lived. New York was a wide-open town, "the modern Gomorrah". How could they have resisted making themselves in this image? The gangs had been developing in sophistication and number since the mid-nineteenth century. By the 1890s, according to their chronicler Herbert Asbury, "Manhattan south of Times Square was divided by the gangs into clearly defined kingdoms, and the boundaries were garrisoned and as carefully guarded as are the frontiers of civilized nations."

Within this urban battle zone, Manhattan's ethnic divisions—from street to street, from ward to ward—were acted out in pitched battles and race riots. However, crime and peer protection were more usual motives. Comprising members aged between ten and twenty, the new gangs subsumed smaller groups, defended their principal product—usually the illegal activity associated with their neighbourhood—and conducted turf wars to establish market superiority. This was delinquency restructured into a barely parodic echo of the corporate consolidation that had begun to dominate American business life.

The consequent carve-up created an alternative map of Manhattan. The Five Pointers commanded the area around Broadway and the Bowery; the Eastmans' patch spread from the Bowery to the East River. Elsewhere the Gas House Gang, the Gophers, the Fashion Plates, the Marginals, and the Pearl Buttons all squabbled over their respective turf. With a high turnover of members, the gangs recruited from the many young men's social clubs that proliferated throughout the East and West sides: set up by local ward bosses, they also had rousing names like the Bowery Indians and the Go-Aheads.

This was a whole world unto itself. All the usual rules were turned upside down, but woe betide those who crossed the new ones. The most successful gang of the early 1890s, the Whyos, offered a detailed price list for blackmail and murder commissions—"punching" only cost $2, but "doing the big job" ran to "$100 and up". The Baxter Street Dudes ran their own basement playhouse, sarcastically called the Grand Duke's Theater. Youngsters and slummers ("elephant hunters") came from all over the city to run the gauntlet of rival gangs and to watch plays performed with stolen scenery and props.

One great attraction of this world was its sexual licence—a definite plus within America's puritan morality—but this only worked for the men. Stephen Crane's scandalous 1896 novel *Maggie: A Girl of the Streets* traced the inexorable momentum of this unequal transaction. Blossoming "in a mud puddle", his heroine has only her youth: "She began to see the bloom in her cheeks as something valuable." Repelled by the prospect of sweatshop slave labour, Maggie enters into a relationship with a local gangster. Once he has used her up, she can do nothing but become one of "the painted cohorts of the city".

Although prostitution was one of the principal gang industries, tough young women could also join the life on their own terms. Apart from the inevitable madams and saloon managers, there were female gangs that arose out of social clubs like the Lady Locusts, the Lady Liberties of the Fourth Ward, and the Lady Truck Drivers' Assocation. The Battle Row Ladies' Social and Athletic Club was affiliated to the Gophers: under the leadership of the ferocious Battle Annie, the Lady Gophers, as they were also known, had proven their worth in "frequent combats with the police".

Virtually all of the gang leaders were male, however: "big men" like Paul Kelly, the Five Pointers' chief, and his henchman Biff Ellison, Dandy Johnny Dolan of the Whyos, and Monk Eastman, so powerful that his gang took his surname. Many successful gang leaders proclaimed their dominance by their dress: Asbury noted that "the really dangerous gangster, the killer, was more apt to be something of a dandy". Kelly was "dapper, soft-spoken", while Ellison "dearly loved to sprinkle himself with scent, of which he had his own private blend especially compounded by a druggist sworn to secrecy".[2]

Within the tenements of Manhattan, this subterranean society offered a theatrical but deadly inversion of all-American values. The successful gang leader was, to all intents and purposes, the mirror image of the successful college athlete, the prince of his own domain. His power meant that many young toughs would seek to emulate his every word and action. During the late 1890s, Eastman became "one of the most celebrated citizens of the East Side, and innumerable young men began to imitate him in speech and manner, so there came into being a Monk Eastman school of hoodlums and brawlers".

This heroic status served to mask the brutal realities of the gang world. For every successful boss, there were thousands of scuffling young toughs. While their chieftain might have been "a big man", his followers were, literally, quite the opposite. Asbury observed that "in the course of years the misery and congestion of tenement life took their toll, and police and prison records show that the average gang member of the time of the Gophers, the Eastmans, and the Five Pointers was not more than five feet and three inches tall, and weighed between 120 and 135 pounds".

These lightweights further compounded the effects of malnutrition and

2. Ellison also ran a saloon that catered to homosexuals, nicknamed Paresis Hall after the medical effects of syphilis.

poor housing by their ready appetite for alcohol and other stimulants, and the sheer danger of their chosen profession. With violence as their major motivating principle, they were more than likely to be knifed, shot, or beaten to death before they attained majority. Indeed, this actuarial probability meant that many were determined to experience what Luc Sante calls "the whole adult order of high and low sensations" during their second decade. By the time they were in their twenties, they were dead, in prison, or all used up.

Riis captured this intensity in his 1890 photograph. His subjects were not static but captured in a brief suspension between one "raid" and another. Their bravado was backed up by their random viciousness. The reformer was careful to note, "lest any reader be led into the error of supposing them to have been harmless young fellows", that no more than half an hour after their encounter three members of the Montgomery Guards were arrested for a violent robbery on an elderly Jewish pedlar. They had tried to saw his head off, "just for fun. The sheeny cum along an' the saw was there, so we socked it to him."

Coming from districts like Poverty Row, a tenement block on West 28th Street, youths like the Montgomery Guards had little chance but to band together to survive, and, once banded, to reproduce the might-is-right ethic that was their social reality. They saw the middle-aged man's approach as a way to reinforce their group identity as a source of pride rather than shame. They hoped that, unlike the brutality of the police mug shot that would be their only other encounter with a camera, Riis's photo would convince the world that they were big men rather than pint-sized, homicidal thugs.

Their heartless bravado, however, reinforced the urgency of the reformers' polemic. In 1893, the historian Frederick Jackson Turner argued in an influential address called "The Significance of the Frontier in America's History" that the continent's wild spaces had been finally tamed. The western migration for land and growth that had fuelled so much of the continent's prosperity during the nineteenth century had reached its limit. There was hardly any more free land, and, after the failure of the Sioux "Ghost Dance" rebellion in the winter of 1890, almost no more American Indians outside their new reservations.

The wild frontier spirit had found its new home in the metropolitan wastes, and, without a socially profitable outlet, had turned malignant. It was as though, just as they finally lost the continent that had been theirs for thousands and thousands of years, the Indians entered the spirits of the savage street children. "A Growler Gang in Session" revealed the uncomfortable truth: the continent held a new set of natives that needed taming. The young gangsters were coming out of the shadows: thousands upon thousands of potential Jesse Pomeroys blinking in the unaccustomed light.

. . .

By the turn of the century, juvenile delinquency had come to international attention as a serious social problem. In *Juvenile Offenders,* published during 1898, the criminologist W. Douglas Morrison observed that "whether we look at home or abroad, whether we consult the criminal returns of the Old World or the New, we invariably find juvenile criminality exhibiting a distinct tendency to increase. It is a problem which is not confined to any single community: it is confronting the whole family of nations; it is arising out of conditions which are common to civilization."

In Britain, youth crime became a national issue as the children of the urban working class elbowed their way into public awareness. As one 1898 newspaper report ran, "No one can have read the London, Liverpool, Birmingham, Manchester and Leeds papers and not know that the young street ruffian and prowler with his heavy belt, treacherous knife and dangerous pistol is amongst us. The question for every man who cares for streets that are safe after dark, decent when dark, not disgraced by filthy shouts and brutal deeds, is what is to be done with this new development of the city boy and the slum denizen?"

However, this was not yet the result of American-style lawlessness but one by-product of the long, slow, and partial march of imperial prosperity. Although one-third of the population existed beneath the poverty line, for the upper working class, things were getting better—with improved housing and diet, more leisure facilities (soccer, holiday resorts, the music hall), and the increased production of consumer items for the new mass market. The growing visibility and increased freedoms of urban youth challenged an anxious bourgeoisie who were determined to see their vision of society prevail.

Rebellious urban youth had been a problem from the mid-nineteenth century. After the garrotting scare of the early 1860s, there were regular press accounts of assaults, bank holiday carnivals, and gang brawls during the 1870s and 1880s. These "outbreaks of rowdyism", as the critic Matthew Arnold called them, "tend to become less and less of trifles, to become more frequent rather than less frequent", threatening "the profound order of settled order and security". Reform had kept pace with this curve, with the institution in the 1850s of separate reformatories and industrial schools for offenders under sixteen.

Education was the most important concern of adults during the 1870s and 1880s as far as youth was concerned. For many children, the new state schools' insistence on religious instruction, compulsory sport, and corporal punishment turned attendance into a battleground. The 1880 Education Act was particularly unpopular because it held children in until the age of eleven: the principal financial burden would now be placed on the older youths who were often the family's principal, if not only, means of support.

Attendance under the new act began well: about 60 per cent during the 1880s. However, by the next decade truancy was the second most common offence committed by juveniles, as family survival came before education. The profusion of unskilled jobs for the fourteen- to eighteen-year-old age group affirmed their economic importance: porters, domestic servants, errand boys, street sellers. To a limited extent, this gave independence and money in the pocket, and at the same time, new consumer products were targeted at the young wage earners: clothes, entertainment, magazines, and comics.

Compulsory school attendance resulted in an increasing pool of literate children, and a cross-class youth reading market grew accordingly. This had long been a battleground between "penny dreadfuls", with their stories of rogues, murderers, vagabonds, and American Indians, and more improving products like the *Boy's Own Paper* (1879), published by the Religious Tract Society. Following on from the success of the irreverent *Ally Sloper's Half Holiday* (1884), a new breed of visual comics like *Comic Cuts* and *Chips* targeted the literate and "subliterate" alike.

These two weeklies featured jokes, social observation, sundry vagabonds, and a high standard of illustration. Their combined circulation reached half a million in 1890, prompting a flood of imitators. In 1893, the first issue of *Larks* featured a front-page story about the Balls Pond Banditti, whose logo included a noose, a mask, and a stake: in six steps, the narrative followed "the enrolment of recruits", "the oath of allegiance", and "the council of war". These tough, foul-mouthed teenage gang members both reflected and inverted their militaristic society: their war was not against a foreign power but adult authority.

These stories, while shocking to many parents, found a ready market because they reflected their adolescent readers' preferred activity: taking to the streets, ganging together, and annoying adults. What to its participants was "larking about", the group experience that sometimes, out of boredom, desperation, or mutual encouragement, tipped into petty vandalism and worse, was to many bourgeois adults the breakdown of the "strong feudal habits of subordination and deference". Their children thought otherwise.

A new type of inner urban gang emerged. In a notorious 1890 incident, the "scuttlers" of Manchester held a free fight involving over five hundred youths.

"AT SEVENTEEN, A FULLY FLEDGED HOOLIGAN",
FROM THE *DAILY GRAPHIC* NEWSPAPER

The term originally came from Lancashire, where "scuttling" denoted the territorial fights enthusiastically held by neighbourhood gangs. During the 1890s, it came to denote a new national youth style, with its own dress and bloodcurdling terminology, that travelled from Manchester (the Forty Row, the Bengal Tiger), to Birmingham (the Peaky Blinders), to Liverpool (the High Rip), and East London (the Monkey's Parade and the Bowry Boys).

According to contemporary reports, the "professional scuttler" wore "a puncher's cap", "narrow-go-wides" trousers, narrow-toed brass-tipped clogs, and heavy customized belts with designs, picked out in metal pins, that included serpents, stars, and pierced hearts. The "boy expert" Charles Russell observed that the Mancunian variant wore "a loose white scarf", with hair "well plastered down upon his forehead", "a peaked cap rather over one eye", and trousers "cut—like a sailor's—with 'bell bottoms'". His girlfriend "commonly wore clogs and shawl and a skirt with vertical stripes".

Observers like Russell might have sought to place the scuttler within the tradition of youthful high spirits, but press reports from the period tell a darker story. In 1892 there was a sensational murder case in Manchester featuring three sixteen-year-old members of the Lime Street gang, who "dosed" a rival gang member with a knife in the back. The killer, William Willan, was led away barefooted from the court, screaming, "Oh, master, don't, have mercy on

me. I'm only sixteen, I'm dying." Violence was also racially directed: in one famous 1897 case, an Armenian immigrant was murdered by a South London
gang.

During August 1898, these disturbances exploded into a national scandal.
It was an unusually hot summer: as *The Times* editorialized, "Does the great
heat fire the blood of the London rough or street arab, with an effect analogous
to that of a southern climate upon the hot-blooded Italian or Provençal?" The
August bank holiday celebrations resulted in a wave of arrests in the capital for
public order offences: drunkenness, fighting, street robberies, and assaults on
the police. Finding their traditional epithets inadequate, the press introduced
a new name: the hooligan.[3]

With its pejorative Irish associations, this offered a useful shorthand that
defined an urgent social problem. Every gang disturbance that summer was
marked by this new term, whether it be the Lion Boys and the Pistol Gang
from Clerkenwell, the Drury Lane Boys, or the Fulham Boys. The participants
themselves readily assumed the press's estimation of their activities. In one
widely publicized incident, members of the Somers Town Boys overturned an
ice-cream barrow belonging to an Italian vendor and assaulted the police. As
they ran away, they were heard to shout, "Look out for the Hooligan gang."

For the first time, English newspapers made an explicit link between dress
and delinquency. The *Daily Graphic* took detailed notes of one Mohicaned defendant during the summer of 1898: "His hair had been clipped as closely as
possible to the scalp, with the exception of a small patch on the crown of the
head, which was pulled down over the forehead to form a fringe." Shortly afterwards, the same paper dissected the hooligan uniform: "All of them have a
peculiar muffler twisted around the neck, a cap set rakishly forward, well over
the eyes, and trousers very tight at the knee and very loose at the foot."

In his 1899 novel, *The Hooligan Nights,* Clarence Rook marked out his hero,
the seventeen-year-old Alf, as "prepared for conflict" by his dress. In this new
type, dandyism coexisted with violence: "Round his throat he wore the blue

3. The exact origin of the term is shrouded in mystery. Writing in 1899, Clarence Rook isolated a
particular individual, Patrick Hooligan, as the "Buddha" or "Mahomet" of this "cult", and gave a
brief biographical sketch of a Lambeth bouncer who killed a policeman and subsequently died in
prison: "There is little that is remarkable in this career. But the man must have had a forceful personality, a picturesqueness, a fascination, which elevated him into a type . . . anyhow, though his
individuality may be obscured by legend, he lived, and died, and left a great tradition behind him."
It seems fair to regard this as more mythmaking than autobiography. In his survey of the term's
origin, Geoffrey Pearson cites various possibilities: a corruption of the American "hoodlum"; two
brothers called Hoolehan who were prizefighters; an adaptation from the name of a swindler—
Mr Edward Hooley—who was in the headlines at the same time.

neckerchief, spotted with white, which my memory will always support him; beneath that a light jersey." The "strong leathern belt" of the scuttler was not his only weapon: "Diving into his breast pocket, and glancing cautiously round, he drew out a handy looking chopper which he poised for a moment, as though reassuring himself of its balance."

Rook delineated a new urban type that did not accord with the thuggish brute of popular imagination. Alf "stands 5 foot 7 inches. He is light, active and muscular. His face is by no means brutal; it is intelligent, and gives evidence of a highly-strung nature. The eyes are his most remarkable feature. They seem to look all around his head, like the eyes of a bird; when he is angry they gleam with a fury that is almost demoniacal." Dealing "from infancy in realities", Alf was a hardheaded, elusive, chameleonlike young man perfectly adapted to the exigencies of contemporary metropolitan life.

Published within months of the 1898 panic, Rook's account of this young South Londoner "who held by the Hooligan tradition" was unusually balanced. His purpose was to offer "a photograph of the young man who walks to and fro in your midst, ready to pick your pocket, rifle your house, and even bash you in a dark corner if it is made worth his while". To those who complained that he was presenting crime in "alluring colours", he offered the defence of reportage: "I do not commend the ways of my young friend, or even apologize for them. I simply set him before you as a fact that must be dealt with."

From their point of view, the hooligans and the scuttlers were attempting to become masters of their own destiny. Ganging together and involving themselves in territorial disputes was a way of asserting themselves, of seeing a bit of excitement, and of transcending a dead-end way of life. However, not all adults were as understanding as Alf's amanuensis. Having been demonized by the press, the scuttlers and the hooligans received condign punishment in the years to come. Once caught, they appeared, as one observer noted, "in droves before the courts, often to receive savage sentences".

The hooligan flared in the press in the late 1890s as a threat to society, but this was a type that reflected the values of its rulers through a barely distorted prism. Clarence Rook's young hero beat up his girl and thought that foreigners were "a class of person" to be held in "great contempt". In a direct echo of Henry Newbolt's public school exhortation, Alf also felt that the policeman, although he might be the natural enemy, "plays the game, and is entitled to be treated accordingly". As he concluded: "You should not kill him, so long as he plays the game, and the game has not lives for stakes."

However, the hooligan scandal gave extra urgency to the calls for the reform of Britain's policy for delinquent youth. General Booth's Salvationist doctrine, which suggested mass shipments out of the slums into the colonies, was not a viable option. By the end of the century this was a problem so pressing that even the fictional Alf was canvassed for his expert opinion. He advised catching "the criminal young": "lift him clean out of his surroundings and teach him a trade. Make him a sailor, a soldier, teach him carpentry, bricklaying, anything that will give him regular employment and regular pay."

* * *

Two years after the hooligan summer, another type of highly visible young villain assumed a national stage. During December 1900, a journalist named Henry Fourquier sarcastically announced in *Le Matin* that Paris was lucky enough to have a tribe of Apaches who appeared to have swapped the Rocky Mountains for a particularly insalubrious district of the capital. He defined them as semi-nomadic youngsters without any obvious parental influence who were helping to muster what the police called an army of criminals.

The Apaches first made the press during the summer as the latest in a number of inner urban gangs with lurid names like Les Coeurs d'Acier (Hearts of Steel), Les Aristos, and Les Riffaudes. The origin of the name was obscure, but according to the crime historian Claude Dubois, it was the inevitable product of a French fascination with American Indians and American culture that had begun with James Fenimore Cooper's 1826 novel *The Last of the Mohicans*. By the 1860s, the term "Peaux-Rouges" (redskins) was used to describe the more visible young denizens of the Parisian underworld.

It was possible that the term "Apache" was a punning play on *Paris*, their city of origin, but it was their extravagant dress that made Apaches stand out. This consisted of a black jacket with a coloured shirt underneath, sometimes worn with a foulard scarf. The most striking element of their garb was their "tummy-ache" pants. These were roughly made felt trousers with watch pockets that were baggy enough to allow the toughs to bunch them from the pockets as if they all had serious stomach ailments. The whole ensemble was topped off with a flat cap, tattoos, and a sarcastic air of bourgeois hauteur.

Until the winter of 1901, the Apache was a local phenomenon. However, the sensational trial of Joseph Pleigneur, a.k.a. Manda, for the stabbing of Dominique Leca helped to broadcast the type to a wider public. It was not an edifying tale: Manda and Leca were both Parisian pimps, and the fight had occurred over a young prostitute, Amelie Helie, also known as Casque d'Or (Head of Gold), who had been both girlfriend and employee to both men. The Parisian press went to town over the affair, and even though the Apaches had not been directly involved, they got roped into this underworld scandal.

During the first few months of 1902, these inner urban savages were rarely out of *Le Matin* and *Le Journal,* dailies with circulations of over a million. The term "Paris Apache" came to serve for all youth misdeeds. Apache parodies sprang up in the clubs of Montmartre, speaking pidgin Indian talk: "Casque à Manda casqua; plaqua Leca, l'apache." By the time the trial of Manda began in late May, the whole affair had become such a circus that Amelie Helie burst out in court, "Les Apaches! Les Mohicans! Casque d'Or! Tout ça c'est des inventions des journalistes. Entre nous, on s'appelle les copains!"[4]

Like the hooligans, the Apaches were essentially a media creation that amplified the criminal activities of a small section of French youth into a generalized climate of fear. However, the furore had an unintended result. While both Manda and Leca were packed off to the French penal colonies in Guyana—never to return—the style with which they had been associated began to spread out of the inner city into the suburbs, from the disenfranchised urban poor to the disaffected young worker. What the press had seen as a juicy scandal, the disaffected young saw as a rallying call.

In her vivid reconstruction, Michelle Perrot describes the Apache as "a young man, eighteen to twenty years old, who lives in the city with a group. He is a young worker from the urban, mainly Parisian peripheries; his gang or group is named for his neighbourhood, and he is in conflict with his family. He rejects salaried work and his parents' proletarian situation, as well as being 'down and out'." Factories and poverty are his nightmare; he has unfulfilled desires for consumption. He likes to wander, to stroll the large boulevards; an outsider, hailing from the suburbs, he wants to be in the heart of the city.

He is well dressed in a silk scarf and a cap, and most important, well shod. An airy elegance causes him to be labelled effeminate by the workers from the city's outskirts. He is always ready to hop into an automobile, a car being the supreme ambition. The Apache dreams of outings, friends, and love. He likes dancing and girls. In Apache gangs, the status of women is ambiguous, both free—they'll gladly switch men if they are no longer satisfied—and subjugated. The men fight for the women, the women sell themselves for the men—who act partly as pimps.

Money counts, but not money alone. Attraction plays a large part in the formation of couples. The Apache is sentimental, a dandy who knows the ropes, has a sense of honour, and a taste for distinction. He doesn't resign himself to anything. He wants to see his name in the papers. An instinctual anarchist, he

4. "Apaches! Mohicans! Golden Head! All of that is the invention of journalists. We call ourselves mates."

considers theft to be fair restitution and practices "individual recovery" on the bourgeois, or "suckers" who fall into his hands. Spending time in the prison of Fresnes, the great Parisian penitentiary that was inaugurated in 1898, is practically a rite of initiation.

Like the hooligan scandal, the arrival of the Apache was used by the advocates of law and order to counter what they called a "crisis in punishment". Embodying a frightening rise in juvenile delinquency, these *voyous* could only be dealt with by whipping and other forms of corporal punishment. They were even invoked to prevent the abolition of the death penalty in France. During the decade after the Casque d'Or affair, the Apache became less attached to a particular type but became a catchall word—like hooligan over the Channel— to denote any kind of ruffian or petty criminal.

While it was designed to raise awareness of a social problem and, therefore, to make solutions possible, the publicity surrounding youth crime in Britain, America, and Europe in the last decade of the nineteenth century had an ambiguous effect. From the reporters' point of view, delinquency was a disturbing new phenomenon that brought savagery, if not actual war, right into the heart of the community. Depending on which side of the fence you stood, the solution was either the improvement of inner urban conditions or a swift dispatch into the army, or, even better, the darkest colonial corners.

CHAPTER 4

"A Sudden Vision of Heaven"

L. Frank Baum and the Dreamland of Oz

• • •

A daytime thought may very well play the part of entrepreneur for a dream; but the entrepreneur, who, as people say, has the idea and the initiative to carry it out, can do nothing without capital; he needs a capitalist who can afford the outlay, and the capitalist who provides the physical outlay for the dream is invariably and indisputably, whatever may be the thoughts of the previous day, a wish from the unconscious.

—Sigmund Freud, *The Interpretation of Dreams* (1900)

ANNA LAUGHLIN AS DOROTHY IN THE MUSICAL
EXTRAVAGANZA *THE WIZARD OF OZ*, 1902

DURING THE SUMMER of 1893, Helen Keller visited the World's Columbian Exposition, the huge fair held on the outskirts of Chicago to celebrate the four hundredth anniversary of America's discovery. She recalled "with unmixed delight those days when a thousand childish fancies became beautiful realities. Every day in imagination I made a trip around the world, and I saw many wonders from the uttermost parts of the earth—marvels of invention, treasures of industry and skill and all the activities of human life."

In Gilded Age America, youth was inextricably intertwined with fantasy, fancy, and commercialized dreamscapes. Helen Keller embodied this connection to a heightened degree: with no hearing, no voice, and no sight, she was locked within her senses and forced to rely, to a considerable degree, on her imagination. By the 1890s, thanks to her courageous surmounting of these adversities, she had become one of America's best-known young people: she was granted an audience with the president and was befriended by Dr Alexander Graham Bell, the inventor of the telephone.

This visit to the Expo was a highlight of her life. Taking in the "glories of the Fair through her fingertips", Keller was transported: "It was a sort of tangible kaleidoscope, this white city of the West. Everything fascinated me, especially the French bronzes. They were so lifelike I thought they were angel visions which the artist had caught and bound in earthly forms." Her rapture was echoed by other young visitors, who were dazzled by the exhibits and the concessions selling souvenirs, popcorn, hamburgers, and soda. For them "it was like getting a sudden vision of heaven".

With 50,000 exhibitors from fifty countries, the size and scope of the Chicago Expo was unprecedented. Between the beginning of May and the end of October 1893, the site was visited by one-quarter of the then total population of the United States. As no other event had done before, it offered a complete snapshot of a continent at its moment of self-definition. This was, above all, the international launch of America, its industry, its culture, and its perception as a way of life to rival Europe. It was, according to the traveller and diarist Henry Adams, "the first expression of American thought as a unity".

With its sparkling white Beaux-Arts architecture and massive scale, the 633-acre Jackson Park site was a staged illusion that had the power to transform reality through sheer force of will. For some Europeans, it had the quality of a hallucination: a German visitor noted that he was afraid to close his eyes because all would "disappear as if in a dream". Most Americans shared this sense of wonder. As Henry Adams remembered, "Here was a breach of continuity—a rupture in historical sequence! Was it real, or only apparent?"

After the 1893 Expo, America would not only be defined by the incredible fertility of its commercial and technological prowess, but also by its ability to create tangible dreams out of thin air. A youthful sense of innocence was an integral part of this showman's trick; indeed, it was the very element that gave it the vital ingredient of sincerity. It also keyed into America's own self-definition as a young country. Within a continent that would be defined by its appetite for pleasure, the intensity of youth was elevated into a national principle.

■　■　■

Among the 27 million Expo visitors was a thirty-seven-year-old travelling sales-man. By 1893, L. Frank Baum had already been through several careers as a playwright, a store owner, and a newspaper editor. Two years previously, he had moved with his wife and four children from the South Dakota wilderness to Chicago. Once the White City was open, Baum visited the site several times. With his highly developed admiration for the fantastic and the childlike, he was dazzled by this walled city where "everyone seemed happy and contented and prosperous".

At the same time, a young illustrator named W. W. Denslow was busy cap-turing the wonder of the Expo: "It is literally stunning, the immensity of the thing," he wrote in his diary. According to Michael Hearn, "Denslow spent nearly every day of the exposition at the White City, sketching the sights and characters for the *Chicago Herald*." Denslow was also fascinated by the artifi-cial, eclectic, and transient nature of the site's apparently monumental build-ings: "My first thoughts were, knowing that they are only intended for short use of six months, was what a magnificent ruin they must make when all is finished."

Both men filed these impressions away for future use. With his interest in the holistic creed of Theosophy, Baum was well aware of "the innate longing in our natures to unravel the mysterious; to seek for some explanation, how-ever fictitious, of the unexplainable in nature and our daily existence". As the decade wore on, he found a new vocation as an author: after the publication of *Mother Goose in Prose* in 1897, he decided to write a new kind of children's story that would also attempt to capture America at a crux moment in its history.

In November 1899, the team behind the year's most successful children's book, *Father Goose,* presented their next project to publisher George M. Hill. *The Emerald City* was to be illustrated by Denslow and written by Baum. Pub-lished the next August as *The Wonderful Wizard of Oz*, the book featured twenty-four colour plates and over one hundred illustrations within an arresting green and red cover. It sold out its first printing within two weeks and became the bestselling children's book of the 1900 Christmas season.

Oz was designed as a break with tradition. Baum wrote in his introduction, "Modern education includes morality; therefore the modern child seeks only entertainment in its wonder-tales and and gladly dispenses with all disagreeable incident. Having this thought in mind, the story of 'The Wonderful Wizard of Oz' was written solely to pleasure children of today. It aspires to being a modern fairy-tale, in which the wonderment and joy are retained, and the heartaches and nightmares are left out." This was an American story, full of "exciting adventures", "unexpected difficulties", and "marvelous escapes".

In his aim to overcome "the old-time fairy tale", Baum opened and closed his story within a recognizable late-nineteenth-century America: the "great gray prairie" of Kansas in the grip of agricultural depression. Dorothy begins the book as an orphan, living with her aunt and uncle; her dog Toto is the one light in her life. Caught up in a twister, she is "suddenly whisked away from her own country and set down in the midst of a strange land". Oz is fantastic, saturated in colour, full of tiny people, anthropomorphic beasts, and all-powerful witches: the plot centres around acts of magic and transformation.

This imaginary land, however, was rooted in American actuality. Just as the grey prairie of Kansas was taken from Baum's hardscrabbling life in South Dakota, the Emerald City that gave the book its first title was inspired by the instant White City of the 1893 Expo. Denslow had been particularly struck by its fantastic architecture, and the original editions of Oz contained a chapter-head illustration of emerald-topped minarets and domes, with the only entrance in the shape of an emerald-eyed face, as well as a long-shot view of the city's domed and towered skyline.

This connection was reinforced by Baum's description of the city with its guards, bustling shops selling "green candy and green pop-corn", and technologically driven comfort. Here illusion became perception: as the Wizard finally admitted, "Just to amuse myself, and keep the good people busy, I ordered them to build this city, and my palace: they did it all willingly and well. Then I thought, as the country was so green and beautiful, I would call it the Emerald City, and to make the name fit better I put green spectacles on all the people, so that everything they saw was green."

Immediately enthralling to children, The Wonderful Wizard of Oz also appealed to adults as a work of psychological depth. Published within months of Sigmund Freud's The Interpretation of Dreams, Baum's narrative was book-ended by powerful evocations of flying and falling: an archetypal dream state within which, according to Freud, "the pleasurable feelings attached to these experiences are transformed into anxiety". Despite Baum's avowed intent to leave out the musty nightmares of European folk tales, Oz was full of trickery, dismemberment, and pervasive fear.

Freud believed that dreams were the product of the conflict between unconscious forces—primitive urges of a sexual or destructive nature—and the conscious controls demanded by civilization. "Since our daytime thinking produces psychical denials of various sorts—judgements, inferences, denials, expectations, intentions and so on—why should it during the night be obliged to restrict itself to the production of wishes alone? Are there not, on the contrary, numerous dreams which show us psychical acts of other kinds—worries for instance—transformed into dream-shape?"

Dreams were, therefore, not just random fantasies but psychic clues into what was repressed by modern civilization. "What once dominated waking life, while the mind was still young and incompetent, seems now to have been banished into the night—just as the primitive weapons, the bows and arrows, that have been abandoned by adult men, turn up once more in the nursery." The keyword, however, was "seems". The sheer incidence of the various pathologies discussed by Freud revealed that this atavism was far from being extirpated: indeed, it threatened to burst out at any moment.

"The unconscious is the true psychical reality," Freud wrote in 1900. His conclusion would have many different applications. Both *The Wonderful Wizard of Oz* and *The Interpretation of Dreams* were published at the moment when American business life was actively seeking to give unconscious drives and visions physical, indeed commodified, form. This was to serve the new economic and social order of materialistic emulation that the Chicago sociologist Thorstein Veblen, in his 1899 polemic *The Theory of the Leisure Class,* called "conspicuous consumption".

. . .

During the late nineteenth century, the public appetite for the printed word rapidly increased, whether in books, magazines, newspapers, or advertisements. Pictorial and verbal imagery became an integral part of the new urban landscape and a vital part of the new mass psychology. As Gustave Le Bon had warned, "The crowd thinks in images, and the image itself immediately calls up a series of other images, having no logical connection with the first. We can easily conceive this state by thinking of the fantastic succession of ideas to which we are sometimes led by calling up in our minds any fact."

The image had been the very thing excoriated by Puritan teaching, and its mass production marked the decline of America's founding religion and its supplanting by a new, secular pantheon. The 1890s witnessed a profound change of values, summarized by T. J. Jackson Lears and Richard Wightman Fox as "the shift from Protestant salvation in the next world to therapeutic self-realization in this one". Within this new morality, the old ideals of abnegation and transcendence were supplanted by "new ideals of self-fulfillment and immediate gratification".

The old certainties were no longer sufficient. In the drive to materialism, the experiences and desires of the country's internal migrants, fleeing the bleak depression of a collapsed rural economy, and its second-generation immigrants, freed from the static European world of their parents, were of vital importance. The White City of 1893 affirmed that the American genius was in showmanship, spectacle, accumulation, and the instant realization of pleasure: a new kind of imaginative vision elevated into a national principle that would bond all these disparate peoples together.

Fulfilling both economic creed and desperate need, dreams came to define America. Visions became money, given tangible form in theme parks, kinetoscopes, tabloids, bestselling books, sheet music, and the cornucopia of consumer goods to be found in department stores or mail-order catalogues. All these new products offered an immediate step outside the exigencies of everyday reality, a consolation for lost freedoms and a celebration of the metropolitan lifestyle. Salvation was to be found through consumption: you became what you bought. You bought your dreams.

Thanks to the great showman/trickster P. T. Barnum, making the product irresistible had already become established as a particular American talent. At the turn of the century, however, advertisers began to work with new film and print technology and the new psychology to go further—into the shaping of conscious and unconscious desires. Underlying this ethos was an attitude to identity that reflected the experience of many Americans, cut off from the past: that identity was not simple and fixed, but fluid and socially constructed—a personal as well as a national becoming.

From a Victorian morality that valued prudence and caution in times of scarcity came a luxuriant, therapeutic ethos that extolled the new abundance of objects. Americans already consumed huge quantities of patent medicines, which proclaimed themselves as tonics for every malady under the sun: "all nervous disorders, bilious complaints, loss of appetite and general debility." Snake oil and American Indian lore were only the rawer version of more mainstream advertising, which from the 1890s on promoted its products in terms of "vim and bounce" to a country obsessed by health and vitality.

Predicated on future wealth rather than scarcity, this new vitalism promised fresh energy in fluid identity, with self-development and self-fulfilment as its ultimate goal, and the intensity of the moment as its keynote. This accorded with the forging of an authentically new American perception in compressed, futuristic urban environments like the Loop, the business district of Chicago.[1] Whereas time for Europeans was seen in a sequence of events, with the present following the past, for more and more Americans time represented a total instantaneity, an infinitely prolongable NOW!

Within these man-made vortices, the young, with their superior cerebral cortices and greater physical strength, would ultimately prevail. Indeed, a major part of what the French philosopher Henri Bergson called this *élan vital* was the attraction of youth. If fitness and health were desirable to American society, then youth, which naturally embodies these qualities, became an attractive ideal to all ages. By the 1900s, advertisers were using upper-middle-class university students to promote fashion garments and sporting goods, in the aspirational ethos that Veblen had so well defined as "pecuniary emulation".

Women played an important part in this new, inner-directed ethos. With the demarcation of the home as "the woman's sphere", most decisions about consumption were left in the hands of the house's "sovereign mistress". The spread of white-collar employment offered freedoms for women that were as yet inconceivable in Europe. Advertisers began to use young, attractive females to sell cosmetics, clothes, and gas stoves. In a turn-of-the-century Quaker Oats campaign, the drawing of a strapping young woman was accompanied by the tagline "It puts off Old Age by nourishing the entire system".

■ ■ ■

An important part of America's vitalist dream economy was the burgeoning music industry. After the unprecedented 1892 success of Charles K. Harris's million-seller "After the Ball", Tin Pan Alley began to expand rapidly: in 1900, two billion copies of sheet music were sold. Popular song became part of America's new national identity. Within this demotic style, actual musical competence was unimportant in the face of intense emotional expression and

---

1. See the 1891 evocation of the Loop by the American writer Charles King: "Collision, shocks, wild plunges for hats that go skimming along the trampling feet; crash in the street, locking wheels, cracking whips, plunging horses, declamatory policemen, blaspheming drivers, slang, billingsgate, uproar, clatter, ear-piercing screams . . . Clang lang, lang. 'Who you shovin'?' Clang lang. Bang, bang, bang. Yells. Shouts. Furious clamour of gongs. Rush, uproar. Hi! hi there ! Look out! LOOK OUT! Bang. Bang. Clang. OUT OF THE WAY! Rush-scurry." This reads like a futurist score from twenty years later.

rhythmic excitement. Like advertising itself, America's popular songs fitted the country's self-definition as an "assertive, pugnacious democracy".

The popular song itself was aggressively advertised from its very inception: Charles K. Harris personally paid to have "After the Ball" inserted into the hit show *A Trip to Chinatown*. In a booklet called *How to Write a Popular Song*, he advised his readers to "look at newspapers for your story-line", to "acquaint yourself with the style in vogue", and to "know the copyright laws". Staffed by recent immigrants and the children of the lower middle class, the popular music industry readily struck a chord with its core audience, being unafraid of raw emotion, sentimentality, and heart-wrenching scenarios.

However, for many young Americans, lachrymose weepies like "After the Ball" did not fit the bill. They wanted something that better accentuated their sizzling synapses, and they began to find it in the new music that was all around them, even if it was still ignored by the music industry. In *Maggie*, Stephen Crane's heroine and her gangster lover enter a downtown saloon where an "orchestra played negro melodies and a versatile drummer pounded, whacked, clattered and scratched on a dozen machines to make noise". The drifting sound of the music "made the girl dream".

Popular music provided one way that blacks could begin to enter American society. Despite the efforts of politicians like Booker T. Washington, who was invited to the White House by Theodore Roosevelt in 1901, life for most Negroes was grim. The lynching statistics—over one hundred a year during the 1890s—were only the tip of the iceberg. "Most had no future nor hope of acquiring any," writes Louis Armstrong's biographer James Lincoln Collier. "They could look forward to nothing but work, poverty, disease and death. A philosophy of *carpe diem* [was] the only sensible position in such circumstances."

A hard core concentrated on pleasure, on the heightened sensations of the moment, in the red-light areas to be found in cities all over America: Chicago, St Louis, Kansas, New Orleans. During the last quarter of the nineteenth century, the spread of these districts provided regular employment for the large pool of travelling musicians. Playing in the saloons and clubs became a viable rite of passage for many young black men and women.[2] The wider American public's taste for Negro music had already been whetted by the popularity of minstrelsy, and by the late 1890s, it was ready for something less ersatz.

During 1898, ragtime exploded as a national craze. A type of music that joined the ragged rhythms of the honky-tonks with the two-step pulse of the classic John Philip Sousa march, it came to take in a lifestyle of dancing (the

[2] See the memoirs of Louis Armstrong and Jelly Roll Morton.

novelty step called the cakewalk), fashions, and even language. As one song observed, "Got ragtime habits and I talk that way / I sleep in ragtime and I rag all day / Got ragtime troubles with my ragtime wife / I'm certainly living a rag-time life." Playing off the old against the new in two-handed syncopation, it captured the ebullient turmoil of a continent in transition.

Ragtime had been heard at the 1893 Expo: not in the walled city, but in the dives surrounding the site. The first rag publication by a white bandleader in January 1897 was followed by more rags by black musicians. Of these, Scott Joplin's 1899 "Maple Leaf Rag" was the best and the most popular. With its contrasting rhythms and hypnotic melodies, ragtime quickly crossed the boundaries of class and race. A snapshot from 1903 had Joplin playing live at a white party, where the young crowd "just loved it and when the party was over . . . asked . . . for his name so they could give a dance and have him play".

However, there was an uneasy trade-off within the exposure of this outcast form to the mainstream. Young white fans responded to the wildness highlighted by the new buzzword, "hot", which denoted sex, glamorous clothes, and above all the sheer intensity of the moment. At the same time an outraged cultural establishment, appalled by the threat of miscegenation, called ragtime a "virulent poison, which, in the form of a malarious epidemic, is finding its way into the homes and brains of the youth to such an extent as to arouse suspicions of their sanity".

The problem was that Americans could not help but take the promises of the Constitution seriously. If this was to be a country that enshrined equality—indeed, if popular music was to be truly of the people—then it should be available to all regardless of creed, nationality, or race. The sheer persuasiveness of the demotic propaganda pumped out by America's popular arts meant that they would become irrevocably charged, to no little degree, with the enfranchising impulse. This would extend not just to Negroes, but to every other group of outsiders, among whom youth would begin to identify themselves.

■ ■ ■

Although it fuelled this surge of popular culture, the American genius for showmanship cloaked urgent social problems. The 1893 Expo was a perfect case in point, a shimmering white city shadowed by its twin, the monolithic black city only a few miles down the lakeshore. By the time of the fair, Chicago had doubled in size within a decade. Although it was the crucible of innovations like the skyscraper, the elevator, and the assembly line, it bore all the scars of unrestricted expansion. With its polluted air and foul stockyard smells, it had overtaken Manhattan in its squalor and its ultra-modernity.

Most of the recent arrivals were immigrants: 78 per cent of the city's population were the children of parents born outside the United States—in Italy,
Ireland, Germany, Eastern Europe. Conditions for most of these new citizens
were grim. The pressures of adaptation from a European past to the city of tomorrow bore down particularly hard on immigrant children. Caught between
two continents, second-generation Americans instinctively itched to break
with what the social worker and writer Jane Addams called "Old World customs" but did not have the parental support to become functioning citizens.

The alienation that existed between the child who had known nothing but
America and the parents who still harked back to the country that they left—
often to the point of barely speaking English—could only increase during puberty. So they went their own way. It was this casting off from all known
moorings that concerned Addams; from the mid-1890s on, she began to record her dealings with the troubled youth of Chicago. "Industrialism has gathered together multitudes of eager young creatures from all quarters of the
earth," she wrote, but there were no facilities to cater to their deeper needs.

One of the first generation of American women to graduate from college,
Addams rejected the then available female career options of medicine, teaching, and missionary work. While in London, she visited Toynbee Hall and took
away its missionary zeal. On her return to the United States, Addams set up
Hull House within a predominantly immigrant neighbourhood in order to
give practical and aesthetic uplift to the women of the district. Although the
settlement's initial focus was cultural, conditions in Chicago soon brought
Addams into direct confrontation with the city's serious social problems.

She found that the perennial problem of pubescent discipline was exacerbated by the fact that the young went to work at the age of fourteen or under.
"In vast regions of the city which are completely dominated by the factory,"
she noted, "it is as if the development of industry had outrun all the educational and social arrangements." The sterility and filth of the work environment curdled the "spontaneous joy" of the young into loneliness, or the
nihilism expressed by Stephen Crane's Jimmy: "After a time his sneer grew so
that it turned its glare upon all things. He became so sharp that he believed in
nothing."

However, their wages gave the working young the freedom to "spend it as
they choose in the midst of vice deliberately disguised as pleasure". Youth was
a "difficult" period everywhere, Addams wrote in the book that collected
her writings on the topic, *The Spirit of Youth and the City Streets*, "but it seems
at times as if a great city almost deliberately increased its perils." Within
the metropolitan sensorium of a continent that was beginning to define itself

through the aptitude for pleasure and its industrial production, the perennial youthful desire for excitement was heightened, if not actively overstimulated.

With its soulless saloons and its huge dance halls that reeked of loneliness, inner-city Chicago offered bright lights in place of real community, exploitation instead of value. "The newly awakened senses are appealed to by all that is gaudy and sensual," Addams wrote, "by the flippant street music, the highly colored theater posters, the trashy love stories, the feathered hats, the cheap heroics of the revolvers displayed in the pawn-shop windows. This fundamental susceptability is thus evoked without a corresponding stir of the higher imagination, and the result is as dangerous as possible."

In some cases, the "perfervid imagination" of the city's young led them into even more dangerous territory. Addams observed that "this same love of excitement, the desire to jump out of the humdrum experience of life, also induces boys to experiment with drinks and drugs to a surprising extent". Cocaine in particular stimulated the "desire to dream and see visions". One user told her that "in his dreams he saw large rooms paved with gold and silver money, the walls papered in greenbacks, and that he took away in buckets all that he could carry".

Drugs were an integral part of American life: the ideal tonics for the citizens of a country that demanded superhuman qualities in its dash for economic growth. The Civil War had introduced the use of morphine on a national basis, while emigrating Chinese had brought opium into the inner cities. Cocaine was then seen as an even poorer high, the preserve of prostitutes, gangsters, and slum children. Offering effects both stimulating and analgesic, hopping them up and making them impervious to pain, it was a drug well suited to their harsh circumstances.[3]

However, dope was not then lashed to a critical generational ideology: rather, it was part of an inner urban culture of deep dissolution that adhered to all-American values as if through a glass darkly. The materialistic visions described by Addams's informant tallied with the artificial paradises invoked by the contemporary folk song "Willie the Weeper". This was a Kubla Khan expressed in New World terms: "Got a ruby-bush, a diamond-mine, / An emerald-tree, a sapphire-vine, / Hundreds of railroads that run for miles, / A thousand dollars worth of coke stacked up in piles."

3. Herbert Asbury notes that a gang called the Hudson Dusters became particular press favourites at the turn of the century. Their fame was directly related to their drug consumption: "While they were never such fighters as the Eastmans, the Five Pointers and the Gophers, they were a rare collection of thugs, and much of their reputation was deserved. Perhaps ninety per cent of the Dusters were cocaine addicts, and when under the influence of the drug were very dangerous, for they were insensible to ordinary punishment, and were possessed of great, if artificial, bravery and ferocity."

Although it attracted much public alarm, this outlaw taste simply echoed America's obsession with patent medicines. During the early 1890s, the cocaine-based soft drink Coca-Cola was promoted as a pick-me-up. At the same time, popular over-the-counter medicines like Ryno's Hay Fever and Catarrh Remedy consisted of nearly 100 per cent pure cocaine. Its unwitting consumers got hooked: "It is ruining our boys," one father wrote to the authorities of the US Bureau of Chemistry. "I have a son that has been using it and have tried for the last year to break him from it, but no use as long as he can get it."

The use of these strong drugs matched the overstimulated environment of the American metropolis, as well as reinforcing the new continent's craving for dreams of any type. At the same time, their overuse further telescoped the lives of young gangsters, already foreshortened by poverty and the danger inherent in their way of life. Cocaine was more troublesome than morphine because its effects were euphoric. Demanding an almost instantaneous replenishment, it turned young criminals into the most avid of consumers at the same time as it jammed them into an eternal present.

This all-consuming concentration on the moment crossed classes and markets. It was the hallmark of the bohemian sensibility that had been inspired by the hell-bent example of Edgar Allan Poe and given an aesthetic boost by Oscar Wilde's controversial year-long tour of America in 1882. The unprecedented 1894 success of George du Maurier's *Trilby*, with its attendant marketing of sausages, ice cream, cigars, and the famous hat, turned bohemianism into a style. It was particularly attractive to young women, who, according to Luc Sante, "derived from it the courage to call themselves artists and bachelor girls, to smoke cigarettes and drink Chianti".

Bohemia showcased a new kind of aristocracy predicated on talent and fame rather than birth. This was the central premise of *Trilby* and Theodore Dreiser's bestselling *Sister Carrie*. In these moralistic novels, however, there was a price to pay for this elevation: the cutting of ties with the environment that nurtured the talent, added to the scars left by years of poverty and struggle. Du Maurier made sure that Trilby, prematurely aged by the hypnosis that made her a star, ended up as surely doomed as Young Werther. She had lived too intensely, had *burned up*.

At the same time, these extreme lifestyles were diluted and promoted for mass consumption within America. "While avant-garde bohemians dramatized the appeal of life in extremis," Jackson Lears observes, the "captains of a nascent 'leisure industry' played to the yearning for intense experience at all social levels. They commodified titillation at cabarets and in amusement parks; they catered to the anxious businessman as well as the bored shop girl;

they assimiliated immigrants and WASPs in a new mass audience. Roller coasters, exotic dancers and hootchy kootchy girls all promised temporary escapes."

There was an undertow to this pleasure-derived ethos that could not be ignored. Intensity might have been youthful and romantic, but it did not make for a long life. The nexus of values between an expanding entertainment industry, the avant-garde, and the dispossessed was full of potential pitfalls. The new media encouraged the short-term thinking, the concentration on the instant, and the fantastic solutions ascribed at the time to children and pubescent youth, at the same time as they excited fundamental human impulses. They promised an alluring but unstable form of mass control.

The new metropolis sucked in thousands upon thousands of people from all over rural America and old Europe. They came fleeing the great grey prairies or worse, in search of a life where they could be freed from the struggle for bare survival. To be a full citizen of these walled environments, however, they not only had to overcome the threat of death by violence or narcosis, but also to collude in the perceptual demands made by the cities' rulers. Having navigated all these temptations and dangers, they found that they lived in a magical world that was nothing less than a conjurer's trick.

All they had to do was take off the emerald glasses, but, as Baum fully understood, the confidence trickster is only successful when he hooks into the dreams and desires of his mark. That's when the fake becomes real. It was no accident that his book was called *The Wonderful Wizard of Oz*. Although his central character was a fraud, he was also the embodiment of this new land, summarizing the American engine of exchange: "In this country, everyone must pay for everything he gets." Indeed with his populist rationale—"I'm just a common man"—the Wizard defined that new capitalist figure: the media magnate.

The twentieth century demanded new myths, and Oz was not only one of the very first, but would be one of the most enduring. Together with *The Interpretation of Dreams,* it stood at a crucial moment in the Western conception of youth. If the new economy of desire had begun to deep-mine the world of the child, then Freud began to open up the hitherto hidden area of infantile sexuality, the drive usually associated with puberty, and the mythic taboo at the heart of the family system. If these fundamental, explosive urges were there to be triggered, then there would be a hitherto unexpected chimera.

Just as the apparent innocence of Oz—defining the childlike sense of wonder that remains part of the American psyche—shaded into complex undercurrents, the onset of a society based on dream commodities had begun to reveal the dark forces that lay underneath. Advertisers might well have sought, as T. J. Jackson Lears notes, "to liberate instinctual life by denying its darker side", but it was impossible to ignore "the towering rages and the insatiable longings in the human subconscious". Appetites, once stimulated, are hard to suppress: once the lid was lifted on Pandora's box, there was no going back.

CHAPTER 5

The American Century

G. Stanley Hall and Adolescence

. . .

Adolescence is a new birth.
—G. Stanley Hall, preface to *Adolescence* (1904)

G. STANLEY HALL, 1890s

WHILE L. FRANK BAUM was preparing the manuscript called *The Emerald City*, the state of Illinois passed a piece of legislation that had profound implications for America's youth. Enacted in July 1899 "to regulate the treatment and control of dependent, neglected and delinquent children", the Juvenile Court Act defined as delinquent "any child under the age of sixteen years" who violated "any law of this State or city or village ordinance" at the same time as it authorized the institution of a separate juvenile court. This was a crucial step in the construction of adolescence as a separate stage of life.

It was fitting that the juvenile court was set up in turn-of-the-century Chicago, not just because of the city's futuristic environment, but because of its vigorous reform movement. The court's institution came after years of lobbying by bodies like Hull House and the Chicago Women's Club. In contrast to the purely punitive approach—which had patently failed to eradicate the problem—the court saw delinquency as the consequence of poor social conditions, a progressive view that countered the deterministic explanations advanced by the criminologists and sociologists of the day.

Chicago's evils played their part as well. Visiting the city during Expo year, the crusading British journalist W. T. Stead thought the forced development of its young a very public scandal. "There is very little reverence for children in Chicago," he observed in 1893. "Messenger boys not more than fourteen years of age, go in and out of the police cells every hour of the night gaining intimacy with the drunken and debased classes, which can hardly be said to tend towards edification." He was amazed that "young children should be introduced so early to the abominations of a great city", and that nobody seemed to care.

This strong taint of corruption helped to focus attention on America's ambiguous legal provisions for its youth. Under civil law, the young were considered to be children until the age of twenty-one, a concept enshrined by the earliest American juvenile reformatory, the New York House of Refuge. However, nineteen- and twenty-year-old delinquents were very difficult to control, and other institutions, such as the New York Juvenile Asylum, began to concentrate on a younger age group. Older youths were thus treated as full adults even though they were still "children" by law.

With juvenile precocity identified as a major problem, the existing age definitions had become inadequate to deal with the complexities of city life. Aiming to protect younger offenders from hardened criminals, the Juvenile Court Act offered a new cut-off point between childhood and adulthood. It also initiated a flexible and preventive approach to the treatment of delinquency. Jesse Pomeroy remained a living, albeit entombed, witness to the principle that condign punishment did not result in reform but in even greater obduracy: during 1899 he made his twentieth and twenty-first attempts to escape.

The court was a great success. During its first year, presiding judge Richard S. Tuthill heard nearly fifteen hundred cases. Of these, the overwhelming number were boys charged with offences like stealing (nearly 45 per cent of the total), "disorderly conduct", and "incorrigibility". This last was a term "apparently coined out of despair" to cover a multitude of everyday urban misdemeanours: "loitering about the streets and using vulgar language", "refusing either to go to work or to school, roaming the street late at night", "keeping bad company, refusing to obey parents, and staying away from home".

Representing only 8 per cent of the caseload, girls were most commonly charged with "immorality", "disorderly conduct", "incorrigibility", and associating with "vicious persons." Most of the young women who appeared before the court were in danger of losing or had already lost their "virtue". Jane Addams was insistent on this topic: "The little girls brought into the juvenile court are usually daughters of those poorest immigrant families living in the worst type of city tenements." She observed that "a surprising number of little girls have become involved in wrongdoing through the men in their own households".

Seventy per cent of the juveniles that passed through the court were the children of immigrants. As a de facto agency of integration, the court made ground-breaking provisions to deal with these new citizens. "Dependent and neglected" children were to be placed either in institutions or in a suitable foster home. Delinquent children could either be sent to the state reformatory or into a foster home, or could remain in their own home "subject to the visitation of the probation officer". The last option was taken up to a surprising degree: Judge Tuthill firmly believed that probation was the best way to deal with the young offender.

In assessing what should happen to each delinquent, the judge required that the court's probation officers take into account three considerations: "the welfare and the interests of the child", "the welfare of the community", and "the intellect and feelings of parents and relatives". This was a remarkably holistic programme that provided for frequent home visits by probation officers at the same time as it aimed to prevent crime before it occurred. "It is the desire of the Court to save the child from neglect and cruelty," Tuthill wrote; "also to save it from the danger of becoming a criminal or dependent."

The court made national news. Although in practice it failed to eradicate the social conditions that bred delinquency, it introduced a progressive approach that elevated the influence of nurture rather than nature on human behaviour. In this, it was out of step with the social scientists of the day, many of whom cleaved to the determinism of Cesare Lombroso and Herbert Spencer. Its success not only spurred on a new generation of sociologists, but also inspired a more accurate definition of that troubled second decade of life. Clearly, calling a young man of sixteen a "child" was no longer adequate.

By the late 1890s, the authorities were seeking actively to corral American youth. Whether it was the wild urban gangs, monomaniacal young murderers, or the sheer incidence of juvenile delinquency, the issue of control had become paramount. At the same time, invested as they were with adult projections for the future, the young had begun to receive an unprecedented level of positive attention. Instead of being sent out to work or allowed to run wild, they were encouraged to stay in school, to delay their entry into adulthood. If they played the game, they would be allowed a circumscribed independence.

However, there was as yet no generally agreed concept to describe this change. During the nineteenth century, puberty had not been thought to form a separate stage of life. Although men attained adulthood by entry into the world of work, the military, or marriage, the time spent in achieving this goal was variable. Young men oscillated between staying at the parental home and living away, as they entered an apprenticeship or further education. This nameless period was recognized as a time of fluctuation, even of "semi-dependence": if it was called anything, it was called "youth".

The definitive term for the elongated hiatus between childhood and adulthood was coined by a genetic psychologist named G. Stanley Hall. During 1898, he was struggling to complete his huge compendium on the second decade of life. He had been collecting data for at least five years, and at a conference held that summer, he gave his first recorded age-related definition of what he called "adolescence". His breakthrough was to realize that, in American and Western society, the intermediate state that Rousseau had both exalted and warned of was not just biologically determined but socially constructed.

"Adolescence is more than puberty," Hall declared, "extending over a period of ten years from twelve to fourteen to twenty-one or twenty-five in girls and boys, respectively, but the culmination is at fifteen or sixteen." Noting the importance of the customs that "savage nations" employed to mark this period, he bemoaned the lack of these rituals within America. The correct transition was all the more important because adolescence was "a period of sex impulse"; it was also "the time of the largest number of arrests for crime in the United States, in England, France and Germany".

Hall proposed nothing less than the creation of a new, generally recognized stage of life that would increase dependency and delay entry into the world of work: "As civilization advances, education broadens. The school years lengthen inevitably as the community tones up its ideals." Any attempt to restrict the time spent in school or college was "an attempt to return to savage conditions, while the ideals are more highly civilized. The estimate of any educational system must be based upon its success in bringing young people through adolescence with [the] greatest perfection of development."

On the face of it, the bearded and middle-aged Hall was an unlikely prophet of youth. He had recently been appointed president of a brand-new American university, Clark, at Worcester, Massachusetts—the culmination of a long academic career. His already rather remote demeanour had not been improved by the accidental asphyxiation of his wife and daughter in the early 1890s. Overcome with guilt and depression, Hall passed through a major crisis at the age of fifty. Suffering with "the early psychic symptoms of old age", he cast around for a new academic enthusiasm.

During the last quarter of the nineteenth century, the dominant trend in American intellectual life had been evolutionary theory. By the 1890s, Darwinism had split into a variety of disciplines, from the deterministic criminology of Cesare Lombroso to the laissez-faire sociology of Herbert Spencer, who believed that, within the survival of the fittest that Darwin had suggested, competition would lead to progress. Any attempt to interfere with that process, like reform, was doomed to failure. The corollary was that the children of the inner cities should be left alone to sink or swim.

Hall had been a favoured pupil of William James, the founding father of American psychology. However, Hall broke with the psychological establishment in the early 1890s. Although austere on the surface, he insisted on the primacy of the feelings that he thought were neglected by James and his acolytes. "The study of soul evolution is just beginning," he wrote in 1894, "but it is becoming already the master-key for every one who is trying to solve the problems of the human will, the emotions and the feelings. The intellect was the beginning and end of the old philosophy. The heart is the beginning of the new."

Searching for another way to integrate evolutionary biology with psychology, Hall fixed on the 1894 book by Henry Drummond, *Ascent of Man*. In this gentler Darwinism, evolution was "the final revelation of the unity of the world": instead of the brutal world of natural selection, the concept of "altruistic Love" was offered, in which the human mother was the highest product of evolution. Drummond also propounded the idea that human beings developed according to the law of recapitulation, which was that "each individual in development recapitulates the form through which the race has evolved".

This accorded with Hall's own visionary tendencies. Adapting Drummond's fusion of evolutionary biology and personal development, he decided that the individual soul was a microcosm of the whole living world, an "echo-chamber" within which the evolution of past generations resounded. The individual psyche was therefore linked to the development of the race. One natural consequence of this was that the correct evolution of each individual had profound implications for their country, indeed for their race as a whole. Incorrect development would result in the death of a civilization.

To implement this new discovery, he returned to the area of research, the Child Study movement, that he had already helped to inaugurate in the mid-1880s. Hall had studied in Germany under the founder of experimental psychology, Wilhelm Wundt, and had sought to apply the techniques of field research to the detailed study of the basic emotional and mental characteristics of child behaviour. Underlying this drive was the belief that, in Hall's own Rousseauesque phrase, "Every child is a little savage": if they were going to evolve correctly, this in-depth research was vital.

Unlike the traditional method of teaching by rote and regimentation, the progressives of the Child Study movement sought to discover what children themselves thought and felt. Using observation and questionnaires, they sought to map a wide range of children's emotions and thought processes: their physical growth, their health, their peer associations, their fear and anger, their art and the nature of their play. Coinciding with the growth of public awareness about education as a whole, the Child Study movement rapidly influenced America's social policy towards its children.

Hall's greatest success with the movement had occurred during the 1893 Expo. Invited to organize one of the many public congresses that marked the event's educational side,[1] he tore up his brief and initiated a new conference on the topic of "Experimental Psychology and Education", during which the entire three days were turned over to Child Study. However, Hall did not rest on his laurels. Ever restless, he announced in 1894 that he was contemplating a whole new field of research, concerning the next stage up the evolutionary scale from childhood, which he defined as adolescence.

In the contemporary elision between childhood and puberty, data on adolescence had already formed part of the Child Study material but had not been explained or identified as something separate. However, the period of dependency formerly associated with the child was on the rise. Increasing numbers

1. It was at another that Frederick Jackson Turner delivered his lecture "The Significance of the Frontier in American History".

of American pubescents were remaining in education, as the number of high schools rose by more than 750 per cent between 1880 and 1900. With a higher percentage of America's young under the control and the observation of teachers, it was possible to expand the Child Study remit upward in age.

Researching puberty accorded with Hall's own enthusiasms. He had been fascinated both by Marie Bashkirtseff's journal—which he called a "precious psychological document"—and by Jesse Pomeroy's motiveless crimes. Further stimulated by his observations of urban gangs, he began to collect material relating to what he called the "teens". It would take ten years for his findings to be published, but in the meantime he travelled throughout America, attending conferences and giving lectures, all the time discussing and refining his understanding of this barely mapped state.

Hall's espousal of adolescence also fitted his own psychology and America's particular stage of development as a new nation. While he was researching his book, he took a holiday and explored the farms where he had lived while growing up. Published in 1899 under the title "Note on Early Memories", his account of the period between his earliest childhood and the onset of puberty at fourteen was full of detailed anecdotal impressions and jottings about the mechanics of memory. For a psychologist, however, he was remarkably opaque about his own feelings during that period.

It was only between the lines that the emotional reality of Hall's adolescence could be detected. A visit to an old graveyard triggered "a depressing sense of loneliness" and "a strange kind of fear". Born into a puritan milieu, with a violent Calvinist father, Hall grew up with a strong sense of his own personal inadequacy and intense sexual guilt. Like Bashkirtseff, he had willed himself out of an untenable situation. He recalled climbing a distant summit while working himself up into a total rage: he vowed "aloud that I would overcome many real obstacles and do and be something in the world".

Immersing himself in the topic of adolescence enabled Hall to revisit and make good an unhappy and unfulfilled period of his own life. Certainly, his passionate identification with the adolescent went beyond the call of duty into wish fulfilment. "Who has made history?" he demanded. "Not the great intellects of the world, but the great hearts—Wesley, Loyola, Buddha, Christ, the great hearts of the world, its prophets. Young men and young women—especially young men as I have learned from my experience of teaching all these years—need first to feel emotion. They must tingle, burn."

As the key element in the new psychology was "the intensity and variety and scope of what we feel", it was not surprising that Hall should turn to the

Bashkirtseff journal for inspiration. As he knew from his own attempts, men who revisited their adolescence wrote "with less abandon" than women. They were "more prone to characterize their public metamorphoses later in life, when they are a little paled, and perhaps feel less need of confessionalism for that reason".[2] Women, on the other hand, surpassed men "in their power to reproduce and describe the great but so often evanescent ebullitions of this age".

What Hall was suggesting was the complete opposite of the rigid masculinity enacted by America's young businessmen and young gangs. He was, however, a contradictory mixture, both visionary and reactionary, and his solution for the excess energy of young men was simple: "Too much can hardly be said in favour of cold baths and swimming at this age." His prescriptions for the education of young girls were informed by his elevation of the mother to the highest stage of evolution. He castigated what he called "the gospel of the feminists": the New Woman's then vigorous agitation for equal rights.

However, his subject inexorably drew him into the future. Hall believed that adolescence was inextricably linked with the rise of a young continent. As he stated in 1898, "We Americans are a mixed race. This makes the period of adolescence in America unique. Where nature is kept pure this period of ferment is accomplished quickly and with little trouble, as among the Jews and the Germans. The period of adolescence is prolonged in America because of mixture of blood, and if we survive the trials and dangers of this period, we will make the grandest men and women the world has ever known."

Born before the holocaust of the Civil War, Hall had witnessed American life accelerate and coalesce into a power such as the world had not yet seen. His country was synonymous with youth: "In the present age of rapid transition and expansion of our race, the future and the ideal must be more dominant than ever before or we are dwarfed as a nation. This is a good age to be young in." Hall began to recast the ringing phrases of the Romantics into a new myth for a new century. "Youth is prophecy," he augured. "The best things have not happened yet, and man is the tadpole of what he is to be."

The new conception of youth was crystallized in 1904, with the eventual publication of *Adolescence*. Hall had announced the project "finished" in 1898, but the lie was given by the description he gave of his methodology. "My intention has been to collect all the available materials and literature," he wrote, "and then to embody in a simple description a composite photograph of the procedure." In fact, the ever-increasing volume of data together with the au-

---

2. Indeed, as Freud was finding in Vienna at the same time, the new psychology was best served by the willingness of women to express, if not indulge, their emotions.

thor's innate prolixity meant that by the time it appeared, the book had assumed monolithic proportions.

A veritable Victorian warehouse of information, *Adolescence* comprised half a million words spread over a two-volume edition of nearly fifteen hundred pages. Its whole tone reflected the multiphrenia that its author ascribed to his subject: "It is the age of sentiment and religion, of rapid fluctuation of mood, and the world seems strange and new." Throughout, Hall the remote, stern educator vied with the romantic visionary still capable, as one of his colleagues attested, of finding boyish delight in the local version of Coney Island.

Today much of the material seems time-locked, but the book still crackles with a barely contained energy that illuminates the pages of barely digested data like sheet lightning: it is a classic of vitalist literature. For all his quirks, Hall was the first to offer a systematic definition of adolescence, and he clearly defined its age: the years between fourteen and twenty-four.[3] *Adolescence* was also one of the first American books to cite Freud approvingly, and indeed, it offered a coherent argument for psychology as the one discipline most suitable for the understanding of this time of "mental and moral inebriation".

Hall thought that "the psychic activities of childhood and youth and of the average common man" were worthy of the highest scientific attention. His explicit linkage of youth as a state to America as a nation made this line of inquiry particularly urgent: "Ephebitis is the term scientists adopt, but we might call it in our country Americanitis, for we are a nation in adolescence." He recognized the youthful concentration of the moment that was coming to define the continent's perception and its industry of dreams: "We hunger for the maximum of life. We want it in all its depth and breadth, now and forever."

His intention was to "collect states of mind", and to Hall, adolescence was above all a volatile condition: "The teens are emotionally unstable and pathic. It is the age of natural inebriation without the need of intoxicants, which made Plato define youth as spiritual drunkenness. It is a natural impulse to experience hot and perfervid psychic states, and is characterized by emotionalism." Alerted by the discovery of the very first youth sexploitation literature, he was quick to note that "sex asserts its mastery in field after field and works its havoc in the form of secret vice, debauch, disease and enfeebled heredity".

Puberty marked the start of this condition: "The dawn of adolescence is marked by a special consciousness of sex." Citing Freud and Breuer's 1895 *Studien über Hysterie*, Hall summarized, "Psychoses and neuroses abound in early adolescent years more than at any other period of life. This causes great

3. Cited by Hall based on an 1898 definition of puberty by the German psychologist Wille, contained in his *Die Psychosen des Pubertsalters*.

emotional strain, which some have described as a kind of repressed insanity."
Concentrating on the extremes of behaviour, he seemed to imply that it was
not possible to establish any norms of behaviour as far as adolescents were
concerned.

Compounding this innate adolescent neurasthenia was the fact that "modern city life, to a degree which is hard to realize, is artificial and unnatural for
youth". Hall took Jacob Riis as his guide: "On the East Side of New York, every
corner has a gang with a program of defiance of law and order, where the
young tough who is a coward alone becomes dangerous when he hunts with
the pack. He is ambitious to get 'pinched' or arrested and to pose as a hero."
American court records showed that adolescence was the peak time of arrests.
Hall concluded that the urban hothouse tended "to ripen everything before its
time".

Reacting against Lombroso, Hall proposed that the increasingly complex
demands of American life made the inherently negative aspects of the adolescent character even worse. As the mass age demanded ever greater social restraints, it made life more difficult for its impetuous and self-absorbed young.
Because they stood out against the grain, they became more visible: "The increase of juvenile crime, so deplored, is not entirely due to city life or growing
youthful depravity, but also to the increasing ethical demands of society."

At the same time Hall reiterated that "these years are the best decade in life.
No age is so responsive to all the best and wisest adult endeavor." His own
prescriptions mixed conservatism with progressive good sense. He favoured
"sympathy, appreciation and respect in dealing with this age", at the same
time as he endorsed the rapidly expanding high school system. He thought
that the school-leaving age should be raised by two years, to sixteen, and that
university undergraduates should be exempted from the exigencies of adult
life: "The student must have the freedom to be lazy."

Most important, he argued for the socially sanctioned prolongation of adolescence. Noting the trend towards "longer and severer apprenticeship and
specialization", he argued for "an ever lengthening probationary period".
Whether primitive or developed, all societies had their rites of passage, their
"objective regimen" to mark the pause between childhood and adulthood, but
in twentieth-century America the increase of this interval would be "another
index of the degree of civilization". Adolescence, indeed, should offer a safe
haven from the insistent demands of industrial society.

Hall recommended that America's institutions should take note of the fact
that "for the complete apprenticeship to life youth needs repose, leisure, art,
legends, romance, idealization, and in a word humanism". These proposi-

tions, redolent of Rousseau's ideal education, slowly infiltrated America's social policy. For *Adolescence* was a surprise hit on its eventual publication: when one of Hall's students visited Brentano's in New York, he was told that the book "was having a remarkable sale for one so high in price".

With a strong academic impact and crossover sales, *Adolescence* accelerated the demand for the widening of educational opportunities and opened up America's eyes to this omnipresent but ill-defined state. At the same time, Hall presented to America a vision of itself as a young country that would be a beacon for the forthcoming century: "The very fact that we think we are young will make the faith in our future curative, and we shall one day attract the youth of the world by our unequalled liberty and opportunity."

PART II

1904–1913

CHAPTER 6

Peter Pan and the Boy Scouts

Imperial British Youth

. . .

What Van Cheele saw on this particular afternoon was, however, something far removed from his ordinary range of experience. On a shelf of smooth stone overhanging a deep pool in the hollow of an oak coppice a boy of about sixteen lay asprawl, drying his wet brown limbs luxuriously in the sun. His wet hair, parted by a recent dive, lay close to his head, and his light-brown eyes, so light there was almost a tigerish gleam in them, were turned towards Van Cheele with a certain lazy watchfulness. It was an unexpected apparition, and Van Cheele found himself in the novel experience of thinking before he spoke. Where on earth could this wild-looking boy hail from?

—Saki, "Gabriel-Ernest" (1909)

"TO DIE WILL BE AN AWFULLY BIG ADVENTURE?"

PETER PAN ON THE ROCK, AN ILLUSTRATION
BY F. D. BEDFORD, 1911

IN THE LAST year of the Second World War, a middle-aged publisher began
to compile his family story. Peter Llewelyn Davies referred to the manuscript
as the *Morgue,* an apt title for a narrative marked by premature death and psychic possession. It was his misfortune not just to share a given name with
the perennially youthful hero of *Peter Pan* but also to be the third of the five
brothers who had inspired "that terrible masterpiece". Peter felt that his soul
had been stolen, and the *Morgue* was a desperate but doomed attempt at
exorcism.[1]

The surviving extracts, however, offer a window into a gilded upper-middle-
class adolescence. To many Britons, the Edwardian era represents the last
golden age, before two cataclysmic world wars and the end of empire: an era
of apparent stability and prelapsarian innocence. Peter Llewelyn Davies's account of the summer of 1908, when he spent a New Forest holiday butterfly
hunting with brother George, appears to bear this out. He recalled "many
happy days with him wandering in the woods and over the commons armed
with net and killing bottle and sandwiches for lunch".

Yet the clouds were already gathering over the eleven-year-old Peter and his
fifteen-year-old brother. In the spring of the previous year, their father, Arthur
Llewelyn Davies, had died from a cancerous tumour in the jaw. Headed by
their mother, Sylvia, the family was being supported by the middle-aged author J. M. Barrie. For the children life went on regardless. Peter remembered
that in 1908 they "lived in the boy world to the exclusion of any other, and
were little troubled by the disappearance of Arthur from our lives or by the
misery which the bereft Sylvia no doubt did everything to hide from us".

A chance meeting in the New Forest revealed that, even in this apparent paradise, there were uncontrollable forces and powerful presentiments of death.
One afternoon, George and Peter encountered a company of soldiers on a remote forest road. Peter later remembered that "they halted and fell out for a
few minutes, unbuckling their equipment and sprawling by the roadside in
the relaxed attitudes of tired men, and George and I got into conversation with
a sergeant and one or two of the privates at the rear of the little column".

The adolescents were fascinated. As young men have always done, they imitated the soldier's regimented gait: "We followed close behind them, enjoying
the rhythm of the marching feet, and moved obscurely by a sense of unity with
the sweating, swearing, back-chatting soldiers." The incident stuck in Peter's
mind "rather like a piece of silent film": "It was a queer little romantic presage

1. Peter Llewelyn Davies abandoned the attempt in 1951. Nine years later, he threw himself under
a subway train, prompting the headline "Peter Pan Commits Death": even in death he could not
escape the association.

of the real marchings of six years later, for which the Highlanders were more or less consciously preparing themselves, [though] nothing could have seemed more remote from the destiny of two small boys."

The first few years of the twentieth century were far from being the perennial golden summer of folk memory, as the imperial European countries expanded their global influence to the point of irreversible conflict. In Britain, Victorian certainties were undermined by the Boer War and presentiments of the greater war to come, while at the same time challenged by the movements for women's suffrage, trade union rights, and the domestic response to European modernism. The century's most successful youth group, the Boy Scouts, was formed in response to the increasing demands of nation and empire.

War and death lay beneath the ordered Edwardian surface, if only in a quickening, irrational impulse. Nowhere is this clearer than in *Peter Pan,* which, first staged in December 1904, has become a twentieth-century archetype.[2] Like its American contemporary, *The Wonderful Wizard of Oz, Peter Pan* was a story aimed at children but adults were hooked in by its deep psychological complexity. It continues to speak so effectively across the generations that it is easy to forget its origins in a particular time, place, and biography.

Peter Llewelyn Davies's account of his encounter with the Highlanders was filtered through his terrible experiences a decade later, but his family's story illustrated the fatal intertwining of fantasy and reality that marked the period. When Sylvia Llewelyn Davies died in the late summer of 1910, Peter and his siblings were entrusted into the full care of the author who had filleted their lives for the play that made his name. J. M. Barrie hinted at this act of transference, if not possession, when he wrote about the Darlings in "Peter and Wendy": "There never was a simpler happier family until the coming of *Peter Pan.*"

When he met the Llewelyn Davies family in 1897, Barrie was already well established, but, beneath the successful façade, he was tormented by doubts and morbid fears. Undersized, haunted by the childhood loss of his brother David, locked into a marriage that he referred to as a "horrid nightmare", Barrie had lost his mother and sister in 1896. During the long walks that he took in Kensington Gardens, he began to turn to other people's children for solace. This was not only a substitute for parenthood but a reflection of his own self-diagnosed dilemma: "He was a boy who could not grow up."

2. After its contemporary success, *Peter Pan* has been routinely sourced in pop-psychological books (like Dr Dan Kiley's 1983 bestseller *The Peter Pan Syndrome*), in big-budget films (like *The Wiz*, 1978, and *E.T.*, 1982), and in the Neverland estate of pop's most bizarre superstar, Michael Jackson.

A chance encounter with George led to a friendship with the whole family. Within a year of their first meeting, he began working on a children's story about the birdlike attributes of babies in general and younger brother Peter in particular. Taking an idea from a contemporary play,[3] he conceived of a character named Peter Pan who escapes from the nursery and attempts to live as a bird. Having cut himself off from human society—"a Betwixt-and-Between"—he becomes an outlaw. When he tries to return to his bedroom, the windows are barred: "There is no second chance, not for most of us."

The idea was further developed in the 1902 novel *The Little White Bird*, where Peter Pan appears as a major subplot. After its success, Barrie set about expanding the character into a full "fairy play": a hasty first draft was finished by April 1904, and rehearsals began six months later. When it opened on December 27, *Peter Pan* was an immediate success with both adults and children. Daphne du Maurier later wrote about her father Gerald's performance as the male lead, "When Hook first paced his quarter deck in the year of 1904, children were carried screaming from the stalls."

Only one critic, Max Beerbohm, noticed the all-too-complete conflation of the adult with the child: "Mr Barrie has never grown up. He is still a child absolutely." On the surface, *Peter Pan* is a play for children: like *The Wonderful Wizard of Oz*, it demands a suspension of adult scepticism and linear thinking, and plays upon the archetypal fears of being lost and orphaned. But if *Oz* is benign and forward-looking—full of the optimism of a new continent—*Peter Pan* is haunted and haunting: if, for Dorothy and the Darling children, there is no place like home, then for Peter there is no home.

The central thrust of Barrie's story was almost exactly the same as the one that Oscar Wilde took for *The Picture of Dorian Gray:* the ideal of eternal youth and the Faustian nature of its *contra naturam* contract. From the moment of his arrival, where he is reunited with his lost shadow, Peter makes clear his outcast status: "I ran away the day I was born," he declares. "Because I heard mother and father talking of what I was to be when I became a man. I want always to be a little boy and to have fun; so I ran away to Kensington Gardens and lived a long time among the fairies."

Peter Pan is in a state of suspension, of permanent becoming. With his ability to fly at will—redolent of the Romantics and Marie Bashkirtseff's visionary dream—he transports himself and the Darling family to a fantastic realm, Neverland. A true *Sonnenkind*,[4] he is endowed with boundless self-

3. Called *Pan and the Young Shepherd*, by Maurice Hewlett (1898).
4. Child of the sun.

confidence and uses his Pan pipes to attract his followers—the Lost Boys—who look to him, amid the dangers of Neverland, for a leadership that is never quite forthcoming. For, despite his magic, he has no morality beyond self-interest: "In the middle of a fight Peter will always change sides."

Despite his represented age—he still has his first teeth—Peter is cryogenically frozen in childhood: however, the age that he acts indicates that he is an adolescent. Peter appears to offer intimacy but always pulls back. Desired by several female characters—Tiger Lily, Tinkerbell, and Wendy—and, perhaps, by that personification of adult cruelty, Captain Hook—Peter cannot even be touched: his whole being is "a frightful sneer at the laws of nature". He thinks that in his magical realm he can avoid the adulthood that he fears most: in his world, nothing could be worse than to become "a man".

However, there is a price to pay for his permanent youth in the curse of arrested development. By the play's end, Peter is alienated from his Lost Boys—now fully grown adults—and the reunited Darling family: "There could not have been a lovelier sight, but there was none to see it except a strange boy who was staring in at the window. He had ecstasies innumerable that other children can never know: but he was looking through the window at the one joy from which he must be for ever barred."

Peter Pan was as uncannily predictive of the youth-centric century to come as *The Picture of Dorian Gray*. Both exploited autobiographical elements to present youth as an abstract principle and to expose its explosive unconscious. Yet Wilde was ostracized, while Barrie became the toast of London, and it wasn't hard to see why. Wilde aimed his book at adults, set it in a recognizable present, and was happy, as a leading decadent, for people to think the worst of him. As a children's author, Barrie's overt fantasy exempted him from criticism, while his personal life was untouched by any hint of scandal.

If Wilde's perversity was up-front—and resolved into a sharply moral tale—then Barrie's was occluded but omnipresent, slipping and sliding through the narrative like his will-o'-the-wisp hero. Writing at the same time as the first explorations of child sexuality, Barrie could not help but reproduce one of Freud's central tenets: the insistence that childhood is not a state that is grown out of and discarded like a snakeskin, but which persists into full adult life. One corollary of this is that these unconscious impulses—once they have been repressed in adulthood—are liable to surface with violent force.

Barrie's final image of Peter, permanently shut out from the world of his youthful friends, was eerily expressive of his own condition: he felt barred from who he wanted to be. There was something not quite right about the author's passionate closeness to the Llewelyn Davies children but, unlike Wilde,

Barrie was both controlled and canny enough to stage his play in a way that cloaked any such ambiguities in theatrical tradition. It was no accident that Peter Pan was first played by an actress in her thirties: desire sublimated into an acceptable form. This age and gender slippage was key.

In having his hero portrayed by a youthful adult, Barrie made sure that its message was relevant not only to children but to adults, and that by implication the arrested development that Peter personified could continue into middle age. Adolescence itself is implicit both in Peter's flighty, solipsistic sensibility, and in the then contemporary elision of all pre-adult states: this was the period when teenaged youths were still called "boys". While overt sexuality is absent, Oedipal hints crop up in the abject status of the play's father figures: Mr Darling in his doghouse, and the damaged, dispatched Captain Hook.

The cross-gender casting of the central role re-emphasized the permanence of Peter's pre-adulthood: he could never grow up into a man because he was already a grown woman. It also placed the play firmly within the traditions of the pantomime, with the transvestism of its lead actress (Principal Boy) and lead actor (the Dame). Despite being presented as a radical departure, with its technological spectacle Peter Pan was a direct continuation of pantomime's theatre of magic and transformation, with an added, Freudian twist: the other worlds explored were not without but within.

Pantomime's original paganism survived intact in Peter Pan. Its hero was not lightly named. Pan was a well-known Greek deity, the goat god of nature who, abandoned as a child, symbolized dance and music—with his Pan pipes, the origin of the European Pied Piper myth. Added to his powers of prophecy were a violent eroticism and a nightmarish appearance. As "the instigator of violent and sudden terror", Pan would have seemed like the right deity to have on your side in an imperial conflict. There was one problem, however: Pan was the only Olympian deity to die in his time, just like a mortal.

This was strange imperial propaganda. One of the most haunting moments in Peter Pan, highlighted by F. D. Bedford's famous illustration, occurs when Peter waits to be submerged in the Mermaids' Lagoon. He hears "a drum beating within him" that repeats the phrase, "To die will be an awfully big adventure." Although it was George Llewelyn Davies who actually uttered this famous epigram—in 1900, during the Boer War—it was Barrie who had planted the idea in his head, thanks to his relentless descriptions of dead children and the paradisical Never Never Land to which they flew.

This is what continues to disturb about Peter Pan. Barrie could not help but bring his own damaged psychology into his relations with the Llewelyn Davies children. It's as though he programmed them, Svengali-like, with his own death fixation. After George, who was killed in April 1915, Barrie's favourite was the fourth child, Michael: their unusually intense relationship was ended by Michael's May 1921 death, at the age of twenty, in an apparent suicide pact. With the brothers' childhood thus subtly contaminated, it's hard to disagree with Peter Llewelyn Davies's belief that Barrie stole their souls.

But *Peter Pan* did not affect just one family: a smash hit in both the United States and the United Kingdom, it was revived year after year and quickly became a staple of children's entertainment. The play inserted the gender exploration of pantomime into the new youth market, helping to make androgyny one of the prime symbols of a coalescing adolescent culture. Within a British context, it initiated a new paganism and recast the perennial youth of the Romantics in terms of premature death. It also encapsulated the ambiguous views of youth that dominated the first decade of the twentieth century.

Youth was seen as an electric harbinger of the future, a force of nature that could either revivify or destroy old traditions. If that were the case, then greater efforts would have to be made to tame this unpredictable and savage beast. In Britain, the public school ideal remained the perfect youth model because it embodied the unthinking self-sacrifice that the empire demanded from its children. "These are my last words, dear boys," Wendy declaims on Captain Hook's pirate ship. "I feel I have a message to you from your real mothers, and it is this: 'We hope our sons will die like English gentlemen.'"

■   ■   ■

One of Peter's most fervent fans was an unmarried man in his mid-forties. Robert Stephen Smyth Baden-Powell was so taken with Barrie's play that he returned the next day to see it again, recommended it to his friends, and developed a relationship with the actress who played Mrs Darling, Dorothea Beard. This might seem odd behaviour for a career soldier and a national hero, but, according to biographer Piers Brendon, Baden-Powell was for the whole of his life "a perennial singing school boy, a permanent whistling adolescent, a case of arrested development *con brio*. He was unabashedly a 'boy-man'."

Born in 1857, Baden-Powell was brought up by his mother after the death of his father in 1860. Educated at Charterhouse public school, he took to the sport ethos of the time like a duck to water: his prowess at games and military activities more than made up for his poor academic record. He also developed a talent for the stage as well as an appreciation for nature stimulated by his many solitary forays into the depths of the countryside. Turned down by Oxford University, he joined the cavalry and was sent out to India, the first in a series of postings that took him to Afghanistan and South Africa.

The British Empire demanded constant vigilance and activity within which individuals were subordinate to the military demands of imperial acquisition and maintenance. Edwardian children's books like *Our Empire Story*, published in 1908, offered detailed accounts of the heroism that followed the British around the globe from North America to Australia and India. The incredible endurance of explorers was matched by constant colonial struggles against native swarms, like the brave "hundred" who held out against the Zulu hordes at Rorke's Drift.

By 1900, Britain was a country of 40 million people and 120,000 square miles attempting to control a population of 345 million spread over 11.5 million square miles. With these odds, a beleaguered tone began to enter imperial ideology: every rebellion was a serious matter to an army and navy stretched to the limit. Baden-Powell literally enacted this mentality, by standing firm during the long Boer War siege of Mafeking. The town's relief was a rare piece of good news in a generally disastrous campaign: when the word came through in May 1900, it provoked wild and spontaneous street demonstrations.

The Boer War marked the moment when the imperial mood changed from confidence to paranoia. The fear was not only that colonial gains might be lost, but that Britain itself might be the subject of invasion. These concerns were promoted in youth magazines like *Boy's Friend* and *Boy's Herald*, which serialized hair-raising stories of invasion by the French, the Russians, the Germans. As one editorial put it, "Will my readers believe that there are at the present time but a few hundred soldiers in this country to resist any attack an antagonistic foreign nation might choose to make on our little island home?"

The increasing level of literacy throughout Britain made its young more susceptible to the flood of alarmist propaganda in these magazines and in bestsellers like Erskine Childers's *The Riddle of the Sands* and William Le Queux's *The Invasion of 1910*. The traditional enemy had been France, but after the 1904 Entente Cordiale, the focus switched to Germany. Public school boys and Boys' Brigade members had long received premilitary training, but now the youth of Britain as a whole were being primed for conflict. But although most of the new white-collar classes and the working classes were patriotic and royalist, the body was not always up to the nationalist spirit.

The hooligan panic of 1898 had made visible the existence of a largely independent youth underclass, addicted to cigarettes, alcohol, and the music hall. When these young urban dwellers enlisted to fight in the Boer War, the first major conflict for thirty years, they were found to be physically substandard. In some poor areas, two-thirds of all volunteers were rejected outright. When it took a British army of 450,000 to quell a rebellion of 40,000 Dutch farmers, it became clear that the great mass of late-Victorian masculinity had fallen far short of the muscular Christian ideal.

The future of the British Empire lay in its youth, and they were not up to the job. According to the "Boy Experts" who proliferated after the Boer War, urban life was to blame, with its "evils caused by drunkenness and gambling, and other forms of vice". With the hooligans fresh in the memory, and with Boer War horror stories like the addiction of soldiers to "the powerful narcotic" cordite, the management of British youth would primarily be concerned with its fitness for battle. The first move was a series of laws aimed at bringing youths out of the limbo that they had so well exploited, into the public sphere.

In a transatlantic echo of the institution of the Illinois juvenile court, the imprisonment of under-sixteens in the same facilities as older offenders was prohibited during 1899, while the 1902 Education Act for the first time authorized state support for secondary education. However, these laws did not begin to address the deeper problems of the urban environment. Philanthropic reformers and church groups had only a limited impact. When the Boys' Brigade or the Church Lads' Brigade marched through working-class districts, they were often met with catcalls, stone throwing, and ribald epithets.

The requisite deference was disappearing. The youth worker Charles Russell observed that "the working class boy is a critic, and by no means a gentle one. He is sharp and stern. He does not see why he should make any allowance for weakness in those who affect to control him, and he makes none." Within his harsh environment, the "boy" could easily become an "ike", the successor to the scuttler: "The ike is a stupid fellow, who, from constant indulgence in vicious habits of many kinds, has lost control over his more brutal passions, and lets them have free play when the opportunity arises."

Poor posture and violent tendencies went hand in hand with a distinct lack of imperial enthusiasm. Russell concluded that "no one who has come into contact with the average boy of the working classes in Manchester can fail to be struck with the almost total lack of *esprit de corps* such as exists amongst boys brought up at the great public schools". If the latter was the British ideal, then the working-class lad was an example of the degeneration that threatened imperial stability by enfeebling the race. His poor physical state meant that he could not fulfil the "ever increasing responsibilities of extending Empire".

As in America, early thinking about adolescence focused on the control of the urban poor. The 1903 governmental "Committee on Physical Deterioration" identified the problem presented by the lad from the "rougher classes" who slipped through the net of church, school, or voluntary organization. Although noting with approval existing youth groups like the Boys' Brigade, the committee recommended a more concerted period of training, with prominent place given to "drill and physical exercises", so that "the male adolescent" could "bear arms with very little supplementary discipline".

Baden-Powell saw his opportunity. In April 1904, he attended the annual drill inspection and review of the Boys' Brigade in Glasgow. Challenged by Brigade founder William Smith to "rewrite the army scouting book to suit boys", the former colonel thought of the Mafeking Cadet Corps, a quasi-military organization of all boys under military age in the besieged town. Aged between nine and eighteen, these cadets provided a ready-made heroic model: as he wrote in *Scouting for Boys,* they "didn't mind the bullets one bit. They were always ready to carry out orders, though it meant risking their lives every time."

Five days before the premiere of *Peter Pan,* this Piper of Pax unveiled his manifesto in the Eton College *Chronicle:* a revealing choice. His letter began with the siege premise: "In England we are a small country surrounded by nations far stronger in arms, who may at any time attempt to crush us. The question is how can we prevent them?" Invoking the knights of the Middle Ages, Baden-Powell proposed a test for "every English boy": "to ask himself on the 1st of every month—'What have I done for the good of the country, apart from what I have done for my own personal amusement or improvement?'"

Baden-Powell decided to form a series of local groups, primed by the reading of adventure stories, who would then be taught "how to shoot with miniature rifles", "how to drill and skirmish", and how to scout. These "corps" would be explicitly charged with a litany of knightly duties: "1. to fear God 2. honour the king 3. help the weak and distressed 4. reverence women and be kind to children 5. train themselves to the use of arms for defence of their country 6. sacrifice themselves, their amusements, their property, and, if necessary, their lives for the good of the their fellow countryman."

The first serious test of these ideas came in 1907 with the inaugural scouting camp, where twenty-one boys between nine and seventeen were instructed in the movement's ethics and practicalities: loyalty to king and empire, camping, cooking, stalking, and tracking. Baden-Powell was most pleased with the class mix, his test group having been carefully selected to include both public school and working-class boys. "The rougher boys were perceptibly levelled up in the matter of behaviour, cleanliness etc.," he wrote, "they watched and imitated the others and improved to a remarkable degree in so short a time."

Scouting had gone through several changes since the 1904 manifesto. Baden-Powell took his ideas from many sources: classical literature, the theories of educationalists like Johann Heinrich Pestalozzi and Frederick Jahn, as well as rituals from the Spartans, the ancient British, and the Japanese Bushido. However, his biggest single influence came from the American Woodcraft Indians, a group developed in the early years of the century by Ernest Thompson Seton. Baden-Powell met Seton on his visit to Britain in 1906: to the latter's chagrin, he adapted the woodcraft ideal into a more regimented form.

Drawing on his fame as the hero of Mafeking, Baden-Powell attracted the backing of the publisher and promoter C. Arthur Pearson, whose principal title was the *Daily Express,* launched in 1900 as a mass-market newspaper with an explicitly patriotic programme—"Our policy is the British Empire." As part of this worldview, Pearson had already instituted a Fresh Air Fund for sending poor children to the country, and during 1907 he gave Baden-Powell's campaign a huge boost with lecture tours and a sustained publicity blitz. He also undertook to publish the movement's house magazine.

Featuring adventure stories and competitions, *The Scout* was an immediate success, rising to a weekly circulation of over 100,000 by the end of 1908. Pearson also helped in the coining of the movement's name: "I do not think the Imperial Scouts is a good name," he wrote in 1907. "It seems to me we should certainly use the word 'Boy'. I do not think you will improve on Boy Scouts." With a cross-media campaign of newspaper articles, lectures, and publications, the market was primed for the launch of scouting with the first serialized appearance of Baden-Powell's book, in January 1908.

This manifesto was an immediate and lasting success. Baden-Powell had a talent for intensity that closely corresponded to the heightened sensations of adolescence. His descriptions of tracking techniques had an almost hallucinatory density, while his insistence on the close observation of nature approached the total involvement with the here and now that is the hallmark of Eastern religion. Most of all, he made it sound like fun: "Camping is the joyous part of the Scout's life . . . living out in God's open air among the hills and the trees, and the birds and the beasts, and the sea and the rivers—that is, living with nature."

Scouting for Boys was arranged around twenty-six "Camp Fire Yarns", which covered relevant topics like "Camp Cooking", "Spooring", and "Self-Improvement". Most of the practical explanation was soundly based on common sense, and contains a wealth of detail—on how to tie nine different types of knot, for instance—that continues to form the basis of today's survivalist handbooks. Within this lively format, Baden-Powell cited the inspirations for the movement: the Knights of St George, the gauchos of South America, the Zulus, and the American Indians.

Baden-Powell also cited famous individuals such as US president Theodore Roosevelt and chivalric exemplars of the Scout ethos, like an eighteen-year-old Scottish lad "named Currie" who attempted to save a young girl from an approaching train. The ideal was self-sacrifice and selflessness. Baden-Powell found his perfect boy in the person of Robert Hindmarsh, a young shepherd who detected a tramp murderer through woodcraft and observation: "you should remember that your acts may be watched by others after you, and taken as an example, too. So try to do your duty the right way on all occasions."

Each Scout was bound by promises that included "loyalty to the king, his country, his scouters, his parents, his employers and to those under him". These also insisted that "a Scout obeys orders of his parents, Patrol Leader, or Scoutmaster without question". Baden-Powell echoed Henry Newbolt in his address to the "younger generation of Britons who are now growing up to be the men of the Empire": "Don't be disgraced like the young Romans who lost the Empire of their forefathers by being wishy-washy slackers without any go or patriotism in them. Play-up! Each man in his place, and play the game!"

Such exhortations revealed that Baden-Powell's manifesto was not as bereft of ideology as it claimed. *Scouting for Boys* was saturated in the imperial ethos of muscular, public school Christianity. There were crude caricature illustrations that inferred essential character from external appearance. "Foreign-looking" people and clothes were automatic targets of suspicion: this at a time when immigrants were alleged, in a Royal Commission document, to harbour "criminals, anarchists, prostitutes and persons of bad character, in number beyond the ordinary percentage of the native population".

Baden-Powell further reproduced the degeneration theories of the time with his frequent injunctions against smoking, drinking, masturbation, and slackers: "There is no room for the shirker and the grouser." Aimed at the young working-class "lad" whom the Boy Experts had identified as a problem, scouting received a mixed reception. Some inner-city youths were delighted to play this new exciting game and to join a peer group that offered adventure, trips into the country, and some release from the demands of parents, teachers, or employers.

By 1910, scouting was not quite the mass movement that it would become in the 1920s and thereafter, but it was already the biggest youth group in the United Kingdom, with over 100,000 members. Like the Boys' Brigade and the other church youth groups, however, it was principally composed of lower-

middle-class and upper-working-class youths. It failed to reach a large proportion of the slum golems who were threatening the empire for two main reasons: the uniform and the subscription payments were too expensive, and many youths were hostile to the movement's insistence on militaristic discipline and drill.

The public school ethos was implanted within the young urban poor through another, unexpected route. The cross-class taste for comics and picture magazines was well established by the time the *Magnet* was launched in 1908, the same year as *Scouting for Boys*. The first issue featured a "complete school tale", written by Frank Richards, that told the story of how a defiant youth is sent away by a "bronzed, grim-visaged old soldier". Having found that his nephew has "run completely wild", Colonel Wharton packs him off to boarding school in an attempt to cure his "wilful and headstrong" nature.

The struggles of Harry Wharton made irresistible reading, not the least because his undoubted "pluck" was tempered by his hair-trigger hostility. Within the first issue of the *Magnet*, there were at least five proper, bloody fights: plenty of savagery to satisfy the most assiduous scuttler. Its depiction of a self-enclosed, peer-dominated society, where boys were badly behaved but eventually brought back into the fold, made the *Magnet* and its Greyfriars stories an instant success, not just with public school boys, but the denizens of the inner cities.

In his memoir of 1900s Salford life, *The Classic Slum*, Robert Roberts remembered he and his peers were addicted: "The standards of conduct observed by Harry Wharton and his friends at Greyfriars set social norms to which schoolboys and some young teenagers strove spasmodically to conform. Fights—ideally, at least—took place according to Greyfriars rules: no striking an opponent when he was down, no kicking, in fact no weapon but the manly fist. Through the Old School we learned to admire guts, integrity, tradition; we derided the glutton, the American and the French."

Compared to their own bleak school, this fictional establishment "became for some of us our true Alma Mater, to whom we felt bound by a dreamlike loyalty".[5] Roberts recognized that "the public school ethos, distorted into myth and sold among us in penny numbers, for good or ill, set ideals and standards. This our own tutors, religious and secular, had singularly failed to do. In the final estimate it may well be that Frank Richards during the first quarter of the twentieth century had more influence on the mind and outlook of young working-class England than any other single person, not excluding Baden-Powell."

5. Roberts remembered that there were "boys so avid for current numbers of the *Magnet* and *Gem* that they would trek on a weekday to the city railway station to catch the bulk arrival from London and buy first copies from the bookstall. One lad among us adopted a permanent jerky gait, this in his attempt to imitate Bob Cherry's 'springy, athletic stride'. Self-consciously we incorporated weird slang into our own oath-sprinkled banter—'Yaro-oh!', 'My sainted aunt', 'Leggo!' and a dozen others. The Famous Five stood for us as young knights, *sans peur et sans reproche.*"

CHAPTER 7

High School Freshmen and Factory Fodder

American Adolescence and Industry

. . .

The young generation has practically brought itself up. School discipline, since the abolition of corporal punishment, has become almost nominal; church discipline practically nil; and even home discipline, although retaining the forms, is but an empty shell. The modern child from the age of ten is almost his own "boss".

—Randolph S. Bourne, "The Two Generations", *Atlantic Monthly*, May 1911

FIVE AMERICAN BOYS, 1900s

WHILE THE IMPERIAL European countries jockeyed for position, America began to stake its claim as the new century's industrial and financial power-house. Its intentions were declared in early 1901, with the creation of the United States Steel Corporation. Capitalized at $1.4 billion, the new company brought into one cartel almost all the American steel producers, in a deal put together by the banker J. P. Morgan. Dwarfing even John D. Rockefeller's Standard Oil Company of New Jersey, it was the biggest company in the world.

America had its own imperial ambitions in the 1900s, but they precluded direct intervention in European disputes. The continent's influence would be exerted through industry. Temporarily freed from the arms race that was beginning to consume its nearest competitors, America pursued its own Manifest Destiny. This was raw capitalism, which was defined not just by industrial production, but by its harnessing, through the flow of money, into ever larger corporations—institutions that were true embodiments of the country's size and potential.

The place of youth within this national project was of paramount importance. Just as the young of northern Europe were being programmed to fight the forthcoming war, the youth of America were to play their full part within the business ideal. This imperative had a considerable impact on American education policy, which drew more and more adolescents out of factory work as it began to fashion a new managerial and service class. With increasing urbanization, the old days of frontier individualism, wanderlust, and self-sufficiency were over.

Businessmen demanded dependability, physical strength, unquestioning obedience, and the ability to work in a group—to develop, in the educational jargon of the day, "a socialized disposition". As in public school Britain, this ethos was best inculcated in the young through sport, and team activities became of prime importance in schools and universities. However, America needed more manpower for its Manifest Destiny than the middle or upper classes could provide. Just as the continent had been tamed, it became necessary to train all American youth out of its "atavistic" behaviour.

The increasing focus on adolescence during the 1900s took the form of official and public concern about youth's most visible manifestation: the savage underclass that ran so wild in the inner cities that it threatened to taint the children of the bourgeois. In a contemporary guidebook entitled *Boys as They Are Made and How to Remake Them*, F. H. Briggs stated that the delinquent did not come "from the home where industry, intelligence and thrift prevail", but was "the boy over the back fence in your alley".

. . .

G. Stanley Hall's *Adolescence* had successfully defined puberty as a separate life stage, but this definition was now used by the business classes to impose their values on America's youth as a whole. From 1905 on, the Problem of Youth became a staple in newspapers and mass-market magazines. *Harper's Bazaar, Good Housekeeping,* and the bestselling *Ladies' Home Journal* ran pieces about "How and when to be frank with boys", "What boys my boy should play with", and "Keeping a city boy straight". Articles about "boys" and "juvenile delinquency" increased tenfold over the previous decade.

The newly developed middle-class market was led to think that young urban toughs represented a serious social threat, that delinquency was contagious and might rub off on their own young. As the country's most famous youth expert, Stanley Hall was thrust into this national debate. He revealed that he had received several hundred letters from concerned parents and friends: "the question in all these letters is, 'What to do?' The parents or relatives are at their wits end, and ready for almost any desperate remedy." He concluded that "never has even the American boy been quite so wild as he is now".

In a January 1906 interview, Hall declared it a national scandal that, out of 27 million young Americans between five and twenty-one, only 12 million were attending school. Even when in full-time education, these children—the boys particularly—were being ruined by a slack syllabus: "Work too often degenerates into a kind of play." Worst of all was that pupils were allowed to select "their own topics of study": "This again depends on the shibboleth of the individual rights of the citizen and even of the child, in whom possibilities of being president are never forgotten."

In his view, American education compared unfavourably with the German system, which not only kept each child in school for longer hours but also made its pupils more suited to the demands of industry. Even language worked in the Germans' favour, with their "technical vocabulary" that could be grasped by a child. The comparison was vitally important because "it is often asked why the Germans are coming so rapidly forward in industrial, mercantile, technical and administrative fields". Education was the key to this "regeneration", backed up by a national sense of purpose that shamed America.

The "sissifying" of American schools had been responsible for creating a generation of unruly adolescents. In a 1908 article, Hall criticized the situation caused by the "rapidly progressive feminization of the teaching force": "Moral suasion prevails, the rod is banished, and a spirit of sugary benignity which does not make the best metal in the soul of boys pervades the school."

In the graphic accompanying the piece, football-playing and sledding groups were pitted against a single long-haired, velvet-suited, lace-cuffed young aesthete: the spectre of decadence.

Hall was not the complete Victorian, but he was a man of his era, and his concentration on the inadequacies of the high schools formed part of a wider national inquiry that ultimately concerned America's international status. The "hoodlumism" that Hall interpreted as a problem of discipline had, for many educators and businessmen, a deeper consequence. The new American mass age would not favour the individual or the dissident. Everyone had their part to play, and that part was not, as in Europe, foredestined by class, but by economics.

The comparisons between America and Germany—both upstart countries— were not lightly drawn. With its unprecedented expansion, Germany was both an inspiration and a cause for concern. The problem for the United States was that greater levels of production were not matched by equivalent consumption. The consequent shortfalls left the economy vulnerable to the disastrous depressions of the mid-1870s and early 1890s. The way out of this impasse was not to cut production, but to expand the potential market for a wider range of products.

The first sign of this solution was an aggressive export drive: after America's shop-window display to the world at the 1893 Expo, it was time to ship and sell. During 1902, the senior banker Frank Vanderlip celebrated the American "commercial invasion of Europe": the country had "sent coals to Newcastle, cotton to Manchester, cutlery to Sheffield, potatoes to Ireland, champagnes to France, watches to Switzerland, and 'Rhine Wine' to Germany". Manifest Destiny was trumping the isolationist Monroe Doctrine.

Unlike their German counterparts, America's youth were not expected to join in the defence against "enemies on all sides". Their task was to work in the factories that they had begun to reject. For businessmen, the equation was simple: every delinquent, every feminized boy was refusing to fulfil their definition of proper manhood. Just when America needed to produce as never before, many of its indigenous young refused to participate in the manufacturing process. Instead of examining poor conditions in the factories themselves, employers chose to blame the schools.

By the 1900s, high school enrolment had reached unprecedented levels, thanks to successive reform campaigns. This removed many adolescents from the labour market, but the children of recent immigrants quickly took their place. However, industrialists soon found that this fresh source of factory fodder was not inexhaustible. Many new American citizens had brought over their socialist politics from the Old World, and were agitating for increased union recognition. The apprentice system was under the control of the American Federation of Labor, which was attempting to increase youth wages.

The movement against child labour had already gathered steam: before 1900, twenty-eight states had passed laws regulating its use. One of its leaders, Florence Kelly, formed the National Child Labor Committee, which agitated for stricter federal controls on "the labor power of youth".[1] In 1906, John Spargo's excoriating exposé *The Bitter Cry of the Children* was published. Jane Addams, inspired by Hall's *Adolescence* to focus on the problem of urban adolescents, wrote a stream of observations and recommendations that were collected in her 1909 book *Youth and the City Streets*.

One of her shocking stories concerned a boy of fifteen who worked in a steel mill: it was his job "to throw a lever when a small tank became filled with molten metal. During the few moments when the tank was filling it was his foolish custom to catch the reflection of the metal upon a piece of looking glass, and to throw the bit of light into the eyes of his fellow workmen. Although an exasperated foreman had twice dispossessed him of his mirror, with a third fragment he was one day flicking the gloom of the shop when the neglected tank overflowed, almost instantly burning off both his legs."

Addams was as guilty of imposing the values of her own class on inner-city youth as any other reformer, but, quite apart from the practical effectiveness of her work and her consciousness-raising, her wish to improve conditions tallied with the desires and needs of the masses. The principle of betterment was ingrained within the American psyche. Having been led to believe that all men were equal, many recent immigrants saw the high school as the first step in that goal, if not for themselves then for their children, who would learn to become true New World citizens. It offered a way out of the factory.

Steadily losing young workers to school enrolment, the employers fought back. They felt that too much time was spent on general subjects, like Latin, algebra, and history, and that the high school had successfully instituted a white-collar education. During 1905, their lobbying organization, the National Association of Manufacturers (NAM), instituted its own Committee on Industrial Education. Its ultimate aim was to combat the twin threats of Germany—the rising industrial power in Europe—and increased union power by creating a new system of education that would prioritize the needs of industry.

---

1. After years of lobbying by the National Child Labor Committee, a federal bill, the Keating-Owen Act, was passed in 1916 with stringent conditions about youth employment conditions: the minimum working age was fourteen, up to sixteen in mines and quarries, and no one under sixteen could be employed at night. The maximum work week was to be forty-eight hours, with a maximum day of eight hours. Although the Supreme Court declared the act unconstitutional in 1918, it provided a framework for many individual state laws.

With the German system of technical-industrial education as their model, the manufacturers' committee sought to train "American boys" to enter the factories in supervisory and skilled capacities. With another lobbying group called the National Society for the Promotion of Industrial Education, they aggressively promoted a segregated system of schooling. It was time, as the dean of the School of Education at Stanford University noted in 1909, to "give up the exceedingly democratic idea that all are equal, and that our society is devoid of classes".

Under this new system, children would be graded at the elementary stage. Those ranked at the top would receive the generalist, classics-oriented high school education. The rest would get a vocational schooling that, according to the 1908 National Educational Association convention, would include "bookkeeping, commercial arithmetic, stenography and typewriting, business correspondence, and commercial law. In manual training students could study mechanical drawing, woodwork, ironwork, pattern making, and advanced ironwork." There would be domestic science courses for girls, including "cooking, sewing and design work, dress-making, household economy".

Although quickly integrated within high school curricula, these reforms did not meet with unanimous approval. The problem was that "the masses", having been offered an educational ladder out of the factory, did not see why they should return there, especially since working conditions were still brutal and inhuman. Much worse was that this graded system of schooling was beginning to result in the kind of segregation already practised against Negroes: for every dollar spent on a Negro child's education, over thirty-three dollars were spent on his white counterpart.

At the same time, gender segregation was becoming part of educational practice, heralded by the many attacks against "feminization". In the 1900s, girls were sneered at if they did well academically. For the daughters of the "masses", marriage was their approved vocation. If not, they would be educated for service jobs in industry: "The graduate in home economics may teach cooking, sewing, bacteriology, chemistry and any of its various branches. She may have supervision of the food and sanitation of institutions such as hospitals, asylums, mercantile establishments, cotton mills, and homes of correction."

In pushing through this system, American businessmen and educators met resistance from teachers and parents alike. They failed to realize that the Prussian system was not the product of a democracy but a feudal empire. As high school numbers continued to rise in the early 1910s, the battle between academics and vocationalists deepened. If the former were committed to "the obligation of the community and the state for a higher and better development of the individual", the latter were simply concerned with making "every individual employee subordinate to the production of his particular institution".

. . .

This ideological conflict hindered the uptake of high school education during the 1910s. Although the number of adolescents aged fourteen to seventeen in school doubled, the figure was only just over 30 per cent of the total cohort by the end of the decade. And the drop-out rate remained high in large cities. In his 1914 survey, *The High School Age,* Irving King noted that in some inner urban areas a massive 88 per cent of high-school-age pupils did not graduate, because they did "not find it possible or perhaps worthwhile to follow out the course".

The high schools might have been attracting more pupils, but they were not holding them. The curriculum might have been responsible, but class was a more pressing reason. Either from necessity or temperament, many poor youths saw no reason to stay in the school environment and left for the world of temporary, low-paying jobs or delinquency. As far as they were concerned, even a few cents in their pockets conferred status and allowed some control over their own lives.

At the same time, the high school was in the process of being promoted as an aspirational institution. Its idealized image, promoted by popular fiction such as H. Irving Hancock's 1910 novel *The High School Freshmen,* was small-town and middle-class: even more so than Frank Richards's stories for the *Magnet,* they were perfectly attuned to business values. However, having had more freedom than their British counterparts, America's slum children were less swayed by these ameliorative documents.

Set in an "average little American city of some thirty thousand inhabitants", *The High School Freshmen* pits Dick Prescott, the straight-up son of a bookshop owner, against the vicious and vengeful Fred Ridley. While "all of Dick's chums were boys belonging to families of average means", "lawyer Ridley usually allowed Fred much more money than that snobbish young man knew how to make good use of." Despite being a lowly freshman of fourteen, Prescott rises through the school through his courage and his proficiency at sports. His reward is to be invited to the senior ball.

Featuring fistfights and dark doings straight out of *Tom Brown's Schooldays* or the *Magnet, The High School Freshmen* is well within the European tradition of schoolboy stories, with which it also shares a propagandist slant. As Dick entreats his mortified enemy, "Come on Fred, be a different sort of chap. Make up your mind to go through the High School, and through life afterwards, dealing with everybody on the square. Be pleasant and honest—be a high-class fellow—and everything will like you and seek your friendship." Peer esteem is not conferred by money, but by being good at sports and a team player.

Hancock's novel shared the same values as the "boy books" that had influenced America's view of children and adolescents ever since the success of Thomas Bailey Aldrich's *The Story of a Bad Boy* and William Dean Howells's *A Boy's Town*. In these late-nineteenth-century works, the natural naughtiness of spirited boys was eventually tamed through outdoor activities and down-to-earth, small-town morality. They were serialized in children's magazines like *Youth's Companion* and *Harper's Young People*, along with more overt boy guides like Ernest Thompson Seton's *Boy Scouts of America*.

The ethos behind the boy books—as encapsulated in Seton's 1903 novel *Two Little Savages*—followed the recapitulation theory explored in *Adolescence*. To the author John T. Trowbridge, the boy was "a barbarian. He inherits not only the mild parental possibilities, but also the cat-like or tigerish traits which enabled his progenitors, in the dim past, to make the struggle for existence. Sometimes it seems as if his humanity were as thin as his jacket, and fitted him as loosely. The wild animal is underneath; strip him and you find the stripes."

These books offered practical solutions to deal with the savagery of eight- to fourteen-year-old boys. These included sports, alert parenting, and vocational education. Physical activity and practical endeavour were also inculcated by the youth group launched by Ernest Thompson Seton, the American Woodcraft Indians. For all its mystical overtones, this was an organization that brooked no dissent: as Seton wrote in *How to Play Indian*, "Don't rebel. Rebellion against any decision of the Council is punishable by expulsion. Absolute obedience is always enforced."

Seton's human ideal embodied self-control and responsibility. With his cleanliness, leadership qualities, and altruism, the Shawnee chief Tecumseh was "the most Christlike character presented on the pages of American history; him, therefore, I select the model of perfect manhood held up for guidance of the young man of America". The movement's first full manifesto, *The Birch Bark Roll of the Woodcraft Indians*, was published in 1906. With its self-governing nature, its system of rewards and ranks, rules and oaths, and the mystical outdoors, it offered a definitive template for the scouting movement.

The most successful voluntary institution that sought productively to channel the energies of American youth was the Boy Scouts of America, founded by a Chicago publisher named William D. Boyce in 1910. Although inspired by Seton, Boyce was a better organizer and took note of Baden-Powell's success: within a few years, his group had subsumed the American Woodcraft Indians as well as other scouting bodies like the Sons of Daniel Boone. Aimed at "boys" between eleven and seventeen, the Boy Scouts of America was organized along the same lines as its British counterpart.

In 1911, the BSA published its manual, *Handbook for Boys*, which included the American Scout Oath: "On my honor, I will do my best, to do my duty to God and my country, to obey the Scout Law, to help other people at all times, to keep myself physically strong, mentally awake and morally straight." The Scout Law delineated the qualities that it demanded from members: "A scout is trustworthy, loyal, helpful, friendly, courteous, kind, obedient, cheerful, thrifty, brave, clean and reverent." Scouts were organized along strict hierarchical lines, from the basic group, called the Patrol, to the larger Pack Troop.

The organization quickly grew into a national force. The BSA magazine, *Boys' Life*, began publication in 1912, the year that Juliette "Daisy" Low formed the American Girl Scouts after witnessing Britain's Girl Guides firsthand. The emphasis in both organizations was on the outdoor life, camping, and woodcraft: merits were awarded for knowledge of Scout skills in an escalating programme designed to encourage personal responsibility, leadership qualities, and community service. In 1916, Congress gave the BSA a federal charter, by which time there were more than 250,000 Boy Scouts throughout America.

For all its teething problems, however, the high school still provided the best answer to juvenile delinquency and child labour. However, novels like the *The High School Freshmen,* which were explicitly aimed at an older age group—at "boys of every age under sixty"—conflated the real institution with its fictionalized counterpart. Hancock's stories of youthful derring-do masked the propagation of business values. "It isn't all play in a High School," Hancock concluded. "A vast amount of study has to be mastered. There are nerve-racking examinations. It is a tremendously busy life despite its sport."

The high school was designed as an assimilation machine from the very beginning. Because of the need to integrate many different races and nationalities, America developed a highly conservative, conformist social structure. The classroom had become an all-important homogenizing instrument. The progressive educationalist John Dewey thought it the ideal place to prepare the young for the particular ethical demands and standards of American society: once the individual had become "a sharer or partner" in group activities, his beliefs and ideas would "take a form similar to those of others in the group".

However, total integration through education was still an elusive dream in the 1910s. As it developed towards a truly mass system, the high school would uneasily juggle the vocational and academic approaches at the same time as it fudged the disparity between American ideals and realities. Proclaiming equal opportunity for all, and indeed, through this rhetoric playing its part in the creation of a peer youth cohort, the high school remained an institution dominated by middle-class values. It was not a true social leveller.

The bitter debates over the national curriculum also highlighted the vexed relationship of American youth to industry. The ruthless exploitation of children and adolescents was, Jane Addams thought, "in danger of quenching the divine fire of youth". The attempted industrialization of education had not been successful: by 1912, only 7 per cent of high school attendees were taking industrial and trade courses. Being a "product" or a man-machine did not adequately fulfil the social role that had already been allotted to America's youth, which was to embody a coalescing nation's latency.

Just as America itself, the land of the free, was in the process of *becoming*, its youth deserved recognition of this special iconic status, one very different from the destructive and sacrificial role being thrust on Europe's adolescents. There was another way of harnessing youth to America's national project. The solution would come from a very pragmatic, if haphazard, marriage of industrial production with a shrewd understanding of the emerging American psyche—that fusing of hardheadedness with the visionary quality already defined and ascribed to youth by Hall, Baum, and other pioneers.

Addams's young steelworker had been unsuited for mechanical work because of his age's biological need for play and for reverie. At the end of his detailed survey of the American educational system, Irving King concluded that "the adolescent is traditionally a dreamer. He longs for that which he can not express even to himself. He feels somehow that he is face to face with a *great thought* which, thus far, no man has ever grasped; he feels he is about to solve the riddle of existence, which hitherto has baffled even the world's greatest minds."

Despite the structural improvements made in youth conditions, it was the dream economy that would inspire adolescents, not only in America but in Europe. It was no little irony that, as American products began to travel across the ocean, their country's implicit promise of equality was being undermined by the imperatives of industry. It was as though the founding American ideals, just as they were on the point of being jettisoned, had became channelled into the essence of the very products themselves, like a tiny homeopathic dose of freedom.

CHAPTER 8

Wandervogel and Neo-Pagans

Europe's Back-to-Nature Movements

. . .

On midsummerday, at night, we'll make a solemn sacrifice again to the gods of Perpetual Youth, to close the cycle and celebrate most worthily his deliverance and birth. I am pondering over the ritual even now: there must be fire; and water, clear spring water poured at sunrise out of a cup of virgin crystal; and wreaths of dog roses and honeysuckle; and there should be a bird in a cage to set free at dawn and a fair prayer to sing as we dance hand in hand round the leaping fire.

—Jacques Raverat, letter to Katherine Cox, January 19, 1910

WANDERVOGEL ON LÜNEBERG HEATH, 1909

IN EARLY 1903, a seventeen-year-old student named Karen Horney recorded her surging emotions in her diary: "I seem to myself like a skipper who leaps from his safe ship into the sea, who clings to a timber and lets himself be driven by the sea's tumult, now here, now there. He doesn't know where he is going." Going into the storm centre, she tried to express her feelings with a "crazy poem" that saw her trapped in an "old masonry stronghold that thousands of years had built for me. It was gloomy and close—I longed for freedom."

Although nearly entombed, she dug herself out with her bare hands: "I breathed life. The brightness of light almost blinded me—yet soon I was used to its brilliance. I look about. The view was almost too wide, my sight could roam to unlimited distances. Oppressive almost the New, the Beautiful invaded me. At that an all-powerful longing seized me, almost bursting my breast, and it drove me forth to wander in order to see, to enjoy, and to know the All." This new freedom, however, did not bring integration but further alienation: "Homeless am I. With no sheltering abode I rove about."

Prevented by a male teacher from joining a class on animal dissection, Karen Horney decided in her fury to dissect herself instead: "That will probably be more difficult, but also more interesting." She was also perturbed by a conversation she had had with her friend Alice, who admitted that she sometimes "went" with "strange gentlemen". She reported the exchange: "*I*: 'I thought such things didn't happen at all in our circles.' *Alice*, laughs: 'In masses. A girl in our class did it—and even with her father.' I was speechless with horror."

Her head filled with Romantic literature and traditional morality, Horney struggled with these realities. Criticizing marriage as a sham, she felt that "all our morals and morality are either 'nonsense' or immoral", deciding that it was "never immoral to give oneself to a man one really loves". She concluded her diary entry by projecting into the future: "Will it ever change? And how? And when? The dawn of a new time is breaking. I hope with all the strength of my young hope. Perhaps even the next generation will not know these battles."

Born into a prosperous middle-class family, Horney was one of the first German women to take advantage of new educational opportunities. In her city of Hamburg, women were only allowed in the gymnasium, the elite school system, after 1901, while the universities only allowed women into their medical schools after 1900. Much of her diary is taken up with the question of women's rights. Horney was a great admirer of the Swedish feminist Ellen Key, who advocated equality for women in books like *The Century of the Child*.

Horney was one of the many middle-class young of northern Europe attempting to forge a "new morality" in the first decade of the new century. "New battles call for our exertions now," she wrote. "We want this freedom for our emotional life and for its expression, freedom not licence, for we feel bound to the demands of Nature." This desire for change was not confined to women, although they were still regarded as second-class citizens. Feminism was but part of the young's revolt against the nineteenth-century world of their parents, which they perceived as a materialistic, hypocritical, and stultifying nightmare.

During the 1900s, new youth movements arose within Britain and Germany in reaction to militarism and industrialism. Their young adherents felt that the only way forward was backward: into the paganism of nature worship. However, in seeking to cast off adult restraints, they left themselves open to the demons lying beneath the ordered, apparently rational surface of European life.

This youthful reaction had a particular charge within imperial Germany, where in the early 1900s the children of the bourgeoisie did not enjoy the comparative freedoms available to their counterparts in Britain, France, and America. Within a system that both expressed and favoured the rigid nationalistic ideology of the German upper classes, these youths found their progress in life blocked by the glass ceiling of Prussian privilege. These tensions were compounded in all classes by the vexed relationship between fathers and sons.

The Prussian ideal of parenting was epitomized by the story of the eighteenth-century Prince Frederick. Rebelling against his martinet father, King Frederick William I, the aesthetically inclined young prince tried to run away but was betrayed and captured: his punishment was to watch the execution of his closest friend, Hans Hermann von Katte, who had escaped with him. Only through this severity did he mature to become the national legend, Frederick the Great of Prussia. This capricious cruelty helped to fuel the murderous father-son hostility that was widespread throughout Germany.

At the same time, the day-gymnasium system of education, with its emphasis on academic hothousing, strict discipline, and its lack of the peer group support that marked British public schools, produced angst-ridden pupils. This was the hypocritical authoritarianism that Frank Wedekind had exposed in *Spring Awakening*, and the spate of schoolboy suicides did not abate. In his study *Le suicide*, the sociologist Emile Durkheim compared rates in France, Italy, and Germany: the highest among the sixteen- to twenty-year-old age group were in Saxony and Prussia.

The depth of disaffection among young Germans was revealed by the extraordinary popularity of the recently rediscovered writer Friedrich Hölderlin. His 1797 novel *Hyperion oder der Eremit in Griechenland* was written in the first person like *The Sorrows of Young Werther*: this direct mode of address helped it to became a cult success during the 1900s. The message of this doomed Romantic was uncompromising: "I can conceive of no people more dismembered than the Germans." For him, "youths" were "no human beings": to attain wholeness, the young had nobody to rely on but themselves.

The inability of Prussian education to deal with "youthful upsurging energies" was explored by Robert Musil in his 1905 army school novel *Young Torless*. Tormented by his physical attraction for another boy, Torless finds himself stripped of his "solid, bourgeois" certainties "in which everything happened in an ordered and rational way". Underneath the ordered surface of European life lie unreckoned demons: "From the bright diurnal world, which was all he had known hitherto, there was a door leading into another world, where all was muffled, seething, passionate, naked and destructive."

If the struggle for young women was to attain social and sexual equality, then the struggle for young men was to find another kind of identity away from the soldier/athlete hammerlock. After Wilde and Nordau's *Degeneration*, the decadent aesthete was both obsolete and vilified. The only option was to explore male sensitivity in a different way. Organized within various groupings, this impulse elevated spontaneity of instinct and emotional expression and the nature mysticism to be found in the outdoor life. This was the "kindling fever" ignited by the twentieth century.

This urge to create a new, discrete youth world was given its first coherent structure within imperial Germany. The *Wandervogel* offered a basic but readily available escape from an oppressive regime. The idea was simple and encapsulated in their name, which means "wandering bird": prolonged group hikes and camping excursions in the countryside. As an early adherent recalled: "the essence of the *Wandervogel* was flight from the confines of school and city into the open world, away from academic duties and the discipline of everyday life into an atmosphere of adventure."

The movement began in the gymnasium of Steiglitz, near Berlin, where a young student and part-time teacher named Herman Hoffman began excursions with his pupils during the spring of 1896. Involving campfires, community singing, and rough sleeping, these prolonged hikes quickly attracted schoolboy adherents. By 1900, the outings had become so popular that they were organized into a national body: in 1901, the charismatic and driven Karl

Fischer assumed leadership and founded a new, official youth group called Ausschuss für Schülerfahrten.

Imperial Germany was hostile to the modern movement, and the terminology of this new group belied its archaic fascinations. Fischer was entitled *Ober-bachant*, the name given to the leader of medieval travelling students, and he demanded absolute obedience from members. There was a probationary system, and a uniform of insignias and caps that harked back to the pre-industrial age. Fischer added will-to-power to Hoffman's nature mysticism. He treated hiking as "a propagandizable idea": "Save yourself, grab your travelling staff, and seek the man you have lost, the simple plain and natural one."

Despite its leader's controlling mentality, the *Wandervogel* appealed because it offered freedom. One of its first members, Hans Bluher, had just entered puberty when he joined in 1901. He saw the movement as an almost instinctive, romantic rebellion that involved the casting off of middle-class conventions: street fighting and, thanks to the popularity of Karl May's western novels, playing at American Indians, were major parts of the movement's appeal. Smoking, drinking, and associating with real vagabonds were the icing on the cake.

For all these allurements, the simple life was at the heart of *Wandervogel* activities. Journeys were undertaken with the minimum of luxury and money: meals were cooked on field stoves and campfires, while accommodation was found in barns and tents. Members were encouraged to record their impressions of the hike and the countryside in prose or pictures, and the results were collected in small magazines. A vital part of the experience was the discovery and group performance of old ballads and airs, accompanied by guitars and lutes, which helped to bring in a renaissance of German folk song.

Unlike the Boy Scouts, *Wandervogel* groups organized themselves, albeit around an older leader. The basic unit typically comprised about seven or eight members. A pyramidal structure later emerged, which expanded to cover a local branch, comprised of all the groups in a particular city, and then a provincial branch, called the *Gau*. Most members were adolescent males: below twelve, they were too young to undergo the rigours of the expeditions, and over nineteen most young men were joining the army or had become students.

In the early days, there was no group identification. This came slowly through the use of badges and pins, and other fashions such as the wearing of flamboyant hats. Group activities were concentrated in the clubhouse, the *Heim*, a shed or a suitable room decorated with club insignia and containing a small library. The most important *Wandervogel* event was the big cross-country expedition. Most of these occurred during the summer, but there were shorter camps and hikes around weekends and major holidays. There was no network of youth hostels, so most of these trips were literally breaking new ground.

The *Wandervogel* attempted to escape from contemporary realities into a prelapsarian idyll, but they could not keep the outside world at bay. Like all other German youth groups, they had a bewildering tendency to split into factions. It was as though the tension between their avowed ideals of freedom and their authoritarian upbringing was too much. Or maybe it was just the German delight in group formation and scissions. There were also other undertones that resulted from the *Wandervogel*'s refusal of overt politics.

The movement's lack of a concrete programme initially worked in its favour: with their medieval dress, openness, and defiant peer group bonding, the movement's early followers shocked Wilhelminian society, who regarded them as rebellious and sexually promiscuous. This archaic romanticism made the movement an accurate expression of a German middle class caught between an increasingly militant proletariat and the Prussian elite. However, it also keyed into the implicit fear of modernism that was then twinned with the *völkische* ideas of blood and race.

As the movement gained popularity, it became more diverse and more ideological. New splinter groups emerged, ranging from the right of the political spectrum, like the Jungwandervogel, to the more urban and cultural, the Hamburg Wanderverein. At one extreme were the visionaries who gathered in the Swiss hill village of Ascona and created the commune that practised vegetarianism, nature cures, and free love. This "constituency of the sensitive" offered a safe haven to anarchists, intellectuals, and *Wandervogel* alike.

The most pervasive new trend, however, was stimulated by the popularity of Hermann Popert's 1910 novel, *Helmut Harringa*, the story of a young man who declares war not only on Germany's Prussian student organizations, but on alcohol and premarital sex. Having contracted venereal disease, Harringa commits suicide because he has squandered the racial stock in "the filthy double-intoxication of a quarter of an hour": "I no longer dare raise my eyes to my forefathers." Linked with racial purity, abstinence became a rallying call among the *Wandervogel* at the turn of the decade.

Two years later, Hans Bluher published the first instalment in his controversial three-volume *Wandervogel* history, which helped further to disseminate the movement's ideas. In the third volume, Bluher uncovered one of the brotherhood's principal fault lines. He had been incensed by the expulsion of Alt-Wandervogel president Willi Jansen for homosexuality. Informed by Freud, the pioneering sexologist Magnus Hirschfeld, and the gay-rights journal *Die Eigene,* Bluher retaliated by suggesting that the movement's male bonding was held together by homosexual eroticism.

This part of his history caused a sensation upon its 1913 publication, not the least because of the homosexual scandals—most notably the 1907 Harden-Eulenberg case—that had exposed the hidden passions underneath the Prussian façade. However, the furore obscured Bluher's belief that the *Wandervogel* comprised a necessary interval before the full responsibilities of adulthood. Karl Fischer had, after all, envisioned "a schoolboys' state", a *"Lebensraum* where boys can be, are permitted, and must be boys, in order to become truly men".

However, Bluher's hostility to women opened up the biggest wound within the *Wandervogel:* the fact that it was an excusively boys' club. In the movement's early years, women were not admitted as a matter of policy. This exclusion remained in force until the successful formation of a breakaway organization for young women, the Wandervogel Deutscher Bund. Other groups allowed limited participation if the girls were chaperoned by their mothers, while others, like the conservative Jungwandervogel, refused to entertain the idea at all.

The pressure was unstoppable, however: by 1911, many youth group leaders agreed that young women should have an equal place in the movement. Even so, there were disputes about whether the genders should be kept separate. Surprisingly, promiscuous sex was not an issue for the *Wandervogel.* One contemporary observer, Elizabeth Busse-Wilson, felt that the youth movement was swamped by "masses of uncourted girls", who had de-sexed themselves and had "found men, if not *a* man in the movement".

As Hall had stated, adolescence was the stage of life "when sex asserts its mastery in field after field", and here was a cohort of Peter Pans, away from parental constraints, attempting to deny the most obvious connection between them. The move towards abstinence placed enormous pressures on each individual. These tensions were forcefully expressed in Karen Horney's diary. Although she strained to free herself "from everyday morality", she was nevertheless bound by the powerful conventions of the time.

Her solution was to be "free of sensuality". She felt that celibacy gave great power to a woman: "Only in this way will she be independent of a man. Otherwise she will always long for him and in the exaggerated yearning of her senses she will be able to drown out all feeling of her own value." However, at the same time as she sought independence, she entertained fantasies of herself as a "strumpet". As she admitted, "In the prostitution wish there is always a masochistic wish hidden; to relinquish one's own personality, to be subject to another." Beneath the overt desire for freedom lay a deeper wish for subjugation.

Young Germans might have wanted freedom with all their hearts, but the reality of their goal was disturbing for adolescents raised in a repressive country. The increasingly hard-line nature of the *Wandervogel* was testament to this paradox. From being a loose grouping of young people who liked to enjoy nature, it became a movement riven by internecine strife. By 1912, the dominant influence was Hermann Popert's group the Vortrupp (the Vanguard), which promoted racial hygiene at the same time as it castigated decadence, alcohol and tobacco, and the mass society.

It was as though the ultimate implications of nature worship were too frightening to contemplate. Following the pagan instincts could lead to accusations of homosexuality in men, and prostitution, if not nymphomania, in women. The *Wandervogel* shared aims and means with the Boy Scouts—the love of the outdoors, the promise of peer bonding—but in the lack of any leadership imposed from above by adults, the youth of Germany chose to police themselves. Their attempts to live outside adult restrictions were subverted from within by the very authoritarianism they were attempting to reject.

. . .

There was no exact parallel to the *Wandervogel* in Britain. For most of the country's young, freedom was a distant chimera during the 1900s. In the upper and middle classes, parents attempted to navigate the gap between Victorianism and the first signs of independence. Even so, plays like Stanley Houghton's *The Younger Generation* showed limited tolerance for youth rebellion. Young men were still expected to conform to their parents' choice of career, while young women were still groomed for the right marriage. Any meetings between them were strictly controlled by an adult chaperone.

In most working-class households, the father remained the absolute authority. In *The Classic Slum*, Robert Roberts remembered that during the 1900s adolescents, "especially girls, were kept on a very tight rein. Father fixed the number of evenings on which they could go out and required to know exactly where and with whom they had spent their leisure. He set, too, the exact hour of their return: few dared break the rule. One neighbour's daughter, a girl of nineteen, was beaten for coming home ten minutes late after choir practice." The restrictions weren't only physical.

Roberts remembered that in Salford, "any interest in music, books or the arts in general, learning or even courtesy or intelligence could make one suspect". The "linking of homosexuality with culture" went right across the classes as the impact of the Wilde trial cut deep. Only within the anonymity of a huge city could the young act out the aesthetic tenets laid down in H. G. Wells's scandalous novel *Ann Veronica:* "If individuality means anything it means breaking bounds—adventure. Will you be moral and your species, or immoral and yourself? We've decided to be immoral."

Although the preserve of a dedicated, if not privileged, few, bohemianism remained one of the few outlets for the nonconformist, relatively privileged young. Another was involvement in the "scientific" socialism of the Fabian Society. For young women of all classes, the most radical choice was involvement in the fight for women's suffrage through the Women's Social and Political Union. However, none of these groups was organized around the specific idea of youth, whether as an ideal or a practical programme.

The one group that did so offered a soft-focus variant of the nature worship practised by the Scout movement and the *Wandervogel.* For the small, elite band of Neo-Pagans, this was expressed in camping out, socialist discussion, nude sunbathing, and an intellectual fascination with sex. As one of the group, Gwen Darwin, later remembered, "We used to loll in armchairs and talk wearily about Art and Suicide and the Sex Problem." For her at least, rebellion was an important impulse: "Sometimes I think everyone should be killed off at the age of 40 when I see the misery all parents are to their children."

The Neo-Pagans were a group of about twenty intellectuals, writers, and artists clustered around Rupert Brooke, Jacques and Gwen Raverat, and the four Oliver sisters. Although they met through a mutual interest in Fabian socialism, they developed a studied youth-consciousness that sought to defy Victorian gender strictures at the same time as it celebrated the intensity of the moment. Their free mixing was heady enough in the era of the chaperone. But they became so intoxicated with their vitality, talent, and beauty that they went much further: how could they, how would they stop time?

In the summer of 1909, Rupert Brooke suggested the scheme that became the Neo-Pagan manifesto. He began with the premise that the world was "imperfectly organized. One fault, one great fault, in it, is that its inhabitants grow old." The worst part of this was not the decay of the body, but of the spirit. So, with breathtaking presumption, he projected the group into the future: "We are twenty-something. In 1920 we shall be thirty-something. In 1930 we will be forty-something, talking to rather fat, rather prosperous, rather heavy, married, conservative, suspicious people who were once young with us."

He observed that London was full of the "dead, top-hatted, ghosts" of those who were once young, "haunting the civilization that was their ruin". But "suppose that a band of the splendid young people in the past had formed a scheme to escape the great destroyer, to continue young, and suppose they had succeeded—wouldn't that have been a wonderful, an unequalled triumph?" Brooke called for the group to meet at Basle Station "on the 1st of May, 1933, at breakfast time". Only that way could they remain forever young: "We'll be children seventy-years, instead of seven. We'll *live* Romance, not *talk* it."

Brooke's enthusiasm quickly spread to the rest of the group. "The idea, the splendour of this escape back into youth, fascinated us," he later wrote. "We imagined a number of young people, splendidly working together, vowing to *live* such an idea, parting to do their 'work in the world' for a time and then, twenty years later, meeting on some windy road, one prearranged spring morning, reborn to make and find a new world together, vanishing from the knowledge of men and things they knew before, resurgent in sun and rain— *We determined to be those people.*"

Brooke was suggesting the simple casting off, by the simple decision to meet twenty-four years hence, of all adult responsibilities and cares in an attempt to erase the intervening years. Instead of being middle-aged, they could, as if by magic, return to the grace and beauty of their adolescent selves. This was a new twist within the Romantic concentration on the child, a philosophy of vitalism and action that echoed the eternal youth obsessions of both *Peter Pan* and *The Picture of Dorian Gray* and enshrined the pagan imperative so pervasive among the double zero generation.

As the golden boy of the group—in Frances Darwin's words, "a young Apollo"—Brooke was restless, driven, vain, and charismatic. The child of a public school housemaster, he began to rebel against his background during his teens. Having been obsessed with *Peter Pan*, he fell under the spell of Wilde and Baudelaire at the age of seventeen. At Cambridge University, he was credited with starting a new style: longish hair, soft shoes, and shirts with open, floppy collars. Scenting the anti-Victorian revolt, Brooke moved quickly from faux-decadence to vegetarianism and Fabian socialism.

With these elements coexisting uneasily in his make-up, Brooke's concentration on an eternal instant helped to dissolve his contradictions. As he concluded, "We have inherited the world. Why should we go crying beyond it? The present is amazingly ours." However, in the lack of any concrete activity beyond spells of Fabian consciousness-raising—like a summer 1910 "caravan" tour in protest against the antiquated Poor Law—the Neo-Pagan programme was rather vague. Youth, privilege, and nature might have been the glue that held them together, but none was sufficient in itself as an organizing principle.

Despite Brooke's exuberance, the Neo-Pagans were caught in a cleft stick.

On the one hand they had the influence of paganism and the sexual licence promoted by influential thinkers like H. G. Wells; on the other, they still cleaved to the middle-class moral insistence that the period before marriage should be a sexual no-go zone. As David Garnett later remembered, "To fall asleep within a yard or two of a lovely girl without a thought of trying to make love to her was natural to me at eighteen. It was simply part of the social climate in which I was brought up."

There were, however, practical considerations. The sanctions were particularly severe for women, as one mistake could result in pregnancy, quite apart from loss of reputation. The Neo-Pagans made a virtue out of necessity and preached abstinence. However, this moratorium on sex meant that they had to divert the wild instincts they had hoped to invoke into a number of prolonged courtships that, with the inevitable jealousies and suppressed longings, helped to tear the group apart within a couple of years.

As the Neo-Pagan figurehead, Rupert Brooke embodied these tensions. His iconic status masked a young man boiling inside with frustration and insecurity. Within a few years, he pursued three Neo-Pagan women, Noel and Brynhild Oliver and Ka Cox, while at the same time flirting with both androgyny and homosexuality. After many Neo-Pagans joined the older and more ideological Bloomsbury movement, with its easy acceptance of homosexuality, Brooke snapped. His curious passivity had led him into circumstances from which he recoiled.

In January 1912, he suffered a near-total nervous collapse that shattered his equilibrium and the group's easy companionship. The illusion of Peter Pan, flying free of all mortal bounds, could not be continued. Within months, the Neo-Pagans dissolved with some acrimony. This event had been predicted by the only married man of the group, Jacques Raverat, who wrote, "Youth is a very deceitful thing; it makes one think so many people so much nicer than they really are, just because of that indolent flush of young blood. Middle age finds them all out in all their nakedness of soul—and body."

From 1912 on, Rupert Brooke began to retreat into an aesthetic and social conservatism. He totally repudiated his former radicalism. When he visited high modernist Berlin and found himself surrounded by the city's bohemians, he reacted by penning that arcadian farewell to his pagan youth, "The Old Vicarage, Grantchester", within which all was subsumed within the unchanging traditions of the English countryside. He began to wish for death as the resolution to his problems: "It is thought by those who know me best (viz myself) that I shall die. Nor do I greatly want to live."

. . .

The impact of the Neo-Pagans and the *Wandervogel* was symbolic, not statisti-cal: they were numerically insignificant compared to the official or political youth organizations of the period. In Britain, the numbers of Boy Scouts dwarfed these children of the sun. Within Germany, the socialist and religious youth groups pulled in the working-class youth that the *Wandervogel* failed to attract. Many of the middle classes joined the new Jungdeutschlandbund, an adult-run group based around military sports, or the German version of the Scouts that was formed in 1911.

However, these two nature-obsessed, would-be pagan groups offered the only organized attempts at defining the adolescent independence that they felt would be a necessary part of the life of the new century. Although already her-alded by a few visionaries, the precise nature of what these youth freedoms would be was unclear to say the least. In their instinctive wish to prolong the state of childhood innocence through the avoidance of sex and emotional com-mitment, the Neo-Pagans and the *Wandervogel* left themselves open to the morbidity that is the inevitable consequence of eternal youth.

That death-instinct, heralded by Wilde and Barrie, was the mirror image of all the talk of sun and light. Like G. Stanley Hall, the pioneers of the 1900s perceived that the complexities of modern life demanded a prolongation of that newly defined state, adolescence. However, by plunging into cults that smacked of irrationality, privilege, and escapism, they failed to carry with them the great bulk of their peers, and themselves fell victim to the tensions between the restrictions of the previous century and the dimly prefigured wildness of the youth century to come.

CHAPTER 9

Nickelodeons and Animal Dances

The American Dream Economy

. . .

Youth's thirst for experience is simply that it wants to be everything, do every-thing, and have everything that is presented to its imagination. Youth has sud-denly become conscious of life. It has eaten of the tree of the knowledge of good and evil.

—Randolph Bourne, *Youth and Life* (1913)

GOING TO THE "MOVIES", 2.30 P.M., JERSEY CITY, NEW JERSEY, BY LEWIS HINE, 1912

DURING THE 1900s, the young in Europe and America adopted new symbols of independence for themselves. Some came from the existing youth market for magazines and books, while others were plucked from the rapidly expanding mass media. The fresh American focus on youth coincided with the growth of commercial psychology and the motion picture industry. The movies found their first market among adolescents, who, according to Stanley Hall, comprised one-third of the total American population. Their enthusiasms rendered them unwitting guinea pigs for the emergent consumer society.

As it spread throughout Europe, American culture's most iconic image was the American Indian. This mythological creature was promoted by many means: Buffalo Bill's Wild West show; "redskin" stories like those written by Edward Sylvester Ellis; hugely popular "western" novels by Zane Grey and, in Germany, Karl May; even the craze for Indian songs that followed the success of Charles N. Daniels's "Hiawatha". Just as the continent was being tamed, Indians were everywhere, a sharp reminder of the individualism that was being steamrollered by the new mass society.

Long a staple of boyhood reading, the American Indian became the identifying symbol of adolescent appeal in the early 1900s. Despite the fact that they usually got the worst of their fictional battles with the cowboys, "redskins" were wild and free. They shared atavistic tendencies with adolescence in general, and their underdog status chimed with an emergent youth class seeking a metaphor for its own situation. Not yet enfranchised yet constantly reminded of their national duty, urban youths in America and Europe saw in the fugitive figure of the Indian a symbol of wide-open space as well as grace under pressure.

This was seen most clearly in early-twentieth-century gang life. In his *Wandervogel* history, Hans Bluher celebrated the rejection of middle-class restraints achieved through Indian play. In France, the Parisian Apaches turned this identification into a national scandal. From the other side of the spectrum, Ernest Thompson Seton and Baden-Powell sought to corral this appeal for their ends. *Scouting for Boys* highlighted the woodcraft skill of Red Indian scouts, who "used to tie a wolf's skin on their backs and walk on all fours, and prowl around the camps at night, imitating the howl of a wolf".

Other outside styles crossed the Atlantic. Minstrelsy had been popular in Britain during the nineteenth century, and the cakewalk arrived in the 1900s. The conquest was made complete by the smash 1912 success of the revue *Hullo Rag-time*. Featuring songs like "Alexander's Ragtime Band", written by the white composer Irving Berlin, this brash all-American show hypnotized its audience through wild music and Negro-style dancing. The future had arrived. To the writer J. B. Priestley, the ragtimers were "drumming us into another kind of life in which anything might happen".

That sense of possibility was the great attraction of the American dream economy. Forget coals, trains, steel, and cutlery—what Europeans wanted from America was its sense of space, its wildness, its pizzazz, its syncopated, crossing rhythms that accelerated the tempo of life in an everlasting present. However, there was a conundrum within this equation. If America was so identified with youth, then presumably it had youthful qualities—and these were both attractive and dangerous. Youth might offer energy and excitement, but it could easily spill over into barbarism and violence.

Within America, the simultaneous commercial exploitation and attempted control of youth gave rise to a paradox. The deep-mining of the psyche encouraged by advertisers began to throw up those very atavistic qualities that they were attempting to channel through the creation of a society based around the accumulation of objects and comforts. Social control through consumerism might have been more benign than through more totalitarian methods, but it set up different kinds of distortions that were increasingly enacted in the deep oscillation between hedonism and puritanism.

. . .

Heralded by the 1893 Expo, America's dream economy began to develop as a major industry during the 1900s. Turning fantasy into hard cash was particularly suited to the national character and the demands of a nation that was still coming together. Born out of the desperate needs of recent immigrants and developed by consolidating corporations, a new mass culture was created that fused basic human psychology with futuristic technological innovations. It was not just a culture but a brand-new way of envisioning the world that quickly became an unstoppable force.

America's technical expertise was the wonder of the world. The 1900s saw the first appearance of many future staple twentieth-century products. These included the first 10-inch gramophone record (1901); the first powered flight (1903); the commercial availability of offset lithography (1904); the first nickelodeon (1905); the first regular radio broadcasts (1906); and the creation of the first car designed for the masses—the Ford Motor Company's Model T (1908). To some considerable degree, these mass products assisted the standardizing tendency insisted on by business. Labour became increasingly atomized.

In 1913, the popularity of the Model T gave rise to the first full assembly-line operation at Ford's Highland Park plant: the principle of labour reduced to the most basic task—a jerk on a screw, a pull on a lever—and endlessly re-peated. The individual worker was a cog in a wheel. Despite continued union agitation, the American economic and social system was fast becoming a fait accompli. If the external world could not be collectively changed, then as far as producers and advertisers were concerned, the individual, internal landscape would be the focus of development.

This project was attractive to a growing nation. In place of the European past, there would be the American present, so vivid that it would appear to last forever. The jerky intercutting between different scenes in Edwin Porter's ground-breaking 1903 film *The Great Train Robbery* compressed perception it-self: as Porter himself commented on his film's rapturous reception, "The future has no end." This intensity, however, would be harnessed to the im-peratives of business: each person could be transformed not by artistic or po-litical activity, but through the acquisition of the requisite product.

Psychology would be the active ingredient in this alchemical process of turning inanimate objects into supercharged, mass-produced talismans. This was, however, not the academic psychology practised by Hall, or Freud's psy-choanalysis, but a simplified variant offered by the new mediators between producer and purchaser: the admen. The advertising industry had expanded tenfold during the previous few decades, and with growth came greater ambi-tion. Seeking direct penetration into the subconscious, advertisers began to fillet the discipline of psychology for their particular brand of spell-weaving.

In the mid-1890s, the trade magazine *Printer's Ink* had looked forward to the time when "the advertisement writer, like the teacher, will study psychol-ogy. For, however diverse their occupation may at first sight appear, the adver-tising writer and the teacher have one great object in common—to influence the human mind." This "enlightened" process of mass education gathered pace in the new century: its most influential proponent, Professor Walter Dill Scott, insisted in 1906 that "the successful advertiser *must* study psychology and he *must* do it at once".

Scott advocated nothing less than the thorough exploitation of atavistic hu-man desires: "We have instinctive responses to act for the preservation and furtherance of (1) our bodies, clothes, homes, personal property and family (also the hunting and constructing instincts which are more complex than others of this class); (2) ourselves as we exist in the minds of others; (3) our mental faculties. We have seen that to secure action along these lines it is not necessary to show the value of such action or the necessity of it, but merely to present the proper stimulus, and the action is forthcoming immediately."

The new ads went beyond the simple delivery of information. In the new abundance therapy, it was not enough for patent medicines or cornflakes to have specific properties: now they were presented, explicitly or implicitly, as having the power to transform everyday life. Therefore Rice Krispies were not sold as having nutritional value but through a sequence of dramatic events: "It pops! It snaps! It crackles!" Claude Hopkins's famous series of "Reason Why" campaigns successfully sold toothpastes and automobiles by suggesting that the purchase of these items would lead in itself to a richer, fuller life.

These techniques were principally aimed at women, but the process began earlier in life. In his influential book *The Psychology of Advertising*, Scott made the link between consumerism and youth: "The young man seems compelled to attempt to be at his best before the young lady, but he does not always know why. The young boy always tries to 'show off' in the presence of young girls. It is often ridiculous that he should do so, and he does not know why he is doing it. When he comes into the presence of the young girl he seems compelled to undertake something *bizarre* which is sure to attract her attention."

Veblen's "pecuniary emulation" had been turned into a multimillion-dollar industry that, as Scott admitted, was rooted in adolescent social psychology: "We are all afflicted as the young man and boy. We consult not only our preference but also the opinions of others in purchasing our clothes and our homes, and in choosing our friends and our professions. We seem compelled to strive for those things which will make us rise in the estimation of others, and in purchasing and choosing we select those things which are approved by those whose esteem we most covet."

By the end of the 1900s, there was already a bewildering number of products targeted at young women. In an article called "The Budding Girl and the Boy in His Teens", Stanley Hall observed the propensity of the adolescent female for "beautiful array". This was "the season of bangs, curls, puffs, pompadours, frills, ribbons, possibly rouges and powders, high heels, flaunting hats, sunshades, ornamental purses, bangles, very long gloves—fashions that fairly smite the beholder; that is to say, such things now loom up into the centre of consciousness. The shop windows are a dream."

Hall was drawn into the popular applications of adolescent psychology almost despite his will. In October 1908, he endorsed a regular new feature set up in the *Woman's Home Companion*, called "Teens and Twenties", and written by the youthful Lucy Norman. Her article was clearly aimed at making useful wives out of adolescent girls: "Our books are welcome, I am sure, to sit there in a row and enjoy the spectacle of the lately graduated Teens and Twenties plying the needle, caring for the house, seeing that the garden is 'tucked in' for the winter and that the house plants have proper warmth."

The popular understanding of psychology was given a boost by the first American visit of Sigmund Freud and his then colleague Carl Jung during the late summer of 1909, invited by Stanley Hall to talk at Clark University. The exchange worked both ways. Hall sought extra support for the academic status of psychology, while Freud was eager for the opportunity to speak outside Austria and, indeed, to seek the academic validation that, despite the publication of *The Psychology of Everyday Life,* he had not yet received. Despite academics who found him a "dirty, filthy man", Freud was very pleased with his reception.

His audience was respectful, as were most of the subsequent newspaper reports. He later wrote, "As I stepped onto the platform at Worcester to deliver my *Five Lectures Upon Psychoanalysis* it seemed like the realization of some incredible dream: psychoanalysis was no longer a product of delusion, it had become a valuable part of reality." The 1909 visit made Freud famous and helped the further spread of his ideas: the importance of sex, the Oedipus complex, repression, the existence of the unconscious in everyday life, the importance of psychoanalysis in the treatment of neurosis.

These theories had an academic and a popular take-up, whether it was in the 1911 founding of the American Psychoanalytic Association or the coinage of the term "Freudian slip". Freud's ideas would be further adapted to the American context by his nephew Edward Bernays, the founder of the public relations industry and the promoter of "mass psychology" as an agent of social control. Freud's insistence on the psychopathology of everyday life reinforced the notion that there could be psychology *in* everyday life, a message that advertisers, producers, and buyers alike took to their hearts.

. . .

The decade before America's entry into World War I saw the increasing popularity of mass entertainment. The most dramatic development came in moving pictures, an industry that came into being as the result of the nickelodeons' astonishing success. By 1910, their hold on the American public had grown to the point where they attracted between ten and twenty million regular visitors weekly. Many of these were children and adolescents, drawn in their hundreds of thousands into a different, futuristic environment that they could call their own.

One by-product of child labour had been the first beginning of youth consumerism, which fed directly into the burgeoning movie business. In her novel about pre-Great War life, *A Tree Grows in Brooklyn,* Betty Smith wrote about how her eleven-year-old heroine, Francie Nolan, felt when she got her wages: "Francie had a nickel, Francie had power." Arriving at a Broadway five-and-dime store, "she walked up and down the aisles handling any object her fancy favoured. What a wonderful feeling to pick something up, hold it for a moment, feel its contour, run her hand over its surface and then replace it carefully. Her nickel gave her this privilege."

Brought up to think that "money was a wonderful thing", American youth associated independence with spending. By the end of the nineteenth century, newsboys, street traders, and schoolchildren hung around candy stores and lunch counters, buying sweets, hamburgers, and ice cream. However, the most popular destination was the penny arcade or the amusement parlour: storefronts or large rooms that contained slot machines and, after the early 1890s, kinetoscopes, machines that displayed moving pictures through a peephole.

From the start, America's youth were entranced by the "movies". There was the novelty of the medium, but the catcher was the fact that the dream-worlds on screen tallied so closely with the developing adolescent psyche. According to G. Stanley Hall, this period "is marked by much emotional intensification of dream life, and that at no age is its influence so marked upon the moods and dispositions of waking consciousness". He felt that puberty was marked by an "inner absorption and reverie" that could end in "narcosis".

Once the peephole had been replaced by the projector, the movies jumped in popularity. It was more pleasurable, and often cheaper, to see images on a large screen: it also gave the young a sanctioned place to go to be together, in the dark. The communal nature of moviegoing was accentuated by the introduction of the nickelodeon during the mid-1900s. These more formalized theatres were so popular that they appeared to observers like Jane Addams to have "sprung up suddenly, somehow, no one knows why". Children and youths were estimated to form between a quarter and a half of "the new movie audience".

Most of these were the children of recent immigrants, as the nickelodeons opened almost exclusively in working-class and inner-city districts. In the movies, young Americans could see their own experience reflected as nowhere else. The "nickel dumps", particularly during the afternoon and early evening performances, also allowed some freedom from adult supervision. Addams noticed that "young people attend the five cent theaters in groups, with something of the 'gang' instinct, boasting of the films and stunts in 'our theater'".

They could do so because many of them were still earning. Compulsory high school attendance hadn't halted adolescent labour. In a 1910s study of Iowa schoolchildren, it was found that more than two-thirds of young men of high school age earned wages outside school hours. The most popular jobs were clerking and delivering newspapers. The figure was lower for young women, just under one-quarter. Attending "movie picture shows" was one of their preferred methods of entertainment: just under half of the boys and two-thirds of the girls sampled saw between one and six movies a month.

By 1910, the new moving pictures were attracting a weekly audience of 10 million. Many reformers thought that the movies had a disturbing effect on the young. Jane Addams quoted "an eminent alienist of Chicago" who stated that he had had "a number of patients among neurotic children" who had "become victims of hallucination and mental disorder" after regular attendance at the theatres. Even more alarming were the "children" who seriously modelled "their conduct upon the standards set before them on this mimic stage".

Addams cited the case of three boys between nine and thirteen who, having seen a stagecoach hold-up on screen, tried to "lasso, murder and rob" the local milkman: "Fortunately for him, as the lariat was thrown the horse shied." In a sensational 1912 trial featuring a teenager accused of cold-bloodedly murdering his friend during a botched train robbery, Edwin Porter's famous film *The Great Train Robbery*—then showing locally—was cited in a press report as the cause of the outrage: the tragedy was "an Exact Reproduction from Movies".

Cases like these, where the perpetrator cited the movies as the inspiration for his crimes, only fuelled adult condemnation of this new form. However, attempts to control the industry foundered on the fact that it was expanding faster than the institutions set up to administer it. A National Board of Censorship had been established in 1909, but until 1914 it passed 95 per cent of all films submitted. The result was considerable freedom not only to dazzle America but also to examine its underbelly: the 1910s saw a range of pictures that depicted the fault lines in American society.

The moviegoing experience was launched by an exploitation picture. In the patents war between established companies like Biograph and the new independents, the upstarts had taken to showing longer, feature-length films in old vaudeville theatres. The pulling power of these larger venues, with their increased audience capacity and greater luxury, was displayed by the unexpected success of one of the very first features, 1913's *Traffic in Souls*. This dramatization of the "white slave trade" was a sensation: 30,000 people saw the film in its first week, many of them young women between sixteen and eighteen.

That same year, juvenile delinquency made its appearance in *Saved by the Juvenile Court*—a rendering of the rehabilitation work performed by the reforming judge Ben Lindsey. This early picture firmly placed delinquent youth within the frame of legal control, but the adolescent street gangs and their more mature counterparts were amply displayed in Raoul Walsh's *Regeneration,* shot with actual gangsters on the streets of the Bowery and the Lower East Side. Based on the memoir of a Bowery gang leader, Owen Kildare, the film captured the slum golems of the 1890s on the point of their disappearance.

Other early pictures tackled youth problems with a reforming gloss. Adolescent intoxication and addiction featured in the 1914 adaptation by Jack London of his novel *John Barleycorn:* with its scenes of child drunkenness, it was hailed as "a compelling plea for Temperance". That same year, *The Drug Traffic* highlighted the necessity for the further control of narcotics by depicting the morphine-related death of a typical American adolescent. However, they were the exception rather than the rule: the movies had never been conceived as a purely documentary or socially conscious form.

Films were an entertainment: even when they dealt with contemporary topics, they were often behind the times or crudely sensationalistic. They were not there to reflect reality, they were a "theatre" where fictional dramas were enacted. Although some confusion between the two might have been unavoidable in their very earliest days, it was obvious by the 1910s that the movies represented a "fairy land" that industrialized the American taste for fantasy into a new medium of unprecedented power. The Wizard of Oz had found the perfect way with which to ensnare perceptually the citizens of the Emerald City.

The relation of the movies to America's youth was psychologically intimate. On the one hand, they represented a fantasy world that offered a pause from everyday life. On the other, they began to produce images reflecting aspects of adolescent life that, subtly fictionalized, fed back into fertile psyches. The consequence was a sophisticated dance between audience and producers: the studios might have held the key as far as making the product, but the audience had the power to bestow or withhold success. Often, as in the case of *Traffic in Souls,* that could be unexpected.

What young moviegoers wanted was a heightened version of reality, one that they could both identify with and at the same time that would take them into another world. These aspirations fused in a new type of public figure that was created by a press hype. Until the 1910s, film actors had enjoyed a low status. They were usually anonymous, and if they were featured, it was as a representative of the company—the "Biograph Girl". In early 1910, to counter deliberately leaked rumours of her death in a street-car accident, Biograph named their "girl" as Florence Lawrence.

Two weeks later, Lawrence was heralded by a newspaper article that noted, "Manufacturers are just beginning to wake to the demand for information by the public of their actors, and are recognizing the value of the personalities of their players." It was predicted that "the time will come when these actors will command the services of press agents as does any other stellar attraction". At the same time, *Variety* described the twenty-year-old Lawrence as the "star moving-picture actress". By early 1912, she had become "The Girl of a million faces".

As one of the first named stars, Florence Lawrence represented a celestial body—Oscar Wilde's Pan-like star-child—materialized in a young, attractive female form, which was then reproduced electronically a thousandfold, blown up beyond its actual size on the screen, and finally consumed by the masses. In this new pagan religion,[1] the star was the god or goddess. In quick time, their characters would emerge as the twentieth-century version of the ancient Greeks' Mount Olympus: an intricate value system of abstracted human impulses that could be applied both to national life and individual needs.

Adolescence was central to this system, exemplifying sexual attractiveness and idealized innocence. Frozen by celluloid, the youth of the star could appear as perennial as that granted to the fictional Dorian Gray or Peter Pan, a quality that could be ascribed to their real lives. The novelist Booth Tarkington observed about the period's most popular male lead, the dashing and muscular Douglas Fairbanks, "He will never be older—unless quicksilver can get old." Indeed, youth was at such a premium that it would be artificially induced, particularly in the early days of the star system.

Films had the power to blur the distinction between reality and fantasy. One of the most popular actresses of the era was Theda Bara, who, following the success of 1915's *A Fool There Was,* was typecast as the classic femme fatale: kohl-eyed and smouldering with "unbridled eroticism". Her studio's press department portrayed her as the "child of a princess, weaned on serpents' blood, given in mystic marriage to a Sphynx", but in actuality she was Theodosia Goodman, a tailor's daughter from Ohio. The masque worked beautifully: when she played against type, her career was over.

This was but one of the pitfalls of the new system. The demands on these industrialized gods were beginning to increase. Apart from the make-over necessary for turning a real person into an abstract, and the corresponding psychological confusion, identities were completely constructed on the studio's terms. In contrast to the lustrously curled twelve- to sixteen-year-old innocent

1. This pagan quality was reinforced by the first blockbuster, D. W. Griffith's 1916 *Intolerance,* which, though based on the biblical story of Belshazzar, made Babylonian decadence sensational, thanks to the massive, spectacularly ornate set. So was Rochegrosse's vision of *Les derniers jours de Babylone* realized.

that she played, the real-life Mary Pickford was in her early twenties, was estranged from her husband, was having an affair, liked wearing long fingernails and smoking cigarettes. The star was becoming Frankenstein's monster.

The elision of actual and fictional age was also embodied in the figure of Charlie Chaplin, who turned the hobo into a comic archetype. To the critic Parker Tyler, Chaplin's famous costume of baggy pants and narrow jacket represented "a paradigm of the adult as seen by the child near his feet and looking up at the envied height". Chaplin began making films in 1914, just before his first major breakthrough, *The Tramp*, which set his image in stone. In choosing this outcast figure as a "Mob-God", Chaplin deliberately represented one of the bourgeoisie's worst nightmares.

The closing of the frontier meant the demonization of the traveller. By the mid-1910s, the hobo was a disturbing holdout of a wild past that many Americans were anxious to put behind them. Scandalous stories about a riot of the homeless in New York during the winter of 1914 reaffirmed the threat posed by the tramp to the orderly fabric of American social life. Assuming the figure of this most despised of all figures, utilizing all the talent and technical facilities at his disposal, Charlie Chaplin brought the underworld to light in the guise of entertainment.

The idea that stars could make outsiders attractive added another twist to the movies' appeal. Outlaws had long been American heroes, and nothing could be more attractive to the young than a figure that your parents hated. In *A Death in the Family*, James Agee described the reaction of his puritanical mother when she first saw *The Tramp*: Chaplin "flicked hold of the straight end of his cane and, with the crooked end, hooked up her [the actress's] skirt to the knee, in exactly the way that disgusted Mama, looking very eagerly at her legs, and everybody laughed loudly, but she pretended she had not noticed".

With their high-wire dance between exploitation and morality, these early movies perfectly embodied the American characteristic that Rupert Brooke defined as the "combination of entire wildness and entire regulation". When San Francisco's "vice district" was closed in 1913, a young cameraman named Hal Mohr shot footage of the final celebrations. The ads for *The Last Night of the Barbary Coast* promoted the pleasure-zone lifestyle at its moment of disappearance: "See the famous Turkey Trot, Texas Tommy, Bunny Hug. See the Negro dance halls with their own styles of dancing never before seen."

. . .

Even more than the movies, American popular music fell foul of the parent society's yo-yoing between hedonism and puritanism. During the early twentieth century, the music industry continued to expand rapidly: between 1890 and 1909, the revenue from sheet music more than tripled, while during the latter year, more than 27 million phonograph records and cylinders were manufactured. By 1914, the figure had risen to 31 million. Hungry for new product, the publishing and record companies continued to release whatever was at hand.

While the bestsellers of the period were big, sentimental ballads, ragtime continued to grow in popularity. Its cultural spread was assisted by a massive internal migration. With European immigration severely restricted after the outbreak of war in 1914, northern industrialists began actively to cast around for a new source of labour, canvassing southern blacks to fill the new jobs created by the demands of wartime production. Within the next few years, nearly one million blacks moved from the South into major urban centres like New York, Chicago, and Detroit, and they brought their life with them.

With many more black performers finding a ready audience outside the South, ragtime and blues continued to move out of inner-city vice districts. This diaspora increased their popularity among young whites. Ragtime might have been percolating throughout the black ghettos since the mid-1890s, but the style's first million-seller was achieved by Irving Berlin, with his 1911 hit "Alexander's Ragtime Band". It took a white man really to sell black music, as previously subterranean styles hit the mainstream as exploitable crazes. That was the deal: the new method of exchange.

Ragtime's crossover success excited unfavourable comment, not the least because of its appeal to youth. The *Musical American* thought that ragtime was like an addictive drug. In 1913, the *Musical Courier* stated that America was "falling prey to the collective soul of the Negro through the influence of what is popularly known as 'rag time' music". This was nothing less than "a national disaster", as ragtime was "symbolic of the primitive morality and perceptible moral limitations of the Negro type. With the latter sexual restraint is almost unknown, and the wildest latitude of moral uncertainty is conceded."

The link between music, race, and sexuality was confirmed in the moralists' eyes by the "animal dances" that flooded the inner cities after the success of "Alexander's Ragtime Band". Beginning with the success of the turkey trot, a very fast and animated dance that evolved out of the nineteenth-century communal cakewalk, a whole bestiary erupted onto the nation's dance floors to the accompaniment of ragtime: dances like the bunny hug, the grizzly bear, the monkey glide, the possum trot, the kangaroo dip. As Irving Berlin noted in his 1911 hit, "Everybody's doing it now."

In the animal dances, participants made up their moves as they went along. Instead of decorously holding each other at arm's length in the formality of the waltz and the polka, dancers whirled around the floor with their arms and legs intertwined. In the turkey trot, the lower half of the woman's body, from waist to knee, was enfolded in the legs of her male partner. The grizzly bear involved a total-body hug that went way beyond previous standards of propriety. This gliding and shimmying was an activity associated with burlesque performers and Negroes, not proper young whites.

America's young didn't care. Like the dreamland offered by the movies, the animal dances were tailor-made for their psyche. "Adolescence is the golden period of nascency for rhythm," Stanley Hall had noted. "Dancing is one of the best expressions of pure play and of the motor needs of youth." More practically, the new taxi-dance halls that had sprouted up to cater to the craze represented public places where America's working adolescents could meet each other away from adult supervision, and where they could court on their own terms.

Young women took the lead. In a 1911 survey of New York entertainment, it was discovered that 88 per cent of girls admitted that they knew how to dance: nearly all said that they enjoyed it. Some Manhattan working girls, according to the youth worker Ruth True, were spending "several nights a week at dance halls". Many of them lived in girls' homes which, as True noted, "were not very advantageous places for entertainment and fun. They are too cramped and too often forlorn." In particular, "visits from gentlemen friends" were "frowned upon".

In the dance hall, women could dance independently. A 1911 report by two adult reformers captured the ritual: "A large majority of the girls came by themselves and the young men by themselves, each finding partners at the hall. Few introductions were seen; two girls dance together and two young men whose fancy they suit pick them out and dance with them. Some fellows chat with them after the dance, and some do not." They concluded that although the girls "were bright and happy and fun-loving", they did not seem to care "what manner of young men they met".

The craze went uptown. *Life* magazine reported in February 1912 that animal dances were flourishing "above, below, and between. The dancing set in our town must be half a million strong." In his 1913 guidebook to New York nightlife, Julian Street observed that dancing had created a "social mixture such as was never before dreamed of in this country—a hodge-podge of people in which respectable young married and unmarried women, and even debutantes, dance, not only under the same roof, but in the same room with women of the town. Liberté—Egalité—Fraternité."

The revolutionary implications of a craze that appeared to stimulate class and race mixing provoked a backlash. Reform groups such as the New York Commission on Amusements and Vacation Resources for Working Girls had already criticized dance halls for promoting "licence and debauch", and they moved their investigators into smart hotels and society dances. Headlines like "Movement Begins to Bar 'Turkey Trot' and 'Grizzly Bear' from Fifth Avenue" tapped into a wider panic about plummeting moral standards.

This was summarized by a hysterical article in the August 1913 issue of *Current Opinion,* which seethed, "It has struck Sex O'Clock in America: a wave of sex hysteria and sex discussion seems to have invaded this country." Animal dances were associated with the increase in blatant prostitution and the prevalence of the white slave trade: the kidnapping and drugging of young girls for sexual purposes. There is little doubt that both did occur in the taxi-dance halls, but not to anything like the lurid extent promoted by the press and films like *Traffic in Souls.*[2] However, the publicity had the desired effect.

"Dance halls nowadays are notoriously great factors in breaking down morality," wrote the penologist William Healy in his encyclopaedic 1915 survey *The Individual Delinquent.* The reformers and the authorities did their best to police the craze. Unable completely to close down the halls or to extirpate this dancing mania, they began to target the urban zones from which all this vice had originated. Just at the time when black American music was finding a greater national and international audience, red-light districts in San Francisco and St Louis were segregated and then totally shut down.

But it was too late as, in defiance of the reformers and the legislators, thousands of American youths continued to throng the dance halls every night of the week. They voted with their feet. The popularity of the animal dances illustrated the fact that, during the first two decades of the twentieth century, adolescents were beginning to find their own culture in gregarious, exuberant urban entertainments. Far from being respectable, these amusements originated in the very outcast groups that were ascribed the same atavistic qualities as they were.

As youth became an integral part of mass American culture, it gave actual adolescents fresh encouragement to explore the very savagery that other

---

2. Congress had already passed the 1910 White Slave Traffic Act, later known as the Mann Act, that forbade, *inter alia,* the transportation of women under sixteen across state lines. This was used to clip the wings of the black heavyweight boxing champion of the world, Jack Johnson, who was convicted on a trumped-up charge in 1913.

American institutions—the school in particular—were attempting to tame. If that contradiction wasn't enough, the national project of linking youth with pleasure had another consequence. "This type of youth is transitory," wrote the radical youthist Randolph Bourne. "Pleasure contrives to burn itself out very quickly, and youth finds itself left prematurely with the ashes of middle age."

The rapid turnover of stars, fashions, and dance styles that marked the new consumer economy enshrined the transitory enthusiasms of adolescence at the same time as they provided an ideal industrial model of quick obsolescence. They also successfully diverted the great majority of America's young from what radicals like Bourne thought their true task: challenging the natural agenda of adults. However, these boons were bought at a price. The industrialized youthfulness of American popular culture, in effectively updating the intensity of the Romantics, also drank deep from their well of morbidity.

PART III

1912–1919

CHAPTER 10

Invocation

The European Generation Gap

• • •

Reproduction is always sacrificial.
—G. Stanley Hall, *Adolescence* (1904)

FRANCES CORNFORD IN NEO-PAGAN ATTITUDE AND ROBE,
AUGUST 1914

DURING 1912, TWO young French intellectuals named Henri Massis and Alfred de Tarde conducted a survey of Parisian males between eighteen and twenty-five, all of whom were in secondary or tertiary education. The sample was not representative of the population, but it captured the way that an influential section of metropolitan youth thought about themselves and their place in society. In turn, the sample had a wider resonance because, looking forward to the time when they would assume power, this elite was more likely than any of their contemporaries to consider themselves a distinct youth class.

The survey had its own bias. Massis and de Tarde were educational traditionalists. In their view, the replacing of classical study by "teutonic" sociology was only one example of a curriculum that failed to address the spiritual needs of French youth. Massis had already published a monograph in celebration of Maurice Barrès, whom he credited with giving his generation, sceptical and searching for a doctrine "that would give us back the energy that comes from will", a renewed sense of purpose. As he concluded, "The day on which we discovered Barrès, we discovered ourselves as well."

Having uncovered a new youth type that rejected the prevailing liberal, technological, and cosmopolitan establishment, Massis and de Tarde decided, like many future market researchers, to hold a survey with a preconfigured result. Collected the next year into the book *Les jeunes gens d'aujourd'hui* and published under the classical pseudonym Agathon—who in Greek history was Socrates' disciple, "brave in war"—the survey amply fulfilled its critical aim. As one of those surveyed bitterly complained, "Everything in their teaching forced us to serve as inert slaves or to exasperate ourselves in rebellion."

Agathon discovered a generation gap. The *enquête* compared the young men of 1912 with those coming to their majority in 1885. The earlier generation had been pessimistic, overtly intellectual, relativistic, and agnostic—qualities that had led them personally into decadence and France itself into its abject position during the 1870s. Tired of what they perceived as France's recent chaos, the rising generation took the opposite position. The young man of 1912 had "exiled self-doubt": it was "his distinguishing characteristic to create order and hierarchy, just as his elders created disorder and ruins".

This offered a fresh twist to the clash of the generations: the sons were rebelling against fathers who were not conservative but liberal, even decadent. It was as though Rimbaud, instead of being a traumatized witness to war, was directly responsible through his poetry for France's ignoble defeat in 1871. There was personal history in this: Massis had become friends with Maurice Barrès's nephew Charles Demange, who committed suicide in 1909. To Massis, Demange "was too much in a hurry to live; and this fever in him had something frightening about it. He had excellent nerves, but he abused them".

Seeking the way out from this adolescent intensity and "cult of self", Massis and de Tarde sought heroic examples to confirm Barrès's nationalism. They found their perfect model in the writer Ernest Psichari, then in his late twenties, and the picture of glowing health and discipline. It had not always been so: in his late teens he had flirted with socialism, and in 1903 had been brought to the brink of suicide. At this crisis point, Psichari entered his compulsory military service and decided to enlist as a regular soldier. For the rest of the decade he served in deepest Africa—an echo of Rimbaud's disappearance.

Published in 1913, the same year as Agathon's survey, Psichari's novel *L'appel des Armes* dramatized the clash of generations, by reversing the "normal relationship within attitudes" with a progressive father and a conservative son. Sent out to Africa on military service, Maurice Vincent falls under the spell of a captain who is "a great authority from the past": "pure, unsullied, uncontaminated by modernity." Progress is a form of Americanism, and "Americanism disgusted him". By the book's end, Vincent has become the perfect soldier, "the very embodiment of France".

Like religion, soldiering enshrined the surrender of the ego for the greater good, defined in this case as the purity and faith of a forgotten France. The linking of religion and militarism was reinforced by another major influence on Agathon, the writer Charles Péguy, who in 1910 published the polemical *Notre jeunesse*. Péguy expressed an apocalyptic disillusion: "We are the last. Almost the ones after the last. Immediately after us begins the world we call . . . the modern world. The world that tries to be clever. The world of the intelligent, the advanced . . . that is to say: the world of those who believe in nothing."

Agathon's principal message was that the generation of 1912 had naturally assumed the qualities that harbingers like Psichari and Péguy had had to strive for. The eighteen- to twenty-five-year-olds of the day were men of action, interested in aeroplanes and sports rather than books. Drawn to Catholicism, they were more sexually conservative than the 1885 generation, and quicker to accept adult responsibility. Disgusted with the corruption of the Third Republic, they sought redemption in the forthcoming war with Germany. Their combination of "battle mixed with prayers" inexorably led to a crusading martyrdom.

Les jeunes gens d'aujourd'hui was a media sensation. One novelist from the very class of 1885 that had been damned as "incapable" retorted by stating that the typical youth of the new generation was "passionately in love with pleasure and violent games, easily duped by the rhetoric of his time, inclined by the vigour of his muscles and the laziness of his mind to the brutal doctrines of the *Action Française*, nationalist, royalist and imperialist". Maurice Barrès, however, thought that "the new generation now ascending announces itself as one of the best that our country has ever known".

. . .

Agathon's survey was one of many European attempts in the immediate pre-war period to construct new youth movements. These sought to translate the vitality of youth and its fresh social importance into an artistic and/or social programme. Hitherto, youth had been a state principally defined by adults: now the subjects of these definitions clamoured to have their own voice. Abstracted in these tracts, youth became a religion in itself, an apotheosis made flesh in May 1911, when the sixteen-year-old mystic Jiddu Krishnamurti, brought to London by the Theosophists, was unveiled as the first adolescent messiah.

These years were the first golden age of the manifesto, as successive waves of angry youths announced their arrival in vaunting invocations of the "eternal dawn" to come and ringing denunciations of the father. There were many reasons for this: the rise in higher education; improved communications and social mobility; frustration at the slow rate of social change. There were also deeper psychological forces at play. While the conflict between father and son had already become a literary trope, Freud's 1910 coinage of the term "Oedipus complex" turned up the heat on a simmering intergenerational conflict.

The manifesto is the classic mode of the impatient adolescent. Living within a world run by elders, youth clearly sees all that is wrong, but is powerless to effect change. Instead, he or she has to continue living by rules that he or she knows with every fibre to be obsolete. The frustration spills out into polarizing rhetoric that admits no grey, just black and white. As the twenty-one-year-old expressionist writer Hans Leybold wrote in his 1913 manifesto *Revolution*, "You respected people! You well-polished ones! You bigwigs! We ought to stick out our tongues at you! Boys, you'll say. Old men! we'll reply."

This was also the first golden age of the "ists": the cubists, the expressionists, the futurists, the vorticists. As group vied with group to be more radical, more controversial, joining meant more than just being part of a movement: it meant total surrender within an ethos so powerful that it was like a religion. This again accorded with Stanley Hall's view of adolescence: he felt that religious conversion was "a natural, normal, universal, and necessary process" at this stage of life. Within an age where some of the avant-garde thought that God was dead, becoming an extremist was a more than satisfactory substitute.

These harder-edged ideologies were marked by the change in meaning of a keyword. In the mid-nineteenth century, "generation" had been used to describe "all men living more or less in the same time". In America, it described immigrant assimilation into society: first or second generation. By 1900, it had assumed a youthful connotation: terms like "the new generation" were common, a usage that returned the word to its Latin root—literally "becoming". It also keyed into the prevalent 1890s discourse of de- and re-generation: that struggle for the future of the nation-race within which youth occupied the front line.

The definition of youth as a discrete class occurred at the same time as the general use of the suffix "generation" as controlling social ideas. However, adults had also promoted the self-consciousness of that newly illuminated class—with unforeseen results, as Frankenstein's monster turned on its creator. Consciously or unconsciously, the new youthists realized that the first step in reclaiming power was to annex the word at the heart of all those adult disciplines. During the 1900s, therefore, "generation" ceased to be a controlling word, and instead became an extremist clarion call.

"Every time a generation presents itself on the terrace of life it seems that the world's symphony is going to have to attack a new tempo," wrote the Italian polemicist Giovanni Papini in his 1912 autobiography, *Un uomo finito*. This offered one of the purest expressions of this period's generational impulse: "For the twenty-year-old man, every old man is the enemy; every idea is suspect; every great man there to be put on trial; past history seems a long night broken only by lamps, a grey and impatient waiting, an eternal dawn of that morning that emerges today finally with us."

However, in these early days the pursuit of freedom was fraught with difficulty. Having forcibly divorced themselves from the experience of their elders and cut themselves adrift from what was known, these young extremists then had to live with the consequences of that separation. Implicit in the idea of the generation gap was the strong feeling that the rising generation was, as Robert Wohl writes in *The Generation of 1914*, "unique, sacrificed, and lost". Within this vacuum, many of these extremists would end up mirroring the values that they so violently rejected.

. . .

The first uses of this generational rhetoric were aesthetic. In 1906, the German painters of the school Die Brücke, the Bridge, called on "all youth to gather" to "create elbowroom and existential freedom against the settled older forces". In practice, however, this resulted merely in a refinement of existing expressionist and fauvist aesthetics. The futurists in Italy, however, presented themselves as a radical rupture. In his journal *Leonardo*, Giovanni Papini had already called on young Italians to throw caution to the wind and live for adventure, dreams, and "eternal programmes".

Coloured by this generational rhetoric and the country's tradition of violent, personally directed polemic called *la stroncatura*, the artist F. T. Marinetti in February 1909 announced his vision of a future world dominated by the youth principle. "The oldest of us is thirty," he declaimed in the futurist manifesto, "so we have at least a decade for finishing our work. When we are forty, other younger and stronger men will probably throw us in the wastebasket like useless manuscripts—we want it to happen!"

However, the most important element in Marinetti's manifesto was its embrace of technology. With the development of the car and the aeroplane, radio and movies, man could now break the bounds of his body and hurl himself into time and space as never before. "We affirm that the world's magnificence has been enriched by a new beauty," Marinetti wrote, "the beauty of speed. A racing car whose hood is adorned with great pipes, like serpents of explosive breath—a roaring car that seems to ride on grapeshot is more beautiful than the *Victory of Samothrace*."

This was a significant break with the nature worship of the *Wandervogel* or the Neo-Pagans: instead of something to be abhorred, the man-machine was to be celebrated. As Marinetti warned, "We already live in the absolute, because we have created eternal, omnipresent speed. We will glorify war—the world's only hygiene—militarism, patriotism, the destructive gesture of freedom bringers, beautiful ideas worth dying for, and scorn for woman. We will destroy the museums, libraries, academies of every kind, will fight moralism, feminism, every opportunistic or utilitarian cowardice."

The futurists cranked up the intellectual and aesthetic acceleration that would inform so much of twentieth-century life. This came at a heavy price, however, as Marinetti and his peers in the bellicose "Young Italy" group thrust themselves into uncharted territory. In their reaction against the perceived "femininity" of decadence, they extolled the rigid certainties of nationalism, the demands of externally imposed discipline, and the trigger-happy violence that marks a particular, defended masculine pathology. There was no place for the female sex in the new youth world of Mars.

Marinetti's rhetoric enshrined the combination of paganism with technology that laced the period: Stanley Hall's "barbarism with electric lights". His brutal polemics, however, bore their own fruit on a visit to London during June 1914, when he was attacked by the adherents of a new art movement. Despite their strong futurist influence, the vorticists and their leader, Percy Wyndham Lewis, were not averse to a spot of patricide. Faced by a group as noisy and as disruptive as any summoned up by his rhetoric, Marinetti entered a climactic argument about speed that broke him "into a hundred angry pieces".

The vorticists issued their first publication in June 1914, a large puce-coloured magazine that encoded its position in the title—*Blast*. Written by the pugilistic Wyndham Lewis, the manifesto's Manichaean opposites, typograph-ically organized into pages headed "BLAST" and "BLESS", injected a new, harsh note into British cultural life. Rejecting the politesse of the Bloomsbury group, the vorticists sought to synthesize European modernism with Polynesian sculpture, and pushed futurist delight in technology and urbanism into a hard-faced, hard-line aesthetic: "We Are Primitive Mercenaries in the Modern World."

The vitality of youth was an integral part of their aesthetic. The introductory "Long Live the Vortex" pronounced, "WE WANT THE WORLD TO LIVE, and to feel its crude energy flowing through us." Wyndham Lewis cursed "The Britannic Aesthete" and advertised "ENORMOUS YOUNGSTERS, BURST-ING EVERYWHERE THROUGH HEAVY TIGHT CLOTHES". Celebrating the contradictory and explosive currents of pre-war life, they themselves would remain calm within the centre of the whirlpool:

> Our vortex is not afraid of the past: it has forgotten its existence.
> Our vortex regards the Future as sentimental as the past . . .
> With our vortex the present is the only active thing.
> Life is the Past and the Future.
> The Present is Art.

There was a distinct sense, in 1912, 1913, and 1914, of everything coming to a point. The vortex began to drag everything within its irresistible momentum, as nineteenth-century certainties began to dissolve. Youth's place in this new savage world was dramatized by one of the period's most sensational *Gesamt-kunstwerke*,[1] so new that it provoked a near riot at its May 1913 premiere.[2] Star-ring the gravity-defying Vaslav Nijinsky,[3] with a score by Igor Stravinsky that carried machine sound into a jarring mechanical repetition, the latest Russian ballet, *Le sacre du printemps*, exalted nothing less than tribal sacrifice.

---

1. Total artworks.

2. The American drama critic Carl Van Vechten attended the ballet's first night at the end of May 1913. He reported that "the French were so startled and offended by this novelty that they hissed it almost without secession".

3. According to the autobiography of Tamara Karsavina, "Somebody was asking Nijinsky if it was difficult to stay in the air as he did while jumping; he did not understand at first, and then very obligingly: 'No! No! not difficult. You have to just go up and then pause a little up there.'"

Sergei Diaghilev's Ballets Russes were notorious both for their lavish, innovative productions and their ability to create scandal: Nijinsky's simulated onstage orgasm in 1912's *L'après-midi d'un faune* had already caused outrage in Paris. Indeed, Diaghilev's productions were high modernist in their fascination with the primitive, their hostility to the new mass civilization, and their exaltation of youthful vitality. *Le sacre du printemps* synthesized visual art, music, text, and dance into an all-out assault on contemporary perception—like a jump cut into the future.

The drive behind techno-paganism was revealed in the narrative that Stravinsky designed to evoke "the creative power of spring". The ballet began with Pan pipes and a ritual of spring regeneration, before moving to "The Great Sacrifice": "All night the virgins hold mysterious games, walking in circles. One of the virgins is consecrated as the victim and is twice pointed to by fate, being caught twice in the perpetual dance. The virgins . . . invoke the ancestors and entrust the chosen one to the old wise men. She sacrifices herself in the presence of the old men to the great holy dance, the great sacrifice."

Stravinsky's first title for the piece—*The Victim*—underscored the idea that there was to be no regeneration without violence. Although *Le sacre du printemps* was coming from the other side of the artistic spectrum than *Peter Pan*, it offered the same brutal prediction. Youth was being energized for conflict, so that they would willingly participate in the sacrifice that was necessary for the twentieth-century world to begin. In July 1914, the critic Maurice Dupont called the ballet "a Dionysian orgy dreamed of by Nietzsche and called forth by his prophetic wish to be the beacon of a world hurtling towards death".

The earlier generation's escapist paganism had no chance against these harsh exigencies. Five months after the sensational premiere of *Le sacre du printemps*, the *Wandervogel* held what was intended to be a climactic gathering at the Hohe Meissner near Kassel. The movement had grown in size and ambit, and had stretched outside Germany's borders to pull in all kinds of youth groupings with political views that ranged from anarchism to anti-industrialism to racism. It had been decided to pull all these disparate groups, or *Bunde*, into one overall organization called the Freideutsche Jugend.

This *Freideutsche Jugendtag* (day for free German youth) was also intended to counteract the many patriotic gatherings held during 1913, the centenary year of the victorious battle of Leipzig, so beloved of German militarists. In contrast to this socially sanctioned beer-hall chauvinism, they wanted the freedom "to give shape and form to their life" apart "from the sluggish habits of the old and from the commandments of hateful convention". However, rambling by itself was not enough to contain all the many ideologies and world theories that the movement was attempting to include.

Many of the speakers delivered contradictory messages, ranging from belli-cose exhortations to the Free School movement founder Gustav Wyneken's thoughtful leftist refusal of nationalism's lure. "We must dare," he stated in the meeting's climactic address, "to keep a certain distance from the Father-land and from the unthinking patriotism in which we have been educated." However, the message did not go in very deep. Contrary to its stated aims, al-most all of the speeches at the *Freideutsche Jugendtag* were by adults, and the audience simply danced right through them.

Despite a general sense of achievement, the Hohe Meissner meeting ended without any clear agreement or definite plan as to how all the different Ger-man youth groups would unite. Very soon afterwards, the scissions started, as the movement split along more traditional left-right political lines. At the same time, alarmed by the *Wandervogel*'s influence, the authorities created adult-controlled youth groups that sought to corral the nature worship and group mentality of German youth into more acceptable forms.

The most successful of these was the nationalistic Jungdeutschlandbund, formed in Prussia during 1911 in order to give German youth proper military training. With its strong links to the army, this new state-approved group of-fered a mixture of fresh-air exercise and "war games": activities included drill, first-aid practice, and full-blown manoeuvres, welded to an explicitly martial ideology. After its initial success, the army and the civil service attempted to bring in all other youth movements under this banner.

By 1914, the Jugendeutschlandbund had swallowed up many *Wandervogel* groupings. Their notions of *Lebensraum* and male bonding were not, after all, too different from the Prussian drive towards expansion and empire. Sacrifice replaced nature worship in the movement's magazine: "War is beautiful. Its greatness lifts a man's heart above earthly things, above the daily round. Such an hour awaits us . . . let that be heaven for young Germany. Thus we wish to knock at our God's door." Mustering about 750,000 members, the Jung-deutschlandbund had become the largest youth group in the world.

CHAPTER 11

Sacrifice

The War Dead and the Young Against the Old

. . .

Nature arms youth for conflict with all the resources at her command.
—G. Stanley Hall, preface, *Adolescence* (1904)

RUPERT BROOKE, 1913, BY SHERRIL SCHELL

NO ONE KNEW when or where the war would begin, but the masses that flocked the streets of European cities in high summer 1914 were suffused with what Wyndham Lewis, commenting on the London throng, called "a sluggish electricity". When the storm finally broke on June 28, the catalyst was patricide: the shooting of the heir to the Hapsburg Empire, Archduke Franz Ferdinand, by the nineteen-year-old Serb Gavrilo Princip, a member of the nationalistic Mlada Bosna (Young Bosnia) group.

As the crisis developed, the demand for war, despite protests, swept all before it in a paroxysm of nationalistic feeling. Gustave Le Bon had warned in 1895 that "the claims of the masses are becoming more and more sharply defined, and amount to nothing less than a determination to utterly destroy society as it now exists". The technological age, as already prophesied, was erupting into the first truly mass conflict, one that would kill millions of combatants and civilians alike.

After six weeks of uncertainty, the war was triggered by Germany's invasion of Belgium on Monday, August 3. In Britain, the previous weekend had been a public holiday and, as *The Times* reported, many "holidaymakers had been attracted to London by a desire to be present in the capital in this moment of grave crisis". By Monday evening thousands of people had gathered in London's public spaces: "The demonstration of patriotism and loyalty became almost ecstatic until at last the enormous crowd eventually dispersed."

"In the afternoon I went up town and wandered about in front of Buckingham Palace and down the Mall," remembered a seventeen-year-old working-class Londoner, Vic Cole. "There was a great crowd of people outside the Palace and other crowds were congregating in Whitehall and towards Westminster. Later on that night, just before midnight, the word went around that, the ultimatum having expired, we were now at war with Germany. I was terribly excited; the thing that people had been talking about for years had at last come about and at any moment (I thought) the invasion of England would begin."

At the age of ten, Vic Cole had witnessed a display at London's Crystal Palace called "The Invasion", which "featured a life-size English village complete with church and pub. Village folk walked slowly from the former and others drank beer outside the latter. Into this peaceful rural scene suddenly a German aeroplane swooped (it ran down a wire) and dropped some bombs which exploded with appropriate noise and a lot of smoke. When the air cleared, it was seen that German soldiers occupied the village. All ended happily when the Territorials arrived and routed the enemy."

Despite being under the minimum serving age, Cole could not wait to sign up: "I wanted to be in the army with gun in hand like the boys I had so often read about in books and magazines." After enlisting, he went home to tell his relatives the news. "Hardly waiting to close the door, I called out, 'I've joined the army!' 'Oh dear! Oh dear!' said Gran. 'My poor boy.' Neither of them were at all demonstrative but when I sat down, Gran put her old arms around me for a moment. My aunt shed a tear and then said, 'Well, I suppose you'd like a cup of tea now.'"

With no idea of what was to come, the youth of northern Europe enthusiastically enlisted. The French regarded the conflict as a chance to make good the national humiliation of the Franco-Prussian War and to reclaim the province of Alsace, lost in 1871. The response to the late July call to mobilization was overwhelming, so much so that when the French Socialist Party leader, Jean Jaurès, called for a concerted working-class effort against the imminent conflict, he was assassinated by a fanatical nationalist. On August 2, Germany crossed the French border for the first time since 1870.

Here was the chance to rewrite history. Ernest Psichari felt that the conflict had "come at the time and in the manner that we required". The bourgeois youth of France agreed. Robert Poustis, then a Parisian student, remembered that in August 1914 "everyone was shouting and wanting to go to the Front. The cars, the railway wagons loaded with soldiers were full of tricolour flags and inscriptions: 'A Berlin, à Berlin.' We wanted to go to Berlin immediately, with bayonets and lances, running after the Germans. The war, we thought, was to last two months, maybe three months."

For their part, the Germans saw war as a chance to flex their muscles on an international stage. Their motto, contained in a contemporary bestseller, was *"Weltmacht oder Untergang"*—World Dominion or Decline. This was backed up by wild crowd behaviour that late July: reason had flown out of the window. As Ernst Junger, nineteen on his enlistment in 1914, later observed, "An interest in the gruesome was of course part of the complex of desires that dragged us so irresistibly into the war. A period of law and order as long as the one our generation had behind it brought a real craving for the extraordinary."

Years of militaristic agitation and preparation by groups like the Jung-deutschlandbund had turned war into a kind of religious experience. The Prussian dramatist and former *Wandervogel* Walter Flex wrote in 1914, "I am no longer myself. I used to be. I am now part of the holy horde which sacrifices itself for you—Fatherland." The first wartime edition of *Der Wandervogel* stated, "Nothing divides the *Wandervogel* from manhood. We are not special. We wish to be considered like all the others, men in the fullest sense of the term."

German youth signed up in an ecstasy of self-immolation. Ernst Junger, one of militarism's most articulate exponents, recalled later in his memoir,

The Storm of Steel, that "we had grown up in a material age, and in each one of us there was the yearning for great experience, such as we had never known. The war had entered into us like wine. We had set out in a rain of flowers to seek the death of heroes. The war was our dream of greatness, power and glory. It was a man's work, a duel on fields whose flowers would be stained with blood. There is no lovelier death in the world."

. . .

The youth of Germany and France were well prepared. By August 1914, the armies of both countries stood at about 3.6 million apiece. In comparison, the British army had been neglected and underfunded, standing at just under 250,000 regular officers and men. With reservists and part-time volunteers, Britain could muster a full military strength of just under 750,000, about a quarter of their fellow combatants. Without conscription, the slack would have to be taken up by volunteers, but the popular enthusiasm was such that 300,000 men enlisted in the first few weeks of war.

Among them were the wards of J. M. Barrie, George and Peter Llewelyn Davies. At twenty-one, George was already attending Cambridge, with Peter, then seventeen, just about to go up. In the first week of August, they were both sent a letter from the adjutant of Cambridge University Officer Training Corps "pointing out that it was the obvious duty of all undergraduates to offer their services forthwith". They found that their school experience was enough to ensure a commission. When the presiding colonel found out that George had played cricket for Eton, he "became noticeably more genial".

It was no surprise that upper-class and upper-middle-class young men thronged the recruitment halls. They had been primed for war on the playing fields, in their self-regulated peer societies, through the ethos of muscular Christianity. Robert Graves, then at Charterhouse, recalled that when an army general visited his school training camp in 1913, he "impressed upon us that war with Germany must inevitably break out within two or three years, and that we must be prepared to take our part in it as leaders of the new forces that would assuredly be called into being".

Shortly afterwards, Graves participated in a school debate on the motion "that this house is in favour of compulsory military service". He recalled that "only six votes out of one hundred and nineteen were noes. I was the principal opposition speaker, having recently resigned from the Officers' Training Corps in revolt against the theory of implicit obedience to orders." Graves was in a distinct minority of about 5 per cent who chose to react against the militaristic ethos of the day, as the overwhelming majority of his peers fell into line.

Other young men from the Boys' Brigade or the Boy Scouts signed up immediately and found that, as designed, their regimented training stood in their favour. As Richard Hawkins remembered, "You had four platoon sergeants which you had to choose from your men, and by Jove if one had been in the Boy Scouts, well, he was a corporal straight away." Jack Davis, then nineteen, enlisted in early September: "I was in the Boys' Brigade and was a member of an athletics club too, so I both accepted discipline and had an organized life. It meant the call of the army quite naturally attracted me."

Just like the *Wandervogel,* the British Scouts adapted quickly to the demands of war. From the early 1910s they had been increasingly affiliated with the Duty and Discipline movement, designed to counteract the "serious social danger" of "present juvenile ill-discipline". This establishment-approved body gave a fresh impetus to the calls for conscription already emanating from the National Service League. For militarists like Lord Roberts and Colonel Baden-Powell, universal military training for all men between eighteen and twenty-three was "the solution to Britain's moral decay".

When the war broke out, Baden-Powell thought that it gave the Scout movement "its greatest opportunity". Apart from getting official recognition for the Scout uniform, he also established a Scout Defence Corps for fifteen- to seventeen-year-olds, in which they would receive special training in basic military techniques like shooting, signalling, and trench building. With his inside track into the boyish mind, he recognized the sheer adolescent appeal of war: "So, too, on the outbreak of war the minds of the boys are obsessed with warlike ideas. It is of little use to fight against this when the fever is on them."

However, 60 per cent of British adolescents had had no contact with any pre-military training, and they were swayed not by war fever alone but by a number of other factors. Some were bored with their jobs and sought adventure. According to the recruitment practice of the time, whole workforces and whole areas were signed up together. This meant that you could remain with your workmates and friends in the same army regiment. To stay at home was all but impossible when all your friends had left to put their lives at risk.

In 1914, exemption was conferred to workers in essential industries and those under nineteen. However this minimum age requirement was often ignored. In that season of war fever, Londoner Reginald Haine went to sign up: "My friend introduced me to the sergeant, who said, 'Are you willing to join?' I said. 'Yes Sir.' He said, 'Well, how old are you?' I said, 'I am eighteen and one month.' He said, 'Do you mean nineteen and one month?' So I thought a moment and said, 'Yes Sir.' He said, 'Right-ho, well sign here please.'"

For the less immediately eager, the attractions of army life increased as unemployment rose during autumn 1914. In the first few months of the war, up to half a million men lost their jobs as the result of blocked trade routes and economic uncertainty. The health of the poor working class had not significantly improved since it had been identified as a national scandal during the Boer War. For a large proportion of Britain's inner-city young, army rations represented a significant improvement on their living conditions. The recruiting sergeants' promise of "meat every day!" struck a chord.

Robert Roberts remembered that recruits returning to Salford on leave were "stones heavier, taller, confident, clean and straight". "Hardly recognizable as the men who went away," they encouraged others to enlist immediately. The officer Charles Carrington remembered that "when they came to us they were weedy, sallow, skinny, frightened children—the refuse of our industrial system—and they were in very poor condition because of wartime food shortages. But after six months of good food, fresh air and physical exercise they changed so much that their mothers wouldn't have recognized them."

The social pressure to sign up was overwhelming. In the early days of the war, this was policed by thousands of young women who went around handing out white feathers to all young men out of uniform in a gesture that imputed cowardice. The idea had been dreamed up by a retired admiral, who created the Order of the White Feather specifically for this purpose, and it was backed up by poster campaigns that asked, "Is your 'Best Boy' wearing khaki? If not, don't *YOU THINK* he should be? If he does not think that you and your country are worth fighting for—do you think he is *WORTHY* of you?"

Bearing in mind that the sexual attractiveness of an army uniform was a factor in many young men's minds, this was a brutally effective campaign. Regardless of whether they were underage or had already enlisted, every apparent "shirker" was a potential victim. A sixteen-year-old Londoner, Norman Demuth, was "astonished" to be given a white feather: "I had been trying to persuade the doctors and recruiting officers that I was nineteen and thought, well, this must give me some added bounce, because I must look the part, so I went round to the recruiting offices with added zeal."

A young art teacher named Harry Ogle recalled that "a wave of fear seemed to have spread over the country and young men not in uniform were presented with white feathers by young women (also not in uniform). Men over forty, thinking themselves safe behind 'important' jobs, urged those to enlist who were too young to have anything to lose but their lives. The elderly and painfully religious couple whose lodger I was were cold to me, loudly praising Ted Pullen, who, as the newspapers had it, had gallantly 'placed his young life at the service of the Nation'."

. . .

These ploys were only the street-level version of a much wider suppression of anti-war sentiment. Opposition was there from the beginning, in speeches by independent socialists, editorials in left-wing magazines, Cambridge intellectuals like Bertrand Russell, and the Bloomsbury group. The rule of law was immediately invoked to suppress them, after the Defence of the Realm Act (known as DORA) was passed on August 8, 1914. Prominent politicians and writers advocated war as a "sovereign disinfectant" against a "national decay", of which the modern movement was the most morbid symptom.

In his bellicose play Der Tag,[1] premiered in December 1914, J. M. Barrie wrote that "Britain has grown dull and sluggish: a belly of a land, she lies overfed, no dreams within her such as to keep Powers alive". In an October 1914 speech entitled, "Art, Morals and the War", Oxford professor of fine art Selwyn Image stated that "we need a cleansing purge, a sharp awakening, a recalling to sanity, to a readjustment of our estimates of things". For him, the war was a "salutary shock". Another populist editor simply expressed his hope for the modernists: "that they may all perish in the war."

Within this overwhelming mobilization of minds and bodies—three million men in the first eighteen months of war—there were very few conscientious objectors: just over sixteen thousand for the whole four-year period. It took considerable conviction to become a CO. Although 80 per cent were granted exemption from military service, a significant proportion were sent to the front to work as ambulance and medical staff, where they were still despised by their fellow countrymen. The more rigorous recusants were among the six thousand or so COs sent to prison, where the unluckier were forced into straitjackets and beaten.

However, that is not to say that many young men did not sign up without misgivings. Beneath the bravado, many were scared of an unknown future. Peter Llewelyn Davies remembered that, on their way to enlist, his brother George "had one of those queer turns, something between a fainting fit and a sick headache, to which he had been prone since childhood, and had to sit for a few minutes on a seat outside the barracks. I would have willingly turned tail and gone back to London humiliated but free. George, however, the moment he recovered, marched me in with him through those dark portals."

The day the Llewelyn Davies brothers arrived at the vast Sheerness barracks for their military training, they found that "eight young officers", who had only joined a week or two earlier, were on their way to France "to replace casu-

1. The German toast to victory.

alties in the Battalions on the Marne and the Aisne. This somewhat abrupt confrontation with the exigencies of the service had, temporarily, a depressing effect, and I remember George, as we undressed in our tent that night, breaking a rather long silence with the words, 'Well, young Peter, for the first time in our lives we're up against something really serious, **** me if we aren't.' "

These misgivings were not misplaced. All soldiers dream of a short, sharp campaign, and this European conflict was no different. In August, almost everyone thought that it would be over by Christmas. As the casualty lists grew, and the two armies became locked in stasis around the Ypres salient, it slowly dawned on the military, if not the public, that this would not be the case. Instead of campaigns fought by small, highly mobile chivalric units, huge forces began to square up to each other over an immovable trench system. This would not be a war of individual heroics, but of slow, mass attrition.

This fundamental change in the nature of warfare came as a huge shock to the idealistic volunteers and conscripts of 1914. Many had already found the transition between peacetime and wartime difficult: this, after all, was one traditional rite of passage between youth and adulthood, and not everyone gave up their youth without some resistance. As a young Yorkshireman, F. B. Vaughan, remembered, "It came rather hard to start to obey commands, but gradually we knew how to form fours, right wheel, left wheel and all the rest of them. We became in other words a disciplined body of men."

Mixing route marches, bayonet fixing, and trench digging, the six-month British infantry training process eliminated individuality and immersed the recruit in the principal army values: to obey the orders of superiors at all costs and to suspend the peacetime taboo against killing another human being. At the same time, the rebelliousness and vitality of youth was subsumed within a world where the elders, the superior officers, unquestionably ruled. This in itself was no different from the classic army training, but wars had previously been fought by a small percentage of the youth population.

In this mass war, millions of adolescents would be involved together in the surrender of their youth, if not their life: a generational holocaust that would have unforeseen and long-lasting consequences. Serving in the first major campaign of the war, the fight for the Belgian port of Antwerp, Rupert Brooke witnessed the new conditions of conflict. "It's a bloody thing," he wrote to an American friend, "half the youth of Europe blown through pain to nothingness, in the incessant mechanical slaughter of these modern battles." He had just turned twenty-seven but continued to define himself by his youth.

On the outbreak of war, Brooke had used his influential contacts like Winston Churchill to get a quick commission. He had finally found his métier. In a brief autobiographical article written just after the declaration of war, "An Unusual Young Man", he revealed that he was the young man of the title, because despite all the horrors to come, "he was extraordinarily happy." Military service and the probability of glorious death offered a cast-iron solution to Brooke's irrevocably tangled emotions. As he wrote, "I expect it will be the best thing for everyone if a stray bullet finds me next year."

After Antwerp, Brooke sought to put his passion for war as the just cause into a long poem called *1914*. In this explicitly youth-oriented tract—"Now, God be thanked / Who has matched us with His hour, / And caught our youth, and wakened us from sleeping"—Brooke converted the ritual sacrifices that the Neo-Paganists had toyed with into the military sacrifice demanded by war. In the third part, called "Death", he celebrated the fallen: "and those would have been, / Their sons, they gave, their immortality." This was "the heritage" that he, and by implication, his generation, had finally grown into.

This sequence struck an immediate chord on its publication in early March 1915. It was the first of many collections that would seek to define an almost inconceivable experience in an intimate, more contemplative language than that of censored news or military communiqué. As the *Times Literary Supplement* stated, "These sonnets are personal—never were sonnets more personal since Sidney died²—and yet the very blood and youth of England seem to find expression in them. They speak not for one heart only, but for all to whom her call has come in the hour of need and found instantly ready."

These flowery phrases, however, did not accord with the actual experience of mass war. In March 1915, George Llewelyn Davies wrote to J. M. Barrie from the trenches. He had seen a soldier put his head above the parapet: "The top of his head was shot off, so he didn't feel it. But it was a dreadful sight." Replying with the news that George's uncle Guy du Maurier had just been killed, Barrie concluded, "I have lost all sense I ever had of war being glorious, it is just unspeakably monstrous now." Three days later, Llewelyn Davies was shot through the head: he had thought it "the finest death one could die".

In early April, the dean of St Paul's Cathedral read out part of *1914* in his Easter Sunday sermon. By this time, however, Brooke was laid up with a severe fever, and on April 23 he died of septicaemia. Already recognized as a significant war poet, his death sealed the pact in marble. The tributes poured in: "He is the youth of our race in symbol" (the *Star*); "He was part of the youth of the world" (the *Daily News*). *The Times* ran a long, unsigned obituary by Ed-

2. The famous soldier-poet of the sixteenth century. On May 3, the *Sphere* wrote of Brooke that he "was the only English poet of any consideration who has given his life in his country's wars since Philip Sidney received his death wound under the walls of Zutphen in 1586".

ward Marsh, which ascribed to him "the sorrow of youth about to die, and the sure triumphant consolation of a sincere and valiant spirit".

This was not the full Rupert Brooke, as his friends attempted to point out in vain: as the *New Statesman* put it, "A myth has been created, but it has grown around an imaginary figure very different from the real man." But these complaints were swamped in an outpouring of national feeling. Aided by a classic profile and the boyish good looks caught in the famous photographs by Sherril Schell, Brooke became the dead poster boy representing every one of the thousands of young men whose deaths were being reported with increasing velocity in *The Times*'s Roll of Honour.

The Germans also celebrated this necrotic ethos of youth immortality. In the early part of the war, many of the first wave of volunteers were killed at the Flemish village of Langemarck. In the reports of this November action, thousands of still untried troops, made up of apprentices, university students, and grammar school pupils, met their deaths in a hopeless advance against heavily defended Allied positions. In the fable, a young voice broke into song—the famous nationalist rallying call, *"Deutschland, Deutschland über Alles"*—and the tune was taken up by successive waves of young Germans.

Out of this needless slaughter a powerful myth was born, one that extolled the principle of self-sacrifice unto death. Many of the dead were former *Wandervogel:* the atavistic irrationality that the movement had toyed with had been easily diverted from nature to battle mysticism. As one young volunteer stated, "We saw the meaning of the war in this inner liberation of the whole nation from its obsolete conventions, in this 'breakthrough' into the unknown, into some heroic venture, no matter whom it devoured. That was what fired our enthusiasm."

This transition was captured in a famous wartime novel. Written by a serving officer named Walter Flex, *A Wanderer Between Two Worlds* celebrated Flex's friend Ernst Wurche, who thought that "all the glory and health of future Germany came from the *Wandervogel*". According to Flex, Wurche "embodied this spirit of pure and bright". From the eclectic nature of *Wandervogel* reading—"a little volume of Goethe, Zarathustra, and a field edition of the New Testament"—Wurche offered a parable about army life: "In the trenches all sorts of alien spirits are forced to rub shoulders. It's the same with books as well as people."

When Wurche was killed, Flex sought to immortalize his friend. He put his thoughts into the mouth of Wurche's ghost, who appeared just at the moment when Flex was losing heart: "That is not old age, as you think, but growing maturity. Your deeds and your dead are making you mature and keeping you young. It is life that has become old and greedy, death remains always the same. Do you know nothing of death's eternal youth? It is God's will that ageing life should become young again in the eternal youthfulness of death. That is the meaning and the mystery of death."

In its conflation of romanticism, *Wandervogel* nature mysticism, and surrender to military ideology, Flex's ideology offered a consistent "moral conviction which can be realized as much in the defeat or in the heroic sacrifice of a nation". Published at the end of 1917, shortly after Flex's death, *A Wanderer Between Two Worlds* helped to make sense out of the senseless. The author had remained true to his vision until the end. As he wrote in his last letter, "I have the tranquil, inner knowledge that everything that happens and can happen to me is part of a living development over which nothing dead has any power."

The works of Walter Flex and Rupert Brooke gave an idealistic gloss to what was becoming nothing less than mass slaughter. Spring 1915 was a time when the horror of this war became apparent. The British offensive at Neuve Chapelle failed, with seven thousand dead. The Germans launched their first chlorine gas attack. The first zeppelin attacks on London occurred. The combatants on the Western Front were bogged down in the trench system that ran from the English Channel to the Swiss border.

During autumn 1915, 80 per cent of the British attacking force in the battle of Loos were either killed or wounded. This was the horror of what the German generals called *Stellungskrieg,* position warfare: a new kind of defensive strategy, where whole battalions went down "like a lot of Charlie Chaplins". Ernst Junger observed that "here chivalry disappeared for always. Like all noble and personal feelings it had to give way to the new tempo of battle and to the rule of the machine." The constant thump of heavy artillery offered nothing but an instant, anonymous death: most of the dead were never identified.

For those who survived, the trench experience was a total assault on the senses. Quite apart from the relentless shelling, troops also had to contend with flame-throwers, gas, snipers, and the everyday conditions of existence: dirt, cold, flood, mud, rats, fleas, and other vermin of all descriptions. In this hell, men aged dramatically. Robert Graves thought that officers were "at their best" between three and four weeks at the front. After then "neurasthenia set in". There was an optimum age for survival: "Officers between the age of twenty-three and thirty-three could count on a longer useful life than those older or younger."

The disparity between the idealism of 1914 and the reality of war was so great that combatants and noncombatants alike had to find myths that would give meaning to the meaningless. The elevation of Brooke and Flex to hero status marked the return of that powerful Romantic nexus of youth, death, and immortality, but not as an expression of freedom. Indeed, both are classic infanticidal victims, Abraham's Isaac—but this time willingly rejoicing in their sacrifice. But although war was a young man's game, it was fought under the terms laid down by older men: youth had no choice but to obey.

. . .

As the war continued without any breakthrough, youth itself became an ideological battleground. This particular conflict, for the soul of a whole generation, was enacted verbally but with no less bitterness. Almost as soon as they had been enshrined, the crystalline abstractions of 1914 were becoming obsolete on the ground. In response to Brooke's death, a twenty-year-old officer named Charles Sorley criticized his sentimental rendering of his military service "as a highly intense, remarkable and sacrificial exploit, whereas it is merely the conduct demanded of him (and others) by the turn of circumstances".

Later that year, another ex–public school serving officer wrote about life in the Loos trenches to his uncomprehending fiancée. Roland Leighton described "the fleshless, blackened bones of simple men who poured out their red, sweet wine of youth unknowing, for nothing more tangible than Honour or their Country's Glory or another's Lust [for] Power". Having enlisted with typical idealism, Leighton sarcastically called on those who promoted war to "realise how grand & glorious a thing it is to have distilled all Youth and Joy and Life into a fetid heap of hideous putrescence".

Youth's central importance was confirmed when the British government finally turned to conscription. The rate of attrition was such that the demand for fresh blood was relentless. In August 1915, a national register had been instituted, which compelled every man and woman between sixteen and sixty-five to provide details of their lives. A further volunteer scheme in October failed to bring the required numbers, and full conscription of single men between eighteen and forty-one was introduced in February 1916. This released two million more soldiers, with more after May, when married men were also conscripted.

That same month, the Germans launched a decisive blow at the Verdun salient, the beginning of a nine-month holocaust that took half a million French lives. In June, the offensive at the Somme began, the first day of which resulted in sixty thousand British casualties. Yet the idealized rhetoric of youth continued, in volumes like *The Quest for Truth*. Published in August 1916, this collected the poems of H. Rex Freston, an Oxford undergraduate killed within ten days of his arrival at the front. "Better to pass away," he had written, "while the limbs are strong and young, / Ere the ending of day, / Ere Youth's lusty song be sung."

For a few combatants, this kind of romantic trope was nothing more than a damnable lie. During 1916, the first attempts were made to counter the prevailing sacrificial ethos. Barely recognized at the time, they were indicative of a change in heart on the part of the class that had been educated for conflict. In the Great War, the officer class led from the front, a military practice that resulted in a greater proportion of officers dying than any other ranks: a disproportionate number of ex–public schoolboys.[3] Some of them began to question the disparity between the idealized image of youth and its smashed reality.

The most direct riposte to Freston's self-sacrificial rhetoric came from a young officer named Arthur Graeme West, who interpreted his front-line experience in terms of "impotent horror". However, he did not have the "martyr stuff" to act on his pacifist leanings. Unwillingly returning to the front, he responded by writing a vitriolic riposte to Freston's "quest for truth". In just over fifty lines, his poem "God! How I Hate You, You Young Cheerful Men!" poured scalding scorn on war romantics, the "sentimental elegies" of home-front propaganda, and the sports-obsessed public school system itself.

West remained unpublished until 1918, the year after his death at Bapaume, but his was an early salvo in what serving soldiers saw as a war for truth. Conscripts and officers alike knew that the official language of war—the vainglorious phrases of most published war poets or the sentimental bellicosity of popular documents like "A Mother's Answer to a Common Soldier"—failed to make any sense of 1917's senseless horror. This was the year of near starvation on the home front, and the year of Passchendaele, a three-month offensive that ended with 250,000 British and 400,000 German casualties.

With public school youth still extolled as the official sacrificial icon, the most sensational British book of 1917 attempted to blow apart the muscular Christian ideal. Written by a serving officer, Alec Waugh, *The Loom of Youth* was the product, as its author later admitted, of "a rebellious mood. The Public School system was venerated as a pillar of the British Empire and out of that veneration had grown a myth of the ideal Public School Boy—Kipling's Brush Wood Boy. In no sense had I incarnated such a myth and it had been responsible, I felt, for half my troubles. I wanted to expose it."

---

3. Harrow recorded 516 former pupils who were killed during the war, just under one year's intake, and an average of one every three days.

On one level, *The Loom of Youth* was firmly in the tradition of 1900s peer group school stories like Rudyard Kipling's *Stalky & Co.* and Horace Vachell's *The Hill*. However, Waugh's anger transformed this overstuffed genre. Entering the fictional Fernhurst in 1911, protagonist Gordon Caruthers immediately learns his new school's overriding ideologies: "to the athlete, all things are forgiven"; "the Public School system . . . loves mediocrity, it likes to be accepted unquestioningly as was the Old Testament." The new boy's overriding feeling is his "fear of doing the wrong thing".

The boys are buffeted by the contradictory forces of "militarism" and the scraps of dissonance provided by Oscar Wilde and American ragtime. Caruthers's friend Tester offers the decadent credo: "I am going to do what I like with my life. Wrong and right are merely relative terms." Preferring to follow their own inclinations rather than "those of a sham twentieth-century civilisation", the more rebellious boys organize several actions to upset the athletes. They perform Stanley Houghton's *Younger Generation* as a patricidal text: "to cut away the shackles of mature thought that are impeding the limbs of youth."

On the outbreak of war, they all sign up, but are not fooled by the prevailing propaganda. As Tester states, "All our generation has been sacrificed; of course it is inevitable. But it is rather hard. The older men have seen some of their hopes realized; we shall see none. I don't know when this war will end; not just yet, I think. But whenever it does, just as far as we are concerned the days of roses will be over." Nothing is left but cynicism: "At the beginning we were deceived by the tinsel of war; Romance dies hard. But we know now. We've done with fairy tales. There is nothing glorious in war."

Sacrifice was promoted as a national ideal, but what did it mean for those who were being sacrificed? How did those who survived make any sense of it? Waugh's prognostications were gloomy. He felt that there would be nothing left for his generation after the war. Even if civilization returned to its former glories in some future, putative peace, he and his peers would be hollow husks, their youth stolen. "We only live once," Tester concludes. "Only once shall we glory in the wind, and the sea, and love and the ecstasy of being alive. And it's all smashed: we shall have never really lived."

The first popular work explicitly to yoke the generational ideal with the reality of sacrifice, *The Loom of Youth* caused a storm. However, it was not the criticism of that ideal that aroused public ire, but the slight hints of homosexuality. This was, of course, the major fault line in the single-gender system and, twenty years after Oscar Wilde, still the ultimate taboo. While some serving officers found the book "exaggerated", it was still potent enough to become a national issue at the end of 1917. It inspired an answering volume, *The Dream of Youth,* which promoted "chivalry" as an antidote to "impurity".

By 1918, the fourth year of the war, any trace of the idealism of 1914 had long disappeared. By this stage, the British army was taking in unprecedented numbers of adolescent conscripts, who had suffered through wartime shortages. They came out to an inferno. The successful Bolshevik revolution of November 1917 led to Russia's withdrawal from the war. Half a million German soldiers were released from the Eastern Front, and with this new army, the Germans planned a once-and-for-all assault on the Western Front line that had hardly moved from its original positions of 1915.

The German attack began in March with the most ferocious artillery bombardment of the war, and the youngest bore the brunt. As one lance corporal remembered, "My section included four youths just turned 18 years, who had only been with our company for three weeks and whose first experience of shell fire it was and WHAT an experience. They cried and one kept calling 'mother' and who could blame him, such HELL makes weaklings of the strongest and no human nerves or body were ever built to stand such torture, noise, horror and mental pain."

Clearly, under such pressure, harsh military discipline was necessary to keep these young recruits holding the line. William Holmes, a private in a London regiment, remembered the arrival of two very young recruits, "between sixteen and seventeen years of age". When ordered to attack, they began "crying their eyes out". Caught running away, they were charged with desertion, stripped of their regimental insignia, and shot. For Holmes, this was consistent with "war facts": "Every man had come out to fight. For the mere disobedience of an officer you could be shot. And so we took punishment as a fact of life."

These incidents were comparatively rare. Although the desertion rate was estimated at 10.26 per 1,000 men, only 266 were executed for this offence. Combatants stayed in place because they had to. This compulsion was enforced by the fear of being shot or of being ostracized by your peers. However, many front-line men put a positive interpretation on their reasons for remaining committed to an insane war. The public school boys still held fast to the "Vitaï Lampada" ideology of playing the game, while, for many workingmen, service was seen in practical terms, of "finishing the job".

The greatest single motivation was the bonding between all ranks. As Charles Carrington remembered, "Men in a trench were like shipwrecked sailors on a raft, completely committed to their social grouping, so that nobody could have any doubts about the moral and physical failings of his pals since everyone's life depended on the reliability of each." These "bonds of mateship", crucially, crossed the previously rigid lines of class in the British army, which until 1916 was a volunteer force as stratified as the wider society. It was only after the middle of the war that officers were taken from among the ranks.

In the cauldron of combat, the classes met each other and learned to get along: they had no choice. Public school boys who had never before encountered the proletariat found that they not only existed on the same plane, but indeed learned much from those whom in other circumstances they might have dismissed. Indeed, the skills of miners and labourers were at a premium in the hard physical world of the trenches. As Harry Ogle was advised by one of his privates, "You'm a schoolmaster an' knows a thing or two that's no use in this bloody place, but when it comes to pick and shovel work, that's *my* job."

This "trust between men" worked both ways. A Lancashire private thought that "our officers and NCO's were wonderful the way they used to do their duty. They were always watching over us and seeing we got a hot drink." Obviously this was not always the case: the war did not eradicate class resentment. But the idea of the bonds between all ranks became the most powerful and workable ideal of the late war years. Replacing the romantic notion of sacrifice and honour, this pragmatic ideal fused with the peer rhetoric that began to appear with greater strength in the last year of the war.

Poets like Siegfried Sassoon, Wilfred Owen, and Richard Aldington began to recast the ideal of generational sacrifice in different terms. Suffused with this new ideal of the deep love between fellow fighting men, poems like "The Blood of the Young Men" and "Anthem for Doomed Youth" did not offer flowery generalities but bitter denunciations—not of the Germans, but the older generation. Here the once respected, authoritative elders were recast as infanticidal maniacs who, like the father in "The Parable of the Old Man and the Young", "slew his son, / and half the seed of Europe, one by one."

These were still minority, barely published voices, but they would grow in stature for sound emotional and demographic reasons. By the last year of the war, Britain was nearing the bottom of its manpower well. The age for service had expanded both upwards—to fifty-five—and downwards. From spring 1918 onwards, many divisions were "largely composed of soldiers who might as well have been at school". By the winter, about half of all the 1.85 million British troops serving in France and Belgium were eighteen years of age. The French and German armies contained a similar age range.

Within military cultures that accentuated peer bonding as opposed to strict class boundaries, it was hardly surprising that a new generational identification should arise. It was as though Agathon's 1912 polemic of a "sacrificed generation" had become a statistical reality, but in 1918 it did not just involve the select few but the great mass of males between adolescence and mid-adulthood. The dreams of 1914 were mere ashes: like the British, the German and French combatants had to make sense of the vast moral and spiritual vacuum consequent on deep disillusion.

In France, the early wartime "generation of 1914" had been superseded by a younger cohort as an earth-shattering rupture. The more vocal would express their visceral rage at incompetent generals and nationalistic youth ideologues. Others used nihilistic black humour, like the serving officer Jacques Vaché. "I'm pleased to live beatifically, like 13 x 18 cameras," he wrote in summer 1918. "It's much like any other way of waiting for the eventual end. I gain strength and save myself for future acts. You'll see what a wonderful helter-skelter our future will be and how it will enable us to kill people!!!"

Germany's young also challenged the war mysticism epitomized by Walter Flex's wanderer-hero. In Fritz von Unruh's banned 1917 novel, *Way of Sacrifice*, the "holy communion" of the sacrificed generation was yoked in service of an idealized, socialist future. Indeed, von Unruh imagined the reversal of power from the old to the united young: "Those who sat on thrones behind sit now at telephones, pale and shaking, and wait upon us. We are the decisive factor. Ours is the initiative! No one will ever again take our heart captive! In us lives youth! Behind us lie the old men!"

Even before its end, the Great War had forever destroyed the automatic obedience that elders had expected from youth. The myth of sacrifice had become a double-edged sword. Young soldiers expected to do their duty, but if they survived, they felt that they had earned the right to dictate their own myth. If they were to be sacrificed, then it would not be on behalf of the elders who remained at home. No, their sacrifice would be offered at the altar of the new youth class, the generation that in their millions had fought each other, suffered together, and who would always be bound by that terrible experience.

CHAPTER 12

The Class of 1902

Juvenile Delinquency and the Great War

• • •

Oh, I know. I know. You all think I'm mad—looking at me like that. [He has completely lost control of himself; his words rush out in an ever growing crescendo.] *But there are millions doing it—millions. The young ones doing it, and the old ones feeling noble about it.*

—Miles Malleson, *Black 'Ell* (1916)

YOUTHS AT AN ANTI-GERMAN RIOT, POPLAR, EAST LONDON, 1915

IN JANUARY 1916, a nineteen-year-old soldier in the Canadian army was faced with a conundrum. Francis Chester had absconded from Canada to New York at the age of sixteen, where he worked as a messenger. He became the "faithful lieutenant" of a middle-aged man who sold cocaine and morphine, and began sampling the goods. By the age of seventeen, he was addicted to morphine and was trafficking to feed his habit. However, the drug had not entirely removed his taste for adventure. Persuaded by his friend "Snuffy", Chester bluffed his way into the Canadian army during the summer of 1915.

The only problem was that both were cut off from their usual channels of supply. Like pigs nosing out truffles, Chester and his partner soon found their way to London's Chinatown. There they satisfied themselves not with their customary morphine injections, but with smoking "hop". Although this was not yet illegal, "the Chinese were taking no chances. They used to smuggle us in, and smuggle us out." Chester was so seduced that he "became an expert in the delights of the pipe, and for three weeks I lived in a room in a Chinese house and gave myself up to it".

This dereliction of his military duties resulted in his return to base at Shorncliffe in Kent. However, the pull of addiction was stronger than any threat of military discipline. Assisted by Snuffy, whose expertise included theft and confidence tricks, Chester immediately acquired a pass to leave the base and the pair made straight for the nearest town, Folkestone. Getting drugs was at the top of their agenda, by force if necessary. Chester recalled that "Snuffy had a pistol that he had bought from somebody in the camp. To this day I believe that the thing would not really shoot."

Fake or not, the firearm looked real enough to serve its purpose: "We stuffed balls of silver paper into the front of the chambers to make it appear as if it was loaded and marched into a chemist's shop. There was a boy in a white coat behind the counter. I pointed the revolver at him out of my tunic pocket. 'Listen kid,' I said. 'We don't want to hurt you. All we want is some junk.' 'Junk? What's that?' he asked, puzzled and terrified. 'All the cocaine and morphine you've got.' 'All right, soldier,' he said. He reached to a shelf and gave us two or three bottles. We left the boy staring."

This incident from Chester's memoir, *Shot Full*, reveals the disturbing effects of the Great War on the European home front. The young chemist's reaction is crucial: not only has he not heard of the North American word for morphine, "junk", but he is left "staring" because he has just faced something completely outside his experience. After sixteen months or so of conflict, it was beginning to dawn on civilians as well as soldiers that nothing would ever be the same again, that people were beginning to behave in ways that they had never done before, that did not yet have a name.

As the Great War progressed, it called into question the West's core values. For the Europhile G. Stanley Hall, obsessively watching its progress in the United States, the only interpretation was a collective "schizophrenia". Following the word's recent coinage,[1] Hall defined this as a term "used by psychologists to describe a divided mind, of which the Jekyll-Hyde personality is one type". Barbarism had returned as civilization devolved. The war had stripped off "the superficial veneer of culture" to immerse "man in the rank primitive emotions".

Nothing was more symptomatic of the new conditions of mass death than the "ZWIIIING, CRASH, CLAAANG! ZWIING, CRASH! CRAASH! CLAAANG!" of constant shelling. "With the first rumble of shellfire, one part of our being hurls itself back a thousand years," the novelist Erich Maria Remarque later observed. "We set out as soldiers, and we might be grumbling or might be cheerful—we reach the zone where the frontline begins, and we have turned into human animals." The overwhelming pressure of this steel storm had devastating psychological effects.

The new war madness was defined by the psychologist Charles Myers, who in February 1915 called it "shell shock". Doctors quickly noted a cluster of symptoms that "followed the shock of an exploding shell": paralysis, stupor, amnesia, an uncontrollable jerking of the limbs in a demented echo of Nijinksy's pre-war dances. In July 1915, the professor of medicine at Oxford recorded an "orgie of neuroses and psychoses and gaits and paralyses. I cannot imagine what has got into the central nervous system of the men . . . hysterical dumbness, blindness, anaesthesia galore."

These symptoms were universal. In Germany, there were over 600,000 cases of "war neuroses" between and 1914 and 1918. Between April 1915 and April 1916, some 24,000 cases of shell-shock were sent back to England. This was a mass "neurasthenia" that only the practitioners of psychology— recognized as a legitimate medical practice in 1913—could interpret. With the sanity of northern Europe increasingly in question, the Great War became the first psychological war. Treatment by psychiatrists was one way of alleviating the unprecedented systemic shutdowns caused by shell-shock.

However, psychology still remained a specialized discipline, applicable only to combatants. Those waiting at home had no such relief. Within the emo-

1. By the famous Zurich psychiatrist, Professor Blueler, in 1911. His definition of the state described a mental disorder "characterized by autistic thinking". The symptoms included: "loss of emotional rapport with the environment, negativism or automatic obedience, and hallucinations."

tional perplex of the time, showing grief and even fear was considered taboo: as one young British woman who lost her fiancé remembered, "I just wanted to hide somewhere where it was quiet and not bother to talk to anybody." What the British called the "stiff upper lip" became a principle of survival, a necessary closing down of explosive emotions that might have otherwise de-stabilized societies already reaching their limits of endurance.

However, the naked fear exhibited by shell-shock victims revealed that this strategy was only partially effective. On the home front, the strict control of overwhelming emotions was generally successful but also resulted in a series of barely explainable symptoms that ranged from occult immersion to drug abuse, juvenile delinquency, and an "overwhelming sexuality". The onslaught of total war precipitated a social and moral revolution: as Magnus Hirschfeld later wrote, "The pleasure of the moment was what decided the action of the individual, for the present moment was the only certain one."

■ ■ ■

This concentration on the present represented, among other things, another nail in the coffin of organized religion. In France, Germany, and Britain alike, the church's unqualified endorsement of the war created resentment from 1916 on. In Britain, civilians turned in increasing numbers to the spiritualists who appeared to offer a direct connection to dead young relatives. Just as the imperatives of American capitalism began to undercut the self-denial pro-moted by Christianity, so the experience of war accentuated the total immer-sion in the present already defined as central to the adolescent psyche.

In previous wars, the status of the soldier and the noncombatant had been kept quite separate. The first mass European war smashed that distinction to smithereens. The sheer numbers of front-line casualties meant that very few civilians were immune from the impact of war. But even more important, civilians were regarded as legitimate military targets. In France, Germany, and Britain, the number of civilian deaths (from malnutrition, disease, and military action) amounted to roughly 10 per cent of total military casualties. In France, the figure was about half a million, in Britain nearly 300,000, and in Germany over 620,000.

This widening of war's ambit meant that the home front became liable to its own strains and stresses. Among the most affected were young women and Europe's most vulnerable cohort, defined by Ernst Glaeser as "The Class of 1902", the younger adolescents who had known little else but war and who were defenceless against its psychosis. Even in early adolescence, the fact of conscription and the likelihood of front-line service loomed large as regular military training became part of the standard curriculum and youth were bombarded with sacrificial propaganda.

With increasing mobilization, working-class adolescents were also drafted into the adult world of work. Previously stringent child labour laws were relaxed as the war continued: in Germany, up to 300,000 young men and women were employed in factories by 1917. In Britain, the figure was estimated at 600,000. Many schoolchildren left before the legal age of fourteen, or were allowed dispensation to work for thirty-three hours a week if they attended school "half-time". In some countryside areas, up to half of school-age adolescents were taken out to work in the increasingly vital task of food production.

At the same time, the authority figures that gave the young structure and discipline began to disappear, as parents, teachers, elder siblings, and policemen were all called up. With schools often closed and relatives involved in the war effort, unprecedented numbers of adolescents were left to their own devices. As early as 1915, they were beginning to live in a peer world largely unsupervised by adults. Together with the adverse effects of malnutrition and the aggression sanctioned by the declaration of war, this lack of control set the stage for an increase in aberrant youth behaviour.

An early indication of this was seen in Britain after the sinking of the passenger liner *Lusitania* in May 1915. According to one inner-city newspaper, "Crowds of young people and women congregated in the vicinity of shops owned by persons with German names and attacked them with some degree of violence." These outbreaks of xenophobic violence were repeated in major cities throughout the country: in Hull, London, and Liverpool. Although socially sanctioned, they pointed to a greater incidence of juvenile delinquency.

In seventeen major British cities, the number of under-sixteen-year-olds charged with offences went up by 33 per cent during 1915. This caused governmental concern: as the police commissioner of London wrote in a report for the Home Office, "The principal increase is, no doubt, the absence of parental control. In numerous cases the father is away on service and the mother has obtained employment in a munitions factory or work of some other description, with the result that no adult is left in charge of the children; this is a factor of very grave importance."

This pattern was repeated in Germany, where juvenile crime figures rose by 60 per cent between 1914 and 1916. The most common offence was truancy: with paid work available and a military future looming, school seemed pointless. A Berlin survey into the problem revealed that 90 per cent of delinquents had a mother who was working or absent. In the lack of adult controls, German adolescents formed informal youth clubs that were often indistinguishable from criminal gangs. The authorities were so concerned by this "moral dissolution" of youth that they attempted to divert these energies into war-related activities.

It's hard to escape the sense that these youths were only acting out what the wider society was doing. At just the age when they were about to enter the outside world, they found that it had exploded in violence. As one of the generation born in the mid-1900s, the Berliner Sebastian Haffner felt that the conflict had an obsessive appeal: "It was a dark, mysterious game and its never-ending, wicked lure eclipsed everything else, making daily life seem trite. It was addictive, like roulette and opium. My friends and I played it all through the war: four long years, unpunished and undisturbed."

In Britain, this found its echo in the street gangs. The hooligans had returned, under a new and more vicious guise. Among the more notorious were Glasgow's Anderston Redskins, one of the many gangs who terrorized the city during 1916. In an article headlined "The Terrorists of Glasgow", the *Sunday Chronicle* painted a terrifying picture: "Each gang outvies the other in savagery and frightfulness. Ladies are held up and robbed; policemen are clubbed and cut with bottles when trying to take some of the ruffians to prison; and old men are beaten and left lying after their pockets had been gone through."

During the first years of the war, a Manchester gang called the Napoo practised their own version of American Indian lore. "They'd creep up behind girls and young women in the street," one of their contemporaries remembered, "then they'd grab the long plaited hair that hung down the back, that was the style of the day, and with a sharp pair of scissors cut off the plaited hair and run off with it as a souvenir." They became "bolder and bolder": "Some used to go upstairs on the trams late at night, and if a woman was sitting on their own, they'd cut off her hair, then, like lightning, dash off without being caught."

Originating in the industrial district of Ancoats, the Napoo were readily identifiable by their group uniform of pink neckerchief. With their very public "scalpings", they quickly gained a fearsome reputation. "They became notorious and every one was talking about them," a Mancunian child of the period remembered. "They did all sorts of things, smashing windows, fighting everybody they could fight, and they had razors stuck out of their waistcoat pockets, cut-throat razors, that sort of business, But you never got to the truth of it. It was always second hand; it was what people said."

Juvenile delinquency did increase in Britain during the Great War, but the public perception of the threat was greater than the reality, as the scare stories in the newspapers had their effect. Adolescent crime was not just a symptom of a world gone mad, but, as the criminologist and reformer Cecil Leeson wrote in his 1917 pamphlet *The Child and the War*, "a waste of life that the nation, situated as it now is, can least afford". Within total war, everyone had to play their part: "The blunt truth is that the state cannot afford juvenile offenders with a population decimated by war."

Leeson acknowledged that "the conditions in which children are now obliged to live preclude healthy moral growth". The rise in vandalism, larceny, and various public disorder offences was explicable in several ways. Thanks to conscription there were far fewer policemen: their replacements, all older men, struggled to contain their wily young opponents. Restricted street lighting assisted criminality, as "wrong loves the dark". Lack of adequate parenting and the interruption of schooling also played their part. The "present abnormal state of society" was also to blame, with its "war talk of craft, guile and revenge".

Working-class adolescents had always borne the brunt of juvenile delinquency scares, but during the war years the fact that many were in full-time employment meant that they had more money to spend and, in turn, this led to increased self-confidence. "Such lads have the wages of men," Leeson wrote, "and are treated like men, though lacking man's experience. Thus they tend to break loose now and then, and in this period of reaction offences are committed." Having entered the world of work, adolescents of fourteen expected to be able to participate in adult pleasures.

This was not possible in wartime Britain, regulated by the endlessly updated DORA. Football, cricket, and racing were banned in the early years of the war, and during 1917, drinking in public houses was severely curtailed.[2] Within an increasingly regulated country, fun-seeking adolescents were seen as a major security problem. The increased focus on youth also arose from the fact that a large proportion of men were off at war: adolescents and women took on an unprecedented visibility, with ambiguous results.

■ ■ ■

War was a man's job: the British secretary of war Lord Kitchener had made it clear that he "didn't approve of women fighting". Young women who wished to do more than hand out white feathers found that they were offered supporting rather than front-line roles. However, they still flocked to join up. For those who wanted to get involved, nursing was the most popular option. Nearly 50,000 young women—some under the minimum entry age of nineteen—

2. Led by David Lloyd George, a former temperance campaigner, the government had long had its eye on public house opening times—up to eighteen hours a day—and in 1917 they were restricted to three or four hours daily right across the country.

flocked to join the Voluntary Aid Detachments. For many young middle-class women, brought up with more ideas of equality, this was the preferred option.

For inner-city girls, factory work brought more spending money and a degree of independence. Robert Roberts remembered that his eldest sister, who worked in engineering, "used cosmetics surreptitiously until one evening the old man caught her with a whole 'dorothy' bag full of the stuff. He threw the lot into the fire. The house, we understood, had been defiled. Hadn't Joe Devine (a neighbour), he thundered, 'turned his daughters into the street for using this muck'. Never again must she dare . . . Jenny stood unperturbed, 'I either go on using it,' she said, 'or you can chuck me out too.'"

At the other end of the class scale, Vera Brittain found that looking after badly wounded soldiers helped to give her an "early release" from Victorian inhibitions. "I had never looked upon the nude body of an adult male," she wrote, but that quickly changed. "Short of going to bed with them, there was hardly an intimate service that I did not perform for one or another in the course of four years, and I still have reason to be thankful of the knowledge of masculine functioning which the care of them gave me".

The greater mingling of the sexes amplified the release of restraints caused by the war itself. Nineteen-fourteen had, according to Magnus Hirschfeld, represented "an outbreak of instinct in sanctioned form" that allowed the mass to do all "that which the state prohibited to the individual". The sanctions against murder and unrestrained sexuality had been overturned. For young men about to die, the urge to have fun was paramount. From the female side, the sexually provocative effect of a military uniform and the wish to make the most of the moment had its own influence.

While not quite approaching the crazed levels to be found in the front-line brothels, this rampant sexual freedom spread to the home front. However, there were consequences. Pregnancies out of wedlock increased at the same time as prostitution and the rapidly rising rate of infection with venereal disease. The problem was deemed so serious that it became a national scandal: in 1916, a Royal Commission estimated that roughly 10 per cent of men in working-class areas of London suffered from syphilis, with many more infected by gonorrhea.

As the war continued, the "girls" got younger: the number of females under the age of twenty-one convicted for prostitution rose by over 50 per cent. Leeson cited the example of "Case D", a fourteen-year-old girl "arrested recently for loitering on a railway station with soldiers". In 1918, the chaplain of London's principal female prison, Holloway, saw "a great deterioration" in the type of prostitute committed there: "The girls for the most part are very young and very ignorant, very vicious and very corrupt. Frequently they come from the provincial towns and country districts. They are distinctly a war product."

The behaviour of young women came under greater scrutiny. Whether sexually active or not, many girls of all classes were assuming the fashions previously associated with prostitutes: cigarette smoking and the public wearing of thick make-up. Confronted with these new phenomena, many adults thought that there was no smoke without fire. With the health of the nation's young men of paramount importance, there issued scare stories about the hundreds of young women who thronged busy ports, public houses, and the entertainment centres of all major cities.

The process of scapegoating began early in the war. In Britain, concerns about female behaviour were yoked to another moral issue: the continued existence of London's nightlife despite the stringent prohibitions of DORA. In the autumn of 1915, a national newspaper story focused on the "Dining Out Girls" thronging London's West End: "Formerly she would never have had her evening meal in town unless in the company of a man friend. But now, with money and without men, she is more and more beginning to dine out." London was becoming "a veritable Eldorado for men with money to burn".

As part of the morality drive against London's debauched nightlife, the young women of "West End Bohemia" were linked with drugs. In a January 1916 column, a journalist named Quex observed the prevalence of "that exciting drug cocaine": "It is so easy to take—just snuffed up the nose; and no-one seems to know why the girls who suffer from this body and soul racking habit find the drug so easy to obtain. In the ladies' cloakroom of a certain establishment two bucketfuls of thrown-away small circular cardboard boxes were discovered by the cleaners the other day—discarded cocaine boxes."

The scandal worsened when, during February 1916, the *Daily Mail* reported the case of one Francis Kingsley, who was caught selling cocaine to an undercover Canadian corporal: Francis Chester was not the only Canadian soldier with supply problems. Cocaine became much more than the self-indulgent preserve of the young women who were already called "flappers": it became a spectre that threatened to affect the war effort. The authorities were forced to act. At the end of July 1916, DORA made "the possession of cocaine or opium" a criminal offence.

During the last two years of the war, DORA—by now anthropomorphized into a bullying female reformer—was everywhere. To combat "khaki fever", more than two thousand units of the Women Police Service patrolled any public place where "dizzy" young girls could become "amateur prostitutes". Church-sponsored organizations like the Social Purity Movement prosecuted a concerted campaign against female drinking. Prostitution was addressed by a 1918 DORA regulation, number 40D, which made it illegal for a woman infected with venereal disease to have sex with any member of His Majesty's forces.

Vigilante moralism reached its peak in the summer of 1918 with the Pemberton Billing libel case. The defendant was a maverick member of Parliament who believed in "the promotion of purity in public life". In early 1918, his magazine, the *Imperialist*, alluded to an imaginary list of "Forty Seven Thousand" public figures whose sexual perversion had led them into treason: many were to be found in the theatre where Oscar Wilde's *Salomé* was being staged. At the trial, Pemberton Billing called Wilde a "social leper" who "had founded a cult of sodomy in this country, and travelled from end to end of it perverting youth wherever he could".

This bizarre trial was only one of many examples of the aberrant behaviour that flourished in northern Europe during the last year of the Great War. The campaigns of 1917 had not brought a breakthrough but an even more lethal stasis. At the same time, the appalling weather that Europe suffered between June 1917 and May 1918 increased the desperate home-front conditions. With supplies and manpower stretched to their limit, malnutrition was rife. Despair followed suit. In Britain, a national newspaper editorialized, "The spirit of the nation is darkening. Its solidarity is crumbling."

Nineteen-eighteen was a year of strikes, mutinies, and riots as the implications of the November 1917 Bolshevik revolution were felt. The "Spanish flu" epidemic decimated already weakened populations. By that time, it had become obvious to many Europeans that the continent could not return to the certainties of the pre-war world that was already beginning to assume the quality of a golden age. As Robert Roberts observed, "1917 was the year when the twentieth century really began. New ideas ran abroad in the world: men were making blueprints for the future."

. . .

This convulsive mixture of war madness and Red revolution informed the period's only European youth art movement. With organized opposition to war almost impossible in all combatant countries,[3] many dissidents had fled to

3. In Germany, the radical socialist Rosa Luxemburg was imprisoned in April 1915 for leading a public protest; in Britain, rolling extensions to DORA made the public expression of anti-war sentiment illegal, punishable by fines, prison, and social ostracism. The cofounder of the No-Conscription Fellowship, Clifford Allen, was tried, sentenced to hard labour, and then immediately rearrested on his release. In January 1918 the conscientious objector Henry Firth died from his prison regime; three days later, Bertrand Russell was sentenced to six months for openly advocating peace negotiations.

neutral Switzerland. As well as revolutionaries like Vladimir Lenin, young artists from across Europe flocked to the safe haven of Zurich. According to the movement's historian Hans Richter, "To understand the climate in which Dada began, it is necessary to recall how much freedom there was in Zurich, even during a world war."

Dada was heralded by a press announcement on February 2, 1916: "Cabaret Voltaire. Under this name a group of young artists and writers has formed with the object of becoming a centre of artistic entertainment. The Cabaret Voltaire will be run on the principle of daily meetings where visiting artists will perform their music and poetry." The advertisement was placed by a group of artists from Germany, Romania, and France: Hugo Ball, Emmy Hennings, Hans Arp, Marcel Janco, and Tristan Tzara. Although aged between twenty and thirty, none had exchanged their youth for a uniform.

The events of the opening night three days later exceeded all expectations: as Ball wrote, "The place was full to bursting; many could not get in." What the packed audience experienced was a new and overwhelming synesthesia. This was described as "noise music, simultaneous poems recited by 4 to 7 people speaking at once, bizarre dances in grotesque masks and fancy costumes, interrupted by readings of German and French sound-verses sounding like nothing on earth". This was, to quote Richard Huelsenbeck's Dada poem, "The End of the World".

In fact, like the movements that it would inspire, Dada was not as radical a break with the past as it would have liked to appear. But war gave its obsessive paganism and provocation a manic urgency: "Pandemonium, destruction, anarchy, anti-everything—why should we hold it in check? What of the pandemonium, destruction, anarchy, anti-everything of the World War?" The performances at the Cabaret Voltaire dramatized a fact that many Europeans were beginning to understand. War had only not smashed illusions, lives, and regimes, it had completely pulverized language, sense, and reason.

The Dadaists transcribed the Western Front's "world of noise" into convulsive verbal assaults, while mimicking the clanging language of the schizophrenic: *"zimzim urallala zimzim urallala zimzim zanzibar zimzella zam elifantolim brussala bulomen brussala bulomen."* Even its name represented disturbance: Dada's nonsensical repetition matched the blind regression that was one major psychological effect of the war, described by Ben Shephard as reverting back "into childhood". The word "Dada" also sounds exactly like a child's call to the father: in this case, however, it was not a call but a curse.

Everything had to be destroyed. "We were ready to sow unrest to the limit of our power," wrote Hans Richter, "and this unrest sprang from various sources. Some felt the possibility or the certainty of a new path; with others it was lack of faith in society, in the nation, in art, in morality, and, in the last resort, in man himself, man the irreclaimable wild beast, man the lost wager. With others it was simply their own inner unrest, whether this was a reflection of the unrest that surrounded us, or just youthful rebelliousness. With every one of us it was youth as well as a mixture of all these elements."

Dada's wartime influence was very small. However, it captured an underlying truth of its place and time. The war had indeed brought about "The End of the World", and the shattering implications of this would be played out in all the combatant countries. Throughout Europe, the war had relentlessly battered home-front populations. The mass brutality had gone into people's souls: it was as though they too had become machines. The great cause of 1914 had been revealed to be a lie, and in the place of idealism came "a recklessness and indifference among people of a kind that they had never known before".

However, the whole point of pagan sacrifice myths is the beginning of a new cycle, as the end of one world presages the beginning of another. Out of the degenerated nineteenth-century imperial system came the regenerative idea of a more equitable, mass society. The war had shattered for all time the unthinking deference that the respective class systems of the combatant European countries had relied upon. Having joined the war effort, hitherto unvalued sections of the population gained some degree of confidence and self-determination.

The Great War forever destroyed the automatic obedience that elders expected from their children. Whether it was the generation of 1914 or the class of 1902, a massive cohort comprising millions of young Europeans had shared similar experiences. Having had prematurely to face adult responsibilities, they were not about to return to their previous invisible state. The war both created and brutalized the new mass society of youth.

CHAPTER 13

Jazz Bands and Doughboys

American Youth Enters Europe

. . .

"I don't want to live to be an old man," said William earnestly; "I'd rather do what I please now and die a little sooner."

—Booth Tarkington, *Seventeen* (1916)

AMERICAN ADOLESCENT, 1910S

TWO YEARS INTO the Great War, America still preserved its neutrality. A tiny percentage of its youth were already involved in the fighting, however. In September 1915, Theodore Roosevelt had called for "every young man just leaving college" to go to Europe "to try to render some assistance". About 25,000 young collegians joined organizations like the French Foreign Legion, the Lafayette Escadrille, or the American Field Service, which attracted figures as diverse as John Dos Passos, Ernest Hemingway, and Harry Crosby.

For many, the motivation was excitement. One of their most articulate representatives, the poet Alan Seeger, wrote as he prepared for an attack in July 1916, "I am glad to be going in the first wave. If you are in this thing at all it is best to be in it to the limit. And this is the supreme experience." Seeger died shortly afterwards, in the battle of the Somme, the Allied attack that wiped out Britain's volunteer army: on the first day of the campaign there were 60,000 casualties. Flanders was saturated in the stench of rotting, dismembered bodies.

An ocean away from this black hell, America's young were being idealized in a "fairy scene" straight out of *Peter Pan:* "Beyond the fence, bright forms went skimming, shimmering, wavering over a white platform, while high overhead the young moon sprayed a thinner light down through the maple leaves, to where processions of rosy globes hung floating in the blue night." This was the idyll of prelapsarian innocence propagated by the continent's bestselling youth book of that year, Booth Tarkington's *Seventeen*.

Already well-known as a novelist, Tarkington had seen his reputation soar after the 1914 publication of his bestselling boy book *Penrod*. By expanding the age of his hero upwards in his new novel, he was attempting to recapture what adolescence felt like: "To the eye of youth, time is not really fleeting," he wrote later; "time is long—so long that for practical uses, the present appears to be permanent." Subtitled *A Tale of Youth and Summer Time*, the episodic nature of *Seventeen* was designed both for magazine serialization and the perception of its young readers.

Booth Tarkington froze his adolescent arcadia in a classic American locus: the small midwestern town free from war, angst, or indeed any sense of the outside world. Within this hermetically sealed environment, the biggest problem facing the seventeen-year-old William Sylvanus Baxter is his frustrated pursuit of the visiting Lola Pratt, a baby-talking nightmare in a white dress. The plot, such as it is, consists of William's attempts to pass through the complicated courtship rituals imposed by a whimsically disinterested Ms Pratt.

Instead of hymns to mass self-sacrifice, William writes bad love poetry. He is a classic American dreamer, inhabiting what Tarkington calls a "roseate gossamer" world. He fantasizes that he is a poet and an actor, and imagines himself ascending the scaffold, like Sydney Carton in *A Tale of Two Cities*, in order to prove the tragic sincerity of his unrequited love. The reality is somewhat different. His younger sister and his female peers mock his elevated feelings, while his neighbour, Mr Parcher, forced to observe William's courting, is driven nauseous to his bed.

These domestic parables of small-town etiquette masked sharp social comment. Tarkington pinpointed in the half-boy, half-man figure of William Baxter the very age that embodied the not yet standardized definition of adolescence. In defining this pivotal year, he also located what would become a perennial theme in the youth culture that would follow. Seventeen would mark that moment when adolescents shook off the shackles of parental control and fully immersed themselves in the peer world that formed the stepping-stone to independence.[1]

Tarkington also inserted psychologically accurate material to strike clear chords within his adolescent readership. William's moodiness is a given: as one of his female peers notes, he "doesn't like much of anything. He's seventeen years old." He is consistently chasing maturity: as he reminds his parents, "I'm going on eighteen," and as far as he is concerned, that is old enough to marry and enter adulthood. This cuts no ice. His parents might indulge his whims, but their word is the final law: as his father says, when refusing the dress suit that would confer maturity, "You're too young, Willie."

Whatever he might imagine, William still inhabits the ambiguous zone between childhood and adulthood: independent in his head, but in reality all too dependent on his parents. Tarkington defined this as "the time of life when it is unendurable not to seem perfect in all outward matters: in worldly position, in the equipments of wealth, in family, and in the grace, elegance and dignity of all appearances in public. And yet the youth is continually betrayed by the child still intermittently insistent within him, and by the child which undiplomatic people too often assume him to be."

With a delicate, sly wit, Tarkington both mocked and empathized with his young hero. *Seventeen* was a transitional but influential document that expanded contemporary definitions of the teens at the same time as it broadcast the idea that middle-class adolescents inhabited a discrete world of their own.

1. Indeed, seventeen would be the particular teen that would mark future generation-defining youth statements. Note the most popular youth novel of 1942, Maureen Daly's *Seventeenth Summer*. Note also, outside the time frame of this book, the Beatles' "I Saw Her Standing There", also titled "Seventeen", and the Sex Pistols' "Seventeen". Note also the age of Pinkie in Graham Greene's *Brighton Rock* (1938): "There was poison in his veins, though he grinned and bore it. He had been insulted: they thought because he was seventeen."

It amplified the sense that youth was a race apart, that it could comprise a separate market, that indeed it could be an object of aspiration, instead of just being a social problem or a piece of malfunctioning machinery that needed proper adjustment.

Most of all, it was a profoundly nostalgic look at an era and a genre that, in 1916, was on the point of disappearing—independently of the events in Europe. After spells in Paris and New York, Tarkington had returned in 1911 to his home-town of Indianapolis to find it scarred by industrial pollution. Railing against big business, which he called "the savage of the world", the author chose to ignore the soot and the acrid smoke, and placed his characters in the unspoiled, pre-industrial Midwest of his own mid-1880s adolescence: "the easy-going old days", which were "gone forever".

In accessing both his own biography and a lost, already golden period, Tarkington was writing in accordance with the dictates of the boy book category—aimed not only at children and adolescents, but also at the prosperous middle-aged. *Seventeen* might have expanded the genre's typical age range upwards from fourteen, but it deliberately omitted any mention of the adolescent sexuality that Freud had already exposed and that American commerce would soon seek to tap. Baxter and his peers are caught right on the cusp of the generational self-consciousness that would soon follow.

On one level, *Seventeen* was obsolete when it was published. It took no account of urban youth culture, animal dances, ragtime, or movies. However, it was not designed as documentary but as fantasy, and through its success it reinforced the particular nature of American adolescence: a state defined not only by its delight in and facility for dreaming, but also by an unquenchable enthusiasm and innocence. Like America itself, Willie Baxter was not yet burdened with the weight of experience, and he looked forward confidently into a future so assured that he was freed to live solely in the present.

.   .   .

This youthful spontaneity could be heard in a very different kind of bestseller that, in early 1917, embodied the nervous system of the urban American adolescent. Despite the morality campaigns, Negro music and the dances that it inspired continued to spread throughout the country and across the classes. Just as the reformers began to close in on the New Orleans red-light district of Storyville, so the music that had originated there—so new that it hardly yet had a name—began to spread with its practitioners around the country.

In March 1917, the Victor Talking Machine Company, then the largest record company in the world, released the Original Dixieland Jass Band's two-sided 78, "Dixie Jass Band One Step" and "Livery Stable Blues". This was quite a coup for the white New Orleans group, who had moved to New York only that January. Other New Orleans groups had played in New York, but they did so as part of a vaudeville show: in contrast, the ODJB were headliners, brought in to cater to the dancers who still thronged Manhattan's nightlife.

New York had heard nothing like their residency in Reisenwerber's, a fashionable establishment on the Upper West Side: the dance floor was quickly filled with "fired-up collegians and adventurous society folk". The city was still the centre of the music industry, and within a month of their arrival the ODJB were invited to audition for the Columbia Graphophone Company. Their music was so loud and harsh that the session ended in mutual incomprehension between the group and the sound engineers. Recording for Victor four weeks later, they got it right, as both sides crystallized the all-out attack of the new jass style.

The term, like the music, had originated in New Orleans's red-light district, deriving from an African word for sexual intercourse. "Jass" was in use by the mid-1910s, although the music had been developing for a couple of decades: as its name suggested, it was much looser and wilder than ragtime. In place of the archaic Sousa marches that rooted the rags in the nineteenth century, jass, or jazz, as it was quickly called, featured several wind instruments playing with and against the melody, with the rag piano giving bottom and the clashing, tribal rhythms ratcheting up heart-stopping levels of intensity.

ODJB cornetist Nick LaRocca and trombonist Larry Shields were both in their late twenties, and had played with Jack "Papa" Laine, New Orleans's outstanding white bandleader. They had been inspired by leading Negro bands like Kid Ory's Brownskin Band, and the Olympia, which featured Sidney Bechet and King Oliver. Like many New Orleans musicians, they had begun to travel outside of the city, moving to Chicago the previous year, where they formed the ODJB: the move to New York came as the result of the vaudeville entertainer Al Jolson's patronage.

To middle-aged Americans, "Dixie Jass Band One Step" must have sounded like chaos, a farmyard cacophony. LaRocca and Shields played with an aerated exuberance, while Eddie Edwards's sliding trombone provided an irresistible momentum. Underpinning this relentless forward drive were the prominent, crashing drums of nineteen-year-old Tony Sbarbaro. The group was promoted as a radical departure, with slogans like "Untuneful Harmonists Playing 'Peppery Melodies'" and quotes from LaRocca claiming that they were musical anarchists and that jazz was "the assassination of melody".

Jazz was in the very first stages of media attention—a transitional phase

THE ORIGINAL DIXIELAND JAZZ BAND, 1919

marked by the ODJB's use of its soon-to-be obsolete spelling—but it took the animal dance craze to a new level: according to *Variety* that March, "this gingery, swinging music is what the dancers want." Like the film companies, the music industry was always liable to be blindsided by the dictates of popular taste. Although Tin Pan Alley was happiest when controlling the market with its patented mix of sentimental and nostalgic songs, it was always interested in novelties—which is how ragtime and the blues were first presented.

This new style might have appeared to have come from nowhere, but once it reached the East Coast it was quickly turned into a new craze. "Dixie Jass Band One Step" might not have been the very first jazz record, but it was the first to strike a chord with the public. Expressly designed for dancing, it flew out of the shops: by the end of April 1917, the month of Scott Joplin's death, it had sold a million copies. There was a very good reason for its success: despite the difficult circumstances of its creation, the record had all the excitement and freshness of first-time exuberance.

. . .

The ODJB's success coincided with America's entry into the Great War: on April 2, 1917, after three years of lobbying and debate, Congress declared against the Central Powers. Public opinion had taken some time to come around to the war. Among the forces rallied against involvement were powerful German and Irish lobbies, pacifists like Henry Ford, and the isolationists who cleaved to the Monroe Doctrine. Also, America was doing very well from its neutrality: by the end of 1916, its factories were supplying 40 per cent of Britain's munitions.

America had to create a mass army from virtually nothing. Lacking the decade-long build-up to conflict that had so exercised Europe, the continent had seen no need for a large standing army: at the time of the declaration, it comprised only 125,000 officers and men. However, the country's organizational will was strong: conscription was immediately introduced when, in May 1917, Congress enacted the Selective Service Act for the registration and classification of all available men between the ages of twenty-one and thirty.

Nearly 10 million men between those ages presented themselves in June 1917, with a further 15 million registering in June, August, and September 1918—nearly half of America's total male population. This astonishing, instant mass mobilization did not, however, immediately translate into troops on the ground. Only 10 per-cent of all those registered were actually inducted into the American Expeditionary Force, and first they had to undergo six months of training in the United States and then a further two months in France.

War was not universally popular among American youth, but most stayed in step. They were assisted in their decision by a relentless barrage of propaganda. Most newspapers and magazines supported the war. Hollywood began production of films like *The Beast of Berlin,* while Tin Pan Alley pumped out war tunes like the spring 1917 million-seller, George M. Cohan's "Over There". Stanley Hall thought that war was a necessary purgative for a "slack, material" nation: he welcomed the fact that America's 10 million young men faced their "acid test".

There was opposition. In the first draft, 50,000 men applied for exemptions and 250,000 failed to register. Principal among the protesters were those who refused on religious and/or political grounds. Dissidents were also to be found among recent immigrants as well as juvenile delinquents and bohemians. Gangs like the Hudson Dusters resented the draft's intrusion into their activities, while for the socialist intellectuals who contributed to the socialist journal the *Masses,* war was nothing less than "an ugly mob madness".

All dissenters were dealt with summarily. Anti-war meetings were violently broken up and prominent figures like Emma Goldman and the socialist leader Eugene Debs imprisoned. Purges of draft dodgers, like the summer 1918 "slacker raid" in New York that netted 16,000 men, were enforced by public humiliation. German books were burned and German nationals tarred and feathered. In East St Louis, the arrival of Negro workers triggered a race riot in July 1917: about a hundred of their number were killed.

The reformist campaigns of the early 1910s were a mere dress rehearsal for the wave of repression that followed April 1917. Capitalizing on this xenophobic and restrictive mood, the prohibitionist Anti-Saloon League harnessed patriotism to their growing crusade. Leading light Wayne Wheeler successfully lobbied the secretary of war to "protect the boys in the army from the ruinous effect of liquor during the war". The ASL went on to sponsor the "Worldwide Prohibition Congress" in Columbus, Ohio, in mid-November 1918, by which time the prohibition of alcohol in America was a foregone conclusion.

However, the Old World did not see this face of America during 1917 and 1918. What war-torn Europeans chose to read into the arrival of the doughboys was health, vitality, and hope. On the Western Front, their sheer physical presence, untouched by four years of war, was seen as nothing short of miraculous. According to one French officer, "We all had the same impression that we were about to see a wonderful transfusion of blood. Life was coming in floods to reanimate the dying body of France."

These "friendly, smiling" paragons, the first Americans that most Europeans had seen in the flesh, offered the hope that had been thought irrevocably lost. It finally seemed as though the war could be won. "So these were our deliverers at last, marching up the road," wrote Vera Brittain on her first sight of the doughboys in April 1918. "There seemed to be hundreds of them, and in the fearless swagger of their proud strength they looked a formidable bulwark against the peril looming up from Amiens."

Apart from the all-important manpower and matériel—which, during the summer of 1918, began to tip the balance against Germany—the American entry into Europe brought a whole set of new ideas, practices, and customs that immediately began to transform the life of the peoples shattered by war. In its combination of industrial might, cultural vitality, and physical confidence, America embodied the future to many Europeans, all the more so because the November 1918 armistice revealed a terrifying vacuum within the combatant countries.

The official cease-fire occurred at the eleventh hour of the eleventh day of the eleventh month of 1918, a suitably numerical-mystical time for such a statistical war. While the Central Powers lost 3.5 million soldiers on the battlefield, the Allies lost over 5 million men. On average, 5,600 men were killed on every day of the war. Reflecting the lack of contemporary youth consciousness, there was no age breakdown of these casualties. But assuming that the fourteen-to-twenty-fours represented even one-third of the estimated war dead—roughly nine million—that means three million adolescents were slaughtered.[2]

This was the destruction of a whole generation: a vast, unhealed psychic scar. The celebrations that followed November 11 did little to fill this void. Although crowds thronged the streets of the Allied capitals, many combatants felt angry, empty, or overwhelmed by loss. "Already this was a different world from the one that I had known during four life-long years," Vera Brittain realized, "a world in which people would be light-hearted and forgetful, in which themselves and their careers and their amusements would blot out political ideals and great national issues."

Young Germans did not even have the consolation of victory. In Berlin, the invalid George Grosz found an outlet for his "hate" in German Dada, a movement that "was completely nihilistic. We spat upon everything, including ourselves. Our symbol was nothingness, a vacuum, a void." For the eleven-year-old Sebastian Haffner, defeat meant that his whole value system had collapsed in an instant. "Where could one find stability and confidence, if world events could be so deceptive?" he remembered. "I stared into the abyss. I felt a horror for life."

. . .

Post-war arrived instantly with a series of electroshock spasms. In Germany, eleven cities flew the red flag of socialist revolution: on the streets of Berlin, radicals battled with the right-wing Freikorps in the power vacuum created by the disappearance of the Kaiser. In London, the death of a twenty-two-year-old actress, Billie Carleton, from a drug overdose just after appearing at the huge Victory Ball at London's Albert Hall,[3] initiated a fresh press panic about "cocaine cigarettes" and a German attempt to subvert the nation with narcotics.

In the first week of January 1919, Jacques Vaché died in Nantes from an opium overdose. Three days after the armistice, he had written to his friend André Breton, "I shall leave the war slightly deranged, perhaps like one of those wonderful village idiots (and I even wish it to happen) . . . or else . . . or else . . . what a film part I will play!—With fabulous automobiles, you know the type, with bridges that give way and giant hands that crawl around the screen towards what document! . . . Useless and insignificant!"

2. This figure does not bring into account all the wounded in mind and body, nor the hundreds of thousands of civilian deaths caused not only by war but by the influenza pandemic that war facilitated.

3. Marek Kohn, in *Dope Girls*, p. 97, notes that Carleton's death was more probably caused by the Veronal she took to come down after a prodigious coke high.

The Old World had been destroyed, and the New rushed in. With its dough-boys, its movies, and its music, America had crossed the Atlantic and Europe would dance to a different piper. In January 1919, the London *Tatler* noted, "They say the night clubs are opening up in rows, and dressmakers say they're dizzy with the order for dance frocks that keep on pourin' in. And they just can't have enough niggers to play jazz music, and I hear they are thinkin' of hirin' out squads of 'loonies' to make the mad jazz noises till there are more ships available to bring the best New York black jazz 'musicians' over."

Three months later, the Original Dixieland Jazz Band came to London for an extended stay that gave Europeans their first experience of authentic American jazz.[4] Their early April debut at the London Hippodrome was previewed by a newspaper article that talked about jazz in terms of "Red Indians and Negroids and West African savages" before assuring its readers that "the players are all white—white as they could possibly be". When they finally played, their reception was so frenzied that the show's star, the comedian George Robey, threatened to quit unless the group were sacked.

Despite the controversy, the OJDB played successful residences at the London Palladium and the Hammersmith Palais: the sense that they regarded themselves as the vanguard of a new style was illustrated by their use of a dancer, Johnny Dale, to display the latest jazz moves. His performances were, according to taste, "clever and marvellously agile" or "like a filleted eel about to enter the stewing pot". Their reception revealed a generation gap: on one side middle-aged critics, who thought that jazz was "impertinent", on the other enthusiastic young fans, augmented by doughboys on leave.

Youth was at a premium in early 1919. Within the void created by four years of death and destruction, there could be no looking back. The only thing left was to go forward, the natural drive of adolescence amply enacted by the shocking novelty of jazz. America epitomized the innocence and enthusiasm of youth, and for Europe's young, there was no question about its appeal. The continent would become the new arcadia, a techno-pagan pleasure world more enticing than anything offered by the youth ideologues of the 1900s—all the more alluring because it was only to be experienced at one remove.

4. Their name had been changed to accord with the generally accepted spelling.

PART IV

———

1919–1929

CHAPTER 14

Post-war Shocks

The Fascisti, the German Bunde, and the Woodcraft Folk

• • •

February 23 [1919]. *Windy and cloudy. Eagerly I watch for every sign of spring. That makes me light up. But the aftermath of war is dark. The future is uncertain—life is swaying. Here are some points. (1) The League of Nations has been launched at the Paris conference and other problems tackled. A true spirit is at work. (2) The late enemy, German, is exhausted, but recovering quickly. Indifference prevails, but Bolshevism has not great hold. (3) Russia is the ulcer of Europe. Chaos and darkness there. (4) In this country strikes are the order. A miner's strike threatens at present. This may mean Bolshevism. (5) What of the new earth? Is the whole world to become a Russia?*

—A Boy, *Eighteen: A Diary of the Teens* (1947)

KINDRED OF THE KIBBO KIFT MEMBERS AT CAMP, 1928

THE ADOLESCENTS OF 1919 stood on the threshold of an uncertain world. For all the slaughter, the conflict was not decisively resolved: as the American Expeditionary Force commander, General Pershing, observed at the time, the Allies' failure to destroy the German army rendered the peace temporary. At the same time, 1919 was marked by further upheaval throughout Europe: more mutinies, strikes by workers in essential industries, riots from city populations faced with food shortages, and increasing political polarization. The new youth groupings would be marked by this extreme instability.

The Treaty of Versailles might have marked the conflict's official end, but it failed to heal the physical and psychic scars. Nor did the many memorials, among which was the ceremony held to honour the one young man who, in the eyes of the British public, epitomized the doomed war generation. Rupert Brooke's *Collected Poems* had already been published to huge sales. In March 1919, his death was commemorated by the public unveiling of a portrait medallion in the Rugby School chapel. The template for this idealized image was Sherril Schell's profile shot of the naked young Apollo.

It was easier to idolize a perennially beautiful young god than to deal with a broken neurasthenic. Brooke embodied the person whom civilians would have liked the returning veterans to be: the fresh-faced, idealistic young men of 1914. The reality was quite different. The British prime minister, David Lloyd George, thought that "the whole world" was "suffering from shell-shock", a crop of symptoms that ranged from amnesia to total catatonia. Shell-shock was both real—as evidenced by many disturbed veterans—and metaphorical, within a Europe that oscillated between forgetfulness and frantic, displaced hedonism.

The journalist Philip Gibbs wrote that the returning veterans "put on civilian clothes again and looked to their mothers and wives very much like the young men who had gone to business in the peaceful days before August 1914. But they had not come back the same men. Something had altered in them. They were subject to sudden moods and queer tempers, fits of profound depression alternating with a restless desire for pleasure." Vera Brittain noticed "a reckless sense of combined release and anti-climax" among her contemporaries, trying to recapture "the lost youth that the War had stolen".

Robert Graves found the abrupt transition from war to peace a huge shock: "Not only did I have no experience of independent civilian life, having gone straight from school into the army: I was still mentally and nervously organized for war. Shells used to come bursting on my bed at midnight . . . strangers in daytime would assume the faces of friends who had been killed." This delayed shock was an indication of the psychological disturbance common to veterans: because it could not be publicly admitted, it would take years to heal.

Within the poles of spasm and shutdown, youth underwent another definition. In his critique of the twenties, *Doom of Youth*, Percy Wyndham Lewis observed that once the war had ended, "every one wished to be, as it were, new-born. To blot out the Past, especially the 'pre-war'—that was the idea." However, this was more easily imagined than achieved. Although men as young as eighteen were returning from the front, they might as well have been eighty from the weight of their experiences. Many sought to obliterate their memories in obsessive hedonism, but the past would always be there.

Although youth was once again idealized as the perfect embodiment of this tabula rasa, the generation born too late to serve in the war found itself in a contradictory position. They had been unable to participate in the conflict that dominated everything at the same time as it was being erased from memory. Although their elders and near contemporaries who had served were held up as role models, the reality of the returning soldier did not come up to the heroic image. There was a huge divide, which bred hostility on both sides.

The post-war generation, Ernst Glaeser's "Class of 1902", had undergone severe privations during the previous four years, of illness, hunger, and neglect. Having grown up without parents and schooling, they had felt themselves compensated by a previously unthinkable degree of freedom. The reimposition of structure in 1919 did not come easily. After years of absence, their fathers were "like strangers to us, huge terrifying and despotic figures with heavy shadows, oppressive as monuments. What did they know of us? They knew where we lived, but what we thought or looked like they knew no longer."

These tensions were exacerbated by the new affirmative value placed on youth and the fact that the war seemed to have confirmed the prophecies of the previous decade's radical anti-adult rhetoric. Nineteen-nineteen heralded the arrival of adolescence as a powerful social and political force within Europe. As a positive, if abstract principle, youth embodied the headlong flight into the future. What that might be mattered less than what it was *not*: the certainties of the nineteenth century, that pre-war world that had flattered to deceive with its ideas of stability and liberal progress.

Youth became an abstract concept, detached from biology. According to Robert Wohl, by 1920 the word "only had a tenuous connection with chronological age. To be 'young' meant only to possess a receptivity to the new and the vitality required to meet and master the ordeal of the crisis." Youth appeared to comprise a new kind of revolutionary force that might offer a third way between capitalism and communism. "Civilisation was about to die," thought the youthful idealist Leslie Paul, "and the future belonged only to us, the young, who were going to build a better one."

Underpinning this was a deep anger. What had once been the preserve of a few dissident poets was fast becoming the accepted history of the conflict. In 1920, the year that Wilfred Owen's poems were collected, Philip Gibbs published an early revisionist account, *The Realities of War*, in which he revealed his true feelings about "that five years' sacrifice of boys of which I was a witness". And who was to blame? "The old men directed their sacrifice, and the profiteers grew rich, and the fires of hate were stoked up at patriotic banquets and in editorial chairs."

. . .

Youth had been betrayed by age, and it was time for reckoning. In the years immediately after the war there was a rapid incidence of aggressive adolescence throughout Europe: whether in the radical, cross-class politics of the new Fascist Party, in expressionist dramas like Arnolt Bronnen's *Vatermord* (Patricide), or in the sociological inquiries that attempted to define these chasms. To be a father in 1919 and 1920 meant being part of the generation that had sent youth to war. The war veterans and their younger cohorts sought to turn the tables and rewrite the infanticidal legends.

With the word "generation" becoming increasingly popular and emotive, there came the need for a more precise definition. In 1920, a forty-three-year-old French sociologist, François Mentre, published an update on Agathon's pre-war survey, which he called *Les générations sociales*. He aimed to address the central problem of generational theory: babies are born every day, so the movement of population is continuous and uninterrupted. There is no obvious biological rupture. So why should one group of people conceive of a different identity from another based on age, and how does the break occur?

Mentre's answer was to formulate the idea of a social generation, defined as lasting for about thirty years, the time span that marked the full working out of the perennial struggle between fathers and sons. This idea explicitly involved collective cohort self-consciousness: "When a man refers to his generation, he uses an expression that is perfectly clear, although it is not chronological. He designates it by those who are more or less the same age as he is, his fellow students and friends, those who were growing up at the same time as he was and who shared with him spheres of activity and influence."

This was a frankly elitist concept: "The majority of men play non-speaking roles in the great human choir and provide the backdrop for the great dress ball of history." Mentre believed that each period had its dominant generational group, an avant-garde that shaped the underlying desires of their contemporaries and the nation as a whole. This group was like an army: "a profound mass" of "male existences that are not rigorously contemporary but that obey a single impulse and are animated by the same ambitions and the same hopes".

While a useful starting point, the problem with this theory was that it failed to take into account the difference between generations then playing out in post-war France. Thirty years was just too long a time frame to account for the rapid rate of change. Mentre admitted that, after the war, the social generations had fragmented into two, three, or four segments. This had occurred, he observed, "because young people are so anxious to get themselves talked about and encroach easily upon the rights of their elders!"

The war represented such a fundamental rupture that several generations were competing for prominence. There were those born in the 1880s, Generation A, the conservative ideologues who had stoked the war fever of 1914. There was a second generation, B, who, born around 1890, had entered war in early adult life. Generation C, born a few years later, had entered combat straight from school, while Generation D, the Class of 1902, had been too young to fight during 1914–18 but were old enough to contest their place in society.

All asserted the primacy of their wartime experience. While Generation A might have been the obvious enemy of Generations B, C, and D, the relationship of the three younger cohorts was uneasy. Generation B had survived an appalling experience but had returned to no glory. Their disillusionment was expressed by their most articulate spokesman, Pierre Drieu La Rochelle, born in 1893. In contrast to 1914's dreams of pride and glory, he felt that returning veterans were "poor children, fascinated and lost". They were "outside of everything".

The most extreme generations were C and D, those who had known no adult life before the war. Initially, the most vocal were the young artists and writers of international Dada. The French wing of the movement went public with the March 1920 variety show at the Théâtre de l'Oeuvre. To a packed, riotous audience the twenty-three-year-old André Breton declaimed the *Manifeste cannibale Dada*: "Dada alone does not smell: it is nothing, nothing, nothing. It is like your hopes: nothing. Like your paradise: nothing. Like your idols: nothing. Like your politicians: nothing. Like your heroes: nothing."

This aesthetic nihilism found a political focus with 1921's *Mise en accusation et jugement de M. Maurice Barrès*, a direct assault on Generation A's spiritual leader. The trial was taken seriously, with prosecution, defence, and witnesses, but the stunt precipitated the break-up of the French group. Its problem was simple: what is the positive after the negative? If there is none, then negative energy turns inwards. The movement's 1919 manifesto, *Dada prophétie*, had already predicted this: "Dada will survive only by ceasing to exist."

The most sensational examination of generational division was provided by the nineteen-year-old Raymond Radiguet's 1923 novel *Le Diable au corps*,[1] designed to cause offence with its storyline of a schoolboy's wartime affair with a soldier's wife. A protégé of Jean Cocteau, the precocious Radiguet was touted as the greatest prodigy since Arthur Rimbaud. His novel lived up to the hyperbole with its taunting opening statement: "Let those already hostile to me consider what the war meant to many young boys: a four year holiday."

Playing upon the serving soldiers' worst fear, the infidelity of the idealized wife, Radiguet rendered his sixteen-year-old protagonist completely uninterested in the war. Instead, he becomes completely obsessed with eighteen-year-old Marthe: "I dreamed of the sort of life one hopes for in later years. We would live in the country; we would remain eternally young." The war does not impinge upon this fantasy, which is destroyed only when Marthe's pregnancy reveals "the thousand contradictions of youth at grips with a man's adventure".

While the serving generations mourned their failure to make headway in the post-war world, Generation D tried to make sense of the apocalypse that had failed to arrive. Radiguet's succès de scandale was followed by several self-examinations that developed his themes of precocious maturity and lack of parental control. Writers like Marcel Arland, André Chamson, André Malraux, and Pierre Luchaire, all born around the turn of the century, saw themselves as maimed by the promise of a revolution that had never come.

Like the Dadaists, they were more certain of what they were against than what they were for. For Luchaire, the war had been "a school of facts" that rendered his peers cynical but above all realistic. Arland felt that his peers' negativism, coupled with their desperate desire for action, would lead to extremism. Malraux wondered what would become of his violent generation, "so marvellously armed against itself and delivered from the vulgar vanity of calling grandeur what is actually disdain for a life to which it does not know how to attach itself?"

. . .

This generational conflict was also enacted in Britain. Many serving soldiers felt that their place in society had been usurped by those too young to serve.

1. *The Devil in the Flesh.*

As Frank Hardy, the unemployed veteran in Philip Gibbs's novel *Young Anarchy*, bitterly states, "You see, we fellows who went through it all had grown four years older without learning anything useful for peace-time jobs. We missed the boat, so to speak. The younger crowd filled up our places, and left us stranded." With the post-war slump, unemployment rose inexorably during the early 1920s, reaching a peak of 2.5 million in the summer of 1921.

Even privileged veterans felt that they were not getting due respect. Returning to Oxford in 1919, Vera Brittain observed the fundamental antagonism "between those who suffered deeply from the War, and the others who escaped its most violent impacts". She became acutely aware of "the many possibilities of misunderstanding which embittered the relations of the war generation and its immediate juniors—a type of misunderstanding that is perhaps inevitable whenever one group has been through some profound experience that another has missed". To her "juniors", the war was already "demode".

The young were not long cowed. In September 1920, Alec Waugh's younger brother Evelyn extolled "the extraordinary boom of youth": "Every boy is writing about his school, every child about her doll's house, every baby about its bottle. The very young have gained an almost complete monopoly of book, press and picture gallery. Youth is coming into its own." In 1921, he noted that "a new generation has grown up; between them and the young men of 1912 lies the great gulf of the war. What will they stand for and what will they do?"

J. M. Barrie observed this generational conflict and made notes towards a play on the topic during 1920. "Age and Youth the two great enemies," he wrote; "the two sides (really old & young—i.e. Before and After War) don't understand (admit) that they have different views of what constitutes immorality. As different as ours from, say, an African tribe (this really the result of war) which at first didn't seem to show itself. It isn't those who fought agst their elders, but those who have been growing up since the war agst outlook of others."

The age war had been declared. The young felt justified in rebellion through the moral vacancy of the elders who had sent them to war or, at least, blighted their adolescence. Despite underlying tensions, the three wartime generations managed to unite on two issues. The first was their shared detestation of the old men, the second was their insistent demand for gratification. From the point of view of the veterans, this was an attempt to recapture their lost youth; from the point of view of those too young to serve, it represented a concerted attempt to have a youth worth calling the name.

The elders did not see it that way. The war had been won. They therefore saw no reason to alter their nineteenth-century morality, formed on duty, authority, and obedience. But the whole thrust of post-war generational rhetoric was to expose age's automatic presumption of authority as a hollow sham. When the authorities did not get the blind obedience from the young that they thought to be their automatic prerogative, they reacted furiously. The police, vigilante committees, and popular press were brought together first to define, then act against a perceived tidal wave of immorality.

A wave of crackdowns followed on drinking, dancing, clubgoing: anything that the younger generations defined as enjoyable. Endlessly refined during wartime, the myriad restrictions of DORA had turned public entertainment into a minefield. The two serving generations looked on in amazement. This was the Victorian morality that they had recognized as their enemy during the conflict: to have it reimposed was too much. Much of the resentment came from the fact that the restrictions of DORA had been thought temporary, a hope that was far from the case.

The response of their younger brothers and sisters was even more basic: if that's how the authorities were going to behave when they were just having a bit of fun, then they'd really do it properly and give them something to complain about. Already characterized by their elders as cynical and coldly realistic, the young men and young women of 1922 had found their cause, something to define themselves against. If drinking, dancing, and jazz were to be excoriated by bishops, generals, and politicians alike, then those activities would be their standard. Hedonism became an ideology.

If pleasure would become the new generation's most visible preoccupation, then politics only played an occasional role. Despite major unrest in the immediate post-war period, which included race riots, strikes, mutinies, and unprecedented levels of unemployment, Britain as a whole remained immune to bolshevism. Revolutionary socialists remained a small minority, although a centrist version of socialism gained power with the election of the first-ever Labour government in 1924. Within party politics, youth was not yet defined as a class.

In lieu of the political, there were other movements to soak up the idealism of the non-cynical young. Dr Frank Buchman's Oxford Group, set up in the early 1920s, instituted an unaffiliated religious revival. With no membership lists or rules, the Oxford Group practised a new kind of Christianity: its young, mainly middle-class adherents attended weekend house parties where they publicly shared their sins. The sect pursued both moral rearmament and pacifism as well as its four-point doctrine of absolute honesty, absolute purity, absolute unselfishness, and absolute love.

At the same time, the League of Nations aimed to assist the reconstruction of shattered countries. By 1923 it had fifty-two member states and real international clout. Although the prime purpose of the League's foundation had been to prevent any return of Germany's power, it provided an ideal model for a future world government. The sheer sweep of the Great War had increased global awareness, and for the idealistic young who joined the League of Nations Union, it represented the best chance for world peace.

The most explicitly youthist British organizations were influenced by the Boy Scouts and the pre-war German *Wandervogel*. The conflict had been good for Baden-Powell's movement. The Scouts had played a useful part in the war effort as agricultural workers, air-raid wardens, messengers, and canteen workers. With Baden-Powell's influence fading, the Boy Scouts successfully adapted to post-war conditions. In the place of imperialism, they promoted class harmony, national reconstruction, and internationalism. By 1925, their membership was nearly double that of 1913, at just under 300,000 Scouts.

However, the history of these groups was marked by splits and breakaways. Critical of Baden-Powell's militarism, Ernest Westlake had founded the Order of Woodcraft Chivalry during 1916. Influenced by the Woodcraft Indians of America and Stanley Hall's *Adolescence*, Westlake aimed to put the theory of recapitulation into practice through ceremonies, rituals, and woodcraft training. The Woodcraft Indians aimed at the utopia of Rousseau's *Emile:* a pantheist search for individual freedom through the appreciation of nature. However, the group failed to expand beyond its upper-middle-class base.

Another group offered a more radical alternative. Expelled from the Boy Scout movement for "disloyalty", John Hargrave formed the Kindred of the Kibbo Kift in 1920: the group was named after the archaic English for "Proof of Great Strength". To the early member Leslie Paul, its manifesto "was like a new wind blowing through our young country. Under the influence of H. G. Wells, it spoke strongly for peace, world unity and a world government." The KK were strongly utopian: "If we envisaged a new society, it must have approximated to that which William Morris describes in *News from Nowhere.*"

Despite the movement's idealistic mix of medievalism and left/liberal socialism, the Kindred of the Kibbo Kift was above all a personality cult, dominated by the powerful charisma of its leader. Hargrave's war record, as a stretcher-bearer and war artist at Gallipoli, made him a "typical Scout 'hero'", and KK members were redesigned in his magnetic image. Paul thought that "he spoke especially to those millions of young men who, like myself, had grown up since earliest childhood in the Scout movement from which we had absorbed hopes and dreams about life our parents could not have understood".

However, the tensions in the movement became quickly apparent. Despite its pacifism, the group celebrated the samurai as a martial ideal. Equally forceful and charismatic, Paul quickly fell out with Hargrave. He focused on the fact that the KK leader had fetishes, models of the dog-headed Egyptian god Anubis, "they reminded me that there was in the new movement a credulous wing ready to tinker with the occult. Perhaps it owed its presence to the many theosophists who were associated with its birth, but I felt then the absurdity of this servant girl stuff as a rugged, open-air movement."

In February 1925, Paul broke away from the Kindred of the Kibbo Kift to form his own group. The Woodcraft Folk were set up along the original socialist and utopian ideals that the KK professed: social reconstruction and spiritual regeneration allied with the teaching of practical woodcraft skills. At the age of nineteen, Paul planned a "small experimental group" on which he and his helpers would "test out afresh what all of us then called 'tribal training' theories of education".

This aim was proclaimed by their founding charter: "It is our desire to develop in ourselves, for the service of the people, mental and physical health, and communal responsibility, by camping out and living in close physical contact with nature, by using the critical facility both of our minds and our hands, and by sincerity in all our dealings with our neighbours: we declare that it is our desire to make ourselves familiar with the history of the world, and the development of man in the slow march of evolution that we may understand and revere the Great Spirit which urges all things to perfect themselves."

In his later memoir, *Angry Young Man*, Paul cited the central influence of *Emile* and *Adolescence* on his nascent group's ideology. The latter's "great vogue" was mainly due to Hall's recapitulation theory. Paul thought that the transition between "the boy-savage and civilized man" was only possible if "the boy recapitulated *everything*. He had to get the thrill and danger of modern war by lying in wet trenches and throwing stones at opposing gangs: he had to be permitted to smoke and drink, and to acquire poise by learning to dance and getting to know girls in a social way."

Allied to these tenets was a healthy dose of utopian socialism mixed with pacifism: Paul thought that "the welfare of the community" could only be assured "when the production of all things that directly or indirectly destroys human life ceases to be". The Woodcraft Folk were designed to play a central part in the holy war against capitalism and industrialism: "We are the revolution. With the health that is ours and with the intellect and the physique that will be the heritage of those that we train we are paving the way for that reorganisation of the economic system which will mark the rebirth of the human race."

The Woodcraft Folk slowly built up its membership from small beginnings: just over one hundred in 1926. In keeping with the internationalist tenor of the time, they made contact with young *Bunde* in Germany, Austria, and Czechoslovakia. They tried to involve working-class adolescents. As Paul recalled, "there is just no doubt that this camping and open-air life that we promoted, which gave a child an opportunity to pit his energy and ingenuity against practical problems, worked wonders for undersized children from the slums."

However, there were problems within this youth utopia. The group's socialist orientation was "window dressing, unconsciously indulged in to satisfy the prevailing 'left' climate of those years. We belonged to a blood brotherhood of the campfire. We pursued an ideal of toughness which made us contemptuous of ease and respectability and involved in us a hatred of the weak, the sick and, above all, the elderly." Behind this spartan vision was the fear that "our youth was slipping away, and that unless we lived now the life we ought to live, the chance would soon be gone forever".

The Woodcraft Folk's rigid programme masked a profound sense of dislocation. Paul later admitted that he and his helpers were "really legislating for ourselves. We felt we had been injured by the process of growing up, and that life had been disfigured for us because of its emotional, sexual and economic miseries. How easy it was for others, too, to make a blind recoil from maturity because of them! We felt the burden of a duty to end this intolerable thing, and it was this that made us read and theorize about pedagogics. Somehow, somewhere it ought to be possible to find a way of growing up gracefully."

Paul externalized all his angst into the organization of his group, which became an end in itself. It was this narrow focus that prevented the Woodcraft Folk from becoming a major force in Britain. Like other post-war generationalists, Paul and his cohorts defined themselves too much by what they were against. They also found that, as a ruling principle, youth had its drawbacks. The Woodcraft Folk leaders might have won a victory over the adults, but even they were vulnerable to their own cult: behind them were "the children, who argued fiercely against the tyranny of the old men of eighteen".

• • •

These issues were thrown into even sharper relief within post-war Germany. The *Wandervogel* had rejected industrial civilization and bourgeois values, but the collapse of the country in the wake of defeat brought the outside world crashing into the fantasy of a free youth brotherhood. The German military surrender ushered in political and social changes with such velocity that, even before the armistice, groups comprised of angry servicemen, disaffected workers, and idealistic young intellectuals—encouraged by the Russian Revolution—had set up soviets in several major cities.

Out of this chaos came Germany's first democratic government, run by the Social Democratic Party, the SPD. However, the new Weimar Republic was immediately tainted when its leaders enlisted the Freikorps, the veterans' militia, to quell the soviets. The leaders of the Berlin uprising, Karl Liebknecht and Rosa Luxemburg, were murdered in cold blood. Reconstruction would not be accomplished simply by a change of regime. There were all too many Germans who, as George Grosz recalled, "could not adjust to a world that was no longer normal, that was in the process of disintegration".

There were no jobs: the "streets seethed with unemployed". Within these uncharted waters, "barbarism prevailed. Morality as such no longer existed. A wave of prostitution and obscenity swept the land. '*Je m'en fous*,' shouted everybody. Shimmying was in style." Like their British counterparts, unemployed German youth looked to the music of the New World for inspiration, forming "small bands that played some kind of imitation American jazz for the few pennies dropped into their hats. Superficially, this all appeared to be very merry, but beneath all was hate and despair."

Youth was at the sharp end of national breakdown, as the bellicose nationalism of the previous four years turned inwards. German adolescents brought the war home, as they engaged in pitched street battles justified by extremist ideologies. George Grosz remembered how "the youth of Germany grouped itself in loose political units, marching in shirt sleeves and singing, 'Croak, Jew,' while behind them another group chanted rhythmically: 'Hail Moscow!' Conflicts inevitably took place. Many skulls were broken, shinbones shattered, and even, occasionally, stomachs riddled with bullet holes."

This polarization infected the *Wandervogel*. The split between militarists and pacifists, leftists and rightists, was already entrenched, and the November 1918 revolution politicized it further. The result was a crazy patchwork of cults and cells within the youth movement. The most powerful pre-war grouping, the Freideutsche Jugend, turned to the left. Their autumn 1920 meeting at Hofgeismar, organized around the proposal to establish "a united front of youth", ended in fundamental disagreements between socialists and communists that paralleled the infighting practised by their adult counterparts.

Disillusion with nationalism and war, together with the news from revolutionary Russia, made revolutionary socialism a magnet for many idealistic youths. As they saw it, capitalism inevitably ended in conflict, as the economy of mass production inexorably reduced down to the mass production of armaments. It was the young and the working-class who bore the brunt of this oppression, and in order for it not to happen, society had to be transformed. The only way to do that was for the people to assume power and run the country. Instead of a nationalist, exploitative elite, the mass would be in charge.

With their insistence on social uniformity and collective action, the Communists were attempting to institute a new society for the mass age. The process that had begun with the French Revolution was reaching fruition, as the crowd flexed its power—no longer the ruled but the rulers. Although materialist, communism was suffused with another kind of mysticism. In their initial enthusiasm, adherents like George Grosz believed that a new kind of man-machine was being born: "Individual destinies are no longer important."[2]

Realizing that there was international support for their regime, Russia's new rulers set up the Communist International, the Comintern, in March 1919. Directed by Moscow, Comintern members actively worked to foment revolution in Europe, with Germany specifically targeted. Although small in number, these sleeper cells had a disproportionate influence. Communism became a powerful new youth ideal, celebrated by artists and intellectuals in new institutions like the Bauhaus, enacted on the streets of German cities by groups like the KPD (German Communist Party).

Despite this creeping polarization, many *Wandervogel* veterans hoped for a return to the movement's pre-war innocence. However, neutrality was no longer possible; at the first great post-war reunion of the *Wandervogel*, at Coburg in 1919, three thousand members witnessed scuffles between left and right. Just as some youth groups preferred radical socialism, others opted for the right-wing militarism of the Freikorps. At a subsequent *Wandervogel* meeting in the Fichtel mountains, the serpentine progress of the old-style ramblers was superseded by the majority of members, walking in military step.

New youth groups attempted to harness the Freikorps brotherhood of force. In 1918, a serving officer named Otger Graff formed a group in the guise of medieval knights. His Jungdeutsche Bund favoured German expansion, denounced Jewish capitalism and Christianity, and proposed a national revival

2. The Communist regime in Russia had not lost time in making plans for their continent's youth. In October 1918, the Komsomol (full title Kom*munisticheskiy* Soyuz Molodiozhi: the Communist Union of Youth) was established as the party's youth wing: it aimed to bring in the vast majority of Russians between ages fourteen and twenty-eight. At the second All-Russian Komsomol Conference in May 1922, it was decided to eradicate any remaining youth organizations, like the Russian scouts, and to create a new group for younger adolescents between ages ten and fifteen—initially called the Spartak Young Pioneers. Under the aegis of Lenin's wife, Nadezhda Krupskaya, the Young Pioneers offered a strict year-by-year age grading hierarchy, before full involvement in the Komsomol at the requisite age. Both organizations reflected the regime's wish to establish a cradle-to-grave structure of total Communist involvement.

"under the sign of the Swastika". Another group, the Neupfadfinder, injected an ideology of "tribal education" and a nationalist philosophy derived from the Kindred of the Kibbo Kift and the poet Stefan George and his circle.

George's concept of the *Bunde*—a hermetic group of true believers hostile to twentieth-century mass society with its "banal beliefs in equality and progress"—was refined by Martin Voelkel's White Knights. With knighthood as their goal, the young men of the *Bunde* would lead the German population out of their chains into the glories of the future "Third Reich". This kind of medieval mysticism added spice to the increasingly authoritarian stew of the male-dominated *Bunde*. The lessons of duty and self-sacrifice to a greater cause had been well learned from the four years of war.

The Weimar regime failed to satisfy a wide section of German youth. Within the confused politics of the period, Germany's young were just as likely to take a position on the right as the left. Their generational conflict began to be enacted in terms of youth against age. The actual old men who had sent the young to war had disappeared after November 1918. In place of Kaiser Wilhelm, the father figure was represented by the Weimar Republic, and it was against this fragile democracy that the hostility of the sons would be directed.

Sebastian Haffner recalled that, after the unsuccessful Kapp Putsch, "interest in politics flagged among all boys. All parties had been compromised and the entire topic lost its attraction." Into this vacuum, extremism rushed. "Only a few remained true to politics, and it struck me for the first time that, strangely enough, they were among the more stupid, coarse and repellent among my schoolfellows. They proceeded to enter the 'right sort' of leagues, the German National Youth Association or the Bismarck League, and soon they showed off knuckledusters, truncheons, and even coshes in school."

Haffner saw one of these bullies "scribble a strange design in his notebook": "Again and again the strange pattern was repeated. A few strokes combined in an unexpected, pleasing way to form a symmetrical box-like ornament. I was immediately tempted to copy him. 'What is that?,' I asked in a whisper as it was during a lesson, boring though that was. 'Anti-Semitic sign,' he whispered back in telegraphic staccato. 'The Ehrhardt Brigade wore it on their helmets. Means "Out with the Jews". You ought to know it,' and he went on scribbling. It was my first acquaintance with the swastika."

. . .

At the dawn of generational politics, it was becoming clear that youth per se was neither progressive nor reactionary. It could be either, both, or worse.

While the Comintern plotted to influence European youth, the right wing had already succeeded in yoking youth to a new kind of extremist politics. Despite being part of the Allied coalition against the Central Powers, Italy had suffered from the same post-war collapse of values. As the returning veteran Adolfo Omodeo wrote in the spring of 1919, "I seem to be living in a world that has lost all moral conscience, whether in the international, the national, or the private realm."

Formed in the spring of 1919, a new party called Fasci di combattimento aimed to focus the anger of the returning veterans into a mass political party. One principal factor distinguished them from the other millenarian groups vying for the veterans' attention. The futurist insistence on the vitality of youth became the central part of the Fascist programme. As the movement's founder, Benito Mussolini, stated in July 1919, "In the *fasci* there is not the mildew of the old ideas, the venerable beard of the old men, the hierarchy of conventional values, but there is youth, there is impetuousness and faith."

Skimpy on details, the Fascist programme was big on rhetoric and spectacle. Using staged events like the November 1919 meeting in Milan, which began with "a magnificent rocket burst" and ended with a torchlight procession, the Fascists harnessed the veterans' *combattentismo* mentality to the revolutionary impulse of many young bourgeois. As one Roman futurist wrote in 1919, "Tomorrow belongs to the young. Let us kneel before the daring military formation that is returning. Their dynamism will dictate the laws that will discipline the world. The world belongs in their hands."

Having united the generations under the banner of the Fascists' trademark song, "Giovinezza! Giovinezza!" (Youth! Youth!), Mussolini—despite being nearer the age of the hated father—was swept to power in October 1922. Although the *fascisti* were not initially as totalitarian as their successors, the precedent was set. By the early 1920s, Mussolini had proved that youth, as an abstract principle and an energetic reality, could be yoked to new parties that, celebrating technology and pagan spectacle, would bypass the traditional nineteenth-century poles of liberalism and conservatism.

The consequence was a seemingly brand-new politics of power and struggle that appealed to the unsatiated violence of the wartime generation at the same time as it activated the as yet untested cruelty of their younger cohorts. To many radicals, the mass brutality of 1914–18 had proved the truth of Nietzsche's most famous dictum. If God was dead, then he would be replaced by the secular religions of communism and fascism. With their innate appetite for what Stanley Hall called "religious conversion", many of Europe's young would join up.

. . .

These polarized politics would prove more and more attractive in Germany as the post-war chaos got worse. When in 1923 the French army occupied the country's industrial heart, the Ruhr, the deutsche mark went into free fall. As Sebastian Haffner remembered, "The cost of living had begun to spiral out of control. Traders followed hard on the heels of the dollar. A pound of potatoes which yesterday had cost fifty thousand marks now cost a hundred thousand. The salary of sixty-five thousand marks brought home the previous Friday was no longer sufficient to buy a packet of cigarettes on Tuesday."

This spectacular devaluation was the final straw. After 1923, there entered into the Germans' soul an "uncurbed, cynical imagination, the nihilistic pleasure in the impossible for its own sake, and the energy that has become an end in itself. In that year an entire generation of Germans had a spiritual organ removed: the organ which gives men steadfastness and balance, but also a certain inertia and stolidity. It may variously appear as conscience, reason, experience, respect, morality, or the fear of God. A whole generation learned then—or thought it learned—to do without such ballast."

During the 1920s, the ideological youth groupings were caught in a fatal cleft. Rejecting the values of the elders, they thought that youth by itself would be enough to transform the world. However, in cutting themselves off from almost all known ties, they projected themselves into dangerous territory. "It was a new paganism that we sought and a new barbarism that we managed to achieve," Leslie Paul later admitted, with the benefit of hindsight. "Denial of civilization became everywhere a cult and an organization, and much European history turns on the mood which my youth movement then typified."

CHAPTER 15

Sheiks and Shebas

The American Youth Market

* * *

I wear bobbed hair, the badge of flapperhood. (And, oh, what a comfort it is!), I powder my nose. I wear fringed skirts and bright-colored sweaters, and scarfs, and waists with Peter Pan collars, and low-heeled "finale hopper" shoes. I adore to dance. I spend a large amount of time in automobiles. I attend hops, and proms, and ball-games, and crew races, and other affairs at men's colleges.

—Ellen Welles Page, "A Flapper's Appeal to Parents", *Outlook*, June 12, 1922

YOUNG AMERICAN FLAPPER, EARLY 1920S

IN *THIS SIDE OF PARADISE*, F. Scott Fitzgerald tabulated a new youth type that marked "the first real break from the hypocrisy of school tradition. The slicker was a definite element of success, differing intrinsically from the prep school 'big man'."

"THE SLICKER"	"THE BIG MAN"
1. Clever sense of social values.	1. Inclined to stupidity and unconscious of social values.
2. Dresses well. Pretends that dress is superficial—but knows that it isn't.	2. Thinks dress is superficial, inclined to be careless about it.
3. Goes into such activities as he can shine in.	3. Goes out for everything from a sense of duty.
4. Gets to college and is, in a worldly way, successful.	4. Gets to college and has a problematical future. Feels lost . . .
5. Hair slicked.	5. Hair not slicked.

Published in 1920, Fitzgerald's first novel announced American adolescence as if fully formed, tracing its history through the idylls of Booth Tarkington to its current, lapsed post-war state: "restless as the devil." With its concentration on the peer worlds of school and college and its defiantly modernist approach, *This Side of Paradise* was a coming-of-age story that typified a generation that was becoming aware of itself and its social power. It also captured the youth obsession that was America's selling point just as its culture began to sweep through the Western world.

Although innocence, of a distinctly American sort, was the most important element in this ideal, both *This Side of Paradise* and the period's other successful coming-of-age novel, Sherwood Anderson's *Winesburg, Ohio*, recognized that the continent's unspoiled quality was already tarnished. Writing about the "revolution" of industrialism, Anderson observed that "much of the old brutal ignorance that had in it also a kind of beautiful innocence is gone forever". Whereas Booth Tarkington's hero remained in the Midwest, Anderson's hero, George Willard, left Ohio as soon as he could: at the age of eighteen.

This Side of Paradise took the boy book to the next stage, from the midwestern arcadia to the corrupting metropolis. Fitzgerald delineated the social activities of upper-middle-class American youth in unprecedented detail: the self-enclosed world of school and college, the sexual experiments, the frenzied dancing and drinking, sudden automotive death. As the book's references to Huysmans,

Brooke, and Wilde made clear, these spasms of booze, sex, and speed offered a new kind of romanticism updated for an age in which illusions had been shattered by the war.

America's entry into the conflict had prompted the same kind of generational antagonism that was being enacted in Britain, Germany, and France. As the twenty-two-year-old soldier John Dos Passos wrote from the front in 1918, "All young men are frightfully decent. If only we governed the world instead of the swaggering old fogies in frock-coats that do!" Another young soldier, Walter A. Hafener, wrote to Stanley Hall in January 1919, "All we want is get out of army clothes and put on civilian clothes and then hide and if anybody tries to tell us what to do, there will be murder done."

Whether they were returning servicemen or college students, nothing would exercise America's young more in the early 1920s than the curtailment of its freedom to, as Hafener put it, "have a drink or two at the Biltmore or Knickerbocker or the Frolic". Between the completion and the publication of *This Side of Paradise*, America's Nineteenth Amendment was passed. The Volstead Act, which prohibited the consumption, the advertising, and the manufacture of liquor, became law on January 17, 1920. Breaking the law would become the ritual for a generation reacting against "the old fogies".

Prohibition might have been one logical conclusion to the pre-war Reform movement, but it also marked the high tide of the illiberalism ushered in by the war. The sweeping powers brought in to help the war were expanded in a campaign against pacifists, dissidents, and especially organized labour. The United States was determined to expunge the Bolshevik virus. The mass trial of 113 International Workers of the World activists in August 1918 was followed at the end of 1919 by a sequence of mass raids and deportations, partly masterminded by an ambitious young lawyer named J. Edgar Hoover.

Just at the point when its freedoms were becoming a beacon to post-war Europe, America was closing up like a clam. The result of intensive minority lobbying, the Volstead Act was unpopular from its inception. It represented the brake of religious morality while most of the country rushed into the more secular values of consumerism. It also marked an arbitrary limit to the licence promoted by that new system and was rightly seen as hypocritical by the young. Indeed, much of the angst in *This Side of Paradise* is the result of the mixed messages that youth receives from its elders about appetites and desires.

At the same time as Prohibition was instituted, consumerism became an important part of American economic policy. It was, as Elizabeth Stevenson writes, "the first time that on a giant scale a society developed a set of manners, a provision of wants and needs, and a faith from the buying and selling of goods". Still charged with representing the future, youth was specially targeted by producers and marketers. As the advertising trade journal *Printer's Ink* observed in 1921: "if you sell the young people of the land, you will at the same time, sell the older people."

In 1918, the total gross advertising in general magazines was $58.5 million; two years later, it reached $129.5 million. Much of this was aimed at the young, who were, as one advertising guru opined, the "radicals in the market". Among the products aimed at youth were clothes, magazines, cosmetics, movies, phonographs, and cigarettes. *Photoplay* magazine made a ground-breaking survey of age-related purchasing habits in 1922, in which it revealed that the most popular items among the eighteen-to-thirty age group were hosiery, underwear, phonographs, and records.

After the false starts and failed experiments of the previous two decades, America's young were granted a new status as the vanguard of the consumer revolution. During the 1920s, high schools doubled their numbers and college entry became a national aspiration rather than the preserve of an elite. Advertising began aggressively to target the new, discrete, pan-youth class created by the eventual successful introduction of mass education. For many young Americans, education became not so much a method of learning as training into their social status as "the customers of tomorrow".

The American contradictions around youth and age, freedom and authoritarianism, choice and coercion were explored in Sinclair Lewis's 1923 novel *Babbitt*. Set in the Midwest of the boy book, it depicted the continent's change from the pre-industrial idyll into a mechanistic, uniform society. George Babbitt, the novel's middle-aged hero, might have fantasized of "the fairy child, a dream more romantic than scarlet pagodas by a silver sea", but his inner, subjective landscape was ever more scientifically yoked to consumerism as it became a secular religion of mass individuality.

Peter Pan had morphed into the peppy, adolescent consumer, as youth became seen in materialist terms. *This Side of Paradise* captured this loss of innocence caused by premature, if not precocious, experience. "Your generation is growing hard," says Monsignor Darcy, one of the few sympathetic adults in a book where they are largely absent; "much harder than mine ever grew, nourished as they were in the stuff of the nineties." At the same time, Fitzgerald's novel was part of this tarnishing process: although it criticized American youth culture, it broadcast the phenomenon to a wider public.

Although he revelled in the descriptions of petting parties and drunken car rides, Fitzgerald was highly aware of the dangers in the elevation of youth as a social ideal. In the words of his protagonist, Amory Blaine, "Youth is like having a big plate of candy. Sentimentalists think they want to be in the pure simple state they were in when they were eating the candy. They don't. They just want the fun of eating it again. The matron doesn't want to repeat her girlhood—she wants to repeat her honeymoon. I don't want to repeat my innocence. I want the pleasure of losing it again."

It was no accident that youth's full arrival in Western society came at the point of historical discontinuity created by the war: with its explicit age division, the generational idea enshrined the sensation of being lost so eloquently evoked in *This Side of Paradise*. But this sense of being lost is inevitably endemic to adolescence: adrift in a world made by adults, not for you. The youth in Fitzgerald's novel act out the insatiable yearning of its author: the actress Rosalinde Fuller felt that "he was one of those people who could never be satisfied with life". But there was another side to the equation.

Fitzgerald wrote his novel at the age of twenty-three as a desperate act of wish fulfilment—to transcend the failure of his father and his own adolescence, and to win the girl of his dreams. His wish was fulfilled when, a week after its publication, he married the nineteen-year-old Zelda Sayre. The book was an immediate succès d'estime and made them both youth celebrities. Scott later observed that, despite his ignorance, he "was pushed into the position not only of spokesman for the time but of the typical product of that moment". To Zelda, the New York of 1920 "was just a lot of youngness".

. . .

The Fitzgeralds were kept busy commenting on the most visible symbol of the new consumer youth. Scott's first book of short stories, published in 1920, was called *Flappers and Philosophers*. In June 1921, Zelda Fitzgerald wrote a "Eulogy on the Flapper", in which she firmly stated that the freedoms for which the "first Flappers" like her had fought, namely to bob their hair, to put on "a great deal of audacity and rouge", and to flirt "because it was fun", had become accepted as the standard of the first mass female adolescent generation.

The commercial media had reflected and shaped the lives of American women since the last years of the previous century, when the housewife was instituted as the model consumer. During the 1920s, advertising began to target a younger cohort of working women, who represented 20 per cent of the total employed. "If I were the manufacturer of notions," wrote a "notions buyer" for the big New York store Gimbel Brothers in 1922, "I certainly would appeal to the young woman of seventeen or eighteen to twenty-six to twenty-seven years, when she is forming the buying habits of a lifetime."

As a type, the flapper explicitly linked youth to the tradition of the female consumer. As Stanley Hall perceptively observed in a 1922 article called "The Flapper Americana Novissima", the war had accelerated the process. It had "completed her emancipation from the chaperon, and it became good patri-otic form to address, give flaglets, badges, and dainties, to young men in the street and, perhaps, sometimes, to strike up acquaintance with them if they were in uniform. Her manners have grown a bit free-and-easy, and every ves-tige of certain old restraints have gone."

The term had first appeared in Europe during the 1890s, when it meant a very young prostitute. That had changed just before the war to describe what the Germans (and Stanley Hall) called a *Backfisch*—an adolescent girl with a boyish figure. During the war, the flapper was redefined in Britain as an inde-pendent, pleasure-seeking, khaki-crazy young woman. Although the more scandalous associations of the type—which included cocaine addiction—disappeared after 1918, the flapper retained traces of the roles that she had passed through in her journey from the margins of society to trendsetter.

Fashion went hand in hand with changing morality. The increased sexual assertion of young women, coupled with the androgyny of the young or the perverse, was reinforced by the slow spread of short haircuts from pre-war Paris and the slow rise of the skirt to just below the knee by mid-decade. In 1920, Hollywood featured one of its brightest new stars, Olive Thomas, in *The Flapper,* a light comedy. The picture made official the American appearance of the type that quickly became the object of an obsessive, unprecedented level of definition in the years that followed.

Writing in 1922, Stanley Hall positioned the type in the teens rather than the twenties, but he also observed a wide range of products and habits associ-ated with this "chic" and up-to-date schoolgirl. They included clothing, soft drinks, perfumes, movies, and anything associated with the "near heaven" of dancing. He felt that the popularity and availability of these consumer items, coupled with the flapper's self-confidence, marked a new kind of social ritual for young women that enabled them to pass successfully through their adoles-cence.

From an insider's perspective, Zelda Fitzgerald observed that flapper styles were originated in the elite schools and were then imitated by "several thou-sand big-town shop-girls". In turn, these were imitated by "several million small-town belles", who got the latest styles "via the 'novelty stores' of their re-spective small towns". Citing a lurid editorial that fixed the blame for all America's social ills "upon the head of the Flapper", she refuted the charge that the type was amoral. On the contrary, she was teaching America's youth "to capitalize their natural resources and get their money's worth".

As the type went mainstream, its signature element was a frank, uninhibited sexuality. Hollywood was quick in developing new stars to satiate the desires of this apparently free and easy new type. The most sensational film of 1921 was *The Sheik*, the torrid tale of a tabooed love affair between an English noblewoman and a sadistic Arab. E. M. Hull, the young female author of this immediate bestseller, concocted a heady fantasy of exotic, rough sex legitimized by the denouement, where it is revealed that the sheik is in fact a viscount of the realm—and therefore of marrying stock.

Premiered that November, the film starred Rudolph Valentino, a twenty-six-year-old Italian who had already made a big splash in *The Four Horsemen of the Apocalypse*. Dark and pampered, scripted and modelled by women, Valentino offered a new, completely un-American masculinity. His effect on both sexes was electric: by the end of 1921, he was receiving nine hundred letters a week from his obsessive female fan base. The film was so popular that it gave its name to a new masculine youth style, the sheik, which aped Valentino's centre-parting, tight waist, and hooded sexual allure.

This was a new pagan world. The ads for *The Sheik* ran:

SEE

**the auction of beautiful girls to
the lords of Algerian harems**

SEE

**matchless scenes of gorgeous
color, and wild free life and love
in the year's supreme screen
thrill—3000 in the cast**

and Valentino was its chief deity. His appeal was laid out in his first press interview for *Motion Picture* in July 1920. In this star-making piece of hyperbole, he was described as "a phenomenal youth" with godlike qualities: "the vitality of Don Juan who would woo; the extravagance of Don Quixote who would exaggerate; the courage of D'Artagnan who would dare . . . the desire of D'Annunzio who would achieve; the strength of Vulcan who would excel; and the philosophy of Omar whose 'yesterday is dead and tomorrow never comes'."

The exploitation of pagan pleasure was further developed by the bestselling 1923 novel *Flaming Youth*. In his introduction, Warner Fabian offered the

YOUNG AMERICAN SHEIK
IN SUIT, 1920S

book as a mirror for the modern woman. He defined his target readership as "restless, seductive, greedy, discontented, craving sensation, unrestrained, a little morbid, more than a little selfish, intelligent, uneducated, sybaritic, following blind instincts and perverse fancies, slack of mind as she is trim of body, neurotic and vigorous, a worshipper of tinselled gods at perfumed altars, fit mate for the hurried, reckless and cynical man of the age".

Warner Fabian's sheiklike pseudonym masked a middle-aged journeyman journalist determined to give his readership exactly what they wanted. *Flaming Youth* exposed premarital sex, abortion, nude swimming parties, illegal drinking, and an adolescent girl's loss of virginity at the hands of an older man. Within this shopping list of shock, youth was the ruling principle: "Don't you wish you were young again?" asked one of the few adults. "To be a desperado of twenty! They're all desperadoes, these kids, all of them with any life in their veins; the girls as well as the boys; maybe more than the boys."

Aimed squarely at modern women, whether they were young or wanted to be young, this titillating hokum was perfect for Hollywood, and the film version of Fabian's novel was rushed out the same year. Its star was the twenty-three-year-old Colleen Moore, selected as the lead because she wore a Dutch bob, trimmed with "bangs, like a Japanese girl's haircut", to the audition. Brazenly marketed with slogans like "neckers, petters, white kisses, red kisses, pleasure mad daughters, sensation craving mothers", *Flaming Youth* cemented the bold new femininity in the public imagination.

The film had an extraordinary impact. Scott Fitzgerald later wrote, "I was the spark that lit up *Flaming Youth*, Colleen Moore was the torch. What little things we are to have caused all that trouble." It also made the bob haircut the symbol of modern woman. In his 1925 survey of the archetypal "Flapper Jane", Bruce Bliven noted that the very latest bob left her with "just about no hair at the back, and 20 per cent more than that at the front—about as much as is being worn this season by a cellist (male); less than a pianist; and much much less than a violinist".

∎ ∎ ∎

By the early twenties, America's dream economy had become a huge, complex, and lucrative industry. The movies had overtaken both vaudeville and the theatre as the country's most popular entertainment form during the mid-1910s and had entered their "golden decade" of artistic and commercial success. During 1922, at least 45 per cent of American adolescents went to the movies once a week. At the same time, record sales were up to a peak of over $100 million, while the medium of radio was expanding nationally—up to 20 million listeners during 1923 and 1924.

The greater sophistication and increasing interconnectedness of these booming industries was illustrated by the cross-media promotion of films like *Flaming Youth*. By 1923, youth styles were being observed, reproduced, and then disseminated throughout the continent by movies, magazines, radio, advertising, or the music industry. The process was so fast, and the sleight of hand so accomplished, that it usually seemed that these media actually set the styles. In fact, they were merely capitalizing on adolescent reality.

America's youth were perfectly complicit in this process: flexing their generational muscle by taking advantage of their new freedoms, then seeing their behaviour reinforced on screen or in popular cartoons like Carl Ed's *Harold Teen*, which started in 1919. Having thoroughly internalized their society's dominant values, America's adolescents entered into a ritual dance with the mass media that made it hard to pick out where modes of behaviour and fashion began and ended. Indeed, mediated youth types like the flapper were, according to Zelda Fitzgerald, "merely applying business methods to being young".

This industrial attention not only increased the generation gap between the mature and the young, it also meant that adolescents were becoming sophisticated ever earlier, at the age of twelve and thirteen. However, this was not just due to the sensationalized influence of Hollywood. The high school was becoming a mass educational system as increasing numbers of adolescent Americans enrolled: 37 per cent of fourteen- to seventeen-year-olds in 1920. Combined with the educational trend of age homogenization within grades, this meant that more of the country's young were joining a discrete peer society.

Babbitt's son Ted epitomized the schoolboy as industrial product: "His suit, the latest thing in Old Eli togs, was skin-tight, with skimpy trousers to the tops of his glaring tan boots, a chorus man waistline, pattern of an agitated check, and across the back a belt which belted nothing. His scarf was an enormous black silk wad. His flaxen hair was ice-smooth, pasted back without parting." Despite this extravagant dress, Ted was an ultra-conformist: a true believer in American business values.

Despite this uniformity, America's adolescents had much to gain from this incipient peer culture. With the radio, gramophones, movies, magazines, and the all-important automobile, they had more opportunities to enjoy themselves away from prying adult eyes. However, going to dance halls, buying clothes, going to the cinema—all of these cost money, and it was here that the real generational tensions were exercised. Although economically dependent on their parents, the young would no longer easily submit to their authority.

For the first time, also, young women had some chance of equality. Increased coeducation along strict age lines also favoured girls: often they were more developed and more confident than their male classmates. Stanley Hall noted that the "Flapper Americana Novissima" treated the boys "as if sex differences did not exist. Toward him she may sometimes seem almost aggressive. She goes to shows and walks with him in the evenings, and in school corridors may pat him familiarly on the back, hold him by the lapel, and elbow him in a familiar and even *de-haut-en-bas* way."

For many adults, the increased sexual frankness of the flapper was a disturbing feature of the new adolescent culture. Not only was an overt sexuality part of youth's commercial hook, it was relentlessly promoted by "sex adventure" magazines like *True Story*, movie fan magazines like *Photoplay*, and major movies like *Flaming Youth*. A report in a midwestern newspaper captured a film opening in 1924: "'Sheiks' and their 'shebas' sat without a movement or a whisper throughout the presentation. It was a real exhibition of love-making."

Despite all this stimulation, full sexual activity before marriage was still a major taboo. The 1920s young had many more opportunities to experiment than their 1890s counterparts, but there were still limits. There was an increase in premarital sex among adolescents, but the new peer culture, with its complicated checks and rituals, gave some control to the very flapper whose make-up, free and easy behaviour, ever shorter skirts, and energetic jazz dancing appeared to unlock a whole world of forbidden sin.

In fact, the high school offered a secure theatre within which the complicated contract of courtship could be safely enacted. It began with ritual teasing and giggling, and was followed by the frank approach, as the female took the initiative. As one high school girl wrote, "Boys, is it fair to make the girls come to a school entertainment unescorted? So far, I have not been to an entertainment without seeing three-fourths of the girls come without escorts. The most disgusting thing about it is, that the boys act as though they do not realize the predicament they've placed the girls in."

Young women made the running in dates, which usually began with a parental introduction, and then involved an evening out that ended with the return home around eleven o'clock. It was understood that a date was a good way of finding out about potential friends, and even boyfriends, but that it did not represent any kind of binding contract. As one Minneapolis girl complained, "Just because a boy is gentleman enough to take a girl home, is no reason that he is in love with her. All we want is common courtesy, not husbands."

Although there were no chaperones on dates, there were brakes on the system. The necessity of parental involvement meant that prospective male dates were vetted. For the young men, the attraction of dates was the prospect of sex, but this too was governed by the rules of what was called petting: the various levels of kissing and fondling that fell short of actual intercourse. At the heart of the matter, however, there was still the old moral hypocrisy, with the sexually active young woman bearing the brunt of strictly enforced criticism.

Dating enshrined popularity as the central ideal of high school life. Fitting in with the qualities desired by your schoolmates became a competitive affair. While researching life in Muncie, Indiana, during 1924 and 1925, Robert S. Lynd and Helen Merrell Lynd interviewed a popular student who stated that the qualities she looked for in boys was "being on the basket-ball or football team. A fellow who's just a good student rates pretty low. Being good-looking, a good dancer, and your family owning a car all help."

The Lynds concluded that education "appears to be desired frequently not for its specific content but as a symbol—by the working class as an open sesame that will mysteriously admit their children to a world closed to them, and by the business class as a heavily sanctioned aid in getting on further economically or socially in the world". This system of peer social grading expanded upwards into America's universities. Despite their professed scholastic ideals, for many colleges academic excellence was not the point: the average man, not the outstanding scholar, was the desired alumnus.

Between 1919 and 1922, the number of university students doubled. This push towards tertiary education was facilitated by smaller family sizes, a large fifteen- to twenty-four-year-old cohort, and the increasing sophistication of American business. Corporatization needed a whole new class of executives, as the number of those working in administration tripled between 1899 and 1929. In Middletown, within one generation the general manager of one glass factory had been succeeded by a "production manager", a "sales manager", an "advertising manager", and an "office manager".

University education became the prerequisite for joining this new elite, and the prime purpose of going to college was to get a step up on the career ladder. Given the upwardly mobile nature of American society, its appeal was cross-class. Although the business class expected their children to go to college, some working-class families decided to make the sacrifices required for an expensive few years. As one Middletown working father complained, "I don't know how we're going to get the children through college, but we're *going* to. A boy without an education today just ain't *anywhere*."

This industrial imperative was reflected in new courses like business and home economics, and in a new consumer culture that promoted college styles and fads not just to students, but to the young at large. With *This Side of Paradise,* Scott Fitzgerald had started an avalanche. The activities and customs of university students had fascinated the American public since the turn of the century, but with the massive proportional increase—over 400 per cent between 1890 and 1924—they became a large industry during the 1920s.

With more money in their pockets from part-time jobs or indulgent parents, students broadcast their difference from the rest of the population with trendsetting clothes and social activities. "If you sell the college man, you sell the many younger lads who are taking the college hero as their ideal," observed the magazine *Sales Management* in the mid-1920s; "the country follows the lead of the college student in matters of dress." Contemporary surveys of students revealed the breadth of their material requirements.

A 1920s study of young Harvard undergraduates revealed that they annually purchased six to eight shirts, eight neckties, six pairs of underwear, twelve handkerchiefs, twelve pairs of socks, two pairs of garters, and three pairs of shoes. All the thirty-five students sampled had phonographs, and most had typewriters. About 85 per cent of the total student population smoked cigarettes. At the University of Pennsylvania, female students bought seven dresses, five sweaters, three skirts, one coat, three hats, four pairs of shoes, twenty-five pairs of stockings, twelve items of lingerie, and four pairs of gloves each year. This Ivy League pattern of spending trickled down to less elite institutions.

Among the styles associated with the college market were, for women, variants on the flapper trinity of bobbed hair, cigarette smoking, and shorter skirts: tubular dresses, open galoshes, yellow raincoats, silk stockings, and bandanas tied at the head and waist. Some women even adopted items normally associated with the opposite gender: waistcoats, ties, and knickerbockers. Male peacocks sported huge raccoon coats, knickerbockers, golf stockings, and very wide "Valentino pants", while their more conservative peers wore soft-collared shirts, low-heeled winter oxford shoes, and non-gartered socks.

College students were also big media consumers. On average, every student went to the cinema once a week—especially once the movies began to reflect university life. The college movie genre was epitomized by the successful 1925 dramatization of Percy Marks's scandalous freshman novel *The Plastic Age*, which starred the future "It Girl" Clara Bow. Music and dancing were high on the list, with the "hot" jazz of the period, whether by King Oliver, Louis Armstrong's Hot Five, or local student bands providing the most popular soundtrack.

College students had been among the first supporters of hot jazz, and the campuses provided a fertile ground for enthusiasts and practitioners alike. At the University of Indiana, the most popular group was the Wolverine Orchestra, featuring the cornetist Bix Beiderbecke. The twenty-year-old had already made a prolonged study of jazz, meeting Louis Armstrong and hanging around Chicago's famous Negro nightclub, the Lincoln Gardens. He became a fixture on campus with his old blue sweater and jug of bootleg booze, as his group serenaded the sorority houses from the back of a truck.

The 1920s college market represented the first time that youth styles were aggressively defined and sold to the nation as a whole. The fact that this was the costume of the new elite, or would-be elite, did not deter many working-class adolescents from becoming what the novelist James T. Farrell described

as "a fake collegian, one of those guys that bought college boy suits on the instalment plan". However, campus life offered freedom within highly circumscribed limits. "You dress your bodies and your minds to some set model,"
cursed one of the characters in *The Plastic Age*.

All too often, the mass standardization of American consumerism was reproduced in the psyches of its young guinea pigs. For all the relaxed adolescent freedoms, colleges were run on very strict peer lines. "A man can never
escape the consequences of his selection of associates," one college magazine
reminded its readers in 1922. "A man is judged by his companions and his organizations." Another observer listed the qualities necessary for popularity:
being good-looking, having money and a car. Just like at high school, being on
the football team was more important than getting A grades.

Despite the presence of working-class students, the pace in college life still
came from the top down. Campus society was ruthlessly enforced by the fraternity system. These societies with their Greek initials worked on the student
from the moment he or she arrived, beginning with the "rushing" of freshmen. Once selection had been made, there was the pledge and then the initiation. This important ritual was marked by what was called "hazing", the
denigration and humiliation of the supplicant, which usually involved physical violence and mental torture.

Fostered by the university authorities, the fraternities offered many benefits to those within the system: guaranteed status and a ready-made social life.
However, their rigid conformity made campus life unbearable for the excluded. "They dress alike, they do the same things at the same time and they
think and speak in the same terms and have practically all the same interests,"
a European visitor noted in 1923. "The standard seems to be a uniformity.
Everyone who is different is 'crazy', perhaps a bookworm or the like."

Campus life was not all it was cracked up to be: one-third of all students
dropped out before graduating. Within such a competitive system, not everyone could be a winner, and students from ethnic groups—such as Jews—and
from lower-income groups were disadvantaged. Known as "grubs" or "grinds",
hard-working or intellectual students had a very low status: one college magazine editor warned freshmen that they had to decide whether to be a scholar
"in isolation from the mass of students" or be "a popular man among his
fellows".

Although "eager capitalists", the pragmatic 1920s college generation did
not entirely lack a critical faculty. Like their younger counterparts at high
school, they relished their generational power. A small but significant minority enjoyed testing the limits of the university system and, by implication, the

world of adults. With avowed and disparate cultural heroes like Emma Goldman, Theda Bara, Rudolph Valentino, and F. Scott Fitzgerald, they aspired at least to some level of nonconformity, and this was principally expressed by having a good time.

Thanks to the spread of jazz, dance halls continued to proliferate across the country in the early 1920s, and they were filled with "college boys whose purpose was to 'sow wild oats'", as well as "high school girls and boys in search of sophistication". In this "emotionally charged atmosphere", American youth could let rip without the worry of interfering adults. However, just as the animal dance craze had brought down the wrath of the reformers in the early 1910s, jazz and dancing continued to attract adverse comment.

In the early 1920s, jazz was generationally divisive. The *Ladies' Home Journal* launched an anti-jazz "crusade": "Anyone who says that 'youths of both sexes can mingle in close embrace'—with limbs intertwined and torso in contact—without suffering harm lies. Add to this position the wriggling movement and sensuous stimulation of the abominable big jazz orchestra with its voodoo-born minors and its direct appeal to the sensory centre, and if you can believe that youth is the same after this experience than before, then God help your child."

The flapper's "pagan attitude to love itself" was shocking enough. However, the fact that jazz and its dances, most notably the Charleston, which premiered in the 1923 musical *Running Wild,* had their origin in Negro society merely compounded the perceived danger to American society. In taking up Negro culture, college students were charged with bringing into white middle-class life the activities more usually associated with the "Black and Tan districts of Chicago or the East Tenderloin in New York". However, the moralists' hysteria only served to increase the appeal of jazz.

More girls were petting—one 1924 study revealed that it was practised by 92 per cent of coeds—but adult criticism only made it clear to the young how out of touch adults were. Even the popularity of group "petting parties", so scandalous to the older generation, represented a "form of exploration" limited by peer mores. Nobody could go too far: as one young Ohio State University student wrote in 1922, the college girl "is secure in the most critical situations—*she knows the limits,* and because of her safety in such knowledge *she is able to run almost the complete gamut of experience* [italics in original]".

Thanks to the tireless efforts of Margaret Sanger, contraception had become more generally accepted in the business classes and their collegiate offspring. However, despite what the Lynds called "some tentative relaxing" among the younger generation, premarital sex was still a powerful taboo. For college girls, the full loss of virginity was a major concern, while male under-graduates were more likely to solve this problem by having "smut sessions" or by going to prostitutes. Being "a fast woman" or "a bad egg with women" was enough to incur peer ostracism, if not actual expulsion.

The central battleground for 1920s college students, as for many of their generation, was Prohibition. Illegal drinking was both accepted and desirable. If a student didn't show at least "a tendency to dissipate", he was considered "wet", but he wasn't wet if he dissipated "to excess". The Anti-Saloon League had specifically aimed the bill at the urban working class and the poor, but its unpopularity meant that illegal drinking, according to one college newspaper, moved "from the saloons and the vulgar cabarets into the social circles and the dance halls of the five hundred".

Imposed upon the country by a minority pressure group, Prohibition brought the very rule of law into disrepute. The collegiate attitude was summed up by the Cornell student newspaper, which called it a "joke" with no "popular accord necessary to its enforcement". This disrespect for the law had a slow radicalizing effect as the illegal economy brought students into contact with ideas, attitudes, and people that their elder brothers and sisters had never encountered. This mood would harden both into an acceptance of "a new pluralism in behaviour" and more overt criticism of the adult world.

● ● ●

Caught between exploitation and condemnation, between pleasure and puritanism, the 1920s generation were early victims of their country's contradictory attitudes. Youth was a volatile subject for an untested mass experiment. Beneath the peppy, pagan, pluralistic image of the sheik and the sheba, there were savage, untamed impulses: the prejudice and violent initiations of college fraternity houses, the physical damage done by unregulated bootleg booze, the hair-trigger violence of youthful gangsters vying for control over the vast illegal liquor market.

In April 1924, the leading bootlegger of the day took control over the Chicago suburb of Cicero in "a chilling public display of power". The twenty-five-year-old Al Capone was unopposed by police and politicians alike. One month later, the dark forces that lay behind America's youth obsession were laid bare by one of the century's most sensational murder cases. It began on May 21 with a ransom demand made to a wealthy Chicago businessman named Jacob Franks, stating that his youngest son had been kidnapped and would be returned for ten thousand dollars.

The next day, the naked body of fourteen-year-old Bobby Franks was discovered in a remote swamp on the outskirts of the city. The press went mad, hyping up "The Danger to the Children of Chicago". After rounding up the usual suspects to no avail, the police traced the culprits through a pair of glasses left at the scene and the distinctive imprint of the typewriter used to write the ransom demand. The perpetrators of this horrific and unprecedented crime were revealed as two college students, both in their late teens, named Nathan Leopold and Richard Loeb.

There could have been no greater shock. Leopold and Loeb were no disfigured slum golems like Jesse Pomeroy. They were handsome, rich representatives of the elite youth class, straight out of Scott Fitzgerald with their snappy clothes and hair slicked back in the sheik style. They appeared to have everything that a young person in a youth-dominated society could want: cars, girls, college hijinks, even the thrills offered by a lawless city. But, having thought themselves above the law and superior to their fellow man, they had crossed the line into murder in an instant.

The police soon discovered that the pair had long planned the perfect crime: after researching ransom drop and body disposal sites, they started searching for a victim in the upscale suburb of Kenwood. Bobby Franks was in the wrong place at the wrong time on May 21: known to Leopold, he got in the pair's rented Willys-Knight and was immediately beaten when he cried out. When he did not stop, the pair forcibly suffocated him. After driving around until it got dark, they poured hydrochloric acid over the dead boy's face and body and dumped him in a culvert.

Within the first shock of discovery, Leopold and Loeb were presented as monsters: "normal persons" could not commit "such a revolting deed". The case excited enormous press and public interest for the reasons stated by the *Chicago Sunday Tribune*: "the diabolical spirit evinced in the planned kidnapping and murder; the wealth and prominence of the families involved; the high mental attainments of the youths; the suggestions of perversions; the strange quirks indicated in the confessing that the child was slain for a ransom, for experience, for the satisfaction of a desire for deep plotting."

Leopold and Loeb had committed a new kind of crime: abstract, almost intellectual, and above all random. They presented an enigma, a puzzle that became a national obsession. The relentless press coverage initiated a national debate about America's relationship to its youth. The pair became the symbols of the "misdirection" of a generation. As the juvenile delinquency expert Judge Ben Lindsey wrote in early June 1924, "It is a new kind of murder with a new kind of cause. That cause is to be found in the modern mentality and modern freedom of youth."

As embodiments of youth's shadow side, Leopold and Loeb were studied and documented to an unprecedented degree. All the attention increased their arrogance, and turned them into a nihilistic version of film stars: "immaculately dressed—the class of fashion and the grace of form," as one female columnist noted. "Dickie saunters along with all the grace and bearing of a Valentino promenading on the screen." While the sob sisters were humanizing the "sheik defendants", crowds flocked around the Leopold, Loeb, and Franks family residences in the upper-crust suburb of Kenwood.

The trial was a major media event, like a Hollywood premiere, or even, as one paper suggested, a Roman gladiatorial contest. The bread-and-circuses nature of the proceedings suited Leopold and Loeb's advocate, the legendary attorney Clarence Darrow, hired by the pair's families to save them from judicial execution. There was, after all, no doubt about their guilt—even if neither had confessed to the actual murder. Darrow decided to base his case on the mitigation of sentence, thus avoiding a jury trial.

Focusing on the issue of mental abnormality, he also avoided the strict legal definitions of insanity, which his charges, busy informing the press about the precise colour and texture of their clothes, patently did not fulfil. Mental abnormality had no clear legal definition and thus offered the chance of mitigation, of life rather than death. Darrow employed three of the country's most eminent psychologists as star witnesses. The result was an airing of psychological theories within the American court system and the mass media such as had not occurred since the trial of Jesse Pomeroy.

Much had changed in the intervening fifty years. Unlike the traditionalists hired by the prosecution, Darrow's witnesses, Drs William White, William Healy, and Bernard Glueck, were all aware of and sympathetic to Freud's theories of the unconscious. At the same time, the defence team hired two physicians, Harold S. Hulbert and Karl M. Bowman, to examine the pair, which they did for fourteen days, compiling an 80,000-word report that went into the details of family, intelligence, and their physical-emotional state. This offered a whole new playground for a content-hungry press.

The newspapers filled their pages with pop psychology, astrology, and Lombroso-like phrenological illustrations of the pair's criminal characteristics. Loeb was dominated by a "great love of sex", while Leopold had a "destructive instinct" and a "dynamic personality". William Randolph Hearst even offered Freud a specially chartered liner if he would come to the United States and write about the trial, while the rival *Tribune* offered Freud $25,000 to psychoanalyse the pair. Already ill, and unwilling to travel to a country he disliked, the founder of psychoanalysis declined.

However, the psychologists hired by the defence revealed what lay beneath the pair's suave façade. Both were at odds with their families and their peers. Raised at a distance by their parents—both had governesses—they both had IQs of over 160. Loeb had completed his first degree at seventeen, Leopold at eighteen. Rooming together at the University of Chicago, they presented an odd couple: Loeb charming and popular, Leopold intellectually arrogant, a convinced Nietzschean. Fellow students liked Loeb well enough, but most found Leopold perplexing and creepy.

The pair had met in 1920. Thrust into a peer world where almost everyone was older, exposed to the temptations of liberty, they began a three-year spree with car theft, which quickly escalated to actual arson and burglary. Loeb, in particular, sought in vain for press coverage of these crimes. After a botched burglary in Ann Arbor, they fell out but agreed to resume the friendship under certain restrictions: Loeb needed Leopold as an assistant in his criminal activities, while Leopold could call upon Loeb for "companionship". They both considered suicide before settling upon murder.

This curious contract masked a complicated, quasi-sadomasochistic emotional and sexual relationship. As Dr White testified, Loeb's interior life included fantasies of being confined: "He would see people peering at him through the bars and commenting upon the fact that he was a great criminal, looking upon him with curiosity. These people were often-times young girls." This is exactly what occurred. The pair were mobbed in court by young women, as Maureen McKernan noted: "The gruesomeness of the crime seemed to have no effect upon the feeling of the giddy little flappers, who begged to get in."

There was a frenzied atmosphere at the trial, already marked by the extreme heat and the months of constant newspaper attention: by the middle of August, the pair "had begun to emerge almost as folk heroes". As celebrities, they posed for a series of photographs, with the police, with Clarence Darrow, where their sleek modernity shone out from the knobbly, misshapen faces of the adults. They became stars: "The attitude of the boys throughout the trial amazed everyone who watched them. Every day newspapers carried pictures of them smiling in the courtroom. When the crowd laughed, they laughed."

Within this carnival atmosphere, Clarence Darrow began his concluding speech: a three-day masterclass on Nietzschean philosophy, the First World War's brutalizing effect on young minds, and the nature of adolescence itself. Darrow argued that "both these boys were in the most trying period in the life of a child". He defined this as "the age of fifteen to the age of twenty or twenty-one", when "the child has the burden of adolescence, of puberty and sex, thrust upon him. Girls are kept at home and carefully watched. Boys without instruction are left to work the period out for themselves."

Darrow concluded that "there is not an act in all this horrible tragedy that is not the act of a child". But neither Leopold nor Loeb *were* children. Their childhood might well have been slow to lift, but if two hallmarks of adolescence are expressions of sexuality and independence from parents, then they had achieved both. Darrow unintentionally highlighted the lacuna in America's treatment of its youth: the still popular elision between childhood and adulthood. In the early 1920s, age definitions were not yet standardized: boys could be men, and adolescents children.

The famous lawyer's eloquence held the day. Judge Caverly summed up by choosing life imprisonment instead of death: "The court is moved chiefly by the consideration of age of the defendants, boys of eighteen and nineteen years." He decided that it was within the court's "province to decline to impose the sentence of death on persons who are not of full age". The pair were quickly shipped to Joliet prison, where there were no female reporters to comment on their colourful fedoras. A long silence followed publicity's glare.

The Leopold/Loeb case took the bloom off twenties youth culture. Despite, or maybe because of their IQ, the pair had failed to fit in with the college culture that was America's youth ideal. Their random murder was fuelled by their wish to revenge themselves on a society from which they felt completely disassociated. This was not Jesse Pomeroy's convulsive rage but a deep, icy alienation. For Leopold and Loeb, other people were not flesh and blood but ciphers. In this way, they internalized all too thoroughly the dehumanizing industrial drive that lay behind the mass society of the 1920s.

CHAPTER 16

The Cinderella Complex

The Problems of America's Mass Culture

. . .

Boy. *"Parents don't know anything about their children and what they're doing."*
Girl. *"They don't want to know."*
Girl. *"We won't let them know."*
Boy. *"Ours is a speedy world and they're old."*

—Robert S. Lynd and Helen Merrell Lynd,
Middletown: A Study in American Culture (1929)

RUDOLPH VALENTINO AS HIS
SPIRIT CONTACT, BLACK FEATHER, MID-1920s

BY THE MID-1920s, it was becoming clear to many writers, academics, and thinkers in Europe and America that the revolution prophesied by *The Crowd* had begun. By definition, the mass did not respond to rationality, but, thanks to its contagious susceptibility, it embodied the very instincts that civilization sought to tame. Le Bon had warned that a crowd thought only "in images": it demanded "a god before everything else". Once whipped up into a state of quasi-religious fervour, the mass was primed to unleash its full destructive power.

Futurologists began to imagine how society could control these eruptions. Writing in the 1890s, Le Bon had missed one essential element of the new age. It was machines that had made the slaughter of the Great War and the mass production of consumer items possible, and the relationship of man to machine was the subject of twenties science fantasy. Man had to be a machine to fit into mass society, but he was also vulnerable to the brutalizing effects of this new, adamantine ideal, as well as its capacity for random malfunction.

Premiered in Britain during 1923, Karel Čapek's play *R.U.R.* introduced the word "robot" with its plot about factory-produced worker-beings turning against their human masters. The dystopian coercion of society through a mixture of harnessed instinct and technological mastery was fully explored by Yevgeny Zamyatin's 1924 novel *We*. With sets straight out of a Dada collage, Fritz Lang's lavish 1926 film *Metropolis* updated *The Time Machine* into a cataclysmic power struggle between Morlock-type workers and an Eloi-like elite, fomented by a monstrous metallic robot, a female Frankenstein.

The man-machine also arrived in the increasingly dehumanized working practices adopted by capitalist, Fascist, and Communist industries alike. By the mid-twenties, Henry Ford's mass production system was entrenched as the potential saviour of America itself. Edward A. Filene, the chain-store pioneer and business ideologue, called for "the application of the mass principle to American industry". He proclaimed that mass consumption, the corollary of mass production, would raise standards of living for all Americans.

However, the American fusion of commerce and deep emotional needs had its violent undertow. The Leopold/Loeb case and Al Capone's takeover of Cicero revealed that what Freud in 1923 defined as the "id"—after Nietzsche's *"das es"*—was not subject to rational controls. In stimulating fundamental desires and primal fears, American business was priming a loaded gun. Freud held that the id could be broken down to two constituents: Eros and Thanatos. The former comprised the life instinct, the latter the sadistic death instinct: "Life itself would be a conflict and compromise between these two worlds."

All the fictional dystopias of the 1920s depicted ideal societies destroyed by the deep death instinct, often invoked by youth. The consumer society was creating its own monsters, and this was where the "mass psychology" promoted by Edward Bernays came in. Prohibition offered a crude, authoritarian model of social control, but as Bernays noted, it was too moralistic to be truly effective in the twentieth century. While Prohibition merely induced a "breakdown in law", he sought to control the "mass mind" through psychological and suggestive techniques that were more in tune to the new machine age.

Like Filene, who contrasted America's "more inclusive social revolution" with "the Russian experiment", Bernays was aware that there was more than one model for the mass society. He attempted to define an alternative to the totalitarianism explored by the futurologists. In his 1928 handbook, *Propaganda,* he proposed a new super-class, an "invisible government" that would organize "the conscious and intelligent manipulation of the organized habits and opinions of the masses". He was not advocating social control by force, but through an industry of perception that would mould the ideal consumer.

If Bernays's ideal was the "public relations counsel", who stood behind the scenes orchestrating the perception of the masses, the place of youth in the construction of this particular Emerald City was central. As the first generation of "human beings" in the mass-produced machine age, they were "radicals in the market", prime targets of advertising and the early swallows of what would surely be a radiant consumer summer. Their importance, furthermore, was not just confined to college entrants and high school students.

Providing cheap and pliable labour, the scions of the working classes could enter the new youth market. With "speed and endurance" at a premium, youth was ideally suited to the accelerating demands of mass production. The Lynds noted that "a boy of nineteen may, after a few weeks of experience on a machine, turn out an amount of work greater than that of his father of forty-five". However, despite their increasingly standardized workplaces, amusements, and education, a section of America's young declined the invitation to surrender their individuality.

Relying as it did on the Wizard's sleight of hand, the new system of mass control provoked profound questions about American society. The Constitution had implicitly promised equality for all: in the new definition of this contract, social inclusion would come through the mass consumerism envisaged by the invisible rulers. According to Edward Filene, the new machine age was not "standardizing human life" but "liberating the masses from the struggle for human existence". This promise would be taken to heart, with unforeseen effects.

. . .

Not everyone could gain admittance to the Emerald City. Its attractiveness was, in part, dependent on its exclusivity. While college students and high school graduates were privileged by the commercial youth culture of the 1920s, inner-city adolescents were ignored. However, they saw no reason why they should not participate in the consumer society. Implanted with the desire but lacking the means, they sought inclusion by fair means or foul. The movies, as one convicted delinquent told the academic Alice Miller, "make you want things, and you take 'em".

Prohibition gave many of them the wherewithal. Within a society that encouraged consumerism, the fact that alcohol could not be legally consumed blew a philosophical hole right through the Nineteenth Amendment. Alcohol's illegality did not stop people from drinking; it just acquired an even greater scarcity value. A huge, billion-dollar criminal industry grew up around its supply, one that, despite its distorting effects on the country's social, political, and moral life, was tacitly condoned by the majority of American citizens.

The centre of this industry was America's urban laboratory, Chicago, "the most corrupt and lawless city in the whole world". Just how lawless was demonstrated by Al Capone's successful takeover of Cicero, which was quickly filled with "arrogant, roistering, swaggering gangsters, and crowded with saloons and gambling houses". It was like the Wild West all over again. Capone became the best-known gangster in America, and his film-star-like ostentation made him an object of emulation: the modern outlaw hero.

One contemporary observer noted that the typical 1920s criminal "was a boy who had taken on the pattern of the successful mobster, the pattern that surrounded him. He wasn't out of step. He was the regular guy. He'd seen what was rated as success in the society he had been thrust into—the Cadillac, the big bank-roll, the elegant apartment. How could he achieve that kind of recognizable status? He was almost always a boy of outstanding initiative, imagination and ability; he was the kind of boy who, under different conditions, would have been a captain of industry or a key political figure of his time."

The Volstead Act was so persistently flouted that it created its own parallel world: a mirror image of dominant American values. The young criminal of the 1920s "hadn't the opportunity of going to Yale and becoming a banker or a broker; there was no passage for him to a law degree at Harvard. There was, however, a relatively easy way of acquiring those goods that he was incessantly told were available to him as an American citizen, and without which he could not properly count himself as an American citizen. He could become a gangster."

For many of the second-generation young, the bootlegging that flourished in their poor inner-city communities represented a valid career structure. Like venture capitalists, their chosen profession was high-risk; like all producers, they were simply supplying the public with a commodity that it wished to buy. Unlike the dissident European youth groups, their rebellion did not reject the modern technological mass society but, having internalized its values, merely inverted them. For the savage violence of their business methods exposed the brutal forces underlying America's laissez-faire economics.

Might was right, and the result was disastrous. Quite apart from its boost to organized crime, Prohibition had served to make reform highly unpopular, and the forward-looking social planners of the 1890s were left high and dry in a harsh, disconnected environment. Still working at Hull House in Chicago in the mid-1920s, Jane Addams observed how her inner-city patch had deteriorated to a disorderly set of blocks that harboured drunks, disintegrating families, gangster-emulating adolescents, corrupt policemen, and gun-toting bootleggers.

The Chicagoan writer James T. Farrell charted this devastation in his *Studs Lonigan* trilogy, which he "conceived as the story of the education of a normal American boy in this period. The important institutions in the education of Studs Lonigan were the home and the family, the church, the school, and the playground. These institutions broke down and did not serve their desired function. The streets became a potent educative factor in the boy's life." Violence and dissipation had become a routine part of everyday life, a deeply ironic twist to the model of abstention and morality intended by Prohibition.

. . .

With youth becoming a lightning rod for the wider problems of 1920s America, new methods of measurement were needed. In May 1924, G. Stanley Hall wrote an essay called "Can the Masses Rule the World?" in which he reasserted his mystical vision. He felt that the one cause for hope in the mass society was an almost worldwide youth movement that "was striving toward a new religion, new light, new man, a new age, a new state, new economic relations and peace". The next month, he died at the age of eighty-one: his many obituaries paid testament to his passion for "youth, freedom, and new knowledge".

However, Hall's romantic vision of youth had become unsustainable. Thanks to his pioneering work, adolescence had become a huge commercial industry as well as a distinct class within Western societies. With the volume of new data about youth, however, it was no longer possible to come to generalized conclusions. When Hall had begun his work, he had been a lone pioneer, but in the intervening thirty years his methodology had been overtaken by new academic approaches that reflected the vastly different adolescent reality that he had helped to bring to light.

The most influential of these originated in America's futuropolis. Opening in 1921, the University of Chicago's Sociology Department developed a radical empiricism. Its first major publication, Nels Anderson's *On Hobos and Homelessness* added "participant observation" to personal involvement to academic rigour. A former hobo himself, Anderson held that hobos were the final holdouts of the original pioneer spirit: "Who hasn't felt that urge to cast off all responsibility and strike out for parts unknown? No grownup can feel it more than the average red-blooded boy."

The department's next book delved further into the city's adolescent life. Published in 1926, Frederic M. Thrasher's *The Gang* surveyed hundreds of youths aged between eleven and twenty-five. He concluded that environment was linked to behaviour, as the great majority of the city's gangs flourished in "a broad twilight zone of railroads and factories, of deteriorating neighbourhoods and shifting populations". This zone was the symptom of a wider problem: "American industrial cities have not had time to become settled and self-controlled; they are youthful and they are experiencing the struggles and instability of youth."

These empty spaces were exploited by urban adolescents: "Boys in gangland enjoy an unusual freedom from restrictions of the type imposed by the normal controlling agencies in the better residential areas of the city." They lived out another version of the pioneer myth: "In some respects, these regions of conflict are like a frontier; in others, like a 'no man's land,' lawless, godless, wild." Thrasher cited romanticism as an important factor in gang life: "Adolescent fancies cast over the world—too often trite and ugly to the adult— the rosy light of novelty and romance."

The basic nature of the gang had changed little since Riis's day. Most congregated along ethnic and neighbourhood lines. However, they had grown in size, number, organization, sophistication, and aggression. This was enacted in violence and sexual predation, in killings and orgies held by gangs like the Knight Riders. One cause of this was the new media. One interviewee told Thrasher how "he used to spend hours at the movies in order to see how the holdups were 'pulled off', and judging from the type of thriller and 'sexy' romance which forms the bulk of the entertainment, there are other attractions too".

What had caused the gangs to become so vicious? Thrasher identified several factors. The mass media's stimulation of fundamental impulses served to detach morality from all known bounds. As he observed, "Demoralizing social patterns confront the gang boy at every hand; they are in the streets and alleys; they come from the older gangs and clubs and from the underworld." This had extra force because there were "conflicting standards with reference to sex, prohibition, gambling and so on. This makes more difficult a conclusive definition of the situation for the boy."

However, the real reason was on the doorstep: "Illicit liquor, gambling and vice have provided the greatest opportunities for the syndicate type of gang in Chicago." The potential profits, the idolization of gangsters, and, indeed, the operation of serious crime "on a basis of business efficiency" made the transition of local gangs into citywide criminal organization ever more likely. Thrasher ended his survey with a series of concrete recommendations that included more active social work and monitoring of the family structure. He retained the reformer's confidence that American society could be improved.

The reforming impulse had not died with Prohibition, just changed its nature. Instead of aggressive moralizing, it revived the concentration on social issues that had marked pioneer progressives like Jane Addams. Believing that environment influenced behaviour, the new generation of reformers advocated a more synoptic approach. In their influential book on the treatment of *Delinquents and Criminals*, the criminologists William Healy and Augusta F. Bronner, like Thrasher, recommended that each young offender should undergo a thorough psychological and environmental study.

This renewed concentration on nurture led directly to a wider critique of American society. *The Gang* appeared coincidentally with another great reformist work, Jack Black's *You Can't Win*, a sensational account of a criminal rehabilitated by sympathetic handling. Black had begun his career while an adolescent in the 1890s, and the book's appeal lay in its exposé of a previously hidden world of "yeggs", "hypos", and "snides". After the book's successful publication, Black toured the United States giving lectures on penal reform, or as he put it, "propaganda against too much law and punishment".

With its historical map of the youth criminal underclass, *You Can't Win* also helped to illuminate the increasingly disturbing problems of the present. During 1926, there were seventy-six gang murders in Chicago alone, as the "slum dictators" fought for supremacy. Even more damaging was the composition of bootleg booze itself: in 1926, 750 people died from its effects in New York. A 1927 analysis showed that 98 per cent of the liquor tested contained compounds like methanol, which causes blindness and paralysis. Many of its consumers died young from what James T. Farrell called "rat poison".

Enquiring minds began to wonder whether the youth problems of gang-sterism, homelessness, and delinquency were not symptoms of the mechani-cal-mystic nature of American life itself. As Robert Herrick wrote in his introduction to *You Can't Win,* "Does modern life offer youth sufficient men-tal stimulus? The motor car, the movie, bootleg liquor, and sex—these are the raw stimuli with which youth tries to infuse some color and movement into the tyrannous drabness of a standardized industrial life." Jack Black himself was in no doubt: "Society was a machine geared to grind me to pieces."

• • •

During the 1920s, adolescents became "the customers of tomorrow": the guinea pigs for the consumer society. However, this social experiment was de-monstrably not all going to plan. According to the anthropologist Margaret Mead, juvenile delinquency was only a symptom of a wider American malaise. "If adolescents are only plunged into difficulties and distress because of condi-tions in their social environment," she wrote, "then by all means let us so modify that environment as to reduce this stress and eliminate this strain and anguish of adjustment."

Mead's first book, *Coming of Age in Samoa,* was a sensation when first published in 1928, but the public furore caused by her descriptions of the Samoans' guilt-free sex life distracted attention from her withering critique of "Western Civilization". Following her mentor Franz Boas, Mead critiqued "the great mass of theorizing about adolescence". Dismissing outright Stanley Hall's characterization of this age as being the "period during which difficul-ties and conflicts were absolutely inevitable", she wondered, "Were these diffi-culties due to being adolescent or to being adolescent in America?"

Her answer was "to go to a different civilization and make a study of hu-man beings under different cultural conditions in some other part of the world". Travelling to Samoa to research the island's female adolescents, Mead discovered a society in which children had "complete knowledge of the body and its functions". Adolescent sexual activity was not repressed, but encour-aged. Furthermore, a more communal attitude to parenting seemed "to en-sure the child against the crippling attitudes which have been named Oedipus Complexes, Electra Complexes, and so on".

Mead's conclusions climaxed in a coruscating polemic: as she later wrote, her book was just as much about "the United States of 1926–1928" as it was about Samoa. Acknowledging that "physiological puberty is bound to be filled with conflicts", she nevertheless felt that the American way of life was to blame for the neuroses of its adolescents. "A society which is clamoring for choice," she wrote, "which is filled with so many articulate groups, each urging its own brand of salvation, its own variety of economic philosophy, will give each new generation no peace until all have gone under, unable to bear the conditions of choice."

Mead thought that the ultimate source of all youthful distress was the "essentially pecuniary nature" of American society, with its "efflorescence of a doctrine of short-cuts to fame". The media made the situation worse: "Moving picture, magazine, newspaper, all reiterate the Cinderella story in one way or another." Films like *It* propagated the idea that anyone, even a "cash girl", could become "head buyer" of the store and marry the boss. Exploiting what Mead called "our American theory of endless possibilities", the Cinderella complex created by these mass-produced visions created a welter of conflicting desires.

■ ■ ■

While Mead was finalizing her research on *Coming of Age in Samoa*, the mob took over Manhattan. The trigger was the death of Rudolph Valentino, just after noon on Monday, August 23, 1926. His sudden illness had been a media event for the previous week, with fans keeping up a hospital vigil. Thousands began to gather at Valentino's place of rest, Frank E. Campbell's Funeral Church on Broadway and 65th Street, where the coffin of their heavily embalmed hero was shrouded by burning incense. By the evening, the area was jammed with people and the police were having difficulty keeping order.

The previous November, female fans had mobbed Valentino and ripped his clothes, but the scenes that followed his death eclipsed anything previously witnessed. By noon on August 24, the crowd was already up to ten thousand and rising. The predominantly female early birds were joined by a boisterous mob of young sheiks "sporting bolero jackets and gaucho hats" as well as "the balloon trousers, spats and the slick hair and long sideburns made popular" by the dead actor. By early afternoon, the crowd—by now 20,000 strong and "psychologically blind"—stormed the doors of the funeral parlour.

Chaos ensued. The police insisted that the building be opened. As the public started to file through, many young women kissed the coffin. However, the relatively slow rate of access did not satiate the crowd, which by mid-evening had increased to 80,000: more disturbances occurred when the parlour was finally closed at midnight. These were repeated the next day when the police tried to shut the Funeral Church after 90,000 had passed through: the several thousand mourners waiting outside struggled to gain entrance, and the resulting pitched battle continued until the small hours.

With the press still pumping out sensational stories, the situation remained highly charged. Valentino's memorial service on Sunday, August 30, was chaotic. By the time the actor's body was finally removed from the funeral parlour, public unrest had subsided, but the frenzy pursued the coffin as it travelled across America. Despite heavy rain, at least fifty thousand people packed Chicago's La Salle Station during a brief stopover, while in Los Angeles thousands more waited outside the Hollywood Cemetery to participate in the burial.

This was not an entirely spontaneous outburst. Rudy's sudden death had created a big problem for his studio. With two Valentino vehicles on the market, *The Eagle* and *The Son of the Sheik*, United Artists was set to lose many millions of dollars unless the star's name could be kept alive. It later transpired that the whole mob drama in New York had been stimulated by Frank Campbell and United Artists publicity man Harry C. Klemfuss, who stayed around the clock at the funeral parlour to make sure that everything was going to plan.

Their campaign succeeded beyond their wildest dreams. Within a few days, both films were doing unprecedented business. Throughout the world, any Valentino film still in the hands of distributors was snapped up and shown to packed houses. The extraordinary volume of letters sent by the public to his studio would not decrease for a decade. The film industry found out for the first time what the newspapers already knew: death sells. Preserved in his prime on celluloid, Rudolph Valentino would never grow old.

This was romanticism updated for the consumer age: the belief, already applied to the young casualties of the Great War, that the gods favoured those who died young. Although he had turned thirty in 1926, Valentino was still associated with virility, potency, and the smouldering sexuality aped by the young sheiks and shebas. His death fixed this forever, like a fly in amber. For the studio bosses, it was ideal. No longer would their star prevent the even flow of business with his moodiness and demands for creative control. Alive, Valentino was a problem; dead, he was the perfect industrial product.

Attracting screaming headlines, the August 1926 riots were a graphic demonstration to the American authorities of the massed power of youth. The fact that the Manhattan mob were rioting over a dead body made their behaviour, if anything, even more irrational to adults, but in fact it was one logical consequence of a dream economy that used psychological triggers to shape and control the mass. Having been encouraged to think of the star as a god, the young Valentino fans were enacting Le Bon's direst prophecies about the destructive power of the crowd—as Eros intertwined with Thanatos.

These mob scenes also revealed that consumerism was an unstable social glue. Mass entertainments like movies, with their particular appeal to youth, might have offered ideals of inclusion and participation, but they also evoked hopes that, because they were so all-consuming, were bound to be dashed. Many reformers and sociologists in the 1920s commented on the movies' intense psychological impact on American youth. Edward Bernays called the "American motion picture the greatest unconscious carrier of propaganda in the world today".

However, the Cinderella complex worked both ways. If the audience could never hope to attain the Hollywood life, many of the Mob-Gods found that the reality of this Olympian ideal did not match up to expectation. Valentino, for instance, had assumed that stardom would wash away the years of poverty and hardship. When he got to the top, however, he found a barren plateau. Although to his rabid fans he was a superhuman deity, to the studio he was a chattel; despite the crowds of frenzied women, both his marriages had disintegrated. He was both deity and human, master and slave, adored and despised.

These contradictions had boiled over in July 1926, when the *Chicago Tribune* delivered a vicious personal attack, headlined "Pink Powder Puffs". It began with a horrified description of finding "a powder vending machine! In a men's washroom!": "We personally saw two 'men' . . . step up, insert coin, hold kerchief beneath the spout, pull the lever, then take the pretty pink stuff and pat it on their cheeks in front of a mirror." As "the prototype of the American male", Valentino was held responsible for "this degeneration into effeminacy". This insult continued to haunt the actor on his deathbed.

The same thing happened to the period's leading female star. In 1927, Clara Bow starred in the definitive flapper film, so archetypal that Mead cited the plotline in her critique of the Cinderella complex: Paramount's adaptation of Elinor Glyn's bestselling novel *It*. If the film's opening titles were to be believed, the "magnetic force" denoted by *It* was defined by the elemental sexuality that Clara Bow embodied. She was, according to Scott Fitzgerald, "the real thing". The public certainly thought so: the film made her one of Hollywood's top draws and "the blazing exemplar of the insouciance of Flaming Youth".

The very impulses that propelled Clara Bow to stardom made her particularly vulnerable once she had attained that dream state. Like Valentino, the It Girl was in flight from a dreadful childhood: "I never had any clothes," she later recalled. "And lots of time didn't have anything to eat. We just lived and that's about all. Girls shunned me because I was so poorly dressed." After winning a talent contest at the age of sixteen, she went out to Hollywood and found success in pictures like *The Plastic Age*. Bow was only twenty-two when *It* made her a star: her problems were not solved, but exacerbated.

As the embodiment of the new sexual directness, Bow was the repository of her audience's hopes and prejudices. The academic Alice Miller quoted a variety of young responses to her most famous film. A "boy scout of fourteen years writes of a motion picture called *It*: 'I believe *It* with Clara Bow is entirely a menace to the community. Pictures of such sort should not be allowed in the community.' An older boy, one of seventeen years, writing of the same film, says: 'I liked *It*. It was a wonderful interpretation of alluring young women.'"

By spring 1928, Bow was hot: her fan mail increased to over 35,000 letters a month. Interviewing her in the first full flush of fame, the journalist and screenwriter Adela Rogers St Johns noted that "there seems to be no pattern, no purpose to her life. She swings from one emotion to another, but she gains nothing, stores up nothing for the future. She lives entirely in the present, not even for today, but just for the moment." Talking to another magazine, she told the truth: "I haven't been happy for many months. The person you see on the screen is not my true self at all; it's my screen self."

Bow sought solace in extravagant spending and sex: indeed, she lived out the siren role a little too enthusiastically for "the moral Kansas" of Hollywood. There was no little hypocrisy here: in the case of male stars, promiscuity was thought merely an addition to their allure. Not so for women, for whom more discretion was required. Her blunt directness was felt to be a severe breach of etiquette. Lacking studio support, Bow became unstuck. Unable to adapt to the new demands of sound, her reputation and psyche were in tatters after a scandalous 1931 court case. At the age of twenty-five, her career was over.

These two high-profile melodramas enacted the paradoxes of the Cinderella complex. Not all stars succumbed: Colleen Moore, the lead in *Flaming Youth*, lived to a ripe and happy old age. But the higher the zenith, the greater the fall. Era-defining icons like Bow and Valentino might well have escaped blasted backgrounds for a glittering realm, but at considerable personal cost. The sexuality that they so successfully invoked aroused emotions that included hostility as well as adoration. Like any other industrial product, they were subject to the law of planned obsolescence.

Yet their luminous presence helped to introduce new archetypes: in their particular case, a blurring of gender roles that evoked the androgyny associated throughout many societies with young deities and talismanic performers. They moved the mainstream in their image, and in doing so, gave hope. Charged with representing an audience of millions, the movies offered a model of social advancement. Here was an arena where the outcast could, in however fantastic a scenario, see him- or herself on screen, where individual stardom could appear to represent the upward move of a formerly marginalized group.

. . .

One unintended consequence of mass culture was that the mass felt that they should be involved in society to a greater degree. Having been granted an unprecedented degree of attention during the 1920s, American adolescents were particularly prone to this assumption. Whether it was the flappers, the gangsters taking over whole sections of American cities, or the college students awakening to their cohort's potential, the country's young began to conflate participation through consumerism into very different ideas of emancipation.

In 1923, an activist magazine called *New Student* had complained about the apolitical nature of America's college cohort: "We are almost the only section of the population which has the leisure and opportunity to study the controversial questions of the day and act accordingly. The power of today is in our hands. But do we study the industrial, economic and international questions and explain them simply to the man on the street, which would seem to be the natural function of the student? We do not. And largely because we are too immature to see this as our role. We have the power but we do not use it."

After the mid-decade, America's students began to do exactly that. Their principal target was Prohibition, as the editors of college magazines began to agitate for a change in the law. A 1926 poll held at the Ivy League University of Princeton showed that 87 per cent of its students were pro-repeal. The *Daily Princetonian* held that Prohibition had "seriously threatened the best traditions of the colleges. Whereas undergraduates once confined their drinking to the Nassau Inn, liquor is now taken and kept in the room or sought in roadhouses. There is but little respect for the law."

Reacting against this adult hypocrisy, America's students began to widen their political ambit. During 1925, the National Student Federation was formed at Princeton at a meeting of 245 colleges gathered together to discuss the World Court that had been instituted by the League of Nations. As part of this pacifist agenda, protests against the compulsory nature of the ROTC—the Reserve Officers' Training Corps—became more strident. While the great bulk of students remained convinced that military training was desirable, many thought that joining the corps should be voluntary.

However, their political sensibilities did not extend beyond their own needs to changing the wider society. College students, for example, tended to parrot normative attitudes to race. This occurred despite their strong taste for hot jazz and frequent visits to the predominantly Negro clubs that were called "Black and Tans". With the increasing proliferation of white jazz groups—formed in sincere, if not fanatical, emulation of their Negro idols—there was little need for the average college student to concern himself overly with one of America's thorniest issues: segregation.

By the later 1920s, jazz had become big business. Its focus had shifted from small combos to huge organizations like Paul Whiteman's thirty-piece orchestra, which was touring the country and attracting the fan hysteria already bestowed upon film stars like Valentino. During a June 1929 performance at a Nebraska train station, the orchestra was mobbed by a 5,000-strong crowd before the musicians had even alighted. Even the brand name had been appropriated for the ground-breaking 1927 sound film *The Jazz Singer*, featuring the definitely not hot Al Jolson.

It did not go unnoticed that jazz had become the lingua franca of American youth. The popularity of the music provided a common ground among the races. Having seen the popularity of Negro music and dancing among young whites and its increasing spread across the mass media, a group of young Negro artists and intellectuals decided to go for some reciprocal emancipation. With jazz becoming an international symbol of modernity and what the writer Alain Locke called "the new democracy in American culture", they felt that it was time finally to step out of the slave era.

The American ideal of transformation appeared to offer genuine inclusion for all the excluded. Locke's ground-breaking 1925 anthology *The New Negro* aimed to provide a framework for a new "Negro Renaissance". The collection showcased a "new generation" of young writers like Claude McKay, Langston Hughes, and Countee Cullen, who employed ultramodernism, traditional patois, and a fresh assertion in their magical conversion of outcast status into social pride. If the idea was to promote "a new aesthetic and philosophy of life", then its central location was Harlem.

This neighbourhood, two-thirds of the way up Manhattan Island, comprised a district of twenty-five blocks and 175,000 inhabitants. With Negro-owned businesses, places of entertainment, and a diverse political and social life, Harlem offered a self-enclosed world to the extent that, as James Weldon Johnson observed, it embodied "a large scale laboratory experiment in the race problem". It was here that, as Locke stated, Negro life was "seizing upon its first chances for group self-expression and self-determination". Youth was central to this ideal of a "race capital".

In May 1926, Langston Hughes declared in *The Nation*, "We younger Negro artists who create now intend to express our individual dark-skinned selves without fear or shame. If white people are pleased we are glad. If they are not, it doesn't matter." The only edition of *Fire*, "A Quarterly Devoted to the Younger Negro Artists", published that November, showcased writers who were, like Hughes, in their early to mid-twenties. The contributions included "Smoke, Lilies and Jade", a prose ode to homosexuality by Richard Bruce Nugent, and Lewis Alexander's exultant poem "Little Cinderella".

Harlem not only provided a beacon for Negroes from all over America, it also acted as a magnet for whites. Entertainment was the draw: the Cotton Club had opened up in 1923 and was followed three years later by the more community-oriented Savoy Ballroom. Thanks to the fashion for jazz and jazz dancing, Harlem and negritude were becoming fashionable not just among the college cohort, but also high Manhattan society. Almost as soon as the Harlem Renaissance was heralded by young Negro writers, it was broadcast to a wider readership by a middle-aged white critic and trendsetter.

Published in late 1926, Carl Van Vechten's *Nigger Heaven* was a classic popularizing document, offering a tourist map to a previously hidden world while containing enough authenticity to appeal to insiders. Despite Van Vechten's sincere interest in Negro culture, the novel was highly controversial on publication. Quite apart from the taboo word contained in the title, the fact that a white man had profited from a movement that was supposed to celebrate Negro parity was hard to bear. Even though "the Negro and all things Negroid had become a fad", the traffic of social inclusion, it seemed, was still one-way.

However, one result of this succès de scandale was the publication, in the late twenties, of several novels by young Negro writers that revealed the complexity of their life from within, a world that parodied the values of white America as if through a looking-glass. Wallace Thurman's novel *The Blacker the Berry* described life at an all-Negro college, where his "all-too-black" heroine Emma Lou Brown is ostracized by her lighter-skinned peers. Like Claude McKay's *Home to Harlem*, it also revealed the level of self-hatred and doubt that often resulted in dissipation and self-destruction.

Despite the illusion of racial harmony, the reality of the Harlem Renaissance was barely ameliorated segregation. Langston Hughes acidly commented that the famous Cotton Club "was a Jim Crow club for gangsters and monied whites": while "the strangers were given the best ringside tables to sit and stare at the Negro customers—like amusing animals, in a zoo"—it didn't work the other way. "The Negroes said: 'We can't go downtown and stare at you in your clubs. You won't even let us in your clubs.'"

The Harlem Renaissance showed the limits of the Cinderella complex. The pluralistic images of the mass media offered the hope of inclusion, but the subjects of that attention had little control over how they were portrayed. In return for this skewed access to the power structure, they were also subject to distortion and exploitation. Many insider accounts of the Harlem Renaissance were flecked with the bitterness of those who witnessed a prolonged process of emancipation turned into a novelty—just another craze to be exploited, and then discarded when the tide turned.

. . .

For those who had cared to study the terms, this had always been part of the deal. During the 1920s, the images of youth promoted by the American media were the medicine-show barker for the consumer society. They made it seem new, attractive, and sexy, but as far as real power was concerned, they were a placebo: they had little or no direct impact on America's social and legal structures. However, the freedom that they contained as a necessary part of their appeal helped to initiate new perceptions and new ideas that would bear fruit in the decades to come.

The increased independence of 1920s youth was not a total illusion. Within a country that prescribed radical agitation, it was expressed in attitudinal rather than political terms. While the college generation and the young gangsters defied Prohibition, their younger counterparts began to assert their independence from their parents. Robert S. Lynd and Helen Merrell Lynd offered an illustration of how this rebelliousness had trickled down to the adolescents of a midwestern American city where, according to a bewildered parent, "children of twelve or fourteen nowadays act just like grown-ups".

Published in 1929, *Middletown* provided a portrait of a midwestern American city where the balance of power had tipped firmly towards the young: "After the age of twelve or thirteen the place of the home tends to recede before a combination of other formative influences, until in the late teens the child is regarded as a kind of junior adult, increasingly independent of parental authority." They quoted a "popular high school girl" who, discouraged from going out with "a young blade in a rakish car", exploded at her father: "What on earth do you want me to do? Just sit around at home all evening!"

During the 1920s, youth began to see itself not just as a market, but as a distinct class. Like the country's other disenfranchised tribes, American youth felt that the attention they had received entitled them to make more demands upon their society. This cohort politics would be expressed in terms of the country's promise of universal equality. However, the fact that they were confusing their status as vanguard consumers with real political power was based on a prosperity that was as febrile as it was fragile.

CHAPTER 17

The Pursuit of Pleasure

The Bright Young People

. . .

BUNTY: *You're getting older.*
NICKY: *God, yes; isn't it foul?*
BUNTY: *Hell, my dear.*
NICKY: *It's funny how mother's generation always longed to be old when they were young, and we strain every nerve to keep young.*

—Noël Coward, *The Vortex* (1924)

BRENDA DEAN PAUL
IN THE ROARING
TWENTIES

AT THE HEIGHT of the 1920s, Brenda Dean Paul went to a Mayfair party held for the cast of *The Blackbirds*, the Negro revue then taking London by storm. Offering the British their first authentic slice of Harlem with its wild dancing and hot jazz, *The Blackbirds* penetrated to the highest levels of society. During its year-long run, its star Florence Mills and the other "blackbirds" were the guests of honour at many parties given by London's gilded youth, who were entranced from the start "with the singing and the dancing of these coloured people".

For the nineteen-year-old Londoner, this radiant evening was a revelation. While a small, select crowd danced to two "superb pianists", she struck up a friendship with Florence Mills, whom she remembered as the "embodiment of natural charm and poise". Having been told by Mills that she could have been "born in Harlem", Dean Paul aspired to become a "coloured dancer": "I felt so utterly at home with these enchanting people that every other white person in the room seemed positively genteel and almost indecently refined."

The *Blackbirds* party was just the start of it, as Dean Paul went to many other events: "fancy dress balls on a grand scale" and "freak parties". Some of the latter had obsessively pursued themes, like David Tennant's "Come as you were twenty years ago" event, which resulted in a crazy children's party: "Even the band were dressed up in Eton suits, Eton collars and school caps." Further freak parties followed: "Pyjama parties, Greek parties, Russian parties, sailor parties, American parties, murder parties, bathing parties and so on."

Recalling those nights of extravagant costumes, cocktails and loud jazz, Dean Paul picked out the most extreme of all: the American party to which guests were "bidden to come as 'hobos', 'gold diggers', 'bums', 'butter and egg men', 'sweet men', 'gangsters', 'yes men', 'sob sisters' etc. etc". Lubricated by "buffets groaning with champagne," the crowd totally let themselves go: "The band had been specially imported from Harlem, and the rhythms were intoxicating without the additional stimulus of alcohol."

This was a life tailor-made for a young woman who had slipped through the cracks of class. The daughter of a baronet, Dean Paul had suffered the indignity of her parents' divorce in her early teens. At seventeen, she was told her mother could not afford to bring her out as a debutante. Dean Paul decided to stay in her mother's studio, and through the contacts that she made there she passed into a new kind of society, that mixture of the bohemian, the upper class, and the clubland lowlife that comprised the Bright Young People, Britain's most visible youth culture of the 1920s.

For these creatures of the media, appearance, charm, and grace were all, and Dean Paul had them in spades. With her natural beauty and a certain headlong recklessness, she became a fixture in the newspapers, one of those individuals whose presence appeared to define the spirit of an era. "For years I never went to bed before four or five in the morning," she later remembered, and the mode was frenetic pleasure with no thought of tomorrow. In the whirl of a freak party, time accelerated and stopped, frozen like one of the many photographs taken of the celebrants in their fantastic clothes.

· · ·

The Bright Young People were only one example of the pleasure-bent youth culture that spread throughout Europe during the 1920s. Concentrating on diversion and on the moment, partying was a way of life directly opposed to the Christian morality of the nineteenth century. It was also an ideal method of signalling the post-war generation's flagrant and public rejection of their forebears' values. Idealism had become a dirty word. All the great themes had been vaporized by the Great War, and in their place came a heedless, headlong hedonism.

Just as Americans still routinely conflated "childhood" with "adolescence", the precise definition of youth in Britain and Europe remained elastic. The 1920s party generation included actual adolescents along with people in their mid- to late twenties. Many of the latter, like Nancy Cunard and Harry Crosby, were rich enough not to have to work. But they had also been damaged by the war to the extent that they had been frozen in 1917 or 1918, at the time when they were still adolescents. Partying was the perfect way to rediscover the youth that the war had stolen. Youth was not an age, but a state of mind.

Partying also suited the new styles percolating across the Atlantic. To young Europeans, dancing the Charleston was novel and exciting; it also embodied the modernity that they assiduously sought. Defined as a social and a commercial animal, the young of the 1920s decided to celebrate freedom on their own terms. In *Adolescence,* Stanley Hall had observed how "savages are nearly all great dancers, imitating every animal they know, dancing out their own legends, with ritual so exact that error means death". Despite its superficial appearance, partying was nothing less than a generational rite.

The combatant countries had demanded an unprecedented level of commitment and sacrifice, and after 1919 the people began to insist on payback. Formerly rigid class structures began to dissolve as the old deference died. The early 1920s saw the beginning of the mass society in Europe. With the spectre of a destabilized and politically polarized Germany, the need to offer a viable social system to Soviet Russia and Fascist Italy became paramount, and America offered the perfect antidote.

American finance had bankrolled the war: now its media and youth culture would set the tone of the peace. This process was boosted by the new eastward migration, as hundreds of American writers, musicians, and bohemians crossed the Atlantic. This was particularly visible in Paris, where the advantageous exchange rate—one dollar bought nearly twenty-seven francs, or one month's supply of bread—meant that it was possible to live cheaply in a culture sympathetic to aesthetic and sexual experiment. With drinking outlawed at home, young American expatriates revelled in guilt-free pleasure.

They went to venues like Boeuf sur le Toit, where Jean Cocteau held court. By the early twenties, there was a strong Cocteau cult, as young men came from all over France to meet the avatar of adolescence. His most famous protégé to date was Raymond Radiguet, who, having shocked Paris with his provocative first novel, *The Devil in the Flesh,* died from typhoid and toxicity at the age of twenty. This was a *génération fichue,* as the American editor Robert McAlmon found out when he met the fashion model Sari at Le Boeuf: "It's no fun to be sixteen," she gravely informed him, "and know too much about life."

For those in the swing, Paris was a city of parties, with private events and annual features in the social calendar like *le Bal Nègre.* The wildest party of all was the annual Four Arts Ball, staged every June by the city's art students. One participant in the 1927 ball remembered bursting into Claridge's Hotel with a crowd of young students: "Half-naked we went screaming through the corridors, into the dining room, pulling the noses of the guests, snatching up their drinks, interrupting the dancing, even rushing upstairs to the bedrooms to open whatever doors were not locked."

Held every year between 1923 and 1929, these bacchanals were irresistible. The poet and Paris resident Harry Crosby, in flight from a repressive Bostonian background, delighted in the chaos. For the 1927 ball, his costume comprised seven dead pigeons and ten live snakes in a sack. "At one o clock it was WILD," he later wrote; "men and women stark naked dancing people rushing to and fro . . . from our loge I opened the sack and down dropped the ten serpents. Screams and shouts. Yet later in the evening I sat next to a plump girl who was suckling one of the serpents. Dear me!"

After the disastrous devaluation of the mark during 1923, Berlin was even cheaper for Americans, as well as being a magnet for other migrants. Sebastian Haffner recalled that Germany's capital became an "international city". He and his friends "were not only friendly towards foreigners, but enthusiastic about them. How much more interesting, more beautiful and richer it made life that the world was not peopled exclusively by Germans! Our guests were all welcome, whether they came voluntarily, like the Americans and the Chinese, or as refugees, like the Russians. Our doors were flung open."

Berlin was well-known for its cosmopolitanism, but during the early 1920s the city became an open house for pleasure-seekers of all kinds. This was accelerated by the events of 1923, when, as Haffner observed, the vertiginous deflation of the mark helped to create a temporary youth takeover: "The young and quick-witted did well. Overnight they became free, rich and independent. It was a situation where mental inertia and reliance on past experience was punished by starvation and death, but rapid appraisal of new situations and speed of reaction was rewarded with sudden, vast riches."

Haffner remembered how "the twenty-one-year-old bank director appeared on the scene, and also the sixth-former who earned his living from the stock-market tips of his slightly older friends. He wore Oscar Wilde ties, organized champagne parties, and supported his embarrassed father. Amid all the misery, despair and poverty, there was an air of light-headed youthfulness, licentiousness and a carnival atmosphere. Now, for once, the young had money and the old did not. Moreover, its nature had changed. Its value only lasted a few hours. It was spent as never before or since."

While this "Hollywood movie" lessened after the mark stabilized, Berlin's status as Germany's entertainment capital was established. As well as the themed restaurants and the jazz dance clubs, there were huge pleasure palaces like the Haus Vaterland, which occupied an entire city block and could accommodate six thousand customers per hour. In its Rhineland Wine Terrace, a calm, sunny panorama of the Rhine was replaced, every hour, by a violent storm that lasted five minutes. This was Yoshiwara, the narcotic auditorium of Fritz Lang's *Metropolis* come to life.

Berlin was an international draw for another reason: it was the sex capital of the world. During the 1920s, it offered intimate cabarets, erotic revues, and pick-up joints like the famous Resi. Then there were the lesbian social clubs, the transvestite balls, and the myriad brothels. The open nature of Berlin's nightlife and adolescent male prostitution, the Doll Boys and the Line Boys hanging around hotels and arcades, made it a magnet for British and American homosexuals. From 1923 on, young Germans flocked to the capital to jump on what one former Line Boy called this "mad carousel ride".

This brazenness was a symptom not of collapse but of stability. After 1924, Weimar was run by its foreign minister, Gustav Stresemann, who ushered in what Haffner called "the only genuine period of peace that my generation in Germany has experienced". The regime mixed socialism with consumerism: "There was an ample measure of freedom, peace, and order, everywhere the most well-meaning liberal-mindedness, good wages, good food, and a little political boredom. Everyone was cordially invited to concentrate on their personal lives, to arrange their affairs according to their own taste."

Haffner turned twenty-one in 1928, and remembered that period as suffused with "something very fine and auspicious" that was "silently ripening among the best of German youth". This new liberalism was characterized by the breaking down of the barriers between the classes: "There were many students who were labourers, and many labourers who were students. Class prejudice and the starched-collar mentality were simply out of fashion. The relations between the sexes were freer and franker than ever."

However, he thought that many Germans were ill-equipped to deal with the freedoms of Weimar. "Accustomed to all the varied sensations of disorder", the country began to follow the lead of its youth, damaged by the war and revolution they had experienced at a formative age. Brought up within an authoritarian system, Germans had never learned how to live with independence and stability: "They regarded the end of the political tension and the return of private liberty not as a gift, but a deprivation. They were bored, their minds strayed to silly thoughts, and they began to sulk."

. . .

Britain was also transformed by the spread of American consumerism. Although victorious, the United Kingdom was in hock to its onetime ally. The real power play between the two nations was laid bare by the question of war loan reparation: the United States was owed £900 million and, in the early 1920s, insisted on a usurious scheme of repayment. Economic control was twinned with cultural imperialism. This fuelled the establishment's hostility to America, which was held responsible by some commentators for making Britain worse than Rome in the days of her decadence.

The age of materialism had arrived. In the early twenties, Britain's traditional heavy manufacturing industries were supplanted by the manufacture of leisure items like cars, wireless sets, gramophones, cosmetics, and artificial fabrics. Large sections of the public were employed in white-collar service occupations like bookkeeping and accounting, selling and advertising—the last of which being an industry that successfully popularized psychology to the tune of a £100 million turnover during 1921. The next year, the British Broadcasting Corporation began to offer a national radio service.

American films dominated the cinema, with icons like Charlie Chaplin and Mary Pickford, while jazz and its assorted dances—the camel walk, the shimmy, and the blues—supplanted ragtime. Although not explicitly aimed at an adolescent market, American movies and music were enthusiastically adopted by Britain's youth, right across the classes. Wanting novelty and fun—and anything that was *not* the war—they unwittingly acted as the spearhead of American-style mass consumption, its laxer moral code and easier social climate having a corrosive impact on Britain's hierarchies.

Young women were at the forefront of the new modernism. This American pattern was heightened by a brutal demographic fact: with one in every seven eligible men killed in the war, there were up to a million surplus women. Marriage was no longer automatic. Suffragette visions had become reality with the granting of partial enfranchisement in 1918. Women had won greater independence by their contribution to the war effort: this was ratified by more relaxed employment and divorce laws, as well as the increased awareness, thanks to Marie Stopes's campaigns, of birth control methods.

A vast, cross-class influx of young, unattached women flooded into the major cities. Those in their late teens or early twenties could find jobs as journalists, shop assistants, waitresses, or secretaries. The working-class girls who had traditionally entered domestic service at the age of fourteen began decisively to reject what they regarded as a system of near slavery in favour of "any kind of job in mill or factory, or even a place with rock-bottom wages like Woolworth's, and freedom—above all, freedom to meet men easily".

This "young emancipation" found its most flagrant expression in the new flappers: "creamed, perfumed and powdered like the 'immoral' actress of 1910, the post-war daughter of the common labourer certainly gloried in the new permissiveness." Fashions like the short haircut and the short skirt might have shocked adults, but it was in the "explosive" post-war dancing boom that the depth of the new youth culture could be fully experienced, as the craze spread from London venues like the Hammersmith Palais around the country.

In Salford, Robert Roberts recalled that "the young from sixteen to twenty-five flocked into the dance halls by the hundred thousand"; "some went 'jigging' as often as six times a week. The great 'barn' we patronised as apprentices held at least a thousand. Almost every evening except Friday (cleaning night at home) it was jammed with a mass of young men and women, class desegregated for the first time. At 6d per head (1s on Saturday) youth at every level of the manual working-class, from the bound apprentice to the 'scum of the slum', fox-trotted through the bliss in each other's arms."

Most ballrooms adhered to the strict steps pioneered during the 1910s by Irene and Vernon Castle: however, they still allowed for an unprecedented level of personal contact. The new dance halls were constructed as discrete

PORTRAIT OF "B.I (AGED 15 $^7/_{12}$)"

youth worlds, pleasure domes with flashing lights and exotic decoration. Roberts remembered that "about the interior of our paradise there hung a faint Moorish air, given off perhaps by the wallpaper, with its minarets, and a narrow gazebo perched high in the angle of an upper wall. From this an excellent band dispensed rhythm almost without cease."

At the same time, younger wage earners found new outlets for their spare cash. Although there had been attempts in the early 1920s to limit what was then called "child employment", inner-city adolescents still had a plethora of temporary jobs or apprenticeships to choose from. The older these "industrial nomads" were, the less they were likely to give most of their earnings to their parents, so from about the age of sixteen they were able to spend their money on new magazines like *Boy's Cinema* (launched in 1919) or *Girl's Cinema* (1920).

While cinemas screened films like *Echo of Youth* and *Blindness of Youth*, these magazines offered a wide range of material of interest to their young readership. In one sample issue from December 1920, *Boy's Cinema* carried ads for a hair-curling potion, a model train set, a gramophone, boxing gloves, and its sister publication, *Girl's Cinema*. The magazine also included general-interest features, including advice to young men (between ages seventeen and a half and twenty-five) on how to get a suitable career, interspersed with gossip and data on the female leads of the day: Mabel Normand, "the popular and dashing film comedienne", or Colleen Moore, "a dainty little maiden" of eighteen.

American culture was very popular among young workers. It went hand in hand with the new values that they sought to live by: greater class equality, less parental control, greater personal and sexual freedom, more mobility. As respect for adults lessened, there was more adolescent drinking, more hanging around street corners. This in turn helped to fuel fears about youth crime, typified by Cyril Burt's 1925 survey *The Young Delinquent*. Opposite the book's title page was an iconic photograph of "B.1 (AGED 15 $^7/_{12}$)", a perfect picture of young insolence with his drooping cigarette and surly gaze.

. . .

The principle of inclusion by consumption worked in Britain during the early 1920s, allied as it was to new measures that aimed to bring underprivileged youth within the institutions of society. The raising of the school age to fourteen in 1918 was accompanied by a strong grassroots movement to create open spaces for inner-city youth. The proof was in the juvenile crime figures, as the number of those charged in the juvenile court fell by 40 per cent between 1917 and 1924. Until the general strike of 1926 there was no serious worker unrest, and that was expressed in Marxist rather than youthist terms.

The modernity that gave many working-class youth some degree of independence and that, indeed, soaked up energy that otherwise might have been politically directed, became, to a small but highly visible minority of the privileged, a flag of rebellion. Hedonism had already been elevated into an ideology, but after his appointment in 1924, Sir William Joynson-Hicks became the century's most repressive home secretary. Under his authority the control of pleasure became a Prohibition-like crusade. Partying became politicized.

Born in 1865, Joynson-Hicks—or Jix as he was quickly nicknamed—came from that very generation that had sent young Britain out to die. When he declared war on sex in general, homosexuality in particular, and London's club life, a section of the young took up the gauntlet with gusto. The generational rhetoric of the war poets had already been assumed by Britain's young modernists, and months before the publication of T. S. Eliot's *The Waste Land,* two adolescent Etonians, Harold Acton and Brian Howard, edited a magazine intended to announce an artistic revolution.

Published in March 1922, the *Eton Candle* contained work by the Sitwell siblings, Osbert and Sacheverell, as well as the young novelist Aldous Huxley. Harold Acton wrote "A Note on Jean Arthur Rimbaud", while Brian Howard's poem "To the Young Writers and Artists Killed in the War: 1914–18" excoriated the "parcel of damned old men" who had murdered "a great Young Generation": "Oh, we will fight for your ideals—we, who were too young to be murdered with you . . . And—we haven't forgotten you."

These two Anglo-American adolescents embodied the ideas that they espoused.[1] Striking in their different ways—Acton solid and inscrutable, Howard lean and bold-eyed—the pair used dandyism to proclaim their difference. Acton was responsible for a variety of new fashions, including the very broad pleated, highly coloured trousers that became known as Oxford Bags. He was also infamous for declaiming modernist poetry, like *The Waste Land,* by megaphone. Acton and Howard were inside-outsiders: educated with the elite but ultimately outcast through birth and temperament.

The fact that they were both homosexual within a society that persecuted the state gave their rebellion extra force: instead of concealment, they chose brazen exposure. The "schoolboy" look taken up by working-class girls might have hinted at homosexuality, but here was the real thing. At another time, their brutal effeteness might have passed unnoticed, but in the 1920s it struck a chord. The slaughter had decimated British masculinity: the rigid physical vigour and martial Christianity of the late nineteenth century had been no match for the reality of mass shelling.

Women had become more powerful, not just because there were more of them, but also because of their vanguard status in the new consumerism. Assuming different masks and roles, experimenting with different ideas and attitudes, Acton and Howard showed that men could slip right into this pliable ethos. Previously, public school men had prepared for war or colonial service. In the 1920s, two of the most influential post-war figures from that class prepared for artistic experiment and, in Howard's case, dedicated partying.

The new masculinity was popularized by Noël Coward's 1924 play *The Vortex,* which caused a sensation through its exploitation of drug abuse.[2] But that was only the most obvious hook. Coward revelled in his leading character's status as a mother-fixated neurotic, recognizing that these were the new youth parameters. From the vorticists to *The Vortex* lay a chasm of sensibility and sexuality: in the 1920s, the most novel youth type would not be the

---

1. Harold Acton's mother was American, his father British. Brian Howard's parents were both American, living in the United Kingdom since his birth.

2. True to modernist form, Coward lived up to the worst possible public perception of him, acting out the principal character's role in a sequence of scandalous press stories. In the *Sketch,* he was pictured in bed "wearing a Chinese dressing-gown and an expression of advanced degeneracy". As he told the *Evening Standard,* "I am never out of opium dens, cocaine dens, and other evil places. My mind is a mess of corruption."

aggressive futurist/pugilist, but the sharp-tongued, overstimulated, androgynous Peter Pan.

This worked both ways. The most visible female rebel of the early 1920s was another Anglo-American, Nancy Cunard, the only daughter of the then current head of the famous shipping family. Born in the very late nineteenth century, Cunard had been brought up to a life of privilege, only to witness it shattered by the war. After a disastrous marriage, she dived into a lifelong quest for novelty, fulfilment, and revenge against her hated mother. Stick thin, thanks to a delicate constitution not improved by "incessant drink", she had an unforgettable impact on all who met her.

Her wildness was backed up by a steely, ice-blue regard, floating walk, and alert posture. Although not conventionally attractive, she presented a new and startling type, with huge eyes, cropped shingled hair, wasp waist, and, in Wyndham Lewis's 1922 portrait, mannish clothes. One of her lovers, Aldous Huxley, thought that she had "the masculine detachment. She can separate her appetite from the rest of her soul." Despite her portrayal as a corrosive vamp in Huxley's novels, she typified herself as "the perfect stranger, outcast and outlaw from the rules of life".

The London club life that Cunard inhabited began to assume an unforeseen importance as the generator of a new youth style. During the early 1920s, nightclubs proliferated in the capital, whether West End venues like the Café Royal and the Embassy, north Soho's Eiffel Tower, the bohemian Ye Old Ham Bone in St James's, or Mrs Meyrick's famous "43" club in Soho. In these clubs, the culture that had originated in wartime spread further: that mix of bohemian, aristocrat, showgirl/prostitute, and the transatlantic influence brought in by Canadian and American soldiers.

Michael Arlen observed this world's underlying vacancy in his 1924 bestseller *The Green Hat*, a roman à clef about café society with a portrait of Cunard, as Iris Storm, at its heart. Despite all the bright lights, the young celebrants "ignored everything but themselves, in whom they were not very interested". "Bored with boredom", this early twenties generation submerged their loss in slow Negro dances like the blues. "It had a beat like a throbbing of an agonised heart lost in an artery of the Underground," Arlen wrote. "You mourned the presence of the dead. You mourned the memory of the living."

Clubgoers might have sought to break loose, but as Arlen shrewdly noted, the pursuit of pleasure was both a secular religion and a chimerical dream. Iris Storm speaks passionately of "the-desire-for-I-know-not-what. They will find it one day when we are dead and all things that live now are dead. They will find it when everything is dead but the dreams we have no words for. It is not chocolate. It is not cigarettes, it is not cocaine, nor opium, nor sex. It is not eating, drinking, flying, fighting, loving." Life's best gift, she concludes, "is the ability to dream of a better life".

The fact that these devouring impulses were fuelled by drink and drugs only increased the authorities' hostility. In the early 1920s, some of DORA's restrictions had been lifted, and clubgoers could enjoy freedoms unthinkable in America. However, the scandal that followed the cocaine overdose of show-girl Freda Kempton in March 1922, coupled with Jix's appointment, resulted in a major crackdown. This failed to stop the popularity of London's nightlife, and the home secretary was amazed to find that, instead of being peopled by whores and drug addicts, these clubs were full of "society".

Jix's moralistic campaigns helped to amplify the restless, devil-may-care attitude of the younger generation just beginning to enter London's clubland. The first public sighting of the Bright Young People occurred in July 1924, when the *Daily Mail* ran a report headlined "Chasing Clues, New Society Game, Midnight Chase in London, 50 Motor Cars, the Bright Young People". This small group was led by a number of upper-class and upper-middle-class young women: specializing in dressing up, hoaxes, and anarchic treasure hunts, it represented "a movement which has captured all smart London".

These apparently trivial activities masked a deep social change that, according to Brenda Dean Paul, could be attributed to "taxation, women's new found independence, and general social laxity. A new class or branch of English society had been born, had sprung out of the war-time upheaval, the 'New Poor'". Her generation "had no inclination to conform to stereotyped private dances and other formal social innovations, and broke gradually away, forming little groups or 'coteries' which came to be known by the press as 'the bright young people'".

Dean Paul cited the massive surplus of young women as one of the reasons why the old formal world of debutantes, private dances, and chaperones had begun to crumble with the emergence of "a new type of host and hostess". These included *Loom of Youth* author Alec Waugh, credited with inventing the cocktail party, or David Tennant, who in 1925 opened one of Soho's longest-running nightclubs, the defiantly modernist Gargoyle. As Dean Paul concluded, "A new camaraderie of youth had arisen, an independence, an equality, which gave birth to a new code of social manners."

Drink was the principal dissolver of class boundaries and, as Evelyn Waugh recorded exhaustively in his diaries, the usual bounds of civilized behaviour. A party wasn't a party unless it was an orgy. In September 1926, for instance, he went to an event hosted by some lesbian acquaintances: "Lulu Waters-

Welch came. He is living in sin with Effingham. Brian O'Brien came; also the leader of the syndicate. Alistair and I both got very drunk indeed. I think I was rude to Bobbie. There was a fight between two men. Also a policewoman who scared everyone and made Joan very pugnacious."

This younger generation lacked the angst of their wartime forebears, and jazz provided the perfect soundtrack for their shrieking exuberance. Americanism was everywhere. "George Gershwin's *Rhapsody In Blue* accompanied every rough-and-tumble on the sofa," Harold Acton recalled; "it seemed to contain all the intoxication of black and chromium cocktail bars." Evelyn Waugh recorded a visit to *The Blackbirds* and an American "monster" actor who "carried around packets of tooth-powder which he said was heroin and everyone took".

Changes in the British media meant that this small group had a disproportionate prominence in the press. In the mid-1920s, national newspapers were developing a new kind of feature: the bylined gossip column. The first diarist to sign his name was a peer of the realm, Lord Castlerosse, and he was quickly followed by columnists like Tom Driberg, Charles Graves, and Evelyn Waugh. This was a new, self-conscious world: these young men would go with their friends to parties and write about both. In turn, the publicity would encourage emulation. This did not go without adult comment.

The Bright Young People's style was a fusion of modernity and Oedipal obnoxiousness organized around what looked like meaningless pleasure. Many of the leading lights had poor relationships with their parents. Evelyn Waugh had produced a memorable woodcut entitled *That Grim Act Parricide*, depicting a young man holding a gun to his ageing father's throat. Brian Howard refused to speak to his father after 1928, while Nancy Cunard caused a scandal in 1930 by publishing a pamphlet making public her quarrel with her mother. Beverley Nichols actually tried to murder his father in 1929.

The rebellion of old money and the new bourgeoisie was all the more shocking because it came from within the very class that had led the charge into battle and had suffered proportionately. As far as the establishment was concerned, to have the younger siblings of war heroes turning into vamps, or worse, was to have sired a generation of traitors. At the same time as the gossip columns trumpeted treasure hunts, the editorial pages delivered splenetic denunciations of modern youth, like the *Daily Express*'s 1925 attack on "The Modern Girl's Brother", that "silken-coated lapdog".

To a considerable extent, however, this reinforced traditional privilege. Young workers had their own pleasures in the large dance halls that had sprouted around the country, but they were not taken up in the press or thought to be fashionable. Emancipation had not gone that far. If the Bright Young People had begun with any ideology, it was the hedonistic and amoral attitude captured by James Laver's famous doggerel: "In spite of Mr Joynson Hicks / We're people of the Aftermath / We're girls of 1926." However, the events of that year showed that they were traditionalists at heart.

The Bright Young People might well have associated with costermongers, rattled away at each other in Cockney as part of their repertoire of voices, and posed with workmen on the way home from one of their costume parties, but when the chips were down, they followed the imperatives of their class. During the general strike of 1926, many of these partygoers joined the fray on the side of the government as strikebreakers, keeping essential services going. When the strike ended in mid-May, the heart was ripped out of the labour movement for a generation.

Their actual contribution was negligible, but as victorious counterrevolutionaries, the Bright Young People's style spread more widely through bourgeois youth: as the commentator Beverley Nichols recalled, after 1926 "Oxford was seized by a hectic gaiety. There was a feeling of *après moi le déluge.*" The parties increased in wildness: as a *Vogue* diarist commented in 1927, "At Hampden House there was more lip-rouge than I have never seen. Lord Portarlington and his son Lord Carlow, as Victorian mother and debutante daughter respectively, were smothered in it."

Nineteen twenty-seven was the high summer of the Bright Young People, and their latest star upped the ante in outrage. The youngest heir to a Glasgow chemical fortune, Stephen Tennant was everywhere in the year that he turned twenty-one: in the gossip columns dressed up as "the Queen of Roumania", or covered "in green rags" in an "impersonation of beggars". Sitting for Cecil Beaton, he epitomized the last word in modernity with his rubber coat and an appearance styled—marcelled hair, lip gloss, and face make-up—on the American actresses whom he so admired.

Tennant did his best to live up to his reputation. In spring 1928, he and Brenda Dean Paul co-hosted a party at the Gargoyle for his brother David Tennant's wedding. With a guest list including Brian Howard, Harold Acton, and the Sitwells, he stole the show by arriving in "an electric brougham of the Edwardian period". The next month, David Tennant held a pyjama party visited by J. M. Barrie: Stephen wore "white satin, but changed halfway through into green"; in June, he was spotted at the Chelsea Arts Ball "in fantastic rags of chiffon and velvet, showing the Picasso scheme of colourings".

The problem with outrage, however, is that it always needs to be trumped. The Bright Young People began to hit the law of diminishing returns. What had begun spontaneously became self-conscious rather than joyous. Brenda Dean Paul thought that the movement "died from two causes, publicity and social blood-poisoning". "The parties became more and more frequent, more and more lacking in originality and amusement," she recalled, "until they became massed drinking orgies, attended by a few bleary-eyed, demoralised bright young pioneers, too tired, too much in a groove to break away."

Pleasure was no longer enough. "I'm heartily sick of London and London parties," Brian Howard declared, "which remain exactly the same as they were five years ago. In London NOTHING changes." His friend Allanah Harper recalled these routs as "a Jerome Bosch hell": "The last party I went to with Brian," she remembered, "resulted in my dress being practically torn off and tufts of my hair held up as trophies." As Norah C. James wrote in her banned novel, *Sleeveless Errand*, "the Crowd are held together by sheer boredom. They run away from themselves into this. We hate each other, but we can't stay away."

■ ■ ■

Like the American collegians, the Bright Young People stoked the media's new obsession with youth. They were the first British youth culture to be defined in aspirational terms, as they heralded the application of adolescence as an ideal beyond biology. By the end of the 1920s, advertisements and newspapers were promoting "Childlike Innocence at 40 Years Of Age" or discussing the conflicts between the war and post-war generations. "There is nothing that big business does not see in terms of £.s.d," Wyndham Lewis observed. "And it has gazed upon 'Youth' and it has found it not *fair*, but *profitable*."

Unlike their American counterparts, the Bright Young People were no Cinderellas, no exemplars of social inclusion. Their antics were only another example of the licence traditionally granted to gilded youth. If the young working class had caused such a disturbance, they would have been quickly arrested. Even the gossip columnists observed the "condescension" of leading figures like Stephen Tennant. And, despite the fact that they were set up for emulation, they also attracted hostility, being heckled and jeered at by the public as they arrived in their costumes at yet another ball.

Disconnnected from society, the Bright Young People had, by the end of the decade, little to show for their partying. Their dissolution was carefully mapped. "Look at our generation," Norah C. James enquired. "And the next; by the next I mean the people who were born just before or during the war. Haven't they struck you as all hopelessly at sea?" Evelyn Waugh thought that the twenties generation had been offered "a chance after the war that no generation has ever had. There was a whole civilization to be saved and remade—and all they seem to do is play the fool."

This harsh reckoning was prompted by the flurry of books and plays that emerged at the end of the decade, as the 1890s generation finally found their voice. Many of these works had a bitter, cathartic tone: R. C. Sherriff's *Journey's End*; Richard Aldington's *Death of a Hero*; Charles Carrington's *A Subaltern's War*; Robert Graves's *Goodbye to All That*; Erich Maria Remarque's *All Quiet on the Western Front*. It was by chance that these memoirs coincided with the exhaustion of the Bright Young People, but the comparisons did not offer any consolation.

The corollary of the veterans' alienation from the present was their celebration of the pre-war years as a golden age, an arcadia of innocence, perfect summers, and youth not yet smashed. The 1890s generation depicted themselves as triply lost: if pre-war life seemed as far away as a fairy tale, then their wartime experience remained as vivid as ever. In turn, the materialist frenzy of the 1920s offered nothing but disillusionment. This influential trope, however, was based on reality: the absence of comrades killed in the war compounded by the survivors' abdication from public life.

Whether they hid themselves away or partied like adolescents ten years younger, they felt lost. "We are superfluous to ourselves," Remarque admitted; "we shall grow older, a few will adapt, others will make adjustments, and many of us will not know what to do." The veterans' need for quiet and shelter also created a vacuum that in turn explained the restlessness of the post-war partygoers, who lacked any meaningful engagement with their immediate elders. Frantic hedonism had failed to eradicate the war's shadow: if anything, it had become deeper and darker.

Some veterans were highly critical of the 1920s generation. In late 1929, a former Freikorps volunteer named Hans Zehrer argued in the influential right-wing German magazine *Die Tat* that his "young generation" of war veterans was comprised of two waves. The first had burnt itself out in dissipation, but the second—which had lived quietly and gained experience of the world—was now poised to revolutionize Germany. Zehrer concluded that Germany would be rebuilt by these "men of the front", not the Americanized twenty-somethings with their "clownish behaviour".

These comparisons revealed an angry reaction against the 1920s youth culture that its self-absorbed adherents could do little to counter. The reckoning had arrived, and it found them wanting. The problem for these perennial adolescents was that they never wanted to grow up, because growing up meant that they would become the hated father. The war's end had provided such a decisive break that it had represented a kind of tabula rasa that allowed the youth movements of the 1920s to think that they could construct a world entirely separate from adults.

In his 1929 novel, *Les enfants terribles,* Jean Cocteau offered the perfect metaphor for this disconnection, in the archetypal adolescent bedroom-cum-shrine of the orphaned Paul and Elizabeth: "The floor was strewn with empty boxes, with towels and various articles of underwear. Every available inch of wall space was stuck with drawing-pins impaling sheets of newspaper, pages torn out of magazines, programmes, photographs of film stars, murderers, boxers." Cocooned within this cell, Paul and Elizabeth enact "the legend of eternal youth" until their premature death by gunshot and opium overdose.

The pair's real-life counterparts were Jean and Jeanne Bourgoint, who were going the same way as Raymond Radiguet: to an early grave. Converting the pair into Paul and Elizabeth, Cocteau observed how the interior explorations of adolescence, without adult control, are condemned to failure, as "to look within requires self-discipline, and this they lacked. Primeval darkness, ghosts of feeling, were all that they encountered."

From bitter experience, Cocteau understood the seductive, self-destructive undertow of excessive youthism: the warping effect of childhood prolonged, the romantic pull of death, the inability to make the transition into adulthood. *Les enfants terribles* was an admonitory parable that also encouraged emulation from its enthusiastic young readership. Despite the fact that they were doomed, Paul and Elizabeth were also magnetic: "Thistledown spirits, tragic, heart-rending in their evanescence, they must go blowing to perdition. And yet all started harmlessly, in childish games and laughter."

Around 1929, many leaders of the hedonistic youth culture came to premature ends. Drink and drugs were responsible: both had been heavily used in the attempt to keep the party going forever, to freeze the parabola forever at its zenith. Bootleg poisons finished off many young Americans, most notably the star cornetist Bix Beiderbecke, while heroin addiction turned Brenda Dean Paul into Britain's most notorious drug addict. Jeanne Bourgoint died from a barbiturate overdose in December 1929, while many others, like Scott Fitzgerald and Brian Howard, began a lifelong battle with alcoholism.

Even more dramatic was the fate of those who could no longer keep up with the constant acceleration. Whether by Brenda Dean Paul, Jean Cocteau, Scott Fitzgerald, Michael Arlen, or Evelyn Waugh, almost all the major youth books of the period include disastrous car crashes. If the destruction wasn't physical, it was mental. Like Waugh's Agatha Runcible, Zelda Fitzgerald ended the decade in a sanatorium, her nervous system jammed into overdrive. Perhaps the most dramatic falling to earth was that of Harry Crosby, who died with his lover in a double suicide pact in December 1929.

By then, the party culture had been overtaken by events. The American stock market crash of October 1929 was one logical conclusion of government-inspired mass speculation. A febrile boom became a negative vortex that began to pull America and Europe into its remorseless grip. However, the Western world did not change overnight. It took time for economics to impact on everyday life, and as there was no precedent for the Depression, there was no expectation that it would occur. As the British writer Ethel Mannin observed, "the Twenties' mood continued into the early Thirties."

The economic foundation of the American mass society had been badly shaken, but it remained potent. In the last of the era's great dystopias, *Brave New World,* Aldous Huxley imagined a nightmare future dependent on seduction and biological determinism rather than brutal coercion. Huxley thought that American-style capitalism would prevail, not the least because it exploited the psychological triggers inherent within every human being. Just as Bernays had suggested, the iron fist of total social control was cloaked within the velvet glove of pleasure.

Capitalism, however, would remain in abeyance over the next few years, while the worst effects of the crash were felt: fascism and communism would rush in to fill the gap. After the October 1929 death of Gustav Stresemann, the first arena in this battle would be an increasingly destabilized Germany. The country's Americanized youth had been unmasked as "the errand boys of a dying age", and the stage was left open to the radical political and pagan youth groups—the various types of *Bunde* and *Wandervogel* that had always disliked modernism in general and the Weimar Republic in particular.

Whether American college students, the Bright Young People, or the Woodcraft Folk, the youth movements of the 1920s had been all too successful in creating their own discrete worlds. In doing so, they had reminded manufacturers, governments, and ideologues that youth comprised a social force that was far too important to be left to its own devices. With the Italian *fascisti,* youth had already been employed as the vanguard of a new kind of national politics. Having demonstrated its capacity to determine the future of nations, youth would become increasingly politicized in the years to come.

PART V

1930—1939

CHAPTER 18

The Soldiers of an Idea

The Hitler Youth

· · ·

With your banners flying, come to us, the German Workers' Youth, fight with us against the old system, against the old order, against the old generation. We are the last fighters for liberty, fight with us for Socialism, for freedom, and for bread!

—Leaflet issued by the Kiel branch of the Hitler Youth, summer 1932

ADOLF HITLER INSPECTING A FORMATION OF THE HITLER YOUTH
AT NUREMBERG, GERMANY, IN 1938, WITH RUDOLF HESS
(WEARING TIE) AND HITLER YOUTH LEADER BALDUR
VON SCHIRACH (TO THE RIGHT OF HESS)

ON JANUARY 30, 1933, a German girl named Melita Maschmann went with her parents to witness the torchlight parade that marked Adolf Hitler's appointment as Reichschancellor. The "uncanny feel" of that Berlin night would remain with her for the rest of her days: "the crashing tread of the feet, the sombre pomp of the red and black flags, the flickering light from the torches on the faces and the songs with melodies that were at once aggressive and sentimental. For hours the columns marched by. Again and again amongst them we saw groups of girls and boys scarcely older than ourselves."

Writing thirty years later, Maschmann remembered her fifteen-year-old self as searching for a "fundamental purpose": "At that age, one finds a life which consists of school work, family outings and birthday invitations wretchedly barren of significance. Nobody gives one credit for being interested in more than these derisory trivialities. Nobody says: 'You are needed for something more important; come!' Where serious matters are concerned one does not yet count. But the boys and girls in the marching columns did count. Like the adults, they carried banners on which the names of their dead were written."

Maschmann had been brought up to revere the war dead and to love Germany "as something mysteriously threatened with grief, something infinitely dear and threatened by danger", the National Socialists "in harmony" with this spirit. She was also attracted by the party's embrace of "the common people", embodied by the family's hunchbacked dressmaker: "For as long as I had known her, she had worn an embossed metal swastika under the lapel of her coat. That day she wore it openly for the last time and her dark eyes shone as she talked of Hitler's victory. My mother was displeased. She thought it presumptuous for uneducated people to concern themselves with politics. But it was the very fact that this woman was one of the common people that made her attractive to me. I felt myself drawn to her for the same reason that I often inwardly took the maids' part against my mother. I realize now that my antagonism to every manifestation of bourgeois snobbery, which I acquired early in life, was nourished by a reaction against my authoritarian upbringing."

Maschmann's mother "expected from her children the same unquestioning obedience that she required of the maids or of my father's chauffeur. This attitude drove me to a rebelliousness which went beyond the purely personal rebellion of adolescence and was directed against the bourgeois values which my parents represented." The fact that her parents witnessed this procession with "an icy blast" of reserve only redoubled her wish "to follow a different path from the conservative one prescribed for me by family tradition".

However, these overt reasons paled before the overwhelming emotions evoked by the event. "I longed to hurl myself into this current, to be submerged and borne along by it," she later recalled: "'For the flag we are ready to die,' the torch-bearers had sung. It was not a matter of clothing or food or school essays, but of life and death. For whom? For me as well? I do not know if I asked myself this question at that moment, but I know I was overcome with a burning desire to belong to these people for whom it was a matter of life and death."

This was exactly the reaction that Adolf Hitler desired. Just like Mussolini's *fascisti*, the Nazis came to power by invoking youth in the abstract as an active agent of change and by mobilizing the actual young through the mystique of conflict, action, and belonging. Major set pieces like the January 30 procession were designed to work on the emotions of disaffected youngsters like Melita Maschmann: "I wanted to escape from my narrow childish life and I wanted to attach myself to something that was great and fundamental. This longing I shared with countless others of my contemporaries."

By the end of 1933, nearly three and a half million young Germans would join the Hitler Youth. This was partly due to the systems of coercion set up by the new regime, but the Nazis also harnessed "the antagonism between the generations". Joining the Hitler Youth gave Germany's aimless adolescents a purpose in life and power against their parents, who were, as likely as not, identified with the despised Weimar Republic. As the Hitler Youth leader Baldur von Schirach stated, "From a National Socialist point of view, youth is always right."

For youth was at the heart of the National Socialists' revolutionary vision. In a January 1933 interview, Germany's new ruler laid out his plans for the future: "I am beginning with the young. We older ones are used up. We are rotten to the marrow. We have no unrestrained instincts left. We are cowardly and sentimental. We are bearing the burden of a humiliating past, and have in our blood the dull reflection of serfdom and servility. But my magnificent youngsters! Are there finer ones anywhere in the world? Look at these young men and boys! What material! With them I can make a new world."

. . .

The crash of 1929 accelerated the arrival of the mass society within northern Europe. The boosters of capitalism had trumpeted mass production's ability to change "the whole social order", but they had failed to foresee its downside. When it worked, everything was fine: wages were higher, prices lower, mass standards of living raised. But when things went wrong, the consequences were disastrous. As the unemployment lines deepened during 1931, it became clear that the damage was systemic. The mass inclusion begun by the 1920s boom would henceforth be driven by politics.

The most important fact in "the public life of Europe" in the early 1930s was, as José Ortega y Gasset observed in his polemical *The Revolt of the Masses*, "the accession of the masses to complete social power". However, this new age had its own totalitarian impulse: "As they say in the United States, 'to be different is to be indecent.' The mass crushes beneath it everything that is different, everything that is excellent, individual, qualified and select. Anybody who is not like everybody, who does not think like everybody, runs the risk of being eliminated."

As the dystopias of the previous decade had warned, the 1930s would exalt the individual who surrendered to the mass. I was not one any more, but only one as part of millions: the ideal Hitler Youth, as Baldur von Schirach stated in 1934, was "the individual soldier of an idea". While the people appeared to be dominating politics in Europe, the actual levers of power remained in the hands of an elite, who began to use the principles of propaganda developed during the 1920s to give a populist gloss to autocracy. At the same time, the methods of social control developed in the 1920s continued at a steady level.

Despite the discrediting of American capitalism, consumerism remained extremely useful to regimes of all hues: helping to palliate greater unrest in Western democracies, sugaring the terror pill in the totalitarian states. But underneath the illusion of mass power lay mass subjugation, with the concomitant psychological effects of infantilism, rage, and violence. Indeed, many of the decade's events would exemplify Gustave Le Bon's curse: "A crowd is a servile flock that is incapable of ever doing without a master."

Politics became the new mass religion and polarization its communion. The struggle between communism and fascism became the "struggle between the forces of good in the world and the forces of evil". Black-and-white thinking comes easily to the adolescent mind, untainted by death, age, or compromise, and indeed offers the welcome certainty of the religious impulse. Many contemporary accounts and histories of 1930s youth from Germany, Britain, France—and even America—all asked the same question: which side are you on?

The most visible members of the 1920s generation had been cynical, pleasure-driven, and materialist. In contrast, those coming of age during the 1930s were mobilized by one overwhelming agenda: to overturn capitalism. However, these youthful impulses would have serious and permanent effects:

as contrasting utopias became national ideologies, the stakes were higher and ruthlessly enforced. The grand ideas of pre-1914, so discredited by the Great War, had returned with a vengeance.

Whether on the left or the extreme right, politics had a mystical quality in the early 1930s, demanding the submersion of the individual ego within the collective ideal: the sacrifice described by the poet Louis MacNeice as "self-fulfilment through self-abnegation". This sincere and idealistic impulse, however, would be channelled within the two opposing totalitarian ideologies of the age. The irony was that these deadly enemies would have the same fundamental belief: *we want the same thing . . . a new system.*

In no European country were these choices starker than in Germany. With the economy in free fall and unemployment escalating, the Weimar government was overwhelmed. Public resentment found its expression in the September 1930 Reichstag elections, where the ruling Social Democrats were outnumbered by the Communists and the National Socialists combined. This election heralded the Nazis' arrival as a serious political party and gave legitimacy to what had been previously considered as little more than a fringe terror group.

Before the crash, the National Socialists' attempts to organize the younger generation had met with little success. Instituted in the mid-twenties, the Hitler Youth had not integrated with the mainstream *Bunde:* they were little more than street fighters. After the appointment of Baldur von Schirach as leader in 1928, the Hitler Youth attracted the freshly impoverished middle class. It became a paramilitary organization dedicated to winning public support by large parades through big cities, with the violence that these events attracted offering a major incentive for the young and restless.

Capitalism's failure had left the stage open for its rivals in the theatre of mass control. Directed by Moscow, the German Communists aimed for nothing less than a final showdown with capitalism. In polar contrast, the National Socialists were heavily influenced by Mussolini's decade-long Fascist government.[1] "The brown shirt would probably not have existed without the black shirt," Hitler stated in 1932, and he took much from the *fascisti:* the construction of the one-party state, the militaristic colour-coded uniforms, the simultaneous regimentation of and appeal to youth.

Combining xenophobia and racial mysticism with the hypnotic power of the mass media, party leader Adolf Hitler began his campaign to capture Ger-

---

1. Mussolini had been sworn in as Italy's youngest ever prime minister in October 1922, at the age of thirty-nine.

many's younger generation. After the 1930 election, the National Socialists' programme of nationalistic engagement, packaged as a quasi-religious mass movement, offered commitment as opposed to alienation. Suicides among young high school students remained as much of a national problem as they had been in the 1890s, and the party's appeal to direct action attracted a large section of German youth hostile to democracy and bored with hopelessness.

In the face of this polarization, the self-styled leaders of the youth movement attempted in vain to establish a democratic or centrist counterweight. The largest of all the independent *Bunde,* the Deutsche Freischar failed to create a strong party of the centre in the elections of 1930. Apart from the party political organizations on the extreme left and right, there were many paramilitary groups which, in their reliance on military discipline, *völkische* theory and anti-Weimar rhetoric, tended towards the right of the spectrum, as did the Protestant youth groups and the Scouts.

This crucial moment was analysed by the conservative *Die Tat* group in a 1931 pamphlet titled *Where Does the Young Generation Stand?* Its writer, Ernst Wilhelm Eschmann, criticized Germany's political obsession with youth as "a magic formula". But this youth mysticism was ultimately a ruse on the part of the country's elders to deny the young their rightful place in national life. This disparity between rhetoric and reality had caused a generational conflict that left "a great mass of unorganized youth".

The anti-democratic impulse underlying much of the German youth movement began to bear its bitter fruit. Emboldened by their 1930 electoral success, the Nazis conducted a successful campaign of terror against the American-produced film of Erich Maria Remarque's *All Quiet on the Western Front.* With its unflinching depictions of war's horror, this revisionist history was anathema to the far right. In December 1930, a group of Nazis halted the premiere. Fearing more violence, the authorities banned the film: for alarmed observers, this capitulation to brute force set a sinister precedent.

■ ■ ■

Violence *worked.* For many of Germany's young, war was preferable to peace: according to Sebastian Haffner, Hitler promised "the revival of the great war game of 1914–1918", and this appeal to this great experience struck a resonant chord. During that year, the unemployment figures reached five million, with adolescents badly affected. Offering a pool of seven million potential voters, Germany's young had unprecedented political power. The race was on to win their hearts. Visiting Germany just after the elections of August 1932, the radical French journalist Daniel Guerin felt that the country had "already shifted to the side of the Nazis. The epidemic was widespread."

Guerin set out on his extended backpacking tour through Germany at this crucial moment. As a revolutionary socialist in his late twenties, he began with great hopes: "Perhaps I would finally find myself at the heart of the action in this youthful, modern and dynamic Germany that I had admired unceasingly since my childhood. It was here that socialism would triumph, or nowhere. It was here that the world's best and most educated working class had taken form. Here economic and social tensions had reached a point of extreme tension."

The Frenchman was attracted by the "happy-go-lucky" camaraderie of the *Wandervogel* that still persisted in the early 1930s. On his first night in Germany, he entered a youth hostel full of "youths aged between fifteen and twenty, blond-haired with virile voices and determined faces. Khaki or green sports shirts with rolled-up sleeves revealed their tan forearms. Sculptured knees emerged from corduroy or leather shorts often held up by a pair of Tyrolean suspenders with a wide rectangular patch of leather forming a kind of bridge between the pectorals. Legs were deeply tanned, muscles taut and hard."

There were undercurrents, however. Guerin picked up the hostel's visitors' book, only to find "this unheeded notice: 'You are requested to keep your politics out of this book.' Yet, as I leafed through it, politics welled up on every page. Politics tormented these youths to the point where they were unable to resist, despite the neutral ambience of the hostel. One hand had written, 'Workers of the world, unite!' But another had obliterated the appeal with a violent stroke of the pen. On another page, the three Socialist arrows pierced a swastika."

The formerly apolitical youth community of wanderers had irrevocably split. The hostel's large common room resolved itself into two competing factions, each chanting and singing at each other, "as if on the eve of battle". One of the combatants explained: "*Deep down we want the same thing* . . . a new world, radically different from today's world that no longer destroys coffee and wheat while millions go hungry, *a new system*. Some believe adamantly that Hitler will provide this, while others believe it will be Stalin. That's the only difference between us [italics in original]."

As he travelled further, Guerin realized that Germany's youth was lost and bitterly divided. The *Wandervogel* ideal had become hopeless vagabondage: "Half a million jobless youths wandered the roads. They had no right to social assistance, most often because at least one of their family was still working.

Fed up with twiddling their thumbs in their grim working-class neighbour-hoods and being a burden on their families, they would set out each spring and knock about in the woods until autumn's end. Some had been drifting like this for several years."

Despite his political beliefs, Guerin felt that the "patient argument" of left-wingers and centrists alike had little chance among the elemental forces stirred up within a country "torn asunder". This was dramatically illustrated by the most striking youth tribe that he saw during his two-month trip: a "strange troupe" encountered by chance on the outskirts of Berlin. Despite superficially resembling the usual *Wandervogel*, this "Wild Clique of homeless youths were very much 'toughs'. They had the depraved and troubled faces of hoodlums."

They wore a bizarre costume of Chaplinesque bowler hats, "old women's hats with the brims turned up in Amazon fashion adorned with ostrich plumes and medals", with "handkerchiefs or scarves in screaming colours". Their ears were pierced with "pendants or enormous rings", while their leather shorts were "surmounted by immense triangular belts—also of leather—both daubed with the colours of the rainbow, esoteric numbers, human profiles, and in-scriptions such as *Wildfrei* (wild and free) or *Räuber* (bandits)".

The Wild Cliques had begun in the chaos of the Great War and multiplied with post-war inflation and post-crash unemployment. Completely without adult control, these "Ring Youth Gangs" ran wild in the outer Berlin districts linked by a concentric ring of avenues. As their numbers were swelled by thousands of homeless youths, these adolescents—mostly aged between six-teen and eighteen—organized themselves into a tribal society that completely rejected civilized morality. They turned their hatred on the society that had abandoned them.

The names that the Wild Cliques chose illustrated their "unbridled in-stinct": "Blood of the Tartars, Blood of the Indians, Blood of the Cossacks, Wild Crime, Girls' Terror, Red Apaches, Black Love, Bloody Carcasses, Pirates of the Forest, and Schnapps Guzzlers". With no legal earnings or state sup-port, these *Wildfrei* lived by homosexual prostitution, car theft, and burglary. Comprised of both sexes—"wild guys" and "gang cows"—the cliques exacted regular financial contributions to support comrades in trouble with the police.

Secret initiation rites—violent, sadistic group orgies—exposed the true sav-agery of the Wild Cliques. Living totally outside society, they were able to give full rein to the rampant adolescent sexuality that successive generations of youth experts had warned against. Guerin concluded that they represented a "spontaneous return to barbarism. Civilisation, after all, is but a very thin, recent, and fragile veneer." He felt "a real anxiety: those who would know how to discipline these masquerade Apaches could make real bandits out of them".

The Wild Cliques represented only the most extreme form of their generation's collective abandonment of rationality. The roots of democracy were not deep: the Weimar Republic had been in existence for thirteen years, and, with seventeen governments during that time, had rarely achieved stability. Even during the relative calm of the Stresemann era, it had conspicuously failed to attract the support of a significant section of Germany's young, who had grown up addicted to crisis and conflict.

Weimar had failed to eradicate imperial structures and attitudes. The universities were unequivocally hostile to democracy, as were traditional religious and militarist youth groupings. As three-quarters of all German youth had passed through one of these groups or another, their influence was enormous. Brought up on a cultural diet of metaphysical nationalism and quasi-religious sacrifice, longing for a resurgence of Germany's imperial greatness, the resentful class of 1918 prepared to avenge the defeat that had accompanied their birth.

Nazi propaganda was designed to exploit this longing for mystical, vengeful regimentation. The party specialized in spectacular mass rallies, like the triumphal October 1932 event at Potsdam. Instead of the expected crowd of 20,000, over 100,000 young men and women congregated on the outskirts of Berlin, swamping the travel facilities. The numbers were so great that the boys' march past lasted from 11 a.m. to 6 p.m. Even non-partisan observers were impressed, while the participants were uplifted to find that they were part of such an unexpectedly large whole.

The appeal that the highly ritualized nature of National Socialist events had for the young was summarized in the popular Nazi novel *Hitlerjunge Quex*. Walking into a woodland glade, the young hero comes across "a circle of young people" that appeared to stretch "to the very edges of the world. Just in front of him, marshalled in lines, stood youths like himself. Each held a long pole with a pennant, rising vertically to the sky, black pennants and brilliant red, with jagged symbols on the field of the cloth. Each of the youths looked like all the others." The narrator found this inspirational rather than horrific.

The highly successful film version of this novel reinforced this sacrificial impulse. Recreating the Nazis' rise to power during 1932, the screenplay dramatized the story of twelve-year-old Herbert Norkus, caught by Communists in the working-class district of "Red" Wedding while posting Nazi handbills.

His attackers stabbed him five times in the back, twice in the chest, and mutilated his face beyond recognition. This was converted into a martyr's parable: the final images of *Hitlerjunge Quex* showed the dying youth reaffirming his faith before the camera cut to marching waves of Hitler Youth.

Despite their avowed hatred of modernism, the Nazis had carefully studied America's experiments in mass control: Guerin observed in 1932 that "all Germany had lost its head over American-style delusions of grandeur". They did not fail to develop further Bernays's theories of mass propaganda: indeed, they elevated the concept to a prime agent of social control, with its very own ministry. It would be one of the peculiarities of their regime that it embodied an apparent paradox: the combination of state-of-the-art technology together with barbaric notions of race and social coercion.

National Socialist propaganda disposed of the checks that the American pioneers of mass manipulation had been obliged to set in place by their democratic system. The party's naked invocation of nationalist emotions and mystical forces gave it an edge in the bitter power struggle of late 1932 and early 1933, not the least because of its appeal to youth. This was augmented by an outlaw allure caused by the Weimar bans on National Socialist organizations, including the Hitler Youth. Ideology gave the party's working-class followers an extra spice in their territorial street brawls with the Communists.

At the beginning of 1933, the Hitler Youth, with over 100,000 members, was numerically stronger than the combined Communist and Social Democratic youth organizations—at 80,000 or so—but was far outweighed by the conservative youth groups, which could muster over one-quarter of a million members. If the non-Nazi youth groups had combined, the Hitler Youth would have had a fight on its hands. But there was a slow drift to the Hitler Youth from right-wing and Protestant youth groupings. For many young Germans, communism was abhorrent: the Nazis were the least worst choice.

They also offered hope and structure to a generation of adolescents who had grown up within seemingly permanent political and social instability. The National Socialists' rhetoric of self-sacrifice and discipline also tapped into powerful German archetypes: the warrior myth of Frederick the Great; the medievalism of the *Bunde* enshrined by many *Wandervogel* groups; the crusading self-sacrifice unto death exalted by the battle of Langemarck. If Romantics like Hölderlin had bemoaned the dismemberment of Germany's young, then the Nazis would make both nation and youth whole and strong.

In desperate circumstances, the lure of irrationality and naked power was too strong. Once Hitler had achieved power, there would be no dissent: there would be no place for those who did not share his vision for this new world which, like that of many adolescents or religious fanatics, was coloured in strictly black-and-white terms: either for or against. After the Reichstag fire of February 1933, which many believed had been started by the Nazis themselves, the National Socialists launched an internal blitzkrieg that, by July, would succeed in outlawing and intimidating almost all opposition.

In March, Hitler was granted the emergency powers that, according to Sebastian Haffner, "abolished freedom of speech and confidentiality of the mail and the telephone for all private individuals, and gave the police unrestricted rights of search and access, confiscation and arrest". After a fresh set of elections, Hitler banned the Communist Party from the Reichstag and passed the Enabling Act that effectively killed German democracy. A week later, on April 1, the Jewish boycott and pogrom began. The regime's internal secret police, the Gestapo, were formed at the same time.

During the spring and early summer, labour unions were taken over, strikes prohibited, and finally, the Social Democratic Party banned. Dr Magnus Hirschfeld's Sexual Science Institute was sacked, and all its contents, including thousands of books, burned in images that went around the world. These official acts were accompanied by a systematic campaign of terror: beatings, shootings, imprisonment without trial in hastily constructed camps. Whole working-class areas were cordoned off and cleansed, most notably left-wing districts like Hamburg's Altona and Berlin's Wedding.

This combination of legality and violence was backed up by the latest technology. Radio was the principal tool of Propaganda Minister Joseph Goebbels, and it was relentless, with "never-ending march music and drums" pumping out of speakers placed on street corners. Within months of Hitler's accession to power, it was becoming clear that Nazi Germany was a new kind of state that aimed for total control over all its subjects. There was to be a complete public commitment to the national community at all times and no life allowed outside the regime's incessant demands.

Most Germans quickly acceded: the beautiful weather and constant celebrations of March 1933 brought so many people into the party that they were called, derisively by long-timers, "March Violets". From a position of increasing opposition, Haffner analysed the reasons for this "million-fold nervous breakdown": "The simplest and, if you looked deeper, nearly always the most basic reason was fear. Join the thugs to avoid being beaten up. Less clear was a kind of exhilaration, the intoxication of unity, the magnetism of the masses." In the end, there was the wish "to be part of a perceived success".

When Daniel Guerin returned to Germany in April 1933, he found his worst fears confirmed. Entering a youth hostel "full of the sons and daughters

of the Essen proletariat", he was "treated with a haughty disdain". In place of
the old freedom songs were militaristic hymns that told of "stormtroopers on
the march". He met some *Wandervogel* holdouts, who told him that the Nazis
were "going to hunt down the musicians and the beggars without mercy". It
was, as he later wrote, the end of a dream: "Soon, the nightingale will be mute
in its cage: in Werther's Germany, only the sound of boots will be heard."

. . .

This prognosis was all too accurate. Youth had a special place in Nazi ideology.
Realizing that there were many born and raised during Weimar who would
not surrender their "innermost being" to the Nazi revolution, Hitler went all
out to indoctrinate the next generation, those whose values were not yet
formed. As he stated in 1933, "When an opponent says, 'I will not come over
to your side,' I calmly say, 'Your child belongs to us already . . . You will pass
on. Your descendants, however, now stand in a new camp. In a short time they
will know nothing else but this new community.'"

Just as the stormtroopers forcibly shut down all political opposition, so the
Hitler Youth began to tackle the previously vibrant and diverse German youth
movement. Initially, many youth leaders thought that it would be possible to
come to terms with the new regime. On February 27, 1933, two hundred representatives of youth groups across the political spectrum—Nazis, Communists, Red Boy Scouts, and Socialist Youth—met at Berlin's Stettiner Station
to try to work out some modus vivendi. But this was instantly nipped in the bud
by the repression that followed the Reichstag fire that very same evening.

The immediate aim of the Hitler Youth leader, Baldur von Schirach, was to
draw as many German adolescents as possible into the monopolistic state system. Many of the apolitical youth groupings attempted to resist this move by
forming a new joint organization called the Greater German League, but even
that was dissolved in June. Only the religious *Bunde* held out: the Protestant
organizations merged with the Hitler Youth in December 1933, while, thanks
to a concordat with Pope Pius XI, Catholic youth groups remained extant, albeit under serious pressure, until 1939.

Underneath his epicene appearance, von Schirach was a good organizer. In
June 1933, he was promoted from youth leader of the Hitler Youth to youth
leader of Germany. The implication was deliberate. The Hitler Youth had become the only permissible activity for German adolescents, and any act against
the official state youth organization was an act against the state. At the same
time, membership became mandatory for various professions—like teaching

or law—and preferment for jobs in general. In a country where unemployment was rife, economic need was as cogent as political ideology.

There were many reasons for joining the Hitler Youth: coercion by peers and state, financial pressures, belief in Nazi ideology, if not the simple wish to belong. And join young Germans did, in their masses: the numbers rose from 108,000 in early 1933 to nearly 3.6 million by the end of the year. Baldur von Schirach immediately set about creating a new structure for this expanding organization. Both genders were grouped by age: boys under ten were Pimpfs, between ten and fourteen Jungvolk, between fourteen and eighteen Hitlerjugend. Girls between ten and fourteen were in the Jungmädel, and between fourteen and eighteen in the Bund Deutscher Mädel.

The leadership of Hitler Youth had a pyramidal hierarchy, with von Schirach at the top. Underneath him were five regional *Obergebiete,* and under them twenty-one *Gebiete,* subdivided into six ranks. At the bottom were the *Schafts,* groups of fifteen youths answerable to their leader, in turn answerable to the next rank up. This system was a replica of the wider Nazi Party hierarchy: a logical and ruthlessly enforced order into which the young were trained at a very early age. By the time they attained majority, it would be so ingrained as to make resistance unthinkable, if not impossible.

Both Hitler and von Schirach envisioned a system of cradle-to-grave control for Germany's young. The Hitler Youth grafted the country's mania for categorization and the Nazi drive for totalitarianism onto the regimented militarism of the early Baden-Powell Scouts. Every recruit was bound to the organization by an oath that, invoking God, made transgression even more serious. After the initiation, the neophyte underwent a trial period that lasted two to six months and ended in an exam involving sport, close combat, and set questions on the party's history.

Once initiated, the Hitler Youth were given uniforms that enforced the homogenization that the regime demanded of its youth. The basic male garb resembled the stormtrooper's uniform with its brown shirt and swastika armband, black shorts, black shoes, and trench cap. The girls wore heavy marching shoes, white blouses, blue skirts, and cotton neck scarves with rings bearing the group insignia. The only differences allowed were badges of privilege and insignia that varied according to which branch of the armed forces the particular group was attached.

Hours of daily sport, physical exercise, and military training were at the heart of Hitler Youth life. In her book *School for Barbarians,* Erika Mann quoted a 1933 Handbook for Hitler Youth curriculum that included "peaceful sport" like "the throwing of bombs". Daniel Guerin warned that "a generation is openly preparing itself. Freed of compulsory military service, it finds it amusing to play soldier by marching along the highways, pack on the back, advancing as if for skirmishes, hugging the ground on exercise fields, and banging old pots to alert the urban population to air attacks."

Military indoctrination began early. As one schoolboy remembered, "A large part of our reading in German lessons was world-war literature. But we also devoured it of our own account." He remembered that most of these books concerned "the comradeship of the front" and heroic deaths in action, but there were variations: "the youth-movement hero, the sensitive wanderer 'between two worlds'; the relentless fighter of the 'bestial Bolshevist hordes'; or the despiser of mankind, the knight in technological armour, the aristocratic freebooting twentieth-century hero of *Storms of Steel*."

The Nazis added a constant round of sporting activities to a curriculum that relied on rote learning and blind obedience. The rationale behind this was stated in Hitler's 1927 manifesto *Mein Kampf:* "The *Völkisch* state has to adjust its educational work not merely to the indoctrination of knowledge but in the first place to the production of bodies physically sound to the very core. The development of intellectual ability is secondary to this. But here again, priority must be given to the development of the strength of will and decision, combined with a training in readiness to assume responsibility."

The perfect expression of this ideal was seen in Leni Riefenstahl's film of the 1936 Berlin Olympics, *Olympiad: Fest der Schönheit*. In a succession of startling tableaux, row upon row of identical blond youths, dressed smartly in sportswear, bronzed by the sun, flexed in their hundreds as one identical glistening, muscled body. Physical indoctrination began for young Germans at the age of ten, when prospective Jungvolk underwent a six-month probation period marked by difficult tests that included running sixty metres in twelve seconds and participating in a thirty-six-hour hike. That was only the start.

Myth was entrained in the service of militarism. The most crucial was the battle of Langemarck. Enshrining the idea that obedience to orders was all-important and that self-sacrifice was an ultimate ideal, this legend was eagerly taken up by Nazi-educated youths. The regime specialized in dramatic and mystical pageantry, and *Triumph of the Will* attested to its success in creating an environment where marches, songs, music, lighting, staging and high-octane rhetoric combined into an otherworldly, supercharged spectacle.

These techniques were also used in the regular initiations held to welcome young Pimpf of both genders into the Hitler Youth. These important rituals, which marked the end of childhood and selfhood, were often held on April 20,

Hitler's birthday, and were usually staged in a great hall or castle festooned with torches, banners, candles, and pictures of German heroes. There the ten-year-olds took an oath: "I promise in the Hitler Youth to do my duty at all times in love and faithfulness to help the *Führer*—so help me God."

This was all part of Hitler's vision for the new race of German supermen, to be forged in the Nazi crucible from childhood. "I want to see once more in the eyes of youth the gleam of pride and independence of the beast of prey," he said in 1933. "Strong and handsome must my young men be. I will have them fully trained in all physical exercises. I intend to have an athletic youth—that is the first and the chief thing. In this way I shall eradicate the thousands of years of human domestication. Then I shall have in front of me the pure and noble natural material. With that I can create the new order."

There was no room for the doubt, softness, or self-indulgence that had marred the Weimar generation: for Hitler, all of Germany's youth had to be "tough as leather, swift as greyhounds, hard as Krupp steel". These words were taken as gospel by the regime's ardent young. Melita Maschmann understood "that the 'hardness' which was required of us was a hardness in 'taking punishment'. I thought we should learn to be hard in bearing privations, punishment or pain." The love of Germany was paramount, and it was in the service of this love that young Nazis "wished to make themselves 'tough, swift, and hard'".

As soon as she could, Maschmann left school and joined the Bund Deutscher Mädel press and propaganda department: "I wanted to educate people politically and, indeed, on expressly National Socialist lines." She was one of the privileged few: in Nazi ideology, women were "intrinsically" different from men and thus ideally confined to homemaking, childbearing, and working on the land. The structure and activities of the Jungmädel and the Bund Deutscher Mädel were underdeveloped. There were no specialized or elite formations for girls—girls were meant only to serve and reproduce.

Life in all branches of the Hitler Youth was relentless: the constant alertness satisfied the adolescent need for action. The ideal was to fill every moment of the day. Whether it was physical training, cultural work, social guidance, or even the obligatory *Heimabend*, home evenings where party aims were discussed in an informal setting, everything was a competition. This incessant tourney had the result of reducing any interior and individual life. The sense of regimentation was increased by von Schirach's policy of naming each year after the desired programme: 1934, the first, was the "Year of Training".

Another vital facet of the organization was the fact that youth was led by youth. More than two-thirds of Nazi youth leaders in 1932 were in their twen-

ties. With everyday life in the Hitler Youth run by cohort peers rather than seniors in the hierarchy, youth occupied a position of central importance in the
new regime, not just as active seeds of the Reich to come, but central pillars of
its social system. The National Socialists, as von Schirach never tired of reiter-
ating, were "the party of youth".

At one stroke, the relationship between the generations was reversed.
Youth was now in charge, and expressed their superiority with "an air of non-
chalant arrogance". Immediately after Hitler's seizure of power, this arrogance
was useful to the new regime: now that "the moment of youth" had come,
many Hitler Youth felt emboldened to repay "the liberal bourgeois hypocrites".
They disrupted school life in the manner of the "beer hall battle", broke the
windows of teachers who had given them bad grades, and assisted in the purge
of Socialists and Communists that occurred both in primary and secondary
education.

With their hatred of reason and suspicion of intelligence, Nazi policy on
education was simple. Every youngster was to be inculcated in the cult of the
Führer and the social Darwinist racial policy of the *Volksgemeinschaft*, with its
Aryan ideal of "culture founders" and hatred of the Jews as "culture destroy-
ers". At every point, Nazi ideology was rammed home, whether in poems il-
lustrating the principle that might was right, or in mathematical questions
about Jews as aliens. Subjects like the classics, art, and most sciences were
quickly dropped, and the difference between the sexes ruthlessly enforced.

Under this explicit policy of reprogramming, the relationship between children and parents became bedevilled. Melita Maschmann had to join the Bund
Deutscher Mädel in secret because her parents disapproved. Dissidents or
wary parents could still, for a while, prevent their children from joining the
Hitler Youth, but in general the traffic was the other way. If parents kept their
children out of the Hitler Youth, they could suffer fines or possible imprisonment. Some parents also had their children taken away from them for being
"politically unreliable"—a definition that included befriending Jews.

This resulted in a mirror-image world where children, not parents, held the
whip hand. Denunciations of parents by zealous adolescents were common. A
young Hitler Youth leader named Walter Hess acquired notoriety and a promotion for reporting his father directly to the Gestapo. A former Communist,
Herr Hess had called the Führer "a blood-crazed maniac" and castigated his
son for his Nazi activities. He was arrested the same night and later died in
Dachau. Hitler Youth informants constantly reported on conversations at
school, at work, and at home. Suspicion became the keynote of family life.

Ostracism was another powerful weapon against non-joiners, all the easier to enforce as Hitler Youth uniforms had to be worn at all times. Backsliders were teased by their peers, humiliated by teachers, and suffered penalties in adult life: for instance, Hitler Youth membership was mandatory for any teaching or civil service jobs. Their parents would also be denied promotion. The more hard-bitten cases were targeted by the special Hitler Youth police force, the Streifendienst, established in July 1934 to combat juvenile delinquency, crime, and undisciplined behaviour.

At the centre of this structure stood the Führer himself, who for many replaced the biological father. At the 1934 Nuremberg rally, the youth parade was held in a frenzied atmosphere. Hitler took the opportunity to reassert youth's place in the new world order: "We want a people that is not soft, but hard as flint, and we want you from early youth to learn to overcome hardships and privations. There must be no classes or class distinctions among our people, and you must never let the idea of class distinctions take root among you. All we expect of the Germany of the future, we expect of you."

The identification between Hitler and his chosen children was reciprocal and total. It was encouraged by von Schirach in pronouncements like, "Your name, my Führer, is the happiness of youth, your name, my Führer, is for us everlasting life." Hitler's deity was reinforced in a relentless stream of youth propaganda: Hitler Youth radio broadcasts and magazines targeted at every age category, by the marketing of Nazi toys, and by the bust of the god himself, an almost ubiquitous fixture in children's bedrooms. The actual experience for those who met the great leader was overwhelming.

· · ·

Despite the weight of the state and the aggressive Hitler cult, some youths still refused to join. There were very few alternative structures for resistance, however. A former Communist youth, J. Georgi, felt "the unforgettable disappointment that in 1933 a large part of the leadership of the youth movement humiliatingly capitulated before the National Socialists". The new law was: adapt or die. This atomization was a deliberate Nazi tactic. In a climate of fear, suspicion, and denunciation, even everyday personal relationships were uncertain.

Dissidence was extraordinarily difficult, if not fatal. According to Karma Rauhut, a young German who managed to avoid service in the Bund Deutscher Mädel, "It was like you were in a spider-web and the spider always noted if something vibrated somewhere and did not ring true. People said, 'Ja, one could flee.' Where should one flee to? You could only do resistance if you took death into consideration. Or horrible torture and also torture for your whole family, and death and KZ (concentration camps). And we are not all heroes. We shat our pants from fear. Not everyone is born to heroism."

Those who refused to submit had to live in a permanent state of anxiety. As Georgi recalled, "Some of us who were not up to this unbearable tension also capitulated although not without rupturing their whole inner being." Resistance could be seen as an exit from this psychological cul-de-sac: in the words of the dissenter Arno Klonne, "It was a healthy rejection of the prison organization forced on youth." In the first few years of their regime, the Nazis had to deal with adolescents who had been brought up during Weimar: unwilling to surrender their freedom, they caused the authorities considerable problems.

Remnants of the old youth groups tried to continue their activities, but they were easy to spot and pick off. In the first year of the regime, a young student named Rudolf Kustermann organized an illegal Socialist youth organization called the Rote Stosstrupp that, too late, united the Communist and Social Democratic youth groups. Based in Berlin, it activated other small groups in major cities but was quickly discovered by the Gestapo. Longer-lasting was the illegal continuation of the samurai-styled d.j.1.11 group that remained in several cities right through the decade.

Some rebelled by heading for the open countryside like the old *Wandervogel*, but in informal groups. This was more successful because it was harder to detect. Adolescents sneaked out of town and set up clandestine dens or mountain retreats. From the frequency of police reports—the main information about these activities—this continuation of the old free-wandering spirit seems to have been a popular option, with 150 Frankfurt dissidents rounded up at one fell swoop after their successful trip to the remote Taunus region.

Working-class affiliations died hard. In the Rhine-Ruhr area, resisters from the Socialist Worker Youth, the Red Falcons, the *Bunde*, and Catholic groups got together in large, ad hoc delinquent groups called the Nerother or the Kittelsbach Pirates. With size and local knowledge on their side, they openly defied the Hitler Youth, to the extent that the organization became "virtually defunct" in some areas. The most consistent irritant for the Nazis, however, were the Catholic youth organizations, which refused to integrate with the Hitler Youth even after they had been expressly ordered to do so.

There were also discipline problems within the Hitler Youth itself. Like many successful monopolies, it had temporarily expanded beyond its organizational capabilities. The fact that youth was led by youth revealed several structural faults. The forcible co-opting of the former youth groups caused the authorities considerable concern about subversives within the heart of the system. Some of these infiltrators conducted a campaign of misinformation and disobedience that led to violent "Jungvolk rebellions" in several large cities during the winter of 1934.

The lack of adult control also resulted in frequent sexual misdemeanours. Cases of homosexuality were severely punished: in one serious "moral lapse", sixteen Aachen Hitler Youth indulged in collective mutual masturbation. The organization's heterosexual promiscuity was tolerated by the regime: as one of von Schirach's assistants stated, "What else are Bund Deutscher Mädel girls for except to take them to bed? It is necessary since otherwise they might become lesbians." The excesses of local groups gave parents the impression that "a certain degeneration" existed within the Hitler Youth.

Yet dissidence still continued, breaking out like a forest fire: dampened down in one city, blazing up in another. Von Schirach therefore decided to make 1936 the "Year of the German Jungvolk", with the aim that every boy and girl born in 1926—turning ten that year—should "volunteer" for the youngest Hitler Youth grouping in time for the Führer's birthday. Having achieved near total enrolment for this age group, von Schirach sought to extend this comprehensive inclusion right up until the age of eighteen, after which members would go into the armed forces, the SA or SS, or compulsory land service.

The result was the "Law concerning the Hitler Youth" passed in December 1936, which made von Schirach "Youth Leader of the German Reich", answerable only to Hitler. The clauses were simple: "1: The whole of the German youth within the frontiers of the Reich is organized in the Hitler Youth. 2: The whole of German Youth is to be educated, outside the parental home and school, in the Hitler Youth physically, intellectually and morally in the spirit of National Socialism for service to the nation and the community." This comprehensive decree represented the zenith of the Nazis' youth policy.

The Hitler Youth was already cemented into the Nazi hierarchy, but after the decree, the organization's links to the elite Nazi echelon, the SS (Schutzstaffel), grew stronger. Heinrich Himmler had been recently appointed National Police Chief, and he aimed at a yearly influx of between 25,000 and 30,000 Hitler Youth, about 10 per cent of the draftable cohort for each year. Hundreds of eighteen-year-olds began service in the SS-Verfügungstruppe, the SS special-duty troops, or in the SS-Totenkopfverbände, the Death's Head Formations, designed specifically for prison-camp work.

At the same time, the links were strengthened between the Gestapo, the state secret police, and the Streifendienst, the Hitler Youth police force, which in the first half of 1937 was given surveillance powers over "all political and criminal activities among German youth". The organization could now bring charges in Hitler Youth courts and furnish information to the regular civil courts. A year later, the ambit of the Streifendienst was increased from over-seeing Hitler Youths to all German adolescents: the two were thought to be synonymous by this stage, and the group became a prime feeder into the SS.

. . .

By the time of the 1936 decree, the Hitler Youth had became respectable, bourgeois even, with two-thirds of the leadership corps coming from gram-mar school and/or university backgrounds: these replaced the workers, peas-ants, roughnecks, and students of the revolutionary days. The organization was further served by a new elite schooling system. This was created in the late 1930s by the institution of the *Nationalpolitische Erziehungsanstalten* and the Adolf Hitler schools, where sport was king and Nazi ideology rammed home twenty-four hours a day, seven days a week.

The heroic phase of the Hitler Youth was over, the battle won. After 1936, there was very little chance for anyone under eighteen to escape from the re-gime's demands. However, during the last years of the decade, this national youth group would suffer unforeseen strains. From being the shock wave of the revolution, it had become the new establishment, with its own bureau-cracy and career structure. There was a sense of anticlimax, as it became hard-ened in a policy of activity for activity's sake that became increasingly militaristic. Faced with more backsliding, the regime sought even greater compliance.

For, despite its mystical appeal and totalitarian methods of coercion, the Nazi regime failed to achieve complete control over Germany's adolescents. In the later 1930s, gangs in major cities like Dresden, Hamburg, and Munich continued the old *Wandervogel* lifestyle, while the Leipzig Meuten collected critical data about the regime and speculated about its violent overthrow. Their greeting was a garbled version of the Russian Pioneer slogan: "Be prepared." The size of this group—up to fifteen hundred—and its overt Communist sym-pathies made it a prime target for a massive crackdown.

Part of the problem lay in the Nazis' rhetoric of youth self-rule, as a 1938 report of exiled Germans noted: "Young people are more easily influenced in terms of mood than adults. This fact made it easier for the regime to win over young people in the first years after the seizure of power. It appears that the same fact is now making it hard for the regime to keep young people in thrall." Citing a general mood of "disenchantment", the report concluded that "young people have reason for special disappointment. They were made particularly large promises which for the most part were incapable of fulfilment."

This disillusion brought a fresh wave of repression. In December 1938, Hitler gave the most chilling expression to his cradle-to-grave strategy for German youth, which began with entry into the Jungvolk at ten. On leaving the Hitler Youth at eighteen, they were to be taken into the Labour Front, the SA, or the SS. If they balked, they would be made to join the Labour Service. Any persisting "class consciousness" would be further treated by two years of military service, after which "we take them immediately back into the SA, SS and so on to prevent relapse and they will never be free for the rest of their lives".

From 1938 on, there was little doubt that Germany was preparing for a much wider conflict within which its youth would play a vital part. During that year, one and a quarter million Hitler Youths were indoctrinated in "defence readiness" and "defence capacity" in explicitly militaristic target shooting and terrain manoeuvre exercises. During that year, Hitler Youth membership stood at 8.7 million, well over double what it had been at the end of 1933. As Baldur von Schirach warned, "Everyone who is of German blood belongs to our group. Below the flag of youth, everyone is the same."

By the next year, only 1.6 million out of 8.2 million German adolescents failed to enrol, but even this level of compliance was not enough. In March 1939, Hitler issued a decree that made youth service compulsory for all sixteen- to eighteen-year-olds and gave Hitler Youth leaders specific powers over every aspect of this age group's life. The decree made non-compliance extremely difficult: the police could enforce enrolment and demand obedience to the local leader. Hitler's vision was nearer fruition: for all of Germany's youth between ten and eighteen, every aspect of their life was subject to the regime's control.

Nazi Germany followed the example of Soviet Russia in applying the principles of mass control to its youth. In keeping with its desire to create an entirely new kind of society, it privileged youth in its institutions, and indeed, for many adolescents this policy offered previously unthinkable freedoms. Intoxicated by this revolution, however, they failed to notice the downside to this Faustian contract: that what appeared to be freedom was slavery, that in the end they would be delivered, bound and gagged, into the hands of a sophisticated and pitiless war machine.

CHAPTER 19

The Children's Army and the New Deal

American Adolescents in the Depression

• • •

He has dressed in rags since the second year of the Depression. His gay young predecessors drove fast cars. He rides blind baggage. His family has moved from a house to a flat to a single room, which, until he takes to the road, he shares with all the generations of his clan. Like as not he spends weary night's decline in a boxcar on a railroad siding. He has nothing to dream on. No past, no present, no future.

—Clinch Calkins, *Youth Never Comes Again* (1933)

"THIS BOY HAD BEEN ON THE
ROAD FOR FOUR YEARS," PHOTOGRAPH
BY THOMAS MINEHAN, 1932

"AUG. 24, 1932. Fight with the old man. He can't boss me. Packed clothes and left. Got a ride on a truck full of furniture going to Louisville. Two men driving. Good guys, bought me my meals. Slept in truck. Men took turns driving. We stole some melons and apples from a farmer." This staccato diary entry, written by a boy tramp named Blink, was typical of the fate shared by the quarter of a million "boxcar boys and girls" wandering through America as the Depression deepened. Like their counterparts in late Weimar Germany, they had no home, no job, no money, and no adult controls.

Blink's terse document of transience was copied for posterity by a young University of Minnesota sociologist named Thomas Minehan, who in 1932 decided to record "the reaction of youth to social change" within America. He plunged into the hermetic world of the young homeless, disguising himself "in old clothes" in order to share their life. He was shocked at how many young boy and girl tramps existed: "Where were their homes? Where were they going? How long had they been on the road? Why did they leave home?"

These diaries were not literary outpourings of feelings or ideas. They were survival documents. Knowledge of conditions on the road could mean the difference between life and death. As Minehan observed, impressions were minimized and facts emphasized, such as "fat woman in a big white house gave me three pork sausages, four cups of coffee, and all the pancakes I wanted for breakfast. . . . A bull socked me as I was leaving the yards. Hostile town. . . . No use standing up for Jesus at——Mission. Nothing but beans and misery."

A Dutch boy from Pennsylvania, Blink was on the way to Seattle when Minehan met him in Ohio. His diary was a bare record of conditions during his aimless odyssey around the Midwest. Some people were kind, others "tight". The Roman Catholics in one small town gave him food but made him "eat outside on the porch". One farmer offered him work, but at a derisory rate: "offer only 25c. Nothing to it. Didn't like him anyway." All the way, he was harassed by the police: "Shelbyville. Cop picked me up. Sent to jail, had to work two hours for dinner and supper. Stayed in jail all night. Six guys of us. N.G."[1]

Blink's relief at getting away from his family had carried him through the first few months on the road. After a year of brutal conditions, he no longer thought that the world "was an oyster". He was both mentally and physically scarred. Minehan recorded that "he had two good eyes when he left his father's farm. Now he has but one. A bloody socket forms a small and ever weeping cave on the left side of his face. Tears streak his cheek, furrowing the dirt and

---

1. Abbreviation for "no good".

coal soot, leaving a strange moist scar alongside his nose. He lost his eye when a live cinder blew into on the Santa Fe."

Minehan was one of the first writers to expose the full extent of youth vagabondage in 1930s America: published in 1934 as *Boy and Girl Tramps of America*, his research deepened the understanding of a serious national issue. The "Youth Problem" presented by the "Children's Army" had hit the headlines during the autumn of 1932, with major magazine articles like Maxine Davis's "200,000 Vagabond Children". Stories like this announced a new generation, emblematic of its period, that could not have been more different from the confident consumer youth of the 1920s.

Adolescents like Blink, or Minehan's constant companion, Texas, represented a new type of wild adolescent, grouped into loose tribes. Unlike the Wild Cliques of Berlin, however, they did not have the opportunity to dramatize their wildness. The harsh conditions of homelessness prevented them from organizing and stole their youth. "Within a year I saw Texas change not only physically but mentally," Minehan wrote. "His frozen ears and stiff fingers were outward symbols of an inner change. From a bright, witty, American schoolboy, full of dreams and vigor, he had turned into a predacious, cunning person."

In the mid-1920s, a college student named Barbara Starke had decided to wander across America in a quest for personal realization. Her experience was unique enough to be turned into a successful book: *Born in Captivity*. What for her had been an outrageous act of nonconformity was, for many of the next generation, a grim necessity. There was no chance to be unique in this mass, and human sympathy became quickly rationed. With no government intervention, these young tramps faced an existence as harsh as that which the early twentieth century reformers had worked so hard to address.

For young radicals like Minehan, this was a scandal that called into question the whole nature of American society: "I had seen pictures of the Wild Children of revolution-racked Russia. I had read of the free youth of Germany after the World War. I knew that in every nation, following a plague, an invasion, or a revolution, children left without parents and homes became vagrants. Before my experiences I had always believed that in America we organized things better. And yet in the face of economic disorganization and social change our own youth took to the highroad."

The young sociologist's quest took place in the depths of an unprecedented national disaster. The depressions of the 1870s and the 1890s had been serious, but nothing on the scale of what ensued after the Great Crash. Between autumn 1929 and summer 1932, stockholders lost $74 billion on the free-falling market, the equivalent of $616 for every American, and nearly five thousand banks failed, wiping out $3.26 billion in deposits. That was just the start of it. The most alarming thing about the Great Depression was that it did not stop, but continued getting worse.

Unemployment increased year by year in the early 1930s, affecting at first the more vulnerable and disadvantaged sections of society: Negroes, blue-collar workers, and women—one-fifth of the total female workforce was made redundant during 1930. By spring 1932, it was firmly entrenched within the middle classes. No one was immune. In July, the *New York Times* reported that in the five boroughs there were ten thousand unemployed graduates from America's most prestigious universities.

For those who were still in work, living standards were decimated by wage cuts: in one survey, the annual average income dropped from $1,499 in 1929 to $960 in 1932. Within the same time frame, professional incomes dropped by 40 per cent. America was a country in shock. The prolonged boom of the later 1920s hadn't been just about money, but about national identity. Industry and business had become mystical attributes in twentieth-century America. The Great Depression became seen as a crisis not only of economics but also of the continent's central belief system.

America began to look outward at the same time as it began a painful process of self-examination. The effect of the Depression in other countries had not gone unnoticed. During 1931 and 1932, talk of revolution became common. Fuelled by news stories like the one that reported 100,000 potential emigrants for 6,000 skilled jobs in Russia, commentators discussed bolshevism while Americans of all classes expressed approval for a different social system. Many people thought that capitalism would totally collapse and that a violent revolution would come from the ranks of the unemployed and the homeless.

The Depression hit American adolescents hard. Among those of high school age, 40 per cent were not in school, while the numbers of those dropping out before graduation were rising. At the same time, youth unemployment rocketed. Four million young Americans between sixteen and twenty-four were out looking for work: about 40 per cent of these were of high school age. By 1932, the "Children's Army" of wanderers was 200,000 strong and rising fast, a very small but highly visible proportion of the 14 or so million Americans aged between ten and twenty.

Disintegration began at home. In her study *The Family and the Depression*, Ruth Cavan observed that the consequence of unemployment was "disorganizing". Families moved to smaller apartments, which meant that parents and children "saw much more of each other than formerly and found themselves

cooped up in a small space. There was little privacy, and friction increased."
Minehan found that most young tramps left home because of "hard times".
As Texas told him, "The big trouble had come and nobody had any money."

Well over 90 per cent of Minehan's sample group of young tramps came
from a home where parents or siblings were unemployed or on relief. Twenty-
five per cent of the boys had endured "frequent whippings". Facing a claustro-
phobic environment in which they were often the nearest scapegoat, American
adolescents hit the road in droves. This impulse crossed all classes. As the
Democratic politician Newton D. Baker wrote in 1932, "The average young
transient of today, we are told by social workers and others who come into
daily contact with him, is a normal boy from a substantial family."

This response was in keeping with the ethos of a country built by mobile labour and guided by a dream of the frontier that was still fresh. As the *Harper's*
writer Lillian Symes stated in late 1933, America had "a radical, even a violently radical tradition. But it is a tradition of individualistic, not collectivistic
radicalism. The individual buccaneer, not the leader of unpopular causes, has
been the American hero. Anarchism is undoubtedly the philosophy most native to our temperament, as it is the most futile in a complicated industrial
world. The country attracts the restless individualist."

■   ■   ■

Young Americans were not the only ones to be affected by the Depression:
many older men and women hit the road, and their numbers were swelled after several successive years of drought in the midwestern and southern plains.
But many wanderers were all-American boys fired with the visions of freedom
offered by the movies and the automobile. At the age of sixteen, Jim Mitchell
decided to run away from his Wisconsin home in 1933: "The quickest and easiest way to get out was to jump a train and go somewhere," he remembered.
"We thought it was the magic carpet—the click of the rails—romance."

The overt reason for leaving was to find work. Seasonal migrations were
triggered by the availability of casual labour. In summer, there would be a
movement west for the harvest fruit-picking jobs. In the autumn, there would
be a general movement out of the country into the larger cities. Thanks to its
warm climate, California was a favoured destination, Woody Guthrie's "Garden of Eden", with up to a thousand adolescents a month pouring into Hollywood at the end of 1933. It became so popular that the city "declared war" on
all transients, blockading the border for several weeks during 1936.

The overwhelming majority rode the rails: at least on the trains there was
the possibility of mutual protection. Even within this primitive community,

however, there was a hierarchy. At the top there were the aristocratic "passenger stiffs", speed-obsessed youths who rode express trains. The vast majority of road bums rode the freights. Those who travelled by the California Fruit Express were one step below the passenger stiffs, followed by those who chose silk trains, then manifest freight trains, then accommodation freights, and finally the majority who rode gondolas, boxcars, or granite cars.

There were many hazards. The trains were dangerous, particularly if not converted for passenger travel. The precariousness of the young transients' purchase made them liable to fall off in cold weather or bumpy conditions. Thousands died anonymously and alone. At the same time, the notoriously violent railway policemen, called "bulls", ruled their domain by whatever means they saw fit. Once the train had stopped in a small town, the young tramp faced being thrown into jail, being conscripted into forced labour, or being given electric shocks and told to get out of town.

Much safer bets were the large cities, where the sheer number of new arrivals made some coherent response necessary. The first port of call was the bread line, which might be a mission, a Salvation Army flophouse, or a municipal welfare station. After registering, the young tramp would receive an identification slip, which usually entitled its bearer to at least one meal. And that was all. The cities might have been safer, but the competition for jobs and money was even more intense. Finding somewhere to rest was also difficult. In the early days of the Depression, thousands slept in parks and public places.

Permanently exhausted, young runaways quickly found that theirs was no yellow brick road. Jim Mitchell had "thought it would be a glamorous life—'By God, we're going to find our fortune. Someone out there needs us.' The hell they did." Within the cut-throat competition for any job, exploitation and ill treatment were rife. Some road kids would even work for no money, just to be able to eat. The work that was available was temporary, usually agricultural, and offered very low payment for gruelling hours.

Young transients aged prematurely. A contemporary study by an Ohio social worker concluded that they "have known no financial security, have come from homes broken for that reason, harried, kicked around, and dazed by things beyond their control. Lost, resentful because they have aged too quickly, they cry for something they cannot get from their own group. They are too old and yet too young. They have seen too much and know too much—have thought too little. They may be sixteen to twenty-one in years, but in some things they are thirty, and in others ten."

Some young runaways took to banding together for mutual support and protection. Groups of up to a dozen would travel together and settle in their own hobo jungles. Locations away from human habitation were preferred. Whether near the outfall of a Mississippi sewer or in a deserted clearing close to the railroad, up to fifty young transients would live in a self-policing micro-society. Minehan found "that the child tramps, left to themselves and living as outcasts of society, develop rules and regulations, elect leaders, and enforce their punishments without the aid of elders".

Conflicts could erupt for any reason. The most common were along racial lines. Negroes formed a small percentage of young transients, nearly a quarter of all the fifteen-to-twenty-four age group in one 1935 survey. For many of their white counterparts, it was their first unsegregated experience: the atmo-sphere was of tolerance at best. Young Negroes were highly vulnerable. There was always the component of sexual jealousy—Minehan reported a group of "black boys, seventeen" boasting about their "relations with white girls or women"—and in the lawless transient world this was an explosive mixture.

Just how much became apparent in 1931, when a group of nine Negroes, aged between twelve and twenty years, were arrested in Alabama. For the Scottsboro Boys, tramping ended in a lifelong nightmare. "All of us were rid-ing the freight for the same reason, to go somewhere and find work," remem-bered Haywood Patterson. "Our families were hard pushed. The only ones I knew were the other three from Chattanooga. Our fathers couldn't support us, and we wanted to help out, or at least put food in our bellies by ourselves. We were freight-hiking to Memphis when the fight happened."

The trouble started when four of the nine boarded a gondola, partly filled with crushed gravel, that also housed two young white women, dressed in men's overalls, and seven other young men. The name-calling started: "Nig-ger bastard, this is a white man's train. You better get off. All you black bas-tards better get off!" Patterson returned the insult in kind and the whites backed off. They returned later, but Patterson had found reinforcements in five other "colored guys", and the aggressors were routed. Patterson even res-cued one of the whites as he was about to fall off the train at speed.

When the train stopped at the next station, however, all the young tran-sients involved in the fight were met by an armed posse and taken to the Scottsboro jail. There the nine young Negroes found that the two white girls, Ruby Bates and Victoria Price, had accused them of rape. Patterson thought this was because "the white fellows got plenty sore at the whupping we gave them". This accusation was dynamite within the depths of Alabama. From the very first moment of their incarceration, the Scottsboro Boys faced near lynch-ings and an almost certain death sentence.

After a farcical trial, during which the prosecutor exhorted the court, "Guilty or not guilty, let's get rid of these niggers," the nine were found guilty and sentenced to death. Despite a storm of protest, the Alabama courts dug in and, in the first retrial, again sentenced the nine to death. By this time, the judicial lynching had became an international scandal: the support of figures as diverse as Nancy Cunard, Albert Einstein, and the author Thomas Mann was followed by a series of demonstrations in Europe and America, culminating in a huge May 1933 protest march.[2]

The Scottsboro Boys case exposed the dark side of America's race relations and the dog-eat-dog life of its wandering adolescents. Sharing the same space with the denizens of the underworld, some road kids began to emulate gangsters by packing guns and extorting money. Even more worrying for the authorities was their anger against the system that had failed them. Like other youth experts, Minehan thought that bolshevism was on the rise: "Practically all boys and girls on the road, whether Communists or not, believe that America is going to have a revolution soon if things do not improve."

In the 1920s, America's adolescents had received unprecedented attention as the standard-bearers of the new mass consumerism: they had been charged with being "embryonic buyers" and "the customers of tomorrow". After the crash, this privilege had evaporated: in the words of one middle-class wanderer, it felt like being "de-princed". Although becoming a hobo was an extreme reaction, the boy and girl tramps represented, within a nation that idealized youth, an unpleasantly direct reminder of the disaster that had befallen the continent.

This was not supposed to happen. The sheer existence of the young tramps, let alone their appearance and demeanour, served as a shockingly public polemic: there is, they appeared to say, no future either for us or for our country. *Boy and Girl Tramps of America* took up this cudgel, heralding the new mood of reform after the Great Crash. The impulse that had withered after Prohibition took hold again with the sudden return to a nineteenth-century cityscape that was "overrun with groups of hoodlums and predators".

With a wary eye on Russia and Germany, the reformers were very concerned about the possibility of revolution. However, the individualistic nature

2. After this march, the Alabamian authorities were forced to order another retrial, with the same result for Patterson and Clarence Neems. Although the convictions were overturned by the US Supreme Court, Patterson was tried a fourth time in January 1936 and sentenced to seventy-five years of "a living death" in an Alabama prison. While four of the nine were finally freed in the summer of 1937, Patterson suffered the death of both parents. "Nothing seemed right after that. I hated to believe anything, hated everybody."

of the American tradition—embodied by the wanderers' own quest for an illusory frontier—militated against collective action. Despite the increasingly violent escalation of the country's labour disputes, like the fatal march against the Ford Motor plant in March 1932, communism failed to take hold as a mass movement. There were young American Communists, but they remained in a tiny minority among their peers.

However, youth experts and parents alike noticed a new mood of intransigence even among the vast majority of youths who still defined their future in terms of work or career (boys) and marriage or domestic life (girls). When they returned to Muncie in June 1935, Robert and Helen Merrell Lynd found that in the decade since their first visit "a more self-conscious sub-culture of the young had grown up". They observed that "adult imposed restraints of obedience to parents, school and public opinion have weakened further as the adult world has crumbled under the depression".

The adolescents born in the later 1910s were emerging into a world very different from what they had been promised. Instead of a youth consumer boom, they were facing unemployment. This predisposed them to a harsh scrutiny of the adult world, which was only exacerbated by the way that all classes and all ages routinely flouted the Volstead Act. Prohibition had, by the early 1930s, eroded respect for the law and all authority. As one high school group told *Parents* magazine in 1932, "You can hardly blame us for distrusting your standards, when some of them . . . have proved so obviously foolish."

Within this climate, the old assumptions of deference were no longer valid. In his 1931 book, *Personality in Its Teens*, the Christian youth worker W. Ryland Boorman quoted one of his high school informants: "You take a lad of seventeen, hold him and rule him with an iron hand. What will happen? It will not be long before you have a sullen, back-biting, stubborn lad, if he is anything like me. This boy may go to Sunday school, stay for church, and take communion. Why? Because he has to do so. Not long after this, he may break all bounds and 'haul freight' for a long sought after freer atmosphere."

This was nothing less than a clash between generations. "It is our impression that no two generations of Americans have ever faced each other across as wide a gap in their customary attitudes and behavior as have American parents and children since the World War," the Lynds concluded. "The cumulating rapidity of social change, including every section of living from industry and business to religion, education, sex and family life, is widening in something resembling a geometrical ratio the gap between the things that were 'right' yesterday and those that make sense to the new generation of today."

American youth had once again become a problem, rather than a market. During the first half of the 1930s, the enthusiastic boosterism of youth that had flourished during the previous decade was replaced by a series of concerned and critical inquiries. The future of the nation was at stake. Thomas Minehan concluded his exhaustive survey of young transients with an impassioned polemic for further state involvement: "Tomorrow American youth must be led. It must be led by men who know where they are going, where the country is going, and where they want youth to go."

. . .

While the Children's Army hit the headlines, many American adolescents continued with their education. Although reduced by the Depression, the number of American seventeen-year-olds remaining in high school had multiplied by at least five- or sixfold since 1900. Within the high school grade system, adolescent immersion in their immediate peer world was total. Just as 1920s college youth had experienced the sense that they were an important social group, their younger, high-school-age siblings began to feel the same.

The institution of youth as a separate class began to reap an unexpected harvest. The Lynds noted that at Middletown's Central High, "The whole range of cultural tolerances and intolerances grind against each other; the child of parents who think it 'cute' and 'attractive' for a daughter to enamel her nails, use rouge, have a crisp 'permanent', and 'learn to handle boys', sits next to the daughter of a family in which the parents are engaged in a quiet but determined campaign to circumvent the influence of the movies and keep their daughter 'simple', 'unaffected' and 'healthy-minded'."

To Ryland Boorman, the peer world of the American high school, while embodying all the hope of the future, also undermined "the influence of the home and the church". He observed that "the increase of leisure time, often accompanied by large amounts of spending money, is leading the way to new forms of mischief. The degree to which the present generation of young people have gone mad over pleasure-hunting is disconcerting to many adults. The new freedom in the relation of girls and boys is the cause also of no little extra confusion."

The strong allure of peer pressure was one of the issues tackled by a whole series of new magazines aimed by church and scouting groups at America's adolescents during the early 1930s: *American Girl, Everygirl,* and *Scholastic.* "How can a girl be pretty and popular," one high school student asked *Everygirl,* if she was forced by her parents to wear "woollen underwear, cotton stockings and flat boyish oxfords?" Rather than proscribe or deny such pressures, these magazines offered sensible advice, assuming that adolescents would share the common sense and conformist values they promoted.

The existence of these magazines reflected the extent to which parents had ceded control over their children's lives. They exposed the real concern that there was little common ground between the generations, but resolved conflicts by reasserting traditional expectations. For boys, the most urgent issue was employment. Magazines like *American Boy* reinforced the competitive ethic: "You will be working for a living and fighting for a career in a competition that is as keen, as remorseless, as subtle as you will ever know." Girls, in contrast, were being prepared to marry and preside over the home.

The greatest source of the tension between parents and children was sex. As the headline in the January 1932 issue of *Ladies' Home Journal* had it: "DOES A GIRL HAVE TO PET TO BE POPULAR?" The young woman who posed this question had found her parents no help: "They, in repentance of their own youth, no doubt, were determined that I should be sweet and chaste and pure." Her dilemma was whether to enjoy her youth "while she had it", or "to turn her back on the Road to Popularity, give up smoking and the rest, for staying home every night gazing fondly and dreamily at the once lively telephone".

The responsibility for enforcing sexual limits was placed not on boys but on girls. Finding their parents oscillating between confusion and prescription, young girls turned to advice columnists like *Everygirl's* Aunt Cherry, who advised abstinence: "Just say to yourself, 'It isn't time yet.'" However, this did not always work. With teenage pregnancy remaining the ultimate taboo, middle-class parents in particular were encouraged to collaborate with these new youth experts in shaping their children's expectations rather than issuing counter-productive orders.

One method was to involve themselves in their children's social life so that they could vet prospective suitors. As one correspondent to *Parents* observed, it was possible to isolate the unsuitable by introducing her daughter to the "right" crowd and letting "the relentless intolerance of youth for one who doesn't fit" take its course. This same approach of suggestion could be used for other contentious issues like smoking and cosmetics. America's parents were being encouraged towards consultation rather than authoritarian control.

This change was enforced by several factors. One problem was the unavailability of sex education at school: "Our high school does nothing about sex education because we don't dare to," a "well-informed" teacher told the Lynds. Outright interdiction could also create defiance, as in the case of a sixteen-year-old girl who, after being warned off by her parents, had unprotected intercourse with the inevitable result. When she took up with a fifteen-year-old boy, "the fact that she felt that she was doing something of which her parents would not approve satisfied her because of the feeling of independence it gave her".

At the same time, traditional methods of control were competing with a media that continued to stimulate basic human drives. The Depression had not eradicated consumerism: the Lynds noticed that, in mid-1930s Muncie, the "more passive, more formal, more organized, more mechanized, and more commercialized" leisure patterns of the 1920s were continuing apace. Of these, the most troubling were the movies: visited by 28 million adolescent Americans a week, they were seen by reformers and moralists alike as "a menace to the mental and moral life of the coming generation".

The psychic power of movies was recognized by the final survey conducted by the Hoover government during 1932. In "The Agencies of Communication", Malcolm Willey and Stuart A. Rice reported that editors of popular motion picture magazines were "deluged" with letters from viewers that were "filled with self-revelations which indicate, sometimes deliberately, more often unconsciously, the influence of the screen upon manners, dress codes, and matters of romance. They disclose the degree to which ego stereotypes may be molded by the stars of the screen."

. . .

A major case in point was MGM's 1931 blockbuster *The Public Enemy*, an "essentially true story" of a young Irishman drawn from street-gang life to bootlegging and gangland execution. In his breakthrough role as Tom Powers, James Cagney was electrifying as a new American demon. Here was the nervy, nihilistic young gangster, with a hint of stylized effeteness under the bravado, whose life—epitomized by the infamous scene where he shoved a cut grapefruit into girlfriend Mae Clarke's face—was one long orgiastic spasm of violence and sadism.

The sheer glee and energy of Cagney's performance undercut the overt moral of the film's end: that crime never pays. Even his protracted, balletic expiration was glamorous. His main foil, Jean Harlow, was similarly outstanding. As opposed to the other feminine leads—the perky good mate offered by Joan Blondell, or the whining doormat played by Mae Clarke—Harlow was Cagney's equal. Her dyed platinum blonde hair and sinuous movements, together with her honking accent, abstracted her from a recognizable youth type into a nervily assertive sex goddess: the Bad Girl incarnate.

It was exactly the blurring of fantasy and reality that made pictures like *The Public Enemy* such a concern. Researchers found that young viewers disregarded the moralistic opening titles and took what they wanted from the picture. One young delinquent, dressed in Cagney style, approved of the actor but not his demise: "'Dat's de boloney dey give you in de pitchers. Dey always die or got canned. Day ain't true. Looka Joe Citro, Pedro Salami an' Tony Vendetta.' The names he mentioned were those of 'big shots', or gangsters, in his own neighbourhood who seemed to thrive unpunished."

The bootlegging gangster of the 1920s had returned as a hero. The reformers also zeroed in on Edward G. Robinson's memorably sinister performance as Rico in 1930's *Little Caesar,* which "swept certain groups of boys of the region like a cyclone". Gangster movies made crime "alluring and criminality distinguished" to the inner-city young: "Almost all of those in this group used Cagney's friendly 'One, two' punch to the rib, chin and shoulder. They imitated his little jig, his big Cagney swagger. They smiled like Cagney and even wore spearhead shirts like Cagney."

The movies' "mass production of flaming youth" became the object of active condemnation, as the moralists sought a new target after Prohibition. The reformer Henry Forman held that the movies promoted the ready assumption among the young "that luxury, extravagance, easy money are the inalienable right of everyone. The recent economic depression has shown us one result of an almost universally accepted concept that wealth is easily attainable. The study of various young delinquents shows to what an extent the same concept derived from the movies has played havoc with the youthful lives."

Published in 1934, Forman's book *Our Movie-Made Children* collected the research conducted in the early 1930s by the Motion Picture Research Council, a pressure group dedicated to movie censorship. One of the central planks of their argument was the sheer number of pictures that dealt with sex and violence. One researcher identified sixteen "goals" depicted in 115 movies: among the top ten goals were "revenge", coming in at number 5, and "crime for gain", at number 7. In 1930, another expert judged that 72 per cent of all movies dealt with the three major themes of "crime, sex and love".

Forman thought that this was like poisoned water entering the mains: "If unwatched, it is extremely likely to create a haphazard, promiscuous and undesirable national consciousness." From one survey of 500 high school students, one-third reported "definite imitation from the pictures in the way of lovemaking". In a round-up of over 250 delinquent girls, more than half declared that "they felt like having a man make love to them" after seeing a hot picture like *The Pagan.* "When I see movies that excite me I always want to go home and do the same things that I saw them do," one sixteen-year-old admitted.

Obviously, Hollywood was not in the business of making documentaries.

But then, it suited the moralists to present youth as a blank slate inscribed with Hollywood's filthy graffiti. In fact, the young audience was far more selective than they allowed. A verbatim transcript between four college girls showed that they had a firm grasp on the movies' ability to shape reality:

"—Her idea of college is Bebe Daniels and Richard Dix."

"*One Minute To Play?*"

"Yes, that combined with *Flaming Youth.*"

"Well, you know a lot of us have that in mind when we come away to college."

"It doesn't take us long to get rid of it, though. But the ones who never get there are the ones who idealize the rah-rah stuff. They really believe college is nothing more than a big house party."

The real problem was that the extreme behaviour of the delinquents surveyed in *Our Movie-Made Children* was but a small amplification of American cultural values. The country's breakdown seemed to be reflected in the behaviour of its youth, and instead of going for the cause, the moralists decided to target the symptom. They felt that the movie industry peddled erotic and violent distortions of youth behaviour with hypnotic skill: successfully deployed, this argument brought renewed calls for movie censorship that resulted, in 1934, in a greatly strengthened Production Code.

Fears that the young were being overstimulated by the American mass media were stoked by the burgeoning pulp magazine industry. "Smashing Cleveland's Opium Ring to Save White Slave Girls" was the way that *Jim Jam Jems*, published in Minnesota, promoted its expose of "drugs, aphrodisiacs and oriental monsters" in this unlikely midwestern setting. From 1932, *Exposed* offered an even more direct denunciation of a "Mad Generation": "Kidnappers at eighteen! Thrill-killers at sixteen! There is something wrong with a civilization that turns so many boys to lives of crime! WHAT CAN WE DO?"

. . .

If America's response to a collective crisis followed the nation's founding frontier spirit, then its restless individualism fuelled new types of lawbreaking. Having established itself during Prohibition, the invisible government of organized crime was not about to disband: instead, it diversified into protection rackets, illegal drugs, kidnapping, and bank robbery. These last two activities were the most visible signs of the changed Depression landscape as, according to the press, the Midwest seethed with dangerous gangs like those headed by Ma Barker, John Dillinger, Machine Gun Kelly, and Pretty Boy Floyd.

The old models of gang and ethnic organization had been supplanted by a new ethic: mobile, atomized, and randomly lethal. Thrill-killers had proliferated in the decade since the Leopold/Loeb trial. During 1933, the crime rate exploded: there were 12,000 murders in the United States, 3,000 kidnappings, and 150,000 robberies. The most famous young criminals of the early 1930s fitted right into this pattern: driving thousands of miles through the back roads of Texas, Oklahoma, Arizona, and New Mexico—a new internal frontier—and killing at will during a series of botched bank robberies.

Born in 1909 and 1910, respectively, Clyde Barrow and Bonnie Parker were not the period's most successful criminals, but they were the most celebrated. Their story was classically simple: a fatal folie à deux between a hardened young delinquent and an intelligent but exhibitionist girl. Within the eighteen months after they went on the run in late summer 1932, Bonnie and Clyde killed twelve people. They were thieves and murderers, but, thanks to their frequent media bulletins, they became legends for their daring escapes, breathtaking speed, and psychopathic violence.

Whether through Bonnie's doggerel poem "Suicide Sal", their posed photos with a gun, or even the cheeky endorsement of the V-8's "sustained speed and freedom from trouble" sent by Clyde Barrow to Henry Ford himself, the two were media-savvy to an unprecedented extent. They even predicted their own demise: "The road gets dimmer and dimmer," Bonnie wrote in "The Story of Bonnie and Clyde", the self-mythologizing poem circulated in the national media after the pair were finally intercepted and killed by the police in May 1934.

What was so galling to the authorities, already hamstrung by laws that prevented the police from pursuing fugitives over state lines, was the fact that so many people celebrated this pair of violent killers as folk heroes. There were mob scenes reminiscent of those at Rudolph Valentino's funeral when their bodies were laid in state in Arcadia, Louisiana: when thousands mobbed the funeral parlour, the owner was reduced to spraying them with embalming fluid.[3] Appalled, the director of the Federal Bureau of Investigation mounted a concerted campaign to stamp out this dangerous glamour.

After the well-publicized exterminations of Bonnie and Clyde, John Dillinger, and Pretty Boy Floyd during 1934, J. Edgar Hoover got his federal powers the next year, removing at one stroke the antiquated legal restrictions. That same year, he launched a whole new breed of crime-busting supermen on the

---

3. The shattered V-8 in which the pair died was still being exhibited forty years later. It was sold in 1973 for $175,000, according to *Time* magazine: $20,000 more than Hitler's Mercedes.

American public: the G-men. With books like Courtney Ryley Cooper's *Ten Thousand Public Enemies,* Hoover turned the fear of crime into an industry. By 1936, millions of American children were consuming G-men products specifically aimed at youth: badges, toy tommy guns, pyjamas, even magazines.

Alarmed by the "mental explosions" of youth, reformers like Will Hays and J. Edgar Hoover sought to control American adolescents in the traditional, moralistic manner even though Prohibition had shown that this was a dangerous route to take. The new generation of progressives also believed that America's young were, as the "products of a psychopathic period", far too vulnerable to "the escape media of movies, radios, fast motors, and alcohol". However, they sought to tackle the effects of the Depression by influencing the reform of youth structures and youth policy.

The angry wanderers and the psychotic gangsters offered a stark warning: the techniques of mass control were failing. President Hoover's laissez-faire approach had brought the country to the brink of disaster, and a new motivating social principle was needed. In August 1932 the economic historian George Soule observed that Americans were "in the midst of a great social revolution". Capitalism had been found wanting, but would be reformed by a new managerial class who rejected its "outmoded" competitive ethos. It was time to inject some socialism into the individualistic heartland.

Soule's prophecy that "a shift in the governing powers will take place, probably by constitutional means", was borne out by the election of a new president, Franklin Delano Roosevelt, in 1932. With a ticket that pledged "a new deal for the American people", Roosevelt instituted a whole set of new programmes during the productive "hundred days" of the 1933 special session of Congress. With measures ranging from agricultural quotas to new labour rights and actual relief, the New Deal was seen as nothing less than a form of "state capitalism".

The New Deal immediately reduced the numbers of unemployed by one-quarter during the spring and summer of 1933. By extending the reach of the state into everyday life, Roosevelt reduced any immediate threat of political and social disruption. With revolution thus averted, capitalism did continue, but with a different face. Instead of the 1920s principle of "crass materialism", the thirties would be run on a pioneer vision of hard work for the future collective good. However, that didn't mean a total change in American aspirations: the consumer ideal had not been totally supplanted, just deferred.

It was one of the new administration's first tasks to deal with transient youth. Within a month of acceding to the presidency, Roosevelt created the Civilian Conservation Corps, available to unmarried men between eighteen and twenty-five, which offered thirty dollars a month in return for working on public projects. Within three months, one-quarter of a million young men were settled in nearly fifteen hundred camps. In general, the experience was positive: as a grateful Jim Mitchell remembered, the scheme "shaped my life, which had no direction".

The corps offered proper food, team structure, and a sense of achievement, invaluable to young men who had previously seen themselves as society's rejects. Its projects included park building, tree planting, beach clearance, and dam construction. Although enthusiasts like Jim Mitchell found "a wonderful social mixture", there were limitations to the scheme. With its lower age limit of eighteen, it failed to pull in more than a small proportion of wandering youth, some of whom—used to their freedom—balked at the regimentation of these "Roosevelt roosts".

Other New Deal provisions began to alleviate the worst aspects of the transient life. The Temporary Emergency Relief Act of 1933 threw the impetus onto local communities to offer transients at least "one free meal, work for the second meal, a bed on the floor, and eviction before the second or third day". At the same time, the government established a Federal Transient Relief Service, which provided for hundreds of transient centres that worked to ship runaways back home or to place them in paid work or Civilian Conservation Corps camps.

The government encouraged American youth to stay in school, where they were under some degree of adult control. Robert and Helen Merrell Lynd observed that "in a world in which the search for jobs has become—and may remain—more difficult than in the past, the schools must effectively delay this participation and become a place where adolescents and young adults may contentedly, and Middletown hopes fruitfully, spend their time as long as possible". By 1936, nearly two-thirds of all high-school-age Americans were in school, although the number of transients was slow to drop.

This was not universally popular: many American adolescents wanted nothing more than to join the adult world. As one sixteen-year-old told a radio audience, "Most people our age want to grow up as fast as they can but their parents don't want them to." Perhaps out of this guilt, parenting during the 1930s became more "democratic": a trend parodied by Sinclair Lewis's novel *Prodigal Parents,* in which adults buckle under their children's insatiable demands. Increased high school attendance, however, had the effect of delaying adulthood and increasing the strength of the adolescent peer society.

The First Lady, Eleanor Roosevelt, also made youth her specific concern. She sponsored the formation of the American Youth Congress in late 1934, which became, according to one of its leaders, Joseph Lash, the "student brain of the New Deal". Sympathetic to student politics, Mrs Roosevelt managed to persuade the AYC left-wingers to work together with the White House instead of deriding established politics and the New Deal. In turn, the patronage of the president's wife helped partially to defuse the threat of youth unrest.

Eleanor Roosevelt was highly aware that America's provisions for youth did not go far enough. "I have moments of real terror, when I think we may be losing this generation," she wrote in 1935. "We have got to bring these people into the active life of the community and make them feel that they are necessary." Five years into the Depression, the threat of revolution had not disappeared. Furthermore, a new kind of Fascist mass youth politics had emerged after Roosevelt's inauguration. As Maxine Brown wrote in her crusading survey of *The Lost Generation*, "The German situation is ever before us."

This failure of the New Deal to improve life for any more than a small percentage of America's lost generation was witnessed by the Lynds in the Midwest. Whether it took the form of cynicism, petty crime, or "smoldering rebellion", "the problem of idle youth was emphatically present in Middletown in 1935". The children of the working classes were the most disillusioned, but they also reported the "quiet bitterness" of "a clean-cut graduate of the local high school and college", who told them, "Our group feel we're thoroughly stopped. There's just no future for our generation."

This situation was repeated throughout the continent: by May 1935, there were 2,877,000 sixteen- to twenty-four-year-olds on relief. The spikes of political polarization were waiting in the wings. On the left, various radical student groups amalgamated into the American Student Union. Joseph Lash recalled that the formation of the ASU coincided with new instructions from Moscow, which, "faced with the growing menace of Hitlerite Germany, made an about face and came into the League of Nations and instructed all its Communists to organize Popular Fronts".

By mid-decade, Fascist politics were being pumped into millions of American homes through the syndicated broadcasts of the Catholic priest Charles E. Coughlin. Having been a rabid New Dealer, Coughlin had followed the populist line all the way to the far right, praising Mussolini and Louisiana governor Huey Long. America also had the Ku Klux Klan, which began to forge links with the various Nazi-sympathetic groups formed by German Americans after Hitler's rise to power—soon collected into the Amerika-Deutscher Volksbund.

For New Dealers like Charles W. Taussig, this polarization made state intervention all the more urgent. "Vendors of gilt substitutes find willing converts to political and social creeds that are destructive to much that this Nation stands for," he wrote. "Now, if ever, we must invoke our cardinal principles of free thought, free speech, and free education. Under the proper direction and leadership, our youth can and will develop a more definite and hopeful philosophy of life. Unless we educate the youth of today to function intelligently in a modern Democracy, democratic government is doomed."

President Roosevelt had hitherto fought shy of spending more government money on America's adolescents. He also expressed the concern that "a special Federal youth agency, as such, might be misconstrued as a step towards the political organization or regimentation of youth". However, with six million young Americans under the age of eighteen living on relief,[4] he changed his mind. After persistent lobbying by Eleanor Roosevelt and Charles Taussig, Roosevelt established the National Youth Administration in June 1935 and allotted $50 million for its use in the next fiscal year.

The National Youth Administration aimed to give financial help to high school, college, and graduate students between the ages of sixteen and twenty-five. But its provisions did not include free relief: like the Wizard of Oz, President Roosevelt held fast to the American rule that "in this country, everyone must pay for everything he gets". In practice, the body's work projects took young unmarrieds between the ages of eighteen and twenty-four and found them employment in exchange for an average monthly pay of $15.73. Eventually, over 150 different jobs were on offer, ranging from clerical to conservation work.

The formation of this body marked a significant change in America's treatment of its youth. Instead of being left to fend for themselves as they had been in the 1890s, American adolescents had come in from the cold as an important part of governmental aims and policy. Just as the Depression had helped to give them a voice—in the many inquiries that sought to discover their feelings and political leanings—it also sealed their status as a valued cohort in American life. However, this would only swell the tide of youthful discontent, as what was offered as a privilege would come to be seen as a right.

4. One-seventh of the total cohort.

CHAPTER 20

Biff Boys and the Red Menace

The Polarization of British Youth

• • •

Every year new generations of schoolboys were appearing, each generation push-
ing him and his a little nearer to that incredible abyss of manhood and the dole.
Why, the supply of boys was inexhaustible; there were millions of them at school;
Marlowe's could keep going for ever. What was to become of him and his when
their time was served? Where would openings occur if every firm was playing
Marlowe's game? If! A horrible suspicion clutched him. Suppose that this
present was an established new order, that once a fellow came out of his time he
remained unemployed for ever!

—Walter Greenwood, *Love on the Dole* (1933)

UNEMPLOYED YOUTHS, THE NORTH OF ENGLAND, 1935

DURING 1935, a left-wing writer came upon a group of British youths called "The Unemployed Gang". One of them recounted exactly how he came to find himself on the scrapheap at seventeen: "OUT at sixteen because the guv'nor wanted to take on an errand-boy who'd do my job cheaper. . . . At a fruiterer's, helped at the counter, cleaned the shop, cycle-delivery boy, hours 8.30 a.m. to 7 p.m., oh, and Saturdays when we started at 8.30 a.m. and worked . . . till we finished. Wages 10s. a week. I had a cycle accident off duty and found the job gone when I got out of hospital. . . . I'll never get another job: I'm too old!"

Just like Thomas Minehan had done in America, W. F. Lestrange travelled for thousands of miles throughout his homeland, England and Wales, to find the stories of the Depression-devastated young. He could barely restrain his rage at what he discovered: "I hope this book will make you realize that some millions of youngsters whom the State (and that means you) is misusing and wasting are practically indistinguishable—except that far too many of them are undernourished—from your own sons and daughters, brothers and sisters."

Lestrange's exposé, *Wasted Lives*, combined government statistics and oral testimony. He recalled one typical case: "A little while ago I was in the Unemployed Rooms (as an honorary member at the time). I was playing table-tennis with Trevor. Trevor is nearly eighteen. I beat him in the fourth game (he had won the other three). To flatter my injured vanity (for I think I can play table-tennis), I said, 'You're jolly good, Trevor.'" The young man had worked as a delivery boy but had been sacked when he reached sixteen: his enormous brown eyes "were emphasised by the hollowness of his cheeks".

"The sing song Welsh intonation was lost in an ugly rasp as he replied, 'So I ought to be. I'm here every day at ten and play til dinner-time unless I go to the Bureau. There's nothing to do in the afternoon, either, so I come up here and play whenever the table's free. Ping-pong: knocking——little celluloid balls about! That's my life. All I'll ever do is play ping-pong. When I was a kid I thought I'd be . . . wanted to be . . .' He ran out of the room and left me to think things out. I rather think he was crying."

Tackling educational policy, the iniquities of the apprentice system, and child labour, Lestrange's polemic was intended, like Minehan's *Boy and Girl Tramps of America,* to shock its readers, and then to have an impact on government policy. This was not the project of a total outsider. Working with the assistance of the Socialist League, a small left-wing group affiliated with the Labour Party, Lestrange contacted government ministries, trade unions, large manufacturers, national newspapers, and city councils in order to present a thorough picture of British youth's hopelessness.

As part of his diagnosis, Lestrange paid particular attention to what were euphemistically called the "Special Areas", the former industrial centres of Britain like South Wales and the North-east that had been worst hit by the Depression. His photographs exposed the filth and the detritus left behind by a totally collapsed economy, most devastatingly in a sequence that showed the boarded-up streets of Tyneside—the bleak locale that would throw up the decade's most famous protest of the unemployed, the Jarrow March of 1936.

These were not "Special Areas" but "Derelict Areas", where degraded living conditions went hand in hand with "the reminders of the horror—derelict steel works, derelict coal mines—rust and slag heaps—ruinous buildings and stagnant, ruined machinery. It is the abomination of desolation—and it is in the midst of all this that little children are living out their heritage, that boys and girls are eating out their hearts in hopeless despair, that the older men and women are asking God why ever He permitted them to be born—why He allowed them to procreate children whose heritage is death in life."

With its innovative layouts and unrelenting concentration on Britain's underbelly, *Wasted Lives* was very much a product of its decade. During the 1920s, the focus of media attention on youth had been towards elites and various forms of pleasure, whether encouraged or condemned. During the 1930s, the focus was on the non-elite, the disadvantaged: the values of the previous decade were discredited and obsolete. This was an inevitable result of the crash, but it also underscored the very real concern that these desperate conditions might help to foster further political polarization.

The signs were everywhere. In America, the young unemployed hit the road, a response that exemplified the energy of a youthful, mobile country: even so, they were seen as the potential incubators of revolutionary feeling. In Germany, they were fodder for Fascist regimentation under the guise of self-rule. In the United Kingdom, if they had some spirit, they went hiking. Otherwise they hung around in defiant groups on deserted street corners. Lestrange's photographs captured them frozen in their boredom and bravado, silhouetted against decayed urban vistas. Were they a revolution waiting to happen?

■ ■ ■

The initial impact of the Great Crash in Britain had been muted. Unemployment had stayed around the million mark in the late 1920s. But as the numbers rose to the eventual peak of three million in 1933, the conditions that had previously been confined to the "Special Areas" spread throughout the whole country. Unemployment and poverty became systemic during the 1930s. Poor diet and unsanitary living conditions bred diseases like smallpox, influenza, and diphtheria, while depression and mental illness flourished: suicides were common.

Youth bore much of the opprobrium directed at the unemployed, as they were considered by the authorities to be responsible for their own fate. As *The Times* pronounced in January 1930, "A large proportion of boys and girls these days are almost being trained to lounge through life, averse from work and impatient of control, taking no more than a tepid interest in anything beyond the spectacles of the football ground and the cinema." However, as writers began to expose the scandal of Britain's living dead, they found that the reality was quite different.

Whereas books about workers had been thin on the ground during the 1920s, a sudden deluge of what the commentator Ethel Mannin called "sociological novels" followed the Crash: F. C. Boden's *Miner*, Walter Greenwood's *Love on the Dole*, A. J. Cronin's *Hatter's Castle*, James Hanley's *Boy*, Alexander McArthur and H. Kingsley Long's *No Mean City*. Both social realist documents and impassioned polemics, they helped to define the style and the preoccupations of the new decade—from ennui to engagement, from Mayfair to Salford. The young were no longer bright but wasted.

As if dammed by a decade of neglect, this flood of books revisited a whole generation of working-class history. They spanned the first wave of unemployment in the early 1920s, the effect of a prolonged and bitter mining strike, and the urban subculture of violent gang life. They not only had "the stamp of truth", they also telescoped past and present into a powerful indictment of a society where it did not matter much whether you were actually employed or not. The result was the same: as Harry Hardcastle, the hero of *Love on the Dole*, came to realize, "Ah may as well be in bloody prison."

Love on the Dole dramatized an institutional problem very prevalent in the 1930s: the casual job or "apprenticeship" that ended when legal protection began, at the age of sixteen. However, the apprentice system was shrinking fast during the 1930s, just as employers began to reduce working hours and ignore workers' rights. New technology and automation were another important factor, combined with the time-and-motion imperatives introduced under the guise of "rationalization". "A handful of men working; crowds of unemployed watching," was how Greenwood summarized "modern progress".

Technology and management combined to create human automata: the robot of *Metropolis*, the Epsilons of Huxley's *Brave New World*. The most notorious new technique was pioneered in America by Frederick W. Taylor and introduced in Britain during the 1930s. The constant surveillance of the Bedaux system—a "scientific" time-and-motion study where any job could be broken down into units of measurement that were used to set hourly and daily targets—resulted in even more dehumanized conditions. As the Trade Union

Congress of 1932 stated, "The worker under such a system is made to feel that he is a cog in a machine for increasing output. The tendency is to obliterate individuality and craftsmanship and make the worker merely a machine."

One of the first acts of the new national government was the introduction of the means test in late 1931: this aimed to deny "transitional benefit" to claimants with savings or support from relatives. The policy of reducing benefit had been suggested by the May Report, which recommended public spending cuts of £96 million, two-thirds of which was to come out of dole payments. The means test was applied "mercilessly" at a local level. In just over two months after its implementation, over a quarter of a million men and women had their benefit cut off.

The means test also reduced the motivation to work, as any extra money would be removed from the benefit claimed by other members of the family. W. F. Lestrange observed that this was a "crushing burden laid on the shoulders" of the youth expected to support their families. He cited the story of Joe, a Londoner:

As a good citizen he had supported his family for four years; he was then nineteen. No, he was not a precious father: his family consisted of his father (out of work indefinitely following an injury which carried no compensation), mother, and brother and sister still at school.

Joe was comparatively philosophic about his inability ever to buy a new suit for himself owing to the remainder of the family—one or other of them—always needing new apparel more urgently than himself.

Joe and I discussed marriage. He said (less philosophically): "A fat chance I'll ever have of getting spliced—with a ready-made family to look after. P'raps Bernie'll get a job next year in a shop—or p'raps there'll be a miracle and I'll get a rise."

The miracle occurred a few days later. Joe was promoted and got an increase of ten shillings a week. He was radiant, talked of a new outfit, spoke about the girl he was "nuts" about. On the Saturday Joe looked like death.

"What's the trouble," I asked.

The boy scowled: he said, "You mighta told me. You're supposed to know all about these things."

"What things?"

"The Means Test. All my rise means is that my old pot-and-pan (*rhyming slang—old man—father*) draws ten bob less off the Committee. So I'm where I was. Any rise I'll get'll never make no difference to me. I got my family hung around my neck—blast 'em!" He flushed and looked a little sheepish. "I don't mean that really. It's not their fault. But . . . oh hell, what's the point of a bloke working when it's never going to do him any good . . . when he'll never be able to have a life of his own."

Within a hostile, labyrinthine system, the options for the young unemployed were very limited. Emigration to the colonies was a possibility: up to 200,000 men per year took this course. Joining the army was another, although 45 per cent of all applicants were rejected on grounds of ill health. The only schemes available for the young jobless were the labour camps that, like the American Civilian Conservation Corps, were designed to instil discipline. However, most young men of any spirit soon learned to avoid these "slave camps", with their brutal, prisonlike regimes.

The most successful initiatives were local "unemployed welfare centres", social clubs that encouraged hobbies and activities like table tennis, choral singing, and football leagues. Hiking was very popular, partly stimulated by the influence of the *Wandervogel* and the growing numbers of youth hostels. However, within the country's confined spaces, the young British unemployed found it harder to lose themselves than their American counterparts. Escape was only for the most daring—like the young brothers who in spring 1936 stole a trawler and sailed her for over eight thousand miles.

Some of Britain's young could still avail themselves of the consumerism that continued its slow march through the areas of Britain, like the South-east, least affected by the slump. This was, as the writer J. B. Priestley observed, the new American-style world "of filling stations and factories that look like exhibition buildings, of giant cinemas and dance halls and cafes, bungalows with tiny garages, cocktail bars, Woolworths, motor-coaches, wireless, hiking, factory girls looking like actresses, greyhound racing and dirt tracks, swimming pools, and every-thing given away for cigarette coupons".

America remained a powerful beacon for Britain's young. George Orwell noted that rental purchase allowed the jobless young man to "buy himself a suit which, for a little while and at a little distance, looks as though it had been tailored in Savile Row. The girl can look like a fashion plate at an even lower price. You may have three halfpence in your pocket and not a prospect in the world, and only the corner of a leaky bedroom to go to, but in your new clothes you can stand on the street corner, indulging in a private dream of yourself as Clark Gable or Greta Garbo, which compensates you for a great deal."

The pattern of youth spending begun in the early 1920s continued during the 1930s. Despite high levels of unemployment, some older adolescents were proportionately well-off. In his exhaustive 1936 survey of working-class families in York, Seebohm Rowntree found that over three-quarters of the fifteen-to-twenty-five age group were over the poverty line that the fives to fourteens or the twenty-fives to forty-fours were struggling to rise above. Old enough to work yet too young to start a family, these wage earners had leisure time—at least a couple of hours each evening—and were catered to by a consumer culture that revolved around the cinema.

In 1933, a young shop girl enumerated her weekly budget in a letter to a film magazine: "Wages 32s—Board and lodging 25s—Saturday visit to cinema 1d—Monday visit 7d—Thursday visit 7d—That makes 27s 2d. Then there is threepence for Film Weekly and three shillings for dress allowance. . . . People consider me smartly dressed, but this is undoubtedly because I copy the clothes I have seen in the films. Powders, soaps and odds and ends are those used by my favourite film stars. When I get a rise in salary, I shall be able to afford another night at the pictures."

Even unemployment could not dent the allure of this dream world. In her 1935–36 survey of adolescent wage earners in Manchester, Joan L. Harley found that all the unemployed respondents went to the cinema at least once a week: half went twice a week, and about a fifth went between three and six times a week. Some were given money by their parents, some used part of their dole, while others were taken by boyfriends anxious to take advantage of the cinemas' dim lighting. It was also the case that in relatively prosperous Manchester, youth unemployment rarely lasted more than a few weeks.

However, even this limited spending was impossible in the Special Areas. But there was one immediate solution: one of Lestrange's photomontages displayed young unemployed men, with tight-waisted suits and defiant expressions, placed next to army posters, pictures of a work camp, and the inside of a jail. Those were the only options for these youths, and turning to crime was quite natural: "To the lounging listless group of youths at the street corner comes one who draws aside his particular pal. 'Things can't be worse than they are. Let's knock off a car and have a bit of fun.'"

The neighbourhood gangs were back, more numerous and more vicious than ever. The renewed public awareness stimulated the success of youth novels like Alexander McArthur and H. Kingsley Long's No Mean City, which sought to frame the story of a Gorbals gang leader within revived concerns about delinquency. At the book's end, the authors reproduced a sequence of contemporary headlines like "PANIC IN GLASGOW CINEMA. VICTIMISED BY GANGS OF YOUTHS." As the authors concluded, "Extracts of the same kind could be quoted ad nauseam from the Glasgow and the national papers of recent years."

Some young criminals continued the hooligan tradition of extravagant dress. One North London gang member remembered that the fashion of his day was "Oxford Bags, that was trousers that were possibly twenty inches across; they were really wide and everybody went for them. They were all in a grey flannel or a soft flannel, and they were quite cheap. And shoes, they'd call 'em winkle pickers. Fortunately I didn't wear them very often, but they're the ones that crippled you, they went right to a point. Sports' shirts were fashionable and when I was eighteen, the fashion was the bowler hat."

These sartorial flourishes fuelled growing concern about adolescent crime during the early 1930s, epitomized by what the authorities called "an epidemic of gangs of idle unemployed youths". Hollywood films were charged with recruiting "hundreds" of slum boys "for the gangs of race-course toughs, motor bandits, and smash-and-grab thieves". Sensational headlines like "TERROR GANGS TO BE WIPED OUT" mirrored a change in British criminal activities. The new public enemies were the dog-track and racetrack gangs that capitalized on the huge British appetite—£400 million a year—for illegal betting.

The comparatively liberal provisions of the 1933 Children and Young Persons Act had tightened up the laws concerning child labour and admitted "care, protection and control" as a possibility for offenders under seventeen, who were not thought to have full adult responsibility for their actions. Instead of an automatic prison sentence, there were a variety of solutions on offer, from borstal to "industrial" school or—the most common solution by far—probation. Young offenders were brought even more within state control at the same time as they were, so critics thought, treated with special leniency.

This more sympathetic approach was promoted by social workers, with their firsthand knowledge of unemployed life. In *London's Bad Boys,* S. F. Hatton advocated a programme of adult supervision up to the age of eighteen. In his descriptions of slum dwellers like "Alf Artful", "Billy Dustup", and "Reggie Smashem", he excused their delinquency as "nothing more serious than the symptoms of a healthy vigorous adolescence". In the same way, inner-city policemen like Harry Daley understood that a certain level of youth delinquency was well within the existing rules of the game.

Political agitation, however, was dealt with severely. Through the winter of 1931, major protests against the means test took place in thirty-one British cities, including London, Glasgow, Birmingham, Leeds, and Newcastle. They were met with baton charges and high-pressure water hoses. In October 1932, a demonstration in Belfast was so out of control that the army shot into the crowd. Two weeks later, a massive rally in London's Hyde Park degenerated into a series of running battles between police and thousands of demonstrators on the streets of central London.

With the increasing number of mass demonstrations, the political map of Britain began to change. In the same month as the Hyde Park rally, Oswald Mosley formed his latest political venture after the failure of the maverick New Party: the British Union of Fascists. At the same time, the Communist Party of Great Britain began to increase in size. The stage was set for a repeat on British soil of the political polarization that had already torn Europe apart, and, with the moral lead given to the unemployed working class, the elite followed suit.

The slump was so deep that it threatened the previously impregnable bourgeois. With capitalism appearing to offer no future, thousands of well-educated young men and women plunged into extremist politics in the quest for salvation and hope. Their older brothers and sisters had expressed their contempt for the "old men" who ran the country by their refusal to grow up. They had appeared to care for nothing and no one, but the generation coming of age in the early 1930s—mindful of the plight of the less fortunate—honed their rebellion into "an almost tangible Oedipal fury" against Middle England.

However, wishing for what W. H. Auden called "the death of the old gang" was only part of it. The most genuine motive was anger at the human cost of the slump and the seeming paralysis of government. Desperate times required extreme solutions, and communism spread through a whole generation of British writers, artists, and intellectuals.[1] Among these were Esmond Romilly, Winston Churchill's nephew, and Rupert Cornford, great-grandson of Charles Darwin. Highly attuned to "the world's vibrations of violence", both led the vanguard in extremist act and deed.

Until 1933, the principal rallying point among students was the campaign for peace: this was the year of the infamous Oxford Union debate that passed the heretical motion that "this House will in no circumstances fight for its King and Country". The spread of communism at Cambridge was boosted by the 1933 Armistice Day anti-war march that descended into violence between the protesters and "patriotic" hearties. The press saw this as unacceptable behaviour on the part of Britain's young elite, whom they dubbed "young hooligans who had got what they deserved for desecrating a holy day".

The Bright Young People had expressed their contempt for the nineteenth-century public school ideal of the muscular Christian through their androgynous hedonism, but the new generation of privileged rebels were more direct. Hating "anti-intellectual jingoism", they decided to take the fight right into the heart of the imperial incubator. Having created a riot at his militaristic school

1. These included the historians Christopher Hill and Eric Hobsbawm, the poets W. H. Auden, Louis MacNeice, and Stephen Spender, and the Soviet spies Guy Burgess and Anthony Blunt—the last a pillar of the establishment who was only unmasked forty years later.

by handing around anti-war propaganda on Armistice Day, Esmond Romilly ran away to join the Marxist-oriented Federation of Student Societies, where he announced the creation of a radical magazine for public school boys.

In January 1933, together with his older brother Giles, Romilly issued the *Out of Bounds* manifesto:

> Disintegration affects in our period the whole of our society. It affects profoundly the public school, showing itself in:
>
> (1) Confusion of thought in the face of modern problems.
> (2) A deliberate attempt on the part of the schools to exclude themselves from genuine contact with political and cultural realities.
> (3) The positive and blatant use of the public schools as a weapon in the cause of reaction.
> (4) The opportunities offered to the Fascist to exploit the situation.
>
> . . . Out of Bounds will openly champion the forces of progress against the forces of reaction on every front, from compulsory military training to propagandist teaching.

This manifesto was barely circulated before the press jumped on it, with headlines like "RED MENACE IN PUBLIC SCHOOLS". Communism appeared to be entering the heart of the establishment, and Churchill's opportunistic "Red Nephew" was quite happy to assist the process. Writing for a national newspaper, Romilly played the extremist card: "Youth has a clear choice, there can be no halfway house. Either they must side with the parasites and exploiters to 'make the world safe for plutocracy', or with the working class to smash the capitalist system and lay the foundations of the classless society."

The vibrations of polarized violence reached their first climax in June 1934, when Oswald Mosley held a mammoth blackshirt meeting in London's huge Olympia hall.[2] This was designed to mark a crucial turning point in his party's history. With the Hitler and Mussolini regimes securely in power, Mosley had adopted key elements of their iconography and worldview: the ritualistic staging, the fears of American mass culture, the scapegoating of designated outsiders. The British Union of Fascists also capitalized on the generational hostility to bourgeois society, full of compromise and decadence.

The BUF was a young movement, with an estimated 80 per cent of mem-

---

2. The extremism of the period was embodied in the three Mitford sisters who embraced extreme politics: Unity, who became the most prominent British Nazi; Jessica, who became a Communist and married Esmond Romilly in 1937; and Diana, who married Oswald Mosley in 1936.

bers under thirty.[3] Its most important constituency was the same class that had provided crucial support for Hitler, skilled and semi-skilled workers. With a significant take-up in the industrial North as well as London's East End, it was designed to appeal to the unemployed. With Nazi brutality as yet unexposed, Mosley set out to seduce the disaffected within a highly charged atmosphere. With his regimented squad of "biff boys" dressed from head to toe in black, Mosley well understood the combination of violence and sexuality.

At Olympia, this highly charged atmosphere erupted. The problem for the protesters was that, according to Harry Daley, the police on duty had been told "not to interfere" in what had been organized as a private event. The result was that every time a heckler or protester stood up, "the ushers in force pounced on the offender and carried him from the hall". Groups of blackshirts then violently attacked "the defenceless hecklers, who could do nothing but stand and cover their bowed heads with their arms and hands until they fell to the ground". Daley recalled that "nobody had ever seen anything like it".

Olympia occurred at the BUF's first membership peak—up to 50,000 in mid-1934—and set a precedent for political violence. Most large-scale BUF events followed a similar pattern: heavy policing outside and "fascist discipline" inside the hall. In Liverpool, the protests were organized by the local Anti-Fascist Committee, comprised of Communists, Labour Party members, and National Unemployed Workers' Movement representatives. This collaboration reflected the Comintern's new Popular Front policy: the alliance of left-wing groups to stop Hitler and even defend democracy.

However, the violence at Olympia finished off any chance of the BUF achieving conventional electoral success: the press coverage cost the party influential backers and the rabid anti-Semites took the ascendancy.[4] The stage was set for the running street battles that would involve the country's youth in the violence that had already spread through Germany and France. Britain had never known such political division. There had been many serious outbreaks of public disorder, but they had never been organized around such clear-cut and diametrically opposing ideologies.

Whether enacted on the streets of the East End, in provincial town halls, or the houses of the privileged, British youth were at war with each other. What began as a neighbourhood dispute or a game became a choice binding until

3. Hard data on the BUF is thin on the ground, as most of its records were destroyed when the party was made illegal in 1940.

4. Chief among these was the most notorious traitor of the Second World War, the Irishman William Joyce, also known as Lord Haw Haw, who was executed in 1947 for his wartime pro-Nazi broadcasts.

death. Jessica Mitford remembered the exchange that occurred when her older sister Unity tried to persuade her to join the British Union of Fascists: "'Don't you *long* to join too, Decca?[5] It's *such* fun,' she begged, waving her brand new black shirt at me. 'Shouldn't think of it. I hate the beastly Fascists. If you're going to be one, I'm going to be a Communist, so there.'"

At fifteen, Jessica faced her fork-in-the-road moment: "This declaration was something more than a mere automatic taking of opposite sides to Boud. The little I knew about the Fascists repelled me—their racism, super-militarism, brutality." The room that the sisters shared became a microcosm of the political forces tearing a continent apart. They divided it down the middle: against Jessica's Communist memorabilia, Unity displayed her Fascist insignia: photos of Mussolini and Mosley and the Nazi swastika. Then they would stage "pitched battles, throwing books and records".

Unity Mitford was then undergoing her season as a debutante. She would have been better suited to the exhibitionist era of the Bright Young People, but the party had moved on and in its place came something more sinister. During her season, she joined the BUF's Oxford branch, but this period of selling the union's newspaper, *Action*, did not last long. "I'm going to Germany to meet Hitler," Unity announced to her sister, and in August 1933 she travelled to Nuremberg to attend the first rally since the Nazis' assumption of power.

In the meantime, Jessica "hardened my resolution to run away and to cast my lot with the anti-fascists". She had to wait for her moment, while "fortress aspects of life at home came to the forefront with a vengeance, virtually drowning out all others. I was in headlong opposition to everything the family stood for, and it was on the whole a very lonely opposition." Reading the scandalous reports of the "Red" public school magazine started by her second cousin Esmond Romilly, she found her admiration "unbounded" and fixed upon him as her escape route.

Having successfully stalked Hitler in Munich, Unity quickly became one of his intimates. She was privileged as a member of the British upper class that fascinated the Führer and that, until the outbreak of war, would offer the Nazi regime considerable support. In 1935, the year of the Nuremberg Decree that stripped German Jews of their rights, she wrote an article for a Munich paper, "Confessions of an English Fascist Girl", which stated that "the British fascist party is a party of front-line soldiers and youth". The tension between the two sisters erupted in "a furious quarrel which ended in a fist-fight".

This bitter antagonism was reduplicated again and again. Communist re-

5. Within the family language, Unity was known as Boud and Jessica, Decca.

sistance to the BUF marginalized the blackshirts and provoked them into further violence. It also helped to reduce membership from the 50,000 of summer 1934 to around 5,000 by October 1935. The BUF decided to exploit their successes in the East End of London—an area with a high immigrant and Jewish population. Months of skirmishes in the area came to a head in early October 1936, when a planned BUF march through a Jewish quarter was opposed by a counter-demonstration of 100,000 people.

As usual, the police were deployed to keep the protesters away from the marchers. When the locals made barricades to prevent Mosley's progress, the police charged but, as one young protester, Charlie Goodman, remembered, "Above there were tenements and the women just leaned out from there, threw everything they could lay their hands on down on to the police, and when I say everything, I mean everything: hot water, boiling water, kitchen oil, fat, urine, lumps of shit, anything they could lay their hands on.

"The rest of the police got very panicked and some of them stood there going 'Heil Hitler' and that sort of thing, which was very provocative. Then somebody threw a brick through this coach and that was when the police started bashing, battering, left right and centre and they pushed the people back a little way. They was just indiscriminately battering people, knocking people through plate-glass windows or shops." When, in the mêlée, Goodman came across a policeman "just about to whack a woman in the head", he punched him in the face and was arrested by a dozen of his colleagues.

Although the protesters had the satisfaction of enacting the commandment "thou shalt not pass", the publicity that surrounded the Battle of Cable Street helped to increase BUF membership in the months that followed. But it became clear to the government that this state of affairs could not continue: on January 1, 1937, the Public Order Act prohibited the wearing of political uniforms in public places and the formation of quasi-military organizations. By then both sides had a much larger theatre for their drama.

. . .

During the spring of 1936, an army-led coup ousted the democratically elected Popular Front government in Spain: one month later, the country erupted into full-blown civil war. The British government's official position was to do nothing: in August 1936, it signed a non-intervention agreement with Italy, Germany, and Russia. The violation of this agreement by Hitler and Mussolini was a clear rallying ground for a generation of young radicals. This was "the whole European issue at its most naked and pure. Democracy versus Fascism."

The politicized young of Europe knew that this was the big showdown. In early August 1936, John Cornford slipped into Spain. Earlier that summer, he had written a paper called "Young Minds for Old": "It is very easy and to some people very comforting to sneer at youthful fanaticism. A movement so young as the Communist movement is inevitably at times naïve, immature, over-enthusiastic, and provides a splendid field for the peddlers of second hand witticisms. But it is nonetheless a serious movement." It was time to test that seriousness, to alchemize theory in the crucible of action.

A few thousand British youths would travel to Spain over the next eighteen months to fight against General Franco's army. The journalist Tom Wintring-ham recalled that most volunteers "had been manual workers, having left school at fourteen—the usual lot of most in those days, no matter how intelligent or able". Only three of the British Battalion's leaders—including Wintringham—had been to university, but they "all had experienced the difficulties and frus-tration of finding work in a period of heavy unemployment. Their anti-fascism was anchored in hatred of the class and social system in Britain."

Working together and fighting together, even dying together, all levels of society could unite in a practical demonstration of Communist tenets. The revolution offered British visitors visions of a new kind of mass society. John Cornford visited the Anarchist-controlled city of Barcelona, where he found that the streets were packed all day: "It's as if in London the armed workers were dominating the streets—it's obvious they wouldn't tolerate Mosley or people selling Action in the streets. And that wouldn't mean that the town wasn't free in the real sense. It is genuinely a dictatorship of the majority."

The Spanish civil war galvanized a generation. The idea of a Popular Front crossed over from the Communist Party to a much wider constituency in the momentum embodied by the success of Victor Gollancz's Left Book Club. For the first time, Britain had a broad-based intelligentsia that was both left-wing and internationalist. Involvement in the Spanish civil war became a rite of passage, an ideal far greater than the comparatively small number of volun-teers who actually went. The utopian vision of the 1930s was exemplified by the way that the classes came together in autonomous, Anarchist Barcelona.

However, the reality was quite different. The enthusiastic young volunteers, from across the classes, quickly realized that they had entered another country altogether, a snakepit of long-standing, highly complex social tensions. They were also pitted against a ruthless foe. The militias within which they served were often ill-equipped with clothing and weapons, and were also prone to in-ternecine struggle. Instead of uniting against the common Fascist enemy, Communists, Anarchists, and Syndicalists often ended up fighting each other. However it was ideologically dressed, this was total war.

The British volunteers joined up out of idealism, but the dangers of political praxis as self-discovery were quickly revealed. In late August 1936, a Communist art student named Felicia Browne was killed, the first British volunteer to die. Just before she left, Browne had testified in a letter to a friend, "You say I am escaping and evading things by not painting or making sculpture. If there is no painting or sculpture to be made, I cannot make it. I can only make out of what is valid and urgent to me." For her, artistic practice paled before "the earthquake which is happening in the revolution".

Realizing that "you can't play at revolution", John Cornford had turned into a professional class warrior: as Esmond Romilly recalled when he met him in late 1936, he had become "a serious person, a rigid disciplinarian". As the leader of a predominantly working-class and Communist English detachment, Cornford had became "a good soldier" and an inspiration to his fellow volunteers. However, as 1936 turned into 1937, he was killed near the town of Lopera on the Cordoba front. With this charismatic youthful death, the Popular Front of the 1930s had its own doomed golden boy.

Named in an explicit homage to Rupert Brooke, Rupert John Cornford suffered a martyrdom as mythic as that Great War icon: a life sacrificed to an idea taken through to its conclusion. Brooke's death had been employed by the establishment to give an attractive human face to technological slaughter. In contrast, Cornford shunned his privileged background: his violence was not veiled but celebrated in the utilitarian, almost gangsterish style of the time. He exalted the people, and in paying the price for his beliefs, affirmed the fact that the elite had to shed their privilege to join the mass society.

However, that realization would be interpreted in ways that the mid-thirties radicals could not have predicted. From mid-1937 on, dissatisfaction and disillusion spread through the International Brigades. Faced with the superiority of the Fascist-backed nationalist forces, the continuing disorganization of the international militias, and the "bloody mess" that either killed or wounded over half of all the volunteers, British intellectuals began to withdraw. For others, the sectarian hard line of the Communists, with their insistence that they and only they should lead the revolution, remained a serious problem.

The agitation did not stop. The late 1930s saw the peak of the Left Book Club, whose many discussion groups[6] and activities—rambling, cycling, and working with the unemployed—offered an entry point into anti-Fascist politics for thousands of middle-class adolescents. As a "university graduate" group convener from Kent wrote in a glowing testimonial to Gollancz about

6. Estimated at over a thousand by 1939.

the organization's inclusive tendencies, "I joined the Left Book Club in the first month of its existence. I belonged to no political party. My outlook, it is true, was left, but it was a very confused, cynical and disillusioned outlook."

The street clashes between Fascists and Communists had become a regular part of British life. In September 1938, a march by Mosley's new party, the British Union, ended in a running battle between police, blackshirts, and left-wing protesters in Parliament Square. As one observer noted, "A line of Fascists now appear with boards held aloft. A young chap with a Communist badge went across and spoke to one of them 'Mosley mugs'. One of the walkers turned and said, 'Get down on your hands and knees, you Communist rat.'"

Although it had begun to recede as a national issue, unemployment rose slightly during 1937: this was partly caused by the baby boom of 1919–20 coming of age. The misery of the North-east and all the other "Special Areas" continued but the unacceptable had become almost normal. In understandable desperation, the National Unemployed Workers' Movement pursued a new policy of stunts: sit-downs in the middle of Oxford Circus, occupying the Tea Room of the Ritz. These got headlines but didn't change the situation: for many of the unemployed young, full mobilization would be the only solution to their problems.

• • •

By late 1937, it had also become obvious that another world war was looming, for which the Spanish civil war had been but a mere dress rehearsal. The last years of the decade were marked by "a deepening sense of gathering storm", as, unchecked and appeased, Nazi Germany annexed the Sudetenland, Austria, Czechoslovakia. The international situation was extremely serious. In March 1937, the first gas mask factories were opened and air-raid sirens tested for the first time, while throughout the year the British army was upgraded and heavily promoted as the "Modern Army".

The oncoming war—or its counterpart, "peace at any price"—began to replace the polarized agenda of the mid-decade as the principal political motivator of the young. The Communists felt justified in their hostility to fascism, while Oswald Mosley tried to reposition the British Union as a party of peace. At the same time, the worst effects of unemployment were reversed by the beginnings of rearmament. There was money around again, and this meant that the introduction into Britain of the consumer society began to quicken its pace.

For those who worked in the new service industries, life was getting better. Even for those on the poverty line, rental purchase made spending possible. By the late thirties, there were over two million cars on the roads. After 1938, eleven million workers became entitled to one week's paid holiday per year, a new leisure opportunity exploited by the first holiday camps in Britain, Butlins. Apart from movies and jazz, other aspects of contemporary American culture filtered over in greater abundance. Pulp magazines like *Fight Stories* and *Action Stories* sold to a "huge" readership.

American consumerism had survived the Depression. The shift from commitment to pleasure was heralded by a new generation of criminals. The young hustler hero of James Curtis's 1936 lowlife novel, *The Gilt Kid*, wants to be a good Marxist but realizes that "all this theorizing is rot". He remonstrates with a Communist in a Soho club: "Listen, you hold demonstrations, meetings, hunger-marches and all that bull. What the hell good does that do? Just a few mugs get nicked and a few more have sore heads where the slops have bashed them with their batons. You can't tell me that brings the revolution any closer."

• • •

The Gilt Kid was an early fictional example of the "wide boy".[7] These new outlaws were not concerned with the class war, but in reducing as far as possible the gap between wanting and getting. They were prepared to back this up, if not with guile, then with cosh, razor, and gun. Their prime locations were the streets and clubs of Soho or Paddington, and their milieu was populated by racetrack gangsters, prostitutes of both genders, and the gay and Jewish underworlds. Cutting a swath in drab late-thirties Britain, the wide boys were harbingers of the new American pleasure world.

At the same time, American methods of mass persuasion and measurement finally found a foothold in Britain. The earliest efforts were readership surveys conducted by newspapers and periodicals, the results of which were then made available to advertisers. This process was boosted by the American pollster Dr Gallup, who after his success in the 1936 American election, opened the British Institute of Public Opinion.[8] These techniques were observed by three young radicals, Tom Harrisson, Humphrey Jennings, and Charles Madge, who decided to inaugurate their own form of mass measurement.

7. See also Ronald Westerby, *Wide Boys Never Work* (1937), Graham Greene, *Brighton Rock* (1938), and John Worby, *Spiv's Progress* (1939).

8. Ever sensitive to the changes in temperature, Jessica Romilly got a job there, and found that "the objective was to compile information for the use of the advertising agency about public reaction to various products, and to this end we were provided with elaborate forms to be filled in the course of door-to-door interviews. The questions, of course, varied widely according to the product. Interviewing for a breakfast food or household cleanser was fairly plain sailing, while the form dealing with a deodorant was likely to contain the question, 'How often do you find it necessary to wash under the armpits?'"

In January 1937, they formed Mass-Observation, which aimed at nothing less than "the science of ourselves". With backgrounds in the arts, journalism, anthropology, and left-wing politics, the founders realized that "ordinary people were being misled by a complacent press and indifferent government". The only possible response to this barrage was "to stick to facts and to set them down as intelligently as is humanly possible". In practice, this meant the detailed observation of the everyday lives usually ignored by the mass media: the idea was to record and dignify what was usually thought to be mundane.

Mass-Observation's initial surveys consisted of three main elements: detailed studies like the Worktown project, where every aspect of life in one northern town, Bolton, was observed over a period of months; a series of reports by hundreds of willing volunteers, the Mass-Observers, collected into books like *May the 12th*, a survey of King George V's Silver Jubilee; and diaries written by contributors who joined up "because they wanted to be of some use in the fight against fascism and against official neglect of ordinary people".

Mass-Observation's relationship to market research was ambiguous. The founders castigated ad agencies and daily newspapers: "These great organisations base their work on the assumption that the human mind is suggestible and they aim their suggestions at that part of the human mind in which the superstitious elements predominate." They aimed to expose these hidden processes in early surveys like *Reactions to Ads*. Despite their critical tone, many of the responses could have been useful to the pollsters that Mass-Observation opposed.

Britain's first modern, picture-led weekly—the domestic equivalent of America's *Life*—was another product of this shift. Set up by the Oxford graduate Tom Hopkinson and Hungarian refugee Stefan Lorant, *Picture Post* published its first issue in October 1938—days after the Munich crisis—with a picture of a young woman, caught in a fairground wind, laughingly displaying her garters. With its innovative layouts and political topicality, the magazine was an instant success: within weeks, it was selling over one million copies.

There was another sense in which *Picture Post* was a creature of its time: it was stuffed with advertisements for Philips radios, "air-floated" face powder, and celebrity-endorsed cigarettes. Despite its political agenda, it also featured popular culture and show-business stories: a feature on the British institution Gracie Fields at home, items about Hollywood stars like Freddie Bartholomew, reports on the latest music and movie sensations from America. Together with "candid" pictures and a colour section, *Picture Post* seduced as it informed.

The success of Mass-Observation and *Picture Post* forced left-wing intellectuals to realize that paying closer attention to the needs and feelings of the mass would remove the threat of class war. The attractions of revolution were beginning to pale in favour of social integration. At the same time, the resurgence of American capitalism offered a third way between fascism and communism. Mass consumerism offered another kind of social inclusion: as the left-wing maverick Claud Cockburn observed, "It could be represented as a kind of democratisation of economic life."

This idea was still new in Britain, and youth was in the forefront. Both Mass-Observation and *Picture Post* took particular notice of Britain's adolescents. The former initiated ground-level investigations of everyday life, like a March 1938 report on "Youth Organisations in Fulham", while the latter explicitly aimed features like "A Glamour Girl's Day" and "Birth of a New Dance Craze" at their young readership. In March 1939, *Picture Post* published an editorial, "Youth at the Helm", which, just as Stanley Hall had done, romantically equated youth with a hopeful future.

"Youth is in the air," argued the *Picture Post* proprietor Edward Hulton; "certainly everyone is talking about it. What journalist fails to write about it? What politician forgets to flatter it, and to make it promises? Leaders and Church and State try to organise it. Even the BBC has instituted a series entitled 'Youth Takes A Bow'." Hulton thought that this concentration on youth was caused by the fact that Britain had entered "an age of transition", but underlying this new focus was the shadow of extremism: "The young, because of their impatience, and their lack of understanding, are highly intolerant."

Published in 1939, Mass-Observation's ambitiously titled *Britain* captured the country's young poised between conflict and consumerism. Its firsthand reports showed that, on the one hand, the violence between left-wingers and Mosleyites was still virulent, while on the other, British youths were flocking to new pleasure domes like "the brand-new-looking, glass-and-chromium Locarno Dance Hall in Streatham". There were also huge open-air dances held in London parks, at which one observer noted "many pairs of youths dancing in unorthodox styles".

By the end of the 1930s, a separate youth culture had become part of everyday life in Britain. Returning to York to review his mid-decade survey, Seebohm Rowntree noticed how almost all the working-class young were "in cinemas, the theatres, the music hall, or dancing". A young man in Manchester, Frank Findley, recalled promenading in the late 1930s: "the boys dressed in their thirty bob suits with 22 inch trouser bottoms would stroll along emulating the screen tough guys of the day." If the weather was too bad, they could "go and fortify" themselves "in Turner's Temperance Bar or in Gottelli's ice-cream shop with a good, hot, highly potent drink of VIMTO at two-pence a shot".

Whether or not they were actually independent of adults, Britain's young began to live in a commercialized world of their own rituals and their own imagining. This account from a Manchester girl in 1939 gives an idea of this self-enclosed world:

MONDAY

4 p.m.	Left school with girl friend, talked about school and film stars . . .
6.10 p.m.	Girl friend called for me. Walked to pictures.
6.30 p.m.	Saw "It's In The Air."
9 p.m.	Left pictures, talked about picture, met two girl friends on the way home.
9.15 p.m.	Stood talking on corner with two girls about clothes, holidays and boys . . .
10 p.m.	Arrived home, had supper, listened to dance music, talked to family about pictures . . .

Despite suffering badly in the Depression, the young unemployed had not erupted in the violence that had torn Germany apart. There were many reasons for this, but spending played an important part. George Orwell observed that between them, "fish-and-chips, art-silk stockings, tinned salmon, cut-price chocolate (five two ounce bars for sixpence), the movies, the radio, strong tea, and the Football Pools" had "averted revolution". This was the beginning of popular culture, for which British youth had already developed a distinct taste. Soon it would become an obsession.

CHAPTER 21

Jitterbugs and Ickies

American Swing and Youth Consumerism

• • •

Adolf Hitler's an ickie and a tin-ear, too. He's a screwball, a bit wacky, but he's full of Schmaltz. A killer, but not a killer-diller. He may weep crocodile tears, but he's no alligator.

—"Outstanding Ickies", *The Jitterbug*, No. 1 (1938)

CALIFORNIA JITTERBUGS GO TO TOWN,
DECEMBER 12, 1939

AT 7 A.M. on March 3, 1937, the members of the Benny Goodman Orchestra arrived at the 3,664-seat Paramount Theater in Times Square to rehearse for the opening show of their upcoming residency. They had no idea that anything special was going to happen, but what they saw at that unmusicianly hour made them wonder whether they were still dreaming. Although the box office hadn't yet opened, there was already a throng of six or seven hundred fans, most of them high school kids from the New York boroughs, dancing, shouting, and lighting fires to ward off the cold.

At seven-thirty, the "fans were multiplying by the minute, pouring up out of the Times Square subway exits like bees from a smoked hive". An hour later, the performance began with the first faint notes of the orchestra's signature theme, "Let's Dance", that slowly became louder as the musicians rose out of the pit. This show-stopping piece of theatre was guaranteed to bring the packed audience to their feet, and that's where they stayed, frantically dancing in the aisles and crowding the bandstand, while the ushers frantically tried to regain control.

These scenes were repeated throughout each of the five shows that day: nobody cared about the co-billed Claudette Colbert film, *Maid of Salem*. By the end of the week, the audience was climbing on the bandstand itself, both to be closer to their idols and to find more space for their acrobatic dancing. The swing kids were, as Goodman later admitted, more than just passive spectators: "We looked at them, I guess, [as if] they were the show and we were the audience."

The Paramount residency marked the moment when Benny Goodman and his orchestra crossed over into the fame that, like the style of jazz that he played, swing, would spread throughout the United States and the Western world. Signalled by powerful riffs, swing fused the exhilarating spontaneity of the classic 1920s "hot" style with the dramatic power of a large orchestra. Goodman numbers like drummer Gene Krupa's forte tune, "Sing Sing Sing", with its pounding jungle beat, offered an invitation to frenzy that the adolescents of the mid-thirties were only too glad to take up.

The popularity of swing was stimulated by radio, the fastest-growing medium of the period. During 1937, Goodman's orchestra was regularly showcased on CBS's *Camel Caravan*, a weekly programme sponsored by the cigarette firm. Using remote recording as well as regular studios, shows like *Camel Caravan* and NBC's *Let's Dance* plugged swing straight into homes throughout America. For the young fans, these "make-believe ballrooms" were a new phenomenon that was "immediately and exhilaratingly real, but at the same time part of the fabric of dream world fantasy".

FANS WITH THE BENNY GOODMAN ORCHESTRA,
NEW YORK WORLD'S FAIR, 1939

Listening in their bedrooms or plugging nickels into a jukebox, American adolescents found that access to swing was easy and quick. Featuring large orchestras made up of top musicians—Goodman's included Lionel Hampton, Harry James, and Gene Krupa in March 1937—swing was meant from the start to be upbeat, physical music that you could participate in. Goodman's vibes player, Red Norvo, summed it up when he told *Variety* that swing "was a tempo that inspires the listener to accelerate in rhythm with an ultra-modern swing. You know, they *swing* with you."

The popular music of the early thirties had been dominated by "sweet" crooners like Rudy Vallee and Bing Crosby. Despite their fanatical female following, they were smooth, coolly assured performers. With swing, the tempo of life sped up, and from 1937 on, it ushered in a whole adolescent world, with its own slang, magazines, fashions, and heroes. This was generated by the fans themselves. "Jazz is a major industry today and depends on mass consumption," the editor of *Jitterbug* noted. "If jazz wants to keep going, it's got to realize that jitterbugs are important."

Swing opened a new chapter in the history of youth and mass communication. The surprise and condemnation that many adult journalists exhibited
when faced with mass swing rallies—"musical Hitlerism" was one comment[1]—only highlighted the fact that American adolescents were operating
on a different wavelength from adults. Swing was not just about musical and
physical freedom, it was about a much wider liberty in all its forms: the true
emancipation, not just of the Negro musicians who pioneered the style, but of
the "teens" whose coming of age the music heralded.

. . .

With their entry to the adult world delayed as a matter of governmental policy,
some of America's young began to make demands of their own. In July 1936,
the American Youth Congress issued a *Declaration of Rights of American Youth:*
"We want to work, to produce, to build, but millions of us are forced to be idle.
We graduate from schools and colleges equipped for careers and professions,
but there are no jobs. We can find us along the highways, or in Army super-
vised camps, isolated from friends and family. We refuse to be the lost
generation."

Rejecting the twenties model of the college consumer, the student activists
of the American Youth Congress staked out a new Bill of Rights, affirming
their solidarity with "the Negro people", striking workers, and progressive
forces everywhere. While not going so far as to state that young people consti-
tuted "a separate social group", they nevertheless stated that "our problems
and aspirations are intimately bound up with those of all the people". Claiming a potential constituency of over a million, they continued to agitate for
practical improvements.

In February 1937, a "Youth Pilgrimage on Jobs and Education" marched on
Washington to protest about the killing of a proposed American Youth Act.
This would have augmented the provisions of the National Youth Administra-
tion by granting free public education for high school students. But the gov-
ernmental youth body was hamstrung by cutbacks and right-wing hostility.
Despite its high-level commitment and its good intentions, the National Youth
Administration did not succeed in eradicating the youth problems of the
Depression.

Many of its provisions were practical and enlightened. It offered a link-up
with adult education programmes and practical courses aiming to orient young

1. Courtesy of Professor Harry D. Gideonse, Columbia University, quoted in the *New York Times*,
November 2, 1938.

people into full-time employment. It also started a nationwide programme of assistance to high school students over sixteen, with the maximum monthly payment fixed at six dollars. Another development was the institution of resident projects in thirty states: camps where the young could stay for up to six months while working, managing themselves, and living with their own peers.

However, the National Youth Administration could reach "only part of the youth who are in the most desperate circumstances". Although 500,000 young people passed through the NYA in its first two and a half years, that was a small proportion of the four million sixteen- to twenty-four-year-olds still unemployed at the end of 1937. As the chairman of the American Youth Congress, William W. Hinckley complained, "To young Americans, living in what should be the heyday of life, the period of golden youth, is offered in the seventh year of crisis, the privilege of working for candy and cigarettes."

For all its socialist inclinations, this governmental youth group did not dent the essential materialism of American life. Clues were given in the NYA documents themselves. Clothes were thought to be "an essential expense" of school. As one supervisor noted, "Usually after about the second pay check, a boy will come into work with a new pair of trousers. They probably cost him two or three dollars, but they're his and he bought them with his own money. Maybe on his next wages he'll get a pair of shoes. The girl will blossom out in a $2.95 dress. You can't possibly know what it means to her."

Despite the Depression, the American definition of successful citizenship remained dependent on the acquisition of commodities. Although American adolescents had had considerable purchasing power during the previous two decades, much of that, particularly below the college age, had been conditional on adult approval and control. Offered government-sponsored youth employment, the children of the 1920–21 baby boom—just turning sixteen and seventeen—decided that if they were to be treated as having their own rights, then they would exercise those rights in the manner they chose.

The first youth market had concentrated on the visible and affluent 1920s college culture. By the late 1930s, with an increasing proportion of America's young remaining in high school, the potential market of adolescent consumers had expanded both in age and class. When the Lynds returned to Muncie, they observed that the pace was still set by "business class girls". From 1935 on a new version of the college girl style was promoted to young American women under the commercial name of "sub-debs"—the contraction of "sub-debutante" reflecting their affluent origin, if not in actuality but in aspiration.

These early attempts at catering to this expanded youth economy were designed to be reassuring. In May 1936, *Vogue* published an examination of

American youth entitled "How Old Is Fifteen?" in which feature writer Ruth Pickering opined, "In New York City, 1936, on a day when conventional formulas are hard to find, the ancient right of youthful exploration spars with the right to adult protection. With the title of sub-debutante, because they attend the private schools and their mothers have gone through the rigmarole for invitations to subscription dances, they are all like all children at adolescence."

With staid pictures and a text that cited Booth Tarkington, the *Vogue* piece nevertheless detected an underlying precocity among its subjects: "The young want early independence, if possible. Visions of storming into Harlem Jungles or Village Pirate's Dens are mirages on the horizons of complete liberty. They crave the outposts of New York because it is rumored that there collegians foregather, those free-moving elderly contemporaries. One dash into such forbidden territory serves as a badge of coming-of-age. Sophistication is the ambition. Sophistication is their own frequently used word."

A quasi-adult independence was the goal of this "restless" group, as was their "craving for the higher age brackets". As usual, the great unspoken in this new precocity was sex, and it was this that the character-building adolescent media continued to police. One of the first media uses of the term "sub-deb" occurred in a regular advice column started during 1935 by the *Ladies' Home Journal*, while during 1936 *Scholastic* introduced a new column, Gay Head's long-running "Boy Dates Girl"—the first of many detailed etiquette primers.

For young women, chastity still remained the ideal. Virgins remained "quality merchandise". They were also expected to tailor their personality to their male dates: "Boys love to run the show and be it." But the burgeoning advice industry went to almost absurd lengths to dampen down adolescent spontaneity—reflecting the side of America that is highly formal and regimented. In *Etiquette for the Teens,* published by the church-backed Home Institute during 1937, "the friendly, sensible, up-to-date advice—written in the language of the teens" stacked up to forty pages of relentless rules.

The etiquette manuals were so obviously an adult projection of how adolescents should act that they highlighted the fact that, in the second half of the 1930s, parents and the authorities were concerned about losing control of America's youth. At the same time, the conservative Home Institute's use of the code word "teens" was an early recognition that there was a discrete youth world that had become enough of a social force to warrant its own brand name. Despite the efforts of adults, however, it would be the swing youth who pulled together all these different strands into a coherent subculture.

• • •

In January 1938, the Goodman Orchestra played its most prestigious date, right in the heart of classical culture, at Carnegie Hall. By then, the animalistic audience behaviour was almost ritualized. *Metronome* observed that the young went crazy during the climactic "Sing Sing Sing": "One kid after another commenced to create a new dance, trucking and shagging while sitting down. Older, penguin-looking men in traditional boxes on the sides went one better and proceeded to shag standing up." At the finale, the crowd "started to applaud, stamp, cheer, yell".

Young women were right at the front. Many fan club presidents were girls still in high school or college. Female swing fans were more identifiable than their male peers, adopting a style that consisted of blouses and sweaters, flat shoes, short white bobby socks, and a short pleated dress that swirled upwards on the dance floor. This was a costume adapted for comfort, practicality, and ease of movement. The Goodman Orchestra vocalist Helen Ward noticed how in the beginning, girls were "all dressed up, but when the lindy really caught on, the gals began wearing saddle shoes".

This was a far cry from the carefully policed sub-deb compound. To the young swing fan Leonard Pratt, more conservative girls who wore "high-heeled shoes, silk stockings, a pretty blue dress" were "out of place". As if rubbishing all those etiquette strictures, the freedoms allowed partaken of by female swing fans also included sex. "The girls would wave at us and many of the single boys in the band would motion to the girls to meet them at the stage door," Goodman's saxophonist Art Rollini remembered. "Fan mail poured into each member of the band, giving telephone numbers."

Male swing fans wore baggy trousers and long jackets, with long chains worn from belt to pocket or swung around the finger. Pork pie hats were also favoured, as well as fake-fur sweaters and bolero sleeves.[2] Much of this was taken from black urban styles, as were the dances performed by jitterbugs: the shag, the Lindy hop, the Suzie-Q. Benny Goodman clearly remembered seeing his first jitterbug in 1934, when a male dancer started to go "off his conk. His eyes rolled, his limbs began to spin like a windmill in a hurricane—his attention, riveted to the rhythm, transformed him into a whirling dervish."

These "neo-African" improvisations had begun when a "folk avant-garde" began improvising on the Charleston in Harlem. In his novel *Parties,* Carl Van

2. There was also Jitterbug Jewellery, sold in Macy's: pins in the shape of different musical instruments.

Vechten cited the Lindy hop's "first official appearance" as having occurred "at a Negro Dance Marathon staged at Manhattan Casino some time in 1928". The most unusual feature was the breakaway from your partner, where you could try "anything you could dream up". As the Lindy hop crossed over into the white audience, it morphed into something else: the most popular term for swing youth, the jitterbug, came from the dance's nervous, jumpy moves.[3]

Schooled in strict rhythm dancing, the late-thirties generation replaced grace and flow with raw, spasmodic energy. As the *New York Times* observed, "The white jitterbug is oftener than not uncouth to look at, but his Negro original is quite another matter. His movements are never so exaggerated that they lack control, and there is a most unmistakable dignity about his most violent figures." This grace was envied by swing fans who, like one Bronx high school student, "all wished we were old enough to go to the Savoy Ballroom, as that was where the really hip jitterbugs showed their stuff".

Like the Lindy hop and the Suzie-Q, jive talk suddenly became mainstream, so much so that it became the easiest identifier of swing culture for the non-converted. Cab Calloway helped the process along with his *Hepster's Dictionary*, first published in 1938. Beginning with the "cats", the band musicians, this glossary covered every facet of the swing life. The fans were "alligators", "jitterbugs", "rug-cutters", who did the Suzie-Q or "blew their wigs" to the "hide-beaters" "beating it out" in a "frolic pad". A "square", also called an "icky", was someone who didn't get the jive, who was "unhep".

These coinages spread like hair grease over the new magazines aimed at the swing market: not just *Down Beat* and *Metronome,* but fan publications like *Swing, Cats Meow, Jam Session,* and *Jitterbug.* This was a world unto itself. In "The Diary of a Jitterbug" the anonymous male narrator recounted his visit to "the big Swing Fest at Orchestra Hall" with "jitterbugs from the Cat's Meow": "Duke Ellington was there, suave and sophisticated, and his band certainly chilled us." The impenetrable outsider code of the late 1920s had been assumed by a large section of American youth.

This had been taken up as a fashion, but the roots came through. For Benny Goodman, the racial mix of his orchestra and the swing style grew "out of our brand of government". The British critic Francis Newton[4] considered that jazz was "a music of protest and rebellion". The progressive politics of the New Deal had a profound impact on swing. The figure at the centre of this link was

3. After the 1929 crash, the word "jitters" replaced "heebie-jeebies" as denoting extreme anxiety. "Jittersauce" was an established term for alcohol during Prohibition, reflecting the disastrous impact of poisoned hooch on the nervous system.

4. In fact the historian Eric Hobsbawm writing under a pseudonym.

the music industry maven John Hammond, who combined political activism with discovering, promoting, and recording artists like Billie Holiday, Bessie Smith, Fletcher Henderson, and Count Basie.

Hammond's influence struck a chord with Goodman, who had grown up in a poor Jewish environment: in 1937, Goodman donated $1,000 to the Committee to Aid Spanish Democracy and organized a benefit called "Stars for Spain". A practical expression of this link-up between swing music and left-wing politics was found in New York's first integrated cabaret and Popular Front nightclub, Café Society in Greenwich Village. Billed as the "Rendezvous of Celebs, Debs and Plebs", the club was attended by stars and celebrities like the boxer Joe Louis, Paul Robeson, even Eleanor Roosevelt.

Black musicians like Duke Ellington and Count Basie offered "an example and a goal" to young Negroes. For the writer Ralph Ellison, the exposure afforded to black musicians at a time when the only available heroes were sportsmen—like world heavyweight champion Joe Louis and the Olympic gold medal winner Jesse Owens—was "news from the outside world". He asked that "all those who write so knowledgeably of Negro boys having no masculine figures with whom to identify would consider the long and international career of Ellington and his band".

The relationship between all these factions was not always harmonious as swing became big business. Many Negroes in integrated bands were adored onstage and treated like dirt once out of the spotlight. The radio networks also feared boycotts by southern audiences and potential sponsors, and thus limited the airtime given to swing pioneers like Count Basie and Chick Webb. Negro bands thus missed out on the exposure, the public acclaim, and the earnings of their white peers. It was a rerun of the Harlem Renaissance.

Nor was the link-up between the left and swing always easy. There was a generation gap between the swing kids and their older counterparts. *Variety* noted that "the adolescents of 1938, thanks to swing and jitterbugging, were vastly different specimens from the serious, depression conscious youths of the early 1930's who had taken their revolt against their elders out by joining unions, and various 'progressive' movements. These youths, now in their late twenties, regarded their adolescent successors with undisguised contempt."

However, swing was unstoppable. In late August 1938, up to 100,000 fans packed Chicago's Soldier Field for a mass event called the Chicago Swing Jamboree. Almost as many thronged outside, pushing and shoving until "with a deafening groan" the gates burst open. Inside the atmosphere resembled "a barrelhouse, boogie-woogie, bacchanal": "It seemed that the whole younger generation of the city—a generation born since the World War and scarred by the depression—let down its hair, lost its hat, and danced wherever there was room to dance to the hot lick rhythms of gutbucket gorillas."

When the Jimmy Dorsey band went into "Flat Foot Floogie", the already rabid crowd erupted, rushing the dance platforms, climbing the stadium stands, sending the band rushing for cover, and breaking stage equipment. While order was restored, the fans made their own rhythms to accompany a group of young Negro men and women who snake-danced through the crowd. The Chicago press was shocked by this mass display of "jitterbug ecstasy": one paper called it "the strangest manifestation of youthful exuberance perhaps ever witnessed since the Middle Ages' ill-fated children's crusade".

But what was most alarming was the fact that the crowd was racially mixed—like the ideals promoted by the music itself. Swing made some inroads into segregation: the large orchestras, for instance, integrated a decade before sport or military organizations. This "melting pot" element was shocking to adult critics. The Catholic bishop of Dubuque denounced swing as "evil" and "communistic": "We permit jam sessions, jitterbug and cannibalistic rhythm orgies to occupy a place in our social scheme of things, wooing our youth along the primrose path to hell."

. . .

The increasing popularity and public prominence of swing represented the fact that, after nearly a decade of being lost and disadvantaged in the Great Depression, America's youth were beginning to regain their privileged status. This was reflected in Hollywood's output. The brutal, doomed outcasts of films like *The Public Enemy* and *Are These Our Children?* were replaced by the street kids of *Boys Town*—a major hit during 1938, starring Spencer Tracy and the ingenue Mickey Rooney—who were seen to respond to fair and sympathetic treatment. They were not essentially bad, just dealt a raw deal.

The Production Code meant that wild depictions of juvenile delinquency became rarer from mid-decade on. Apart from the Dead End Kids—the "derelict no good kids" who, alternating between cheek and menace, stole the otherwise stagey *Dead End*—Hollywood's principal adolescents were to be found in the Henry Aldrich and the Andy Hardy series. Set in that classic locus of the boy book, small-town America, these films were extremely popular: the star of the Andy Hardy series, Mickey Rooney, was the top US draw of 1939.

Unlike Hollywood, the music industry had no externally imposed code of conduct. It was not possible to ban the music because of its associations. Instead, the authorities began to look even more closely at the link between musicians and drugs, thrust into the spotlight by Louis Armstrong's high-profile arrest for marijuana in 1931—which occurred only a few months after Harry Anslinger had been appointed as the US commissioner of narcotic drugs. Lawmen have their own job-creation schemes just like anyone else: with the Volstead Act dead and buried, it was time for a new demon.

Anslinger specifically targeted marijuana as linked to jazz, and his campaign was furthered by widely circulated scare stories. The most famous was the July 1937 article that Harry Anslinger co-wrote with J. Edgar Hoover's amanuensis, Courtney Ryley Cooper, "Marijuana: Assassin of Youth". They set out to establish the increased popularity of the drug that they claimed was as dangerous as a "rattle-snake". In pulp confessions like *True*'s "I Was a Dope Fiend" and movies like the sensationalistic *Reefer Madness,* marijuana was implicated in a fresh explosion of juvenile delinquency, suicides and thrill-killing.

Anslinger's promotion of the drug as the new public enemy number one was highly successful. In 1937, the passing of the Marijuana Tax Act made non-medical possession illegal. He also sought to extend the link between musicians and the drug: during the 1930s, almost every major swing band recorded at least one reefer, or "viper", number. However, marijuana did not cross over into the white audience to any great degree. Even Courtney Ryley Cooper's synoptic, if not hysterical, late-thirties survey of juvenile delinquency, *Designs in Scarlet,* found very little hard evidence of its use.

These campaigns did not succeed in preventing swing from becoming an acknowledged part of the American adolescent mainstream. *Life*'s survey of the "Youth Problem: 1938" featured, among its carefully chosen representative types, an eighteen-year old "white collar boy" from Maryland, Kenneth Jones, who neither smoked nor drank and wanted to be "a Republican politician". However, this everykid spent the free time from his insurance job drumming in a swing band and playing Jimmie Lunceford records with "his girl".

To some commentators, the enthusiasm of these young jazz fans offered much-needed optimism and oomph: a tonic for a tired country. "Swing is the voice of youth striving to be heard in this fast-moving world of ours," the *New York Times* opined in early 1939. "Swing is the tempo of our time. Swing is real. Swing is alive." As American culture continued to travel across the Atlantic, swing's musical excitement and siren freedom calls struck a chord with the young Europeans who, facing the living death of fascism or the dead-end greyness of unemployment, began to a dream of something more.

· · ·

Swing began to arrive in Europe during the later 1930s. The British and French taste for hot jazz had been established during the 1920s, and the flame had been kept alive by a hard core of student fans who flocked to see visiting stars like Louis Armstrong. Cab Calloway's 1935 visit to the United Kingdom was marked by a gig in Manchester where "people climbed all over the stage and then tried to tear our clothes off as we left the theater". By the mid-1930s, there were magazines devoted to *Hot Music* and *Swing*, and the French critic Charles Delaunay published his ground-breaking *Hot Discography*.

Swing's entry into Britain was hindered by the 1935 Musicians' Union ban on visiting American bands. The prevailing fashion was for prescribed steps—the foxtrot, the waltz, the quickstep—but towards the end of the decade freestyling swing began to become more popular. In November 1938, a Mass-Observation reporter at the Streatham Locarno noted a new dance style called "trucking": "The idea of swing music is that you make it up as you go along; these people are doing swing with their feet, freelance shufflings and jigging; it's all a long way from the formalised foxtrotting steps." The animal dances had returned under a different guise, and as in the 1910s, they were, for many ballroom-goers, an alien interruption.

In neither Britain nor France was the assumption of the swing style thought exceptional. However, in Germany, being a swing fan was more dangerous. The regime had despised jazz from the beginning. Their view was summarized by a Hitler Youth leader in summer 1936: "The Nigger has a very pronounced feeling for rhythm, and his 'art' is perhaps indigenous but nonetheless offensive to our sentiments. Surely such stuff belongs among the Hottentots and not in a German dance hall. The Jew, on the other hand, has cooked these aberrations up on purpose."

Nazi Germany had been a heavily censored state from its very early days. In September 1933, Propaganda Minister Joseph Goebbels had instituted the Reichskulturkammer, with six separate sections for radio, theatre, film, creative writing, the press, and music. The Reichsmusikkammer set out to control the activities of every single musician in Germany, introducing membership cards, without which playing in public was forbidden. In December 1937, "alien" music was officially proscribed.

The Reichsrundfunkkammer censored radio. This medium was integral to Goebbels's propaganda, and apart from Nazi speeches and songs, he filled it with quality light-entertainment music. Jazz presented a thorny problem, having enjoyed considerable success in Weimar Germany in the hands of visitors like Josephine Baker or Sidney Bechet, or home-grown bands like Stefan Weintraub's Syncopators. Although seen by many Nazis as "the rot of a decaying society", hot jazz was part of the technological, consumerist society that the regime continued to promote right up until the late 1930s.

Controlling the mass media was easier said than done. The remaining hot clubs made full use of the gaps in their totalitarian state. Until late 1937, small groups in Düsseldorf (the International Rhythm Club), Berlin (the Melodie Klub), and other cities like Leipzig were still able to buy German-produced jazz records. At the same time, they could travel within Germany to see bands. Thanks to the powerful transmitter of Radio Luxembourg, they could also hear uncensored shows and, as international travel was not restricted until 1938, even go abroad to meet their idols.

The status of jazz remained ambiguous. It was actively targeted by the Hitler Youth police group after the law of 1936. There were frequent scenes like the destruction of records that occurred when some stormtroopers found a group of adolescents listening to jazz on a Baltic beach. Reichsmusikkammer spies, easily recognizable by their shabby dress, were regularly spotted in nightclubs and ballrooms. At the same time, Goebbels was forced to bow to the German taste for jazz by showcasing, late at night, a minimum of tepid home-grown productions on the German network.

The difficulties of being a jazz buff were willingly endured because the music held the promise of another world. The cohort born between 1920 and 1925 had borne the brunt of the pressure to join the Hitler Youth, but a small but persistent number of hot clubs continued to live the jazz life as far as was possible. The members of Werner Daniels's International Rhythm Club, based in Düsseldorf, all adopted Anglo-American names and hailed each other with the greeting "Swing high". Identifying with Harlem Negroes rather than the Hitler Youth, they formed an amateur jazz band before land service duty claimed them.

The biggest group was the Hamburg Swing Youth. Centred around cosmopolitan adolescents like the half-Cypriot Demetrius "Kaki" Georgiadis and the Dutch-born Greek Andreas Panagopoulous, an "ice-rink clique" formed during the winter of 1937. They first gathered at their wealthy parents' houses, wearing outrageous clothes and displaying an insulting predilection for English music. At this stage, their impulse was nothing more than to have fun. However, when they started to go public, parading up and down the city's most fashionable streets whistling swing refrains, the trouble started.

The introduction of the "social dance" called "swing" in the second half of 1937 brought jazz fans into open conflict with the authorities. Loosely based on the Lindy hop seen in the American film *Broadway Melody of 1936,* the swing dance emphasized loose-limbed pair movement. There was cheek-to-cheek dancing, but, according to the historian Michael Kater, the partners "usually followed the hectic speed of the propulsive band, jiving to and away from each other and exuding sexuality". Compared to the ersatz Nazi version, this wild dance was more exciting to its "Swing Heini" or "Swing Baby" practitioners.

However, it contravened the rigid, militaristic discipline that the Nazis sought to inculcate in all German youth. During 1937, the SS explicitly denounced Benny Goodman and George Gershwin. This was followed up by local interdictions against public jazz dancing. In Hamburg, the local warden condemned the swing dance as "one of the most terrible outgrowths of the Negro dance period". In Berlin, the Moka Efti ballroom was posted with similar *verboten* signs. However, these attempts at control were successfully ignored by the Swing Heinis. Goebbels's panopticon was not yet all-seeing.

. . .

In turn, the Nazi virus had crossed the Atlantic. In February 1939, the German-American Bund held its largest rally yet in Madison Square Garden. "The great hall was jammed with 20,000 men, women and many children," wrote the undercover investigator John Roy Carlson. "High above the speakers' platform towered a huge figure of George Washington, flanked by giant swastikas. From somewhere in the rear of the hall came the muffled sound of drumbeats as a uniformed Nazi legion, 1200 strong, marched in behind the swastika flags and the banners of the German National-Socialist Party!"

Despite the avowed intention by Fascist organizations to form youth groups in colleges around the country, the young men to whom this course of action appealed were mostly "from broken or demoralized homes, and had records of sex crimes, incorrigibility, petty theft or other unsocial behaviour". Carlson noted the dialogue of a "typical" follower of Father Charles E. Coughlin, dialect and all: "'Read Social Justice and loin how to solve the Jewish question.' 'How?' I turned to the pimply youth in his early teens. 'Line them up against the wall and give 'em the rat-tat-tat!'"

The bitter street battles formed the setting for James T. Farrell's novel about a young Coughlinite, *Tommy Gallagher's Crusade*. His young Fascist might have been little more than a nuisance, but the German-American Bund was a more serious political threat. Formed by Fritz Julius Kuhn, a veteran of the Munich putsch,[5] the Bund's aim was to whip up support for Hitler in the United States and to give German Americans, victims of prejudice during the Great War, an opportunity to learn about their heritage. In its youth programmes, children were taught to speak German and to salute the swastika.

5. He had emigrated to Detroit to work at the Ford plant, and was encouraged by the anti-Semitism expressed by Henry Ford in the *Dearborn Independent*.

When Carlson infiltrated a Bund camp in Long Island—one of twenty-four in America—he found a mini-Nazi state: "At three o'clock a car drove up and twelve uniformed members of the *Jugendschaft* filed out. The *Jugendschaft* (male Youth Division of the Bund) was modeled directly on the Hitler Youth. They wore swastika buttons and carried their emblem—a short flash of jagged lightning set against a black background. The short daggers they carried were inscribed *'Blut und Ehre'*—Blood and Honor—signifying eternal allegiance to the Fatherland."

These malign phenomena took place against the worsening international situation. By the summer, America's mood was as tense as the humid weather: the daily papers were full of the Danzig crisis, with columns advocating the isolationist position. In August, a *New York Daily Mirror* front page pictured a nineteen-year-old Brooklyn Bund member named Helen Vooros giving a Nazi salute. Her testimony to the Dies un-American Investigating Committee was unequivocal: "Germany," she said, "hoped to conquer the United States in the future."

This threat resonated because, ten years after the crash, over a quarter of all school-leavers were failing to find work. The 1920s baby boomers were dangerously adrift. A major American Youth Commission survey, *Youth Tell Their Story*, reported that America's adolescents "do a lot of loafing and would rather do something else". Courtney Ryley Cooper estimated that "four and five million young persons between the ages of sixteen and twenty five are out of school and out of work and wandering aimlessly about their communities looking for some outlet for their energies".

America's youth was apparently ripe for anything—murder, riot, or revolution—and at this crux moment there was, according to the essayist and journalist Walter Lippman, "no sure faith" that would enlist their support. Writing a keynote essay for *Life* magazine's June 1939 cover story on "America's Future", Lippman invoked John Fiske's idea of America's Manifest Destiny. "Our personal preferences count for little in the great movements of history," he concluded. "What Rome was to the ancient world, what Great Britain has been to the modern world, America is to be to the world of tomorrow."

The impetus behind this crystal-ball gazing came from the opening of the 1939 World's Fair in Flushing Meadows, New York. Ever since the Chicago Expo of 1893, America had excelled at these theatrical events. Entitled "The World of Tomorrow", the 1939 fair was a genuinely global exhibition, with contributions from over sixty nations (excepting Germany). At the same time, the streamlined shapes of the pavilions and the twinned fair logo of the Perisphere and the Trylon were reproduced throughout the world: dream symbols of the forthcoming technological utopia.

The World's Fair attracted a lot of pre-publicity. "Once you have glimpsed the World of Tomorrow," enthused *Harper's Bazaar*, "you can never look back." The *Harper's* story sold the fair to an adolescent readership: "On April 30, 1939, we are going to start looking into the future. Not the future as evoked by old ladies in gypsy tea rooms but the real future, told by scientists, architects, artists, inventors, and lighting experts in a fantastic new world, risen from a dump heap on the Flushing plains. You may enter it a girl of today. You'll come out a girl of tomorrow."

. . .

During this hot, listless high summer, Metro-Goldwyn-Mayer premiered *The Wizard of Oz* in New York. It had taken two years for this version of Baum's classic to reach the screen, nearly forty years after the book's first publication. The studio had planned the film as an epic to compete with the market domination of Fox's Shirley Temple, the biggest box-office draw of 1936, 1937, and 1938. It was also designed to coincide with the contemporary Hollywood mode that screenwriters Florence Ryerson and Edgar Allan Woolf called "a stampede back to the simple, untroubled hours of childhood".

To achieve this idyllic simplicity, *The Wizard of Oz* had been a remarkably complex shoot. With many set pieces, a huge cast of extras, and sweeping technological innovations, the production lasted nearly six months and went way over budget, ending up at nearly double the cost of a typical major MGM picture. The studio had some serious recouping to do, and set in motion a massive promotional blitz that began in May 1939 and continued building over the next three months up to the saturation booking of the film nationwide.

All media were included, whether free postcards, giveaway flyers, cinema lobby banners, posters, tie-in products, and lavish campaign books, or a multitude of different stills and stories each precisely targeted at different mainstream magazines and newspapers. The film's theme tune, "Over the Rainbow" had been intended by writers Yip Harburg and Harold Arlen as "a song of yearning". Performed by the film's sixteen-year-old female lead, Judy Garland, it was, by August, the most frequently played tune in the country.

MGM decided to send Judy Garland out on tour to coincide with the film's premiere in each city. The rising star would be accompanied by the country's top juvenile: Garland and Mickey Rooney had already been established as a duo in 1938's *Love Finds Andy Hardy*, and the studio wished to promote their forthcoming musical *Babes in Arms*. Both were accomplished and popular vaudeville veterans, but no one could have predicted the response that began with the pair's first appearance—in Washington on August 9—and that built over the next three days in Connecticut.

In New York, the pre-hype reached a crescendo. The competition to be one of the 150-strong "official welcoming committee" had attracted 250,000 replies. When Garland and Rooney arrived in Manhattan at midday on Monday, August 14, the selected few were swamped by a "screaming, delirious, perspiring roped off mob" of 10,000 fans who filled Grand Central Station. The *New York Daily News* pictured Judy Garland stretched in a crucifixion pose between two rescuing policeman, her face contorted in a rictus of pain and shock.

On the day of the official opening at the Capitol Theater, Thursday the seventeenth, the queue began forming on Broadway at 5.30 a.m. By the time the 5,000 tickets went on sale at 8 a.m., police estimated that 15,000 were outside the theatre, eventually forming a line that went five and six deep around the block between 50th and 51st Streets, Broadway and Eighth Avenue. This time, reporters took a closer look at this predominantly female swarm and observed that "about sixty per cent of the multitude were minors".

Stunned by their reception, Garland and Rooney quickly recovered themselves and gave their professional best in the dance and vocal numbers that interspersed the performances of the film itself. By the end of the day, they had given seven shows to 37,000 customers: according to the *Hollywood Reporter*, "The overflow filled almost all the other Broadway houses, jammed the restaurants, soft drink parlors, and candy stores." With rave notices, this pattern continued for nearly two weeks until Rooney's final appearance on August 30: packed performances, jammed streets, mobbed stars.

There had been other mass demonstrations for film actors: most notably after Rudolph Valentino's death in August 1926. However, this particular takeover of Manhattan's streets was marked by the nature of the crowd—not ghoulish and not violent—and the nature of the stars, this time very much alive. It happened almost despite Hollywood, which had very little idea of the adolescent market. Despite the hype, *The Wizard of Oz* had not been planned as a youth film, but as a fairy tale that had become subsumed within the rising popularity of its two stars.

Nor were they typical adolescents. Judy Garland and Mickey Rooney were highly specialized products of an insecure, itinerant vaudeville upbringing: hardly the kids next door. They also embodied the age elision that had marked adolescent marketing thus far. Although honoured by Hollywood as "the spirit and personification of youth", Rooney was five feet three inches tall, small for his age. At seventeen, he could look twelve, as he did in his 1938 vehicle *Boys*

Town: "Most boy actors reach an age where they start growing and reach what they call the gangling age," he said, "then they have to quit. I didn't grow that way."

His co-star was just as freakish. Signed to the "feudal kingdom" of Metro-Goldwyn-Mayer in 1935, Judy Garland had been made over from the age of thirteen. Her body—deficient from Hollywood's perspective—was ruthlessly reshaped: corsets for the waist, caps for the teeth, benzedrine in 1937 when the weight became too much. Sixteen during the *Oz* filming, Garland had her breasts taped so that she would look twelve—somewhere between the child Dorothy of the book and the full adolescent of the 1902 *Oz* stage show. But the industrial process of turning humans into stars meant nothing to the fans.

The hunger of the young crowd—for something of their own, for an excuse to act out—made the event. Once they got inside the Capitol, they found what they wanted: dazzling new technology that gave the colour sequences "a strange, heightened quality" and offered a metaphor for their own situation. As the film jumped from monochrome sepia to hyper-vivid colour, they saw Dorothy's drab life opening out into a quest for freedom, friendship, and transformation, where you could find friends like yourself and become who you wanted to be.

On August 27, Judy Garland and Mickey Rooney visited the World's Fair, specially kept open for the freshly crowned royalty of the new youth culture. For a couple of hours, they rode the Stratoship, the Aerial Joyride, the Road of Tomorrow around the Ford Building. They visited the Theater of Time and Space, and the Theme Exhibit of the World's Fair, where you could gaze down at "Democracity," the "planned and integrated garden city of tomorrow". It was, Garland later remembered, "the most wonderful night of my life".

On August 29, Macy's of New York splashed out on full-page ads for the "Judy Garland Dresses" that were on sale in their special "Youth Centre". There was also a tie-in to the Capitol shows and a sidebar showing a "Wizard of Oz" hat. "Designed for and selected by Judy Garland herself," these waisted crepe and wool items were targeted at "Teen Age girls who are exactly Judy's age . . . growing girls with grown up ideas. They firmly believe that no one is too young for a certain amount of glamour." Three days later, Europe went to war.

PART VI

1939-1943

CHAPTER 22

Conquerors and Overlords

The Hitler Youth at War and at Home

• • •

In every era of history one law has invariably proved its unchanging truth: youth will always triumph over age. The old nations must disappear when the hour strikes. Who can reasonably expect any other outcome at this time when one nation, become conscious of the power of its youth, sees in another merely a group of quarrelsome old men who lost faith even in their own people? To express it another way, the secret of our military victories lies in our conquest over the symptoms of age.

—*Schwarze Korps*, SS publication, August 1940

HITLER YOUTH AS FIREFIGHTER
POSTER, 1940s

IF TOTALITARIANISM WAS one of the key inventions of the twentieth century, then Nazi Germany was its most vigorous manifestation: a quasi-occult state built around the principles of war, sacrifice, death, and total control. As the government's organizational head, Dr Robert Ley stated, in "National Socialist Germany, such a thing as a private individual does not exist". In the Nazis' world, there was no grey, no in between. Everything was black and white, for or against. This was National Socialism reduced to a stark choice, victory or annihilation, and Germany's adolescents were on the front line.

Although the vast majority of young Germans were Hitler Youth in September 1939, that was not enough. Soon after the outbreak of war, there were at least four bodies with responsibility for youth policing, punishing dissidents or backsliders with a variety of escalating forfeits: weekend arrest, labour camp, concentration camp, or execution. Of the eighteen hundred or so inmates killed for political reasons during the Second World War in one prison, the Zuckthaus Brandenburg, seventy-five were under twenty, twenty-two were students and school pupils, and one was just over sixteen.

The mobilization entailed by total war demanded even more controls, even more fanaticism, as the Nazis' obsessive tinkering with education reached new heights. In December 1940, Adolf Hitler outlined his vision for the new elite institutions of Nazi Germany. These were to admit the sons of workers and peasants who would not have previously entered higher education: "It is marvellous that we imagine a state in which in the future every position will be occupied by the ablest sons of our people, irrespective of their origin, a state in which birth means nothing and achievement and ability everything."

But, as ever, there was a mortal enemy. In the same speech, Hitler railed against democracy: "These two worlds are the ones that confront each other today. On their side we can see a state governed by a thin crust, the upper class, who send their sons automatically to specific institutions like Eton College. On our side we see the Adolf Hitler schools and the National Political Education Institutes. Two worlds. In the one case the children of the people, in the other only the sons of a financial aristocracy. I admit one of the two worlds will have to break."

After 1939 the Fascist Germany was pitted against the capitalist democracies. Before then, the Führer had damned the third element in this global power play, the Soviet Union, and indeed, had risen to power on the back of his party's rabid anti-communism. After the Soviet-German pact of August 1939, however, the Nazi war machine was free to set its sights on Western Europe. The Stalinist regime, meanwhile, began the war by participating in the carve-up of Poland. Between the opposing forces of the three mass societies, the youth of Europe was caught in an unyielding vise.

. . .

In September 1939, German youth were better prepared for war than any others in the world. With their general pre-military training and specialized expertise in marine, motor, and air formations, the Hitler Youth passed effortlessly into the highly drilled fighting machine that, for a few seasons, swept all before it. Down the countries fell like ninepins: Poland in October 1939, the Netherlands in May 1940, Belgium two weeks later, France just under four weeks later. Successful campaigns were also undertaken in Norway, Denmark, Finland, North Africa, and western Russia.

At the outbreak of war, the Hitler Youth numbered 8,870,000 boys and girls. The youngest of these had been born in 1929, the eldest in 1921, and they had already undergone years of harsh training. Militarism and expansion had been part of Nazi ideology from its very beginnings in Hitler's *Mein Kampf*: "Oppressed countries will not be brought back into the bosom of a common Reich by means of fiery protests, but by a mighty sword." The honing of that instrument had accelerated in the late 1930s, with Hitler's successful annexations and the refinement of the Nazi educational system.

The great majority of German adolescents had virtually no experience of democracy, free expression, or free movement. The regime had a deep understanding of what motivated German youth, its need for activity and independence, which they satisfied with a system of education that emphasized romantic national myths as well as promoting sport, quasi-military activities, and an extreme racist ideology. As Adolf Hitler wrote in *Mein Kampf*, "He who wants to live should fight, and he who does not want to battle in this world of eternal struggle does not deserve to be alive."

Selfless enthusiasm and reckless idealism had been a part of German youth culture since the early days of the *Wandervogel*. The continuum between Hitler Youth service and armed service was so seamless that most young Germans made the transition without question. Many signed up for adventure, as a Luftwaffe radio operator remembered: "I was only 17 and hadn't started to shave—political considerations weren't determining my choice. We were troublemakers, tough kids, and we wanted experience and adventure."

Even doubters like Melita Maschmann, old enough to remember the last conflict's aftermath, were swayed by war fever. Travelling eastwards by train to the occupied territories, she had a revelation: "A voice inside me suddenly said: 'It is war: now you have nothing more to fear.' 'What do you mean?' I asked. 'I don't understand.' For some time there was silence within me and then the voice replied: 'When you are dead you have nothing more to fear—have you?' 'No,' I said, 'I haven't.' 'Well, for yourself you are now dead.' Everything that was *I* had been absorbed into the *Whole!*"

Germany's young were swept along by a seemingly unstoppable wave of nationalist euphoria. The stunning victories of 1939 and 1940 totally legitimized Nazi ideology for most Germans. Not only had the humiliations of 1918 been reversed, but Hitler's wildest pronouncements had also been given concrete reality. The establishment of the thousand-year Reich appeared imminent—not just within Europe but throughout the world—and this would be an empire of German youth. At the turn of the 1940s, they felt themselves invincible, part of an unstoppable juggernaut.

. . .

After the outbreak of war, any pretence that the Hitler Youth was not a military organization completely disappeared. Baldur von Schirach immediately set about directing the vast resource of nearly nine million young Germans into the many and varied demands of blitzkrieg. During the last few months of 1939, over a million Hitler Youth were actively deployed in the war effort. At least a quarter of all their leaders had been immediately called up so the position of *Unterbannführer,* responsible for five to six hundred boys, was granted to sixteen- to seventeen-year-olds: youth truly leading youth.

The pre-war frenzy of activities was now concentrated in assisting the fatherland's *Kampf.* All fit sixteen- and seventeen-year-olds were immediately drafted in to help bring in the harvest, as part of obligatory land service. In the cities, Hitler Youths delivered call-up cards and ration papers. Bund Deutscher Mädel and Jungmädel girls helped to evacuate young children from the war zone in Germany's east. Some also staffed field hospitals and state kindergartens, and acted as greeting girls at railway stations, offering drink and food for in-transit troops.

All Hitler Youth pitched in by calling on every residence to collect materials required for the war effort: copper, razor blades, scrap metal, paper, brass, and bottles. These mundane tasks were undertaken as passionately as any sporting competition. One former Hitler Youth remembered an enthusiastic colleague: "On the back, a satchel stuffed with bottles, in the left hand, a basket full of them, balanced only by a massive net on the right hand, also full of bottles. And all that beneath a face looking as though through him and his bottles the war would be won."

In 1940—designated as "The Year of Trial" for the Hitler Youth—Baldur von Schirach was replaced as *Reichsjugendführer* by Artur Axmann, who set about streamlining the organization and further adapting the Hitler Youth to military requirements. The new training schedules required Jungvolk to spend two hours a week in physical exercise and four in team sports on Sunday mornings. For those adolescents nearing combat age, there were four hours a week of marksmanship training and terrain exercises.

The biggest task specifically entrusted to the Hitler Youth was the administration of the rapidly expanding German empire. In Western Europe, the conquerors set up sympathetic governments and allowed them to rule with a reasonable amount of autonomy as long as they followed the Nazi line. Many posts were filled by long-term Fascist organizations, like Anton Mussert's Nationaal-Socialistische Beweging in the Netherlands. France was divided up. The Southern Zone was headed by Marshal Pétain, while the north's Occupied Zone was run by the Nazi general Otto von Stulpnagel.

In these countries, life carried on as normally as possible after an invasion, unless you were a Jew. In Holland and France, Jews were subject to an increasing amount of controls and restrictions until the universal introduction of the yellow star in the summer of 1942. In the east, however, the full nature of Nazi terror was instantly unleashed. The Polish campaign was marked by the extreme savagery of the *Einsatzkommandos*: the aim was to wipe out Poland's ruling and professional classes, and so priests, intellectuals, teachers—indeed anyone of local prominence—all were simply taken away and shot.

The Nazis' plan was aimed to repopulate whole swaths of Europe with their chosen race, the German minority groups from eastern Central Europe and ethnic Germans from the long-disputed areas of Upper Silesia, the "corridor" of Danzig and West Prussia, and East Prussia. The section of western Poland renamed the Warthegau was specifically earmarked by Hitler as the testing ground for the establishment of racially pure German satellites. He chose Himmler and Axmann to implement these policies, in tandem. This was the new frontier, and the Hitler Youth were the pioneers.

Melita Maschmann arrived in Posnan as chief press officer during October 1939. She found the land cold and hostile, the towns smelly and archaic, and the people stupid and degraded. However, she supported the mission to colonize Poland with ethnic Germans. In contrast to some of her fellow "Reich Germans", who she felt were "working off personal neuroses in their political behaviour", she believed in her "noble and difficult service", as she later wrote, "by which we believed ourselves to be fulfilling our duty towards the Reich. For the individual it meant more than an increase of self-esteem."

Despite the hostile environment, the "colonisation work" helped to heal "the wounds which our sense of honour had suffered in our childhood and early youth". Travelling through the Warthegau as a "cultural missionary", Maschmann found compensations for the difficult conditions: "Bureaucracy was not yet in command there: almost everyone was a little king in his own field of action. There was room for boldness, imagination and enterprise." As the months went on, she realized that her work symbolized an opportunity for German women to prove themselves as equals.

However, that immediate task was not yet accomplished. Sent in the summer of 1941 to an "Eastern Venture" camp in a remote district, Maschmann submitted to her Führer's edict that "we must not spare our strength for a single minute". She found herself besieged by adult responsibilities: "Excessive demands were being made upon us all the time. We had to force ourselves to adopt an air of outward superiority, irrespective of whether we were inwardly mature enough to deal with a situation, and so one found that the things one attempted generally 'came off'."

The heady days of blitzkrieg were nearly over, as the battleground changed from the "civilized" west to the barbarous east. In June 1941, Hitler tore up the Nazi-Soviet pact and sent three million Germans east over the old Polish and Romanian borders. This would be a war of total destruction. One of those caught in the advance was a sixteen-year-old German Jew named Solomon Perel: "Whenever the suspicious soldiers had the slightest doubt about a man, they ordered him to drop his trousers. If he was circumcised, they cursed at him and made him join the group headed for the forest. There he was shot."

. . .

The opening of a second front also cemented the increasing influence of the SS within the Hitler Youth. For the ambitious young, joining the SS was a favoured option. By the end of 1940, the Waffen-SS strength stood at 150,000— a separate army specifically selected for the war in the east. During 1941, the SS recruitment tsar Gottlob Berger began to target the seventeen- and eighteen-year-olds of the class of 1923. In February 1942, Himmler issued a secret directive to the effect that the Waffen-SS could forcibly recruit under-age youth without permission from guardians or parents.

In the occupied territories, the initial SS involvement was in administration, leaving the Hitler Youth and the Bund Deutscher Mädel to do the groundwork. But after 1940, the back-to-the-land imperative pioneered by the Artamanen, the agrarian-racist youth group to which Himmler had belonged, became top priority. The Landdienst, yoked to the SS since 1938, became a prime focus. "Good defence-peasants" were what Himmler wanted: in October 1940, Artur Axmann entrusted the Landdienst with putting the Artamanen "declaration of war on a liberal world" on a "much wider and broader base".

The importance of this policy was spelled out in 1942, designated as the "Year of Service in the East and on the Land": according to Axmann, "Youth must be closely tied in with this annexed territory. The East is Germany's fate." That year 18,000 Hitler Youth leaders served in the Ukraine and Poland while 30,000 boys and girls carried out their service in the east. Like Maschmann, they worked as colonizers, teachers, and farmers, helping to create an infrastructure within a depopulated, blasted region. An important part of this land service was to indoctrinate the Germanic youth from the occupied territories.

Most did what their new overlords told them in order to survive. However, a small minority throughout north-western Europe actively supported Nazi aims and activities: a few were committed Fascists, but many more believed in the Nazi vision of a newly united Europe. In this, the fight against the hated Bolshevists was a crucial selling point. Youths from Denmark, Holland, Belgium, Estonia, Latvia, Norway, and Alsace-Lorraine poured into the newly expanded Reich. Once passed as racially pure, they were put through the *Nationalpolitische Erziehungsanstalten* for full indoctrination.

These elite schools had been given the green light for expansion after Hitler's December 1940 speech, and they became more aggressively ideological as they became increasingly dominated by the SS. As the war continued, many experienced *Nationalpolitische Erziehungsanstalt* teachers were replaced by SS nominees. These schools also began to spread throughout the eastern territories, initiating selected youth from the whole of occupied Western Europe in the doctrines of racial superiority and extreme violence. The ultimate career option was service in the Waffen-SS.

Although lesser in number, the Adolf Hitler schools were even more rabid. The central tenet of their curriculum was an unquestioning acceptance of National Socialist doctrines and mythology, which vitiated the schools' professed principle of pupil "self-government". Their prime purpose was to create a new class that would administer the rapidly expanding Nazi empire—in an echo of the rapid development of the British public school system in the mid-nineteenth century. This bureaucracy, however, would not involve any hint of Christian ideals but the brutality of total racial subjugation.

Solomon Perel, renamed Josef Perjell, arrived at one of these elite schools in 1942. He had convinced his German captors that he was an ethnic German and so was a prime candidate for Nazi fast-tracking. As he recalled, "The courtyard was bordered by two-storey residential houses. There was an Olympic-sized swimming pool, a cinder track, and various areas for gymnastics and team games. At the far end of the courtyard, on the gable of a tall neo-gothic structure, was the inscription *Kraft durch Freude* (Strength through Joy). This building housed the dining room."

Youths from all over the new German Reich attended the school, which was designed to "train new generations of leaders for the various party organizations". The students were grouped into several homes, each with a special sphere: navy, air force, communications, motorized Hitler Youth, and the SS. Even the furnishing and fittings were ideological: in the bedrooms were mottoes about "how 'the purity of German blood' was being preserved primarily in the rural farm areas". Another poster reproduced Hitler's "hard as Krupp steel" exhortation to German youth.

Armed with his "blood and honour" Hitler Youth dagger, Perjell entered the regime, studying *Mein Kampf* and Alfred Rosenberg's *The Myth of the 20th Century*, and participating in Race Studies classes that taught "the Characteristic and Distinguishing Feature of Jews". The seventeen-year-old was terrified at being "a lone fighter in a sea of swastikas": "I realised that I had entered the lion's den. If—God forbid!—they had discovered I was Jewish, they would have surely have torn me to pieces like beasts of prey. Once this terrible fear became lodged in me, I could never quite rid myself of it."

Perjell had to sing one refrain translated as "We'll be better off once Jewish blood spurts from our knives": "Something terrible, a barbaric inhuman odium, clung to this song. The tramping of German hobnailed boots could be heard far and wide. Millions of terrorized people were fleeing before them. The words of another of their songs heralded occupation and destruction: '*Wir werden weiter marschieren, bis alles in Scheiben fällt / Heute gehört uns Deutschland und morgen die ganze Welt.*' (We will march onwards until everything is destroyed / Today Germany is ours, tomorrow the whole world)."

The youths marched into the dining hall, which was festooned with flaming swastikas: "Nobody sat down right away. They were all standing stiff and straight as pokers, their eyes directed to a small gallery below the high ceiling at the front of the hall. There, behind a microphone, sat the home leader getting ready to speak. Solemnly he waited until the last whisper had died down. . . . A deathly silence reigned. And the home leader spoke: the acoustics of the hall, which were comparable to a cathedral, amplified his voice. . . . I picked up a few words: 'Keep the race pure . . . be strong.'"

Within this elite, the Waffen-SS represented the crowning pinnacle. As one member recalled, this privileged cohort "were the first to receive camouflage jackets; they had outstanding equipment; and they knew they had the honour of being used where they were desperately needed. The overriding thought on everybody's mind was, 'When are we going to get to the front: where will the next mission, the next test at the front be?'" These were the shock troops of Nazism, the ultimate embodiment of the sacrificial demands made upon adolescence by the regime. They were born to die.

September 1942 saw a huge convocation of all Europe's Fascist movements in Vienna for a rally to found the "European Youth League". This was intended to cement the new German order. Participants included Italy's Fascist youth movement, the youth movement of the Spanish Falange, the Walloon Rexist Youth, the Flemish National Socialist Youth, the Norwegian Nasjonal-Samling Youth, the Finnish Youth Movement, the Romanian State Youth, the Hungarian Levente Youth, the Dutch and Danish National Socialist Youth, as well as representatives from Japan, Bulgaria, and France.

The new world order of Fascist youth seemed imminent. However, as Melita Maschmann was beginning to discover on the ground in the Warthegau, the everyday practice did not quite come up to the crusading ideal. First, the bureaucrats had arrived, and with them, the corruption that she had feared. Her frequent encounters with higher functionaries affronted her perfectionism: "One day, I believed, these third rate Party Bosses would die out and then a generation would take charge who had learned to practise voluntary self-discipline as youth leaders."

She was also forced to realize that not all her fellow Germans shared her fervent beliefs. Maschmann was baffled by the attitude of her working-class charges: "These girls were furious to be sent so far from their homes. They had been earning good money in the armaments industry and now they were supposed to do a job for which they had not the slightest inclination, in return for pocket money consisting of—I believe—of thirty *pfennigs* a day. In addition they had to put up with never being allowed to do what they wanted after work in the evenings, and only rarely at weekends."

This was a true clash of the classes: "They were bored by every kind of instruction. Most of them thought our folk dances and the songs we sang with them ridiculous. What they wanted were pop songs and American dances. Their conversation revolved around sex, and despite their youth some of them already had considerable experience in this field." For Maschmann, this was a true failure. As she admitted, "I was all the more disheartened because when I first became a youth leader in the National Socialist movement, fellowship with the young working class was the one thing I had romantically yearned for."

Even this fervent disciple of Nazism could not help noticing the Jewish ghettos, but she firmly closed her mind: "If I had enquired further, I should have become inextricably entangled in conflicts which would have caused the total collapse of my 'world'. Clearly our subconscious energies—and I can speak here for my companions—were fully concentrated on protecting us from such crises. It is from such experiences that one can recognise the terrible power which so called ideologies can exercise over young people. Once they have surrendered to them, they see without seeing and hear without hearing."

During late 1942, the Nazi state reached its zenith. Its military machine had fulfilled almost every one of Hitler's wildest promises and, with Moscow in sight, appeared set to achieve the ultimate prize. However, for all the regime's extraordinary success in subjugating a large swath of Europe, including its own population, there was a void at its centre. Once the tide of war began to ebb away from Nazi Germany, the invulnerability felt by Germany's youth would be replaced by fear, anger, or blind sacrifice unto the end.

CHAPTER 23

Reluctant Conscripts and Socialist Heroes

British Youth at War

. . .

By the time the children of today are grown up, it should be about time to have another war.

—"Garage girl, 19" from "US 12", *Mass-Observation Weekly Report*, April 19, 1940

WOMAN WORKER ROLLING A BOMB, UK, EARLY 1940s

BRITAIN MOBILIZED LATE. It was only after the Munich crisis in September 1938 that the Nazi threat became widely apparent and thousands flocked to join the Territorial Army. In April 1939, the government introduced peacetime conscription for the first time in British history: this applied to young men of twenty and twenty-one, who were called up for six months. On the outbreak of war, with 400,000 men in both the regular and the territorial armies alike, all men between eighteen and forty-one became liable for military service.

By the end of the year, over one and a half million men were in the armed forces, the vast bulk in the army. Unlike their German counterparts, their mood was neither overtly enthusiastic nor jingoistic. Britain's youth signed up for a number of reasons: a sense of duty, the realization that the Nazis had to be stopped, and the spirit of adventure. "For myself," wrote one them, Richard Hillary, "I was glad for purely selfish reasons. The war solved all problems of a career, and promised a chance of self-realisation that would normally take years to achieve."

An upper-middle-class Oxford graduate, the twenty-year-old Hillary had experienced Nazi arrogance on a summer 1938 trip to Europe. Participating in a regatta, his "untrained" and "quite hopelessly casual" crew was harangued by one of the "stupid looking giants" on the rival team. "He had been watching us, he said, and could only come to the conclusion that we were thoroughly representative of a decadent race. No German crew would dream of appearing so lackadaisical if rowing in England: they would train and they would win."

Hillary saw himself as part of an "Oxford Generation" whom he typified as "selfish and egocentric without any Holy Grail in which we could lose ourselves. The war provided it, and in a delightfully palatable form. It demanded no heroics, but gave us the opportunity to demonstrate in action our dislike of organised emotion and patriotism, the opportunity to prove to ourselves and to the world that our effete veneer was not as deep as our dislike of interference, the opportunity to prove that undisciplined though we might be, we were a match for Hitler's dogma-fed youth."

In general, upper-middle and upper-class youth were highly motivated. There was no question that the vast majority would go into the armed forces. As a grammar school headmaster wrote during 1942, "The War has done the boys good. I believe that it has made them face up boldly to genuine facts and problems, it has emphasised duties rather than privileges, and it has given them a wider outlook on their own future responsibilities. As one boy remarked to me some weeks ago 'We have finished with "Safety First". We've got to live dangerously . . . and don't we know it!'"

Many of Hillary's peers were still in full-time education at the age of twenty, by which time many of their less privileged contemporaries had been at work for half a decade. Many of these conscripts were afflicted with "a half-cynical boredom, as remote as possible from the high crusading fervour which their situation authorises and requires. They are not pacifists, or disloyal, but 'bored stark'." Their "acquiescence in an absurd and unwelcome necessity" had its roots in the poor conditions of the 1930s and the betrayed promises of the First World War.

The deep scepticism of Britain's conscripts was revealed by the regular wartime Mass-Observation reports on youth. Commissioned during 1940 by the Ministry of Information to survey morale, Mass-Observation observers conducted regular polls on the home front. In these questionnaires or field reports, the social classes were ranked, *Brave New World* style, between "A" and "E". Most sampled came from "C" and "D", a bias that reflected both the availability of interviewees and the compilers' left-wing origins.

A November 1939 visit to a North London registration point produced a variety of responses ranging from "just signed my bloody death warrant" to "I wish I had the guts to be a conscientious objector". However, very few young men of call-up age took the conscientious objector's option: despite the pre-war popularity of the Peace Pledge Union, the imminent threat of invasion and the sheer resentment against Hitler was strong enough to overcome most qualms. Grudgingly or not, British youth submitted to uniform: there was a job to do.

■ ■ ■

During late spring 1940, the American journalist William L. Shirer was invited by the Nazis to witness blitzkrieg in Belgium. Coming across a group of British prisoners near Maastricht, he went over to talk to them. He was struck by their poor physique: "They were hollow-chested and skinny and round-shouldered. About a third of them had bad eyes and wore glasses. Typical, I concluded, of the youth that England neglected so criminally in the twenty-two post war years when Germany, despite its defeat and the inflation and six million unemployed, was raising its youth in the open air and the sun."

Shirer's observations bore out the truth of W. F. Lestrange's *Wasted Lives*. In comparison to the Germans, who had lived under a militaristic regime for several years, the young British conscripts had only had a few months to prepare for war. As adolescents, they had also been blighted by poor diet and lack of exercise. The Germans were "bronzed, clean-cut physically, healthy-looking as lions, chests developed and all. It was part of the unequal fight. The English youngsters, I knew, had fought as bravely as men can. But bravery is not all: it is not enough in this machine age war."

Although nominally neutral, Shirer was thoroughly disgusted with the Nazi regime after six years in Berlin. He was charmed by the British soldiers: "Despite the shell-shock, despite the black future as prisoners, they were a cheery lot. One little fellow from Liverpool grinned through his thick glasses: 'You know, you're the first American I've ever seen in the flesh. Funny place to meet one for the first time, ain't it?' This started the others to make the same observation, and we had a good laugh. But inside I was feeling not so good."

In the mid-thirties, W. F. Lestrange had called for a revolution in public attitudes in order to safeguard the future of Britain's adolescents. The shocking discovery that a large section of recruits were unfit and unprepared to deal with the German master race hastened this transformation. Now that youth was needed, the deficiencies in state provisions became quickly apparent. Mindful of the previous war's juvenile delinquency problem, child experts, youth workers, and left-wing crusaders began to correlate a mass of data that would, by the middle of the war, influence government policy.

Having trained as an anthropologist—when he lived with "the last practising cannibals in the world"—Mass-Observation's Tom Harrisson was well placed to do this. In 1940 he made an unfavourable comparison between the way that the cannibals and the "Cockneys" brought up their adolescents: "After fourteen, at which age three-quarters of our population leave school, youth is largely allowed to look after itself. This period is critical, since it includes the changes from childhood to manhood. The cannibal knows it, and takes the greatest care of his children in those years. We do not."

War precipitates great social changes, and along with the renewed focus placed upon Britain's hitherto forgotten youth came the partial dismantling of an anachronistic social hierarchy. Much of the truculence shown by Britain's adolescents during the early days of the war was due to class resentment: the sense of "Them" and "Us". Harrisson felt that the services would get "better and keener fighters if they didn't make the young men feel like cyphers waiting their turn to go through the tabulating machine".

An October 1940 questionnaire highlighted "The Problems of the 18–20 Age-Group", defined as those young men who found themselves in "a curious dead-end sort of position" between the world of work and the armed forces. Ten questions were posed, ranging from "What are your plans for the next twelve months?" to "What do you think of the present Government?" to "Has war affected your sex-life at all?" The responses were not encouraging. One twenty-year-old Class C male, when asked about his post-war expectations, replied that he would "go in the gutter along with all the other fellows".

A white-collar male of eighteen retorted, "What's the good of making plans? All you've got ahead is the army, the navy and the airforce." Asked whether he was saving during wartime, another "M18C" simply stated that there was no point: "If you're alive when the war's over the government will take all your dough." One "M20C" was particularly terse. He thought that the war would stop "the moment it's killed me". And, in response to the question "Has war affected your sex-life at all?" his answer was blisteringly direct: "I fuck a different woman every night instead of a different one every month."

The compilers detected "a lessening in self-discipline" among the youth polled and concluded that there was a "deep-rooted impression among the younger men that soldiers never come back". The lessons of the First World War had become part of popular mythology: as Harrisson observed in 1940, "There is always the possibility that after the war, Youth will blame Age for the whole business. There are already signs of a growing antagonism of this sort. It would pay the old to think about the young."

During the late thirties, life in Britain was often drab for young people without means. The poverty, lack of mobility, dead-end jobs, and poor wages delineated by Lestrange had not changed much for a significant proportion of the population. There were very few organizations and services for youth outside commercial outlets: as Harrisson noted, "About two-thirds of our young people had no strong ties or interests of a cultural sort, and no contact with any club or organization, except Football Pools." Youth had been "largely left to its own devices".

What little fun there was came principally from British and American popular culture. Without the possibility of direct experience, however, American films and magazines and music had the quality of an unattainable dream in the early war years. For instance, although dancing was still the key leisure activity, jitterbugs were thin on the ground.[1] Instead, the ballrooms were filled as never before with young people performing foxtrots and British "party dances" like the conga and the Lambeth Walk.

Britain's adolescents were not being catered to, but they were being called upon to support the war, "even to die". The youth worker Pearl Jephcott observed that "Great Britain has more than two million working boys and girls under eighteen, a sufficiently large part of the population to be very valuable from the point of view of manpower". She thought it "necessary that such boys

1. A May 1941 "Jitterbug" contest at the Streatham Locarno attracted under a quarter of the expected participants.

and girls should be made to realize, quickly, by conversation, by formal teaching and by specially written youth newspapers and magazines, that the way in which the war goes will have a direct and speedy effect on their own lives".

However, there would be a price to pay for that support. Adolescent involvement in the war was part of a deal that promised greater social inclusion for British youth once the job was done. The Second World War in Britain would be fought as a war of social democracy against fascism, of emancipation instead of slavery. Youth had been little valued, but steps would now be taken to correct this situation. As Jephcott concluded, "We can make young people aware, and not merely impatient of the war, if we show them that their youth does not stop them from being a genuinely important part of the state."

. . .

The first salvos in the struggle for social democracy occurred during the evacuation of September 1939. Fearing the complete destruction of all major cities by German aircraft, the government put into practice a long-planned scheme that moved one and a half million women, children, and school-age adolescents out of the cities and into the outer suburbs, market towns, and the deepest countryside. Together with the other two million who made their own private arrangements, that month saw three and a half million people migrate within the British Isles, the largest mass movement ever.

However, despite the alacrity with which the plan was executed, several basic misconceptions became quickly apparent. The first came in the reception areas where the billeting officers and host parents selected the young that they would take. A twenty-one-year-old kindergarten teacher described the process as "more akin to a cattle or slave market than anything else". The prospective foster mothers "just invaded us and walked about the field picking out what they considered to be the most presentable specimens". In the resulting chaos, "It was some hours before all the children were disposed of."

These scenes were repeated throughout the country. Part of the problem was that the first evacuation occurred right at the end of the summer holidays, before the pupils could be put through the regular delousing parades at the start of term. In the highlands of Scotland, prosperous hosts "raised Cain" when they saw the lousy and infested state of the children and adolescents who arrived from Edinburgh's slums: "They were delightfully oblivious to the fact that other people had to take what they were refusing to deal with: the children did not cease to exist because they were undesirable."

There was an enormous divide between town and country. A Blackpool landlady complained about her slum charges that "if you say two words to them they turn round and swear at you. I've seen a lot of dogs with better manners." A seventeen-year-old transplanted North London girl wrote that "the main problem between evacuees and hosts seems to be the difficulty of adapting the one to the other. A few of the hosts treated their evacuees as guests or as they would their own children, but the majority treated the girls as unpaid maids."

The classes looked at each other and did not like what they saw. Although, as an eighteen-year-old doctor's daughter observed, the different strata of the population were now "aware of each other's existence", the evacuation policy was not a success: when, during the period known as the "Phoney War", the expected destruction from the skies failed to materialize, one million evacuees returned to the cities. When Britain was finally blitzed in the late summer of 1940, many parents refused to leave again and were caught with their children in the devastation.

In the early years of the war, London was heavily targeted by German bombers: between September and November 1940, the capital was visited nightly. By May 1941, about two million Londoners—one-sixth of the total population—had been made homeless. Nobody was immune from this mass destruction, but urban youth were particularly vulnerable to its psychological effects. Reports from inner London boroughs in the winter of 1940 describe an epidemic of looting, accompanied by petty vandalism and general "rowdyism".

A Mass-Observation survey of conditions in Paddington and Bermondsey observed that "the youth problem has moved away from the club towards the darkened street". Since the blitz started, there had been "practically no home life for youngsters", who grouped together in wild gangs. These were the "wild type of young people always running amok from shelter to shelter, with opportunities for promiscuous sexual relationships, drinking and gambling, many of which are taken". Another observer in the East End recorded "a general slackening of moral sense among the young, owing to the complete devastation of life".

The juvenile delinquency of the First World War had returned, but this time the authorities were ready to describe, explain, and cure these urban symptoms. One immediate cause of the problem was the fact that many schools were shut, damaged, or requisitioned, as many as one in five in some London districts. Clubs, night schools, and other youth venues were also closed. There were almost no amenities for those between school and army age, except the public shelters. These were shunned by adolescents because they were full of old people.

Between 1939 and 1941, there was an increase of 33 per cent in delinquency among the under-seventeens: most of this was malicious damage, with about 20 per cent of the convictions for petty theft. Contemporary analysts suspected that, because it had been anticipated, the problem was slightly exaggerated: it was suggested "that 'mischief', rather than serious offences, accounted for a large part of the rise". But the surveys detected the almost total lack of facilities for adolescents: "Youth is 'nowhere' in particular, youth is doing 'nothing special'."

In the early 1940s, Britain's under-military-age adolescents could hardly do anything right. As in the First World War, any sign of increased youth visibility attracted adverse comment. If they didn't help the war effort they were damned, and they were criticized if they did. As one justice of the peace wrote in 1941, "Since the outbreak of war high wages paid to boys for unsuitable and unskilled work have led to gambling and then to delinquency. Cases brought before the juvenile courts have revealed that lads of 15 and 16 are earning £4 or more weekly."

Sensational press stories linking high wages with juvenile delinquency stated that young workers were earning between £5 and £7 a week. But it was revealed in a summer 1941 survey that in fact, adolescents up to twenty-one earned on average about £2 per week. Working conditions were also poor: although the most recent legislation provided for a maximum forty-eight-hour week, many boys and girls were working over seventy hours in dangerous industries. The "causation" between high earnings and delinquency was "very difficult to establish".

However, there was still enough money for Britain's adolescents to spend on themselves. Targeting boys between fourteen and twenty and girls between fourteen and nineteen, a Mass-Observation "Youth Survey" of Paddington and Bermondsey in January 1941 found that half the young polled spent their leisure time in "serious" pursuits like reading, sewing, and ARP (Air Raid Precautions) work. Others were using their hard-earned money on dance records, entertainment, books, cigarettes, pictures, and clothes. The observers' tone indicated that this was thought to be rather frivolous and selfish.

Public venues had increased to satisfy this "great rise in the proportion of spending on leisure outlets". Adolescents favoured snack bars and billiard halls. The observers found no public dances, but a few informal dance clubs were still operating and private parties were frequent. Fun fairs were also popular. Many cinemas were bomb-damaged, but films were "very well supported by youth, who go mainly with groups of their own sex, not with their girl friends or boy friends. Simple homely comedy and detection is preferred to love."

Clothing was also important, as "the youths nearly all had a far greater regard for personal appearance than the older people" and "the men of 17–20 were *very* clothes conscious". These youths wore predominantly muted colours—black, blue, brown, and grey—with a few roll-neck sweaters. Their hair was usually brilliantined. Mass-Observation turned up only one real dandy of seventeen, who was spotted sporting a brown zigzag-patterned jacket and trousers with brown shoes.

Young women were far more stylish. One Bermondsey "Fi8C" wore "a half length black coat, waisted, without a collar. A plain black frock, decorated with a chromium clip at the neck, and a patterned collar. Black patent shoes with rather high heels. Sheer black stockings. A large shiny black bag. No hat, auburn hair in a low page boy bob." A seventeen-year-old sported "a plain black coat with golden filigree work on the shoulders. A brown check frock underneath. A golden coloured bandeau hat on golden hair. High fur bootees." The report noted that "the buying of cosmetics by girls can be considered an interest in itself".

As in America, girls were at the forefront of British youth spending. With almost every young man of over eighteen off in the armed forces, young women began to enter white-collar occupations and heavy industry in order to fill the manpower shortfall. Under the rigours of war Britain expanded to full employment in 1943—a labour pool of 22 million in total.[2] The question for young women therefore was not "when will I get a job?" but "which one of the various, rather unpleasant and rather unsuitable jobs which exist shall I take?"

However blasé the young women polled in late 1940 might have been—"the atmosphere is one of boredom and slight defiance"—the proliferation of new jobs enabled many to escape domestic service for laundry work, filing and clerking, and factory work. There were so many posts available that even a short spell of unemployment was welcomed as a "pleasant interlude". Younger women were privileged in this employment bonanza: fourteen- and fifteen-year-old girls were highly prized in factory work for their good eyesight and attention to detail.

This was the cohort studied by Pearl Jephcott in her 1941 survey of young women's social habits, *Girls Growing Up*: "Boys and girls are prepared to spend what free time they have in an effortless and irresponsible way, largely because the work they have to do is in so many cases largely beneath their powers. No compulsion has been on them to use their brains to anything like the full extent since the day they left school. Many of them have done nothing but

2. Out of a total population of 47 million.

routine work, packing sweets, assembling battery parts, machining trouser pockets, or nailing cases, from the time they were fourteen."

Girls Growing Up captured the emergent British adolescent market. A "typical" factory girl of sixteen owned "an attache case, a brush and a comb set, a watch (broken), seven children's books and some magazines, a pair of scissors, three boxes of face powder and one of face cream". Cosmetics were the favourite spending item, along with "romance magazines" like *Oracle, Miracle, Girl's Crystal,* and *Glamour.* The staple content of these and other "erotic bloods" was the standard Cinderella complex fantasy.

Of twenty-seven city girls surveyed in autumn 1941, few read books or went to evening classes. By far their most popular activity was going to the pictures. Newsreels were extremely unpopular, while historical pictures were favoured. Most girls expressed approval for adolescent stars like Judy Garland and Mickey Rooney, "people like ourselves". The only radio programmes they listened to were variety and dance band shows: dancing was found to be "extraordinary popular among adolescents. They spend an amazing amount of energy on it."

By the second year of the war, hot jazz music was increasing in popularity because, Jephcott thought, "The hot rhythm and syncopated music seem to be in the same tempo as the noise and speed of the factory and make an easy appeal to people who live in a continual din. Dance-band music is essentially the music of to-day, and young people are concerned with to-day, not yesterday or tomorrow." She observed that "the one occasion on which a very noisy group of fifty boys and girls may be willing to be quiet for an hour will possibly be in order to hear a talk on jazz and swing music".

Jephcott was responding to a 100 per cent increase in female juvenile delinquency and a 70 per cent rise in venereal disease rates between 1939 and 1941. Alerted by sensational headlines like "Camp Followers; Girls 16–18 Running Wild", the authorities struggled to comprehend how thousands of girls could be adjudged as "morally at risk". According to one authority, this serious social problem was caused by "earlier maturity" and the "jungle rhythms heard by juveniles from morning till bedtime, and slushy movies are in part responsible for an increase in sex delinquency among youths".

The causes, however, went a little deeper: the disruption caused by evacuation, the lack of proper sex education, and the aphrodisiac nature of war itself. With the reduction in parental restraint and the general "live for today" attitude caused by the war, many young women plunged into sex at an early age. Girls of fifteen were "rushing rather than growing up, and are suffering the effect of a war which has uprooted large numbers of older men from their own surroundings and almost limited their contacts with the opposite sex to the casual encounters of the dance hall".

Basic urges might well have been responsible for this wave of perceived delinquency, but at the same time, many young women considered that they had a contract. Having prematurely entered the world of work, they thought they had the right to live their own lives. Stuck in "the last generation", many parents misread this wish as rebellious precocity. Most girls wanted to be thought older, but if they were to be considered "a genuinely important part of society" at such a young age, then they could not be blamed if they confused adult licence with adult responsibility.

These tensions highlighted the ambiguous status of adolescents. The very word "girl" presupposed the retention of childhood that was not supported by the facts of wartime life. A "girl of sixteen" complained to Jephcott that she had "to lead a kind of Alice in Wonderland existence, her height ten inches one moment and 'rather more than nine feet' the next. 'You are grown up at fourteen if you want a railway ticket, at sixteen if you want to get into an "A" film. At home you are a child if it is convenient for them but the moment that they want to put something on you they say that you are grown up.'"

The demands of war, as they had done twenty years previously, inadvertently precipitated greater female emancipation. Unlike the Nazis, who regarded most women as simple baby-making machines, the British authorities sought to draw them into the kind of jobs that would have been unthinkable or impossible during the 1930s. In March 1941, the minister of labour, Ernest Bevin, called for "a great response from our women to run the industrial machine. Women made a tremendous contribution to the winning of the last war and will be equally effective in this struggle."

By 1943, some seven million women were working in essential war production, up to 40 per cent in some industries, or serving in the forces. This was a sudden change within a society where girls were "still inferior creatures in many homes". The reaction of the newly liberated was also mixed. The working hours were long, up to twelve-hour shifts six days a week, and the tasks dangerous. One eighteen-year-old earned £10 a week, twice the national average, assembling bullet detonators, but "the cordite used to fly about, fly up into your face. It caused a rash, impetigo, and would come up in big lumps."

Away from home, young women could become emotionally vulnerable and ground down both by heavy industry's male ethos and the repetitive boredom of the tasks. Set against that were the good feeling of proper money in your pocket and the sense of release from family responsibilities and restrictions.

One young aircraft worker remembered her delight at having a room of her own at a specially built women's hostel: "There was a main block down the road where all the social activity took place. It seemed like paradise really, it was the beginning of the fun we had during the war."

. . .

The youth problems of 1939 and 1940 continued into the third and fourth years of the war. A report from the winter of 1941–42 noted how many children "have become sullen and aggressive. Fearful for the disintegration of their normal lives they are forming themselves into gangs, with a strong leader whose morals may be doubtful, but whose presence seems secure. Child delinquency is increasing. It was in just such a breeding ground of fear and insecurity that Hitler planted the seeds of Nazism, a philosophy for frightened, downtrodden, neglected people."

To prevent such an eventuality, efforts were made to overhaul the whole nature and structure of youth service in Britain. Before the war, only a third of Britain's school-leavers had come into contact with any of the voluntary organizations. Despite the 1939 institution of the National Youth Committee, which had greater powers than the previous Juvenile Organization Committees, the situation was still unsatisfactory. Many public buildings had been destroyed, and any good work was performed on a piecemeal basis.

In October 1940, the government issued a circular concerning "Youth Physical Recreation and Service", with the understanding that the service of youth had now become youth service, in other words that "to help youth now is to enlist the help of youth". Inculcating a sense of responsibility and "cooperative living", youth clubs and youth groups were seen as the solution to wartime juvenile delinquency, and the number of voluntary and civic youth organizations began to expand during 1941 and 1942.

The most popular were the Boy Scouts and the Girl Guides, with their full range of outdoor activities. Their programmes were tailored to the demands of war: the Guides, for instance, trained in first aid and map reading. Pre-military units comprised the Sea Cadets, the Army Cadet Corps, the Girls' Training Corps, the Messenger Corps, with the most popular being the Air Training Corps, the junior section of the RAF. These combined exercise, drill, and teaching in the specific skills required by each branch of the armed forces.

Boys' and girls' clubs were very much dependent on the personality of the organizer and his assistants. In one typical northern town, there was a civic youth club in each council school, offering debates, lectures, first-aid courses, dancing, cycling, football, and canteens. With an average membership of about 170, these organizations did not reach most local youth, but they were popular. One boy of seventeen thought it was "fun. You make a lot of pals. Besides, I get fed up of sitting around listening to the old men running the war."

In December 1941, the government ordered the compulsory registration of all boys and girls between sixteen and eighteen, with no further compulsory action. A few months later, there was a "positive intention" of enlisting the registered young into a pre-military corps. But this ran into difficulties. Voluntary bodies were "violently opposed to 'the state' taking over the supervision of youth in its leisure time". Adults also expressed displeasure at this Nazi-style regimentation: "real Gauleiter stuff I call it." The scheme was quietly dropped.

Governmental involvement was not to be checked, however. By 1941, almost every conceivable aspect of British life was centrally regulated, from food, media, jobs, wages, military service, housing, transport, right down to the CC41 symbol on the state-supplied Utility brand of clothes and furniture. This was a practical recognition that some form of overall planning was necessary to maximize labour and fighting strength in a mass war. However, there was another side to this unprecedented organization: the drive towards socialism.

The lessons of the Depression had returned to haunt the government. Having been adjudged vital to the war effort, the mass of people decided by the third year of the war that involvement was a two-way process. The people's future was proposed in pamphlets about social conditions, army discussion groups, and in *Picture Post* specials like the January 1941 *Plan for Britain,* where 1930s slums were pictorially contrasted with idealized images of a socialist future, with the slogans "Work for All", "Health for All", and "Education for All": "The new Britain is the country we are fighting for."[3]

Even Britain's public school boys were not immune from this virus. A group of fourteen- to sixteen-year-olds wrote that "schools such as Eton and Harrow should be abolished, as they give rise to snobbishness". Their practical suggestions for the post-war future included slum clearance and better conditions for the poorer classes. As one young essay writer concluded, "Working men should be allowed to enter the Government, if they are fit for the position, because most of the present members are either too old to be allowed out without a nurse or they have not enough sense to keep goats."

One of the most impassioned pleas for the new order came from the twenty-

---

3. This was given concrete form by the December 1942 publication of the Beveridge Report, which offered practical templates for the former left-wing utopias of child benefits, free medical treatment for all, and full employment. Stimulating a passionate debate, it was favourably received by about two-thirds of the population.

three-year-old who emerged as the inheritor of Rupert Brooke's mantle. Richard Hillary was a member of the elite who had joined up in the very first stages of the war and had been seared by death. As a Battle of Britain pilot, he had joined those men described by Winston Churchill as the new Knights of the Round Table. In comparison to other theatres, air combat still offered one-on-one jousting and, at this early stage, the chivalry of a bygone era. Published in 1942, Hillary's memoir about the experience touched a popular nerve.

Fighter pilots were young—nobody over twenty-six could lead a squadron—and highly motivated. Although crack warriors, they curbed their arrogance through a powerful peer culture that relied on "black humour and a sport-derived team spirit". With death likely at any time, the stiff upper lip was not a sign of emotional paralysis but a vital strategy for survival. However, youthful high spirits could not be damped down for long. As one pilot remembered, "It was just beer, women and Spitfires, and a bunch of little John Waynes running around the place. When you were 19, you couldn't give a monkey's."

Hillary was different from his comrades, and tortured by that difference. When the success of the Battle of Britain made RAF fighter pilots national heroes,[4] he attempted to refuse the role. Explaining the genesis of his memoir, he wrote, "I got so sick of the stuff about our Island Fortress and the Knights of the Air that I determined to write it anyway in the hope that the last generation might realise that, while stupid, we were not that stupid, that we could remember all too well that this had been seen in the last war but that in spite of that and not because of it, we still thought this one worth fighting."

The Last Enemy is couched in the form of a spiritual journey: the surrender of an elitist youth to the human empathy required by a truly mass society. This tension pervades the book, from Hillary's selfish excitement at the declaration of war to the realization that he was just the same as everybody else. The break from his former life occurred in September 1940, when he was shot down and badly burned: "You should be glad this has happened to you," his mother told him. "Too many people told you how attractive you were and you believed them. You were well on the way to becoming a cad."

Having received this shattering blow, Hillary could still not forget himself. However, trapped with the working-class dead in a bombed public house, he finally realized that "it was impossible to look only to oneself, to take from life and not to give except by accident, deliberately to look at humanity and pass by the other side". His solution was to write *The Last Enemy* as a hymn to the cross-

---

4. As exemplified by Churchill's August 20, 1940, speech: "Never in the field of human conflict was so much owed by so many to so few."

class, technocratic RAF pilots who had been his comrades and to the "Humanity" that he had formerly despised and scorned. Only then would he have justified his "right to fellowship with my dead".

Published in June 1942, *The Last Enemy* became an instant classic. Hillary's socialist conversion enabled readers to interpret the meaninglessness of war in a way that confirmed the inexorable leftward drift of British society. Proving the sincerity of this transformation, he then attempted to erase his privilege as a Battle of Britain veteran and a successful author. Inspired by Wilfred Owen and T. E. Lawrence's *The Mint*—in which the First World War legend described his anonymous return into the RAF—Hillary prematurely returned to active service, and crashed fatally in January 1943.

Like Rupert Brooke, Hillary was a golden boy who died in his mid-twenties, just at the point when adolescence shaded into adulthood. Like that First World War icon, he wrote about the brutality of war in a way that made his life mythic and that helped to define contemporary attitudes to that conflict. Hillary fulfilled every possible qualification of an establishment hero, but British society had changed in twenty-eight years. Instead of being the sacrificial victim of a remote and static oligarchy, he was democratically egalitarian—a harbinger of the post-war age to come.

CHAPTER 24

Sub-Debs and GIs

American Adolescents in School and in Uniform

. . .

*That night, lying in bed, I couldn't help wishing that there wasn't so much sad-
ness in growing up. It was all so confused in my mind.*

—Maureen Daly, *Seventeenth Summer* (1942)

HIGH SCHOOL STUDENTS, IN THE TULARE MIGRANT CAMPS, VISALIA,
CALIFORNIA, 1940, PHOTOGRAPH BY ARTHUR ROTHSTEIN

WHEN WAR BROKE out in Europe, many American adolescents did not want to be involved. As one editor of a high school newspaper wrote: "War!!—Three little letters, the symbol of what might be the destruction of civilization . . . we do not want war." "Youth should storm the gates of heaven, live and create," wrote another. "No great painting, great music, great writing was ever created by youth while he was starving in a muddy trench. No freedom, peace or happiness has ever come out of war."

Europe seemed very far away. Influenced by the peace propaganda of the 1930s and struggling with the lasting effects of the Depression, many American youth held the non-interventionist position. Some revelled in their country's neutrality, like the high school student who, "seeing evidences of the war abroad", thought that "the American is more than ever elated at his lot in life". Others thought that the country's "prosperity and economic, social and living standards" were being "threatened by the presence of war in Europe".

But the battle for hearts and minds was on, with some authorities seeking to attribute youth's pacifism to agitation and subversion. In October 1940, the *Reader's Digest* offered a guide to treasonous activities in an article called "Yes, We Have Fifth Columnists", which isolated six separate approaches used by the isolationists: "nihilist", "terror", "You can't win", "neo-pacifist", "separatist", and "appeasement propaganda". The reader was encouraged to report any suspicious behaviour "to the nearest office of the F.B.I.".

Despite John Roy Carlson's vivid exposé of the many Bundist and KKK groups working within the United States in 1939 and 1940, Nazi ideology remained ethnically confined to German Americans and only reached a tiny proportion of American adolescents. On the other side of the coin, the pro-Communist American Youth Congress had its heart ripped out by the August 1939 Nazi-Soviet pact. Once war seemed inevitable, the congress switched from its anti-militarist position to agitation for the rights of adolescents in American society.

However, the European conflict could not be ignored. In anticipation of America's involvement, the Selective Service Bill was signed in Congress during September 1940: it allowed for a maximum of just under one million young men between twenty-one and thirty-five to serve in the armed forces for just one year. This was called, for the first time, "the draft". The first nationwide register was held during October 1940, and only a handful refused. At the same time, the process of rearmament began: this would boost the economy and finally take America out of the Depression.

Autumn 1940 also marked the turning point in young America's view of the war. Press reports, the introduction of Selective Service, individual contacts with Europeans, and the sheer unstoppable drive of blitzkrieg changed the non-interventionist mood. America suddenly appeared under threat and thus more precious: as one high school student wrote after the fall of France, "Today the word 'democratic' is on everyone's lips and in everyone's thoughts— it has suddenly become very important during this war period."

In October 1940, Dr George Gallup published a poll called *American Youth Speaks Up*. His task was to impress anxious American adults that they could set their "mind at ease about the younger generation". He polled a controlled group designed to represent "an accurate cross section of the 21,000,000 Americans between the ages of 16 and 24". A wide range of locations and classes were sampled: college youth, workers in factories and offices, the unemployed, and "reliefers". It was also "the first Gallup poll to reach individuals below voting age".

Those sampled were asked ten questions, all "carefully framed to bring out the attitude of the young people towards life and towards our democratic institutions, and to reveal their opinion on America's vital foreign and domestic policies". The results were encouraging, as they were designed to be: 87 per cent supported the American way of life, believing that they had just as good a chance in life as their parents had, if not better. They were also immune to polarized politics: "Stalin, Hitler and Mussolini are three of a kind."

The principal purpose of the poll was to determine youth's attitude to war. Fifty per cent thought that the United States should fight Germany if England was defeated. Asked whether "every able-bodied young man 20 years old should be made to serve in the Army, Navy or air force for a year", 68 per cent of the boys and girls agreed. Over 75 per cent of the young men sampled denied that they would have any objection to spending a year in military service under selective conscription. "If I'm likely to be called on to fight, I'd rather know how" was a typical response.

Poised almost exactly at the halfway point between the outbreak of war in Europe and Pearl Harbor, Gallup's poll revealed a generation reconciling itself to military service. Apart from their desire to keep America out of the war, many of the youth surveyed held firm to New Deal principles. When asked what they would do if they were president, the young respondents stated that they would, *inter alia*, "reduce unemployment; strengthen Government finances; help the poor; halt the trend away from undemocratic principles".

Democracy was what America would be fighting for, and as a governing idea, it would be put under careful scrutiny by a large swath of the country's population during the next few years. Much of this debate would be critical. As the American Youth Commission stated in summer 1940: "We must face the realities of our situation, but we must face all the realities, including the very pressing question as to whether democracy is willing to be sincere about its own purposes to the extent of carrying out the things for which democracy stands.

"The hope and faith of our own young people are in danger," it concluded, "precisely at the time when the nation stands in the greatest need of that hope and that faith. It is therefore the considered opinion of this commission that if as a people we are to adopt a measure providing for compulsory military training and service, we should at the same time bring to an end all partial and hesitant handling of the immediate needs of youth within the civil population." The deal terms were set out: conscription in exchange for respect, attention, and, most important, recognition as adults.

· · ·

By 1940, there were record numbers of youth in American high schools: around 75 per cent of the total fourteen-to-seventeen cohort of nearly 10 million. This was twice the number of students in 1930. Going to high school had become the norm rather than the exception. Prophesied by Jean-Jacques Rousseau and G. Stanley Hall, adolescence had arrived as a separate stage of life. Although still economically dependent on their parents, high-school-age adolescents began to create a new youth class that took its cues not from adults but from peers.

The products of the mid- to late-1920s baby boom were reaching adolescence. While four million of their older counterparts were still unemployed and looking for work, America's fourteen- to seventeen-year-olds were staying in school longer to avoid the fierce competition for jobs. With unemployment in mind, federal policies and programmes had for several years fostered a policy of keeping older adolescents in full-time education. At the same time, the emerging commercial youth culture—fuelled by the success of swing—gave young Americans a sense that they were special.

The American system of education shaped this youth class. The British anthropologist Geoffrey Gorer wrote in the 1940s that the high school was "in the first instance, a social device, and an extremely successful one, for stamping the American character on children, whatever their background and origins may be". The mixture of age-group organization and social blending, seasoned with the country's insistence on the striving for success, meant that "by adolescence most Americans have inextricably confused the two ideas: to be successful is to be loved, to be loved is to be successful".

This conformist adolescent culture was centred around cliques. While researching adolescent social behaviour in a "Middle Western Corn Belt community" during 1940 and 1941, August Hollingshead found that these groups were "voluntary and informal; members are admitted gradually to a pre-existing clique and dropped by the mutual consent of the inhabitants. Although there are no explicit rules for membership, the clique has a more or less common set of values which determines who will be admitted, what it does, and how it will censure some member who does not abide by its rules."

With students in school for at least seven hours a day for two-thirds of the year, these cliques assumed an overwhelming importance in adolescent life, so much so that their group loyalties usually triumphed in the "conflicts between the clique and the family, between the clique and the school, or between the clique and the neighbourhood". This was a self-enclosed peer world that had the power to make or break reputations, and to govern almost every aspect of an adolescent's life: friends, slang, clothing, leisure activities. The great majority of Elmtown's young bought into it.

A "white collar" Elmtown girl named Joyce Jenson told Hollingshead about her best friend: "She influences me almost as much as my parents do. I listen to them, especially when choosing friends, but I don't agree with everything they tell me. I've had them really give me the dickens about going around with some girls I wanted to go with." However, she admitted that "when my folks put their foot down on me I listen. I know that the folks give me good advice, but sometimes they just don't understand what kids want to do, and they think we ought to act like they acted twenty years ago."

Clique styles were broadcast back at high school youth by a media already alerted to the spending power of this emerging class. In January 1941, *Life* magazine—one of the picture-based publications very popular with adolescents—ran a feature with the full title of "Sub-Debs—They Live in a Jolly World of Gangs, Games, Gadding, Movies, Malteds and Music". The breathless copy trumpeted a new type who "speak a curious lingo . . . adore chocolate milk shakes . . . wear moccasins everywhere . . . and drive like bats out of hell".

The early 1940s, as the researcher Richard Maring Ugland writes, was "a propitious time to test" the idea of specialized age merchandising on adolescents. High school students still got money from their parents, which, supplemented by readily available temporary jobs, sent them out into department stores in search of clothing and cosmetics. Although their purchasing power was not individually significant, their numbers when placed together in relation to the slightly older, unemployed college-age cohort, gave them a new economic importance. Advertisers and producers took notice.

In February that year, *Parents* magazine started a "Tricks for Teens" column that exploited the sub-deb fashion for costume jewellery. As the editors wrote, "High school girls have a fashion language all of their own. A language mothers might find difficult to understand. Their customs might look strange to you but they are only the fads that sweep periodically through high schools from coast to coast. Be tolerant of them."

Later in 1941, the publishers of *Parents* started an explicitly youth-oriented publication, *Calling All Girls*. Subtitled as "the Modern Magazine for Girls and Sub-Debs", this sold at ten cents and was the first magazine to use swing culture as its calling card. Shirley Temple and Judy Garland were on its "junior advisory board", while Benny Goodman wrote an article called "Music as You Like It". Its major innovation was a monthly report on high school fads. At the same time, newspapers began to run new youth-oriented comic strips: *Archie Andrews*, or the typical bobby soxer with boy trouble, *Teena*.

The ideal location for these early products of the adolescent market was the suburb or the small town. The values were middle-class, reflecting the adult fantasy of the naughty but ultimately upstanding all-American adolescent. This was seen in the run of youth movies that began after *Love Finds Andy Hardy* and *The Wizard of Oz*, and in swing—still the prime American popular music. After the summer of 1939, Glenn Miller replaced Benny Goodman and Artie Shaw as the top bandleader. The bespectacled and mature-looking Miller epitomized the small-town midwestern boy made good.

Instead of coming out like debutantes, the sub-debs went to the drugstore. In *Seventeenth Summer*, written during 1941, Maureen Daly described the anxiety that her heroine Angie Morrow felt on her first visit to Pete's: "In our town that is the crucial test. Everyone is there and everyone sees you. I know of a girl once who went out to Pete's with her cousin and no one else asked her to dance or paid any attention to her, and so she went away to college in the fall and never had dates at home for any of the dances at Christmas or Easter. If you don't make the grade at Pete's, you just don't make it.

"Once two girls came in with the same hesitant air. They were palish girls, about my age, with their hair very carefully set in neat waves and very little lipstick. One of them had on flat black oxfords—and everyone knows that no high school girl should wear anything but saddle shoes or collegiate moccasins! All the booths were filled but they walked down the aisle between them, peering over the high sides, looking for a place to sit down. No one said hello or offered to move over to make room so the girls turned, talking to themselves and giggling a little, and walked out. Their faces had a stiff, hurt look."

With social ostracism turning on the style of a shoe, the adolescent need for money was paramount. Hollingshead drily observed that "long before a young Elmtowner is able to earn money, he knows that he must have it to buy the things his culture teaches him he must have if he is to be 'successful'". This was the contradiction in the new cross-class youth culture. Although apparently democratic, the sub-deb world, through its very etymology, enshrined an upper-middle-class vision of American youth, with its conspicuous consumption and infinitesimal snobberies. What if you couldn't buy in?

This was one principal ambit of Hollingshead's survey, later published as *Elmtown's Youth*. Working in the same depth as the Lynds had in *Middletown*, but concentrating purely on those of high school age, he aimed to test the hypothesis that "the social behavior of adolescents" betrayed their parents' social origins. He found that, despite Hall's influential concept of youth as a discrete biological stage of life, and despite the then current consumer fantasy, the young people of this small midwestern town were sociologically determined and thus riven by class distinctions as rigid as any of those in the Old World.

Identifying five classes,[1] Hollingshead revealed that school life was dominated by the top three groups. One Class IV girl described "a group of girls here who think they are higher than us. They look down on us. I won't mention any names, but they are a group of girls from the higher families. They have a club that is supposed to be outside of school, but it's really in the school. They just go from one club to the other and hog all the offices. They're in all the activities. They talk about what they're doing, what they're going to do, and they won't pay any attention to us. They snub us and they won't talk to us."

Despite "official denials" of any class system, these distinctions were ruthlessly enforced. For a student to cross more than two class lines was very rare. Failure to observe these rules resulted in ostracism, as in the case where a Class III girl named Joan Meyers, who had risen to become a member of a Class II group called the GWGs, dated a Class IV boy. She was "cut" by her erstwhile friends: as one explained, "We do not have anything to do with her *now*!" This was a method of social control that was "almost like a secret police system—no one escapes being checked on. At least no one who counts."

Elmtown's young men also had their own rituals: "Most boys wear 'dress pants', white shirts and ties, with jackets or suit coats; very few, however, wear hats. Standard head gear is a visored, cloth cap adorned with a dozen or more metal buttons, miniature toys, and animal tails. Such a cap marks a boy's low class in Elmtown, but those who wear them consider them the height of fash-

1. Class I : Old Money, the "Society Class"; Class II: Upper Middle Class; Class III: Lower Middle Class—the pivotal class; Class IV: The Working Class, Blue Collar; Class V: Unskilled or semi-skilled, or on relief: the "really low class".

ion. The higher-class boys either go bareheaded or wear hats." Many spent their money on their cars, or in less sanctioned pursuits like gambling, cigarette smoking, and drinking.

The reality of this tense, coiled society mocked the breezy images of freedom and transformation propagated by the American popular culture that Hollingshead thought was failing to supply adequate guidance for its young. This was a nationwide problem for the large social group who still found themselves in an "ill-defined no-man's-land" enshrined in the law. For instance, adolescents could get a job at fourteen, but not vote until eighteen. They needed parental consent to marry until eighteen if female, twenty-one if male. Even the laws regulating alcohol consumption varied from state to state.

This push-me-pull-you state was compounded by a lack of adult communication: America's "clandestine complex". Premarital sexual activity across all class lines was more frequent than ever before, with one-quarter of eighteen-year-olds indulging by the early 1940s. The conspiracy of silence between adults and adolescents around the topic made things even more difficult: "The maturation of sexual capacities several years before society allows young people to marry presents adolescents with a serious dilemma. They must repress their sexual desires or violate the mores."

With very little to lose, some Class IV and nearly all Class V adolescents freely indulged in taboo pleasures. Having begun working before the other classes, they construed independence in strictly financial terms. Staying in school was hardly an option either, as they were "made to feel unwanted in the classroom, on the playground, or in the clubs and extracurricular activities". The high school dropout statistics bore this out; none from the top two classes, 41.3 per cent from Class IV, and 88.7 per cent of Class V. Ejected prematurely into the adult world, Class V adolescents pursued adult sensations.

It was these adolescents who were most seduced by the Cinderella complex. One girl dreamt of becoming a screen siren like "Joan Crawford". Hollingshead also cited the case of another student, a "cross-eyed, seventeen-year-old Class V girl who came from one of the lowest ranking families in Elmtown". She "was known for her 'B.O.', poor clothes, dirty skin, and her habit of singing while she worked. She had been fired from at least three jobs because she sang 'all the time'. She said, 'I am always practicing the latest thing,' in order to realize her hope to become a torch singer in a night club."

Although it criticized the lack of American rituals to ease the passage between childhood and adulthood, Hollingshead's data[2] also provided an exhaustive survey

2. Finally published in 1949 as an exposé of America's "class system".

of the country's youth consumer culture in that culture's prime location, the small town, just at that very moment when it was becoming a national force. In the same way, Maureen Daly's best-selling *Seventeenth Summer*—with its deliberate echoes of Booth Tarkington's idyllic adolescent classic—captured America's high school society in its first full flush, only months before its innocence had been darkened by the experience of war.

. . .

By the autumn of 1941, America's involvement in the war was inevitable and mobilization began to impact on the high schools. Some adolescents recognized their future responsibility and believed that "it is to the American youth, you and me, that the leaders of our country look for the preservation of democracy". Others remained totally oblivious. Asked by a psychologist how she felt her life would be affected by war, one young high school student stated, "I had never thought about it, and I doubt whether many other students had."

America's young were caught between the security of the known and an uncertain, dangerous future. "Students seem to be waiting for something to force the issue," observed an Ivy League professor, "for whatever is going to happen, whether it's war or not, to become more *imminent*." Despite this expectancy, the news of the December 7 attack on Pearl Harbor came as a huge shock. American isolation and security had been brutally violated. According to one high school student, "War has come to America, the America that was impregnable, the America that was neutral and trusting."

After Pearl Harbor—and Germany's declaration of war against America on December 12—recruiting offices were swamped. Like a lumbering machine, the American armed forces took a while to get up to speed: those called up in 1942 would not be fully trained until a year later. The strains of adaptation to army life were considerable: by the summer of 1942 about 14,000 men a day were flooding reception centres and training camps. Many of these were fresh out of high school, after the draft age was lowered to eighteen.

American youth had a new value. The New Deal academic Howard McCluskey thought that "young people are still the prize resource of the nation. They are the vanguard of defense. Their bodies can deliver and take punishment, and their segregation into regiments and squadrons is of all ages the least disrupting to the normal life of society." The rules of engagement had changed for draft-age American males, required to make the transition between a "fun-loving eighteen-year-old son" to a pilot "manipulating a bomber over Tokyo".

Joining the army meant the end of adolescence. As a drafted sociologist wrote, "The essential fact about induction, reception centre and basic training is the knifing off of past experience." Required to bond into another clique—his immediate army buddies—the recruit was remodelled by months of extreme physical exertion and military indoctrination. His previous identity meant nothing. No longer a college student, farm boy, office worker, he became a number, harassed by "sadistic sergeant overseers", thrust together with the kind of people whom he had never met before—part of a new mass.

The nature of military training remains constant, but American youth had changed since the First World War. The new recruits were better educated: 30 per cent were high school graduates, as opposed to 4 per cent in 1917. Many were college students and graduates, independent and not prepared to be victimized by the often poorly educated standing army sergeants and officers. Although many realized that toughness was necessary for the task that they had undertaken, there was a vocal rump that considered "the Army tradition bigoted and medieval, utterly out of keeping with our democratic ideals".

The American GI was very different from his European counterparts. He was, according to the playwright Arthur Miller, "a much more complicated character than he is ever given credit for. He cannot be written into the script as though he were a civilian wearing a brown suit with metal buttons, nor can he be regarded as a 'soldier', a being whose reactions are totally divorced from civilian emotions." The GI remained a civilian at heart, with an obstinate insistence on democracy expressed in the loose marching style that characterized the American army as it spread around the world like a beacon of freedom.

America's adolescents were expected to share in this collective endeavour, even if under military age: eighteen for young men, twenty for young women. "War forces boys and girls to grow up overnight," wrote Caroline B. Zachry in *The Family in a World at War*. "The more responsibilities that they can assume, the more naturally can they and their families accept their sudden maturity. Those still in school should have definite courses directed toward war and relief training and should have jobs in the community and at home that will satisfy their urge to be of service and their need for adult responsibility."

Published in 1942, *The Family in a World at War* was a record of the fresh importance placed by America's government on the country's young. The lessons of the 1930s had not been forgotten: "A lot of thinking has been going on between the last war and this one, a lot of thinking about America's young people. Government and private agencies alike have spent millions in the study of youth problems and it is not very likely that we will go ahead and work in terms of the emergency while disregarding all that we have learned."

One of the first changes to hit home was the introduction of rationing—of petrol, sugar, candy bars, chewing gum, and even Coca-Cola—during the spring of 1942. As a high school student wrote in a local Indianapolis newspaper, "Nearly every student has been affected by the war. The shortage of commodities such as sugar and rubber, the sale of bonds and stamps, the higher cost of living, the entrance of our fathers and brothers into the armed forces and war industries and the daily newspapers are constant reminders that we are at war."

High schools entered the war effort with a series of activities with slogans like "Study, Sacrifice, Save and Serve". Air-raid drills were regularly held to preserve alertness and awareness of wartime dangers. During the first year of war, scrap drives and salvage campaigns collected myriad items for recycling into war matériel: books, bobby pins, iron, and phonograph records. New courses were introduced during 1942: more science, maths, and physical education, after the poor performance of the first batch of Selective Service draftees.

Moralistic youth experts like Anna Wolf thought that "sound discipline" was required of the "soft" and overprivileged American adolescent. To inculcate "iron in their systems", the Office of Civilian Defense suggested a ten-point programme for public schools during February 1942. These included one hour of physical education daily and practical courses in first aid. Many of these classes assumed a pre-military character, as gym teachers put pupils through a "commando drill" of obstacle courses, rope climbing, and pull-ups. Students were also encouraged to participate in boxing, wrestling, and other team sports.

That onetime bugbear of the American Youth Congress, the Reserve Officers' Training Corps returned to prominence. Its purpose, according to one recruit, was "to awaken in the adolescent appreciation of all the obligations of citizenship, to prepare him to discharge his duties as a citizen, and to qualify him as a military leader". During the "tough" three-year course, cadets took lessons in marksmanship, military courtesy, guard duty, hygiene, first aid, American citizenship, and rifle training, with regular drill. This relentless activity eventually resulted in a very high—up to 90 per cent—drop-out rate.

Another scheme promoted by the Office of Education aimed to accelerate the schooling of adolescents to make them available for the draft or essential war work. Instead of the usual minimum three-and-a-half-year high school course, students could graduate in three years if they attended summer sessions. In 1942, the most popular classes were history, maths, and English, but for a price—up to ten dollars for a shop class—other subjects more suitable to the armed services were on offer: navigation, military maths, physics, aeronautics, and radio.

Student publications also promoted patriotic involvement. This was inevitable, given that the purpose of these magazines was to interpret the life of the school for the broader community: "Only the student publications," advised one student journalist adviser, "remain as lines of mass communication with the adults of your city." Although censored, these magazines gave students necessary information about the war effort, with articles about draft law, curriculum changes, and summer courses punctuating school gossip.

In November 1942, *Life* celebrated the lowering of the draft age with its cover story of an "18-Year Old". Featuring Bob Berger, an undergraduate at the University of Nebraska, the cover shot displayed a smart, serious youth with cardigan, collar, and tie, and an armful of textbooks, flanked by institutional pillars. The text inside placed Bob and roommate George Schmelzer as typical representatives of the 2.5 million newly draftable adolescents, pondering "the prospect of going to war" against a "collegiate backdrop of pin-up girls".

Life's cover boy fitted the ideal GI promoted by influential war correspondents like Ernie Pyle: down-to-earth soldiers, "the boys". In his account of the late 1942 North African campaign, *Here Is Your War*, Pyle offered thumbnail sketches of some "boys": "Private Frank T. Borezon, of 631 Payne Avenue, Erie, Pennsylvania said the worst part of being in Africa was that he couldn't find a bowling alley." *Life*'s description of Bob Berger highlighted this laconic everyman quality: "If you ask him why this war is being fought, he shuffles his feet and mutters something about the rights of all free men."

However vague, these principles had a terrific charge in 1942. The president of the National Conference of Christians and Jews, Everett R. Clinchy, thought that the goal facing American youth was "to become missionary-minded in sharing the American Idea with the rest of the world. American youths can be very proud of the great experiment that is going on in America. What is this experiment? It is the adventure of sons and daughters of all of the old-world peoples living together on one continent, to create one nation of many nationalities, including all racial strains and all religious persuasions."

This American Idea was enshrined in the Constitution and the Bill of Rights. Youth was entrusted with the challenge of propagating the democratic ideal because it epitomized the country's own self-definition, as expressed in 1942 by Mark McCloskey: "America has been the land of hope and therefore the land for youth." But there was the other side: "It will not do to refer constantly to 'the American way of life' without attempting systematically to give that phrase concrete meaning for the boys and girls who are to continue this nation when the fighting is over."

The American Youth Congress held that "the salvation of this country will not be advanced by the conscription of life that is underprivileged and unhopeful. This country can only be defended enthusiastically by people who expect just treatment from it." The deal was on the table. Greater expectations meant greater inclusion. This involved not only adolescents but all the other neglected groups in American society suddenly found to be of value in the mass mobilization. The contradiction between the rhetoric of freedom and the reality of oppression would become a constant wartime theme.

. . .

Negroes began to agitate for a bigger slice of the democratic pie. During early December 1941, one of them wrote to the president, "If there is such a thing as God, he must be a white person, according to the conditions we colored people are in. Hitler has not done anything to the colored people—it's the people right here in the United States who are keeping us out of work and keeping us down." Anna Wolf understood this contradiction: "Though we are fighting a war against Hitler and the selfish doctrine of race superiority, we ourselves are riddled with race prejudice and religious intolerance."

This resentment had been building since the 1930s, when Negroes had been barely touched by the New Deal. This sense of injustice was compounded by the fact that the usually liberal FDR had failed to pass anti-lynching legislation, even after the fate of the Scottsboro Boys had revealed the desperate situation in the South. When rearmament began to mop up the white unemployed in 1940 and 1941, Negroes remained without jobs. Even when they flocked to enlist, the army put them in segregated units and assigned them to menial tasks.

As the army, so the society. The young voices collected in E. Franklin Frazier's *Negro Youth at the Crossways*—prepared for the American Youth Congress—partook of this newly aggressive mood. Fired by the examples of Booker T. Washington and Joe Louis, some of the high school and college students interviewed found their feelings of alienation transforming into militancy. However, many found that their first reaction was the internalization of prejudice into self-doubt: "I don't believe I or any other Negro can help but feel inferior," a seventeen-year-old college freshman stated; "sort of an Indian sign on me, you know."

Some of the adolescents interviewed strongly felt that the system was weighted against Negroes. According to a twenty-one-year-old "laborer's son",

"White people don't treat us fairly and even white policemen seem to get a great kick out of beating up Negroes, not only because of the things they do, but because they happen to be Negroes and can't fight back." A sixteen-year-old named Warren Wall opined that "Negroes don't get as good chances as white people". Some of those interviewed found release in intoxicants and "heterosexual activity".

Others pursued the policy defined by one twenty-year-old "lower class" man: "Be as courteous as possible to white people, don't talk back to them, and do your work as well as possible." Another technique was defined as "clowning" or "acting like a monkey". Underneath these survival strategies, however, there were "expressions of resentment toward subordination to whites" and "sullen and 'mean' dispositions". Even in the black middle class, which endeavoured at all times to differentiate itself from the lower class, there was a "nascent race consciousness".

"I'd like to see all segregation wiped out," stated an eighteen-year-old high school senior. "I'd like to be able to go where I please and do the things I want." However, it was becoming increasingly clear that these rights would not be granted but would have to be fought for. And yet, despite all the prejudice, there were several interviewees who wanted nothing more than to enter American society on their own terms. The seventeen-year-old Dick, an officer in the high school cadet corps, thought that "the army is the greatest thing a Negro can get into. That's one place a Negro can get the respect a white man can get." In fact, the reality of the segregated army was woefully different.

During the summer of 1941, the Negro March on Washington Committee planned a mass demonstration of over 100,000 in the capital. In the negotiations that resulted in the march being called off, the president issued a government directive that "there shall be no discrimination in the employment of workers in defense industries or government because of race, creed, color or national origin". The army was next in line for agitation: as the National Association for the Advancement of Colored People's journal put it, "A jim crow army cannot fight for a free world."

But then, some Negroes felt that they were already at war, and not with the Axis. In *Twelve Million Black Voices*, the novelist Richard Wright—famous for his excoriating 1940 bestseller *Native Son*—delivered a pictorial meditation on Negro life. He observed that "even in times of peace some of the neighbourhoods in which we live look as though they had been subjected to an intensive and prolonged aerial bombardment". He extended the bitter mood with a minatory premonition about the new generation: "We watch strange moods fill our children, and our hearts swell with pain."

AT THE SAVOY IN HARLEM,
EARLY 1940s

On one page, however, there is a snapshot of a young man, bathed in light, with a curiously shaped, high-buttoned long jacket and pegged trousers. Stepping out of the Savoy Ballroom with a soft smile of anticipation, he appears beamed in from the future. Wright contextualized this extraordinary image by celebrating the universal appeal of jazz: "We play our guitars, trumpets and pianos, beating out rough and infectious rhythms that create an instant appeal among all classes of people." He concluded with a statement of fact that sounded like a boast: "Our music makes the feet of the whole world dance."

CHAPTER 25

German Swing Kids and French *Zazous*

Swing in Nazi Europe

· · ·

I don't want you to feel that there might be differences in political opinion which kept me away because I really feel that two souls like ourselves with such a common decent interest as swing know of no barriers. When it comes to art, and swing is an art, there are no lines.

—Henry Sklow, New York, letter to German pen pal, Kurt "Hot-Geyer" Michaelis,
August 1939

FRENCH *ZAZOU*, c. 1942

AS SWING SPREAD through Europe in the early 1940s, its most fervent adherents were youths in Germany and the Nazi-occupied countries. Barely heeding the wider implications of their actions, they instinctively responded to the freedom that they heard in their forbidden records. Swing spoke to the secret desires of the young who wanted more than blood and soil: it was, as the French Hot Club founder Charles Delaunay noted, a reaction "against the oppression under which we were living. Jazz had the taste of forbidden fruit."

These passions were dangerous in wartime Europe, as the Nazis sought complete compliance from their subjects and their own people. At the same time, youth was destabilized by the demands of total war: the chaos of mobilization, the disruption of family life, and the deranged psychology of war itself conspired to double the figures for juvenile delinquency in Nazi Germany during 1940 and 1941. At the time when confidence in the regime was at its height, there were over 17,000 recorded youth crimes, of which two-thirds were committed by members of the Hitler Youth.

The full weight of the Nazi state had not eradicated the hard rump that resisted joining the Hitler Youth. These refusers were few in number—up to 95 per cent of German youth would remain in thrall to the regime until 1943— but they created a significant problem simply because the regime demanded total subservience and obedience. Within this police state, any attempt at or hint of deviant behaviour would "be visited by terror". With Germany at war, the actions and attitudes of youth took on a new importance, and the cycle of dissent and repression escalated throughout the war.

Pre-war problems reappeared with a vengeance. Germany's major cities and towns had never been total Nazi strongholds, and in the early war years some of the generation socialized under Hitler began to form their own dissident groups. From predominantly working-class if not proletarian origin, these neighbourhood gangs added subtle anti-Nazi touches to the garish wide boy (*Stenzen*) style. Loud checked shirts and battered hats were topped off with metal edelweiss badges or coloured pins worn on the collar, together with "gruesome signet rings" topped with the skull and crossbones.

These groups of fourteen- to eighteen-year-olds evolved spontaneously out of a desire to avoid Hitler Youth service. Many of them had left school at fourteen and were thus outside the immediate influence of the state youth organization. In the few years before they were conscripted, they began working and found independence in the high wages of the booming wartime economy. Having assumed an adult role, they were not about to be bossed around like children: "It's the Hitler Youth's own fault," one Düsseldorf gang member stated. "Every order I was given contained a threat."

A continuation of pre-war groups like the Edelweiss Pirates, these gangs existed throughout industrial Germany: in Düsseldorf, the Shambeko Band and the Kittelsbach Pirates,[1] in Essen the Travelling Dudes, in Cologne the Navajos, in Ahlberg the Snake Club. Their names indicated the kind of life they wanted: freedom from the constant harassment of the Hitler Youth and the police. These "Wild Cliques" of boys and girls travelled around the country, hitchhiking and walking as far as the Black Forest, Berlin, or Vienna in direct contravention of police controls and travel restrictions.

In the Third Reich, overt political opposition was quickly detected, and the penalties were so severe as to discourage all but the very bravest. So the Edelweiss Pirates employed sarcasm and humour. One of their favourite tactics was to alter the lyrics of popular hits: "Hark the hearty fellows sing! / Strum that banjo, pluck that string! / And the lasses all join in / We're going to get rid of Hitler, / And he can't do a thing." Or in another example: "We march by banks of Ruhr and Rhine / And smash the Hitler Youth in twain / Our song is freedom, love and life / We're Pirates of the Edelweiss."

Pirates encounters with the ubiquitous Hitler Youth "flying patrols" were common. These wild gangs would enthusiastically "clobber" the young agents of the regime. By 1941 a mining instructor found that, among his trainees, "every child knows who the Kittelsbach Pirates are. They are everywhere; there are more of them than there are Hitler Youth. And they all know each other, they stick close together. They beat up the patrols, because there are so many of them. They never take no for an answer."

The rising level of delinquency both within and without the Hitler Youth represented a direct challenge to the authorities. In June 1940, Heinrich Himmler's Police Order for the Protection of Youth initiated several new restrictions: a curfew to keep under-eighteens off the streets and out of restaurants and bars, while under-sixteens were not allowed in cinemas, variety shows, and cabarets after 9 p.m. Under-sixteens were also not allowed to drink and smoke. The penalties were three weeks in prison and a fifty-reichsmark fine.

Enforcement of this new order was undertaken by the expanding Streifendienst, the Hitler Youth police force. Fifty thousand members were used to patrol cafés, bars, and cinemas in tandem with the police and the SS. Many worked in police stations, writing reports on wild clique behaviour as well as sexual and political felonies. Rewired through special brainwashing courses at SS camps, the young Streifendienst robots—many of whom relished their

---

1. Named after a brook that flows between Düsseldorf and Duisburg.

role—enthusiastically participated in the mass sweeps of Wild Cliques that began after 1940.

Three months later, Himmler and Hitler Youth leader Artur Axmann introduced another punitive measure. The Youth Service Arrest gave Hitler Youth leaders power to detain boys between fourteen and eighteen for up to ten days. These "service arrests" had to be made within twenty days after the alleged offence, and were "tried" in quick hearings. Avoiding the final sanction of expulsion, which would have suited die-hard rebels, the Youth Service Arrest was a highly effective way of ensuring obedience: there would be no serious Hitler Youth rebellion during the war.

After 1940, any young rebels had to contend with a hydra-headed system of surveillance. Everyday life in Nazi Germany was so highly controlled that activities that might have been unremarkable in free countries became crimes against the state. There were many police raids: 1,715 offenders were arrested in Dresden during the spring of 1940, 400 in Mainz, 600 Navajos in Cologne during 1941. Around the same time an SA unit in Mühlheim asked "the police to ensure that this riff-raff is dealt with once and for all. The Hitler Youth are taking their lives in their hands when they go out onto the streets."

The Edelweiss Pirates were marked out partly because of their free and easy sexuality that offended the puritanism of the authorities in general and Himmler in particular. This was stratified in the Nazi youth system, which was based on strict gender segregation from the age of ten. Because they banded together in groups of boys and girls outside state surveillance, the Edelweiss Pirates and the other Wild Cliques were assumed to be getting up to the kind of uninhibited sexual expression that sent the authorities into a frenzy.

This was the fault line that the swing youth also exposed: reports on their activities were full of phrases like "sexual intercourse among minors", "group sex", and "homosexuality". Although the Swing Heinis were relaxed, their vaunted decadence was rather innocent. As one member of a Kiel swing club called the Plutocrats wrote to a travelling friend, "Be a proper spokesman for Kiel, won't you? I.e., make sure you're really casual, singing or whistling English hits all the time, absolutely smashed and always surrounded by really amazing women."

. . .

Swing clubs continued to exist in several large German cities in the early war years, in Breslau, Kiel, Berlin, Frankfurt, Dresden, Stuttgart, and Hamburg. These were mainly composed of middle-class or upper-middle-class boys and girls determined to retain their freedom. Holding on to their precious, forbid-

HAMBURG SWINGS, C. 1939—
TOMMIE SCHEEL IS SEVENTH FROM THE LEFT, BACK ROW

den swing records, even managing to adapt the ersatz article peddled in variety shows, they managed to persist with the hot jazz lifestyle. Growing their hair outrageously long for Nazi Germany, they cultivated an air of defiant individuality.

While most of their cohort was in uniform, the Hamburg swing kids sported treasonous fashions: checked English sports jackets, shoes with thick light crepe soles, Anthony Eden hats, and an umbrella on the arm "whatever the weather". The girls wore their hair long, with lavish make-up and lipstick. In contrast to the Bund Deutscher Mädel, they wore provocative clothes. A young Leipzig swing kid, Jutta Hipp, remembered going out "with a pair of blue silk stockings, with a red heart on the knee" just to be different. If anyone got upset, she would walk back and "then smile at him".

This nonconformity was seductive but dangerous. In Frankfurt, a group of young fans formed the Harlem Club: wearing English clothes and long hair, they succeeded in making a couple of records. They continued to listen to the BBC—an activity that after September 1939 carried severe penalties—and hailed each other in the street by whistling their signature tune, Eddie Carroll's "Harlem". This habit soon spread to Frankfurt youths who were not members of the club, as a kind of rebellion that was under the Gestapo's radar.

The Frankfurt clique had their own nemesis, a Gestapo agent nicknamed Ganjo, who hounded its more visible members. In the first two years of the war, there were no major arrests. Some of the activities of the police verged on farce, like their use of speedboats to chase youngsters playing banned records on small vessels in the Main River. But they were indicative of the Nazis' increasing determination to stamp out the swing lifestyle. In Hamburg, the skirmishes between the Swing Heinis and the authorities ended in a full-scale campaign of terror orchestrated by the city's own swing tsar, Hans Reinhardt.

Protected by their parents' wealth and their own daring, the Hamburg swings continued to party on regardless. Secretly attending a February 1940 dance in an Altona hotel, the Gestapo agents were horrified: "There was only swing of the worst sort. Sometimes two boys danced with one girl; sometimes several couples formed a circle, linking arms and jumping, slapping hands, even rubbing the backs of their heads together; and then, bent double, with the top half of the body hanging loosely down, long hair flopping into the face, they dragged themselves round practically on their knees."

It got worse: "The band played wilder and wilder items; none of the players was sitting down any longer, they all 'jitterbugged' on the stage like wild creatures. Several boys could be observed dancing together, always with two cigarettes in the mouth, one in each corner." This frenzy was not only perverse but seditious. As the report concluded, "The Swing dance was being executed in a completely hideous fashion. English music was played with English vocals, while our soldiers are engaged in battle against Britain."

This Gestapo testimony laid out in detail what so appalled the authorities about the swings: their explicit Anglophilia, their imputed perverse sexuality, and, worst of all, a "wild ecstasy" directly opposed to the martial movement favoured by the Nazis. The swings' lifestyle reversed almost every Nazi tenet. Instead of uniformity, they proclaimed difference; instead of aggression, overt sexuality. They also refused to take the war seriously: they played their jazz records in public shelters, listened to the BBC, and covered up the Führer's portrait in public places.

The battle was on, but the swings didn't understand the rules of engagement: they didn't realize that having fun or being obnoxious was totally *verboten*. Another big public dance was halted in the spring of 1940. The participants were invited by printed invitations, with all guests checked at the door. However, at 11 p.m., when the music was at its height, the police rushed in. They locked all the exits and harassed and searched all the four hundred or so swings present for several hours. Almost all the arrested were under twenty-one, but most were quickly set free. A follow-up party planned two weeks later was instantly cancelled.

At the same time, the Hamburg swings continued to test the boundaries of the regime. Tommie Scheel and two friends dressed as gangsters and committed a fake robbery at a friends' villa, photographing the process. Scheel and his friends also disrupted newsreels at the local cinema with sarcastic comments and made snide comments in cafés when the Gestapo were present. He remembered that "we were going to tell these dumb bastards that we were different, that was all". With this attitude, he was one of the first leading swings to be arrested by the Gestapo in autumn 1940.

Inside Hamburg's Stadthaus, Scheel was repeatedly beaten. In between these bouts, he had to sit facing the wall for hours. If he moved, one of the Gestapo would smash his head repeatedly against the wall. Although only seventeen, he was charged with being a leader of the swings, an organizer of "hot feasts", and, after the Gestapo found the pictures of the fake robbery, of burglary. He was later moved to Hamburg's notorious Fuhlsbüttel prison and sentenced to hard labour. His fate was shared by several other swings arrested by the Gestapo that autumn: some of the unluckier over-eighteens were also sent to the front.

With public venues closed, the swings continued their activities in clubs and private parties. European bands passed through what was still an international city. In early 1941, the swings congregated at a large, glass-roofed casino on the river in Hamburg's centre, where the featured attraction was John Kristel's Dutch swing band. The mood there "was great", remembered one of the participants, "and it escalated. People went mad with excitement. What was happening was unbelievable. John Kristel's band had a fabulous trumpeter. Whenever he stood up to blow his solos, the entire house broke down."

However, the Gestapo quickly got wind of what was going on. At another show at the end of February, they turned up en masse: John Kristel and his musicians were locked into a basement room, then whisked out the back door. The assembled swings were informed that the band had suddenly had to leave Hamburg, a transparent fiction. Although Kristel returned to the Alsterpavillon a few months later—licensed to entertain troops on leave—the magic had gone: the musicians had been warned by the authorities to tone things down. The music was "not all that great".

By then the Gestapo had new powers against this "degenerate music". Their principal weapon against swing had been the ban on public dancing, which fluctuated according to the fortunes of war and was thus difficult to enforce. During August 1941, however, the Reichsmusikkammer issued an interdiction of "hot and swing music in the original or copied". After this live music and public events were patrolled by Reichsmusikkammer functionaries and the Gestapo, who installed specialized spies in Hamburg and Frankfurt.

After this ban, the Hamburg swing movement moved underground into the basements of their parents' expensive villas that were, for a while, no-go zones even for the Gestapo. There they could sip cognac and listen to swing records, in rooms with "murals on the walls, and fitted carpets", together with "bright-red leather cushions on the floors". This "warm and inviting" environment was an oasis. Nevertheless, there was another big sweep of the swings in autumn 1941, during which one of the leading figures, Kaki Georgiadis, was arrested and placed in solitary confinement for several weeks.

The Gestapo's campaign was extremely effective against a group of young people unprepared for such brutality. They used stool pigeons, pressuring vulnerable swings to inform on their friends. The Hitler Youth informed on swing pupils in local schools and acted with directors to expel the rebels. However, the subculture persisted to the extent that, in the summer of 1941, an appeal for help was made to the head of the Central Security Agency, Reinhard Heydrich. In January 1942 the net was drawn even tighter with a new decree that banned dancing in semi-private locations like sports clubs.

That same month, Himmler intervened. He was determined that there would be no "mere half-measures" against this contagion: "All the ringleaders, and I mean ringleaders both male and female, and all teachers with enemy views who are encouraging the swing youth, are to be assigned to a concentration camp. There the youth should first be given thrashings and then put through the severest drill and sent to work. I think that any sort of labour camp or youth camp would be inappropriate for these youths and worthless girls. The girls should be put to work weaving and do land work in the summer."

Himmler thought that a spell of "2–3 years" in a concentration camp would deal with these offenders. Their studies and their youth would be immediately curtailed. At the same time, he recommended a thorough investigation of "how much encouragement they have had from their parents. If they have encouraged them, then they should also be put in a KL [*Konzentrations lager*: concentration camp] and their property confiscated. It is only by intervening brutally that we shall be able to prevent the dangerous spread of this anglophyle[2] tendency at a time when Germany is fighting for her existence."

One climactic event tipped the scale against the Hamburg swings. During a

2. Spelling as in original document.

June 1942 dance on a private estate just outside Hamburg, a lavish buffet dinner was followed by a cabaret that featured impersonations of Hitler and Goebbels. The person responsible, Kaki Georgiadis, was betrayed to the Gestapo. Exposed as traitors, the leading Hamburg swings were arrested, brutally beaten, and sent either to concentration camps like Uckermark, Neuengamme, and Moringen, or to the eastern front where as "effeminate cowards" they were put in the most dangerous situations.

However, the Nazis did not succeed in eradicating the Swing Heinis. At the end of the summer, the SS attended a Hamburg concert by the Willi Artelt band, whose "leader was performing in an apparent state of ecstasy. He was conducting with his back hunched and with rolling eyes; the audience was roaring in accompaniment." The subculture spread to Berlin, Hanover, and Dresden, as young audiences spurred on the bands to play proper jazz: "The wilder, 'hotter' and more jazzified the music they play, the more unrestrained the applause they obtain from people of this type."

The authorities' actions drove the swings into more overt anti-regime displays. A report on a summer 1942 Hamburg jazz show noted that the wild clapping for English tunes "was in sharp contrast to the applause bestowed on the German numbers. Among other items, the English hit 'Sweet Sue' was performed, using the words 'read the midday paper, read the daily paper'. Since the 'swing youth' have always sung the words in the amended form, 'read the midday paper, read the daily paper, all lies, all rubbish', and that is how they are always known, this piece reaped particularly loud applause."

· · ·

The same trajectory of repression and radicalization occurred in the Nazi-occupied zone of northern France. During the spring of 1941, press reports circulated about misbehaviour at jazz concerts: "petits Swings" were accused of wriggling uncontrollably and mocking the serious national situation. Later that year, the Fascist youth paper *La Jeunesse* detailed the "ultra-swing 1941": "They wore deliberately tousled hair down to the neck, sported small Clark Gable moustaches, jackets without lapels, striped trousers, thick crepe-soled shoes, and alternated their syncopated walk with Sioux war cries."

French swing had a symbiotic relationship to the occupation. According to the historian Jean-Claude Loiseau, "The excessive ecstasies that accompanied each concert by 'swing' orchestras both good and bad, increased step by step as the occupation grew more and more serious." Within a year of France's fall, swing became a pop fashion. A singer named Johnny Hess started it with "Je Suis Swing", and others leapt in with tunes like "Êtes-vous Swing?" and "Swing

Partout". But there was another side to this fad, an emotional response to the occupation: "What could you do when you couldn't stand it?"

The new regimes of occupied France made strenuous attempts to impose their own order on youth. After the defeat of summer 1940, the Germans had carved up the country into eight separate zones, including the Southern Zone and the Occupied Zone in the north, which ran from Reims to Bordeaux and included Paris. With a vigorous pre-war Fascist movement complemented by the inevitable opportunists, the French were quick to take up the Nazi standard—symbolized by the *Blutfahne,* the blood banner, which the Germans hung on the Eiffel Tower after Paris fell.

Control in the Southern Zone was vested in the Vichy regime. Headed by the eighty-four-year-old World War I hero Marshal Pétain, with Pierre Laval as deputy prime minister, Vichy began to pursue a "National Revolution" that aimed to replace the old French Revolution slogan of "Liberté, Egalité, Fraternité" with a fresh trinity, "Travaille, Famille, Patrie"—work, family, homeland. With Joan of Arc as a symbol, this revolution aimed to reintroduce what Pétain saw as the eternal verities: the family as the "essential cell" of the social order and land work as the highest form of human endeavour.

Youth's place in this agrarian utopia—not dissimilar to the Nazis' plans for the Warthegau—was simple subservience. As Pétain stated soon after his accession to power, "The spirit of youth has been overtaken by the spirit of sacrifice." The young no longer had rights but duties. To Vichy ideologues, the French defeat was the result of a breakdown in moral order caused by the Communists, the Jews, and intellectuals. To combat this, Vichy passed new laws against alcohol, venereal disease, and abortion: *dénatalité,* the reduction in the birth rate, was considered the "collective suicide of the nation".

Vichy's educational policies emphasized sport at the expense of literature. Instead of materialistic individualism, duty, discipline, and faith would be the cornerstones of the new national spiritual community. Two youth groups promoted this ideal. The Compagnons de France was a Scout-like voluntary movement for young men between fifteen and twenty: entrants began as apprentices and graduated to "journeymen" by fulfilling the strict requirements of camp life. Countryside activities like forestry were alternated with choral singing and drama.

Through the *Chantiers de la Jeunesse,* "Youth Work Sites", Vichy youth were to be rebuilt as peasants. Membership was compulsory for all twenty-year-olds in the Southern Zone as a substitute for military service. This was seen as the best way to inculcate the new national character: "Before the young sought to wriggle out of their obligations, they brutalized animals and obeyed nothing but their basest instincts. After: the young speak with one voice, the young love all of France, the young have confidence in their leaders, the young are clean in their thoughts, their words and their deeds."

The rare travellers from the Occupied to the Southern Zone found a "strange land, a sort of principality where everyone, from children of six upwards, were regimented into groups from *Jeunesses* to *Anciens Combattants*, wearing *Francisques* or symbols of the Legion, seemed to be in uniform". A religious fervour underpinned Vichy's policies for youth. This wish for a new chivalry that would save European civilization reached its apotheosis in the mass August 1942 pilgrimage organized by the Catholic Scouts to celebrate the Black Virgin at Le Puy.

To Simone de Beauvoir, observing from Paris, the marshal's phrases about the family, God, and the "reign of virtue" was the "same violent prejudice and stupidity that had darkened my childhood—only now it extended over the whole country, an official and repressive blanket". In comparison to the Vichy's return to a non-existent religious agrarian past, conditions in the Occupied Zone were both more modern and more serious. Although Vichy was the capital of the new France, Paris was the seat of power and under the direct rule of the Nazis.

The most enthusiastic French collaborators were pre-war Fascists, writers like Henri de Montherlant, Drieu La Rochelle, and Robert Brasillach, as well as younger ideologues like Lucien Rebatet and Alain Laubreaux. Collaborationism was vigorously pursued in a series of small magazines, mostly funded by the Germans. These began with *La Gerbe* (the Wreath) in July 1940, followed by *La Jeunesse*, a weekly paper aimed at youth, during December 1940, and the relaunch of *Je Suis Partout* in February 1941.

Presided over by the talented and vicious Robert Brasillach, *Je Suis Partout* (I Am Everywhere) promoted the Fascist vision of youth: "We have to give youth the cult of the hero, the virtues of force, courage, enthusiasm, responsibility, sacrifice, a taste for brutality and energy." It quickly became the most popular *collabo* magazine:[3] the house organ of the *ubiquistes,* the denouncers who were everywhere. The column "Partout et ailleurs" (Everywhere and Elsewhere) printed the names and addresses of those hunted by the Nazis and thus actively assisted in their arrest and, on occasion, murder.

These shrill voices represented an extreme reaction to the Nazi occupation, but the impact of Nazi rule in the Occupied Zone was all-pervasive. Almost every aspect of daily life posed a moral dilemma. As Jean-Paul Sartre later

---

3. And as such was derisively called *Je Chie Partout:* I shit everywhere.

wrote, "Everything we did was equivocal; we never quite knew whether we were doing right or doing wrong; a subtle poison corrupted even our best actions." In her diary for the period, a Parisian schoolgirl noted her contrasting reactions: "I detest and will always detest the Boche," she exclaimed, "but Germans taken individually are very nice, usually well brought up and correct."

Resistance was difficult and punished with instant execution. With political action seemingly impossible, some French youth found a response in the mannered sarcasm first rehearsed by Baudelaire. From 1940 onwards, a number of "petits Swings" began to dress up in an act of deliberate provocation. This was the foppish revolt later described by Albert Camus in L'homme révolté: "The dandy can only play a part by setting himself up in opposition. He can only be sure of his own existence by finding it in the expression of others' faces. Other people are his mirror."

Getting their inspiration from America, the "petits Swings" changed into "Ultra Swings", and then, during the winter of 1941, into the Zazous. By that time, the occupation had become more oppressive. After America's entry into the war, jazz and swing were heavily censored. A Sorbonne bookshop was bombed when it exhibited works by Henri de Montherlant. Afterwards, the cafés in the Boulevard St Michel were closed: a direct response by the authorities to "le mauvais esprit" of the Latin Quarter, typified by the Zazous, who "danced on the edge of the volcano, marking out the tempo with a raised index finger".

The Zazous were principally middle- or upper-middle-class, at the upper range of what the occupiers called, for rationing and identity card purposes, the J3 age group: thirteen to twenty-one. They set themselves apart by their clothing and their attitude. Like Camus's dandy, they provoked, and when the authorities and the collabos struck back, they provoked again, all the while preserving a blank, sarcastic façade. Although they avoided direct confrontation with the Germans, they mocked "Greta Gestapo". When La Jeunesse called for all the young "to bring us your twenty years", they replied: "for what, exactly?"

The word Zazou came from jazz slang. Cab Calloway, whose watch chains and checked jackets were highly influential on the style, recorded "Zah Zuh Zah" in 1933, and embellished it with the chant "zazouzazou—hey!" The scat singer Slim Gaillard developed this clanging surrealism in songs like "Tutti Frutti" and "Flat Foot Floogie". Others cited an expatriate American trumpeter named Freddy Taylor, who recorded a version of "Viper's Dream" before the war. However it started, the term soon achieved a pejorative status in the hands of the collabos, who regarded the Zazous as "imbeciles" and worse.

In March 1942, the magazine L'Illustration made a detailed survey of this new type. The male Zazous wore long checked jackets riddled with pockets and belts. Their shirts had high collars, with long sleeves covering manicured, beringed hands. They were often decorated with woollen and string ties. The trousers were straight, the socks of bright primary colours. The whole effect was topped off with huge crepe-soled shoes and hair, "oiled like a salad", that hung over the collar. As a final, dandyish touch, they fixed handkerchiefs in their buttonholes.

The women wore suede coats, roll-neck sweaters, and bum-freezer jackets with boxy shoulders. They tied their hair up into a bun on the front of the skull, and made themselves up with scarlet lips and nails. Their skirts were short and pleated and revealed legs that culminated in Minnie Mouse shoes: flat with stacked soles, "large as ships". The whole effect was accessorized with chains, earrings, bracelets, and square shoulder bags. With their signature umbrellas and sunglasses, worn after dark, the Latin Quarter *Zazous* blended American, British, and continental fashions into something unique.

La Jeunesse placed the origins of the movement in a section of bourgeois youth, "a generation of morons" who promenaded around the Left Bank, "the world a canvas for their narcissism". Their headquarters were two cafés, La Capoulade and Le Dupont-Latin, where they ostentatiously smoked English cigarettes. There was a second *Zazou* zone, centred on the Champs-Elysées, with its HQ a café called the Pam Pam. These central *Zazous* were more high-fashion, as befitted their proximity to the heart of haute couture: their taste for luxury gained them the epithet of "spoiled little scumbags".

Living under curfew and surveillance, the *Zazous* took their culture under-ground, reviving a 1920s tradition of "surprise parties"—illegal, unlicensed gatherings. Behind thick shutters and under soft lights, they could listen to New Orleans jazz and swing without fear of interruption. In this heady air of freedom, they behaved like obnoxious adolescents rather than dutiful Nazi slaves: sometimes they ended the night by smashing everything up, an act of gleefully wilful destruction within a regime that preached repentance and mortification.

They also idolized American culture. After the Germans censored all Eng-lish and American films made after 1937, the *Zazous* felt bereft. "We deplored the disappearance of the old M.G.M. lion like that of a friend," one remem-bered. "All that mythology of American cinema still lived within us, was our world, was our key to a secret existence." American culture became a lost para-dise, a kind of Eldorado. Seemingly innocuous lines became commandments of faith, like Jimmy Stewart's speech in *Mr Smith Goes to Washington*: "I am free, to think and speak."

The Germans couldn't censor everything. The *Zazous* plucked phrases out of the air to express forbidden emotions. "The decrypting of hidden messages in even bad films was," according to *Zazou* Jean-Louis Bory, "a question of attitude." Forced to undergo the interminable costume dramas and patronizing pronouncements pumped out by the Southern Zone, the *Zazous* perfected an appreciation of Vichy kitsch, the riper the better. Deciding that a government headed by a man in his mid-eighties had very little to say to youth, they hunted for *Pétainismes* like pigs sniff out truffles.

Denounced by the Vichy minister of education, Abel Bonnard, as "the last vestiges of an individualistic society", the *Zazous* got their revenge by ridiculing his statement that Joan of Arc was the perfect example to all young France. This was the perfect example of the "crystallised perfume of stupidity" that sent them scouring the Vichy newspapers for the latest nugget that they passed around for fun. Inspired "with the spirit of contradiction, we could not stomach the trinity of *'Travail-Famille-Patrie'* that they were trying to force upon France. We got energy from the absurdity of the situation."

The *Zazous* not only perfected a negative aesthetic, but also took energy from their enemies. The *collabos* had begun with dismissals but quickly became more proscriptive. Lucien Rebatet linked swing with Gaullism and Jewishness. Robert Brasillach excoriated them for not "having the fascist spirit, which is the spirit of joy". In April 1942, *La Jeunesse* decided that the *Zazous* combined "all at the same time, the madness of jazz, the rhumba, and the Lambeth Walk, while playing with their yo-yos, showing their legs and flirting like there was no tomorrow". According to *La Gerbe*, they "were not Frenchmen".

Above all, the *Zazous'* sarcastic attitude symbolized their mute resistance[4] to the occupation. As *La Gerbe* concluded, "These young idiots are playing with fire." There were many ways in which the *Zazous* infuriated the regime's termagant spokesmen. Their extravagant clothes and flagrant smoking contravened rationing and led to accusations of black-market involvement. Like the Hamburg swings, they mocked what they thought was a ludicrous national rhetoric: they were not the generation who had lost the war, so why should they be involved in sacrifice and reparation?

To the ultra-*collabos*, who had become obsessed with this small youth cult, the *Zazous* embodied the decadence that had cost France its national pride. In July, *La Jeunesse* accused "these young citizens of free France" of waiting "for the victory of de Gaulle and the return of Coca-Cola". Most of all, they drove the Fascist journalists wild with a disengagement—*"l'attentisme"*—that, al-

---

4. Silence was the preferred option for many French writers during the occupation. The apparently meaningless yet obstinate refusal to explain his crime by the unnamed hero of Albert Camus's *L'étranger* can be seen as a parable of this facet of French life during the war.

though not illegal, was nevertheless detected as a particularly obstinate kind of defiance. As a critical Simone de Beauvoir noted, the *Zazous'* "Anglophile and anarchic attitude did stand for a kind of opposition to the regime".

Matters accelerated during spring 1942. After *La Gerbe* advocated a public beating for the *Zazous,* the Jeunes Populaires Français—a brand-new *collabo* youth group—took up the cudgel. For founder Jacques Doriot, dress was "the sign of the race", and he told his followers, "You will be hard, you will be strong, you will be violent, but you will be correctly dressed." In their uniforms of blue shirt and black tie, hundreds of Jeunes Populaires Français swarmed through the Boul' Mich' at the end of May, all the while shouting, "Vive Pétain, Vive Doriot!" Any *Zazous* or Jews that they found were beaten up.

This was a prelude to the police sweep held in mid-June, when about a hundred *Zazous* were arrested. In July, *La Jeunesse* made its headline of the week: "RASEZ LE ZAZOU, RASEZ LE ZAZOU, RASEZ AIR CONNU, DEPUIS PEU, GRACE AUX J.P.F." This was the way to correct the decadents: shaving their heads. Although they were busy assisting the Nazis with the first big round-up of Jews, the Jeunes Populaires Français fell to their tonsorial task with gusto. For a brief period, any *Zazou* who found himself in the wrong place at the wrong time had his head scalped, none too gently.

As well as being targeted by Fascist bully-boys, the *Zazous* were picked up in regular police sweeps and sent off to work in the harvest. Reinforcing their status as public enemy number one, some *Zazous* responded to the introduction of the yellow star that summer by creating their own star "to show their sympathy for the Jews". This was "exactly like the official one, except for one detail: at the centre, there was a word of five letters: Swing". Outcasts by dress, these *Zazous* identified with the ultimate racial outcasts: once discovered, they were summarily arrested and pitched into forced labour.

These events occurred just at the moment when swing became a national fad. The summer 1942 film *Mademoiselle Swing* popularized the style and everything became swing: cocktails, aperitifs, fashions. By the autumn, however, the *Zazous* were disappearing: the boldest continued to frequent their old haunts, but many others toned down the excesses of their costume. "We had to regroup amongst ourselves," remembered Jean-Louis Bory, "to avoid getting our faces smashed." If clothes meant real trouble, then change them. Discretion became the rule, rather than provocative display.

In October 1942, the forced-labour drafts began in earnest. With over-eighteens liable for the Service du Travail Obligatoire (STO), stray youths could be arrested if found in any public place during the day, and sent straight to Germany. It was not a time to stand out. In November, *La Gerbe* profiled a new type of *"zazou triste"*, wearing sombre clothes and steel-rimmed glasses, but many former *Zazous* had joined the ranks of *"les refractaires"*, the youths who went underground to avoid forced labour. The most stubborn of these joined the armed liberation movement of *maquisards*.

The *Zazous* appeared on the French stage and then disappeared, as if in a puff of smoke. Although they cultivated a blank façade, they left the authorities in no doubt about their total contempt for "The National Revolution". They also revelled in their bad press to the point of delirious abjection. Turning adolescent obnoxiousness into street theatre, they offered a symbolic resistance to the occupation's "ambient, abstract horror" that also mirrored its ultimate vacancy. However, they learned that in Nazi states everything was politicized, and that defiance was punishable by violence, imprisonment, and death.

CHAPTER 26

Zoot-Suiters and Victory Girls

American Unrest in 1943

. . .

No American can as yet have much to say about the extent of the emotional damage done to children in countries that experienced war at its grimmest. The story within the story—of how children think and feel and act in countries where homes are laid waste again and again and death and destruction are the rule, of how under such conditions they still manage to stride forward to maturity, or on the other hand, regress to brutality or mere passivity—is still to be heard.

—Anna Wolf, *Our Children Face War* (1942)

ZOOT-SUITERS ON PARADE, NEW YORK CITY, 1943

AMERICA WAS AT WAR: but where was the enemy? Several thousand miles away, over the Pacific and the Atlantic oceans. Throughout the first two years of the war, very few Americans were actually engaged in combat. For the vast majority of the population, the enemy would be a person that they would never see except in newsreels or photographs: an abstract. This left the vast reservoirs of hostility released by war—those impulses defined by Freud as "selfish and cruel"—all dammed up with nowhere to go.

All the aggression usually repressed in peacetime was summoned up and then focused on the national enemy. This process, however, was impossible to control fully. During 1942, America was a pressure cooker: "It was the look on the white people's faces when I walked down the streets," wrote Chester Himes, "it was that crazy, wild-eyed, unleashed hatred that the first Jap bomb on Pearl Harbor let loose in a flood. All that tight, crazy feeling of race as thick in the street as gas fumes." These tensions quickly boiled over.

The first to suffer were the Nisei, Americans born of Japanese parents. "The moment the impact of the words solemnly being transmitted over the several million radios of the nation struck home," John Okada wrote in *No-No Boy*, "everything Japanese, and everyone Japanese, became despicable." Okada's novel explored the situation of the 100,000 Japanese Americans who were forcibly deported and placed in special camps: overnight, they had become the most despised group in America, "Jap-Jews".

In Detroit there was a major disturbance at the end of February 1942. When the authorities attempted to move black families into new houses right next to a Polish-American area, a riot ensued. The Sojourner Truth Homes did not offer their first tenants a warm welcome. "Hundreds of whites blocked the roads, stoned cars and trucks and brutally beat unsuspecting Negroes," wrote a Detroit newspaper. The police just stood by and "allowed the whites to congregate and openly display weapons".

In Los Angeles, the problems of wartime dislocation were projected onto the figures of seventeen young Mexican Americans, accused of murdering a young gang member in the cause célèbre named the "Sleepy Lagoon" case after Harry James's current hit. The tune evoked an island idyll, but the lagoon in question was a swimming hole popular with Mexican youths barred from segregated pools. When the body of José Díaz was found nearby, the press and the police had a field day with these new enemies within.

At the same time, juvenile delinquency escalated. With their parents either called up or beginning to find war work and their nerves jangled by war fever, many adolescents revelled in the lack of adult controls. In April 1942, *Variety* noted that unsupervised youngsters were running amok in cinemas. This was only the most obvious sign of a wider problem covered by *Life* that autumn: "Suddenly the country is aware of what war is doing to children. American youth is on the same kind of lawless rampage that swept England during 1940."

In the first years of the war, America's young found themselves both liberated and freshly scapegoated. The main problem that they faced was the lack of a clear role in the national effort. Unlike under-army-age adolescents in Germany, France, and Britain, they did not have to suffer bombs, forced labour, or the other horrors of total war. Nor were they required to enter pre-military organizations. Instead, American adolescents had to make their way in a continent turned upside down by mass migration and war fever: they were, as one youth expert wrote, "more affected by the war than any other group".

Many quit school and went to work. During 1942 and 1943, enrolments in high school dropped with the "avalanche of youngsters" into industry. While in 1940 only, just over one million boys and girls between fourteen and seventeen were employed, the figure would rise to nearly three million by 1944, nearly 30 per cent of the total US cohort. In summer, traditionally a boom time, the number of working adolescents between fourteen and seventeen was estimated at between four and five million. Of these, the number between fourteen and fifteen entering the labour market was over double that of the sixteen- to seventeen-year-old age group.

The motivation for dropping out varied. The authorities treated adolescents as a pliable labour pool and made direct appeals: "While the war lasts, *every* girl must be taught that it is her patriotic duty to work at some essential job. America's critical manpower shortage cannot be solved unless this is done." Industry was, as one high school student observed, "clamoring for outstanding boys and girls in the younger age classification. Boys are wanted immediately in the shops and offices; girls, in the offices as stenographers and typists."

There was also the uncertainty caused by war itself. "The adolescent feels that the foundations of his universe has changed overnight," wrote the director of the Institute for Personality Development; she felt that America's young oscillated between fear, guilt, resentment, and restlessness. For boys, the temptation to quit school was considerable. The whole culture was full of propaganda that stressed excitement and thrills. Whether it be movies like *Flying Tigers*, starring John Wayne, or boys' books like *Flying Wildcats*, the feeling was the same: hyperstimulation and overexcitement.

The social definition of adolescence changed again: from the Depression-era imperative of staying *in* school and *out* of the labour market to the promotion of full employment. With most eighteen- to thirty-year-olds temporarily removed from public life, pre-army-age youngsters had a social and economic importance that they had never before enjoyed. Conditioned to the likelihood that they would have to join in the fighting and given confidence by their average ten dollars per week, America's adolescents began to step out on the streets and into the headlines.

This unprecedented visibility attracted adult criticism and renewed controls. Responding to the 1942 press reports of juvenile delinquency, many local authorities introduced 10 p.m. curfews for non-working youth under seventeen, which brought greater amounts of juveniles into the crime statistics. In Indianapolis, where an after-dark curfew was instituted in February 1943 for boys under sixteen and girls under eighteen, police "took special notice of adolescents loitering in groups, especially near taverns and dance halls or while school was in session".

The curfews were very unpopular. "Our whole way of life will be affected," one high school student observed. "On the other hand, there might as well be a curfew, since even couples strolling, heretofore the only pleasure left to daters after gas rationing, tire rationing, candy rationing, coke shortages etc., will no longer be seen due to shoe rationing." "I'll bet that when the ones on that council were fifteen they stayed out later than 10," another complained. "Now, after they've had their fun, they want to take it away from us. I know that a lot of teen-agers are going to be damned mad if something isn't done."

. . .

Pearl Harbor initiated convulsive changes. From a nation in depression, America soon became a booming industrial powerhouse. Seventeen million new jobs were created, triggering a migration on a scale unseen since the nineteenth century. Thirteen million men were mobilized, while nine million workers and their families left home for the war industries in the West and South-west—at over twenty million, about 16 per cent of the total population. At the same time, 1920s-style mass production returned as the economy's driving motor.

Mobilization triggered a year of "frantic construction" of which $12 billion worth was financed by the government. The new principle was that of "cost-plus". Overproduction didn't matter any more, as Uncle Sam ate up everything that the humming factories could turn out. The New Deal, with its centrally planned and socially regulated economy, was finished: the new industrial kings demanded an end to what they considered socialist "nonsense". The boom days of unrestricted growth and employer domination were back.

The good part of the deal was that there were plentiful jobs for the long-term unemployed. The downside was that the huge new industrial units, epitomized by the Ford-run bomber plant at Willow Run, Michigan, were built with scant regard for worker rights and amenities. This was the Gold Rush and the Dust Bowl all over again, as the disadvantaged from all over America descended on cities and small towns like Seneca, Illinois, where the population rose by a factor of 27 in a matter of a few months.

Young women, adolescents, and children were particularly vulnerable to these changes. In the first three months of 1942, the sales of wedding rings rose by 300 per cent, as young couples quickly sought to make firm bonds. While their husbands were away, the new brides had to live, and work was an acceptable solution. During the four years of war, 6.5 million women entered the labour force, irrevocably altering the way that America saw its female population—the change embodied by the popular figure of Rosie the Riveter.

"Women are bursting out of the mold in which we have sought to fix them," the journalist Max Lerner wrote in early 1943. Attempting to define the "emerging American woman", he gauged that "when she works in an aircraft factory day after day doing a man's work, or in the railroad roundhouses, or driving a cab, or welding a submarine, it is unlikely that her ways of thinking and behaving will stay frozen. The traditional maidenly modesty, I am told, shows signs of cracking. A group of girls coming out of a war factory behaves very much like a gang of young fellows."

Lerner pointed out just how unprepared the authorities were for this change: "Here we let a major revolution take place in the lives of women and children, but fear to assume any responsibility for it, because that would be 'socialism'." As Mark McCloskey wrote in his survey of America's upheavals, "Some of the women living in these new defense towns have said that it was just like life in a concentration camp. They have not been able to develop any feeling of solidarity. They have no community ties."

Childcare became a major problem. The journalist Agnes Meyer described how, near the war plants of the San Fernando Valley, "a social worker counted 45 infants locked in cars of a single parking space. In Vallejo, the children sit in the movies, seeing the same film over and over again until mother comes off the swing shift and picks them up. Some children of working parents are locked in their homes, others locked out." A social worker caught a twelve-year-old girl in a beer hall at midnight: asked what she was doing there, she replied, "I'm just waiting for 12 o'clock. My bed isn't empty until then."

Public places of entertainment became the new child-minders. A reporter in Muncie described the scene in the local cinema one Saturday midnight: "Down in the entrance, sleepy, tired youngsters are awaiting their parents. One little boy, whose small, pinched face already shows signs of age, whose too large coat hangs loosely and whose torn buttonholes won't hold the varied assortment of buttons, waits. He has picked up a cigarette and has a few puffs while he waits."

Young GIs were also subject to these convulsions. Moulding their recruits into a ganglike clique while inculcating the likelihood of death and sacrifice, the armed forces disgorged thousands of lonely and combustible young men on leave or weekend passes into cities and towns already bursting at the seams with migrants of all hues. Depersonalized and reprogrammed to fight an as yet invisible enemy, the GI was no longer a civilian but had not yet assumed his full role. Before shipping out, he was a stranger in a strange land.

This carpe diem psychology reaffirmed the conscript's adolescent status in the midst of adult duties. GI drunkenness and violence were tolerated. Sex was up-front, stimulated by the Vargas beauties and the cheesecake featured in army newspapers like *Yank*. "In every issue," the writer James Jones remembered, there was "an obligatory full-page 'pin-up' of some known or unknown star or starlet (and many oh-so-familiar names: Paulette Goddard, Ann Sheridan, Barbara Stanwyck, Jane Russell, the ubiquitous Betty Grable)".

As soon as the GI was off duty, he felt free "to release his impulses and feelings". Gangs of GIs roamed through the main streets and urban centres close to army bases or embarkation points. In major cities, downtowns became an electric, neon environment of a jagged intensity. Many of these areas still retained the marginality associated with the hobo days: they were full of peep shows, burlesque theatres, and fleapit cinemas showing exploitation films with lurid posters. Here the come-on was all, the sense that anything could happen.

The result was a carnival of drunkenness, violence, and sexual aggression. The army canteen worker Donald Vining saw the disparity between the patriotic rhetoric of the healthy GI and the desperate reality. As he wrote in his diary during May 1942, "I cannot help thinking of the soldiers roaming the streets in various stages of intoxication at all hours of the nite, of soldiers cutting the meals in the mess halls for a dinner of pie and coke in the canteens. I think too of the many calls for sanitubes and ointment for crabs, not to mention the hospitalized cases of venereal disease, and the injured."

The large proportion of the armed forces waiting to be shipped out added more pressure, and by the second year of the war the tensions were building. The patriotic bloom had worn off, and enthusiasm replaced by grumbling and discontent. In May 1943, the country's miners went out on strike amid scenes of violence. That same month, the FBI executed its first nationwide crackdown on draft dodgers, netting a mere 638 fugitives. A few weeks later, several hundred servicemen ran amok in Los Angeles in the second major riot of the war.

Their targets were zoot-suiters, young Mexican-American *pachucos* and *pachiquitas* marked out by their clothing as enemy aliens. What was thought to have begun with GIs harassing a few *pachiquitas* developed into a ten-day riot during which the United States lost control over thousands of its servicemen. As the senior patrol officer for the area reported to his superior on June 8, "Groups vary in size from 10 to 150 men and scatter immediately when shore patrol approach. Men found carrying hammock clues, belts, knives, and tire irons when searched by patrol after arrest."

"Marching through the streets of downtown Los Angeles, a mob of several hundred soldiers, sailors and civilians proceeded to beat up every zoot suiter they could find," wrote the journalist Carey McWilliams. "Streetcars were halted while Mexicans, and some Filipinos and Negroes, were jerked out of their seats, pushed into the streets and beaten with sadistic frenzy. Huge half-page photographs showing Mexican boys stripped of their clothes, cowering on the pavements, often bleeding profusely, surrounded by jeering mobs of men and women, appeared in all the Los Angeles newspapers."

Like the *Zazous*, the zoot-suiters displayed their difference through their costume, but they were not outcast by choice. As recent immigrants, these young Mexican Americans recast the perennial second-generation problem in a new guise. Many of their parents had arrived in Southern California during the 1920s to work in the mines and on the farms, but the Depression had forced them to relocate into the inner urban areas of Los Angeles. Debarred from many jobs and most amenities, young Mexican Americans began to form neighbourhood *pachuco* gangs in the late 1930s.

They were caught between their parents' culture, where "a boy of sixteen was ready to assume responsibilities of family and a life in the community", and American society, which sought to prolong adolescence. Crammed into their barrios, these adolescents rebelled, according to one observer, "against not one but two cultures. They neither understood nor wanted any part of either. Being lost, they looked for a means to express their group solidarity. They found it in hostility to the established order and in the pleasures of shocking public opinion."

Outrageous clothing was their flag of dishonour, as the zoot suit became the proudly born standard of *pachiquismo* in the early 1940s. The style came from the same root as the *Zazous'* costume: mid-thirties Negro fashions. During

POLICE OFFICERS TAKE A ZOOT-
SUITER INTO CUSTODY ON THE
SIXTH DAY OF UNDECLARED WAR
ON THE REET PLEAT IN WATTS,
CALIFORNIA, JUNE 11, 1943

that time, Malcolm X saw his first zoot in Boston's ghetto, Roxbury. He quickly
went hunting for his own off-the-peg number. It was "just wild: sky-blue pants
thirty inches at the knee and angle narrowed down to twelve inches at the bottom, and a long coat that pinched my waist and flared down to my knees".

As with any street style, the zoot's true origin was shrouded in mystery. It
seems to have begun around 1935 among urban hipsters in Harlem nightclubs like the Savoy Ballroom and was popularized by Clark Gable's drape-
shape jacket in *Gone with the Wind,* released at the end of 1939. The suit's first
explicit media mention occurred in early 1940, when a young busboy named
Clyde Duncan ordered what was reported in the *Men's Apparel Reporter* as "the
newest model, known in South Georgia as the Killer Diller".

Like *Zazou,* the word "zoot" originated in hipster slang: the New Orleans
patois for "cute" filtered through the clanging rhymes beloved of Cab Calloway
and Slim Gaillard. As the 1942 song went, "I wanna zoot suit with a reet pleat /
With a drape shape and a stuff cuff / To look sharp enough to see my Sunday
girl." By the beginning of that year, off-the-peg zoots were available under the
trade name of "extremes". They were principally aimed at jitterbugs: the looseness
of jacket and trouser perfectly suited the swirling motion of the Lindy hop.

Although official production of the zoot was curtailed after the introduction
of cloth rationing in 1942, illegal suits remained popular in New York, Chi-

cago, Detroit, and Los Angeles. In June 1943 the *New York Times* reported that high school children were flocking to Harlem to buy zoots priced between $18 and $75. Those who could not afford it simply bought an extra-large suit and had it tailored down. The zoot also appeared in films like *Stormy Weather*, which featured Cab Calloway in a resplendent canary yellow specimen.

The *pachucos* took to the style like a duck to water. According to a September 1942 *Newsweek* story, they wore polka-dot shirts with outlandish trousers and jackets in yellow and purple, as well as "string ties, pearl buttons as big as silver dollars, and trousers so tight they have to be zipped". By this stage, the Sleepy Lagoon case had tagged all Mexican-American youth as murderers. There had also been simmering bad feeling between the *pachucos* and the police, who objected to their hanging around street corners as well as their egregious dress and volatile demeanour.

Los Angeles could be a very hostile place. As well as the ministrations of the LAPD, the *pachucos* also had to deal with the local press, who followed their pitched "midnight battles" with considerable interest. There were at least thirty-five *pachuco* gangs in Los Angeles during the early 1940s. They were no angels. As one member later recalled, "We were kids, anxious to be wanted but we just couldn't make the grade. We were openly discriminated against in public swimming pools. There were no recreational facilities to speak of. We could only raise hell in the streets."

The gangs were hooked into the Sleepy Lagoon case because the victim, José Díaz, had been in a scuffle the night before his death. Members of the 38th Street Club were involved, and twenty-four of them were later arrested: nineteen were charged with conspiracy, manslaughter, and assault. Ten days after the murder, the LAPD conducted a drive against young Mexican Americans: "Approximately six hundred persons were brought in. There were approximately one hundred and seventy-five arrests for having knives, guns, chains, dirks, daggers, and any other implement that might have been used in assault cases."

When the verdicts were announced in January 1943, seventeen of the defendants were found guilty of murder. That there was an injustice was in little doubt. As Carey McWilliams protested, the trial was more like a "ceremonial lynching". The defendants were typified by the police as racially subhuman, Aztec "wild cats" who harked back to the "Indian" who showed "many of the oriental characteristics, especially so in his utter disregard for the value of life". Bizarre clothing was yoked to racial characteristics to construct a picture of a savage fifth column.

Never mind that many Mexican Americans were already serving in the armed forces; the problem had been defined and needed solving. The solution was graphically illustrated in a nationally syndicated cartoon series. Written by the conservative Al Capp, *Li'l Abner* was read by up to 50 million people every day. For a month in spring 1943 the strip featured a bizarre storyline about the imminent takeover of America by zoot-suiters. Published at the end of May, the final frame simply contained a newspaper headline: "ZOOT-SUIT HATING MOBS CONTINUE TO SMASH UP ZOOT-SUIT STORE!!"

The flashpoint finally occurred on June 3, 1943. The police thought it was the result of a sexual advance. The navy thought it was retaliation against zoot-ers who "rolled" drunken sailors. Mexican Americans thought it was a planned attack. As Beatrice Griffith wrote, "The sailors walked out of Chavez Ravine with rocks, sticks, clubs, belts, heavy weights in their handkerchiefs, and palm saps. They walked out, got into cars, and drove over to Alpine. One naval offi-cer later said, 'we knew where they were going and the guards looked the other way. Most thought it was high time something was done.'"

The next night, two hundred sailors cruised through the barrio attacking zoot-suiters at will. The police arrested the victims. The violence continued, but did not make the press until the sixth. Among the reports was a guideline on how to locate and deal with the quarry: "Grab a zooter. Take off his pants and frock coat and take them off and burn them. Trim the 'Argentine Duck-tail' that goes with the screwy costume." Thus encouraged, thousands of white Americans packed downtown Los Angeles during the evening of June 7, ad-ministering summary and symbolic justice to any zoot-suiters they found.

The crowd was composed of both servicemen and civilians. Seven truck-loads of sailors came from Las Vegas, while taxis provided free transport to this "mass lynching". The normal rules of law and order broke down as gangs chased and indiscriminately attacked zooters, Negroes, and Mexicans alike. Holding that the problem was a matter for the military police, LA's finest made no attempt to control the rioters. The whole affair was described in terms of a military operation, a "blitz", or a "punitive task force".

For servicemen, press, and civilians alike, the zooters were the perfect tar-gets for their martial aggression.[1] However, the disturbances represented a se-vere breakdown of military discipline. After another night of disorder, the

---

1. Note the escalating headlines in the *Los Angeles Times:* "Zoot Suiters Learn Lesson in Fights With Servicemen" (June 7); "Riot Alarm Sent Out in Zoot War" (June 8); "Zoot-Suit Fans Find Out That Life's Getting Tough" (June 8); "City, Navy, Clamp Lid on Zoot-Suit Warfare" (June 9); "Warren Orders Zoot Quiz; Quiet Reigns After Rioting" (June 10); "Brass Knuckles Found on Woman Zoot Suiter" (June 10); "Ban on Freak Suits Studied by Councilmen" (June 10); "Zooters Escape San Diego Mob" (June 10); "Punishment of All Urged to Break Up Zoot Suit War" (June 13).

authorities took the problem in hand. The whole of downtown Los Angeles was declared off-limits to service personnel and charges were preferred against those arrested for inciting or actually participating in these riots. However, justice was not unbiased, as members of the armed forces could count on the support of the authorities. A mere twenty servicemen were arrested.

The victims were routinely vilified as "kids running together bent on devilment"; they were addicted to marijuana, "the passion-inflaming narcotic weed"; their clothes reflected "mental abnormality". According to one psychologist, "Your zootsuiter is not old enough to get into the services or he's in 4-F or will not be accepted because he already has a delinquent record." On June 9, the Los Angeles city council banned the zoot as "a badge of hoodlumism". "We prohibit nudism by ordinance," one councillor stated, "and if we can arrest people for being underdressed we can do so for being overdressed."

After that, the riots subsided. Although they did not publicly admit mutiny, senior service officers issued specific instructions for greater discipline. The zooters lay low and licked their wounds. In one incident, several cars packed with *pachucos* drove past the LAPD HQ with American flags and white truce banners, proclaiming that "we're good Americans". The zooters did not disappear as bogeymen, being explicitly targeted by press reports linking the clothes with violence in Chicago, Detroit, Baltimore, and New York. But with the outlawing of their suit, the correct punishment had been administered.

■   ■   ■

Just under two weeks after the Los Angeles disturbances, there was a much more serious riot. For seven days, Negroes and whites took over the streets of Detroit in a race riot that left thirty-four Americans dead and the nation's reputation tarnished. As Alfred Lee observed, "This is a picture of one part of the Land of the Free on Monday, June 21, 1943, in the midst of a global war fought for the Four Freedoms: Shootings. Beatings. Looting. Property destruction. Car-burnings. Maimed and wounded innocents. A terrified populace. A horrified minority, inadequately protected and besieged in an American city."

Detroit had already erupted during the Sojourner Homes fracas. By 1943, the city's population had risen by a third in three years. Of these, about 60,000 were Negroes, and over 400,000 were whites from the Deep South, who felt that Negroes had become "too uppity". These migrants had caused friction in war plants. Their young had also contributed to a growing juvenile delinquency problem. Rejected by both industry and the army, they formed themselves into gangs that enacted the hostility of their elders: in May 1943, one hundred white and Negro youths fought a pitched battle in a city playground.

The "spontaneous combustion" occurred on Sunday, June 20. After a confrontation between two rival girl gangs at Belle Isle in the Detroit River, thousands of whites and Negroes fought each other and the police. No quarter was expected or given. The unpatriotic implications of these vicious riots were not lost. The mayor of Detroit observed that the only ones to benefit from the strife would be the "Nazis and the Japs". A few weeks later, Vice-President Henry Wallace gave a speech in Detroit, in which he admitted that we "cannot fight to crush Nazi brutality abroad and condone race riots at home".

Youth played their part in the violence. Detroit had very few facilities for the mass of new immigrants: schools were swamped and recreational facilities were non-existent. Adolescents were left to find their own amusement: bored, they were ripe for indoctrination by the pro-Fascist groups operating in the city. A local newspaperman observed how "the kids particularly get tired of the bars and the juke joints. You go into those places any night and you see them sitting around with perfectly vacant faces. They don't know what to do with themselves. They don't even talk . . . aren't they ready for any kind of excitement?"

For the adolescents involved, this was their own war. One "19-year old hoodlum" bragged about taking the day off from his factory job "so I could be in the thick of it downtown. Jesus, but it was a show! We dragged niggers from cars, beat the hell out of them, and lit the sons of bitches autos. I'm glad I was in it!" Four white youths between sixteen and twenty gunned down a fifty-eight-year-old Negro who was quietly waiting for a bus: they murdered him "just for the Hell of it". As one of them later admitted, "We didn't know him. He wasn't bothering us. But other people were fighting and killing and we felt like it, too."

On July 14, the president criticized the recent unrest: "I join you, and all true Americans in condemning mob violence, whatever form it takes and whoever its victims." The summer of hate continued. On August 1, Harlem erupted after the false rumour spread that a black soldier had been killed by a white cop. Tensions had been building after the June closure of the Savoy Ballroom. The official reason given was that it was a haunt of prostitution, but the police hated the fact that it was an integrated venue. The riots were quickly contained, after six deaths and hundreds of injuries.

The revelation that American adolescents were behaving like Fascist thugs fuelled the summer's other scandal. The "juvenile delinquency" issue that had also been simmering finally boiled over in the summer of 1943. "You see it in the papers every day," stated Look in "Are These Our Children"; "five boys caught stealing automobiles; a 15-year-old girl charged with thirty sex offenses;

in Detroit, a juvenile mob invades night clubs, bars, movies, smashing windows and furniture; a father reproves his 17-year-old son, and the next day the father's mutilated body is found beside a railroad track."

"War unleashes powerful social and psychological forces," stated the pictorial magazine *Click* in a spring 1943 article: "Symptomatic of these is the 21 per cent nationwide increase in juvenile delinquency reported in 1942's first nine months by FBI director J. Edgar Hoover. Yet it has been only recently that delinquency has been recognized as an important problem on the home front . . . with fathers changing from job to job, mothers either going to work or going crazy in an effort to carry on family life with all normal schedules wrecked by unprecedented working hours, children left to roam the streets."

During 1943, American adolescents seemed to go crazy. Gangs of young hoodlums terrorized New York City. In the streets of Indianapolis, slum gangs called the North Side Dukes and the Rinky Dinks held pitched battles in the street and vandalized cinemas and streetcars. A Massachusetts boy and girl killed a man for 48 cents. Middle-class children disrupted high school events, showed a lack of respect for their teachers, and acted noisily in restaurants and drive-ins. In one extreme case, a thirteen-year-old boy attempted to dynamite a railway line in a bid to become the local "dictator".

. . .

What really shocked America, however, was the unrestrained behaviour of adolescent girls. An April 1943 Harry James show at the New York Paramount resembled combat conditions, as the fourteen- and fifteen-year-old audience enacted its own Dionysian tribal rite: "The children wriggled ecstatically in their seats, moved convulsively each time that Harry James 'sent them' . . . they surged out of their places, bore down on grim ushers and danced in the carpeted aisles. Hours later, as they departed, hundreds of girls—Hep Jills—left lipstick imprints on the glass protecting the band leader's photograph in the lobby."

American pop music had changed since swing, but crowd behaviour had become even more extreme. The pendulum had swung back to a romantic style that also suited more conservative emotional conditions. Ballads had become very popular among girls, as they expressed the hopeless yearning that appeared to be part of their lot. Harry James described the archetypal situation faced by every seventeen-year-old girl with a soldier boyfriend: "Tomorrow he will have gone back to duty and you to the dull, lonely routine of your life without him—waiting, waiting, for the day of his return."

The increasing prominence of women in American life had already attracted adverse attention with the scandals about lax working mothers: now their younger siblings were coming under increasing scrutiny. It wasn't just the eruptions at concerts by Harry James but the much thornier problem of adolescent female "sex delinquency of a non-commercial character". In July 1943, the head of the Federal Office of Community War Services stated that "there is no dodging the fact that this is a nationwide problem, and that the urgency increases with every added day of war".

The popular term for these delinquents was Victory Girls, "khaki-whacky" young women. A National Recreation Association pamphlet from 1943, called *Teen Trouble*, summarized their MO: "They walk down city streets, six or seven abreast, breaking as they pass civilians, but holding on to each other's arms as they approach a soldier or a sailor, forming a very flattering net around him. As the walk progresses, the line gets shorter and shorter, as girl and boy pair off and leave the group. It's a childish, very effective get-your-man plan used by girls around fourteen and fifteen years old!"

Sometimes as young as thirteen, the V-Girls were, according to the historian Richard Lingeman, "easily recognizable in their Sloppy Joe Sweaters, hair ribbons, anklets or bobby-sox and saddle shoes, trying to look older with heavily made-up faces and lipstick". Many got jobs that enabled them to come into contact with servicemen, as barmaids or waitresses. In various American cities, they became so persistent that the authorities had to act. Due to their inexperience, venereal disease became a big problem: in the South-east naval district, it was estimated that 80 per cent of VD cases were caused by amateurs.

The V-Girls were responding to wartime conditions in their own way. As one of their peers explained, they picked up servicemen "because they are trying to regain some of the fun that the war has deprived them of". Life was hard for females under the conscription age of twenty: as one complained, "Being sixteen or seventeen, we're considered too young for the armed forces and too young for work in war factories." With no immediate part to play, and with the disappearance of many male contemporaries, the result was "a continual sense of frustration".

These were precocious children, according to a wartime commentator: "Girls who would normally be developing a healthy interest in boys their own age, seem to mature overnight and become unabashed uniform chasers." With attention focused on the issue, the statistics for delinquency among girls showed a dramatic increase during 1942–43: in Indianapolis, the number going through the juvenile courts rose by 27 per cent. However, the overall statistics did not quite bear out the panic: sex delinquency involved only 1 to 2 per cent of America's adolescents.

Much of the outrage was caused by a perceived loss of innocence. "I was exposed to a lot of young men, seventeen, eighteen years old," a former Victory Girl told Studs Terkel. "If there hadn't been a war, I would have stuck to my twelve- and thirteen-year-old school mates. The war absolutely ruined me. The more men I had, the more my ego was fed. I had no attachments at all." She admitted that the war had stolen her youth: "On December 6th 1941, I was playing with paper dolls: Deanna Durbin, Sonja Henie. I had a Shirley Temple doll that I cherished. After Pearl Harbor, I never played with dolls again."

The anguish at this "spurious maturity" was highlighted by the April 1943 trial of seventeen-year-old Josephine Tencza, charged with the "compulsory prostitution" of girls between twelve and fifteen. The case had only come to light when schoolteachers became suspicious about the girls' spending money. Max Lerner contrasted Tencza's actual age with the fictional idylls of *Seventeen* and *Seventeenth Summer*. "From Tarkington's Willy Baxter and his lisping baby talk to this Rivington Street 'madam' is a long stretch," he wrote, "but it encompasses all the agony and degradation of one phase of American life."

The spectacle of underage girls having sex added fresh spice to the juvenile delinquency scare. In July, *Pic* magazine carried the Josephine Tencza story under the headline of "TEENAGE VICE": "one of our most perplexing and ghastly social problems." The next month, it ran another article about girl delinquency with "Boston's Morals Problem", which delineated V-Girl activities. Since the previous year, the magazine alleged, sex offences involving teenage girls had risen by 200 per cent: "The average age of offenders is fifteen. The number of runaway girls is up 48% over 1942. Truancy cases are up 400 per cent."

In a typically American dynamic, the identification of a social problem—particularly one involving sex and youth—was quickly followed by exploitation, as Hollywood studios released a flood of low-budget films. RKO bought the rights to the *Look* story and rushed out *Youth Runs Wild*, a film promoted by the tagline "The Truth About Modern Youth!" Monogram issued a couple of shockers called *Are These Our Parents?* and *Where Are Your Children?*, the latter boosted by fake headlines like "INCREASE IN JUVENILE DELINQUENCY ALARMS NATION" and "YOUNG THRILL SEEKERS ENDANGER THE NATION".

Adults relished enumerating just how America's youth had gone wrong. One correspondent to an Indianapolis newspaper thought that "the biggest trouble with children these days is that instead of doing what their parents tell them to do, they tell their parents what to do, and their parents do it". Another writer thought they were "given too much money, too much leisure, too much coddling, and are not required often enough to rely on themselves. And the result many times is that we have youngsters to whom the everyday things are repugnant. They must have thrills, speed, excitement."

Simultaneously exploited and condemned, America's adolescents had every right to feel misunderstood. They hadn't started the war, but they were being used as a litmus test for all of America's social problems, "the creeping rot of moral disintegration" that, as J. Edgar Hoover warned, was placing the nation in "deadly peril". Among the reasons advanced for the outbreak of juvenile delinquency were a breakdown in family life; war psychosis, with its culture of violence; and all the youth media—comic books, jukeboxes, movies, and "the style of boogie woogie which appeals to hep cats".

During 1943, the juvenile crime statistics soared, in some cities by nearly a third. This was a reflection not only of a genuine increase in lawlessness but also increased police activity and media attention, much of which oscillated between titillation and overheated censure. Certainly, when the hand of J. Edgar Hoover was involved, suspicion was advisable. Hoover had long coveted the adolescent market, and with the dire prophecies of 1939's *Designs in Scarlet* apparently coming true, he rammed home the message with lurid tales of reefer-smoking gangs in Los Angeles and teacher-killers in Brooklyn.

The FBI's statistics for the first half of 1943 stated that although the general crime rate rose by only 1.5 per cent, the rate for boys and girls under eighteen rose by 40 per cent. These were disputed by the Children's Bureau. "We cannot say with certainty whether juvenile delinquency is increasing or decreasing throughout the country as a whole," a representative wrote, "because of the absence of reliable and comprehensive data over a period of years. Such statistics as are available have shown no alarming tendency to increased 'juvenile crime' as newspapers perennially claim."

This bickering continued in the Pepper Committee's "Hearings on Wartime Health and Education" held in autumn 1943, which focused on juvenile delinquency. The FBI's agenda was punitive: locate the problem, overstate it if there isn't a big enough furore, crush it with greater force. The Children's Bureau sought to understand the underlying issues and to work with professionals to eradicate the causes of delinquency. However, despite days of detailed testimony, the committee could not reach any definite agreement.

One conclusion the committee did come to was that "rather than discourage delinquent acts, sensational reporting glamorized and encouraged them". If the titillating media stories alarmed adults, then they also thrilled adolescents and encouraged copycat behaviour. The scandal of 1943 was another example of wartime hysteria, this time involving the youth who represented the future of America. From the idealized apple-cheeked midwesterner, America's adolescents had turned into that disturbing phantasm, "the psychopath".

A book published in early 1944 spent nearly three hundred pages attempting to unravel this conundrum. Written by the psychologist Robert M. Lindner, *Rebel Without a Cause*[2] reproduced the results of a forty-five-hour-long hypnoanalysis course practised on "Harold", an adolescent imprisoned for a serious crime of violence. Faithfully transcribing the youth's own words, Lindner revealed a story of childhood trauma, weird blocked sex, and escalating violence that created a sensation at the time.

Lindner defined the psychopath as "a rebel without a cause, an agitator without a slogan, a revolutionary without a programme". The psychopath, "like the child, cannot delay the pleasures of gratification"; his state was "in essence a prolongation of infantile patterns and habits into the stage of physiological adultism". With a very low "limen of satiety", he could not abide "the preliminaries demanded by conventional community life, ie gradualness, perseverance, and the flavoring of increasing anticipation". When thwarted, he resorted to a sadistic, infantile, and highly dangerous aggression.

A certain precociousness was part of this paradigm: "Like the play-pattern of the very young, he shows an intensiveness, even a brilliance, at the outset of work; but the performance rapidly falls apart into a fitful type of behavior." The young criminal bemoaned the lack of his relationship with his father, his ambiguous feelings about homosexuality, and how violence resolved his inadequacies: "'When I had a gun on me I thought I was better than other people.' As he continued, 'perhaps that's the reason I committed all those crimes— sex, masturbation. I don't know. I didn't give a damn.'"

Harold manifested many of the impulses coursing through wartime America. His concentration on the present and propensity towards violence were reflected in the wider culture. An army psychiatrist later found that many outstanding combat soldiers "were hostile, emotionally insecure, and extremely unstable personalities who might well be termed clinically 'psychopaths' whatever that might imply, who fully enjoyed the opportunity of taking out hostilities directly in a socially acceptable setting of warfare and who in the absence of such an outlet not infrequently end up in penitentiaries".

The violent events of 1943 changed America's attitude towards its youth. Just as GIs had revealed themselves as vicious thugs, so America's young were

---

2. Lindner's book was the source for the title of James Dean's classic film, as well as providing the basis for the screenplay.

in danger of becoming "embryonic Storm-Troopers" rather than the future standard-bearers of democracy. The year's many scandals led to a fresh public and governmental focus on the rights of adolescents, in a return to the New Deal ideas that had been temporarily jettisoned. To prevent the creation of more monsters, reformers, youth experts, and marketers sought to channel youth's new independence into socially acceptable, if not useful, forms.

PART VII

1942–1945

CHAPTER 27

The Peaceful Invaders

American Soldiers and British Youth

· · ·

I cannot say that flims [sic] have even made me dissatisfied with life but I can safely say that flims [sic] do make me dissatisfied with my neighbourhood and towns. From what I have seen they are not modern for instance there are no drug stors on the corner of the street where you can take your girlfriend and have some ice creem or a milk shake. In our town there are no sky scrappers or really high buildings and there are not half as many buildings which are as those on the flims [sic] are such as Broadway.

—"Fourteen-year-old son of a welder", British film magazine survey, 1945

BRITISH LAND ARMY GIRLS AND AMERICAN US EIGHTH ARMY
AIR FORCE MEN AT A DANCE HELD AT A WOMEN'S LAND
ARMY CAMP, SUFFOLK, ENGLAND, MID-1940s

DURING JULY 1942, Mass-Observation reported on a unique youth club called the Dead End Kids' Institute. Situated in a working-class housing development in the north-west of England, the Institute had a full-time resident warden and was open every night between 7 p.m. and 10 p.m. (except Sundays) to boys and girls between fourteen and twenty. The entrance fee was one shilling for those over sixteen, sixpence for younger members. Unlike many clubs run by voluntary organizations, this one had facilities "unequalled anywhere in the city".

Funded by a local philanthropist, the building offered a large hall "with a perfectly appointed" stage, a gymnasium with showers, billiards and table tennis, a canteen "with glass topped tables and comfortable chairs", a restroom, and a library. There were minor snags, such as "the absence of cloakrooms and the height of the showers", but all in all this innovative mix of private and public initiatives was "a youth Warden's dream". But there was an unexpected hitch in this perfectly planned youth utopia.

Britain's policy for its adolescents during the early 1940s was haunted by the memory of how they ran amok during the First World War. The favoured official solution was "the ideal school", a youth club of diverse interests "where social activities would bring together people with differing tastes and interests". However, the observer noted that at the Dead End Kids' Institute, "Every effort that has been made to interest the members in cultural activities—lectures, debates, discussion groups—has failed."

Unsurprisingly, the clientele rejected uplift for fun: "Ballroom dancing is the main attraction, and the members are very sophisticated, the 15 year old girls made up like Ginger Rogers and the boys passable imitations of Cagney and Rooney at their toughest. The resemblance between these boys and the raw material upon which Spencer Tracy, as Father Flanagan, had to work in the film Boys' Town is uncanny. The observer instinctively looked around the lovely building for a raw-boned Irish priest, but unfortunately he wasn't there. He should have been."

The observer identified the problem: "All these young people, even the youngest, are workers. So are the young people in the Civic Youth Clubs, but these youngsters undertake some of the hardest and roughest types of work, the boys in engineering shops, the girls in clothing factories. It can therefore easily be seen why such pursuits as knitting socks for soldiers do not appeal to the girls, nor studying the construction of aeroplanes to the boys. They want relaxation, and physical relaxation rather than mental stimulation. Their idea of letting off steam consists of doing the Conga."

This clash between the paternalistic and the hedonistic views of youth had a particular urgency during the early 1940s. While middle-class professionals thought that slum adolescents were "deserving of special study, care and treatment", the working youth at issue felt completely free to reject civic duties that felt like more war work and cultural activities that felt like going back to school. While both sides agreed that youth should have more attention and, indeed, respect, their respective solutions couldn't have been more different.

There were two separate streams of thought. The first, promoted by left-wing commentators and planners, was the social-democratic ideal of inclusion and fairness, given tangible form by Sir William Beveridge's plans for the Welfare State. The other strand was American popular culture. This was a democracy of consumerism that appeared to offer a whole set of new freedoms, or at least an escape from England's static class system. The social democrats were extremely suspicious of American culture, which made it even more attractive to the spirited young.

Although the boys and girls of the Dead End Kids' Institute were offered a carefully calibrated ideal of education and "co-operative living", they shunned the reformers' anti-materialist utopia. Instead of "a permanent sense of well-being", they wanted "transitory pleasure": excitement, release, and instant gratification. Having entered the workplace, they had crossed the threshold of adulthood. If that meant that they wished to interpret their partial enfranchisement in the way that they saw fit, that was hardly surprising. If democracy was to be for everyone, then participation would be on their own terms.

■ ■ ■

Self-determination was on the minds of Britain's youth during the summer of 1942. In a representative sample taken by Mass-Observation, 61 per cent of those under forty thought that "it would be a good thing" to have "more young people in some of the most important positions running the war", while 71 per cent thought that those running the war were too old. "We have got some old people in the government," said one F20C; "we could certainly do with some more brains." Even Churchill was criticized: "Put a younger man in altogether than what's in it now."

The national government had been successful in busying the country's premilitary youth. When Mass-Observation returned to the topic of adolescents in 1943, it found that, compared to 1941, they "were much more occupied". When the bombing raids were at their height, youth had been fractious. But "now there was little question of boredom" as they knuckled down to evening work and, in the case of young women with mothers out at work, housekeeping and child-minding. But these paragons were getting tired of endless duties.

Another 1943 report canvassed the attitudes of fourteen- to sixteen-year-old girls. One fourteen-year-old from Bolton worked in a grocery between 9 a.m. and 6 p.m., then came home and did housework. Most of the girls polled wanted "a mixed club with dancing". "I'm working now," complained one fourteen-year-old, "and I want some fun at nights, not something like school." As the report concluded, "The factory girls don't mind doing P.T. or learning something, but also they want to dance with older boys, make up, and not have too much supervision or regulations."

By the summer of 1943 at least a third of Britain's adolescents were spending their hard-earned wages on "recreation". A quarter did so on clothes and cigarettes—a category that had not been "prominent in 1941". Movies, dance music, glamour magazines: the fun stuff came from America and that's what Britain's youth—like the *Zazous* and the Hamburg swings in occupied Europe—couldn't get enough of. With 30 million attendances a week, the cinema was the most popular and the most direct way of escaping somewhere else.

Hollywood had a powerful effect on young minds, as Pearl Jephcott discovered when she met a Carmen Miranda fan: "She acquires further enlightenment about her heroine from Picturegoer for 20th September 1941 (No. 537) which fills the child with stuff like this: 'naked midriffs and swirling skirts . . . Is hot tempered . . . nude-centred dresses . . . Is Miranda entertaining? Fascinating? Overbearing? Revolting? The answer is it all depends on one's tastes.'" This fourteen-year-old was "already beginning to think that Carmen is 'very nice' and to wish that she could resemble her in a remote and humble way".

Jephcott thought that adolescents were "basing their conception both of worthwhile entertainment and a life that is worth living on the standards set by the film corporations. On the whole these are standards which exalt violence, vulgarity, sentimentality, and false psychology. Veronica Lake and Lana Turner do more for the girl of fourteen than merely set her hair style." Movies and dancing meant that "the sex instinct is being over-stimulated precisely at the age when this should be avoided".

The trickle of American culture into Britain confirmed the worst fears of thirties leftists. An anti-American ethos pervaded much of Britain's intellectual activity throughout the 1940s. "There is much to be said for the Soviet Government's regulation of picturegoing," Jephcott observed, "which does not allow children under sixteen to attend evening performances at the cinema or theatre, but which does attempt to cater for the needs of young people by providing special children's cinemas and Theatres for Youth."

Low-grade imports—"Yank mags"—and their popularity among the working class skewed the leftists' opinion of American culture. They found it highly disturbing that American violence was travelling over the Atlantic, and focused their distaste on the then popular *No Orchids for Miss Blandish,* by the British writer James Hadley Chase. Jephcott thought this "most sadistic and hard-boiled of American tough tales, in which there is a rape for every ten pages and a murder nearly as often, seems unfortunate reading matter for girls who have no standards of literature by which to judge such books".

The brutality of Hadley Chase's novel was also criticized by George Orwell. He was no lover of the United States: at the beginning of 1942, he observed that "up till about 1930 nearly all 'cultivated' people loathed the U.S.A., which was regarded as the vulgarizer of England and Europe". However, "the younger intellectuals have no objection to the American language and tend to have a rather masochistic attitude to the U.S.A., which they believe to be richer and more powerful than Britain. Of course, it is exactly this attitude that excites the jealousy of the ordinary patriotic middle class."

On the other hand, he felt that "English working-class people nearly always dislike Americans when in actual contact with them, but they have no preconceived cultural hostility. In the big towns they are becoming more and more Americanized in speech through the medium of the cinema." However, he could not deny that the American influence had gone much deeper and that the process of colonization had begun: "There are great numbers of English people who are partly Americanised in language and, one ought to add, in moral outlook."

American and British relations have always been seen through the distorting prism of the 1776 rebellion and the illusion of a shared language. "Americans are supposed to be boastful, bad-mannered, and worshippers of money," Orwell wrote, "and are also suspected of plotting to inherit the British empire." On the other hand, the famed radio correspondent Ed Murrow admitted that, before the war, he had thought Britain "a relatively unimportant island off the coast of Europe . . . a sort of museum piece".

America's entry into the war made the British more appreciative. Mass-Observation noted in early 1943 that the "widespread feeling in the early stages of the war that the Americans *ought* to be helping us" had changed into a deep gratitude. "Today the Stars and Stripes symbolise a brother nation," said one correspondent, while another held that "the Americans are warm-hearted, enthusiastic, idealistic". Britons expected "a higher standard from the US than from most Europeans": "If Frenchmen are looked on as a chance acquaintance, then Americans are looked on as relatives."

The arrival of the GI on British soil was a turning point. Singapore, Rangoon, and Tobruk had just fallen, but, just as there seemed no comeback against the Axis, the tables were turned. The peaceful invasion began in February 1942 with the staged arrival of Private First Class Milburn H. Henke, a handsome young man from Minnesota who got sacks of fan mail. The very purpose of sending GIs to the United Kingdom was symbolic of a fresh hope: they were there to prepare for the invasion of the Nazi continent.

With the time lag involved in mobilization and training, and the inevitable logistical problems, it would take over two years for the requisite muster of 1.5 million troops to be reached: 3 per cent of Britain's total population. There were often severe strains of adjustment within this colonization, but on balance the reception given to the US servicemen was very positive. After two and a half years of war, they offered novelty, a taste of the outside world, and a much-needed boost of energy to a flagging nation—a taste of a tangible future.

GIs had been warned of potential difficulties by a US War Department pamphlet.[1] The principal barrier was language itself: "At first you may not understand what they are talking about and they may not understand what you say." As a British journalist wrote, "When American soldiers landed in Great Britain we made the mistake of thinking that because they spoke English they were just like ourselves. The attitude of the American soldiers was naturally the same. They expected a home from home and what they found was, to all intents and purposes, a foreign country."

The invaders and their hosts tended to come across each other in public places: pubs, cinemas, dance halls, clubs, and train stations. With so many gangs of young men, fired up for combat, conflict was inevitable. Much of this was triggered by the facet of the American character that the British found the most obnoxious: bragging and boasting. However, there were many successes. The first people to be won over by the GIs were children, a relationship cemented by the exchange of chewing gum, chocolate, cigarettes, and leftovers from the overflowing post exchange (PX) canteens.

American popular music made the most dramatic impact. A fourteen-year-old Sussex girl thought that "Britain seemed so dull and corny; the Yanks gave us cigarettes and chewing gum and the music was fantastic. I loved jitterbugging. I won a contest. We used to make these dresses with short, pleated skirts and when we danced they'd flare up right around our waists, so we couldn't

1. Titled *Instructions for American Servicemen in Britain 1942*.

stop the leg-make up (or the eyebrow-pencilled 'seams') at our knees. Who wants to listen to some schmaltzy sentimental music when they're young and can dance to the 'A-Train' with the Yanks?"

. . .

In December 1943 *Picture Post* illustrated the "show steps" of the "coloured" swing style. As well as giving the lingo—a "hep-cat who's solid" was translated as an "enthusiast who's good"—the text gave a history of the style. "Its heights are reached by an intensity of feeling rather than by technical virtuosity," the article stated, "and this is where white dancers, however good, fall short as they encroach on so racial an idiom as swing." However, there was no harm in trying to perform "the Suzy Q, Peckin', the Shag, the Jockey and the Jig-Walk", and the accompanying photos showed how.

With the GIs, jitterbugging—formerly a minority interest—became an obsession among Britain's youth. Its individualistic and unrestrained aerial flights were in total contrast with the then popular "party dances" and slow foxtrots. But most of all it was fun, as a Liverpool girl remembered: "Once you had learned how to do the jitterbug, there was just nothing else for it, it was marvellous. They'd throw you over their shoulders and throw you under their knees and it was absolutely fabulous, really lovely."

An RAF serviceman remembered a concert in an aircraft hangar filled with "uniformed boys and girls swaying gently or 'jiving' wildly according to the dictates of that essential commodity, the dance band, the vocalist, his (or her) face almost obscured by an enormous microphone, singing of love not war. The dance was on and all we were conscious of was the music (and what music it was), the exhilarating rhythm, and of course, the girl in our arms. She may have been a little WAAF cook, or an ATS orderly, but as the orchestra wove its spell, she was Alice Faye, Betty Grable, Rita Hayworth."

Touring internationally with his American Air Force Orchestra, Major Glenn Miller played seventy-one concerts to nearly a quarter of a million listeners in the United Kingdom during 1944. The band reached thousands of others through regular radio broadcasts. A twelve-year-old girl bluffed her way into a local show: "I was *determined* to hear him play. So I stood outside the gate all dressed up and waited while the boyfriend of an older girl took her in and then came out to escort me in. Of course, my mother never knew . . . whenever I hear 'Perfidia' now, I can remember that evening. It was *wonderful*."

Although swing spread all over the country, London was the principal rendezvous for American culture. Glenn Miller played four nights at the capital's

Rainbow Corner, on the junction of Shaftesbury Avenue and Piccadilly Circus. The Hammersmith Palais became a favourite with GIs, staging jitterbug marathons and swing contests. As one officer remembered, "The trips by special train to London for two days off each month had the supercharged aspect to be expected, given the pent-up—not to put too fine a point on it—social and physical energies, and the unspent pay, of healthy young men."

If London was the American beachhead, Rainbow Corner was its HQ. Opened in November 1942 in the heart of London, this GI facility symbolized the depth of the US presence and the penetration of its incessant rhythms within a country where "time was slow". Open twenty-four hours a day, it offered recreation, first aid, and other facilities including sightseeing tours of London. In the lobby, the poles of the GIs' existence were marked by three arrows: one for Leicester Square, only a few yards away; another for Berlin, 600 miles; the third reminded the GIs that New York was 3,271 miles away.

Rainbow Corner aimed to recreate that staple of American adolescent life, the corner drugstore. In the recreation rooms, GIs shot pool, played pinball, or listened to a jukebox stocked with the latest hits. The two dining rooms could seat two thousand men, while the basement snack bar, which stayed open long after nearby British establishments closed at 9 p.m., served waffles, hamburgers, doughnuts, coffee, and endless Cokes. The club was extremely popular with local youth, so much so that the authorities had to close the doors to the girls who thronged outside.

The GIs were irresistible to many young British women. A seventeen-year-old Londoner remembered "these gorgeous men walking in. They had beautiful uniforms that made them all look like officers, but the whole point was they seemed like film stars. There was this great magic about America. It was to do with the films—we used to go to the pictures three times a week. We were so drab and it was another world, so glossy and clean, with picket fences and pretty white houses and Betty Grables and they all had lovely clothes."

Americans epitomized freedom and space. A young Londoner named Odette Lesley realized that "there was a very big new world out there that we knew nothing about at all. All I knew, for instance, was my little bit of North London, where I'd been brought up; the local streets, my neighbours and the local dance hall. But I was hearing these marvellous stories, and they opened up horizons to such an extent that I thought I might even see those places one day, I might go there. And I felt a strong sense of independence as a girl that I'd never felt before. It was so exciting, I thought anything was possible."

Despite the fact that GIs were often "aggressive and undiscriminating in their pursuit of British girls", they also, as a Red Cross Club worker remembered, "brought with them colour, romance, warmth and a tremendous hospitality to our dark, shadowed island". With more money and better health, the GIs represented stiff competition for young British soldiers. As one grudgingly conceded, the GIs were "in general taller, bulkier and handsomer than we were. Many were blond giants with hair cut short in 'combat crops'. In general, I think they looked superior to the very plebeian British servicemen."

It was, however, nineteen- to twenty-three-year-old women who were hit hardest by the inevitable consequences. During the war, one-third of all babies born were illegitimate. With up to 80 per cent of all American troops being sexually active while stationed in Europe, the arrival of the GIs had a strong impact on the figures. Many girls and women in their twenties were left pregnant with no hope of marriage, and one-fifth of these pregnancies ended in an abortion. However, those who decided to keep their babies without the protection of marriage were no longer subject to pre-war stigmas, and instead of censure they received minimal child support and maternity rights.

Just as they attracted girls, the GIs attracted crime. The American forces brought over a vast reservoir of highly desirable rationed items. American PXs were money pits: as one manager told Studs Terkel, "I did forty thousand dollars a month in beer, I did over one hundred and twenty five thousand dollars a month in PX supplies, and that's just with cigarettes and candy." For those prepared to siphon off excess rations, there were rich pickings: thousands of dollars a week from the sale of chocolate, cigarettes, nylons, or petrol. This helped to fuel an already thriving local black market.

With fewer police, the crime statistics for the capital shot up: the figures for 1944 showed an increase of 50 per cent from 1938. "Everybody made hay," John Wain wrote in his evocation of wartime London, "everybody was out for some fun *now*, this minute. Which exactly suited that large category of citizens who had quietly opted out of the war, and in consequence had to live without identification papers or fixed addresses. Deserters, or people who got sick of their lives and decided to disappear quietly, or just plain criminals—it made no difference. There was a place for everybody, and no questions asked."

Soho was the focal point for these twenty thousand or so refugees: an "improvising, floating, free-wheeling population" of writers, artists, drunkards, musicians, prostitutes, drug addicts, and adolescent runaways like the hero of Wain's novel *Strike the Father Dead*. This bohemian mixture was powered by crime, as few had any legitimate means of support. With thousands of willing consumers, a new breed of contact man arose, "a recognisable type who could be approached in the same way that a prostitute was approached—with a certain confidence that illicit requests would not be rejected".

This type was the spiv. While the origin of the term was lost in the mists of thieves' cant, the style was far from mysterious. The duck's arse haircut, Clark Gable moustache, rakish trilby, drape-shape jacket, and loud garish tie like "a giant tongue poking vulgarly out at life"—these all represented a deliberate snook cocked at wartime austerity. With these American-style clothes grafted onto the flashy costume of the 1930s wide boy, spivs embodied New World values. They were associated with the forbidden and the exotic, and they facilitated the instant gratification that the British government sought to defer.

The spiv's costume was the nearest equivalent to the zoot suits that they could see in films like *Hellzapoppin'* or on black GIs in the centre of London. But this sartorial visibility also highlighted one of the thorniest social issues thrown up by the American occupation. "Negro troops are already a familiar sight in dozens of towns in Britain," stated *Picture Post* in October 1942. "They fitted into our grey, unexotic background with surprising ease." Behind the positive propaganda gloss, however, the reality was different: prejudice and interracial violence on a level that Britain had never witnessed.

As part of an army that was still heavily segregated, black troops were denied a combat role, serving mainly as labourers, transporters, and kitchen staff. US Army policy was to keep the two races completely separate. However, the potential for trouble was always there. Sex was often the flashpoint, with many local women finding "a peculiar fascination in associating with men of colour". There were serious disturbances in Manchester, and shootings in Cornwall, Bristol, and Newbury, where a gun battle developed outside a pub: two black GIs were shot dead.

The British attitude was mixed. With a long colonial past, many of the population shared the prejudice expressed by the Duke of Marlborough, that it was "unwise and dangerous to go out into the roads and country lanes after dark" near black bases. However, many people thought that the Negro GIs were well behaved and less boastful than their white counterparts. There was a gut-level sense that blacks, within the new democratic ideal, should have fair treatment. A 1943 Mass-Observation poll revealed that the British were "overwhelmingly opposed to racial discrimination".

Segregation was challenged. A Bristol girl remembered that when black GIs came into her father's pub, a white GI told him not to serve them. Infuriated, her father "told the coloureds that they were welcome to stay, however they drank up immediately and left. I went outside to tell them that they need not have done so. They told me that the reason they left was that my father had treated them so well, it would have been a scene of considerable damage had they remained. Their parting words were, 'it's like this in the States, but things will be different after the war.'"

Emancipation was the promise that Britain and America held out to its youth as a reward for their war efforts: the problem for the US military authorities was that, as at home, they had been caught out by their own rhetoric of freedom. Within Britain, this contract was enshrined by new social-democratic legislation like the 1944 Education Act, which, enacting the Beveridge Report, instituted free secondary schooling up to the age of fifteen. Through the eleven-plus examination, it also gave brighter pupils the chance to enter grammar schools.

At the same time, the American ideal had been given a huge boost by the arrival of the GIs. American consumer products were freely spreading through the United Kingdom for the first time, and provided a huge morale boost in the midst of a dirty war that, even at the close of 1944, seemed to be never-ending. Of all the imports, dance music was the most widespread and the most popular among British youth: it was, quite literally, the sound of a freedom so compelling that even formerly hostile social reformers and youth workers began to take heed of the American model.

Late in the war, *Picture Post* ran an article about Rainbow Corner: "the perfect example of what a club for young people should be." This US establishment shamed most wartime British efforts to cater to its youth: "The Americans have come and created fine centres of recreation for their men. What is going to happen to them after the war?" The answer was simple: Rainbow Corner should become the shining model for the new voluntary service response for the needs of "British youth in peace".

By then the battle for the hearts and minds of Britain's adolescents had been won. The social planners stood little chance against the dreamland of American consumerism. To many of Britain's youth, discussions and lectures were like school. The experience of war had accelerated their development, and after sampling the transatlantic delights brought by the GIs, they wanted more. By 1945, British youth was not partly but completely "Americanized". As one eighteen-year-old girl wrote to a film magazine, "I always talk to myself in an American accent, and often think that way too."

CHAPTER 28

Helmuth Hübener, the White Rose, and Anne Frank

Resistance in Nazi Europe

. . .

The German people are in ferment. Will we continue to entrust the fate of our armies to a dilettante? Do we want to sacrifice the rest of German youth to the base ambitions of a Party clique? No, never! The day of reckoning has come— the reckoning of German youth with the most abominable tyrant our people have ever been forced to endure.

—The White Rose, *Fellow Fighters in the Resistance!*, February 1943

HANS SCHOLL, SOPHIE SCHOLL, AND CHRISTL PROBST, 1942

ON OCTOBER 2, 1942, crowds five or six deep lined the pavements of the Boul' Mich' for the launch of an autobiography by the star writer of *Je Suis Partout*, Lucien Rebatet. *Les décombres* (The Rubble) was a huge success for its author, the most rabid of the *collabos:* his philosophy was "hate until death". In an interview earlier that year, he expressed his "joy at having seen in Germany the first Jews marked by their yellow star. It will be an even greater joy to see this star in the streets of our Paris where, only three years ago, that dreadful race trampled us underfoot."

Hidden in an Amsterdam attic, Anne Frank noted a week later that "many Jewish friends and acquaintances are being taken away in droves. The Gestapo is treating them very roughly and transporting them in cattle-trucks to Westerbork, the big camp in Drenthe to which they're sending all the Jews. Miep told us about someone who'd managed to escape from there. It must be terrible in Westerbork. The people get almost nothing to eat, much less to drink, as water is available only one hour a day, and there's only one lavatory and sink for several thousand people."

That wasn't the worst of it. "Men and women sleep in the same room," she continued, "and women and children have their heads shaved. Escape is almost impossible, many people look Jewish, and they're branded by their shorn heads. If it's that bad in Holland, what must it be like in those faraway and uncivilised places where the Germans are sending them? We assume that most of them are being murdered. The English radio says they're being gassed. Perhaps that's the quickest way to die. I feel terrible."

Summer 1942 had seen the high point of the Third Reich; during the autumn the tide started to ebb. In October, the German armies received their first major setback at the hands of the British in the North African desert at El Alamein. In the Russian campaign, General von Paulus's army was stalled at Stalingrad. Major German cities were bombed with greater frequency and force. However, with their philosophy of victory or annihilation, the Nazis were not about to loosen their controlling grip. Life became unbearable for large sections of the population in Nazi-occupied Europe.

The campaign to exterminate all the Jews was stepped up after the approval of the "final solution" at the January 1942 Wannsee Conference. Very few of those travelling to their unknown destinations knew what they would face. On arrival, they were filtered left or right. Left meant instant extermination; right meant work duties. This was the point at which many youngsters were separated from their families. They were left in no doubt as to their status. "We had no rights," remembered Jack Mandelbaum, a fifteen-year-old Polish Jew. "The *only* right we had was to die."

Inducted prisoners were issued with a striped uniform displaying a number. No longer a name but a cipher, their dehumanization was complete. Beatings were frequent and savage: "They wanted to terrorize us so we would do what we were told. It worked. From that moment on, I was always afraid." Conditions in Mandelbaum's camp, on the Polish-German border, were very harsh: inmate facilities were minimal, the food almost non-existent, the hard physical labour almost beyond normal endurance. Failure to work meant death.

No youth in the occupied countries was exempt from the tightening of the screw. In October 1942, Himmler reinforced the 1939 Youth Service Order with a circular called "Enforcement of Youth Duty": as the manpower situation became more serious, so did the regime's attempts to coerce *everyone* into military service. Many of these caught by the new sweeps were placed in the new *Wehrertüchtigungslager,* SS-run camps that put boys of sixteen to eighteen through twenty-one days of intensive indoctrination. Secreted in total isolation, these camps were an assembly line for the mass production of hate-filled robots.

One Cologne-area trainee wrote back to his masters, "These three weeks were for all of us a living hell. If I should ever meet one of you trainers at night, I would beat the shit out of you, so that you would never again dare to mishandle freedom-loving people. A time will come when we will even the scores with you SS swine. Then no SS big-shot will escape with his life. It would have been better for you to have stayed on the Eastern Front. But it always happens that the biggest pigs and dogs bum around behind the front and enslave people."

The fact that this letter was sent anonymously showed the rarity of dissent. Most of the testimonials from the Cologne trainees delivered glowing testimonials about how they had been rescued from "soft and dreamy tendencies" and turned into someone "harder, more self-assured, and courageous". The Nazis were specialists in indoctrination: morale in the camps was higher than in the civilian population. Those who rejected the totalitarian system constructed by these "artists of death" found that passive withdrawal was the safest option.

One week after Himmler's latest youth circular, a young man was decapitated in Hamburg's Plotensee prison. The process took twenty seconds. At seventeen and a half, the youth was still a minor, but because of the severity of his offence he had been sentenced to death. Part of his punishment was not to know the time and date of his execution: he was only told at 1 p.m. on October 27 that he would face the guillotine that evening. In his last surviving letter, he wrote, "I am very thankful to my Heavenly Father that this agonizing life is coming to an end this evening. I could not stand it any longer anyway!"

RUDI WOBBE,
HELMUTH HÜBENER, AND
KARL-HEINZ SCHNIBBE, 1941

The story of Helmuth Hübener and his tiny group of rebels illustrated the extreme dangers of explicit resistance within the Third Reich and the fierce moral courage of those who attempted it. Up to 800,000 German citizens were imprisoned for resistance during the twelve years of the Third Reich. Many of these were Communists and Social Democrats attempting to continue their political opposition. However, little is known about the full range of dissident activities because of the need for total secrecy, the destruction of documents, and the deaths of the people concerned.

The fact that most Germans supported the regime made active opposition extremely difficult. It was even harder for adolescents who had known nothing but Nazi rules: most resistance cells were formed by adults, like the Stauffenberg group behind the July 1944 plot. There was some youth resistance, however: during 1942 Edelweiss Pirates linked up with Communists to produce over fifty leaflets in Düsseldorf, Stettin, and Dortmund. Two cells in particular—Helmuth Hübener's group and the White Rose—have become known because of the testimony given by surviving members and relatives.

In the book *When Truth Was Treason*, Karl-Heinz Schnibbe recalled that he and his friends Rudi Wobbe and Helmuth Hübener were all between fourteen and fifteen at the start of the war. They were already sick of the Nazis: "I did not like it anymore. The pressure and the coercion did not appeal to me." He was also upset by the way the Nazis treated the Jews. Backed up by his father, who saw the Nazis as a satanic, "competing religious system" to Christianity, Schnibbe punched his bullying Hitler Youth leader and lost all contact with the organization.

By the time the three met at their local Mormon church, Schnibbe was an apprentice in a printing firm and Hübener a white-collar apprentice. Brought up by his grandparents because he refused to live with his Nazi stepfather, Hübener was "the smartest kid in the bunch". He was a working-class auto-didact, tough, quiet, and persistent, and informed by a strong Christian faith. Like his friends, he had been radicalized by the bullying compulsion of the Hitler Youth and the regime's treatment of the Jews.

In the third year of war, Hübener decided to act. Working in local government, he had access to many forbidden documents. "He read books about foreign policy, domestic policy, and the economic situation," Schnibbe remembered. "We did not know anything, because we were not supposed to know." Hübener became convinced that Germany could not win the war. "Just think about it," he told his gang. "England, France—it is strategically impossible! It just can't be. Germany is cut off, has no raw materials, everything will collapse."

Hübener decided to assist the process. When his brother returned from occupied France with a radio that could pick up the BBC, he began to compare Nazi and Allied propaganda and quickly worked out that Nazi news reports were full of lies. The truth was shocking to Schnibbe and his young friends: "The German people were being duped. Anyone who was not yet totally castrated intellectually and blind, shuffling along through this glorious period, must have noticed it. 'Comrades, we are conquering ourselves to death.'"

The small group was already well aware that by listening to the BBC they were indulging in an illegal activity. However, according to Schnibbe, "The anxious feeling that we were doing something perverse or committing a crime abated gradually. Nevertheless it was a certain thrill." In the summer of 1941, Hübener made small leaflets, printed on red paper with swastikas, with slogans like "Down with Hitler", "Hitler the Murderer", and brief reports about the war in the east. These were produced in small numbers and left lying in telephone boxes with the notice "This is a chain letter, pass it on".

Incensed by the brutality of the Russian campaign, Hübener asked his friends to distribute the leaflets in phone booths, mailboxes, and apartment blocks. Schnibbe fretted, "Those little handbills burned in my hand like a hot iron. I said to Helmuth, 'If they catch us, we'll be in deep, deep trouble.' You could read in the newspapers nearly every day about death sentences or imprisonment because of conspiracy to commit high treason. I tried to speak to Helmuth about it to see if there was some other way, but he was completely convinced and would not be moved by any arguments."

As summer turned into autumn, the leaflets got longer, bigger, and more and more frequent: from one a month to twice a week. Offering information about current events—like the flight of Rudolf Hess—that were unavailable to most Germans, and countering German propaganda with astonishingly detailed strategic and economic reports, Hübener slowly moved to more direct, emotional appeals. "Do you want to tolerate having the happiness of your life taken from you," he wrote, "and your children cheated out of the most beautiful years of their lives? Do you want to tolerate this?"

Hübener directly tackled the subjugation of his peers, insisting that the Hitler Youth was "a compulsory organization of the first order for the recruiting of Nazi-enslaved national comrades. Hitler and his accomplices know that they must deprive you of your free will at the beginning, in order to make submissive, spineless creatures out of you. For Hitler knows that his contemporaries are beginning to see through him, the suppressor of free nations, the murderer of millions. Therefore we are calling out to you: Do not let your free will, the most valuable thing you possess, be taken away."

Dodging air raids and congregating in a small café to plot their next move, the youthful group began to lose their "terrific anxiety" about distributing these seditious leaflets. Although still sure that "someone would come out of the next house and seize me", Schnibbe became "more daring. I even took the opportunity to stick a few flyers into coat pockets in a cloakroom. It was possible to recognize the coats of high party functions, because they had a thing hanging from them we called the golden pheasant. After a while we weren't afraid anymore, though we were really playing Russian roulette."

Although the group "needed to be cautious about what we said and to whom we said it", their leaflets reached too few people. They needed extra help. This proved to be their downfall, when in early February 1942 Hübener asked a workmate to translate a leaflet into French for distribution among Hamburg's prisoners of war. The translator informed the office "overseer", who then told the Gestapo. Hübener was caught the next day with the carbons of his final leaflet, *Who Is Inciting Whom?* The Gestapo had been in the dark: if it hadn't been for Hübener's rashness, he would not have been discovered.

Five days later, Schnibbe and Wobbe were arrested and the three entered the Nazi criminal justice system with its "absolute presumption of guilt". Kept apart from each other, they suffered an almost unbearably punitive and violent regime. "If you did not go for interrogation in the Gestapo headquarters, then you were subject to the harassment in the prison. They had you either way. They never left us in peace." However, the small group did not crack: Hübener took all the blame to minimize the penalties to his friends: Schnibbe and Wobbe were respectively sentenced to five and ten years' imprisonment.

The Gestapo couldn't believe that just one seventeen-year-old had been responsible for the leaflets. Discovering no wider conspiracy, they transferred the adolescents to an investigative prison. When the indictments arrived in May, the group realized that they faced a long sentence of imprisonment or the death penalty: they were charged with listening to a foreign radio station and conspiracy to commit high treason. None of them had ever thought it would come to this, but they all realized that "to speak the truth" in those days was "a fatal luxury".

The trial was held in Berlin during August 1942. With their guilt predetermined, the trio received no legal help. Facing nine enraged Nazi dignitaries, Hübener maintained his poise in his exchanges with the judge:

"Would you have us believe that the British are telling us the truth? Do you really believe that?"

"Yes, surely, don't you?"

"You don't doubt Germany's ultimate victory, do you?"

"Do you actually believe that Germany can win the war?"

Having already worked out that he would be sentenced to death, the young man felt free to tell the truth. After the sentence was pronounced, he was asked if he had anything else to say.

"Now I must die even though I have committed no crime. So now it's my turn, but your turn will come."

Hübener's remaining two months were grim. The death row cell had no heating. There was only a small stool, a table, and a bed made of planks. Every ten minutes, a guard peeped through the spyhole. Expecting death at any moment, Hübener kept his Christian faith. As he wrote in his final letter to his parents, "I have only two hours left, then I have to appear before my God." His execution was publicly announced the next day by blood-red placards. The next summer, his mother and grandparents died in the Allied bombing of Hamburg.

Operating around the same time—although they had no knowledge of Hübener's arrest and trial: so effective was Nazi control—another resistance cell shared this visceral disgust and deep religious faith. "Germans," they wrote, "do you and your children want to suffer the same fate as that suffered by the

Jews? Do you want to be judged by the same standards as your traducers? Are we to be forever the nation which is hated and rejected by all mankind? No. Disassociate yourselves from National Socialist gangsterism. Prove by your deeds that you think otherwise. A new war of liberation is about to begin."

The White Rose was formed in early 1942 by a group of middle-class Munich University medical students. Hans Scholl, Alexander Schmorell, Christl Probst, and Willi Graf were all in their early twenties and were undergoing compulsory military service on the eastern front. They had religious and dissenting backgrounds. Scholl's father loathed Hitler, whom he called "the Pied Piper of Hamelin", and was imprisoned after a workmate heard him expressing those views. Graf had belonged to one of the surviving Catholic youth organizations, but had been caught and arrested in a 1938 clampdown.

The prime instigator, Hans Scholl, turned twenty-four during 1942. All the others were about the same age, except Hans's younger sister Sophie. At university they had access to sympathetic elders, like Kurt Huber, the professor of psychology and philosophy at Munich's Ludwigs Maximillian University. Outrage and religious conviction fired their resistance: "Whoever today still doubts the reality, the existence of demonic powers," they wrote in a summer 1942 leaflet, "has failed by a wide margin to understand the metaphysical background of this war."

With his older sister Inge, Hans had originally entered the Hitler Youth with enthusiasm: they both found there "a sense of belonging that carried us safely through the difficulties and loneliness of adolescence". Doubts crept in after they heard about the concentration camps: "What was really happening to our Fatherland? No freedom, no flourishing life, no prosperity or happiness for anyone who lived in it." Hans joined an outlawed *Bund,* and when he and Inge were arrested, his doubt turned to anger. He wrote in one of his forbidden books, "Tear out our hearts—and they will fatally burn you."

Although Inge was terrified, Hans continued in his dissident activities. He was encouraged by his father, who held that a regime that outlawed basic freedoms had "lost every spark of respect for man". Hans slowly gathered together a group of like-minded medical students during the early war years: the carefree, humorous Alexander Schmorell; Christl Probst, the only married member; and the thoughtful and reserved Willi Graf. Like many students, they enjoyed late-night intellectual discussions, but their backdrop was forced military service, and the tighter grip of the terror state.

Two separate events gave them inspiration. In early 1942, leaflets appeared in Munich mailboxes reproducing the protests of Count Galen, the bishop of Münster, against the euthanasia of the mentally ill. According to Inge, Hans

Scholl was electrified: "I can still see Hans standing there, with the leaflet in front of him, saying, 'if only I had a mimeograph machine.'" The students' outrage was given a deeper focus by the forty-nine-year-old Professor Huber, whose lectures on theology shed light "on the present moment, when man was not only trampling on the divine order, but also trying to annihilate God himself".

In spring 1942, the first White Rose leaflets appeared. Although produced in editions of only a hundred, they created an extraordinary stir at Munich University. Their hostility to the regime was backed up with practical suggestions: "offer passive resistance—resistance—wherever you may be, forestall the spread of this atheistic war machine before it is too late, before the last cities, like Koln [Cologne], have been reduced to rubble, and before the nation's last young man has given his blood on some battlefield for the hubris of a sub-human. Do not forget that every people deserves the regime it is willing to endure."

Taking their name from a Spanish novel, the White Rose produced three other leaflets in early summer 1942. In these extraordinary documents, anger was given shape by intellectual rigour. Quoting from the Bible, Lao-tzu, Friedrich Schiller, and Aristotle, they protested the murder of 300,000 Polish Jews, the deepening cost of the Russian campaign, and the total loss of civil liberties within a "dictatorship of evil". As they concluded, "After all, an end in terror is preferable to terror without end."

In high summer, the four students returned to the Russian front: before they left, they decided to step up their campaign as a matter of duty. As Christl Probst declared, "We must gamble our 'No' against this power which has arrogantly placed itself above the essential human values, and which is determined to root out all protest. We must do it for the sake of life itself—no-one can absolve us of this responsibility. National Socialism is the name of a malignant spiritual disease that has befallen our people. We dare not remain silent as we watch its course, as the German people suffer its ravages."

After his return from the front in the early winter of 1942, Hans Scholl travelled to Berlin to hook up with another resistance fighter, Falk Harnaek. It was then that he developed the plan "to establish illegal student groups in every university". It was at this point that Hans's younger sister became involved. A pretty and determined twenty-one-year-old, Sophie Scholl had been a Bund Deutscher Mädel leader, but her loathing for the regime deepened when she began her studies at Munich University. Feeling that the war was already lost and fired by her religious convictions, she joined the group's campaign.

Meeting in a secluded garden studio, the White Rose planned more leaflets and explicit anti-Nazi graffiti. The ground in Munich was fertile: the local *Gauleiter* had appeared at the university to criticize the students' low morale and to announce that women had no business being at university, as they would be better employed in producing children for the Reich. He was shouted down and publicly humiliated by the students. When the graffiti "Down with Hitler" and "Freedom" appeared on walls near the university at the turn of 1943, the authorities were both alerted and outraged.

After the German Sixth Army surrendered at Stalingrad on February 2, 1943, the White Rose's next leaflet, *Fellow Fighters in the Resistance!*, went straight to the heart of the matter. The Nazi state had always gambled on its appeal to Germany's youth, but the White Rose had seen through the regime's promises of self-determination: "In the name of German youth, we demand restitution by Adolf Hitler's state of our personal freedom, the most precious treasure that we have, out of which he has swindled us in the most miserable way."

On February 18, Hans and Sophie set off to distribute their latest bulletin in the main university hall. This time, the omens were malign: Sophie had had a dream the previous night in which both she and Hans were arrested. After completing their task, the pair spontaneously returned inside the building to throw the remaining sheets down the light well of the main stairs. They were spotted by the superintendent, who immediately locked all the doors: the pair were summarily arrested and their fate was sealed.

Expecting execution, Hans and Sophie Scholl retained a dignified calm. Neither they nor Christl Probst suffered the brutality meted out to the Helmuth Hübener group. When Sophie was asked if she would have done what she did if she'd known the full implications, she replied, "I would do exactly the same next time, for it is you, not I, who have the mistaken *Weltanschauung*." The two left written testaments. On the back of the indictment sheet, Sophie had scrawled the word "Freedom"; on the wall of his cell, Hans wrote a quotation from Goethe: "Hold out in defiance of all despotism."

To stop the contagion from spreading further, the authorities hastened the trial. Beginning only three days after their arrest, it was presided over by the notoriously vindictive president of the People's Court, Roland Freisler. With nothing to lose, Hans and Sophie Scholl gave no ground. As their sister Inge wrote later, "It was as if in these days their many unlived years were compacted into a heightened level of activity." The three defendants replied openly and deliberately to the court's questions: at one point, Sophie stated, "What we said and wrote is what many people are thinking, only they don't dare to say it."

They were executed hours later, defiant until the last. The night before she died, Sophie had another dream: "It was a sunny day. I was carrying a child in a long white dress to be baptised. The way to the church led up a steep slope, but I held the child in my arms firmly and without faltering. Then suddenly the footing gave way and there was a great crevice in the glacier. I had just enough time to set the child down on the other side before plunging into the abyss. The child is our idea. In spite of all obstacles, it will prevail. We were permitted to be pioneers, though we must die early for its sake."

The authorities were not finished. Shortly afterwards, Graf, Schmorell, and Huber were arrested, along with eleven others who had helped to distribute the leaflets. Held in mid-April 1943, the trial resulted in the death penalty for the three remaining principals. Freisler reserved his contempt for Huber, because of his age and his fiduciary position; as he yelled at the professor, "The days when every man can be allowed to profess his own political 'beliefs' are past. For us, there is but one standard: the National Socialist one." All three had "disgraced German youth—especially the youth who fought at Langemarck".

News of the executions spread internationally. Later in 1943, there was a mass meeting held in New York, attended by luminaries like Eleanor Roosevelt. A witness later remembered how "hundreds and hundreds of New Yorkers came to pay tribute to the six heroic victims of the 'other Germany'. Their names meant little to them at the time, but their deeds very much. Their sacrifice proved that Hitler was not the master of all Germans and their conscience; there was resistance, and their tragic deaths represented a glimmer of hope for the future."

For all their bravery, the White Rose had little immediate effect in Nazi Germany: the penalties for dissidents were too severe. However, their critique was uncannily prescient: they saw how Hitler's mesmeric popularity, so dependent on the moods of the masses, could be threatened by serious reversals. They also saw through the false consciousness of the Nazis' youth policy: "We grew up in a state where all free expression is unscrupulously suppressed. The Hitler Youth, the SA, the SS, have tried to drug us, to revolutionise us, to regiment us in the most promising young years of our lives."

● ● ●

The White Rose struck at a key point in the history of the war. Stalingrad was a disaster, and as the news came back from the front, it increased the regime's obsessive impulse to bring everyone under its control. Goebbels shut down all popular entertainment for a few days in February 1943, stating that personal freedom did not matter within the *Volksgemeinschaft*. From then on, the Gestapo's net was cast wider and wider. If the members of the White Rose had been executed as "typical outsiders", what of the ultimate outsiders, the Jews?

In February 1943, Goebbels initiated the "Factory Operation" to cleanse Berlin completely of its remaining 27,000 Jews before Hitler's birthday. On the day that this operation began, Anne Frank recorded an episcopal letter sent out by the local bishops: "People of the Netherlands, stand up and take action. Each of us must choose our own weapons to fight for the freedom of our country, our people and our religion! Give your help and support. Act now!" Although she found this intervention inspiring, she thought that it was "definitely too late to help our fellow Jews".

By then, Anne Frank had been in hiding for nearly six months. During the previous summer, her family had received an SS notification requiring her older sister Margot to report for forced labour in Germany. Alerted to the Germans' plans for Holland's Jews, Otto Frank had decided to resist in the only way possible: to join the ranks of the "divers" and go underground. On July 5, 1942, Otto moved his family and his friends the van Pelses into the two-floor attic space—called the Annexe—above his business premises at Prinsengracht in the centre of Amsterdam, and sealed the door.

With the later addition of the middle-aged Fritz Pfeffer (Albert Dussell in the diary), there were eight adults and children in the Annexe: Otto and Edith Frank, with their daughters Margot and Anne, Hermann and Auguste van Pels (van Daan in the diary), and their son Peter. Apart from the fear of discovery and denunciation, everyday life in the cramped space was hard on all its occupants, but particularly so for an inquisitive and restless adolescent. Being cooped up was more than Anne could bear, and she exploded in her diary, "Let me out, where there's fresh air and laughter!"

As the youngest of the eight and the family's "mischief-maker", Anne took her incarceration hard. As another "diver", Eva Schloss, remembered, "I was thirteen, and had so much energy, but I just couldn't do anything. I was very afraid and very upset. I used to have wrestling matches with my mother to get rid of my energy." Even worse than anger was the sense of isolation: "I am surrounded by too great a void," Anne wrote in November 1942. "I never used to give it much thought, since my mind was filled with my friends and having a good time. Now I think either about unhappy things or about myself."

Forced to develop her inner resources at a very young age, she poured out her feelings in her one confidante, her diary, which she anthropomorphized as Kitty, a character from an extremely popular series by the novelist Cissy van

A LATE PHOTOGRAPH
OF ANNE FRANK, 1942

Marxveldt called *Joop ter Heul*. Finding space to be alone and write in her diary, which she called "her true friend", was a lifeline. Her incarceration had forced her into a clear-sighted candour way beyond her years, and her diary contained an intimate record of an intelligent young girl forced by extraordinary circumstances to accelerate her adolescence.

Many entries, however, contain the chatter you might expect. In the world that had existed before her incarceration, Anne had been a diligent student, anxious to learn, albeit slightly spoiled and mischievous. She was sociable and popular with her peers: when possible she liked to play the class comedian. Her moods changed like quicksilver, but she was already aware of this and capable of moderating their worst effects. Even at this young age, her gaze was fixed outside her family and her immediate circumstances: she wanted to be "different from what I am".

Her ambition was to be a journalist and "to spend a year in Paris and London learning the languages and studying art history": as she wrote, "I still have visions of gorgeous dresses and fascinating people." She participated in the period's limited youth culture, plastering her wall with pictures of Deanna Durbin, the Hollywood star. She continued to read and emulate the young heroes in a popular series of girls' books. She fantasized about shopping in Switzerland, where she would buy foundation and cleansing cream, bath salts, and eau de cologne as well as sensible schoolwear.

At the same time, Anne was enough of an adolescent to be at odds with her parents: "Every day I'm growing cooler and more contemptuous of Mother, less affectionate to Father and less willing to share a single thought with Margot; I'm closed up tighter than a drum." In another entry she exclaimed that she wanted "nothing better than to do without their company for a while, and they don't understand that". Even worse, both she and her older sister felt that they were "treated like children when it comes to external matters, while inwardly, we're much older than other girls our age".

However, although Anne railed in turn at every one of them, the five Annexe adults helped her development and her "self-knowledge": "I can watch myself as if I were a stranger. I can stand across from the everyday Anne and, without being biased or making excuses, watch what she's doing, both the good and the bad." Anne revised the diary in 1944, and in a key entry from that March, she looked back at her "unreal" former life and the eighteen months that had followed: "The Anne Frank who enjoyed that heavenly existence was completely different to the one who has grown wise between these walls.

"When I was at home, my life was filled with sunshine. Then, in the middle of 1942, everything changed overnight. The quarrels, the accusations—I couldn't take it all in. I was caught off guard, and the only way I knew how to keep my bearings was to talk back. The first half of 1943 brought crying spells, loneliness and the gradual realisation of my faults and shortcomings, which were numerous and seemed even more so. I filled the day with chatter, tried to draw Pim [her father] closer to me and failed. This left me on my own to face the difficult task of improving myself."

Turning fourteen marked a turning point. A few months before her fifteenth birthday, Anne began to conceptualize her adolescence: "Girls my age feel very insecure about themselves and are just beginning to discover that they are individuals with their own ideas, thoughts and habits. I just turned thirteen when I came here, so I started thinking about myself and realised that I have become an 'independent person' sooner than most girls. Sometimes when I lie in bed at night, I feel a terrible urge to touch my breasts and listen to the quiet steady beating of my heart."

Anne had reached the crucial stage of puberty. Breaking away from her parents, she became attracted to the only male adolescent in the Annexe, the shy but kind Peter van Pels: "After New Year the second big change occurred: my dream, through which I discovered my longing for . . . a boy; not for a girlfriend, but for a boyfriend. I also discovered an inner happiness underneath my superficial and cheerful exterior. From time to time I was quiet. Now I live only for Peter, since what happens to me in the future depends largely on him!"

Outside in occupied Holland, things were getting steadily worse. For any Jews not already in the camps, life was even more dangerous: as the payments for finding Jews escalated, more and more "divers" were discovered. Anne was aware that discovery and arrest might be imminent, but she was also fascinated by the onset of puberty. She explored her vagina: "You can barely find it, because the folds of skin hide the opening. The hole is so small I can hardly imagine how a man could get in there, much less how a baby could come out."

Her obsession with Peter precipitated a family crisis in spring 1944. When her father objected to their necking, Anne wrote him a letter: "Don't think of me as a fourteen year old, since all these troubles have made me older; I won't regret my actions, I'll behave the way I think I should!" The next day her father gave her a good talking-to. Anne's reaction was shock and contrition: "Yes, Anne, you knew full well that your letter was unkind and untrue, but you were actually proud of it! I'll take Father as my example once again, and I *will* improve myself."

Yearning for emancipation but living within enslavement, Anne was—like the adults—in an impossible position, and her diary reflected her mood swings. On May 3, 1944, she railed against the "destructive urge in people, the urge to rage, murder and kill. And until all of humanity, without exception, undergoes a metamorphosis, wars will continue to be waged." Two paragraphs later, she was resurrected: "Every day I feel myself maturing, I feel liberation drawing near, I feel the beauty of nature and the goodness of the people around me. Every day I think what a fascinating and amusing adventure this is!"

During the spring and summer of 1944, Anne also thought hard about the role of the adolescent in society. She began to conceive of a possible future after the war: "I finally realized I must do my schoolwork to keep from being ignorant, to get on in life, to become a journalist, because that's what I want. I *know* I can write." She was encouraged by a broadcast from London calling for "diaries and letters dealing with the war": "Just imagine how interesting it would be if I published a novel about the Secret Annexe. The title alone would make people think it was a detective story."

In June, D-Day month, she turned fifteen and received "quite a few gifts", including a five-volume art history book, a gold bracelet, and a bouquet of peonies from Peter. She continued to write about feminism, the imminence of liberation, and the position of youth in society. In July, she discussed a youth book called *What Do You Think of the Modern Young Girl?* that criticized "today's youth from head to toe": "In some passages I had the strong feeling that the writer was directing her disapproval at me, which is why I finally want to bare my soul to you and defend myself against this attack."

Anne felt that the war had placed intolerable burdens on her generation: "We're much too young to deal with these problems, but they keep thrusting themselves on us until, finally, we're forced to think up a solution, though most of the time our solutions crumble when faced with the facts. It's difficult in times like these: ideals, dreams and cherished hopes rise within us, only to be crushed by grim reality. It's a wonder I haven't abandoned all my ideals, they seem so absurd and impractical. Yet I cling to them because I still believe, in spite of everything, that people are truly good at heart."

• • •

The opening up of the second front in June and July 1944 ratcheted up Nazi oppression to an unbearable pitch, as the Hitler regime revealed the death cult that lay at its heart. That summer saw "an orgy of killing" at Auschwitz: "The furnaces in the crematoria became so hot that firebricks cracked, and additional burning pits had to be dug. Once started, the flames were fuelled with the fat that had run off the burning bodies." In Jack Mandelbaum's camp, "prisoners died of disease and starvation in ever greater numbers."

Germany's youth were primed for total war. The forcible draft of under-military-age adolescents continued during 1943, designated as the "Year of War Service of the German Youth". The classes of 1926 and 1927, then sixteen- and seventeen-years-old, were packed off into Waffen-SS units along with multinational volunteers. It was as though Nazi Germany was becoming one vast camp and the prophecy of the White Rose was coming true: "Gradually one bond after another was clamped around Germany, until finally all were imprisoned in a great dungeon." However, the Nazi system of youth organization held firm.

Most German youth still believed in the *Volksgemeinschaft* ideal, in the total rightness of Germany's cause, and most of all in the head of the cult, Hitler himself. The indoctrination had become more extreme. During the summer of 1943, the Allied bombing of German cities had escalated to the extent that the authorities began a systematic campaign to pull half a million adolescents out of the industrial heartland in the west and north. They were sent to *Kinderlandverschickung* camps in East Prussia, Upper Silesia, and the Warthegau. These were not schools, but Hitler Youth factories.

These evacuated adolescents were extremely vulnerable to Nazi extremities: far away from home and in shock, they could be freely indoctrinated without any fear of outside influences and distractions. Many Hitler Youths already presented fertile ground for hate doctrines. Most of the referents of normal life had disappeared. With schooling disrupted, and the beloved *Volksgemeinschaft* under serious threat, many of Germany's young transmuted the psychological damage caused by the Allies' bombing into an even greater disregard for human life, including their own.

For most German adolescents, the identification of self with Hitler became complete during the last two years of the war. If there was to be no victory, then there would be total annihilation. Their natural home was the *Wehrertüchtigungslager,* which became the prime Nazi unit of youth organization by the end of 1943. These camps featured three weeks of brainwashing. The first, "We Fight", promoted war as a natural law; the second, entitled "We Sacrifice", reinforced the Langemarck myth; while the final week, "We Triumph", trumpeted the inevitability of German victory in the east.

Nineteen forty-four was designated by Artur Axmann as the "Year of the War Volunteers". By then, young Germans of fourteen and fifteen were entering the SS system. This under-age mobilization made international news. An American journalist noted in 1944 that "many boys and girls thirteen to fifteen years old work in war industries. With iron consistency the Nazi Party has organized the life of German youth for its own purposes. The individual lives of these young people are being swallowed up in the common life of the organizations to which they belong."

The crème de la crème of this system were concentrated within a special Waffen-SS unit, called the 12th SS Panzer Division Hitlerjugend. About 10,000 boys between sixteen and eighteen began their period of intensive training in the summer of 1943. They were bound together by a regime that placed great emphasis on the informal relationship between officers and men: the priniples of the youth movement finally adapted to total war. The unit combined battle inexperience with a death-defying recklessness that epitomized Nazi youth education's nihilistic final phase.

The 12th SS Panzer Division Hitlerjugend saw its first action after the D-Day landings in June 1944. At Caen, they fought "like wolves". By September, there were only 600 left of the original 10,000. The fate of this division highlighted one of the most shocking things about the Nazi regime: its complete lack of regard for its adolescents. As Melita Maschmann wrote about her comrades, "They did not wish to spare themselves: they would stand their ground wherever their command summoned them to do so, and it was expected that this would be given in a responsible manner."

However, by 1944, even diehards like Maschmann realized that the Nazi leaders had made "no attempt to protect" their youth. Just at the moment when they believed that they had emancipated themselves, German youth had "succumbed to the fateful domination of the technological era". She realized that the "dehumanization—of the victory of technology over the soul, if I may use this old-fashioned word—which was expressed in the institution of apparatuses for mass murder (the concentration camps) could also be seen in the way the National Socialist state over-organised its young people".

The Hitler Youth monolith was breaking down under the depredations of the SS and the eastern evacuations. This had an unforeseen effect. With most of the youth police funnelled off into SS combat divisions, juvenile delinquency increased in the blacked-out cities of western and central Germany. Emboldened by the chaos, the wild gangs began to organize in greater numbers and continued the campaign of sabotage and civil disobedience advocated by the White Rose. The authorities reacted with even greater severity.

These late dissident youth groups were usually known under the collective name of that earlier Wild Clique, the Edelweiss Pirates. "These youngsters, aged between 12 and 17, hang around into the late evening, with musical instruments and young females," observed a July 1943 surveillance report. "Since this riff-raff is to a large extent outside the Hitler Youth and adopts a hostile attitude towards the organization, they represent a danger to other young people. It has recently been established that members of the armed forces are also to be found among them."

After Stalingrad, the Edelweiss Pirates merged with the Kittelsbach Pirates, groups comprised of Hitler Youth renegades, working-class youth, and the remains of youth cliques. Their activities included daubing graffiti like "Down With Hitler", public brawling, and roaming the streets en masse. Infuriated by this gang behaviour, the regime initiated even more severe crackdowns. A 1943 criminal law for youth specifically instructed juvenile judges to hand over offenders for unlimited detention in protective custody camps—like Moringen, home to an unbearably punitive and lethal regime.

In April 1944, Himmler ordered that all inmates of juvenile protective custody camps were to be classified by the Criminal Biological Institute run by the security police. After arrival at camps like Moringen, inmates were to be placed in an observation block for six months. Those who could be rehabilitated were to be sent off into land service or the army, with asylums or concentration camps for the unregenerate. Later that year, Himmler, Artur Axmann, and the minister of justice decided on further action against "the constantly increasing number of cliques".

Offenders were to be punished by being sent to a protective custody or concentration camp. Cliques were defined by the Central Security Agency as "collections of young people outside the Hitler Youth" who were "particularly indifferent to the demands of war". Three basic types of offender were identified: urban street gangs, political opponents of the regime, and in the final category the swing rebels who continued to practise their Anglophiliac obsession with hot music and sexual experimentation.

As the regime entered its last full year, it reached new heights of vindictiveness. In October 1944 the fourth and final White Rose trial took place. This involved a Munich group, led by the medical student Hans Leipelt, which had attempted acts of sabotage and had links to a second generation of more politicized Hamburg swings. As one of them, the fifteen-year-old Thorsten Muller, was told during an interrogation, "Anything that starts with Ellington ends with an assassination attempt on the Führer!" Leipelt was sentenced to death.

That same month, Himmler issued his final youth directive: yet another ordinance for the "combating of youth cliques". This was specifically aimed at the Edelweiss Pirates who had turned to armed resistance. In Cologne, they linked up with prisoners of war, deserters, forced labourers, and escaped concentration camp prisoners. Their escalating partisan-style campaign climaxed with the murder of the Cologne Gestapo chief. The authorities took revenge by publicly hanging thirteen Edelweiss Pirates in the city centre, including Bartel Schink, the sixteen-year-old leader of a local group called "The Navajos".

CHAPTER 29

The Arrival of the Teenager

The Launch of Seventeen

■ ■ ■

You are the bosses of the business.
—"Seventeen Goes On Record", *Seventeen*,
issue no. 1, SEPTEMBER 1944

THE FIRST ISSUE OF *SEVENTEEN*, SEPTEMBER 1944

ON THE DAY before the fourth White Rose trial began, Frank Sinatra opened his third season at New York's Paramount Theater. It was October 12, Columbus Day, and the premiere was a wow even before it began. Weegee was there with his camera and notebook, capturing the scene for the *New York Daily News*: "Oh! Oh! Frankie. . . . The line in front of the Paramount Theater on Broadway starts forming at midnight. By four in the morning there are over five hundred girls . . . they wear bobby sox (of course), bow ties (the same as Frankie wears) and photos of Sinatra pinned to their dresses."

By eight in the morning there was a huge milling mob: "A big blow-up picture of Sinatra in front of the theatre is marked red with lipstick impressions of kisses, endearing messages of love, and even telephone numbers. The theatre is soon filled. The show starts with the feature (*Our Hearts Were Young and Gay*). This is the most heckled movie of all times . . . not that it's a bad movie . . . just the opposite . . . but the girls simply didn't come to see that . . . as far as they are concerned they could be showing lantern slides of the screen.

"Then the great moment arrives. Sinatra appears on the stage . . . hysterical shouts of Frankie . . . Frankie . . . you've heard the squeals on the radio when he sings . . . multiply that by about a thousand times and you get an idea of the deafening noise . . . as there is no radio control man to keep the noise within ear level. Sinatra does a few numbers and leaves the stage hurriedly." But that wasn't the end of it: "A big mob is waiting at the stage entrance . . . he dares not leave . . . so he's marooned inside the theatre. . . .

"At two in the morning the theatre closes up . . . the porters come in to clean up . . . some of the girls, having been in all day and night and having seen the five shows, refuse to leave . . . and try and hide in the ladies room . . . - but the matrons chase them out . . . so those having had some sleep during the picture go outside and wait in line again." For Weegee, this was yet another example of the human extremities that he documented with his unerring instinct for the climactic moments in the life of New York City: what he didn't mention was the fact that, after each performance, the Paramount was drenched in urine.

Like Valentino's funeral in 1926 or the 1939 *Wizard of Oz* opening, the Columbus Day riot was a generation-defining media event acted out on Manhattan's streets: some 30,000 frenzied girls taking over Times Square. The writer Bruce Bliven called it "a phenomenon of mass hysteria that is only seen two or three times in a century. You need to go back not merely to Lindbergh and Valentino to understand it, but to the dance madness that overtook some German villages in the Middle Ages, or to the Children's Crusade."

Sinatra's fame had been steadily building for three years or more. His first major breakthrough came during his first Paramount season in December 1942, when he was billed as "Extra Added Attraction" to the Benny Goodman Orchestra: the moment he was introduced, the theatre erupted with "five thousand kids stamping, yelling, screaming, applauding". These scenes were amplified when Sinatra returned to the Paramount in May 1943: "This time, they threw more than roses," remembered his factotum, Nick Sevano, "they threw their panties and their brassieres."

The furore overtook the hype. The media might have called Sinatra "Mister Swoonatra" but his audience did more than that. His press agents remembered "hiring girls to scream when he sexily rolled a note. But we needn't have. The dozen girls we hired to scream and swoon did exactly as we told them. But hundreds more we didn't hire screamed even louder. Others squealed, howled, kissed his pictures with their lipsticked lips and kept him prisoner in his dressing room between shows at New York's Paramount Theatre. It was wild, crazy, completely out of control."

The hysteria continued throughout 1943 and 1944, boosted by cameos in films like *Higher and Higher*. Sinatra's rise was unstoppable, for he filled an industrial and an emotional need. In concert, he seduced his young audience with a ferocious intensity only accentuated by his gaze. His bright blue eyes raked the crowd, singling out individuals and thus appearing to be singing for them alone, just one in a crowd of thousands. Matched to the ethereal kitsch of slow ballads like "Embraceable You" and "Over the Rainbow", "The Voice"— as Sinatra was known—cast a spell that appeared to suspend time.

Hysteria rushed in to fill the vacuum. Bruce Bliven observed Sinatra at the Paramount: "When he sings sadly, I'll walk alone, the child sitting next to me shouts in seemingly genuine anguish, 'I'll walk wid ya, Frankie,' and so on, in various words, do several hundred others. When the song says that nobody loves him, a faithful protagonist on my right groans, 'Are you kiddin' Frankie?' Then the whole audience falls into an antiphony with him, Frankie shouting 'No!' and the audience 'Yes!' five or six times."

Although nearly twenty-nine by October 1944, Sinatra was slightly built, nervous, and young-looking for his age. Married with a child, he was still a Peter Pan figure: as he later stated, "It was the war years, and there was a great loneliness. I was the boy in every corner drugstore, the boy who had gone off to war." Bliven thought that the bobby-soxers at the Paramount "found in him, for all his youthfulness, something of a father image. And beyond that, he represents a dream of what they themselves might conceivably do or become."

FRANK SINATRA HYPNOTIZES HIS YOUNG AUDIENCE, MID-1940S

Sinatra was both at one with his audience yet forever out of reach: "He earns a million a year, and yet he talks their language; he is just a kid from Hoboken who got the breaks. In everything he says and does, he aligns himself with the youngsters and against the adult world. It is always 'we' and never 'you'." Not everyone was so understanding. The *Herald Tribune* held that his concerts were in no way an "artistic manifestation." The education commissioner of New York blamed Sinatra for making young people lose "control of their emotions".

Much more controversial was Sinatra's draft status: he was classified 4F during 1943, rejected for service because of an ear injury sustained at birth. To patriotic Americans, this was a red rag to a bull. Sinatra was constantly attacked by the press for being out of uniform. GIs resented any man not in uniform and hated the photographs of the singer being mobbed by "all these enthusiastic girls". After a much-publicized incident where a young man threw eggs at Sinatra, a group of sailors threw tomatoes at the enormous blow-up of the singer outside the theatre—a symbolic desecration enacted for the cameras of the press.

But there was an added thrust to the vitriol directed at Sinatra. Like Valentino, the singer was not traditionally masculine: he was designed to appeal to young women. This not only excited jealousy but also dramatized the split between the GIs' expectation of home life and the reality. The land that they had left was not the same. A new generation had come up, and—in the vacuum caused by the drafting of two million young men during 1944—was claiming its time. The fact that the bobby-soxers did not desire battle-hardened GIs but a seemingly effete "feather merchant" was an index of that change.

Whether anyone liked it or not, Sinatra had become a national figure. His status was confirmed in September 1944 when he went to the White House and met the president: "I was a little stunned when I stood alongside him. I just thought, here's the greatest guy alive today, and here's a little guy from Hoboken shaking his hand." Roosevelt had already made public pronouncements linking American politics with its popular music, but this meeting was a shrewdly taken opportunity to reaffirm publicly the fact that adolescents were an important part of American society.

. . .

American women had always been in the forefront of the country's consumer culture, but during the later stages of the war events conspired to amplify this importance. Most young men above eighteen were among the seven million or so army draftees; with the eighteen-to-thirty age group removed from public life, adolescents in general were much more visible on a day-to-day basis. Most of those were female, and they were in full-time employment, up to three million fourteen- to seventeen-year-olds during 1944: while their jobs were often menial, they also included responsibilities and long hours.

This cohort had prematurely crossed one of the main thresholds between adolescence and adulthood, and yet did not have a clear role assigned to them within the war effort. In addition, many of these young working women were not receiving much family support and had their traditional route to adulthood—usually defined by marriage—blocked. Sensational articles about female delinquency amplified adult fears about a younger generation of fourteen- to eighteen-year-olds who, despite being the most affluent in American history, seemed to be running amok and adrift.

The events of 1943 encouraged many Americans to be fearful of their young, who were offered up as a blank canvas onto which adults could project their fears about the war and its impact on American society. The disparity between the media hysteria and the more prosaic reality was highlighted by a 1944 film called *Youth Runs Wild*. Presenting its young delinquents not as

hardened criminals but as lost victims, this sober (albeit sensationally promoted) account ended with a direct address to the audience: "We're not going
to waste them anymore, we need them. After all, they're what we're fighting for."

This inclusive approach accorded with what many young Americans felt:
not all of them were zoot-suiters, bobby-soxers, or Victory Girls. As one young
woman informed a summer 1944 *New York Times* forum about juvenile delinquency, "We want to work, we don't want to be interested only in juke boxes
and cokes. There's a lot of youth power in the country that can make up for the
shortage in manpower. The adults must help us organize it into a voluntary
corps. Young people want a chance to do things and to have responsible jobs."

However, America's booming economy did not allow for anything but the
most minimal social welfare: to do anything would have smacked of the New
Deal state socialism that was an anathema to the cost-plus corporations. Indeed, the great youth bodies of the Depression era—the CCC and the NYA—
had ceased operation by 1944. Some action was needed, but thirties-style
paternalism and public good works were desirable neither to big business nor
to the young themselves, who wished to be catered to on their own terms.

The way forward was shown by a May 1944 feature in *Look,* which described
the successful campaign run by Ruth Clifton, editor of the high school paper
in Moline, Illinois, to open a youth centre. Concerned about the number of
adolescents drinking in saloons, she successfully petitioned the city council to
renovate an empty warehouse. Picturing the new centre full of adolescents
drinking Cokes, the copy noted "how juvenile delinquency can be decreased
by mobilization of the energies and creativeness of young people. Young
America knows its own difficulties; it will solve them, given a chance."

The Moline club was part of the American state's most creative solution to
wartime delinquency: the nationwide system of Teen Canteens. From the outset, they were designed as a more enlightened approach to youth work. As the
scheme's author, Mark McCloskey, stated in March 1944, "This world has
been full of trying to do all the things that kids don't want to do." Believing
that most agencies had failed to update their programmes, McCloskey canvassed America's young about what they wanted—something every previous
youth service organization had failed to do.

A committed vitalist like G. Stanley Hall, McCloskey refused to enter into
the hysterical condemnation that followed the events of 1943. "I understand
perfectly why the kids dance down the isles in the Paramount Theater when
Harry James blows a great trumpet," he said at the time. "It's what I call a
neo-Dionysian revel." When the congressional hearings on youth problems
identified the lack of recreational facilities as the principal cause of juvenile

delinquency, McCloskey, as recreational director for the Office of Community War Services, was empowered to act.

McCloskey felt traditional youth organizations had not confronted contemporary adolescent realities: "Your Boy Scouts, your Girl Scouts, your YMCAs, have never dealt with the delinquent child." Other wartime programmes like the Senior Service Scouts and the Junior Police Organization were too authoritarian. The Office of Community War Services began from the premise that "a large group of tween-teens, the 14–18-year-olds have long been socially, often educationally adrift, and too often, as police blotters testify, morally adrift".

Teen Canteens mushroomed during 1944. They offered a delicate balance between adolescent independence and discreet adult input. If the scales tipped too far either way, the centre would not be a success: too much wildness on the one hand, too much control on the other. Usually located in YMCA rooms, churches, empty shops, and community centres, their names reflected the adolescent culture of the day: the Jive Hive, the Buzz Bucket, the Swing Haven, Hep Cat Hall, Rhythm Rocker, Boogie, and the Strut Hut.

Canteens like Indianapolis's Jive Hive needed several months of planning, with involvement from adults and the local council. Its opening was attended by two hundred adolescents, along with their parents and the city's mayor. These canteens were neighbourhood-based, with strict age and residency requirements, and opened several nights a week: weekdays until 9.30, Fridays and Saturdays until 11 p.m. They usually featured a jukebox, ping-pong tables, a dance floor, and a Coke machine: alerted to this movement's marketing potential, Coca-Cola distributed pamphlets on how to start a centre.

The Teen Canteen catchment age customarily ranged from thirteen to nineteen: saloon-age patrons of twenty-one were unlikely to be impressed by soft drinks and adult chaperones. These youth clubs were dominated by high school adolescents, potential inductees into the kind of life envisaged by the club constitution of Hep Cat Hall: "clean, wholesome recreational facilities and entertainment based on the American Republican form of government." The Teen Canteens represented an official attempt to apply the wartime rhetoric of freedom and democracy to adolescent lives.

This bore fruit in race-torn Detroit, where in 1944 black and white teenagers joined the same clubs, and supported a citywide, biracial Youth Council. Other Teen Canteens were not so harmonious. High school cliques tended to dominate their social life, while ethnic and racial divisions were often upheld. Trouble usually occurred for these reasons: the crossing of neighbourhood boundaries that might have been invisible to an outsider but were as real to locals as if they had been marked in white paint on every street corner.

This self-enclosed adolescent world was disturbing to parents, many of whom complained about the amount of time their children spent away from home. Traditional youth workers also bemoaned the elevation of "hang-out recreation" at the expense of more improving programmes. However, the balance of power had swung away from paternalism. In its *Youth Service* pamphlet, the Office of Community War Services celebrated the fact that adults had been forced to take the lead of "the teenage movement". Government recognition of greater adolescent independence had become a fact of life.

. . .

In September 1944, a magazine was launched that pulled together the strands of democracy, national identity, peer culture, target marketing, and youth consumerism into an irresistible package. After all, as its pre-launch ad copy advised, American youth had an estimated spending capacity of $750 million: untold riches awaited those who plugged into this still virtually untapped market. If the Columbus Day riot dramatized the emotional intensity of young women, then *Seventeen* celebrated their economic importance with its mix of "Young fashions & beauty, movies & music, ideas & people".

Harking back to the age idealized by Booth Tarkington and Maureen Daly, the magazine continued the twinned thrust of the Teen Canteens. On the one hand, it treated adolescents as quasi-adults, aware of their future responsibilities, and eager for information about current affairs. As the magazine's inaugural editorial ran, "You're going to have to run this show, so the sooner you start thinking about it the better. In a world that is changing as quickly and as profoundly as ours is, we hope to provide a clearing house for your ideas."

But it was also a commercial package, explicitly aimed at the most affluent young generation thus far: "SEVENTEEN is your magazine, High School Girls of America—all yours! It is interested only in you—and everything that concerns, excites, annoys, pleases or perplexes you." In the new era of democracy and emancipation, it explicitly encouraged reader participation: "Write us about anything and everything. Say you disagree with SEVENTEEN or disagree violently, say we're tops, say we're terrible, say anything you please—but say it!"

Launched out of editor Helen Valentine's deep-seated conviction that high school girls needed a magazine of their own, *Seventeen* excluded adults and directly addressed its target market. The first issue's editorial copy included a celebrity feature on Harry James, a Frank Sinatra photomontage, a Hollywood gossip column, film, book, and record reviews, a "First Date Quiz", and other

AD FOR THE BLUM STORE'S TEEN CANTEEN
IN *SEVENTEEN*'S FIRST ISSUE

etiquette columns. Another regular slot, "Why Don't Parents Grow Up", offered common-sense suggestions on how to bridge the generational divide.

Seventeen aimed to shape its young readers into acceptable adults. "Growing up and earning your living has its compensations," Alice Beaton wrote in the college-age section, "For Seniors Only"; "It's a lot like jitterbugging. It keeps you plenty busy, gets you out of breath, doesn't always seem to take you very far—but it's fun, exciting, challenging." Responsibility was also inculcated by articles like "What Are You Doing About the War?" and an explicit instruction to stay in high school: "Remember one thing . . . you're an adult-in-training."

But the magazine's main hook was fashion. Features on inexpensive items were interspersed with home dressmaking tips and fashion spreads with price details. The advertisements were more alluring: the Blum Store took out a big ad for its "teen-age" clothes entitled "Teen Canteen", while Saks Fifth Avenue promoted its "Young Circle" range with the copy, "Teenagers love this smooth little wool, pure and simple." Teen-Timers Inc. heralded its school frocks with the clanging rhyme line "Reet for Neet Teens", offering at the same time a full list of "potent Teen Shops" in locations around the nation.

Seventeen was a smash because it both shaped and reflected the desires of its readership: the initial print run of 530,000 rose to nearly 650,000 within six months. "We are proud of SEVENTEEN because it does not distort our outlook on things, baby us, or make our habits seem ridiculous to adults," wrote "F.M.C." from Texas. Another, younger reader from Michigan revealed her pleasure at getting her "sophisticated" subscription card: "I felt that I must use Mom's stationery to tell you how grown up it feels to get SEVENTEEN for Christmas when one is only thirteen."

Like many apparent overnight successes, *Seventeen* synthesized existing trends. In 1941, *Parents* had launched *Calling All Girls*—a good idea let down by its overreliance on childish comics: adolescent girls wanted to be treated as older than they were. The next year, *Good Housekeeping* introduced a column called "Teens of Our Times" that ran updates on adolescent slang and dating etiquette. Nineteen forty-four also saw the launch of *Miss America*. At the same time newspapers began to publish columns like "Sub-debs and Squires" and "Jive Journal", and to cover youth music in the entertainment pages.

A reliable index to the upward graph of youth coverage in the mass media was to be found in the pages of the glossy weekly news magazines. *Life*'s coverage reflected this rapidly developing market. In one of two 1944 articles about "sub-debs", *Life* counted nearly seven hundred clubs in Indianapolis: many of these had acronymic names, like "WITCH" (We In This Club are Hell-cats) and "JERKS" (Junior Elite Receive Kind Servicemen). If you were outside this magic circle, you were referred to as a "square", These articles were popular with many young readers, who thought them "hep".

A May 1944 *Life* article about "High-School Fads" described new crazes that included stitching "Alcatraz '44" and "Sing-Sing '45" on the back of denim shirts and jackets. In keeping with the continuing spread of hipster jive through the high school crowd, many fads were music-based: responding to a popular tune called "I'd Rather Have a Paper Doll to Call My Own", high school boys pinned paper dolls to their clothing. The popularity of Frank Sinatra sparked a craze for bow ties among young men, while lipstick-smeared pictures of the singer regularly adorned girls' school lockers.

These spontaneous fashions were the purest manifestations of American youth's desire for novelty, excitement, and self-identification. Fads also keyed in to the clique conformity that underlay these apparently anarchic and novel styles. In December 1944, *Seventeen* approvingly advised its readers, "You buy loafer moccasins because your friends do . . . you go to Joe's Grill . . . or Doc's for cokes, not because those places are charming, or the food is good—but because the crowd goes. Most of your surface habits are picked up from people your own age."

Fads also offered manufacturers, retailers, and the media a fast track into the youth market. As *Parents* magazine observed in its "Tricks for Teens" column, high school fads "keep your daughter interested in her appearance; they make going to school more fun; and they give her the assurance that she is 'one of the crowd'". By 1944 the magazine was receiving nearly two thousand letters a week from high school girls. Syndicated nationally, the "Tricks for Teens" column spawned its own clubs, where adolescents put on gadget jewellery shows in department stores.

The seamless segue between market, media, producer, and retailer was epitomized by the success of one clothing manufacturer. Recognizing that 25 per cent of its "junior" dresses were marketed in special youth sections of department stores, this New York firm adopted the name Teen-Timers Inc. in 1943. Its first lines, called "OHriginals", were heavily cross-marketed: clubs were formed in Teen-Timers retailers for high school girls to stage fashion shows and advise on current youth styles. The company's monthly sales nearly quadrupled over the next three years.

This new teen arena "brought public attention down from debutantes and college girls" to the high school cohort. Helen Valentine actively chased this democratically richer market, commissioning a well-known firm, Benson and Benson, to conduct pioneering demographic research. Published in a pamphlet called *Life with Teena*, the conclusions were crystal clear: "Teena . . . has money of her own to spend . . . and what her allowance and pin-money won't buy, her parents can be counted on to supply. For our girl Teena won't take no for an answer when she sees what she wants in *Seventeen*."

Using this everyteen, Valentine and her promotional director, Estelle Ellis, were able to talk up the vanguard spending power of adolescence to the right parties. As the pamphlet advised, Teena could be counted on "to convince her parents she needs a new hat, a new dress, a complete spring wardrobe—before anyone else in her family. Watch her go into the nation's stores surrounded by her friends . . . Hear her tell the saleslady exactly what she wants. Suspect her influence when father says she's old enough for black, mother says she's big enough to shop on her own."

Discovering that Teena was extremely style-conscious, *Seventeen* worked with manufacturers to design fashions that represented her "time of life". Lines like Pert and Pretty Teenage Hats and Hi-Girl Campus Caper Sweaters were sold in special youth sections of department stores, with teenage girls in

an advisory role. At the same time, Valentine and Ellis stressed the peer conformity that powered this market: "Teena and her teenmates come in bunches,
like bananas . . . sell one, and the chances are you'll sell them all." Within a
few months, the magazine was blocked solid with advertisements.[1]

This upsurge of youth consciousness was ameliorist. *Seventeen* was, after
all, a mass-market publication. It offered some recognition of everyday problems in features like "Ugly Ducking—Don't Despair". However, the message
that youth was full of possibility and hope fuelled its target market's self-
esteem and self-awareness. As one correspondent attested, "I love being seventeen. Wish I could stay just this age for a while. Seventeen is the perfect spot
between that strange state called adolescence, which means you are going
somewhere, and adulthood, which means that you are on the downgrade."

. . .

At the very moment that *Seventeen* was launched and Sinatra became a national figure, the age that they brought to public prominence found its definitive terminology. The increasing importance of youth demanded a new name.
That America had a unique way of organizing its adolescents had already been
recognized by the sociologist Talcott Parsons. In an October 1942 article titled
"Age and Sex in the Social Structure of the United States", he coined the term
"youth culture" to describe the particular "set of patterns and behavior phenomena" that was unique to American society.

Admitting that "a tendency to the romantic idealization of youth patterns
seems in different ways to be characteristic of Western society as a whole",
Parsons contrasted German and American adolescence. Compared to the
"comradeship" of the *Wandervogel,* he found that "in the American youth culture and its adult romanticization a much stronger emphasis has been placed
on the cross-sex relationship. It would seem that this fact, with the structural
factors which underlie it, have much to do with the failure of the youth culture
to develop any political significance in this country."

However, the "comradeship" of the *Wandervogel* had prepared German
youth for their enslavement in the Hitler Youth. Parsons observed that, in

1. In one sample issue from spring 1945, there were advertisements for Neiman Marcus's "Teen-
Age Shop"; Elgin American cigarette cases and compacts; 7-Up; "April Showers—The Fragrance
of Youth" by Cheramy; Minx Modes Dresses at Filene's of Boston; Junior Clique Frocks; Flexnit
Foundations—girdles, panties, and corsets; Jantzen swimming costumes; Swan soap; Coca-Cola;
Schiaparelli nail polish; Keepsake engagement rings; and Medicated Noxzema for those "Skin
Problems".

America, "at the line between childhood and adolescence, 'growing up' consists precisely in the ability to participate in youth culture patterns, which are not for either sex, the same as the adult patterns practiced by the parental generation." He felt that American youth culture was "irresponsible. One of its dominant notes is 'having a good time' in relation to which there is a particularly strong emphasis on social activities with the opposite sex."

Parsons's coinage confirmed the fact that, by the early 1940s, American adolescents had succeeded in creating a world quite distinct from both adults and children. Despite its apparent lack of politics, it had been considerably affected by war's upheavals and its patriotic rhetoric of emancipation. Already defined as an ideal and a market, adolescents had begun publicly to assert their independence, a development that had caught government and industry by surprise. At the same time, their upbeat culture was beginning to spread through the youth of war-torn Britain and northern Europe.

During 1944, the words "teenage" and "teenager" became the accepted way to describe this new definition of youth as a discrete, mass market. Teenagers were neither adolescents nor juvenile delinquents. Consumerism offered the perfect counterbalance to riot and rebellion: it was the American way of harmlessly diverting youth's disruptive energies. Of the existing terms, "adolescent" was a forty-year-old coinage. The term "sub-deb" smacked of class distinction and was on the point of obsolescence, while the word "bobby-soxer" was too identified with a musical style, swing, that was passing.

The term's origin lay in the inflected form of "ten" that, according to the *Concise Oxford Dictionary*, was "added to the numerals 3 to 9 to form the names of those from 13 to 19". From Tarkington to Daly and the magazine itself, *Seventeen* had long been the apotheosized adolescent age: old enough for self-determination yet still not adult. The suffix "teen" had also had a long life, occurring in *Adolescence* and in the 1920s with *Harold Teen*. "Teenage" had been freely used after the mid-1930s, often hyphenated as "teen-age", while attempts to promote clunky alternatives like "teener" and "teenster" had failed.

Teenage it was, then. The general take-up of the term marked the full introduction of a concept as utopian as Stanley Hall's adolescence. The changes within America had borne out Hall's prophecy of a hiatus between childhood and adulthood: already institutionally recognized, this liminal state was, during 1943 and 1944, harnessed to quick-turnover mass production. Naming something helps to bring it into being: assumed both by youth marketers and youth itself, the Teenage was clear, simple, and said what it meant. This was the Age—the distinct social, cultural, and economic period—of the Teen.

CHAPTER 30

Year Zero

The Teenager Triumphant

• • •

We are the generation without ties and without depth. Our depth is the abyss.
We are the generation without happiness, without home and without farewell.
Our sun is narrow, our love cruel and our youth is without youth.

—Wolfgang Borchert, "On the Move: Generation Without Farewell" (1945)

AMERICAN TEENAGERS IN A RECORD STORE IN WEST GROVE, MISSISSIPPI, 1944,
PHOTOGRAPH BY NINA LEEN

IN THE FIRST WEEK of January 1945, the *New York Times Magazine* published "A Teen-Age Bill of Rights", the result of a study proposed by the Jewish Board of Guardians in New York. The proposer, Elliot E. Cohen, thought that "in the current debate about 'teen-agers', the pendulum has swung between 'What is wrong with our children?' and 'What is wrong with us?'" Aiming to enlighten bewildered parents and leading with the brand-new buzzword, his "ten point charter framed to meet the problems of growing youth" ratified the new Teen Age with bold headings that deliberately invoked the American Constitution:

I   THE RIGHT TO LET CHILDHOOD BE FORGOTTEN.
II   THE RIGHT TO A "SAY" ABOUT HIS OWN LIFE.
III   THE RIGHT TO MAKE MISTAKES, TO FIND OUT FOR ONESELF.
IV   THE RIGHT TO HAVE RULES EXPLAINED, NOT IMPOSED.
V   THE RIGHT TO HAVE FUN AND COMPANIONS.
VI   THE RIGHT TO QUESTION IDEAS.
VII   THE RIGHT TO BE AT THE ROMANTIC AGE.
VIII   THE RIGHT TO A FAIR CHANCE AND OPPORTUNITY.
IX   THE RIGHT TO STRUGGLE TOWARD HIS OWN PHILOSOPHY OF LIFE.
X   THE RIGHT TO PROFESSIONAL HELP WHENEVER NECESSARY.

These Teen Commandments were a manifesto for the new youth world. They flatly demanded that parents took pains to see their children's point of view. Some appeared to insist that teenagers were equal to adults: the right to professional help, the right to a "say" about one's own life, "the right to question ideas". But most of all, the Teen Age was seen as a journey towards "a philosophy of life": "Each generation feels that it is the future," the article concluded. "To the 'teen-ager' nothing is more important to find out where he fits in relation to life around him. It is a serious quest, often a painful one."

This Bill of Rights assumed teenagers were part of the mainstream of American life. They had achieved this position not just because of their purchasing power but because they appeared to epitomize America's democratic ideals: "The teenager wants opportunities, in education and vocation, and he wants to be able to compete for them, regardless of sex, race, color or creed." This zeal reflected the agitation of the other groups for whom the war had opened doors formerly bolted shut: the working women, Negroes, and Mexican Americans.

That had been the explicit contract under which the war was fought. Despite lacking any class basis except the accident of common age, American teenagers were encouraged to see themselves as part of this emancipation. As Barbara Gair wrote in the February 1945 issue of *Seventeen*, the Declaration of Independence "says that all people—not only the rich, or the highly cultured, or the aristocratic—but *all* people have the right to 'life, liberty and the pursuit of happiness'". With American soldiers so near victory, the possibilities for the further development of democracy were "infinite".

Racial prejudice was explicitly targeted in the emerging Teen Age. The alternative, as the Teen-Age Bill of Rights warned, was a recurrence of the "deep" frustrations that had exploded in 1943. After reading Gunnar Myrdal's exposé of American racism, *An American Dilemma*, Frank Sinatra appeared in *The House I Live In*, a short film promoting racial tolerance. "I'll never forget how it hurt when the kids called me 'dago' when I was a boy," he stated. "It's a scar that has lasted quite a long time and which I have never quite forgotten."

Another 1945 short, Warner Brothers' *It Happened in Springfield*, dramatized an early attempt at integrated schooling in Massachusetts. *Seventeen* reported that "Anti-Semitism and Anti-Negroism have been labelled for what they are—a menace to America and all that our country stands for. The secret of the Springfield plan is its recognition that learning to live together successfully is a habit that can't start too early in life. In the Springfield schools even the youngest children are made aware of the truth that there can be no real democracy if there is suspicion and distrust between neighbors."

Seventeen also published a story about anti-Semitic prejudice, "The Way the World Ends" by Anne Clark, that was enthusiastically received by its readers. "No story I have ever read or ever will read will stick with me and do me as much good as this one," wrote "J.K." from Cincinnati. For "C.H.P." from New York, it was "unfortunate" that there were "people here who call themselves one hundred per cent Americans but who have swallowed the completely unscientific racial prejudices invented by Hitler's soothsayers and cultivated here by native fascists!"

Much of this rhetoric could have come straight from Anne Frank's diary. However, despite the optimism of the New World, the war was not yet over. An ocean separated Anne Frank from the Jewish teenagers who proposed the Teen-Age Bill of Rights, but it might as well have been several thousand years. The forward-looking teenager who had written only a few months before, "I am afraid of prison cells and concentration camps," was forced to live through her worst fears, in conditions of barbaric brutality.

In the week that the Teen-Age Bill of Rights was published, Frank was incarcerated in Bergen-Belsen extermination camp, where she had no name, no clothes, no food, no youth, and no hope. Belsen had become the dumping ground for sick prisoners from other Nazi camps: it was awash with the excreta of human beings dying from typhus, tuberculosis, and diarrhoea. Arriving within this "disorganised hell" during the November ice, all Anne Frank had was her sister Margot: "The two were inseparable," another inmate remembered, "they looked like two frozen birds."

The hammer had fallen on August 4, when the Gestapo stormed into the Annexe after a tip-off. In the chaos of the arrest, Anne's diary pages were strewn across the floor: one of the family's Dutch helpers, Miep Gies, salvaged the notebook and a few of her possessions. The eight were quickly transferred to the holding camp at Westerbork, a journey that offered them a momentary release. As Otto later remembered, "It was summer. Meadows, stubble fields and villages flew by. The telephone wires along the right of way, curvetted up and down along the windows. Like freedom."

At Westerbork it was possible to have some semblance of a normal life. An acquaintance named Rootje de Winter recognized the family: "I did speak to Anne, and to Margot, but I did not want to become real friends. That was a form of self-preservation I had learned. You never knew what was coming next." Though anxious, the eight were still together, and remained so on the last train out to Auschwitz. This journey, in a bare cattle truck, was not so benign: the Franks were jammed against fellow prisoners suffering with dysentery.

After three days, the train arrived at Auschwitz: as an inmate later recalled, "It was so insane—that moment of realization, 'Yes, this is an extermination camp.' It was dreadful . . . the horrible effect of that very bright, dirty looking neon light, a bluish light, and that grey sky above." They had entered a world "created and governed according to the principles of absolute evil. Its only function was death." The prisoners were immediately separated: Otto Frank later stated that he would "remember the look in Margot's eyes all my life".

The women attempted to survive by sticking together. A fellow inmate observed that "they gave each other a great deal of support. All the things that a teenager might think of her mother were no longer of any significance." Anne herself was "very calm and quiet and somewhat withdrawn. The fact that they had ended up there had affected her profoundly—that was obvious." A couple of months after their arrival, they had the chance to go to work in a forced-labour factory, but Edith and Margot refused to leave Anne, who had scabies.

Shortly afterwards, the sisters were put up for selection in front of the notorious Dr Mengele: "fifteen and eighteen years old, thin, naked but proud, approaching the selection table with the SS men . . . Anne encouraged Margot, and Margot walked erect into the light. There they stood for a moment, naked and shaven-headed, and Anne looked over at us with her unclouded face, looked straight and stood straight." They were sent the next day to Bergen-Belsen: inconsolable, Edith died weeks later. When Otto Frank was liberated in January, his two children awaited death several hundred miles away.

Convinced that their parents were dead, the sisters gave up. After Margot died from dysentery, Anne developed typhus, which was endemic in Bergen-Belsen. Another inmate's final encounter with Anne revealed her wrapped in a blanket: "She told me that she had such a horror of the lice and fleas in her clothes that she had thrown all of her clothes away." Still unaware that her father was alive, Anne felt totally alone, and towards the end of March 1945, she died alone. She was buried in an unmarked grave.

By that time, it was obvious that the Germans had lost the war. The seat of Nazi power, Berlin, suffered almost non-stop bombing. Nothing worked anymore. After her parents died in a raid, Melita Maschmann lost hope. "I understood, though indeed barely consciously, that this terrible mass death could no longer be regarded as a meaningful sacrifice. Something senseless was happening, not merely that—something insane. Surely now the worst was bound to happen, which would prevent a recovery. But what could this worst be?"

The once continent-wide Greater Reich had shrunk to a slice of land between the Rhine and the Oder. The rapid Russian advance trapped half a million adolescents evacuated to the *Kinderlandverschickung* in the "safe" east. Into this "vortex of disaster", Axmann and Himmler poured a "third wave" of seventeen-year-olds as an "iron reserve". They faced a Red Army consumed by hatred for the brutal invaders. The eastern front had always been the most bitter theatre of war, but the gang rapes and murders that occurred in the winter of 1944–45 sent 8.5 million Germans fleeing west.

By this stage, the Hitler Youth infrastructure had disappeared. In early 1945, SS recruitment tsar Gottlob Berger was authorized to call up one-fifth of the seventeen-to-eighteen cohort. During the next few months, 150,000 adolescents were pressed into SS service. After the rest were recruited into the Volkssturm, normal life for Germany's adolescents was suspended as they were dressed in ill-fitting uniforms and sent into combat with their *Panzerfausts*—crude anti-tank weapons. With conscripts as young as twelve, this children's crusade marked the ultimate "barbarization of warfare" under the Nazi regime.

In the first week of March, the Rhine was breached at Remagen: of the Nazi force attempting to hold the bridge, at least 20 per cent were adolescents. On the twenty-eighth, Hitler Youth leader Artur Axmann declared that "from the Hitler Youth has emerged a movement of young tank-busters". He told his adolescent charges that "there is only victory or annihilation. Know no bounds in your love to your people; equally, know no bounds in your hatred of the enemy. It is your duty to watch when others are tired; to stand when others weaken. Your greatest honour, however, is your unshakeable faithfulness to Adolf Hitler."

These child soldiers were completely fanatical. Melita Maschmann recalled that "for them the call to the 'ultimate sacrifice' was no empty phrase. It went straight to their hearts and they felt now that their hour had come, the moment when they really counted and were no longer dismissed because they were still too young. They shovelled away day and night on the East wall or the West wall—the system of earthworks and tank traps which was built along all the frontiers during the last few months. They looked after refugees, they helped the wounded. Finally they went in."

The fighting was without quarter. At the end of March, a nineteen-year-old tank gunner, John P. Irwin, was advancing through the Ruhr Valley when he encountered a twelve-year-old running towards his tank with a *Panzerfaust*. Forced to shoot the boy "quite deads", he felt nothing but "relief". Entering Germany in early April 1945, a Free French doctor attended a fourteen-year-old boy with multiple shrapnel wounds: "I leaned over him and said in German, 'You dummy! Look at what this has gotten you!' Well that boy suddenly heaved himself up, spat in my face, and shouted, 'Long Live the *Führer!*'"

The advancing Allies uncovered the regime's horrific secrets. John Irwin's regiment liberated a forced-labour camp at Nordhausen in the Ruhr, where they found "fourteen-year-old boys and men aged beyond their years and dying of tuberculosis, dysentery and starvation". Irwin was amazed at the guards: he had expected "twisted, ugly, vicious countenances but saw instead only handsome, unrepentant young men". His world was turned upside down: "World War II was in black and white with shades of gray—no trace of the Technicolor that transformed Dorothy's movie-Kansas into Oz."

In early April, Artur Axmann authorized 4,000 boys to act as tank-destroyer troops. These were pledged to the final defence of Berlin, an act that appalled the battle-hardened Wehrmacht general Wiedling. A week after the final Berlin Philharmonic performance—at the end of which young ushers offered cyanide capsules to the audience—Melita Maschmann attended the final induction of ten-year-old boys and girls into the Hitler Youth. "While the distant thunder of battle could be heard in the eastern suburbs," she wrote, Axmann "called upon his 'youngest comrades' to fight for the victory of Greater Germany."

The next day was Hitler's fifty-sixth birthday. As the Allies encircled Berlin, the crippled Führer made his last public appearance, reviewing a line of Hitler Youth decorated for attacking Soviet tanks. Many of these twelve-year-olds were subsequently thrown to the flames. But then Hitler had never shirked from sacrificing his subjects. His madness arose from a hypertrophied identification between himself and his people. If he was going to die, then Germany would die, and pride of place would be given to the beloved youngsters who had formed the basis of his rise to power.

With Hitler's words ringing in their ears—"I am convinced that we shall be victorious in the struggle above all because of German youth, and in particular because of you, my boys"—the last few thousand Hitler Youth were committed to the defence of Berlin. "They burned with the desire to prove themselves as soldiers," Maschmann wrote; "they wanted to stand by the promises made in their songs. But I dread to think what despair and misery must have overcome them as they saw their comrades bleeding to death beside them and when their own intoxication gave way to sober consciousness."

The cynicism of the Nazi Youth leadership was beyond bounds. Artur Axmann fled to the Bavarian Alps on the first of May. The previous day, Hitler had committed suicide. But their brainwashed youth fought on until the final German surrender on May 7. A Silesian Hitler Youth leader remembered that his group of children "died in atrocious agony. . . . They believed in their fatherland, remained faithful to him whom they called Führer; they carried his name in their hearts. . . . And he who gave them his name and promised that the future was theirs, he has long since betrayed them."

The Nazis had bewitched, trained, and finally sacrificed their youth. As one German girl later explained, "We believed in Hitler. We believed in the whole system, the entire leadership. There we were, already half-dead, still believing in victory. We could not do anything else. That was our generation and he was our idol." The last Hitler Youth cohort were "hard on the outside, hard in heart and thought": "There existed for them only shortage and deprivation, the rationing of foodstuffs, of clothes, and all the little things which children still love even when a hard education has taken from them the fear of death."

For many Hitler Youth, the Führer's suicide and the revelation of Nazi genocide were shattering. One young prisoner was taken to the liberated camp at Dachau: "We entered a hall and, for a moment, we thought we were in a boiler room with a number of big furnaces. That idea was immediately dispelled when we saw before each furnace a stretcher of metal with iron clamps. Some of these were still half-way in the furnace, covered by the remnants of burnt bodies. That night was a sleepless one. The impact of what we had seen was too great to be immediately digested. I could not help but cry."

However, the Nazis had one last trick up their sleeves. At the end of 1944, the SS had created a small but elite organization of 200 or so Hitler Youth, called Werewolves, to act as a guerrilla force in the event of Germany's defeat.

Unable to countenance the collapse of her world, Melita Maschmann joined them in the Bavarian Alps at the end of April: "I sought salvation in the idea that now a new period of illegal activity would begin, although no one knew what its political purpose would be. So we adjusted ourselves to the idea of fighting on. We deliberately overlooked the fact that all was already lost."

In mid-May, she left the Werewolves and wandered alone through the Tyrolean Alps. One day she found herself "watching children at play on the edge of a village. They were throwing a turnip to one another like a ball and shaking with laughter. Suddenly a window in the house behind them opened and I heard, faintly at first, the great *Ricercare* from the *Musical Offering*. As I absorbed the music, along with the scent of the flowering bush and the children's laughter, I felt as if I had awoken from an evil enchantment, in which I had been tormented by terrible phantoms and demons of hell."

· · ·

The German surrender was made official on the afternoon of May 8, 1945. In London, huge crowds went wild in Trafalgar Square, Leicester Square, and Piccadilly Circus. However, in the days that followed, euphoria gave way to several cold realizations. First, the war was not yet over. Although the mainland of Japan had been pulverized by American bombing raids, the Japanese had still not surrendered. The war had destroyed great swaths of Britain's cities, had killed or maimed over half a million people, and had virtually bankrupted the country.

But most of all, it was the Americans who were emerging as the true victors, as their culture and their mass consumption economy began to sweep through Europe in the vacuum left by the collapse of Nazism. Having already conquered the youth of Britain, American GIs performed the same trick throughout Europe. "The G.I. found it easy to establish rapport with people his own age," their historian Lee Kennett wrote, "especially girls, because Hollywood films and American music had preceded him as ambassadors."

This "humanism for millions" offered a future for young Germans living through Götterdämmerung. Teenage culture was inclusive: that spring, the editors of its flagship magazine, having received a glowing testimonial from Australia, had announced themselves "delighted to discover 'Seventeen' has international appeal. It bears out our firm belief that teen-agers the world over have much in common." The snaps taken in occupied Germany by the US Army photographer Tony Vaccaro caught the moment when Coca-Cola replaced the swastika, as young Germans shed *Panzerfausts* for baseball gloves.

Back in the United States, the new era was still being ratified. A June 1945 *New York Times* article, entitled "Teen-Agers Are an American Invention", held that "defining young persons as 'teen-agers', that is, not ready for the serious matters of adulthood, invites their absorption in the frivolous matters of 'teen-age culture', and the leisure and the unprecedented affluence of teenagers predispose them to accept the invitation". A *Life* cover on "Teen-Age Boys" displayed a range of outfits together with an amazing daily diet of that included "soda, ice cream, candy, two bottles of pop, crackers, cereal, fruit, jam, butter".

On July 1, Glenn Miller's AAF Orchestra played in front of 40,000 Allied servicemen at Nuremberg Stadium. This symbolic moment marked a fitting tribute to the most emblematic wartime musician, missing and presumed killed on a flight to Paris during December 1944. Before his death he had made Allied Expeditionary Forces radio shows explicitly aimed at Nazi youth, linking his music with the American democratic ideal. The appearance of this big band at the seat of Hitler's spellbinding power represented the final victory of swing over its mortal Nazi opponents.

Four days after the Nuremberg show, a general election was held in Britain. This was the first opportunity since 1939 that the British had had to vote, and they spurned the man who had led them to victory. When the result was called on July 26, Labour had beaten Churchill's Conservative Party by 393 seats to 213. The deep democratic rhetoric of the previous six years had borne fruit: "Among the servicemen, there was a feeling that they were as good as anybody else, and they wanted the right to tell the officers off when the war was over."

The GIs had played their part in this muted revolution. "The Americans changed England more than the English like to realize and admit," one female enthusiast remembered. When the US armies left for Europe, no one missed them more than the young. For Averil Logan, an adolescent evacuee from London, "It was so drab when they had gone. The whole world had been opened up to me and then it was closed down again. . . . We realized how confining England was, how dull the weather was . . . there always seemed to be clouds on top of my head . . . and the men, how small the gene pool was."

At the end of July, US *Vogue* ran a cover story on "Beauty and the Younger Generation", which stated that "the time is overdue for a teen-age revolution in this country. In America, this generation is something to be reckoned with. Entire magazines are published for its readership; entire shops and departments seek its custom. It has evolved for itself a style as nearly perfect as exists in this imperfect world—successfully avoiding the twin pitfalls of childishness and sophistication." Most of all, it carried "its youth like a banner".

On August 2, authorization was given to use the first atom bomb against Japan. Despite their hopeless situation, the country's leaders refused to surrender: they still had two million combat troops and nine thousand kamikaze planes to pitch into a last-ditch defence. Fearing the suicidal nihilism that had marked the last days of Nazi Germany, President Truman gave the order to drop "Little Boy", a weapon capable of creating "an explosion of gigantic dimensions". Having beaten Germany in the fission race, the Americans were the sole possessors of the most powerful weapon the world had ever seen.

At 8.15 on the morning of August 6, people in Hiroshima watched a single object fall from a high-flying silver fish into the centre of their city. Its impact was instant and devastating beyond human imagination, as a Japanese reporter later testified: "Suddenly a glaring whitish pinkish light appeared in the sky accompanied by an unnatural tremor which was followed almost immediately by a wave of suffocating heat and wind which swept everything in its path. Within a few seconds the thousands of people in the streets and the gardens in the centre of the town were scorched by a wave of searing heat."

Three days later, Nagasaki got the same treatment. The following week, *Time* magazine ran a cover story on the architect of the air force, strategist Major-General Curtis LeMay, whose pugnacious pose was reflected in the coverage of Hiroshima's hecatombs: "Once again, President Truman applied the psychological squeeze on Japan: 'We are now prepared to obliterate more rapidly and completely every productive enterprise the Japanese have above the ground. . . . If they do not now accept our terms, they may expect a rain of ruin from the air, the like of which has never been seen on this earth.'"

In the "Business & Finance" section at the back of the same issue, a small feature celebrated a new kind of market researcher. Unlike the editors of *Seventeen,* this self-made man was still a teenager: "In Chicago, some retailers think they now know that high-school students prefer colored toothpaste, eat three times as many candy bars as their parents, heed Lifebuoy's 'B.O.' slogan oftener than Ivory's 'It Floats'. This and other sales-stimulating information is the merchandise they buy from Chicago's newest pollster: 19-year-old jive-jumping Eugene Gilbert, president of Gil-Bert Teen Age Services."

The Chicago department store Marshall Field employed Gilbert to "learn the clothing preference of 7,700 high-school boys (gabardines & denims, single-breasted suits, two-tone sport coats). Next, the Joseph Shoe Salon, which once employed Gene as a part-time clerk, paid him $500. He found out where bobby-soxers bought their shoes and why. Other firms ordered surveys on chewing gum, cosmetics, perfumed soap. Tall (6ft. 1in.), dark and hefty

(192lb.) Gene learned organization and promotion at Senn High School, running clubs and parties.

"Hep to the kid mind as well as to business," Gilbert decided that "if the advertisers wanted to spend money for the teen-age market, they should know what the kids want." *Time* reported that "for his key workers he appointed the 'Joe Guns' (most popular students) of Chicago high schools as 'research supervisors', gave them 75¢ an hour to poll students. He now has a staff of 350 adolescent aides and a pert, blonde fashion director, 18-year-old Shirley Rappelt." Having just appointed representatives in Indianapolis and New York, Gilbert also had plans for "28 other cities".

On August 14, the Japanese surrendered, and the Second World War was over. Roughly 20 million combatants and 38 million civilians had died, with 11 million murdered—6 million of whom were European Jews—in the German death camps. What was left of European civilization, Lewis H. Lapham wrote, "passed into the American account. The war had also prompted the country to invent a miraculous economic machine that seemed to grant as many wishes as were asked of it. The continental United States had escaped the plague of war, and so it was easy for the heirs to believe that they had been anointed by God."

• • •

Nineteen forty-five was Year Zero, the start of a new era heralded by the revelations of Nazi inhumanity and the unleashing of the ultimate terror weapon. The mass production of arms and commodities had resulted in an acceleration of life. The A-bomb's apocalyptic revelation precipitated a new kind of global consciousness and a new kind of psychology. Faced with the prospect of instant vaporization, many humans began to focus totally on the present, if not the instant. This did not mean that the structures of life altered overnight, more that what people wanted from life began to change.

The new psychology—soon to be culturally interpreted as existentialism—privileged living in the moment and was materially oriented. The old world was dead and the best-placed group to flourish in the uncertain post-war era were the young—who had always been held to embody an auspicious future. "Their lives are lived principally in hope," Aristotle had written, while for Stanley Hall, adolescence was nothing less than "a new birth". In the act of forgetting necessary for the Western world to continue, youth was once again—as it had been after the Great War—exalted as a tabula rasa.

The definitions of youth had gone through many twists and turns since Marie Bashkirtseff and Jesse Pomeroy had surprised and shocked the late nineteenth century. European nations and regimes had tried to organize adolescents for their own ends, efforts that almost always ended in regimentation and militarism—the syndrome that, at its most extreme, had led the Hitler Youth into suicidal fanaticism. Many artists and writers had tried to imagine what youthful independence might be like, while psychologists had made strenuous efforts to map and control this volatile, stressful state.

Thanks to Stanley Hall's pioneering research at the turn of the century, America had led the way both in its youth cultures and in the way that it attempted to include youth within society. It had seen the first mass adolescent consumer culture during the 1920s, and the first governmental attempts, during the 1930s, to treat adolescents in a humane rather than a coercive way. The two approaches had come together during the Second World War, when the demands of the burgeoning youth market were integrated with social policies that offered adolescents some degree of freedom.

The name given to this new synthesis was the Teenager. The many possible interpretations of youth had been boiled down to just one: the adolescent consumer. Coming to prominence through an intricate ecology of peer pressure, individual desires, and savvy marketing, the Teenage resolved the question posed by the war: what kind of mass society will we live in? In contrast to fascism, the American future would be ordered around pleasure and acquisition: the harnessing of mass production to disposable leisure items like magazines, cosmetics, and clothes as well as military hardware.

The Allies won the war at exactly the moment that America's latest product was coming off the production line. Defined during 1944 and 1945, the Teenage had been researched and developed for a good fifty years, the period that marked America's rise to global power. The post-war spread of American values would be spearheaded by the idea of the Teenager. This new type was the ultimate psychic match for the times: living in the now, pleasure-seeking, product-hungry, embodying the new global society where social inclusion was to be granted through purchasing power. The future would be Teenage.

GLADYS PEARL GRANT, 1926

ACKNOWLEDGEMENTS

ALTHOUGH I AM named as the author and the final result is my responsibility, many people have been involved in the making of this book. I would like to thank the following:

For the provision of ideas, information, informed commentary, and rare materials (in alphabetical order): Vince Aletti, Alan Betrock (RIP), Adair Brouwer, Martin Chalmers, Steve Chibnall, Colin Fallows, Simon Frith, Mike Gallagher of Gallagher Collectibles, Paul Gilroy, Philip Hoare, Stephen Humphries, Ian Sinclair, Neil Spencer. Thanks also to Michael Hearn for data on L. Frank Baum and the world of Oz; Sheila Jones at Beaumaris Library for locating several rare books; Mott R. Linn, Coordinator of Archives and Special Collections at the Robert Hutching Goddard Library at Clark University; Dorothy Sheridan and Joy Eldridge at the Mass Observation Archive (the University of Sussex).

For friendship, emotional, and/or practical support (in alphabetical order): Vince Aletti, Nicola Barker, Stuart Baxendale, Ian Birch, Dorothy Bleakley (RIP), Michael Bracewell, Fudge Bradley (RIP), Liz Bradley, Amanda Brown, Peter Brown, Peter Burton, Murray Chalmers, Caroline Cowell, Colin Fallows, Stuart Ferraris, Paul Fletcher, Simon Frith, Laurence and Gabriel Gane, Paul Gilroy, Dave Godin (RIP), Penny Henry, Raymond Hughes, Brian Jackson, Harri Jones, Joanna Laxton, Ged Lynch, Ian MacDonald (RIP), Gillie Mc Ewen, Johnny Marr and Angie Marr, Rhys Mwyn, Renate Noller, Thom Oatman, Patti Palladin, Penny Perrin, Lucy Pilkington, Geoff Powell, Henry Priestman and Jackie Priestman, Gwyndaf Pritchard, Arthur Roberts, Markie Robson-Scott, Peter Rogers, Chris Salewicz, Tracey Scoffield, Neil Spencer, Neil Tennant, Jenny Thomas, Ben Thompson, Paul Tickell, Nest Tomos, Chloe, Mike, and Sarah Walczak, John Wardle, Stuart Williams, Sharon Wilson, Jon Wozencroft.

For commissioning the book way back in the twentieth century: Jonathan Burnham and Wendy Wolf. For picture research, Marshall Walker and Lily Richards. For her book design, Carla Bolte; for the jacket design, Greg Mollica; and for keeping track of it all, Sharon Gonzalez. For doing such a good job on the copyediting, Roland Ottewell, and finally for transcribing and typing under duress, Marc Issue Robinson.

For their assistance, encouragement, criticism, and all their hard work, I would especially like to thank my editors, Wendy Wolf and Jenny Uglow, and my agents, Tony Peake and Ira Silverberg. Your help was invaluable.

Finally, I'd like to mention some of the members of my family who were alive during the period covered by the book: Malcolm James Grant, Dorothy Louise Grant, Joseph Leslie Sage, Margaret Dorothy Sage, Dorothy Bleakley, and the great-aunt whom I never knew, Gladys Pearl Grant. This was your time.

VIRTUE AND VICE, FILM STILL, 1920s

INTRODUCTION

G. Stanley Hall's age definition of "the years between fourteen and twenty-four" occurs in *Adolescence* (London: D. Appleton and Company, 1920), preface, p. xix. The subsequent quotes, "a fiat nation" and "the very fact", come from the same source, p. xvi and p. xvii.

The John Lennon quote, "America used to be the big youth place", comes from *The Beatles Anthology* (London: Cassell & Co., 2000), "John Lennon", p. 10; Dick Hebdige's *Subculture: The Meaning of Style* (London: Methuen, 1979). For details of the shop at 430 Kings Road, see Jon Savage, *England's Dreaming: Anarchy, Sex Pistols, Punk Rock, and Beyond* (London: Faber and Faber, 1991), chapters 1, 5–8, 14, and 20. See also Jane Mulvagh, *Vivienne Westwood: An Unfashionable Life* (London: HarperCollins, 1998), chapter 3, "Prankster Retailing", and chapter 4, "Cartwheeling to Casualty".

J. M. Greenwood's review of *Adolescence* appears in the April 1905 issue of the *Educational Review*, pp. 342–364, "President Hall's Work on Adolescence" (reproduced in the Collected Papers of G. Stanley Hall, Robert Hutching Goddard Library, Clark University, Worcester, Mass.).

1 HEAVEN AND HELL

The extracts from Marie Bashkirtseff's diary come from the latest English translation, *I Am the Most Interesting Book of All*, by Phyllis Howard Kernberger with Katherine Kernberger (Chronicle Books, 1997). This is a well-presented volume that restores all the cuts that Marie's mother made in the original edition. As the first volume, it ends in May 1876. Extra data came from Dormer Creston's *Fountains of Youth: The Life of Marie Bashkirtseff* (New York: Dutton, 1937), including details of Marie's correspondence with Guy de Maupassant.

During recent years, Marie Bashkirtseff has become a feminist icon and many of the search hits on her name follow this line of enquiry. http://perso.wanadoo.fr/marie.bashkirtseff/1GREAT%20BRITAIN. htm offers a good bibliographic résumé, including details of an article by Kabi Hartman that compares the different English translations of the 1887 French edition by Mathilde Blind (1890) and Mary J. Serrano (1891). There are also details of William Gladstone's 1889 review.

Many of Marie Bashkirtseff's pictures were destroyed during the Second World War, but a "virtual gallery" at www.geocities.com/mbashkirtseff contains reproductions and gallery attributions of those that survive—including *Un meeting* and the haunted *Les saintes femmes au tombeau*. Marie was also the subject of a 1935 Austrian film, made in German and directed by Henry Koster: the fortune-teller gets a good billing. In 1999 a British play by Carlo Arditi called *Brief Candle* resumed her life to indifferent notices.

G. Stanley Hall's *Adolescence* (New York: D. Appleton and Company, 1904) contains a detailed résumé of Marie's diary in chapter 8, "Adolescence in Literature, Biography, and History". He considered it "in some sense a feminine counterpart of Rousseau's confessions, but is in some respects a more precious psychological document than any other for the elucidation of the adolescent ferment in an unusually vigorous and gifted soul". He also cites a book by the adolescent Ada Negri, *Fate* (Boston, 1898), which contains a gothic hymn to Marie "in her coffin among worms, her skull grinning and showing its teeth".

In chapter 5, "Juvenile Faults, Immoralities, and Crimes", Stanley Hall also cited Jesse Pomeroy as an outstanding youth type: a "notorious pubescent murderer" who epitomized childish bullying taken to the nth degree. Joseph M. Hawes's *Children in Urban Society: Juvenile Delinquency in Nineteenth-Century America* (New York: Oxford University Press, 1971), chapter 1, "The Awful Tragedy of Jesse Pomeroy," uses the story of Jesse Pomeroy to introduce his subject: how the threat of juvenile delinquency hung heavy over nineteenth-century America and the different approaches that were used to combat this threat. Taking in Hall, Lombroso, Dickens, and Carpenter, this is both a readable and invaluable book.

Hawes is also the source for the dialogue between Pomeroy and James T. Fields (chapter 7, "Ragged Dick and Huck Finn: Juvenile Delinquency and Children's Literature"). The rest of the data comes from Harold Schechter's detailed and well-researched *Fiend: The Shocking True Story of America's Youngest Serial Killer* (New York: Pocket Books, 2000). Schechter carries the story through to Pomeroy's death—still incarcerated—in September 1932. Pomeroy also makes a cameo appearance in Caleb Carr's bestselling 1994 novel *The Alienist*.

A full discussion of pre-1870s youth literature is outside the theme of this book, but the following were useful. Norman Kiell's *The Universal Experience of Adolescence* (Boston: Beacon Press, 1964) arranges quotations and selections from writers as diverse as Aristotle, Jean-Jacques Rousseau, Marie

Bashkirtseff, Goethe, Simone de Beauvoir, and Anne Frank into themed chapters that make a convincing, albeit general and subjective case for adolescence as a physiological as well as a cultural state.

The topic of youth and the Romantics would fill several books, but I have confined myself to the following. I used the 1911 Barbara Foxey translation of Jean-Jacques Rousseau's *Emile* (reprinted by Everyman, London, 1993) and the 1989 Penguin edition of Goethe's *The Sorrows of Young Werther*, translated by Michael Hulse. Both have informative introductions, while the latter remains a founding document of what is now called youth culture: parts of it still read like they were written yesterday.

Richard Holmes's *Coleridge: Early Visions* (London: Hodder and Stoughton, 1989) looks at the Romantic poet in relation to the cross-currents of circa 1780—a revolutionary time and place. Coleridge was inspired by the American Declaration of Independence as well as the French Revolution, and was one of the pioneers of the Romantic youth obsession. Mary Shelley's *Frankenstein* (London: Penguin, 1985) can be understood as a parable about the parent-child relationship as it undergoes the stresses and strains of puberty.

The two-volume *A History of Young People in the West*, edited by Giovanni Levi and Jean-Claude Schmitt (Boston: Harvard University Press, 1997), contains a wealth of data. In volume 2, Michelle Perrot's "Worker Youth: From the Workshop from the Factory" (chapter 4) is excellent on changing work and social patterns in the nineteenth century, while Sergio Luzzato's "Young Rebels and Revolutionaries, 1789–1917" (chapter 6) is a useful summary of revolutionary youth activity from the French Revolution through the Chartists to the Paris Commune and the Nihilists.

Robert Baldick's *The First Bohemian: The Life of Henri Murger* (London: Hamish Hamilton, 1961) tells the story of the struggling Parisian writer whose *Scènes de la vie de Bohème* became a mid-century bestseller. The struggling artist could become a beautiful swan, although not without difficulty. Baldick observes that, a decade before his premature death, Murger glorified material success and turned "his back on Bohemia, heaping scorn and success on those artists and writers who follow their vocation in poverty and obscurity without ever trying to achieve fame".

For those who want to delve further, Simon Schama's *Citizens: A Chronicle of the French Revolution* (London: Penguin, 1989) is a magisterial 900-page overview of 1789 and all that. Subtitled *Russian Radicals and Revolutionaries in the Reign of Alexander II (1855–81)*, Ronald Hingley's *The Nihilists* (London: Weidenfeld and Nicolson, 1967) is a brief but fascinating account of the young group who succeeded in assassinating Tsar Alexander II. For those seeking illumination about the roots of terrorism, as well as a summary of mid-nineteenth-century revolutionary groupings, this is very informative.

Kellow Chesney's *The Victorian Underworld* (London: Pelican, 1972) is a standard text for those who want to understand the disastrous effects of unrestrained urban expansion in the nineteenth century. Chapters like "Gonophs, footpads and the swell mob" examine the youth reality behind Dickens's fiction. Finally, Michael D. Biddiss's *The Age of the Masses: Ideas and Society in Europe Since 1870* (New York: Harper Colophon, 1977) is a definitive exploration of the social, political, and cultural changes undergone by Europe in the late nineteenth and early twentieth centuries.

2 NATIONALISTS AND DECADENTS

The question of youth occupies a small part of W. L. C. von der Goltz's *The Nation in Arms* (London: Hodder and Stoughton, 1906). The phrase "the strength of a nation lies in its youth" was pulled out of context to adorn the punk exploitation shop Boy (King's Road, London, 1977), where it was widely assumed to be a Nazi quote. In fact, von der Goltz's book was influential in Britain as well as in Germany, being published twice during the 1880s and 1890s—not the least because the German theorist pointed out the United Kingdom's strategic deficiencies.

There is a wealth of material on the nineteenth-century British public school. *The Victorian Public School*, ed. Brian Simon and Ian Bradley (London: Gill and Macmillan, 1975), contains eleven essays by a variety of contributors. Particularly useful were Patrick Scott's "The School and the Novel: Tom Brown's Schooldays", Norman Vance's "The Ideal of Manliness", and Geoffrey Best's "Militarism and the Victorian Public School". For more details on Thomas Arnold's educational revolution, see J. B. Hope Simpson, *Rugby Since Arnold* (London: Macmillan, 1967).

After the success of Thomas Hughes's *Tom Brown's Schooldays* (1857), the public school novel became a minor but significant subgenre. Examples include: Dean Farrar, *Eric, Or Little by Little* (1858), Rudyard Kipling, *Stalky & Co.* (1899), and *The Hill* by H. A. Vachell (1906). By the turn of the twentieth century, the pious approach of clergymen like Farrar was being supplanted by the peer bonding in Kipling's novel. The suggestion is that this leads to enlistment rather than any appeals to muscular Christianity.

The attempts to define and control youth during this period are dealt with in John R. Gillis's *Youth and History: Tradition and Change in European Age Relations 1770–Present* (London and New York: Harcourt Brace Jovanovich, 1974). Chapter 3, "Boys Will Be Boys: Discovery of Adolescence 1870–1900", covers the public school system, the German gymnasium, and the Boys' Brigade. It quotes the immortal street chant riposte to a Brigade march: "Here comes the Boys' Brigade / All smovered in marmalade / A Tup'ny-'apenny pill box / And 'arf a yard of braid."

John Springhall's equally thorough *Youth, Empire and Society: British Youth Movements, 1883–1940* (London: Croom Helm, 1977) contains detailed accounts of the institution of the Boys' Brigade and the various religious brigades to the Boy Scouts and beyond. The link between religion and pre-military preparation was explicit. As Boys' Brigade founder Alexander Smith stated in 1887, "by associating Christianity with all that was most noble and manly in a boy's sight, we would be going a long way to disabuse his mind of the idea that there is anything weak or effeminate about Christianity."

Rimbaud has been well served by generations of biographers, each of whom recast this protean youth for their time. They include: *Rimbaud: The Boy and the Poet* by Edgell Rickword (New York and London: Knopf, 1924); *My Poor Arthur* by Elisabeth Hanson (London: Secker and Warburg, 1959); *Somebody Else: Arthur Rimbaud in Africa, 1880–91* by Charles Nichol (London: Vintage, 1998); and *Rimbaud* by Graham Robb (London: Picador, 2001). All have something to recommend them, although the later biographies have more data and more up-to-date research.

Graham Robb's book is particularly clear in its attempts to go beyond the romantic mythologizing that has made Rimbaud the avatar for the century of rebellious youth. As he says in his introduction, "For many readers (including this one), the revelation of Rimbaud's poetry is one of the decisive events of adolescence." However, in constantly accessing "the poet's own savage cynicism", Robb has tried "to allow Rimbaud to grow up". For the poetry, I have used the translations in the Paul Schmidt *Complete Works* (London: Picador, 1988).

For decadence in general, Joris-Karl Huysmans's *Against Nature*, translated by Robert Baldick (London: Penguin, 1959), is still outside time and place. James Laver's biography *The First Decadent* (London: Faber and Faber, 1954) traces Huysmans's inspirations—Edgar Allan Poe, Charles Baudelaire, Rimbaud, and Edmond de Goncourt—as well as fellow decadents like the proto-hippie Joseph Aimé "Sar" Péladan, who, with his long hair and occult incantations, had "sworn to deliver the soul of the world from materialism".

While it concentrates on the visual arts, Philippe Jullian's *Dreamers of Decadence: Symbolist Painters of the 1890's* (New York and London: Praeger, 1971) contains much memorable data about the wilder shores of late nineteenth-century aesthetics. It reproduces many memorable images by painters like Odilon Redon, Gustave Moreau, and Fernand Khnopff, as well as Georges Rochegrosse's *Les derniers jours de Babylone* (now lost except in reproduction). It is also the source of the "hair-raising contributions from fake Rimbauds" quote.

With its thematic bent, Jullian's book ends with a sequence of 114 quotations that encapsulate fin-de-siècle turbulence. One of the most memorable comes from the magazine *Le Decadent* in 1890: "The future belongs to Decadism. Born of the world-weariness of a Schopenhaurian civilisation, the Decadents are not a literary school. Their mission is not to found but to destroy, to demolish the old order and prepare the embryonic elements of the great national literature of the twentieth century."

Other books referred to include: Roger Shattuck's justly celebrated *The Banquet Years: The Origins of the Avant-Garde in France between 1885 and World War 1* (New York: Vintage, 1968); Richard Gilman's *Decadence: The Strange Life of an Epithet* (London: Secker and Warburg, 1979), which shows how late-nineteenth-century aesthetes readily assumed the pejorative name for their activities; and, for apocalypsism right across the spectrum, see *1900: A Fin-de-Siècle Reader*, edited by Mike Jay and Michael Neve (London: Penguin, 1999).

Like Rimbaud, Wilde has become a litmus test for biographers. Richard Ellman's mammoth *Oscar Wilde* (London: Hamish Hamilton, 1987) is a veritable Victorian warehouse of information: a mammoth achievement, albeit light on the subject's homosexuality.

Alan Sinfield's *The Wilde Century* (London: Cassell, 1994) discusses Wilde in terms of nineteenth-century socialist and gender politics as well as Victorian norms, while Elaine Showalter's *Sexual Anarchy* (London: Virago, 1992) amplifies this theme to encompass feminism, androgyny, and contemporary fears of sexual disease. H. Montgomery Hyde's *The Trials of Oscar Wilde* (London: William Hodge, 1948) contains a blow-by-blow account of the three trials, while Michael S. Foldy's *The Trials of Oscar Wilde* (New Haven and London: Yale University Press, 1997) clearly elaborates on what was at stake in the spring of 1895.

"The Star-Child", *The Picture of Dorian Gray*, "The Soul of Man Under Socialism", and "Phrases and Philosophies for the Use of the Young" are collected in *The Complete Works of Oscar Wilde*, introduced by Vyvyan Holland (London: Collins, 1990). The Aubrey Beardsley "rabid puritanism" quote comes from Stanley Weintraub's biography, *Beardsley* (London: Pelican, 1972). For a guide to aestheticism in the fin-de-siècle British capital, including venues, cafés, brothels, etc., see Antony Clayton's *Decadent London* (London: Historical Publications, 2005).

Gustave Le Bon's *The Crowd: A Study of the Popular Mind* (London: Fisher Unwin, 1896) was very influential in its day: it remains intermittently prophetic. Max Nordau's *Degeneration* was sourced from the reprint (Nebraska: Bison Books, 1993) of the 1895 translation, which contains a useful introduction by George L. Mosse. Nordau's epic polemic was "the most sensational attack upon the atmosphere of malaise which seemed to have engulfed so many of that generation". Nordau's comments about Wilde occur in *Degeneration*, book 3, "Ego-mania", chapter 3, "Decadents and Aesthetes". Frank Wedekind's *Spring Awakening* (London: Methuen, 1990, trans. Edward Bond) was indicative of this malaise. Nordau's comments about Wilde occur in *Degeneration*, book 3, "Ego-mania", chapter 3, "Decadents and Aesthetes".

The Albert Mathiez speech is mentioned in Sergio Luzzato's "Young Rebels and Revolutionaries, 1789–1917": Luzzato places it within the context of 1789 revolutionary populism. John Neubauer's *The Fin-de-Siecle Culture of Adolescence* (New Haven and London: Yale University Press, 1992) is an extremely useful account of how European culture was preoccupied with youth at the turn of the century: it discusses, *inter alia*, *Spring Awakening* and Maurice Barrès's *Les déracinés* trilogy.

"Vitaï Lampada" is mentioned in many cultural histories of the Great War, for example, Modris Eksteins's *The Rites of Spring* (London: Black Swan, 1990), chapter 3, "In Flanders Fields". In *A War Imagined: The First World War and English Culture* (London: Bodley Head, 1990), chapter 2, "The Arts Enlist", Samuel Hynes mentions that Newbolt penned the first published war poem in the United Kingdom—called "The Vigil". For the origin of the Sudan conversation, see *My World as in My Time: Memoirs of Henry Newbolt* (London: Faber and Faber, 1932). Newbolt does not mention his most famous poem anywhere in this three-hundred-page book.

3 HOOLIGANS AND APACHES

The recent reprint of Jacob Riis's *How the Other Half Lives* (New York and London: Penguin, 1997) contains an introduction by Luc Sante; Riis's description of the Montgomery Guards comes from chapter 19, "The Harvest of Tares". Herbert Asbury's justly celebrated *The Gangs of New York* (New York: Paragon House, 1990) was first published in 1927, just when the events it was describing were far enough away to seem nostalgic. It remains both intimate and immediate. Luc Sante's *Low Life: Lures and Snares of Old New York* (New York: Farrar, Straus and Giroux, 1991) refashions this protean material from a late-twentieth-century viewpoint. It crackles with ideas and good stories.

Stephen Crane's *Maggie: A Girl of the Streets* is, as Jayne Ann Phillips writes, "an unrelenting explosion": of Bowery dialect, of the brief flower of youth ruined, of rage at a vast, uncontrolled metropolis where unheard-of wealth can coexist with brutal, lethal poverty. The story was so shocking that it took Crane five years to get it published, albeit in a toned-down form. The more common paperback edition currently available (New York: Bantam, 1986) restores Crane's original 1891 manuscript.

Theodore Dreiser's *Sister Carrie* (New York: Bantam, 1992, with an introduction by E. L. Doctorow) justly retains its reputation, remaining vivid and evocative. Moving to a rapidly expanding Chicago in 1889, Carrie Meeber epitomizes a continent and a people in the state of becoming: "The city had laid miles and miles of streets and sewers where, perhaps, one solitary house stood out alone—a pioneer of the populous ways to be. There were regions open to the sweeping winds and rain, which were yet lighted throughout the night with long, blinking lines of gas-lamps, fluttering in the wind."

The Urbanization of America 1860–1915 by Blake McKelvey (New Brunswick, NJ: Rutgers University Press, 1963) gives the sweep of America's urban growth. Michael Lesy's memorable *Wisconsin Death Trip* (New York: Pantheon, 1977) makes it clear what was involved in this migration: "The people who left the land came to the cities not to get jobs but to be free from them, not to get work but to be entertained, not to be masters but to be charges. They followed yellow brick roads to emerald cities presided over by imaginary wizards who would permit them to live in happy adolescence for the rest of their lives."

Jane Addams collected her impressions and conclusions from her work at the Hull House settlement in *The Spirit of Youth and the City Streets* (New York: Macmillan, 1912). For general information about American life and politics in the 1890s—including the rise of Theodore Roosevelt and the Spanish-American War—see H. W. Brands, *The Reckless Decade* (New York: St Martin's, 1995). For the importance of sport in the American colleges, see E. Anthony Rotundo, *American Manhood* (New York: HarperCollins, 1993), chapter 10: "Passionate Manhood: A Changing Standard of Masculinity".

W. Douglas Morrison's *Juvenile Offenders* (New York: D. Appleton and Company, 1898) is a compendium of the then current thinking on this pressing topic. Geoffrey Pearson's ground-breaking *Hooligan: A History of Respectable Fears* (London: Macmillan, 1983) is mandatory reading for anyone who wishes to research the hooligans and official responses to juvenile delinquency from the mid-nineteenth to the mid-twentieth century: chapter 4, "The Traditional 'Way of Life' ", and chapter 5, "Victorian Boys, We Are Here!" Pearson's source notes and illustrations are particularly thorough and useful.

Stephen Humphries's *Hooligans or Rebels?* (Oxford: Basil Blackwell, 1981) contains vital oral testimony as well as extra source material on the hooligan scandal as well as groups like the scuttlers; see chapter 7, "Street Gangs: Revolt, Rivalry, and Racism". *The Hooligan Nights* was reprinted in the late seventies (Oxford: Oxford University Press, 1979) with an introduction by Benny Green that includes a brief biography of the little-known Clarence Rook. For another late-nineteenth-century juvenile delinquency classic, see *Mord Em'ly* by William Pett Ridge (London: Robin Clark, 1992), the fictional story of Alf's female counterpart.

E. S. Turner's *Boys Will Be Boys* (London: Michael Joseph, 1948) is subtitled "The story of Sweeney Todd, Deadwood Dick, Sexton Blake, Billy Bunter, Dick Barton, et al." and offers a very entertaining résumé of a century of youth magazines. Turner's text is perfectly poised between fandom and amused critique. For more details of the comics of the 1880s and 1890s, *The Penguin Book of Comics*, by George Perry and Alan Aldridge (London: Penguin, 1967) has full-page reproductions of *Ally Sloper's Half Holiday, Comic Cuts, Dan Leno's Comic Journal,* and *Chips*.

The bulk of the Apaches' history comes from the rollicking and lavishly illustrated *Paris gangster: Mecs, macs et micmacs du milieu Parisien* by Claude Dubois (Paris: Editions Parigramme, 2004), chapter 2, "*Les Apaches, pourquoi les Apaches?*" and chapter 4, "*Les hommes*". The recreation of the climactic fight between Menda and Leca—staged for the newspapers—is particularly amusing. Michelle Perrot's detailed delineation of the Apache type comes from her essay "Worker Youth: From the Workshop to the Factory" in Levi and Schmitt, eds, *A History of Young People in the West*, volume 2.

4 "A SUDDEN VISION OF HEAVEN"

As a defining event in American history, the 1893 Expo has created a publishing industry in itself. *City of the Century: The Epic of Chicago and the Making of America* by Ronald Miller (New York: Simon and Schuster, 1997) tells the story of the 1890s boomtown and the fair that it showcased. Arnold Lewis's *An Early Encounter with Tomorrow: Europeans, Chicago's Loop, and the World's Columbian Exposition* (Chicago: University of Illinois Press, 1997) concentrates on Chicago as a futuropolis and European reaction to its synesthesia.

The Helen Keller material comes from her autobiography, *The Story of My Life* (Boston: Dover, 1997): "In the three weeks I spent at the Fair I took a long leap from the little child's interest in fairy tales and toys to the appreciation of the real and the earnest in the workaday world." The Henry Adams quote comes from *The Education of Henry Adams: An Autobiography* (Boston: Houghton Mifflin, 1961). For more details of the exhibition site as a whole, see the maps and photographs provided by the University of Virginia on their Web site at http//:xroads.virginia.edu/~MA96/WCE/introduction.html.

For a distaff view of the Expo, read *The Reason Why the Colored American Is Not in the World's Columbian Exposition* by Ida B. Wells, Frederick Douglass, Irvine Garland Penn, and Ferdinand L. Barnett (Chicago: University of Illinois Press, 1999), originally published in 1893. For a dark-side exploration of the time, see *The Devil in the White City* by Erik Larsen (New York: Random House, 2003), which counterpoints the story of the fair with that of the mass murderer H. H. Holmes, who preyed on the millions attracted to Chicago like moths to a flame.

Among the visitors to the Expo were Stanley Hall, Scott Joplin, and L. Frank Baum. The details of how the fair influenced both Baum and W. W. Denslow are contained in Michael Hearn's lavish and scholarly *The Annotated Wizard of Oz* (New York: W. W. Norton, 2000). Baum's interest in Theosophy is expressed in January 25, 1890, article by him in the *Aberdeen Saturday Pioneer*—kindly furnished by Michael Hearn. I also referred to the second American edition, *The New Wizard of Oz* (Indianapolis: Bobbs-Merrill, 1903).

Sigmund Freud's *The Interpretation of Dreams* is well served by the current British edition (London: Penguin, 1991); it contains a sketch of Freud's life and ideas by James Strachey, as well as Freud's own prefaces to the book's many subsequent editions. Although very long, it is a masterly piece of writing.

Useful background was provided by Morton Hunt, *The Story of Psychology* (New York: Doubleday, 1993), chapter 7, "Explorer of the Depths: Sigmund Freud". For those wishing further elucidation, there is the excellent Freud Museum in London: contact freud@gn.apc.org.

Thorstein Veblen's maximally sarcastic *The Theory of the Leisure Class* (London: Penguin, 1979) is a deserved classic. *The Culture of Consumption: Critical Essays in American History 1880–1980*, edited by Richard Wightman and T. J. Jackson Lears (New York: Pantheon, 1983), contains two crucial essays: Jackson Lears's "From Salvation to Self-Realization: Advertising and the Therapeutic Roots of the Consumer Culture, 1880–1930", and Christopher P. Wilson's "The Rhetoric of Consumption: Mass-Market Magazines and the Demise of the Gentle Reader, 1880–1920".

For the history of snake oil, patent medicines, et al., see Gerald Carson's entertaining and lavishly illustrated *One for a Man, Two for a Horse* (New York: Bramhall House, 1961). *Was There a Pepsi Generation Before Pepsi Discovered It?* by Stanley C. Hollander and Richard Germain (Chicago: NTC Business Books, 1993) offers a résumé of "youth-based segmentation in marketing". Chapter 2, "A History of Marketing to Youth: 1880–1940", is particularly useful. For more material, see Richard S. Tedlow, *The Story of Mass Marketing in America* (New York: Basic Books, 1990).

Charles King's memorable description of the Loop comes from Lewis's *An Early Encounter with Tomorrow*, part 1, "Chicago: Laboratory of the Future", chapter 3, "The Urban Transformation of Time and Tempo". In *Sister Carrie*, chapter 3, "We Question of Fortune, Four-Fifty a Week", Carrie Meeber goes to find work in one of Chicago's department stores. She is dazzled by its scale and the attitude of both the "fine ladies" and the "shop girls": "A flame of envy lighted in her heart. She realized in a dim way how much the city held—wealth, fashion, ease—every adornment for women."

There is a vast reservoir of information about American popular music. Nicholas E. Tawa's *The Way to Tin Pan Alley: American Popular Song 1866–1910* (New York: Schirmer, 1991) is a masterful history of the development of this truly demotic form that examines the constitution of the early American music industry as well as the underlying emotions, desires, and fears that created this huge market. The "assertive, pugnacious democracy" quote and the details of Charles K. Harris's marketing techniques come from this source, chapter 3, "The Publishers of Popular Songs".

Ian Whitcomb's classic *After the Ball: Pop Music from Rag to Rock* (London: Penguin, 1973) remains an excellent and readable introduction to the topic. Those persuaded by his approach will enjoy the double vinyl album of the same name, released on Starline (EMI Records) during 1972. For details of the music industry of the time, and the relevant software formats, Russell Sanjek and David Sanjek's *American Popular Music Business in the 20th Century* is very useful (New York: Oxford University Press, 1991), chapters 1 and 2.

Having been a prophet without honour in his own time and country, Scott Joplin has been the recipient of much attention since the 1970s. In 1970, the musicologist Joshua Rifkin released the bestselling long player *Piano Rags by Scott Joplin*. A couple of years later, there was the first ever full production of Joplin's opera, *Treemonisha*, the plot line of which—the overcoming of superstition in the black American community—was reproduced that same year by Stevie Wonder's chart-topping 45 "Superstition". Through a complicated chain of circumstances, a Joplin rag called "The Entertainer" was used in 1973 as the title theme music for George Roy Hill's film *The Sting*.

The success of this Academy Award-winning movie helped to turn Joplin's rags into a pop fad. Scholarly works like Peter Gammond's *Scott Joplin and the Ragtime Era* (London: Abacus, 1975) and Edward A. Berlin's *King of Ragtime: Scott Joplin and His Era* (New York: Oxford University Press, 1994) are a product of this deserved revival. Berlin is the source of the quote about Joplin playing at a white party (chapter 7, "A Guest of Honor"). For the hysterical reaction against ragtime, see Berlin, chapter 6, "The King of Ragtime Writers, 1901–1902".

They All Played Ragtime by Rudi Blesh and Harriet Janis (New York: Knopf, 1950) was for many years the standard text and remains a mine of information. In the same way, although Blesh's *Shining Trumpets: The History of Jazz* (London: Cassell, 1955) has been superseded—and indeed, remains highly contentious on the topic of white jazz musicians—it was a ground-breaking document. Blesh was close enough to the original events to carry out the research on which successive generations of music historians have built.

For the stories of individual New Orleans musicians, Donald M. Marquis's *In Search of Buddy Bolden: First Man of Jazz* (New Orleans: Louisana State University Press, 1978) tells the short and sad story of the unrecorded jazz pioneer, who was consigned to a segregated mental hospital in 1907. Bolden's forte number was called "Funky Butt". James Lincoln Collier's *Louis Armstrong* (London: Michael Joseph, 1984) is thorough and excellent on context, what he calls the New Orleans "philosophy of *carpe diem*".

Two autobiographies: Louis Armstrong's essential *Satchmo: My Life in New Orleans* (London: Ace Books, 1957) has been thoroughly updated by the 1999 Oxford University edition, which contains his manuscript as originally typed. *Mister Jelly Roll* by Alan Lomax (Berkeley: University of California Press, 1973) was redacted from the mammoth interviews that Jelly Roll Morton gave to the Library of Congress during 1938. Jazz historians have cast doubt on some of Morton's assertions, but the book is a compulsive read, especially on his youthful travels.

Immigrant statistics come from Blake McKelvey, *The Urbanization of America*, cited above. The Addams quotes are from *The Spirit of Youth and the City Streets*. The Hudson Dusters are cited in Asbury, *The Gangs of New York*, chapter 12, "Kingdoms of the Gangs", while "Willie the Weeper" is quoted in full in Sante, *Low Life*, part 2, chapter 3, "Hop". Richard Davenport-Hines's *The Pursuit of Oblivion: A Global History of Narcotics 1500–2000* (London: Weidenfeld and Nicolson, 2001) gives a good account of late-nineteenth-century American drug use—including the Ryno's Hay Fever quote, in chapter 6, "Degeneration".

For American bohemianism, see Philip Lindsay, *The Haunted Man: A Portrait of Edgar Allan Poe* (London: Hutchinson, 1953), and *Edgar Allan Poe: His Life and Legacy*, by Jeffrey Meyers (London: John Murray, 1992). For the American impact of Gerald du Maurier's *Trilby* (London: Everyman, 1994), see Sante, *Low Life*, part 4, chapter 3, "Bohemia", and the first chapter of *The Improper Bohemians* by Allen Churchill (London: Cassell, 1961). The latter includes George Sterling's 1904 definition of bohemians "as young, as radical on their outlook on art and life, as unconventional".

5 THE AMERICAN CENTURY

Joseph Hawes devotes two chapters (10 and 12) to the juvenile court in *Children in Urban Society*. Hawes is also the source for the W. T. Stead quote, which comes from his 1894 pamphlet about corruption—spiritual, ecological, and political—in the Windy City: *If Christ Came to Chicago*. Jane Addams's observation about "little girls brought into the juvenile court" comes from *A New Conscience and an Ancient Evil* (New York: Macmillan, 1912).

Stanley Hall's *Adolescence* was first published by D. Appleton and Company of New York in 1904; I have used a reprint from 1920. His papers are held at the Clark University Library at Worcester, Massachusetts. Although none of his working materials for *Adolescence* remains, the library does have copious bound volumes that contain almost all of Hall's major articles between the mid-1890s and his death in 1924. They give a good indication of the progress of his thought.

The earliest age definition of adolescence that I could find comes from item number 118, in volume 7 of Hall's collected works mentioned above: an abstract of an address given to the American Institute of Instruction on July 5, 1898. Another similar set of definitions was given in Santa Rosa, California, at the end of December in the same year (GSH Papers, vol. 8, item 122): this includes his linking of adolescence the state to America the nation. A February 1896 Boston lecture, "Modern Methods in the Study of the Soul" (GSH Papers, vol. 7, item 102), illustrates these ideas in embryo: here Hall describes adolescence as a "kind of physical regeneration".

For Hall's relation to Lombroso and William James, see Hawes's *Children in Urban Society* and Morton Hunt's *The Story of Psychology*. "The study of soul evolution" quote comes from Hall's account of the Child Study movement given to the *Journal of Education* in December 1894: "Practical Child Study" (GSH Papers, vol. 6, item 93). The fullest account of Hall's life and thought, including the influence of Henry Drummond, is given in Dorothy Ross's definitive biography, *G. Stanley Hall: The Psychologist as Prophet* (Chicago: University of Chicago Press, 1972).

The "every child is a little savage" quote comes from "Practical Child Study". Hall's thoughts on Marie Bashkirtseff are contained in *Adolescence*, vol. 1, chapter 8, "Adolescence in Literature, Biography and History". "Note on Early Memories", dating from December 1899, is to be found in Hall's collected papers, vol. 8, item no. 135. The "who has made history" quote comes from a November 1895 article called "Pedagogical Methods in Sunday School Work" (GSH Papers, vol. 6, item 100). The linkage of adolescence and America is contained in "Adolescence" (GSH Papers, vol. 8, item 122).

Hall had pronounced the project finished in an October 1898 lecture called "Initiations into Adolescence" (GSH Papers, vol. 7, item 119), which also contains the "composite photograph" quote. The reminiscence of Hall at the White City, a "diminutive Coney Island near Worcester", comes from an appreciation by A. E. Hamilton in the *American Mercury*, July 1924. The age definition of fourteen to twenty-four occurs in the preface to *Adolescence*, as do "the age of sentiment" and the "sex asserts its mastery" quotes.

"Psychoses and neuroses" is from *Adolescence,* chapter 4, "Diseases of Body and Mind". "We hunger for the maximum of life" is from *Adolescence,* chapter 16, "Intellectual Development and Education". Hall's mention of Jesse Pomeroy and citation of Jacob Riis—"On the East Side of New York"—is contained in *Adolescence,* chapter 5, "Juvenile Crime". His statement that "modern city life . . . is artificial and unnatural for youth" comes from chapter 15, "Social Instincts and Institutions", as does his assertion that the "student must have the freedom to be lazy".

Hall's comments about high schools occur in *Adolescence,* chapter 14, "Intellectual Development and Education". "These years are the best decade in life" occurs in the preface. *Adolescence,* chapter 13, "Savage Pubic Initiations" is the source for the "objective regimen" and the "index of the degree of civilization" quotes. For the sales of *Adolescence,* see the August 17, 1904, letter by David Gibbs (GSH Papers). Hall's recommendation that "youth needs repose" comes from the preface to *Adolescence,* as does his vision of America as a young country: "We shall one day attract the youth of the world."

6 PETER PAN AND THE BOY SCOUTS

The source for J. M. Barrie's relationship with the Llewelyn Davies family is Andrew Birkin's compulsive *J. M. Barrie and the Lost Boys* (London: Constable, 1979). Details about Peter Llewelyn Davies's family history, the *Morgue,* are contained in chapter 6, as well as the source notes. Birkin suggests that the compilation of the *Morgue* was so distressing to Llewelyn Davies that it was "a contributory factor" in his eventual suicide—in 1960, at the age of sixty-three. A typical headline ran: "BARRIE'S PETER PAN KILLED BY A SUBWAY TRAIN".

Peter Llewelyn Davies's account of the summer 1908 meeting with the Highlanders comes from chapter 11 of *J. M. Barrie and the Lost Boys,* as does the quote that begins "lived in the boy world". My main sources for the story of Peter Pan itself are *Peter Pan or The Boy Who Would Not Grow Up* (London: Hodder and Stoughton, 1928), in a uniform edition of Barrie's plays, and Barrie's novelization *Peter and Wendy* (London: Hodder and Stoughton, 1911), adorned with F. D. Bedford's memorable illustrations.

The literary origins of *Peter Pan* are explored in *J. M. Barrie and the Lost Boys,* chapter 5ff. The reaction of Daphne du Maurier and Max Beerbohm is contained in Bruce K. Hanson, *The Peter Pan Chronicles* (New York: Birch Lane Press, 1993), which also contains detailed notes about the original production. The concept of the *Sonnenkind,* the perennially adolescent male child of the sun, comes from chapter 1 of *Children of the Sun: A Narrative of "Decadence" in England after 1918,* by Martin Green (New York: Wideview, 1980).

For the wider implications of Barrie's play, Jacqueline Rose's *The Case of Peter Pan* (London: Macmillan, 1994) considers Peter Pan in relation to psychoanalysis, pantomime, and end of empire. For the mythological and archetypal psychology of Pan the deity, see *Pan and the Nightmare* (Spring Publications, 1979), which contains James Hillman's extended essay on Wilhelm Heinrich Roscher's 1900 discursion on Pan, "Ephialtes". For Peter Pan and androgyny, see Marjorie Garber, *Vested Interests* (London: Penguin, 1993), chapter 7, "Fear of Flying, or Why Is Peter Pan a Woman?"

Baden-Powell's adoration of *Peter Pan* is mentioned in Garber, *Vested Interests,* chapter 7. For more on Baden-Powell, see Piers Brendon, *Eminent Edwardians* (London: Pimlico, 1993). For Baden-Powell as "boy man", see Michael Rosenthal's *The Character Factory: Baden-Powell's Boy Scouts and the Imperatives of Empire* (New York: Pantheon, 1986), introduction, "The Imperilled Island". Baden-Powell's military career, including his role in the relief of Mafeking, is considered in chapter 1, "The Chief Scout".

For imperial propaganda and jingoistic manifestations, see H. E. Marshall *Our Empire Story: Told to Boys and Girls* (London: Thomas Nelson and Sons, 1908); Richard Price, *An Imperial War and the British Working Class* (London: Routledge Kegan Paul, 1972); John R. Gillis, chapter 3, "Boys Will Be Boys", from *Youth and History;* for the Mafeking celebrations and early-twentieth-century public disorder, "mafficking", see chapter 4, *Hooligan,* by Geoffrey Pearson; for details of the invasion scares, see chapter 11, "Britain Invaded", in E. S. Turner, *Boys Will Be Boys.*

For boy experts like Charles Russell and data on the attempted controls on British youth in the early 1900s, see Gillis, *Youth and History,* chapter 3, and Rosenthal, *The Character Factory,* chapter 3, "Working Class Lads and Public School Ideals"—this chapter also mentions Henry Newbolt's ubiquitous "Vitai Lampada". Russell's invaluable *Manchester Boys: Sketches of Manchester Lads at Work and Play* was first published in 1905 but was reprinted with all its illustrations intact in 1984 (Neil Richardson, Manchester).

Chapter 5 of *The Character Factory* is the source for the 1903 Committee on Physical Deterioration: Baden-Powell's Eton College manifesto is reproduced in chapter 2, "Fortifying the Wall of Empire". This chapter follows the story until the first publication of *Scouting for Boys* in 1908. I have used a later edition of Baden-Powell's *Scouting for Boys* (London: Scout Association, 1980). The first issue of the *Magnet* was reprinted in 1965 by Fleetway Publications. For Robert Roberts on the *Magnet*, see *The Classic Slum* (London: Pelican, 1973), chapter 8, "Culture".

7 HIGH SCHOOL FRESHMEN AND FACTORY FODDER

The Randolph Bourne quote comes from Marcia Jacobson, *Being a Boy Again: Autobiography and the American Boy Book*, chapter 1 (Tuscaloosa: University of Alabama Press, 1996). This is an excellent survey of youth literature from Thomas Bailey Aldrich to Booth Tarkington, by way of William Dean Howells and Stephen Crane. A radical and a bohemian who opposed the American entry into the Great War, Bourne died from the Spanish flu epidemic in late 1918. He is a figure deserving deeper study.

America's imperial ambitions and corporatization are covered in H. W. Brands, *The Reckless Decade*, chapter 2, "In Morgan We Trust", and chapter 8, "Democratic Imperialism". Frank Vanderlip is cited by David Nasaw in *Schooled to Order: A Social History of Public Schooling in the United States* (Oxford: Oxford University Press, 1979), chapter 8. Chapter 6 of this clear and invaluable book is the source for the F. H. Briggs quote and the data about the Problem of Youth articles.

For the Stanley Hall quotes "the question in" and "never has even the American boy", see "The Awkward Age" (GSH Papers, vol. 17, item 276). He also contributed the introduction (GSH Papers, vol. 9, item 147) to William Byron Forbush's *The Boy Problem* (Albany, NY: Sabbath Literature Company, 1901). Hall's 1906 interview was given to the *Worcester Telegram* (GSH Papers, vol. 15, item 234e). For "The Feminization of Boys", see GSH Papers, vol. 16, item 260.

For the movement against child labour, see Nasaw, *Schooled to Order*, chapter 7, "The War Against the Wards"; John Spargo, *The Bitter Cry of the Children* (New York: Quadrangle, 1968, with a good introduction by Walter I. Trattiner); and Jane Addams, *The Spirit of Youth and the City Streets*. The move to reform the high schools and the consequent conflict between the vocationalists and the academics is detailed in Nasaw, *Schooled to Order*, chapters 8 and 9.

The Irving King quote comes from *The High School Age* (Indianapolis: Bobbs-Merrill, 1914). King states in his introduction, "There is no season in the life of a boy or a girl which, to parent and teacher, is more interesting and more baffling than are these which we may roughly consider as lying between thirteen and twenty." H. Irving Hancock's *The High School Freshmen* (Philadelphia: Henry Altemus Company, 1910) was subtitled *Dick & Co.'s First Year Pranks and Sports*. It was the first in a long-running series.

For wider context of the boy book, the details of Ernest Thompson Seton's *Two Little Savages*, and the John T. Trowbridge quote, see Jacobson, *Being a Boy Again*, chapter 1. For more material on Seton and the Boy Scouts of America, see Michael Rosenthal, *The Character Factory*, chapter 2. The John Dewey quote, "a sharer or partner", comes from his 1916 book *Democracy and Education*, cited by Nasaw in *Schooled to Order*, chapter 6.

8 *WANDERVOGEL* AND NEO-PAGANS

The Jacques Raverat letter comes from Paul Delany's stimulating survey *The Neo Pagans: Rupert Brooke and the Ordeal of Youth* (New York: Free Press, 1987), chapter 5, "Ten to Three". For the Karen Horney diary entry, see *The Adolescent Diaries of Karen Horney* (New York: Basic Books, 1980), and for more contextual material, see John Neubauer, *The Fin-de-Siecle Culture of Adolescence*, chapter 7, "The Adolescence of Psychoanalysis".

The standard work in English on the *Wandervogel* and other German youth movements is Walter Z. Laqueur's *Young Germany* (London: Routledge and Kegan Paul, 1962). Although a mine of detail, it is as complex and as baffling as its subject. Neubauer's *The Fin-de-Siecle Culture of Adolescence*, chapter 10, "Youth Organizations and Movements" contains much useful data. For the story of Frederick II and the father-son relationship, as well as the background to the popularity of Hölderlin's *Hyperion*, see Peter Gay, *Weimar Culture: The Outsider as Insider* (New York: Harper and Row, 1968), chapter 3, "The Secret Germany: Poetry as Power", and chapter 4, "The Hunger for Wholeness: Trials of Modernity".

For details of the commune at Ascona, see Martin Green, *Mountain of Truth: The Counterculture Begins Ascona, 1900–1920* (Hanover, NH: University Press of New England, 1986)—a great story with some astonishing photographs of the long-haired *Naturmensch* Gusto Graser among others. Hermann Popert's *Helmut Harringa* is mentioned in both *Young Germany* and *The Fin-de-Siecle Culture of Adolescence*. The latter also gives a clear account of Hans Bluher's scandalous *Wandervogel* history.

For the homosexual undertow in German militarism and in the *Wandervogel*, see Robert Musil, *Young Torless* (London, Picador, 1987) and *Homosexuality and Male Bonding in Pre-Nazi Germany*, edited by Harry Oosterhius and Hubert Kennedy (Binghamton, NY: Harrington Park Press, 1991). The latter examines the pioneering gay magazine *Die Eigene*. Elizabeth Busse-Wilson's *Wandervogel* critique can be found in *The Fin-de-Siecle Culture of Adolescence*, chapter 10. Her "masses of uncourted girls" quote is contained in Neubauer's notes for that chapter.

Stanley Houghton's *The Younger Generation* (London: French, 1910) is subtitled "A Comedy for Parents in Three Acts". For material on the suffragettes, see Liz McQuiston, *Suffragettes and She-Devils: Women's Liberation and Beyond* (London: Phaidon Press, 1997), chapter 1. The full invitation to meet in Basle Station, contained in his October 1909 letter to Jacques Raverat, can be found in Christopher Hassall's *Rupert Brooke: A Biography* (London: Faber and Faber, 1964), chapter 6, "The Orchard". This Neo-Pagan neo-manifesto is also discussed in Delany's *The Neo Pagans*, chapter 4, "At Granchester, Where the River Goes".

Delany also covers in detail the early 1912 split between Brooke and his group. *The Neo Pagans* is the source for the "youth is a very deceitful thing" quote, as well as Brooke's statement that he did not "greatly want to live". For Brooke's anguish and confusion about his sexuality, see *inter alia* the account of his seduction of Denham Russell-Smith in *Friends and Apostles: The Correspondence of Rupert Brooke and James Strachey 1905–1914*, edited by Keith Hale (London: Yale University Press, 1998).

9 NICKELODEONS AND ANIMAL DANCES

For details about Buffalo Bill and Edward Sylvester Ellis, see E. S. Turner, *Boys Will Be Boys*, chapter 15, "Wild West". Karl May's stories are mentioned by John Neubauer in *The Fin-de-Siecle Culture of Adolescence*, chapter 5, "Literary Adolescence: An Overview". Charles N. Daniels's "Hiawatha" is cited in Rudi Blesh and Harriet Janis, *They All Played Ragtime*, chapter 6, "An Album of Old Portraits". For Bluher, see Neubauer, *The Fin-de-Siecle Culture of Adolescence*.

Ian Whitcomb's *After the Ball* cites *Hullo Rag-time* as a major event, and highlights J. B. Priestley's reaction. Priestley was shocked into prophecy: "Out of this ragtime came fragmentary outlines of the menace to old Europe, the domination of America, the emergence of Africa, the end of confidence and any feeling of security, the nervous excitement, the frenzy of modern times." Both Rupert Brooke and J. M. Barrie were *Hullo Rag-time* enthusiasts: see Christopher Hassall, *Rupert Brooke*, chapter 10, "Enter Perdita", and Andrew Birkin, *J. M. Barrie and the Lost Boys*, chapter 13.

For American industry, see David A. Hounshell's *From the American System to Mass Production, 1800–1932* (Baltimore: John Hopkins University Press, 1984), in particular its introduction and chapter 6, "The Ford Motor Company and the Rise of Mass Production in America". Porter's comment on *The Great Train Robbery* is quoted in Kevin Brownlow's excellent history of the early movies, *Hollywood: The Pioneers* (London: Collins, 1979), chapter 3.

Several books cover the growth of advertising and its psychological techniques in the early twentieth century: Stuart Ewen's *Captains of Consciousness: Advertising and the Social Roots of the Consumer Culture* (New York: Basic Books, 2001), particularly chapter 2, "Mobilizing the Instincts"; E. S. Turner, *The Shocking History of Advertising!* (London: Michael Joseph, 1952), chapter 6; and Stanley C. Hollander and Richard Germain, *Was There a Pepsi Generation Before Pepsi Discovered It?*

Walter Dill Scott's *The Psychology of Advertising*, 4th edit. (Boston: Small, Maynard and Company, 1912), is a founding statement of intent: the two quotes come from chapter 5, "Human Instincts". Stanley's Hall's lecture "The Budding Girl and the Boy in His Teens" can be found in the GSH Papers, vol. 18, item 287; "Teens and Twenties" comes from the *Woman's Home Companion*, October 1908 (GSH Papers, vol. 17, item 283).

For the full story of the September 1909 lecture series by Freud and Jung at Clark University, see Saul Rosenzweig, *The Historic Expedition to America: Freud, Jung and Hall the King Maker* (St Louis: Rana House, 1994). See also William A. Koelsch, *Incredible Daydream: Freud and Jung at Clark, 1909* (Worcester, MA: Clark University Press, 1984). For Bernays, see his autobiography: *Biography of an Idea: Memoirs of a Public Relations Counsel* (New York: Simon and Schuster, 1965).

David Nasaw's two excellent books on the social history of early-twentieth-century inner-city America are the principal source for adolescent consumerism and the early movies. *Children of the City: At Work and at Play* (New York: Anchor Press, 1985) covers, *inter alia*, the jobs that they took and how they spent their money. Gangs of different ages were empowered by the few cents that they had earned from their work as rag-pickers, junkers, or newsboys to roam the streets and enter restaurants, candy shops, and nickelodeons. The Betty Smith quote is in chapter 7, "The Little Mothers".

Nasaw's *Going Out: The Rise and Fall of Public Amusements* (New York: Basic Books, 1993) covers vaudeville, burlesque, and of course the nickelodeons and early movie houses. He cites Jane Addams's critique of the movies, in particular the "gang instinct" and the "eminent alienist" quotes, which can be found in full within *The Spirit of Youth and the City Streets*, chapter 4, "The House of Dreams". Stanley Hall's "is marked by" comes from *Adolescence*, chapter 4, "Diseases of Body and Mind".

The details of the 1912 botched train robbery come from Brownlow, *Hollywood: The Pioneers*. His subsequent *Behind the Mask of Innocence: Sex, Violence, Crime: Films of Social Conscience in the Silent Era* (Berkeley: University of California Press, 1992) is a mine of information about sensational silent pictures and the attempts to censor them. The details about *Saved by the Juvenile Court, Regeneration*, and *Traffic in Souls* come from this source. For the "Biograph Girl", see Nasaw, *Going Out: The Rise and Fall of Public Amusements*, chapter 14, "Combination Shows, Stars and Features".

Oscar Wilde's "The Star-Child" comes from *The Complete Works of Oscar Wilde*. The material on Theda Bara and Mary Pickford came from Brownlow, *Hollywood: The Pioneers*, chapter 15, "The Cult of Personality". For more on stardom in early Hollywood, see Alexander Walker, *Stardom: The Hollywood Phenomenon* (London: Penguin, 1974), and Kenneth Anger's fascinating and beautifully written *Hollywood Babylon* (San Francisco: Straight Arrow, 1975): never let it be said that Anger lets the facts stand in the way of a good myth.

Parker Tyler's *Chaplin: The Last of the Clowns* (New York: Vanguard Press, 1948) is a typically wayward and penetrating biography by this most underrated of all film writers. Kenneth S. Lynn's thorough *Charlie Chaplin and His Times* (London: Aurum Press, 1998) is the source of the James Agee quote and the phrase the "Mob-God". For *The Last Night of the Barbary Coast*, see Brownlow, *Behind the Mask of Innocence: Sex, Violence, Crime: Films of Social Conscience in the Silent Era*, chapter 2, "Matters of Sex".

Ragtime's spread is covered in Edward A. Berlin's *King of Ragtime: Scott Joplin and His Era*, Ian Whitcomb's *Irving Berlin and Ragtime America* (London: Century, 1987), and Nasaw's *Going Out*. For the animal dances, see Whitcomb, *After the Ball*. Nasaw's *Going Out*, chapter 9, "Laughter and Liberty Galore: Early Twentieth-Century Dance Halls, Ballrooms and Cabarets", is the source for the Ruth True and Julian Street quotes. Hall's "nascency for rhythm" is from *Adolescence*, chapter 2, "Growth of Motor Power and Function".

For the reformers' reaction against ragtime and the dance halls, see Whitcomb, *After the Ball*, Nasaw's *Going Out*, chapter 9, and Berlin's *King of Ragtime*, chapter 5, "The Ragtime Dance". The *Current Opinion* "Sex O'Clock" quote comes from Nasaw, *Children of the City*, chapter 10, "The Children and the Child Savers". For William Healy on dance halls, see *The Individual Delinquent* (Boston: Little, Brown and Company, 1915), chapter 6, "Environment Factors", paragraph 219, "Social Allurements".

For more background with regard to youth, see Lucy Rollin's *Twentieth Century Teen Culture by the Decades: A Reference Guide* (Connecticut: Greenwood Press, 1990), chapter 1, "The Early Decades 1900–1920"—an extremely useful sourcebook. Randolph Bourne's quotes at the beginning and the end of the chapter come from an essay called "Youth and Life" that gave its title to his first book, published by Houghton Mifflin in 1913. It was reprinted in *The Cult of Youth in Middle-Class America*, edited by Richard L. Rapson (Massachusetts: D. C. Heath and Company, 1971).

10 INVOCATION

The Stanley Hall epigraph comes from *Adolescence*, chapter 11, "Adolescent Love". The details of Agathon's *enquête* are contained in Robert Wohl, *The Generation of 1914* (Cambridge, MA: Harvard University Press, 1979), chapter 1, "France: The Young Men of Today". This fascinating and unjustly forgotten book contains a synoptic view of youth extremism and sociology during the 1900s and 1910s in France, Germany, England, Spain, and Italy. The seeds of fascism are to be found here, as well as vital data on the thoughts and deeds of the generation that went to war in 1914.

For more on Péguy and Psichari, see Tim Cross, *The Lost Voices of World War I* (London: Bloomsbury, 1988). Subtitled *An International Anthology of Writers, Poets and Playwrights*, this essential book contains thumbnail sketches of fifty-nine writers from Serbia and Hungary as well as France, Germany, England, and Italy—all of whom died during the First World War. Cross's excellent introduction also includes essays about what he calls "the battle of the generations" and "the lure of politics". For the data on Krishnamurti, see Mary Lutyens, *Life and Death of Krishnamurti* (India: Nesma Books, 1999).

Sigmund Freud coined the term "Oedipus complex" in *The Psychology of Love*, published during 1910. He had already discussed the Oedipus story in *The Interpretation of Dreams*, chapter 5, "The Material and Sources of Dreams: Typical Dreams". For more on Freud and the Oedipus complex, see Morton

Hunt, *The Story of Psychology*, chapter 7, "Explorer of the Depths: Sigmund Freud". The Hans Leybold manifesto, *Revolution*, is contained in Cross, *The Lost Voices of World War I*.

Stanley Hall's observations on religious conversion come from *Adolescence*, chapter 14, "The Adolescent Psychology of Conversion". For a discussion of "generation" as a keyword, see Raymond Williams, *Keywords: A Vocabulary of Culture and Society* (London: Fontana Press, 1988). For the extreme polemics of Giovanni Papini and F. T. Marinetti, see Wohl, *The Generation of 1914*, chapter 5, "Italy: Giovanezza! Giovanezza!"

The manifesto of Die Brücke is contained in Bernard S. Meyers's *Expressionism: A Generation in Revolt* (London: Thames & Hudson, 1963), section 3, "Die Brücke", chapter 12, "The Brücke Group and Followers". For the futurists, see Wohl, *The Generation of 1914*, chapter 5, and Cinzia Sartini Blum, *The Other Modernism: F. T. Marinetti's Futurist Fiction of Power* (Berkeley: University of California Press, 1996). F. T. Marinetti's futurist manifesto is contained in *"The Founding and Manifesto of Futurism"* (trans. R. W. Flint), in Umbro Apollonio, ed., *Futurist Manifestos* (London: Thames and Hudson, 1973).

Wyndham Lewis's account of his confrontation with F. T. Marinetti comes from *Blasting & Bombardiering* (London: Calder and Boyars, 1967), chapter 2, "Mr W. L. as Leader of the 'Great London Vortex' ". Lewis commented that Marinetti "certainly made an extraordinary amount of noise". The first issue of *Blast*, edited by Wyndham Lewis, was reprinted in full, with an introduction, by Black Sparrow Press (Santa Barbara, 1981). For more about vorticism in general, including the work of artists like Christopher Nevinson, Edward Wadsworth, William Roberts, Henri Gaudier-Brzeska, see *Vorticism and Its Allies* (London: Arts Council of Great Britain, 1974).

Le sacre du printemps is dealt with in detail by Modris Ekstein's *Rites of Spring: The Great War and the Birth of the Modern Age* (London: Black Swan, 1989), act 1, chapter 1, "Paris". For more details about Diaghilev and Nijinsky, see Richard Buckle, *Nijinsky* (New York: Simon and Schuster, 1971), chapter 6, "Autumn 1912–September 1913". Buckle quotes the eyewitness Valentin Grosz: "Nothing that has ever been written about the battle of *Le Sacre du Printemps* has given a faint idea of what actually took place. The theatre seemed to be shaken by an earthquake. It seemed to shudder. People shouted insults, howled and whistled, drowning the music."

The climactic *Wandervogel* meeting at the Hohe Meissner is detailed in Walter Z. Laqueur, *Young Germany: A History of the German Youth Movement*, chapter 5, "Metapolitics". See also John Neubauer, *The Fin-de-Siecle Culture of Adolescence*, chapter 10, "Youth Organizations and Movements". Laqueur mentions the Jungdeutschlandbund in *Young Germany*, chapter 8, "Other Youth Movements".

11 SACRIFICE

For Wyndham Lewis's "sluggish electricity", see *Blasting & Bombardiering*, part 2, chapter 4, "The War—Crowds". For the demonstrations in London in August 1914, see Richard Van Emden and Steve Humphries, *All Quiet on the Home Front* (London: Headline, 2003), chapter 1, "A Nation in Arms". For the disturbances in Germany, see Modris Ekstein's *Rites of Spring*, act 1, part 2, "Berlin".

For Vic Cole's story, see Van Emden and Humphries, *All Quiet on the Home Front*, chapter 1. Other accounts of the build-up to war are contained in Martin Gilbert, *The First World War* (London: Harper-Collins, 1994), and Niall Ferguson's revisionist *The Pity of War* (London: Penguin, 1998). Ernest Psichari's quote comes from Tim Cross, *The Lost Voices of World War I*, and the Robert Poustis quote is from Max Arthur, *Forgotten Voices of the Great War* (London: Ebury, 2003), chapter 1, "1914". For Ernst Junger, see *The Storm of Steel* (London: Constable, 1994).

Walter Flex's story is detailed in Cross, *The Lost Voices of World War I*, and in John Neubauer, *The Fin-de-Siecle Culture of Adolescence*, chapter 11, "Adolescence: The Fiction of Reality". For George and Peter Llewelyn Davies, see Andrew Birkin, *J. M. Barrie and the Lost Boys*, chapter 14. For militarism in the British public school and his reaction, see Robert Graves, *Goodbye to All That* (London: Penguin, 1971), chapter 8. For Richard Hawkins on the Boy Scouts' suitability for military service, see Van Emden and Humphries, *All Quiet on the Home Front*, chapter 1. For Baden-Powell on the war, see Michael Rosenthal, *The Character Factory*, chapter 7.

The stories of early recruitment come from Arthur, *Forgotten Voices of the Great War*, chapter 1, and Van Emden and Humphries, *All Quiet on the Home Front*, chapter 1. Robert Roberts's memories about the recruits returning to Salford as new men is contained in *The Classic Slum*, chapter 9, "The Great Release". For the white feathers, see Arthur and Van Emden and Humphries. The Harry Ogle quote comes from Richard Holmes, *Tommy: The British Soldier on the Western Front 1914–1918* (London, HarperCollins, 2004), part 2, "Flesh and Blood", "New Army".

For the reaction against modernism and the enlistment of the arts, see Samuel Hynes, *A War Imagined: The First World War and English Culture* (London: Bodley Head, 1990), part 1, chapters 1, 2, and 3. For Rupert Brooke as establishment icon, see Christopher Hassall, *Rupert Brooke*, chapter 14, "Man into Marble"; Robert Wohl, *The Generation of 1914*, chapter 3, "England: Lost Legions of Youth"; and Tim Cross, *The Lost Voices of World War I*. H. W. Koch's *The Hitler Youth: Origins and Development 1922–1945* (New York: Cooper Square Press, 2000) gives an excellent account of the Langemarck myth in its preface.

Walter Flex's *A Wanderer Between Two Worlds* is cited in Walter Z. Laqueur, *Young Germany*, chapter 5, "Metapolitics"; in Neubauer, *The Fin-de-Siecle Culture of Adolescence*, chapter 10; and in Cross, *The Lost Voices of World War I*. Cross's invaluable book is also the source of the Charles Sorley material. Roland Leighton's description of conditions at the front come from a letter written to Vera Brittain on September 11, 1915; it is contained in *Letters from a Lost Generation*, edited by Alan Bishop (London: Abacus, 1999).

For H. Rex Freston's poems, and Arthur Graeme West's response, see Hynes, *A War Imagined*, part 2, chapter 7, "Descent at the Turn". West's poems are also contained in Cross, *The Lost Voices of World War I*. "A Mother's Answer to a Common Soldier" is reproduced in Graves, *Goodbye to All That*, chapter 21.

For Alec Waugh, see *The Loom of Youth* (London: Cassell and Company, 1928). The answering volume, *A Dream of Youth*, subtitled *An Etonian's reply to* The Loom of Youth, was written by Martin Browne (London: Longmans, Green and Company, 1918). For details of recruitment policy in 1917 and 1918, see Arthur, *Forgotten Voices of the Great War*, and Holmes, *Tommy*. The story of the deserters told by William Holmes comes in Arthur, *Forgotten Voices of the Great War*, chapter 4, "1917". The Charles Carrington quote, "shipwrecked sailors on a raft", comes from the same source.

The Harry Ogle quote comes from Holmes, *Tommy*. The familiar story of Siegfried Sassoon and Wilfred Owen is well told in Hynes, *A War Imagined*, part 3, "Waiting for Daylight", chapter 8, "Dottiville". For Jacques Vaché, see *4 Dada Suicides: Selected Texts of Arthur Cravan, Jacques Rigault, Jean Torma & Jacques Vaché* (London: Atlas, 1995). Fritz von Unruh's banned novel *Way of Sacrifice* is detailed in Wohl, *The Generation of 1914*, chapter 2, "Germany: The Mission of the Younger Generation".

12 THE CLASS OF 1902

The Miles Malleson quote from *Black 'Ell* comes from Samuel Hynes, *A War Imagined*, part 2, "The Turning Point", chapter 7, "Descent at the Turn". Francis Chester's story is contained in *Shot Full: The Autobiography of a Drug Addict* (London: Methuen, 1938), chapter 8, "Fighting for My Country". Stanley Hall's comments about the war come from "Have You Got a Schizophrenia", an article from the *New York Evening World*, July 1916, GSH Papers, vol. 22, item 353b. The quotes about the sound and the psychological impact of shellfire come from Erich Maria Remarque, *All Quiet on the Western Front* (London: Penguin, 1969), chapter 4.

Ben Shephard's *A War of Nerves: Soldiers and Psychiatrists 1914–1994* (London: Jonathan Cape, 2000) is the source for Charles Myers's definition of shell-shock: prologue, "The Shock of the Shell". Chapter 2 of Shephard's book, "Shell-Shock in France", deals with the statistics of this mass "neurasthenia". For the "stiff upper lip", see Richard Van Emden and Steve Humphries, *All Quiet on the Home Front*, chapter 4, "It Is My Painful Duty . . ." For the "overwhelming sexuality" precipitated by the war, see Magnus Hirschfeld's superheated and sensational *The Sexual History of the World War* (New York: Panurge, 1934).

For attitudes against the church, see Van Emden and Humphries, *All Quiet on the Home Front*, chapter 4. For spiritualists, see Robert Graves, *Goodbye to All That*, chapter 21. For more on the relationship of the church and religion to the fighting, see Richard Holmes, *Tommy*, part 6, "Heart and Soul, Man and God". The military casualty figures come from the general histories: Martin Gilbert, *The First World War* and Niall Ferguson, *The Pity of War*.

Ernst Glaeser's unjustly neglected *Class of 1902* (New York: Viking, 1929) is a riveting account of the war from a young adolescent's point of view. For adolescence in wartime Germany, see Roger Chickering, *Imperial Germany and the Great War 1914–1918* (Cambridge, UK: Cambridge University Press, 2004). For the *Lusitania* disturbances in the United Kingdom, see Van Emden and Humphries, *All Quiet on the Home Front*, chapter 3, "The Enemy Within".

The statistics for offences committed by the under-sixteens come from Cecil Leeson, *The Child and the War* (London: Howard Association, 1917), and are reproduced in Van Emden and Humphries, *All*

Quiet on the Home Front, chapter 8, "Toil and Trouble". The latter is also the source for the quote from the police commissioner of London. Chickering is the source for the German juvenile crime statistics, *Imperial Germany and the Great War 1914–1918,* chapter 4, "The War Embraces All: Young and Old". For Sebastian Haffner on the war as a "dark, mysterious game", see *Defying Hitler: A Memoir* (London: Weidenfeld and Nicolson, 2000), prologue.

The activities of the Anderston Redskins and the Manchester Napoo are cited in Van Emden and Humphries, *All Quiet on the Home Front,* chapter 8, and Stephen Humphries, *Hooligans or Rebels?,* chapter 7, "Street Gangs, Revolt, Rivalry and Racism". For juvenile delinquency as "a waste of life", and the subsequent two paragraphs, see Cecil Leeson, *The Child and the War.* DORA's restrictions are mentioned in Van Emden and Humphries, *All Quiet on the Home Front,* chapter 8.

Lord Kitchener's quote that he "didn't approve of women fighting" comes from Van Emden and Humphries, chapter 1, "A Nation in Arms". For the status of women in war, see Vera Brittain, *Testament of Youth* (London: Victor Gollancz, 1933), chapter 3, "Oxford *versus* War"; Hynes, *A War Imagined,* part 1, chapter 3, "The Home-Front Wars", section 4, "The Women's War"; and Van Emden and Humphries, *All Quiet on the Home Front,* chapter 5, "Caring for the Wounded". For greater female independence, see Robert Roberts, *The Classic Slum,* chapter 9, "The Great Release", and Brittain, *Testament of Youth,* chapter 4, "Learning *versus* Life".

For prostitution, see Roberts, *The Classic Slum,* chapter 9, and Leeson, *The Child and the War.* That the behaviour of young women came under greater scrutiny is well covered by Marek Kohn, *Dope Girls: The Birth of the British Drug Underground* (London: Lawrence and Wishart, 1992). For the cocaine scare of 1915 and 1916, see Kohn, *Dope Girls,* chapter 2, "Snow on Their Boots".

For the endless restrictions of DORA and the vigilante moralism of 1918, see Hynes, *A War Imagined,* chapter 11, "The Last of the Home-Front Wars"; Philip Hoare, *Wilde's Last Stand: Decadence, Conspiracy & the First World War* (London: Gerald Duckworth & Co., 1997); Van Emden and Humphries, *All Quiet on the Home Front,* chapter 9, "The Darkness Before the Dawn". "1917 was the year when the twentieth century really began" comes from Roberts, *The Classic Slum,* chapter 9.

There are many Dada histories, but I have used Hans Richter, *Dada: Art and Anti-art* (London: Thames and Hudson, 1978), and Willy Verkauf, *Dada: Monograph of a Movement* (London: Academy Editions, 1975). The following three essays within Verkauf's book are particularly useful: Willy Verkauf, "Dada: Cause and Effect"; Richard Huelsenbeck, "Dada and Existentialism"; and Hans Kreitler, "The Psychology of Dadaism". For reverting back into childhood as a psychological response to the war, see Ben Shephard, *A War of Nerves: Soldiers and Psychiatrists 1914–1994,* chapter 8, "Arguments and Enigmas, 1917–1918". Roberts, *The Classic Slum,* chapter 9, is the source for the "recklessness and indifference" quote.

13 JAZZ BANDS AND DOUGHBOYS

"I don't want to live like an old man" comes from Booth Tarkington, *Seventeen: A Tale of Youth and Summertime and the Baxter Family, Especially William* (New York: Amereon House, n.d.), chapter 18, "The Big Fat Lummox". For Theodore Roosevelt, see Gary Mead, *The Doughboys: America and the First World War* (London: Penguin, 2000), chapter 3, "Easeful Death". For details of the American Field Service experience, see Geoffrey Wolff, *Black Sun: The Brief Transit and Violent Eclipse of Harry Crosby* (New York: Vintage, 1977), chapter 4.

Alan Seeger's quote, "I am glad to be going in the first wave," is reproduced in Mead, *The Doughboys,* chapter 3. Some of Seeger's poetry is also reproduced in Tim Cross, *The Lost Voices of World War I.* For the "fairy scene" from Booth Tarkington, see *Seventeen,* chapter 25, "Youth and Mr Parcher". For details about Tarkington's life and work, see James Woodress, *Booth Tarkington, Gentleman from Indiana* (New York: J. B. Lippincott, 1955), and Keith J. Fennimore, *Booth Tarkington* (New York: Twayne, 1974).

"To the eye of youth" comes from Fennimore, *Booth Tarkington,* chapter 6, "The Juvenile World". For the "roseate gossamer" quote, see Tarkington, *Seventeen,* chapter 17, "Jane's Theory"; for *A Tale of Two Cities,* see Tarkington, *Seventeen,* chapter 20, "Sydney Carton". Sister Jane's comment that William "doesn't like much of anything" comes from Tarkington, *Seventeen,* chapter 28, "Rannie Kirsted"; his father's refusal of the dress suit comes from chapter 23, "Fathers Forget"; and Tarkington's disquisition on the contradictions of adolescence come from chapter 4, "Genesis and Clematis".

Tarkington's polemic against big business is cited by Woodress, *Booth Tarkington, Gentleman from Indiana,* chapter 9, "The Major Phase"; for "the easy-going old days", see Marcia Jacobson, *Being a Boy*

Again, chapter 7, "Booth Tarkington"; for the ambiguous target market of the boy book, see Jacobson, chapter 1, "The Boy Book".

The initial impact of the Original Dixieland Jazz Band is well covered by Arnold Shaw in *The Jazz Age: Popular Music in the 1920s* (New York: Oxford University Press, 1987), chapter 4, "King Oliver, Jelly Roll and Satchmo", and Ian Whitcomb, *Irving Berlin and Ragtime America*, chapter 8, "Mr Jazz Himself". For wider context, see Francis Newton, *The Jazz Scene* (London: Penguin, 1961), Louis Armstrong, *In His Own Words* (New York: Oxford University Press, 1999), and for a detailed deconstruction of "Dixie Jass Band One Step", see Rudi Blesh, *Shining Trumpets: A History of Jazz* (London: Cassell and Company, 1955), chapter 9, "Black and White Rag".

The first recordings of the Dixieland Jazz Band have been released on a CD called *Original Dixieland Jazz Band 1917–1923* (Paris: Jazz Archives, 1995). For the "Untuneful Harmonists" quote, see Whitcomb, *Irving Berlin and Ragtime America*, while the "assassination of melody" quote can be found in www.redhotjazz.com; for the *Variety* quote, see Whitcomb, *Irving Berlin and Ragtime America*.

America's entry into the Great War is covered in Mead, *The Doughboys*, chapter 1, "No More Sleeping Treason". For conscription, see Mead, *The Doughboys*, chapter 4, "Enter the Doughboys", and H. C. Peterson and Gilbert C. Fite, *Opponents of War 1917–1918* (Connecticut: Greenwood, 1986), chapters 1 and 2. Chapter 9 of this fascinating book contains the details of how the American media joined the war effort; for the suppression of anti-war sentiment, see Peterson and Fite, *Opponents of War 1917–1918*; for the *Masses* "ugly mob madness" quote, see Alan Churchill, *The Improper Bohemians*, chapter 5, "Trials and Tribulations". For the repression in America and the East St Louis race riots, see Mead, *The Doughboys*, chapter 18, "The Cost".

Vera Brittain's reaction to her first sight of the doughboys is contained in *Testament of Youth*, chapter 8, "Between the Sandhills and the Sea". For the casualty statistics in the Great War, see Niall Ferguson, *The Pity of War*, and Martin Gilbert, *The First World War*, and data from the Imperial War Museum. For accounts of November 11, 1918, see Robert Graves, *Goodbye to All That*, chapter 25; Samuel Hynes, *A War Imagined*, chapter 13; Philip Hoare, *Wilde's Last Stand*, chapters 9 and 10; and Brittain, *Testament of Youth*, chapter 9, "This Loneliest Hour".

George Grosz's account of German Dada can be found in *A Little Yes and a Big No: The Autobiography of George Grosz* (New York: Dial Press, 1946), chapter 13, "Dadaism". For Sebastian Haffner's "stared into the abyss", see *Defying Hitler*, prologue. For the death of Billie Carleton, see Marek Kohn, *Dope Girls*, chapter 6, "Unholy Rites". For Jacques Vaché, see *4 Dada Suicides*. The *Tatler* quote from January 1919 comes from Kohn, *Dope Girls*, chapter 8, "Cocaine Girls in the West End". For the UK visit of the Original Dixieland Jazz Band, see Jim Godbolt, *A History of Jazz in Britain: 1919–1950* (London: Northway Publications, 2005), chapter 1, "When I Hear That Jazz Band Play".

14 POST-WAR SHOCKS

The chapter epigraph is from A Boy (pseudonym of Aubrey Fowkes), *Eighteen: A Diary of the Teens* (London: Fortune Press, 1947). For General Pershing and the temporary peace, see Gary Mead, *The Doughboys*, chapter 18, "The Cost"; for the immediate aftermath of the war, see Martin Gilbert, *The First World War*, chapters 26–28. Rupert Brooke's deification is well treated by Christopher Hassall, *Rupert Brooke*, chapter 14, "Man into Marble". Lloyd George's quote about the whole world suffering from shell- shock comes from Ben Shephard, *A War of Nerves*, chapter 11, "Will Peace Bring Peace?" This is also the source for the Philip Gibbs's returning veterans quote.

Vera Brittain's "reckless sense" comes from *A Testament of Youth*, chapter 10, "Survivors Not Wanted". For the continuation of war in peace, see Robert Graves, *Goodbye to All That*, chapter 26. The Wyndham Lewis quote comes from *Doom of Youth* (London: Chatto and Windus, 1932), part 1, chapter 5, "Slimming and the Profile of Youth". This extraordinary rant on twenties youthism contains, among the usual bluster, some arguments that are still relevant today. Particularly useful is the "gallery of exhibits" that reproduces many headlines and magazine articles on the topic of youth towards the end of the 1920s. Typical exhibits include articles with titles like "The Revolt of Youth", "Battle of the Generations", and "Youths Who Really Matter".

For the war generation obliterating their memories with obsessive hedonism, see Brittain, *A Testament of Youth*, chapter 10. For the status of the generation who were children and early adolescents during the war, see Ernst Glaeser's *Class of 1902*, passim. The quote about the fathers being "like strangers" comes from the same source, part 2, chapter 5, "Homer and Anna".

For the idea that youth became detached from biology, see Robert Wohl, *Generation of 1914*, chapter 6, "Wanderers Between Two Worlds". For Leslie Paul's "civilisation was about to die", see *Angry Young Man* (London: Faber and Faber, 1951), chapter 3, "O Young Men, O Young Comrades". Philip Gibbs's *The Realities of War* is quoted in Gilbert, *The First World War*, chapter 29; for the original book, see *The Realities of War* (London: Hutchinson, 1923). For the aggression of post-war adolescents in Germany, see Peter Gay, *Weimar Culture*, chapter 5, "The Revolt of the Son: Expressionist Years". For François Mentre's 1920 survey, see Wohl, *Generation of 1914*, chapter 1, "France: The Young Men of Today".

For the conflict of French generations, see Wohl, same source. The Drieu La Rochelle quote comes from *La suite dans les idées* (Paris, 1927). For Breton's *Manifeste cannibale Dada*, see Hans Richter, *Dada: Art and Anti-art*, chapter 6, "Paris Dada 1919–1922". For *Dada prophétie*, see Richter, as above, chapter 6, "Paris Dada 1919–1922"; Envoi. For Raymond Radiguet, see Francis Steegmuller, *Cocteau: A Biography* (Boston: Nonpareil, 1992), chapter 5, "Inventing the '20s", and Raymond Radiguet, *The Devil in the Flesh* (New York: Signet, 1959). For details of other Generation D writers, see Wohl, *Generation of 1914*, chapter 1.

For Philip Gibbs, see *Young Anarchy* (London: Hutchinson, 1926), chapter 4. For the fundamental antagonism between the war generation and the post-war generation, see Brittain, *Testament of Youth*, chapter 10: this is also the source for the war being "demode" quote. For Evelyn Waugh on the "extraordinary boom of youth", see *The Diaries of Evelyn Waugh* (London: Weidenfeld and Nicolson, 1976), diary entry for Saturday, September 25, to Thursday, September 30, 1920. For "a new generation has grown up", see *The Essays, Articles and Reviews of Evelyn Waugh* (London: Penguin, 1986), part 1, "First Steps: 1917–28", "Editorial: The Youngest Generation". J. M. Barrie's notes on "Age & Youth . . ." are contained in Andrew Birkin, *J. M. Barrie and the Lost Boys*, chapter 16, "1917–1921".

For DORA and the post-war crackdowns, see Marek Kohn, *Dope Girls*, chapter 8, "Cocaine Girls in the West End", and Ronald Blythe, *The Age of Illusion: England in the Twenties and Thirties 1919–40* (London: Penguin, 1964), chapter 2, "The Salutary Tale of Jix". For a fictional window into the youthful adherents of revolutionary politics, see Gibbs, *Young Anarchy*. For the League of Nations, see Beverley Nichols, *The Sweet and Twenties* (London: Weidenfeld and Nicolson, 1958), chapter 1. For the Boy Scouts after the war, see John Springhall, *Youth Empire and Society*, and Michael Rosenthal, *The Character Factory*, chapter 8, "Predecessors and Successors": this is also the source for the data on Ernest Westlake's Order of Woodcraft Chivalry.

For Leslie Paul on the Kindred of the Kibbo Kiff, see *Angry Young Man*, chapter 3; this chapter is also the source for Paul's disillusionment with the Kindred of the Kibbo Kiff leader John Hargrave, and the institution of Paul's own group, the Woodcraft Folk. The subsequent quotes come from this chapter. For Weimar and Germany after the war, see John Willett, *The New Sobriety 1917–1933: Art and Politics in the Weimar Period* (London: Thames and Hudson, 1978), chapter 6, "Revolution and the Arts: Germany 1918–1920", and George Grosz, *A Little Yes and a Big No*. For the split in the *Wandervogel*, see Laqueur, *Young Germany*, chapter 11, "1919: Left v. Right". For the Freideutsche Jugend and the meeting at Hofgeismar, see Walter Z. Laqueur, *Young Germany*, chapter 12, "Years of Disillusion", and chapter 13, "The End of the Beginning".

For the reunion at Coburg in 1919 and for the new youth groups that attempted to harness the Freikorps's Brotherhood of Force, see Laqueur, *Young Germany*, chapter 11. A wider examination of the psychology of the Freikorps is given by Klaus Theweleit in his masterful two-volume *Male Fantasies* (Cambridge, UK: Polity Press, 1987 and 1989). For the Neupfadfinder and the White Knights see *Young Germany*, chapter 14: "The White Knights". For the thought and influence of Stefan George, also see Gay, *Weimar Culture*, chapter 3, "The Secret Germany: Poetry as Power".

For Haffner's first sight of the swastika, see *Defying Hitler*, part 1, prologue, chapter 8. For the returning veterans in Italy and the start of fascism, see Wohl, *Generation of 1914*, chapter 5, "Italy: Giovinezza! Giovinezza!" and R. J. B. Bosworth, *Mussolini* (London: Arnold, 2002), chapters 5, 6, and 7. For Haffner on the rampant inflation of 1923, see *Defying Hitler*, part 1, prologue, chapter 10. For Paul on "a new paganism", see *Angry Young Man*, chapter 3.

15 SHEIKS AND SHEBAS

For the Ellen Welles Page quote that makes up the chapter epigraph, go to www.geocities.com/flapper_culture, and hit the link "A Flapper's Appeal to Parents". This page provides a basic introduction to what it calls "Flapper Culture and Style". For F. Scott Fitzgerald's contrast between the "slicker" and the "big man", see *This Side of Paradise* (London: Penguin, 2000), chapter 1, "Amory, Son of Beatrice". The phrase "restless as the devil" comes from *This Side of Paradise*, "Interlude: May 1917–February 1919". Also note Sherwood Anderson, *Winesburg, Ohio* (Minneola, NY: Dover, 1995).

For the generational antagonism within America, John Dos Passos is quoted in Geoffrey Wolff, *Black Sun*, chapter 6. For Walter A. Hafener, see Stanley Hall, Selected Papers, letter of January 16, 1919. For the introduction of Prohibition, see Elizabeth Stevenson, *Babbitts and Bohemians: The American 1920s* (New York: Macmillan, 1967), chapter 4, "The Unresolved Peace: 1919–21"; Edward Behr, *Prohibition: The Thirteen Years That Changed America*, chapter 5, "Prohibition's First Victims", and chapter 6, "America Goes Dry"; and Kenneth Allsop, *The Bootleggers* (London: Arrow, 1970), chapter 1, "The Mud-hole of the Prairies".

For the introduction of the consumer society as national policy, see Robert S. Lynd and Helen Merrell Lynd, *Middletown: A Study in American Culture* (New York: Harcourt, Brace and Company, 1929), chapter 8, "Why Do They Work So Hard?", and Stevenson, *Babbitts and Bohemians: The American 1920s*, chapter 8, "A Sufficient Freedom—1924". For the quotes about youth marketing, and the 1922 *Photoplay* magazine survey, see Stanley C. Hollander and Richard Germain, *Was There a Pepsi Generation Before Pepsi Discovered It?*, chapter 2, "A History of Marketing to Youth, 1880–1940".

For George Babbitt and the "fairy child", see Sinclair Lewis, *Babbitt* (London: Jonathan Cape, 1956), chapter 1. For "your generation is growing hard", see F. Scott Fitzgerald, *This Side of Paradise*, "Interlude: May 1917–February 1919". For "youth is like having a big plate of candy", see *This Side of Paradise*, chapter 5, "The Egotist Becomes a Personage". Rosalind Fuller is quoted in James R. Mellow, *Invented Lives: F. Scott and Zelda Fitzgerald* (New York: Houghton Mifflin, 1985), chapter 2, "Never the Same Love Twice". For the success of *This Side of Paradise*, see the same chapter, and Nancy Milford, *Zelda Fitzgerald: A Biography* (London: Bodley Head, 1970), part 2, chapter 6, "The Twenties". The Zelda Fitzgerald quote cited by Milford, "just a lot of youngness", comes from her novel *Save Me the Waltz*.

Fitzgerald also referred to his early success in two separate essays, "Echoes of the Jazz Age" and "My Lost City", collected in F. Scott Fitzgerald, *The Crack-up, with Other Pieces and Stories* (London: Penguin, 1965). It should also be noted that the title of *This Side of Paradise* was taken from a Rupert Brooke poem titled "Tiare Tahiti". Zelda Fitzgerald's article "Eulogy on the Flapper" is cited in Milford, *Zelda Fitzgerald: A Biography*, chapter 6, and is contained in full in *The Collected Writings of Zelda Fitgerald* (Tuscaloosa: University of Alabama Press, 1997).

For advertisers targeting younger women, see Hollander and Germain, *Was There a Pepsi Generation Before Pepsi Discovered It?*, chapter 2. This chapter is also the source for the "If I were a manufacturer . . ." quote. Hall's article "The Flapper Americana Novissima" was published in the *Atlantic Monthly*, June 1922 (GSH Papers, item 389). For the evolution of the flapper, see Stevenson, *Babbitts and Bohemians*, chapter 6, and Robert Graves and Alan Hodge, *The Long Week-end: The Living Story of the Twenties and Thirties* (London: Penguin, 1971), chapter 3, "Women".

Valentino is well covered by a number of biographies. The most informative is Irving Schulman's *Valentino* (New York: Trident Press, 1967). Michael Morris's *Madame Valentino: The Many Lives of Natasha Rambova* (London: Abbeville Press, 1991) is also useful. Reference has also been made to Alexander Walker, *Stardom: The Hollywood Phenomenon*, chapter 10, "Enter the Great Lover: Valentino"; Norman A. Mackenzie, *The Magic of Rudolph Valentino* (London: Mitre Press, 1974); Kevin Brownlow, *Hollywood: The Pioneers*, chapter 16, "Great Lover of the Silver Screen"; and David Thomson, *A Biographical Dictionary of Film* (New York: Knopf, 1994).

Warner Fabian's *Flaming Youth* (New York: Boni and Liveright, 1923) went to fourteen printings in the first ten months of 1923. The dedication to the "woman of the period" comes from the introductory "A Word From the Writer to The Reader"; "Don't You Wish You Were Young Again?" comes from *Flaming Youth*, chapter 1. For the film version of *Flaming Youth*, see www.geocities.com/flapper_culture. For the Scott Fitzgerald quote "I was the spark", see Brownlow, *Hollywood: The Pioneers*, chapter 15, "Cult of the Personality". For the Bruce Bliven article "Flapper Jane", see Stevenson, *Babbitts and Bohemians: The American 1920s*, chapter 9, "The Evolution of the Flapper".

For the expansion of the American dream economy, see Brownlow, *Hollywood: The Pioneers*, preface; Russell Sanjek and David Sanjek, *American Popular Music Business in the Twentieth Century*, chapter 2, "The Formation of ASCAP and the Diversification of the Radio and Recording Industries". For the flapper "merely applying business methods to being young", see Zelda Fitzgerald, "Eulogy on the Flapper". See also Lucy Rollin, *Twentieth-Century Teen Culture by the Decades: A Reference Guide*, chapter 2, "The 1920s", for the comic strip *Harold Teen*.

The increase in high school enrolment is cited in David Nasaw, *Schooled to Order*, chapter 11, "Between the World Wars: To School or to Work—College for Whom?" Ted Babbitt's extravagant dress is delineated by Sinclair Lewis, *Babbitt*, chapter 2. Lynd and Lynd, *Middletown: A Study in American Culture*, chapter 5, "Who Earns Middletown's Living?", contains much excellent data and source quotes about high school peer culture and parental attitudes to increased adolescent demands. They also include data on "sex adventure magazines" in chapter 17, "Inventions—Making Leisure". For the qualities sought by popular students in high school, see chapter 16, "School 'Life' ". The "education as a symbol" quote comes from the same chapter.

For the increase in university education, see Paula S. Fass, *The Damned and the Beautiful: American Youth in the 1920s* (New York: Oxford University Press, 1977), chapter 2, "The Family Redivivus 1880–1930". The increase in college enrolments in *Middletown* is dealt with in chapter 13, "Who Goes to School?" See also Nasaw, *Schooled to Order*, chapter 11. For the Middletown father complaining about the cost of college, see Lynd and Lynd, *Middletown*, chapter 11, "Childrearing".

The 400 per cent increase in college students between 1890 and 1924 is cited in Hollander and Germain, *Was There a Pepsi Generation Before Pepsi Discovered It?*, chapter 2, "The History of Marketing to Youth, 1880–1940" subsection "The College Market". This is also the source for the college marketing quotes in the next two paragraphs, including the survey of Harvard undergraduate fashion requirements. For more on college fashions, see Fass, *The Damned and the Beautiful*, chapter 5, "Competition and Conformity in the Peer Culture".

The college student taste for hot jazz is detailed in Fass, chapter 7, "Symbols of Liberation", and Richard M. Sudhalter and Philip R. Evans, *Bix: Man and Legend* (London: Quartet, 1974), chapter 8. James T. Farrell's description of the "fake collegian" comes in *The Young Manhood of Studs Lonegan* (New York: Modern Library, 1934), chapter 17. The "You dress your bodies" rant comes from Percy Marks, *The Plastic Age* (New York: Century, 1924), chapter 17. For campus uniformity and the quote "A man can never escape . . . ", see Fass, *The Damned and the Beautiful*, chapter 4, "Work and Play in the Peer Society". For the qualities necessary for popularity, see Fass, chapter 3, "The World of Youth: The Peer Society".

For hazing, see Fass, chapter 4. For the denigration of bookworms and hard-working students, see Fass, chapters 3 and 4. For college student heroes in the 1920s, see Fass's conclusion, "Change and Stability". For the *Ladies' Home Journal* anti-jazz crusade, see Fass, chapter 1, "The Children of Our Discontent". For petting among coeds, see Fass, chapter 7, "Symbols of Liberation". For premarital sex as a powerful taboo, see Lynd and Lynd, *Middletown*, chapter 10, "Marriage". For smut sessions and being a "bad egg", see Marks, *The Plastic Age*, chapter 15. For Prohibition and its disregarding, see Fass, chapter 7.

For Capone's takeover of Cicero, and the phrase "a chilling public display of power", see Stevenson, *Babbitts and Bohemians*, chapter 9, "Evolution of the Flapper, 1920–26". For the details of the Bobby Franks murder and the arrest of Leopold and Loeb, see Hal Higdon, *The Crime of the Century: The Leopold and Loeb Case* (New York: G. P. Putnam & Sons, 1975), part 1. The *Chicago Tribune*'s "diabolical spirit" quote is cited in Higdon, part 2, chapter 11, "Anguish"; Judge Ben Lindsey quote is cited in chapter 15, "Plea"; for the pair as nihilistic film stars, the use of psychologists, and Hearst's offer to Freud, see chapter 13, "Condemnation"; for the psychological assessment of Leopold and Loeb, see chapter 17, "Mitigation"; and for the pair being mobbed by young women as "folk heroes", see chapter 18, "Alienists".

For Clarence Darrow's concluding speech, see Higdon, *The Crime of the Century*, chapter 19, "Showdown", and chapter 20, "ABCD". The full speech is cited in the University of Missouri–Kansas City (UMKC) School of Law, Famous American Trials Web page, written by Douglas O. Linder (http://www.law.umkc.edu/faculty/projects/ftrials/leoploeb/leopold.htm). For Judge Caverly's summing up and consideration of the defendants' age, see Higdon, chapter 21, "Judgement". For more reading, see Maureen McKernan, *The Amazing Crime and Trial of Leopold and Loeb* (New York: Signet, 1957), and Nathan Leopold, *Life + 99 Years* (London: Four Square, 1960).

16 THE CINDERELLA COMPLEX

The epigraph comes from Robert S. Lynd and Helen Merrell Lynd, *Middletown*, chapter 11, "Child Rearing". For the crowd thinking only in images, see Gustave Le Bon, *The Crowd*, chapter 2, "The Sentiment and Morality of Crowds", and chapter 4, "A Religious Shape Assumed by All the Convictions of Crowds".

Karel Čapek's play *R.U.R.* is mentioned in Ethel Mannin, *Young in the Twenties* (London: Hutchinson, 1971), chapter 2, "A View from the Stalls". Yevgeny Zamyatin's novel *We* (London: Penguin, 1972) was the inspiration for both George Orwell's *Nineteen Eighty-Four* and Aldous Huxley's *Brave New World*. For more information, see Zamyatin's book of essays, *A Soviet Heretic* (London: Quartet, 1991). For

Metropolis, see the full script contained in *Metropolis: A Film by Fritz Lang* (London: Lorrimer, 1973): this booklet contains an excellent essay by Paul M. Jensen, "Metropolis: The Film and the Book".

For Henry Ford and mass production, see David A. Hounshell, *From the American System to Mass Production 1800–1932*, chapter 8, "The Ethos of Mass-Production and Its Critics". For Edward Filene, see *Successful Living in This Machine Age* (New York: Simon and Schuster, 1931). For Eros and Thanatos, see Sigmund Freud, *The Ego and the Id* (London: Hogarth Press, 1962). See also Morton Hunt, *The Story of Psychology*, chapter 7, "Explorer of the Depths: Sigmund Freud". For "mass psychology", see Edward Bernays, *Propaganda* (New York: Horace Liveright, 1928), chapter 4, "The Psychology of Public Relations".

For mass production as a more inclusive social revolution, see Filene, *Successful Living in This Machine Age*, chapter 23, "Social Planning". For Bernays on the invisible government, see *Propaganda*, chapter 3, "The New Propagandists". For more information, see also Stuart Ewen, *Captains of Consciousness*, chapter 5, "Consumption and Social Change". For the phrase "radicals in the market", see Stanley C. Hollander and Richard Germain, *Was There a Pepsi Generation Before Pepsi Discovered It?*, chapter 2, "A History of Marketing to Youth". The original quote was given by Albert. T. Poffenberger in *Psychology in Advertising* (New York: A. W. Shaw Co., 1925).

Lynd's data about the fresh value placed on youth—who represented a cheap, strong, and adaptable labour force in the new machine age—is contained in chapter 5 of Lynd and Lynd's *Middletown*, "Who Earns Middletown's Living?" The Filene quote about liberating the masses comes from the introduction to his *Successful Living in This Machine Age*, "A Definition". The delinquent's quote, "make you want things," comes from Alice Miller Mitchell, *Children and Movies* (Chicago: University of Chicago Press, 1929), chapter 13, "Delinquents and Movies".

For Prohibition in general, see Kenneth Allsop, *The Bootleggers*, Edward Behr, *Prohibition: The Thirteen Years That Changed America*, and Elizabeth Stevenson, *Babbitts and Bohemians*, chapter 6, "Harding's Time—1920–23". The quotation about "the typical 1920s criminal" comes from Allsop, *The Bootleggers*, chapter 20, "The Tidelands of City Life". For the relationship between gangsters and business, see Max Lerner, *America as a Civilisation* (London: Jonathan Cape, 1958). Jane Addams is cited in Stevenson, *Babbitts and Bohemians*, chapter 6, "Harding's Time". The James T. Farrell quote comes from the introduction to the Modern Library edition of the *Studs Lonegan* trilogy (New York: Modern Library, 1938).

G. Stanley Hall's "Can the Masses Rule the World?" is contained in his Collected Papers (item 455). The tribute to his passion for "youth, freedom, and new knowledge" comes from a July 1924 article in the *American Journal of Psychology*, "Granville Stanley Hall", by Edmund C. Sanford. For details about the University of Chicago Sociology Department and Nels Anderson's quote "participant observation", see Nels Anderson, *On Hobos and Homelessness* (Chicago: University of Chicago Press, 1998), introduction by Raffaelle Rauty. For the Anderson quote "red-blooded boy", see *On Hobos and Homelessness*, chapter 10, "The Juvenile and the Tramp".

Frederic M. Thrasher's musings on the urban interzone are contained in *The Gang* (Chicago: University of Chicago Press, 1963). The original introduction is now in part 1, "The Natural History of the Gang". The quote about American cities and the instability of youth is contained in chapter 20, "Attacking the Problem", as is his remark that "boys in gangland enjoy an unusual freedom". For "adolescent fancies", see chapter 6, "The Role of the Romantic". For violence and sexual predation in the gang, see chapter 9, "Sex in the Gang". The influence of the movies is tackled in chapter 14, "The Structure of the Gang", and "demoralizing social patterns" comes from chapter 12, "Social Patterns and the Gang".

Thrasher's summary of the adverse impact of bootlegging comes in chapter 18, "The Gang and Organized Crime". For his conclusions, see chapter 20 and chapter 21, "Crime Prevention and the Gang". Also see William Healy and Augusta F. Bronner, *Delinquents and Criminals: Their Making and Unmaking* (New York: Macmillan, 1926), part 4, "Conclusions".

Jack Black's criminal classic *You Can't Win* was first published with an introduction by Robert Herrick (New York: Macmillan, 1927). The quote "society was a machine designed to grind me to pieces" comes from chapter 19. *You Can't Win* has been recently reprinted with an introduction by William Burroughs (San Francisco: AK Press, 2000). For Chicago gang murders, see Allsop, *The Bootleggers*, chapter 4, "The Old-Fashioned O'Donnells". For the disastrous effects of bootleg booze, see Behr, *Prohibition*, chapter 16, "A Fatal Triumph".

For Margaret Mead on the impact of environment on adolescents, see *Coming of Age in Samoa* (New York: Morrow Quill, 1973), chapter 14, "Education for Choice". Her critique of G. Stanley Hall and her reasons for going to Samoa are mentioned in chapter 1, "Introduction". For her findings in Samoa about adolescent sexual activity and parenting, see chapter 10, "The Experience and Individuality of the Average Girl", and chapter 13, "Our Educational Problems in the Light of Samoan Contrasts". Her description of the book being as much about Samoa as about "the United States of 1926–1928" is contained in the preface to the 1973 edition. "A society which is clamoring for choice" is in chapter 14. This chapter is also the source for the quotes in the next paragraph: the "essentially pecuniary nature" of American society, "efflorescence of a doctrine", and "the Cinderella story".

For a full description of Valentino's death, the riots in Manhattan, and the aftermath, see Irving Schulman, *Valentino*, "Act One: Scene One." For his being adored and mobbed in London, see Schulman, "Act Three: Scene Thirteen"; for the "Powder Puffs" article and Valentino's reaction, see Schulman, "Act Three: Scene Sixteen". See also Alexander Walker, *Stardom*; Norman A. Mackenzie, *The Magic of Rudolph Valentino*; and Michael Morris, *Madame Valentino*. For a lurid account, see Kenneth Anger, *Hollywood Babylon*, which also reproduces the full text of the July 18, 1926, "Powder Puffs" article in the chapter called "Rudy's Rep".

For the impact of the movies in American culture, and criticism of, see Alice Miller Mitchell, *Children and Movies*; Lynd and Lynd, *Middletown*, chapter 18, "Inventions—Making Leisure"; and Bernays, *Propaganda*, chapter 11, "The Mechanics of Propaganda".

For Clara Bow, see David Stenn, *Clara Bow: Runnin' Wild* (New York: Cooper Square Press, 2000), particularly chapters 15, 16, and 17. See also David Thompson, *A Biographical Dictionary of Film*. For the youthful response to *It*, see Mitchell, *Children and Movies*, chapter 11, "Movies Children Like". Adela Rogers St John's article is quoted in Stenn, *Clara Bow: Runnin' Wild*, chapter 15. Kenneth Anger's take is preserved in *Hollywood Babylon*.

For the *New Student* magazine quote, see Paula Fass, *The Damned and the Beautiful*, chapter 8, "The Politics of Cultural Liberalism". For the college student attitude to Prohibition, see chapter 7, "Symbols of Liberation". For the details of the National Student Federation, see chapter 8. This chapter also includes accounts of the students' attitude to race. For details of the June 1929 performance by the Paul Whiteman Orchestra, see Richard M. Sudhalter and Philip R. Evans, *Bix: Man and Legend*, chapter 18. For *The Jazz Singer* and the popularization of jazz, Arnold Shaw, *The Jazz Age: Popular Music in the Twenties* (New York: Oxford University Press, 1987).

For the Negro response to this popularization, and fresh ideas of democracy, see Alain Locke, ed., *The New Negro* (New York: Touchstone, 1997), foreword and "The New Negro" by Alain Locke; for linking the Harlem Renaissance and youth, see *The New Negro*, "Negro Youth Speaks"; for Harlem as a race capital and for the "large scale laboratory experiment in the race problem", see *The New Negro*, James Weldon Johnson, "Harlem, the Culture Capital". For more general data, a useful timeline, and some excellent music, see *Rhapsodies in Black: Music and Words from the Harlem Renaissance* (Los Angeles: Rhino Records, 2000).

The single-issue magazine *Fire*, "devoted to younger negro artists", has been reprinted (no publishing details). For Langston Hughes on the Black Renaissance quote, see *The Big Sea: An Autobiography* (London: Pluto Press, 1986), "When the Negro Was in Vogue", and "Harlem Literati". Carl Van Vechten's *Nigger Heaven* has been recently reprinted (Chicago: University of Illinois Press, 2000). For the quote "the Negro and all things negroid had become a fad", see Wallace Thurman, *The Blacker the Berry: A Novel of Negro Life* (New York: Collier, 1970), part 5, "Pyrrhic Victory". For Langston Hughes on the Cotton Club and for his disillusion, see *The Big Sea*, "When the Negro Was in Vogue" and "Patron and Friend".

For the precocious adolescence of American children in the 1920s, see Lynd and Lynd, *Middletown*, chapter 11. For the "popular high school girl" quote, see *Middletown*, chapter 18, "Inventions—Making Leisure".

17 THE PURSUIT OF PLEASURE

The Noël Coward epigraph comes from *The Vortex*, act 1, in *The Collected Plays: 1* (London: Methuen, 1999). For Brenda Dean Paul and *The Blackbirds*, see her extraordinary autobiography, *My First Life* (London: John Long, 1935), chapter 6, "Today We Live". This chapter is also the source for her comments about parties. For her background, see chapter 3, "A New Life". Dean Paul's account of the "Bright Young People" is contained in chapter 6. For the 1920s partygoers, see also Ann Chisholm, *Nancy Cunard* (London: Sidgwick and Jackson, 1979), and Geoffrey Wolf, *Black Sun: The Brief Transit and Violent Eclipse of Harry Crosby*, chapters 7–10.

Stanley Hall's definition "savages are nearly all great dancers" comes from *Adolescence*, chapter 3,

"Growth of Motor Power and Function". For Americans in Paris, see Wolf, *Black Sun*, and William Wiser, *The Crazy Years: Paris in the Twenties* (New York: Athenaeum, 1983), passim. For Boeuf sur le Toit, see Francis Steegmuller, *Cocteau: A Biography*, chapter 5, "Inventing the Twenties", and for the Sari quote, see Wiser, *The Crazy Years*, chapter 14, "The Ox on the Roof".

For descriptions of the Four Arts Ball, see Wolf, *Black Sun: The Brief Transit and Violent Eclipse of Harry Crosby*, chapter 10, which is the source for the Claridge's Hotel quote. The original citation comes from Jimmie Charters, *This Must Be the Place: Memories of Montparnasse* (New York: Lee Furman, 1937). For Sebastian Haffner on Berlin in the later 1920s, see *Defying Hitler*, prologue, chapter 13. For Berlin as pleasure city and the description of the Haus Vaterland, see Mel Gordon, *Voluptuous Panic: The Erotic World of Weimar Berlin* (Los Angeles: Feral House, 2000), "Girl Culture and the All-night Bummel". For male prostitution, see *Voluptuous Panic*, "City of Whores". The "mad carousel ride" quote comes from *Voluptuous Panic*, "Berlin Means Boys". John Henry MacKay's *The Hustler* (Los Angeles: Allison Publications, 1985) is an evocative period novel set in this milieu.

For American consumerism in post-war Britain, see Noreen Branson, *Britain in the 1920s* (London: Weidenfeld and Nicolson, 1977), chapter 14, "New Enjoyments", and John Montgomery, *The Twenties* (London: George Allen and Unwin, 1970), chapter 3, "The Changing Scene". For war loan reparation, see Robert Graves and Alan Hodge, *The Long Week-End: A Social History of Great Britain, 1918–1939* (London: Penguin, 1971), chapter 5, "Post-War Politics". For the establishment's hostility to America and to youth consumerism, see Ronald Blythe, *The Age of Illusion: England in the Twenties and Thirties* (London: Penguin, 1964), chapter 2, "The Salutary Tale of Jix".

The popularizing of psychology in early 1920s advertising is cited in E. S. Turner, *The Shocking History of Advertising!*, chapter 7, "The Technique Changes", and Graves and Hodge, *The Long Week-End*, chapter 5. For the importance of young women, see Noreen Branson, *Britain in the 1920s*, chapter 13, "Women", and John Montgomery, *The Twenties*, chapter 12, "Emancipation". For increased employment opportunities and women's move to the major cities see Robert Roberts, *The Classic Slum*, chapter 10, "High Days and After". This chapter is also the source for the quotes about the dancing craze. For the spending of young wage-earners and the data about *Boy's Cinema* and *Girl's Cinema*, see David Fowler's excellent *The First Teenagers: The Lifestyle of Young Wage-earners in Interwar Britain* (London: The Woburn Press, 1995), chapter 4, "The Teenage Consumer in Interwar Britain". For fears about youth crime, see Cyril Burt, *The Young Delinquent* (London: University of London Press, 1925). For youth policy in the 1920s and 1930s, see Geoffrey Pearson, *Hooligan: A History of Respectable Fears*, chapter 3, "Past Perfect". For the war on pleasure and the importance of William Joynson-Hicks as Britain's home secretary, see Blythe, *The Age of Illusion: England in the Twenties and Thirties*, chapter 2, and Graves and Hodge, *The Long Week-End*, chapter 3, "Women".

The stories of Harold Acton, Brian Howard, and the *Eton Candle* are well told in the following books: Martin Green, *Children of the Sun*, chapter 3, "The New Dandies Arrive", and Marie Jaqueline Lancaster, *Brian Howard: Portrait of a Failure* (London: Anthony Blond, 1968), chapter 4, "1922: A Great Ephemeral, the Eton Candle". See also Humphrey Carpenter, *The Brideshead Generation: Evelyn Waugh and His Friends* (London: Weidenfeld and Nicolson, 1989), part 1, "The Eton Candle", chapter 1, ". . . Thought They Must Be Foreigners". For the background and early life of Howard and Acton, see Lancaster, *Brian Howard: Portrait of a Failure*, chapter 3, "Eton by Candlelight", and chapter 5, "Signs of Promise". See also Green, *Children of the Sun*, chapter 4, "1918–1922: Eton", and chapter 5, "1922–1925: Oxford".

For Noël Coward and *The Vortex*, see *Collected Plays: 1*, and Philip Hoare, *Noel Coward* (Chicago: University of Chicago Press, 1995), chapter 8, "The Vortex". For Nancy Cunard and "incessant drink", see Chisholm, *Nancy Cunard*, chapter 6, "A Year in Close-up"; for Wyndham Lewis's portrait, see *Nancy Cunard*, illustrations, section 1, page 12, and for her description as a vamp, see chapter 8, "Aldous Huxley". Her self-description as "the perfect stranger" comes from her book of poems titled *The Outlaw* and is cited in *Nancy Cunard*, chapter 9, "Travels and Poetry".

For early 1920s club life, see Graves and Hodge, *The Long Week-End*, chapter 8, "Amusements". For Nancy Cunard and Michael Arlen, see Chisholm, *Nancy Cunard*, chapter 7, "Michael Arlen". The "bored with boredom" quote and the description of "the blues" comes from Michael Arlen, *The Green Hat* (Suffolk, UK: Boydell Press, 1983). The "Iris Storm" quote, the "desire-for-I-know-not-what" comes in *The Green Hat*, chapter 1, "The Green Hat". For DORA in the 1920s and Jix's moralistic campaigns, see Graves and Hodge, *The Long Week-End*, chapter 8, and Blythe, *The Age of Illusion: England in the Twenties and Thirties*, chapter 2.

Marek Kohn's *Dope Girls*, p. 129ff., is the source for Freda Kempton's cocaine overdose. The origin of the Bright Young People is described in Graves and Hodge, *The Long Week-End*, chapter 8, and also Charles Graves, *The Bad Old Days* (London: Faber & Faber, 1961), chapter 5. Dean Paul's account of the movement is contained in *My First Life*, chapter 6. Alec Waugh's invention of the cocktail party is cited in Green, *Children of the Sun*, chapter 6, "1925–1932: Brian and Harold in London", and David Tennant's *The Opening of the Gargoyle* is cited in Philip Hoare, *Serious Pleasures: The Life of Stephen Tennant* (London: Hamish Hamilton, 1990), chapter 4, "Napier & Eloise".

Evelyn Waugh's September 1926 description of a wild party comes from The *Diaries of Evelyn Waugh*, ed. Michael Davie (London: Weidenfeld and Nicolson, 1976), chapter 3, "The Twenties Diary 1924–28". Harold Acton's quote about George Gershwin's *Rhapsody In Blue* comes from Carpenter, *The Brideshead Generation*, part 3, "1924–1929: Bright Young People", chapter 3, "A Sort of Cumulative Futility". For Evelyn Waugh and the "monster" actor, see the diary entry from September 19, 1925, from *The Diaries of Evelyn Waugh*, chapter 3, "The Twenties Diary 1924–28".

For the rise of the gossip columnist, see Graves, *The Bad Old Days*, chapter 5; Dean Paul, *My First Life*, chapter 6; Graves and Hodge, *The Long Week-End*, chapter 4, "Reading Matter"; Carpenter, *The Brideshead Generation*, part 3, chapter 3; and Green, *Children of the Sun*, chapter 6, "1925–1932: London, New Friends and Allies".

For the Bright Young People's Oedipal obnoxiousness, see Chisholm, *Nancy Cunard*, chapter 17, "The Breach with Lady Cunard"; Lancaster, *Portrait of a Failure*, chapter 14, "Ups and Downs of the Bright Young People"; and Beverley Nichols, *Father Figure* (London: Heinemann, 1972). The Evelyn Waugh woodcut *That Grim Act Parricide* is illustrated in Carpenter, *The Brideshead Generation*, between pages 190 and 191. The *Daily Express*'s attack on "The Modern Girl's Brother" is cited by Graves and Hodge, *The Long Week-End*, chapter 8. For the James Laver doggerel, see Blythe, *The Age of Illusion: England in the Twenties and Thirties*, chapter 2.

For the Bright Young People as strikebreakers, see Evelyn Waugh, *The Diaries of Evelyn Waugh*, chapter 3, "The Twenties Diary 1924–28", entry for May 11, 1926; Branson, *Britain in the 1920s*, chapter 12, "General Strike"; and Hoare, *Serious Pleasures*, chapter 5, "Overture . . ." The spread of the Bright Young People is covered in Montgomery, *The Twenties*, chapter 14, "The Bright Young Things". For the Beverley Nichols quote, see *The Sweet and Twenties* (London: Weidenfeld and Nicolson, 1958), chapter 9, "Home of Lost Causes". The 1927 *Vogue* "lip-rouge" quote comes from Lancaster, *Brian Howard: Portrait of a Failure*, part 2, "1927–1940: The Years of Waste", chapter 11, "A Taste of the Twenties".

For Stephen Tennant as the latest star of the Bright Young People, see Hoare, *Serious Pleasures*, chapter 7, "Stage Centre". For Tennant's love of American actresses, see chapter 2, "The Never-land". For the spring 1928 parties, see chapter 8, "Intermezzo". For Brenda Dean Paul and the death of the Bright Young People, see *My First Life*, chapter 6. For Brian Howard's "I'm heartily sick of London", see Lancaster, *Brian Howard: Portrait of a Failure*, chapter 14. This chapter is also the source for the Allanah Harper quote.

For Norah C. James, see *Sleeveless Errand* (New York: William Morrow, 1929). The Wyndham Lewis quote about big business and youth comes from *Doom of Youth*, part 1, chapter 1. The headline "Childlike Innocence at 40 Years of Age" comes from Lewis, *Doom of Youth*, part 3, "Exhibits". For the condescension of Stephen Tennant, see Hoare, *Serious Pleasures*, chapter 8; the quote comes from a *Daily Express* article of September 14, 1928.

For the 1920s generation playing the fool, see Evelyn Waugh, *Vile Bodies* (London: Penguin Classics, 2000), chapter 8. For the appearance of the war books, see Samuel Hynes, *A War Imagined*, chapter 21, "Myth-making". For the dissolution of the 1890s generation, see Robert Graves, *Goodbye to All That*, Richard Aldington's *Death of a Hero*, and Eric Maria Remarque's *All Quiet on the Western Front*. The Remarque quote comes from *All Quiet on the Western Front*, chapter 12. For the disillusionment of the postwar generation seen from within, see Noël Coward, *Post-Mortem* (London: Heineman, 1931).

For the Hans Zehrer article, see Robert Wohl, *The Generation of 1914*, chapter 2, "Germany: The Mission of the Young Generation". Paul and Elizabeth's bedroom shrine is described in Jean Cocteau, *Les enfants terribles* (London: Harvill Press, 1999), part 1. For the background to *Les enfants terribles* and the story of the Bourgoint siblings, see Francis Steegmuller, *Cocteau, A Biography*, part 6, "Opium, Orpheus and *The Blood of a Poet*". For more twenties disillusionment and death in general, see Lancaster, *Brian Howard: Portrait of a Failure*; Richard M. Sudhalter and Philip R. Evans's Bix Beiderbecke biography, *Bix: Man and Legend*; Dean Paul, *My First Life*; Waugh, *Vile Bodies*; Wolf, *Black Sun*; and Nancy Milford, *Zelda Fitzgerald*.

For the continuation of the 1920s mood into the 1930s, see Ethel Mannin, *Young in the Twenties*, chapter 14, "Overflow to the Thirties". *Brave New World* was published by Chatto and Windus in 1932. Sebastian Haffner's musings on the impact of Gustav Stresemann's death are contained in *Defying Hitler*, prologue, chapter 13. The "errand boys of a dying age" quote is from Hans Zehrer, and comes from Robert Wohl, *The Generation of 1914*, chapter 2, "Germany: The Mission of the Young Generation". For the *Bunde* and the *Wandervogel* in the later 1920s, see Walter Z. Laqueur, *Young Germany*, chapter 16, "Panorama of the Bunde", and chapter 18, "National Bolshevism".

18 THE SOLDIERS OF AN IDEA

The Kiel leaflet is reproduced in H. W. Koch, *The Hitler Youth: Origins and Development, 1922–45* (New York: Cooper Square Press, 2000), chapter 5, "Dominance". The Melita Maschmann quotes over the next few paragraphs come from *Account Rendered: A Dossier on My Former Self* (London: Abelard-Schuman, 1964), chapter 1. The figure of three and a half million Hitler Youth comes from Koch, *The Hitler Youth*, chapter 5.

The antagonism between the generations quote comes from Maschmann, *Account Rendered*, chapter 1. The Baldur von Schirach quote "From a National Socialist point of view, youth is always right", comes from Erich Michaud, *Soldiers of an Idea: Young People Under the Third Reich*, from Levi and Schmitt, eds, *A History of Young People in the West*, volume two, chapter 8. Hitler's statement that he was "beginning with the young" is reproduced in Gerhard Rempel, *Hitler's Children: The Hitler Youth and the SS* (Chapel Hill: University of North Carolina Press, 1989), chapter 1, introduction.

For the crash in general, see John Kenneth Galbraith, *The Great Crash of 1929* (London: Penguin, 1975). For the ability of mass production to change the whole social order, see Edward A. Filene, *Successful Living in This Machine Age*. For the José Ortega y Gasset quote, see *The Revolt of the Masses* (New York: W. W. Northam and Company, 1932) chapter 1, "The Coming of the Masses". For the Hitler Youth being the individual soldier of an idea, see Koch, *The Hitler Youth*, chapter 5. For Gustave Le Bon on the crowd as a "servile flock", see *The Crowd: A Study of the Popular Mind*, chapter 3.

For the "struggle between the forces of good in the world and the forces of evil", see Julian Symonds, *The Thirties: A Dream Revolved* (London: Faber and Faber, 1975), chapter 12, "Spain". For the accounts of youthful polarization, see for instance: Sebastian Haffner, *Defying Hitler*; Symonds, *The Thirties*; Maschmann, *Account Rendered*; David Pryce-Jones, *Unity Mitford: A Quest* (London: Weidenfeld and Nicolson, 1976); Kevin Ingram, *Rebel: The Short Life of Esmond Romilly* (London: Weidenfeld and Nicolson, 1985); and Jessica Mitford, *Hons and Rebels* (London: Victor Gollancz, 1960).

The Louis MacNeice quote about "self-fulfilment through self-abnegation" comes from Miranda Carter, *Anthony Blunt: His Lives* (London: Macmillan, 2001), chapter 5, "Don". The italicized quote *"we want the same thing"* comes from Daniel Guerin, *The Brown Plague: Travels in Late Weimar and Early Nazi Germany* (London: Duke University Press, 1994), "Before the Catastrophe".

For the countdown to the Nazis assuming power from the 1930 election onwards, see Sebastian Haffner, *Defying Hitler*, prologue, chapter 14, and Koch, *The Hitler Youth*, chapter 4, "Birth". For the influence of the *fascisti* on the National Socialists, see Eric Michaud, *Soldiers of an Idea*. For the failure of the *Bunde* to create a coherent opposition, see Walter Laqueur, *Young Germany*, chapter 15, "Ernst Buske and the Freischar". For the Ernst Wilhelm Eschmann quote, see Robert Wohl, *The Generation of 1914*, chapter 2, "Germany: The Mission of the Young Generation".

The anti-democratic impulse of the *Bunde* and the German youth movements as a whole is brilliantly delineated in Peter Gay, *Weimar Culture: The Outsider as Insider*, chapter 6, "Revenge of the Father: The Rise and Fall of Objectivity". For the demonstrations at *All Quiet on the Western Front*, see Koch, *The Hitler Youth*, chapter 4. For Hitler promising a return to "the great war game of 1914–1918", see Haffner, *Defying Hitler*, prologue, chapter 14.

For the impact of unemployment on Germany's youth, see Laqueur, *Young Germany*, chapter 18, "National Bolshevism". For the Nazi epidemic spreading, see Guerin, *The Brown Plague*, "Before the Catastrophe". The Daniel Guerin quotes over the next few paragraphs are from the same source. This includes his description of the political polarization in the youth hostel, the fact that Germany's youth was lost and bitterly divided, and his description of the "Wild Cliques". The Duke University Press edition of *The Brown Plague* also contains Christine Fournia's extraordinary 1931 article "The Ring Youth Gangs" as an appendix.

For the relationship of the youth movement and the Nazi accession to power, see Laqueur, *Young Germany*, chapter 18 and chapter 19, "In Hitler's Shadow". For youth unemployment in Germany, the failure of the youth movement, and the predisposition of German youth towards the Nazis, see Koch, *The Hitler Youth*, chapter 5. This chapter is also the source for the details of the triumphal October 1932 Potsdam rally.

For the importance of *Hitlerjunge Quex*, the film and novel, see Detlev J. K. Peukert, *Inside Nazi Germany: Conformity, Opposition and Racism in Everyday Life* (London: Penguin, 1993), chapter 2, "The Rise of National Socialism and the Crisis of Industrial Class Society", and Siegfried Kracauer, *From Caligari to Hitler: A Psychology of German Film* (Princeton, N.J.: Princeton University Press, 1970), chapter 21, "National Epic". The real story of Herbert Norkus is detailed in Koch, *The Hitler Youth*, chapter 4.

For the relation of the Nazi regime to American experiments in mass control, see Guerin, *The Brown Plague*, "Before the Catastrophe", and Peukert, *Inside Nazi Germany*, chapter 2 and chapter 4, "The Führer Myth and Consent in Everyday Life". For early Nazi propaganda, and the banning of the Hitler Youth in 1932, see Koch, *The Hitler Youth*, chapter 5.

For the relative size of the Hitler Youth against the Communist and Social Democratic youth organizations, see Rempel, *Hitler's Children: The Hitler Youth and the SS*, chapter 1. For the relationship of Nazi rhetoric to existing German cultural myths, see Gay, *Weimar Culture*, chapter 3, "The Secret Germany: Poetry as Power", and chapter 4, "The Hunger for Wholeness: The Trials of Modernity". For the activities of the Nazis when they came to power, see Koch, *The Hitler Youth*, chapter 5, and Peukert, *Inside Nazi Germany*, chapter 7, "The Working Class: Everyday Life and Opposition".

For a first-person account of the Enabling Act, see Haffner, *Defying Hitler*, "The Revolution", chapter 19. For the banning of trade unions and the burning of books, see Guerin, *The Brown Plague*, "After the Catastrophe", chapter 10, "The Swastika over the Trades Unions", chapter 13, "Their Prisons", and chapter 15, "Underground". See also Haffner, *Defying Hitler*, "The Revolution", and "Leave Taking", chapter 28, and Koch, *The Hitler Youth*, chapter 5. For the trashing of Dr Magnus Hirschfeld's Sexual Science Institute, see Mel Gordon, *Voluptuous Panic: The Erotic World of Weimar Berlin*, "World in Flames".

The combination of barbarism and technology is detailed in Peukert, *Inside Nazi Germany*, chapter 3, "Contradictions in the Mood of the 'Little Man'". and Guerin, *The Brown Plague*, "After the Catastrophe", chapter 12, "The Other Germany". The "never-ending march music and drums" quote comes from Haffner, *Defying Hitler*, "Leave Taking," chapter 34. For the Nazis' aim of total control, see Koch, *The Hitler Youth*, chapter 5: "As in all sectors of National Socialist Germany, total control of all Germans was the ultimate aim of the government."

For the "March Violets" quote as applied to those who joined the Nazis after their accession to power, see Maschmann's *Account Rendered*, chapter 1. They were also called "the Casualties of March". For Haffner's analysis of this "million-fold nervous breakdown", see *Defying Hitler*, "The Revolution," chapter 19. For Guerin's visit to a youth hostel in April 1933, see *The Brown Plague*, "After the Catastrophe", chapter 1, "The Tidal Wave". For the *Wandervogel* holdouts, see chapter 12, "The Other Germany".

For the youth of Germany surrendering their innermost being to the Nazi revolution, see Haffner, *Defying Hitler*, prologue, chapter 1. Hitler's 1933 statement "Your child belongs to us" is contained in Jennifer Keeley, *Life in the Hitler Youth* (San Diego: Lucent Books, 2000), chapter 5, "Home Life". For the closing down of the German youth movements, see Koch, *The Hitler Youth*, chapter 5, and Rempel, *Hitler's Children: The Hitler Youth and the SS*, chapter 3, "Unifiers, Delinquents, Enforcers".

Baldur von Schirach's appointment in June 1933 is covered in Koch, *The Hitler Youth*, chapter 5, and Peukert, *Inside Nazi Germany*, chapter 8, "Young People: Mobilisation and Refusal". The membership figure of 3.6 million Hitler Youth comes from Koch, *The Hitler Youth*, chapter 5, as does von Schirach's new structure for the Hitler Youth. For the Hitler Youth oath, see Keeley, *Life in the Hitler Youth*, chapter 1, "Joining the Hitler Youth".

The Hitler Youth programme of activity is detailed in Koch, *The Hitler Youth*, chapter 5. For the uniform, see Keeley, *Life in the Hitler Youth*, chapter 1. That the uniform was designed by Hitler is mentioned by Eric Michaud in "Soldiers of an Idea: Young People Under the Third Reich", in Levi and Schmitt, eds, *A History of Young People in the West*, volume two.

Erika Mann's quote about "peaceful sport" is contained in Guerin, *The Brown Plague*, "After the Catastrophe", chapter 8, "War or Peace". This is also the source of Guerin's "a generation is openly preparing itself". For military indoctrination and the quote "a large part of our reading", see Peukert, *Inside Nazi Germany*, chapter 8. Adolf Hitler's "the *Völkisch* state" is cited in Koch, *The Hitler Youth*, chapter 8, "Education".

The description of the Hitler Youth initiation ceremony and the full oath is contained in Keeley, *Life in the Hitler Youth*, chapter 1. Adolf Hitler's quote "pride and independence of the beast of prey" is cited by Rempel in *Hitler's Children: The Hitler Youth and the SS,* chapter 7, "Contestants, Boxers, Combatants". Hitler's famous dictum "hard as Krupp steel" comes from the same source. Melita Maschmann's reaction to that statement is contained in *Account Rendered,* chapter 2, as is her decision to join the Bund Deutscher Mädel.

For the Nazi attitude towards women, see Peukert, *Inside Nazi Germany,* chapter 8, and Keeley, *Life in the Hitler Youth,* chapter 1, and chapter 4, "The School Day of the Hitler Youth". For the relentless Hitlerjugend schedule, see Koch, *The Hitler Youth,* chapter 6, "Ideology", and Peukert, *Inside Nazi Germany,* chapter 9, "Brown Revolution". For the naming of years, see Koch, chapter 5.

For the fact that youth was led by youth, see Koch, *The Hitler Youth,* chapter 6; for the relationship between the generations, see chapter 8. The general Nazi policy on education is detailed in Keeley, *Life in the Hitler Youth,* chapter 2, "The Race War", and chapter 4; see also Rempel, *Hitler's Children: The Hitler Youth and the SS,* chapter 7, "Contestants, Boxers, Combatants".

For Melita Maschmann on the disapproval of her parents, see *Account Rendered,* chapter 3. For the bedevilled relationship between parents and children, see Keeley, *Life in the Hitler Youth,* chapter 5, "Home Life". For the sanctions against non-joiners, see Keeley, chapter 1, and Rempel, *Hitler's Children: The Hitler Youth and the SS,* chapter 3. For the formation of the special Hitler Youth police force, see Rempel, chapter 4, "Police Boys, Informers, Rebels".

For Hitler's 1934 Nuremberg rally quote, see Koch, *The Hitler Youth,* chapter 5. This chapter is also the source for von Schirach's pronouncement, "Your name, my Führer, is for us everlasting life." For Hitler marketing, see Peukert, *Inside Nazi Germany,* chapter 10, "Public Show and Private Perceptions", and Koch, *The Hitler Youth,* chapter 5. For the experience of meeting the great leader, see Keeley, *Life in the Hitler Youth,* chapter 1.

For resistance and the J. Georgi quote, see Koch, *The Hitler Youth,* chapter 10, "Dissent". For the Karma Rauhut quote, see Keeley, *Life in the Hitler Youth,* chapter 7, "Resistance". For the quote "It was a healthy rejection of the prison organisation forced on youth", see Rempel, *Hitler's Children: The Hitler Youth and the SS,* chapter 3. For the old youth groups trying to continue their activities and the Rote Stosstrupp, see Koch, *The Hitler Youth,* chapter 10.

The continuation of the old *Wandervogel* lifestyle is detailed in Rempel, *Hitler's Children: The Hitler Youth and the SS,* chapter 3. This chapter is also the source for details of the Nerother and the Kittelsbach Pirates. For the Nazis' problem with the Catholic youth organizations, see Peukert, *Inside Nazi Germany,* chapter 6, "The Middle Classes and the Nazi State". For the discipline problems within the Hitler Youth, see Rempel, *Hitler's Children,* chapter 3.

For 1936 and the year of the German Jungvolk, see Koch, *The Hitler Youth,* chapter 5. This chapter is also the source for the 1936 decree. The full text of this decree concerning the Hitler Youth is reproduced in full by Keeley in *Life in the Hitler Youth,* chapter 1. For the greater affiliation of the Hitler Youth with the SS, see Rempel, *Hitler's Children: The Hitler Youth and the SS,* chapter 2, "The Formation of a General Alliance", and chapter 3. For the Hitler Youth becoming respectable, see Eric Michaud, "Soldiers of an Idea: Young People Under the Third Reich", and for the institution of the NPEAs, etc., see Koch, *The Hitler Youth,* chapter 9, "Elites".

The increasing militarism and compliance demanded by the regime is described in Koch, *The Hitler Youth,* chapter 10, while Peukert's *Inside Nazi Germany,* chapter 8, "Young People: Mobilisation and Refusal", contains details about the Meuten and the 1938 report of exiled Germans. For Hitler's December 1938 cradle-to-grave strategy for German youth, see Koch, *The Hitler Youth,* chapter 9. This chapter is also the source for the Hitler Youth's indoctrination in defence readiness and defence capacity, as well as the 1938 Hitler Youth membership figures.

For the 1939 Hitler Youth compulsory youth service decree, see Koch, *The Hitler Youth,* chapter 5, and Rempel, *Hitler's Children: The Hitler Youth and the SS,* chapter 3. For Nazi ideals of sacrifice and militarism, see Keeley, *Life in the Hitler Youth,* chapter 3, "Ideology of Activities", and Koch, chapter 6 and chapter 8.

19 THE CHILDREN'S ARMY AND THE NEW DEAL

The Clinch Calkins epigraph comes from Errol Lincoln Uys, *Riding the Rails: Teenagers on the Move During the Great Depression* (New York: TV Books, 1999), part 1, introduction, "When School Was Out". The diary entries of Blink, the young tramp, come from Thomas Minehan, *Boy and Girl Tramps of America* (New York: Grosset and Dunlap, 1934), chapter 14, "Two Diaries". The figure of a quarter of a million boxcar boys and girls comes from Uys, *Riding the Rails,* part 1, introduction.

Minehan's decision to join the young homeless is contained in *Boy and Girl Tramps of America*, introduction. For his comments on the tramp diaries, see chapter 14. For the youth problem and the Children's Army, see Uys, *Riding the Rails*, introduction. This is also the source for the citation of Maxine Davis's "200,000 Vagabond Children", a September 1932 article in the *Ladies' Home Journal*. Maxine Davis went on to publish a crusading volume called *The Lost Generation: A Portrait of American Youth Today* (New York: Macmillan, 1936).

For Minehan on the deterioration of the boy tramp Texas, see *Boy and Girl Tramps of America*, chapter 15, "Their Tribal Life". Barbara Starke's account of her wanderings through America was published in both England and America: in the United States as *Born in Captivity* and in the United Kingdom as *Touch and Go: The Story of a Girl's Escape* (London: Jonathan Cape, 1931). For Minehan on the Wild Children of revolutionary Russia (the *bensprizorni*) and the free youth of Germany, see *Boy and Girl Tramps of America*, introduction.

For details and statistics of the effect that the Great Crash had on America in general, see David A. Shannon, *The Great Depression* (New Jersey: Prentice Hall, 1960), part 5, "The Middle Classes, Bank Failures and Unemployment", chapters 32–38.

For the impact of the Depression on the working class, Negroes, and women in particular, see Robert S. Lynd and Helen Merrell Lynd, *Middletown in Transition* (New York: Harcourt Brace and Company, 1937), chapter 2, "Getting a Living"; Marjorie Rosen, *Popcorn Venus: Women, Movies and the American Dream* (New York: Avon, 1973), part 3, chapter 8, "The Whole Town's Talking"; Louis A. Erenberg, *Swingin' the Dream: Big Band Jazz and the Rebirth of American Culture* (Chicago: University of Chicago Press, 1998), part 1, chapter 1, "Just One More Chance: The Fall of the Jazz Age and the Rise of Swing 1929–1935".

For the dropping of professional incomes by 40 per cent, see Grace Palladino, *Teenagers: An American History* (New York: Basic Books, 1996) part 1, "Adolescence", chapter 3, "A New Deal for Youth: 'Progressive' Education and the National Youth Administration". For talk of revolution in America, see Shannon, *The Great Depression*, part 7, "Will There Be a Revolution?", and chapters 43–50. For the figure of four out of ten high-school-age children not in school, see Uys, *Riding the Rails*, introduction, and Palladino, *Teenagers: An American History*, part 1, chapter 3.

America's population statistics are contained in *The Report of the President's Research Committee on Social Trends, Recent Social Trends in the United States* (New York: McGraw-Hill, Company, 1933), chapter 1, "The Population of the Nation", by Warren S. Thompson and P. K. Whelpton. For the Depression's impact on the family, see Ruth Shonle Cavan and Kathleen Howland Ranck, *The Family and the Depression: A Study of One Hundred Chicago Families* (New York: Books for Libraries Press, 1969), chapter 6, "Adjustment to the Depression".

For Minehan on why tramps left home, see *Boy and Girl Tramps of America*, appendix, table 12, "Reasons for Leaving Home Given by Boy or Girl Tramps". Texas's quote comes from Minehan, chapter 2, "Before the Big Trouble". For the home status of young tramps, see *Boy and Girl Tramps of America*, appendix, table 15, "Economic Conditions in Homes of Boy and Girl Tramps", and table 16, "Emotional Situation in Homes of a Certain Number of Boy and Girl Tramps". Newton D. Baker is quoted in Shannon, *The Great Depression*, part 4, "Nomads of the Depression", chapter 27, "Anxiety about the Vagrants".

Lillan Symes is quoted in Shannon, *The Great Depression*, part 7, "Will There Be a Revolution?", chapter 49, "A Revolutionary Post-mortem". Jim Mitchell's story is told in Uys, *Riding the Rails*, part 5, "The Way Out", the interviews. For migration to California and the closing of the frontier, see Uys, part 1, introduction, "In Harm's Way", and Palladino, *Teenagers: An American History*, part 1, chapter 3.

For the hierarchy of boy and girl tramps, see Minehan, *Boy and Girl Tramps of America*, chapter 12, "Prestige, Standards". For the hazards of travel, see Uys, *Riding the Rails*, part 1, introduction, "In Harm's Way"; for the violent railway policemen, see Uys, part 3, "Travellin': The Bulls". For arriving in a city, see Uys, part 1, introduction, "In Harm's Way", and Minehan, *Boy and Girl Tramps of America*, chapter 5, "How They Get Food". The Jim Mitchell quote comes from the source cited before.

For the premature ageing of young transients, see Uys, *Riding the Rails*, part 4, "Hitting the Stem". Note also this Jan van Heé quote from the same source: "We went from childhood to being adults. We never thought about being teenagers. We only thought about surviving." See also Minehan, *Boy and Girl Tramps of America*, chapter 15.

For the Ohio social worker quote, see Uys, *Riding the Rails*, part 2, "Catching Out, Go Fend for Yourself". Details of the hobo jungles and the child tramps' rules and regulations are contained in Minehan,

Boy and Girl Tramps of America, part 1, "The Seasons in the Life of a Boy Tramp", chapter 7, "Where They Sleep", and chapter 17, "Conclusions".

For the racial composition of transients, see Uys, *Riding the Rails*, introduction, "The Wrong Side of the Tracks" and personal testimony from part 3, "Hard Travellin", interview with "Clarence Lee, 1929–31", and part 4, "Hitting the Stem", interview with "Clydia Williams, 1932–35". For the combustibility of the young transient world, see Minehan, *Boy and Girl Tramps of America*, chapter 12, "Prestige Standards", and chapter 9, "Sex Life".

The Scottsboro Boys case is covered in Uys, *Riding the Rails*, part 1, introduction, "The Wrong Side of the Tracks", and Haywood Patterson and Earl Conrad, *Scottsboro Boy* (London: Victor Gollancz, 1950), part 1, "The Big Frame", chapters 1 and 2. This book also contains a timetable of events in the Scottsboro case. For Nancy Cunard's involvement, see *Scottsboro Boy*, chapter 6, and Ann Chisholm, *Nancy Cunard*, chapter 18, "The Black Cause", and chapter 21, "The Publication of Negro".

For young transients and guns, see Uys, *Riding the Rails*, part 1, introduction, "Bitter Harvest"; for the "America is going to have a revolution" quote, see Minehan, *Boy and Girl Tramps of America*, chapter 11, "Political and Social Philosophy". For youth feeling "de-princed", see the quote by James San Joule in Uys, *Riding the Rails*, part 2, "Catching Out". The quotes about adolescents as "embryonic buyers" and the "customers of tomorrow" come from Stanley C. Hollander and Richard Germain, *Was There a Pepsi Generation Before Pepsi Discovered It?*, chapter 2, "A History of Marketing to Youth".

Minehan's vision of America's cities being overrun with groups of hoodlums comes from *Boy and Girl Tramps of America*, chapter 17, "Conclusions". For the violence at the Ford Motor plant, see Robert Lacey, *Ford: The Men and the Machine* (New York: Ballantine Books, 1987), chapter 21, "Overpass". For the American adolescents still defining themselves in terms of work and marriage, see Palladino, *Teenagers: An American History*, part 1, "Adolescence", chapter 2, "Advice and Consent: Building Adolescent Character". For Robert S. Lynd and Helen Merrell Lynd's "a more self-conscious subculture of the young", see *Middletown in Transition*, chapter 5, "Making a Home: The Arena of Private Adjustment".

For the 1932 *Parents* magazine quote, see Palladino, *Teenagers: An American History*, part 1, "Adolescence", chapter 1, "The High School Age". For the "you take a lad of seventeen" quote, see W. Ryland Boorman, *Personality in Its Teens* (New York: Macmillan, 1931), part 4, "His Life Principles", chapter 7, "Morals and Ideals". For the generation gap quote, see Lynd and Lynd, *Middletown in Transition*, chapter 5. For Minehan on state involvement, see *Boy and Girl Tramps of America*, chapter 17.

For peer pressures and the new adolescent magazines, see Palladino, *Teenagers: An American History*, part 1, chapter 2. For the lack of sex education in schools, see Lynd and Lynd, *Middletown in Transition*, chapter 5. For the power of movies, see *The Report of the President's Research Committee on Social Trends, Recent Social Trends in the United States*, chapter 4, "The Agencies of Communication", by Malcolm L. Willey and Stewart A Rice.

The film *The Public Enemy* has recently been reissued on DVD in *James Cagney: The Signature Collection* (Warner Home Video UK, 2005). (The others are *Angels with Dirty Faces*, *The Roaring Twenties*, and the apocalyptic *White Heat*.) For the young gangster copying James Cagney, see Henry James Forman, *Our Movie-Made Children* (New York: Macmillan, 1934), chapter 15, "Movies in a Crowded Section". This chapter is also the source for the quotes about Edward G. Robinson and James Cagney.

The phrase "mass production of flaming youth" comes from Forman, *Our Movie-Made Children*, chapter 13, "Sex—Delinquency and Crime". Chapter 11, "The Path to Delinquency", is the source for the "luxury, extravagance, easy money" quote. For another moralistic view on this topic, see also Herbert Bloomer, *Movies, Delinquency and Crime* (New York: Macmillan, 1933), cited in David M. Considine, *The Cinema of Adolescence* (Jefferson, NC: McFarland, 1985), part 4, "Juvenile Delinquency", chapter 8, "Dead Ends and Death Row 1931–1949".

For the goals depicted in movies, see Forman, *Our Movie-Made Children*, chapter 3, "What Do They See?", and for "undesirable national consciousness" and "definite imitation from the pictures in the way of love-making", see chapter 9, "Movies and Conduct". The dialogue between the college girls is contained in Forman, *Our Movie-Made Children*, chapter 10, "Moulded by the Movies". For the new Production Code, see Considine, *The Cinema of Adolescence*, part 1, chapter 1. See also Rosen, *Popcorn Venus*, part 3, "The Thirties", chapter 9, "Gentlemen Prefer Blondes". The copies of the pulp magazines *Jim Jam Jems* and *Exposed* came from the Alan Betrock archive.

For the diversification of organized crime after Prohibition, see Edward Behr, *Prohibition*, chapter 17, "The Aftermath". For the new type of murderous gangs, see Anthony Summers, *Official and Confidential: The Secret Life of J. Edgar Hoover* (New York: G. P. Putnam and Sons, 1993), chapter 5. See also Courtney Ryley Cooper, *Ten Thousand Public Enemies* (Boston: Little, Brown, 1935). For the explosion of the crime rate during 1933, see John Treherne, *The Strange History of Bonnie and Clyde* (London: Grafton, 1985), chapter 15, "The Hunters Prepare".

Bonnie Parker's doggerel poem "Suicide Sal" is cited in Treherne, *The Strange History of Bonnie and Clyde*, chapter 12, "Snake Eyed Killer, Cigar-Smoking Moll". Clyde Barrow's endorsement of the Ford V-8 is contained in Robert M. Lacey, *Ford: The Men and the Machine*, chapter 18, "Depression". Bonnie's self-mythologizing poem is contained in Treherne, *The Strange History of Bonnie and Clyde*, chapter 20, "Distrust and Disagreements". The mob scenes at the funeral come from the same source, chapter 22, "Tears and Burials". For J. Edgar Hoover's reaction, see chapter 24, "From Hoover to Film Noir".

The origin of the G-men is covered by Summers, *Official and Confidential: The Secret Life of J. Edgar Hoover*, chapter 6, and for G-men paraphernalia, see the same source, chapter 9. The assertion that America's young were the "products of a psychopathic period" is contained in Maxine Davis, *The Lost Generation: A Portrait of American Youth Today*, part 1, "Trustees of Posterity", chapter 1, "Focus on Youth". For George Soule on America "in the midst of a great social revolution", see Shannon, *The Great Depression*, part 7, "Will There Be a Revolution?", chapter 50, "The Revolution: A Sophisticated Dissent".

For the impact of the New Deal, see Lynd and Lynd, *Middletown in Transition*, chapter 2. For the impact of the New Deal on youth, see Palladino, *Teenagers: An American History*, part 1, chapter 3, and Uys, *Riding the Rails,* part 1, "A New Deal for Youth". The Jim Mitchell quote comes from part 5, "The Way Out".

The increasing numbers of America's youth remaining in high school as part of American policy is well covered by Palladino, *Teenagers: An American History,* part 1, chapter 1, and Lynd and Lynd, *Middletown in Transition,* chapter 2. For the changed relationship between the generations, see Sinclair Lewis, *The Prodigal Parents* (Canada: Doubleday, Doran and Company, 1938). The book is subtitled *The Revolt of the Parents Against the Revolt of Youth.*

Eleanor Roosevelt's involvement with the American Youth Congress and the New Deal, and the "moments of real terror" quote, are cited in Uys, *Riding the Rails,* part 1, introduction, "When School Was Out", and Betty and Ernest K. Lindley, *A New Deal for Youth: The Story of the National Youth Administration* (New York: Viking, 1938). For Maxine Davis's worries about the German situation, see *The Lost Generation,* part 2, "Mope—Hope—Grope", chapter 2, "Why Get Sore?", and part 1, "Trustees of Posterity", chapter 1, "Focus on Youth".

For "smoldering rebellion," see Lynd and Lynd, *Middletown in Transition,* chapter 2. For the quiet bitterness of the local graduate, see also chapter 12, "The Middletown Spirit." For more concern about Germany, see also Uys, *Riding the Rails,* part 1, introduction, "Bitter Harvest", and Palladino, *Teenagers: An American History,* part 1, chapter 3. The statistic of 2,877,000 sixteen- to twenty-four-year-olds on relief comes from Betty and Ernest K. Lindley, *A New Deal for Youth,* chapter 2, "Youth Inherits the Depression". For the Joseph Lash interview about the American Student Union, see http://newdeal.feri.org/students/lash.htm.

For the Fascist Catholic priest Charles E. Coughlin, see *The Aspirin Age,* ed. Isabel Leighton (London: Penguin, 1964), "1934: The Radio Priest and His Flock" by Wallace Stegner; Win Craig Wade, *The Fiery Cross: The Ku Klux Klan in America* (New York: Simon and Schuster, 1987), book 3: 1930–1937, chapter 9, "The Klan Is an American Institution"; John Roy Carlson, *Under Cover: My Four Years in the Nazis Underworld of America* (New York: E. P. Dutton, 1943), book 1, "Before Pearl Harbor", chapter 4, "Coughlin's 'Christian Crusade'".

The quote by Charles W. Taussig comes in Betty and Ernest K. Lindley, *A New Deal for Youth,* foreword. For details of how the National Youth Administration worked, see Uys, *Riding the Rails: Teenagers on the Move During the Great Depression,* part 1, introduction, "A New Deal for Youth", and Palladino, *Teenagers: An American History,* part 1, chapter 3.

20 BIFF BOYS AND THE RED MENACE

The epigraph comes from Walter Greenwood, *Love on the Dole* (London: Jonathan Cape, 1933), chapter 4, "Fine Feathers". For "The Unemployed Gang", see W. F. Lestrange, *Wasted Lives* (London: George Routledge and Sons, 1936), p. 71. (Note that this book is not divided into chapters or parts, therefore page references will be given instead.) For Lestrange's motivation, see "Brief Preface and Explanation", pp. 5–7. For the story of Trevor, see p. 120ff. His preface also cites the government, professional, and union organizations that he contacted while researching the book. For the "Special Areas", see pp. 108–112. For the photos of young men, see pp. 83, 109, and 117.

For the effect of the crash on Great Britain and the peak unemployment figures, see Claud Cockburn, *The Devil's Decade* (London: Sidgwick and Jackson, 1973), chapter 1, "After the Crash (1929–1931)", and chapter 2, "Britain 1931"; see also Robert Graves and Alan Hodge, *The Long Week-End*, chapter 15, "The Depression, 1930". For the effect of the Depression, see Lestrange, passim, and George Orwell, *The Road to Wigan Pier* (London: Penguin, 1962), chapters 1–6, passim.

The January 1930 article in *The Times* is quoted in Cockburn, *The Devil's Decade*, chapter 2. For the rush of "sociological novels", see Ethel Mannin, *Young in the Twenties*, chapter 15, "The Sobering-Up". The quote from *Love on the Dole*, "Ah may as well be in bloody prison", is from part 3, chapter 6, "A Man of Leisure". For Harry Hardcastle's realization that he is on the scrapheap, see Greenwood, *Love on the Dole*, part 2, chapter 1, "Revelation".

For the problem of apprenticeships, see Lestrange, *Wasted Lives*, p. 74ff., and Members of Merseyside Socialist Research Group, *Genuinely Seeking Work: Mass Unemployment on Merseyside in the 1930s* (Liverpool: Liver Press, 1992), part 1, "Unemployed Lives", chapter 2, "Who Were the Unemployed of the 1930s?" For the rationalization of industry, see the same source, and for the Walter Greenwood quote about modern progress, see *Love on the Dole*, part 3, chapter 6, "A Man of Leisure".

The details of industry's increased reliance on time-and-motion and the Bedaux system are contained in Members of Merseyside Socialist Research Group, *Genuinely Seeking Work*, part 2, "Class Rule and the State", chapter 8, "Are You Working?: Discipline Then Speed-Up". (In a bizarre postscript, Charles Bedaux became involved with the Windsors, and tried to use this connection to tout business with the Nazi Party. When the United States finally went to war—he was a US citizen—he was arrested in North Africa. In December 1943 he was flown to Miami for investigation, but took a drug overdose and died in his cell before he went to trial.)

For the means test, see Members of Merseyside Socialist Research Group, *Genuinely Seeking Work*, part 2, "Class Rule and the State", chapter 5, "'God Helps Those Who Help Themselves': The Law, the State and the Unemployed"; Cockburn, *The Devil's Decade*, chapter 4, "Counter-Offensive (1932–35)"; Lestrange, *Wasted Lives*, p. 123ff.; and Ronald Blythe, *The Age of Illusion: England in the Twenties and Thirties*, chapter 9, "Jarrow".

For emigration and the labour camps as a possible outlet for the unemployed, see Steve Humphries and Pamela Gordon, *Forbidden Britain* (London: BBC Books, 1994), chapter 4, "Slave Camps and Skivvy Schools". For the popularity of hiking and the stealing of the trawler, see Blythe, *The Age of Illusion*, chapter 9. For Orwell on cheap clothes and the dreams of Clark Gable and Greta Garbo, see *The Road to Wigan Pier*, chapter 5. The material about youth spending, including the 1933 shop girl quote and the Joan Harley research, comes from David Fowler, *The First Teenagers: The Lifestyle of Young Wage-earners in Interwar Britain*, chapter 4, "The Teenage Consumer in Interwar Britain".

Lestrange's photomontage of young unemployed men is on p. 126 of *Wasted Lives*. For contemporary headlines of violence, see Alexander McArthur and H. Kingsley Long, *No Mean City: A Story of the Glasgow Slums* (London: Longmans, Green and Company, 1935), appendix. For extravagant dress among the young unemployed, see Harry Daley, *This Small Cloud: A Personal Memoir* (London: Weidenfeld and Nicolson, 1986), part 3, "Metropolitan Police 1925–50", chapter 18, "Young men in places like Hammersmith scraped and pinched to buy gay clothes, then stood about like peacocks with empty pockets, possessing nothing but what they stood up in, and not at all down-hearted."

The Oxford Bags quote comes from Steve Humphries, *A Secret World of Sex* (London: Sidgwick and Jackson, 1991), chapter 6, "Street Gang Sex". The quote "an epidemic of gangs" comes from Members of Merseyside Socialist Research Group, *Genuinely Seeking Work*, part 2, "Class Rule and the State", chapter 6, "Policing the Slump". For the influence of Hollywood films, sensational delinquency headlines, the 1933 Children and Young Persons Act, and details of S. F. Hatton's *London's Bad Boys*, see Geoffrey Pearson, *Hooligan*, part 1, "The Decline and Fall of the British Way of Life", chapter 3, "Since the War—Past Perfect". Also see S. F. Hatton, *London's Bad Boys* (London: Chapman and Hall, 1931), chapter 1, "Hooliganism", and chapter 2, "Adolescence".

As for the rules of the game as understood between the police and criminals, see Daley, *This Small Cloud: A Personal Memoir*, part 3, chapter 15. For protests against the means test, see Cockburn, *The Devil's Decade*, chapter 4; Members of Merseyside Socialist Research Group, *Genuinely Seeking Work*, part 2, chapter 6; and Pearson, *Hooligan*, chapter 3. For the Hyde Park demonstration, see these sources, and Graves and Hodge, *The Long Week-End*, chapter 10, "The Depression, 1930".

For Mosley and the British Union of Fascists, see Robert Skidelsky, *Oswald Mosley* (London: Macmillan, 1981), chapter 14, "Part-time Saviour"; see also Thomas Linehan, *British Fascism, 1918–1939: Parties, Ideology and Culture* (Manchester: Manchester University Press, 2000), chapter 4, "The British Union of

Fascists"; and Ann De Courcy, *The Viceroy's Daughters: The Lives of the Curzon Sisters* (London: Phoenix, 2002), chapter 18, "Diana Guinness, Trophy Mistress". For the slump affecting the bourgeois, see Graves and Hodge, *The Long Week-End*, chapter 10, and David Pryce-Jones, *Unity Mitford: A Quest* (London: Weidenfeld and Nicolson, 1976), chapter 5, "The Big Push".

The "almost tangible Oedipal fury" quote comes from Miranda Carter, *Anthony Blunt: His Lives* (London: Macmillan, 2001), chapter 4, "Angry Young Man". For the move to the left by British intellectuals, see Blythe, *The Age of Illusion*, chapter 12, "The Crucible of Grief", and Julian Symonds, *The Thirties: A Dream Revolved*, chapter 3, "The Old School and the New Freedom".

The infamous Oxford Union debate is mentioned in Kevin Ingram, *Rebel: The Short Life of Esmond Romilly* (London: Weidenfeld and Nicolson, 1985), chapter 5, "Another World". For the violence at the Armistice Day march in Cambridge, see Carter, *Anthony Blunt: His Lives*, chapter 5, "Don". For the quote "the world's vibrations of violence", see Peter Stansky and William Abrahams, *Journey to the Frontier: Two Roads to the Spanish Civil War* (New York: Little, Brown, 1966), part 2, "John Cornford", chapter 3, "London".

For Esmond Romilly's *Out of Bounds* manifesto, see Ingram, *Rebel*, chapter 7, "A Bang—Not a Whimper", and Jessica Mitford, *Hons and Rebels* (London: Victor Gollancz, 1960), chapter 10. The climactic June 1934 Olympia rally is covered in Blythe, *The Age of Illusion*, chapter 10, "Thugs, Trunks and Things"; Ingram, *Rebel*, chapter 9, "Out of Bounds"; and Linehan, *British Fascism*, chapter 4. Harry Daley's detailed account comes in *This Small Cloud*, part 3, chapter 21.

Details of anti-Fascist action in Liverpool are contained in Members of Merseyside Socialist Research Group, *Genuinely Seeking Work: Mass Unemployment on Merseyside in the 1930s*, part 3, "The Fight Back?", chapter 11, "Styles of Reaction: Orangeism and Fascism on Merseyside in the 1930s". For the Popular Front policy of the Comintern, see Antony Beevor, *The Spanish Civil War* (London: Castle, 2002), chapter 3, "The Second Republic". For the downturn in the fortunes of the BUF, see Linehan, *British Fascism*, chapter 4.

For the political struggle between the Mitford sisters, see Jessica Mitford, *Hons and Rebels*, chapter 8. For Unity and the BUF, see Pryce-Jones, *Unity Mitford: A Quest*, chapter 5. As Pryce-Jones writes, fascism for Unity was "debutante life in reverse, literally in black instead of white". The quote "I'm going to Germany to meet Hitler" comes from *Hons and Rebels*, chapter 8. Jessica Mitford's quote about fortress aspects of life comes from the same source, chapter 9, as does her reaction to Esmond Romilly.

Unity Mitford's friendship with Hitler is covered by Pryce-Jones, *Unity Mitford: A Quest*, chapter 6, "Pick-up in the Osteria Bavaria". For details of her article "Confessions of an English Fascist Girl", see the same source, chapter 7, "Storm-Troop Maiden". For Jessica's description of the furious quarrel and the fistfight between the two sisters, see *Hons and Rebels*, chapter 13. For details of the Cable Street march, see Linehan, *British Fascism*, chapter 4, and for Charlie Goodman's quotes, see Humphries and Gordon, *Forbidden Britain*, chapter 3, "Bloodshed and Burning".

For the Spanish civil war, see Blythe, *The Age of Illusion*, chapter 12, and Symonds, *The Thirties: A Dream Revolved*, chapter 12, "Spain"; and for the non-intervention policy of the British government, see Antony Beevor, *The Spanish Civil War* (London, Cassell, 1982), chapter 11, "Arms and the Diplomats". John Cornford's article "Young Minds for Old" is cited in Stansky and Abrahams, *Journey to the Frontier: Two Roads to the Spanish Civil War*, part 2, "John Cornford", chapter 4, "Cambridge".

Many excellent oral histories from the Spanish civil war are displayed on the following site: http://www.geocities.com/HCHill-9820/spain/5.html. For John Cornford on revolutionary Barcelona, see Stansky and Abrahams, *Journey to the Frontier: Two Roads to the Spanish Civil War*, part 4, "Spain", chapter 1, "John Cornford". For the reality as opposed to the ideal, see Beevor, *The Spanish Civil War*, chapter 14, "The Battle for Madrid".

For Felicia Browne, see spartacus@pavilion.co.uk. For John Cornford as "a serious person", see Ingram, *Rebel: The Short Life of Esmond Romilly*, chapter 14, "Madrid!" The fact that Cornford was named after Rupert Brooke is cited in Stansky and Abrahams, *Journey to the Frontier: Two Roads to the Spanish Civil War*, part 2, "John Cornford", chapter 1, "Rupert John Cornford". For a distaff view of this 1930s icon, see the quote from his contemporary Stephen Runciman: "He was an extremely clever, forceful, merciless, rather inhuman boy"—from Carter, *Anthony Blunt: His Lives*, chapter 5.

For the disillusion of British intellectuals and the International Brigades, see Beevor, *The Spanish Civil War*, chapter 20, "The Brunete Offensive and the Mediterranean"; Symonds, *The Thirties: A Dream Revolved*, chapter 12; and Blythe, *The Age of Illusion*, chapter 12. For the Left Book Club, see Blythe, chapter 6, "Comrades! O Comrades!", and for the Kent Group convener testimony, see Tom Jeffery, *Mass-Observation: A Short History* (Sussex: University of Sussex Library, 1999), Mass-Observation Archive,

Occasional Paper No. 10, part 1, "The Need to Know", chapter 3, "The Left Book Club and Political Education".

The September 1938 clash between Communists and Fascists is contained in *Mass-Observation: Britain* (London: Penguin, 1939), chapter 2, "Crisis", part (g), "Hub of the Universe". For the rise of unemployment in 1937, see Cockburn, *The Devil's Decade*, chapter 11, "Rearmament (1937–8)". For the National Unemployed Workers' Movement stunts, see Graves and Hodge, *The Long Week-End*, chapter 23, "Social Consciences". For the sense that the forthcoming war was inevitable, see Cockburn, *The Devil's Decade*, chapters 7, 8, 11, and 12.

For the British army being promoted as the "Modern Army", see Jeffery, *Mass-Observation: A Short History*, part 1, chapter 2, "The Crisis of the Late Thirties", For the entitlement of workers to paid holidays, see Cockburn, *The Devil's Decade*, chapter 9, "Britain 1936". For the rise of consumerism in general, see Graves and Hodge, *The Long Week-End*, chapter 22, "Keeping Fit and Doing the Lambeth Walk". For pulp magazines, see George Orwell's famous March 1940 *Horizon* article about "Boys' Weeklies", presented in *The Collected Essays, Journalism and Letters of George Orwell, Vol. I* (London: Penguin, 1971), item no. 163.

For "all this theorizing is rot", see James Curtis, *The Gilt Kid* (London: Penguin, 1947), chapter 3, "Hazy". For increasing Americanization and the reaction to it, see Pearson, *Hooligan*, chapter 3. For the origins of the "wide boy", see Robert Murphy, *Smash and Grab: Gangsters in the London Underworld* (London: Faber and Faber, 1993), chapter 3. For details of Dr Gallup's British Institute of Public Opinion, see Graves and Hodge, *The Long Week-End*, chapter 23, "Social Consciences", and Jeffery, *Mass-Observation: A Short History*, part 1, chapter 1, "Social Investigation Between the Wars".

The origins and context of Mass-Observation are dealt with in Blythe, *The Age of Illusion*, chapter 6; Symonds, *The Thirties: A Dream Revolved*, chapter 11, "Mass Observation"; and Jeffery, *Mass-Observation: A Short History*, part 2, "Mass-Observation: History and Development", chapter 1, "Objectives". For details of "Work Town", see the same source, part 2, chapter 3, "Work Town and Holiday Town". For Jessica Romilly and the British Institute of Public Opinion, see Jessica Mitford, *Hons and Rebels*, chapter 20.

Mass-Observation's critical relationship to advertising and mass media is discussed in Jeffery, *Mass-Observation: A Short History*, part 2, chapter 2, "First Year's Work". The survey about advertisements is in the Mass-Observation Archive at Sussex University: FR (file report) A10, "Reactions to Ads", November 1938. For *Picture Post*, see Jeffery, *Mass-Observation: A Short History*, part 1, chapter 4, "Documentary"; Robert Kee, *The Picture Post Album* (London: Barrie and Jenkins, 1989); and Jon Savage, *Picture Post Idols* (London: Collins and Brown, 1992).

The complete *Picture Post* archive is kept at the Hulton Getty archive in West London; for Gracie Fields at home, see vol. 1, no. 5; for Freddie Bartholomew, see vol. 1, no. 10. For American consumerism as a kind of democratization of economic life, see Cockburn, *The Devil's Decade*, chapter 5, "The New Consumer".

The Mass-Observation report "Youth Organisations in Fulham" is contained in the Mass-Observation Archive, TC (Topic Collection) Youth, 1937–1940, 1/2, March 1938. For *Picture Post's* "A Glamour Girl's Day", see vol. 1, no. 14; "Birth of a New Dance Craze", see vol. 2, no. 1; Edward Hulton's editorial "Youth at the Helm" is also contained in vol. 2, no. 1. For the Locarno dance hall in Streatham and the unorthodox dancing at the huge open-air dances in London parks, see *Britain by Mass-Observation*, chapter 5, "Doing the Lambeth Walk". For the separate youth culture, including the Seebohm Rowntree material and the quotes from the young Mancunians, see Fowler, *The First Teenagers: The Lifestyle of Young Wage-earners in Interwar Britain*, chapter 4. For George Orwell's quote about consumerism averting revolution, see *The Road to Wigan Pier*, chapter 5.

21 JITTERBUGS AND ICKIES

The epigraph comes from an article titled "Outstanding Ickies", in *The Jitterbug*, no. 1 (New York, 1938). For a full description of Benny Goodman's Paramount Theater engagement, see James Lincoln Collier, *Benny Goodman and the Swing Era* (New York: Oxford University Press, 1989), chapter 13, "Finally, Success", and Lewis A. Erenberg, *Swingin' the Dream: Big Band Jazz and the Rebirth of American Culture* (Chicago: University of Chicago Press, 1998), part 2, "Now They Call It Swing, 1935–42", chapter 2, "The Crowd Goes Wild: The Youth Culture of Swing".

The quote about the audience being the show comes from Erenberg, *Swingin' the Dream*, part 2, chapter 2. For the impact of "Sing Sing Sing", see the same source. For swing on radio and the "make-believe ballrooms", see Collier, *Benny Goodman and the Swing Era*, chapter 13; Erenberg, *Swingin' the Dream*, part 2, chapter 2; and Abel Green and Joe Laurie Jr, *Show Biz from Vaude to Video* (New York: Henry Holt, 1951), chapter 56, "Disk Jocks and LP versus 45s." See also Russell Sanjek and David Sanjek, *American Popular Music Business in the Twentieth Century*, chapter 4, "The Fall and Rise of the Record Business".

For the development of swing and the Goodman band, see Collier, *Benny Goodman and the Swing Era*, chapter 11, "The First Victor Records", and chapter 12, "Making It at the Palomar". The Red Norvo quote comes from Abel Green and Joe Laurie Jr, *Show Biz from Vaude to Video*, chapter 7, "Hep to the Jive". For the crooners, see Erenberg, *Swingin' the Dream*, part 1, "From Jazz to Swing, 1929–35", chapter 1, "Just One More Chance: The Fall of the Jazz Age and the Rise of Swing"; see also Charles Thompson, *Bing: The Authorised Biography* (London: W. H. Allen & Co., 1979), and Rudy Vallee, *Vagabond Dreams Come True* (New York: Dutton, 1930).

The details of swing as a whole adolescent world are contained in Collier, *Benny Goodman and the Swing Era*, chapter 14, "The Swing Band Phenomenon", and Erenberg, *Swingin' the Dream*, part 2, chapter 2; this chapter is also the source for the "musical Hitlerism" quote.

For the American Youth Congress declaration, see Errol Lincoln Uys, *Riding the Rails*, part 1, introduction, "A New Deal for Youth". This chapter is also the source for the February 1937 "Youth Pilgrimage on Jobs and Education" march on Washington. See also Grace Palladino, *Teenagers: An American History*, part 1, "Adolescence", chapter 3, "A New Deal for Youth: 'Progressive Education' and the National Youth Administration".

More details on the NYA are to be found in Betty and Ernest K. Lindley, *A New Deal for Youth: The Story of the National Youth Administration*, chapter 1, "A New Deal for Youth", chapter 2, "Youth Inherits the Depression", chapter 3, "Out of School and Out of Work", and chapter 4, "Spare Time Put to Use". The quote "only part of the youth who were in the most desperate circumstances" comes from Lindley and Lindley, *A New Deal for Youth*, chapter 10, "The Balance Sheet for NYA". The William W. Hinckley quote is cited by Uys, *Riding the Rails*, part 1, introduction.

For the figure of half a million adolescents passing through the NYA, see Lindley and Lindley, *A New Deal for Youth*, chapter 9, "A Challenge to Education". For the 1920s baby boom, see *Report of the President's Research Committee on Social Trends, Recent Social Trends in the United States*, vol. 1, chapter 1, "The Population of the Nation", by Warren S. Thompson and P. K. Whelpton. For the importance of the high school market, as opposed to the college market, see Erenberg, *Swingin' the Dream*, part 2, chapter 2.

Robert S. Lynd and Helen Merrell Lynd's observations about the pace in high school being set by "business class girls" are contained in *Middletown in Transition*, chapter 5, "Making a Home: The Arena of Private Adjustment". Note also the Lynds' comments in chapter 7, "Spending Leisure": "The wives of the business class, gaining nowadays relatively little status from the arts of the housewife, throw themselves into leisure and have become the leisure-innovators of the culture." For the term "sub-debs", see Palladino, *Teenagers: An American History*, chapter 4, "Swing-Shift: Bobby Soxers Take the Stage".

The article "How Old Is Fifteen?" comes from *Vogue*, May 1, 1936 (New York: Condé Nast Publications), pp. 51–53. For the first regular advice columns in the *Ladies' Home Journal* and *Scholastic*, see Palladino, *Teenagers: An American History*, chapter 2, "Advise and Consent: Building Adolescent Character". This is also the source of the quotes "quality merchandise" and "boys love to run the show and be it". The booklet *Etiquette for the Teens* was published by the *Pittsburgh Sun-Telegraph* in collaboration with the Home Institute Inc. during 1937. It was written by Elizabeth Eldridge.

For the Benny Goodman Orchestra's famous concert at Carnegie Hall, see Erenberg, *Swingin' the Dream*, part 2, chapter 3, "Swing Is Here: Benny Goodman and the Triumph of American Music", and Collier, *Benny Goodman and the Swing Era*, chapter 17, "The Famous Carnegie Hall Concert". For Helen Ward on girls wearing saddle shoes, see Erenberg, *Swingin' the Dream*, part 2, chapter 2; this chapter is also the source for the Leonard Pratt quote. For Art Rollini on fan mail, see Collier, *Benny Goodman and the Swing Era*, chapter 14.

For swing fashions, see the pages of *Jitterbug* magazine (New York: 1938 and 1939) as well as Collier, chapter 14. Benny Goodman's "off his conk" quote comes from Erenberg, *Swingin' the Dream*, part 2, chapter 2. This chapter is also the source for the "folk avant-garde" quote, and the descriptions of Negroes dancing the Lindy hop. For the origins of the Lindy hop, see Carl Van Vechten, *Parties: Scenes from Contemporary New York Life* (New York: Alfred A. Knopf, 1930), chapter 14.

For the phrase "jitterbug ecstasy", see Collier, *Benny Goodman and the Swing Era*, chapter 14. For jive talk, see *Jitterbug* no. 1 and no. 2. For Cab Calloway's *Hepster's Dictionary*, see *Of Minnie the Moocher and Me* (New York: Thomas Y. Crowell, 1976), "The Cotton Club and The World"; a reprint of the sixth edition of Cab Calloway's *Hepster's Dictionary* is contained as an appendix in this volume, p. 252ff. For an excellent account of the origins of jive, see Mez Mezzrow and Bernard Wolfe, *Really the Blues* (New York: Citadel, 1990), chapter 12, "Tell a Green Man Something".

The idea that swing as grew "out of our brand of government" is cited in Erenberg, *Swingin' the Dream*, part 2, chapter 3. For the quote jazz as "a music of protest and rebellion", see Francis Newton, *The Jazz Scene* (London: Penguin, 1961). For John Hammond's influence on Benny Goodman, see Erenberg, part 2, chapter 5, "Swing Left: The Politics of Race and Culture in the Swing Era". For musicians as role models for the black community, see Erenberg, part 2, chapter 4, "News from the Great Wide World: Count Basie, Duke Ellington and Black Swing Bands". For the business of swing, see Erenberg, part 2, chapter 6, "The City of Swing: New York and the Dance Band Business in Black and White".

The uneasy relationship between the twenties and the thirties generations is mentioned in Green and Laurie Jr, *Show Biz from Vaude to Video*, chapter 47, "Hep to the Jive—Birth of Swing". For details of the Chicago Swing Jamboree see Erenberg, *Swingin' the Dream*, chapter 2. For youth movies and Hollywood in the 1930s, see David M. Considine, *The Cinema of Adolescence*, part 2, chapter 2, "From Skid Row to Middletown 1930–1949", and chapter 8, "Dead Ends and Death Row 1931–1939".

For the war on marijuana in the 1930s, see Harry Shapiro, *Waiting for the Man: The Story of Drugs and Popular Music* (London: Mandarin, 1990), chapter 5, "Hey, Hey, Harry J—How Many Guys Did You Bust Today?" The July 1937 article by Harry Anslinger and Courtney Ryley Cooper is cited by James A. Inciardi in *The American Drug Scene* (Boston: Roxbury Publishing, 2004). For songs about marijuana and "vipers", listen to the fifty songs contained in the double CD *Dope and Glory: Reefer Songs from the Thirties and Forties* (Munich: Trikont, 2002).

For marijuana not crossing over into the swing audience to any great degree, see Jill Jonnes, *Hep-Cats, Narcs and Pipe Dreams* (New York: Scribner, 1996), chapter 7, "The Sky Is High and So Am I", and Courtney Ryley Cooper, *Designs in Scarlet* (Boston: Little, Brown, 1939), chapter 8, "The Ghost Comes Back". For *Life* magazine and Kenneth Jones, see "Youth Problem: 1938" (*Life*, June 6, 1938), pp. 14–15. For the *New York Times* quote "Swing is the voice of Youth", see Erenberg, *Swingin' the Dream*, part 2, chapter 2.

The arrival of swing in Europe is covered in Newton, *The Jazz Scene*, chapter 13, "The Public", and Jim Godbolt, *A History of Jazz in Britain 1919–50*, chapter 7, "Duke and Lesser Mortals", and chapter 8, "Pundits, Record Companies, Rhythm Clubs". For Cab Calloway's 1935 visit, see *Of Minnie the Moocher and Me*, "The Cotton Club and the World". For the *Picture Post* article "Dance Madness in U.S.A.", see vol. 1, issue 6. For the Streatham Locarno description, see M-O A: MDJ, 1/4, Streatham Locarno, November 17, 1938, p. 2.

For swing in Germany, and the Hitler Youth quote "the Nigger has a very pronounced feeling for rhythm", see Michael H. Kater, *Different Drummers: Jazz in the Culture of Nazi Germany* (New York: Oxford University Press, 1992), chapter 1, "On the Index: The Third Reich's Pre-war Campaign": "Ideological Foundations and Polemics". For the controls on music and the media, see chapter 1, "On the Index: The Third Reich's Pre-war Campaign": "First Public Controls" and "Broadcasting and Recordings". For the continuation of the hot clubs, see chapter 2, "Jazz Defiant: The Re-assertion of a Culture": "The Jazz Congregation and Its High Priests".

For the destruction of records and the availability of Radio Luxembourg, see Kater, chapter 1, "On the Index: The Third Reich's Pre-war Campaign": "Broadcasting and Recordings". For the tepid German version of swing, see chapter 1, "On the Index: The Third Reich's Pre-war Campaign": "Attempts at German Jazz". Details of the International Rhythm Club are contained in chapter 2, "Jazz Defiant: The Re-assertion of a Culture": "The Jazz Congregation and Its High Priests", and for the Hamburg Swing Youth, see chapter 2, "Jazz Defiant: The Re-assertion of a Culture": "Jazz Within Politics". This chapter is also the source for the description of social dancing. For the SS denunciation of Benny Goodman and George Gershwin, see Kater, chapter 1, "Broadcasting and Recordings", and for the Hamburg condemnation of the swing dance, see chapter 2, "Jazz Defiant: The Re-assertion of a Culture": "Jazz Within Politics".

The description of the February 1939 German-American Bund rally in Madison Square Garden is to be found in John Roy Carlson, *Under Cover*, chapter 2, "School at Stahrenberg's". For the description of young fascists from broken or demoralized homes, see *The Aspirin Age*, ed. Isabel Leighton, "1938: The Radio Priest and His Flock", by Wallace Stegner. For the "rat-a-tat-tat" quote, see Carlson, *Under Cover*, chapter 4, "Coughlin's 'Christian Crusade'". See also James T. Farrell, *Tommy Gallagher's Crusade* (New York: Vanguard, 1939).

More details of the German-American Bund are contained in Carlson, *Under Cover*, chapter 7, "Puppets of Adolf Hitler". The Helen Vooros quote comes from the *New York Daily Mirror*, Saturday, August 19, 1939, p. 8. For school-leavers failing to find work, see *Life*, "Youth Problem 1938", p. 11, and Courtney Ryley Cooper's statistic in *Designs in Scarlet*, chapter 3, "The Crazy Things They Do". For the Walter Lippman article, see *Life*, "America's Future", June 5, 1939, p. 47ff.

Good descriptions of the 1939 World's Fair are to be found in Wolfgang Friebe, *Buildings of the World Exhibitions*, p. 156ff, and the official guidebook, *New York World's Fair: The World of Tomorrow, 1939* (New York: Exposition Publications Inc., 1939). The *Harper's Bazaar* article comes from issue 7219, February, 1939, pp. 45–47.

For MGM and the market domination of Shirley Temple, see Aljean Harmetz, *The Making of The Wizard of Oz* (London: Pavilion, 1989), chapter 4, "Casting". For more about Shirley Temple, see Norman J. Zierold, *The Child Stars* (London: Macdonald and Company, 1965), chapter 3, "What Was Shirley Temple Really Like?" The quote "a stampede back to the simple, untroubled hours of childhood" comes from *The Wizard of Oz: The Screenplay* (New York: Delta, 1989), introduction by Michael Patrick Hearn.

Oz's complex shoot is detailed in Harmetz, *The Making of The Wizard of Oz*, chapter 1, "The Studio, 1938", chapter 3, "The Brains, the Nerve, the Heart and the Music", and chapter 4, "Casting". The process is also covered by John Fricke, Jay Scarfone, and William Stillman, *The Wizard of Oz: The Official 50th Anniversary Pictorial History* (London: Hodder and Stoughton, 1989), part 1, "The Oz Diary: Creating a Classic", chapters 1–7. For the media campaign, see the same source, part 2, "The Oz Diary Continued: Promotion and Reception", chapter 8, "The Oz Campaign".

For the "song of yearning" quote in relation to "Over the Rainbow", see Harmetz, *The Making of The Wizard of Oz*, chapter 3. For Judy Garland and Mickey Rooney in 1938, see the same source, chapter 4, and Zierold, *The Child Stars*, chapter 5, "The True Judy", and chapter 8, "The Mick". For the "official welcoming committee" competition, see Fricke, Scarfone, and Stillman, *The Wizard of Oz: The Official 50th Anniversary Pictorial History*, chapter 10, "Capitol Times in Manhattan".

The arrival of Garland and Rooney in Manhattan was well covered: see the *New York Daily News*, Tuesday, August 15. For descriptions of the fans, and the quote "about sixty per cent of the multitude were minors", see the *New York Post*, Thursday, August 17. For the construction of Mickey Rooney and Judy Garland, see Norman J. Zierold, *The Child Stars*, chapter 8 and chapter 5. See also Jerold Frank, *Judy* (New York: Da Capo, 1989), chapters 10–11. For the benzedrine, see Frank, *Judy*, chapter 14.

For the quote about the "strange, heightened quality" of the colour sequences, see Harmetz, *The Making of The Wizard of Oz*, chapter 8, "Below the Line". For Judy Garland and Mickey Rooney visiting the World's Fair, see Fricke, Scarfone, and Stillman, *The Wizard of Oz: The Official 50th Anniversary Pictorial History*, chapter 10. For the Macy's of New York Judy Garland dresses advertisement, see the *New York Daily Mirror*, Tuesday, August 29, 1939, p. 11.

22 CONQUERORS AND OVERLORDS

The opening quotation from the *Schwarze Korps* comes from Jennifer Keeley, *Life in the Hitler Youth*, chapter 8, "The Hitler Youth at War". For the Robert Ley quote "such a thing as a private individual does not exist", see Blair R. Holmes and Alan F. Keele, *When Truth Was Treason: German Youth Against Hitler* (Chicago: University of Illinois Press, 1995), notes, introduction, note 17. For the vast majority of young Germans being in the Hitler Youth, see Gerhard Rempel, *Hitler's Children: The Hitler Youth and the SS*, chapter 1, introduction.

For the intricate system of youth policing and all those acronyms (helpfully decoded in the book's opening pages: pp. xi–xii), see Rempel, *Hitler's Children*, chapter 3, "Unifiers, Delinquents, Enforcers". Among the bodies with responsibility for youth policing were the Gestapo, the KRIPO (Kriminalpolizei), the SIPO (Sicherheitspolizei), and the SRD (Streifendienst). For the executions in Brandenburg, see H. W. Koch, *The Hitler Youth*, chapter 10, "Dissent". Adolf Hitler's December 1940 speech about education is contained in Koch, chapter 9, "Elites".

The preparedness of German youth for war is covered in Koch, *The Hitler Youth*, chapter 11, "War", and Keeley, *Life in the Hitler Youth*, chapter 8. See also many of the interviewees contained in Johannes Steinhoff, Peter Pechel, and Denis Showalter, *Voices from the Third Reich: An Oral History* (New York: Da Capo, 1994), part 1, "The Master of Europe", For the rapid German advances, see Mark Arnold Forster, *The World at War* (London: Pimlico, 2001), chapter 2, "The Phoney War", and chapter 3, "The Fall of France".

The figure of over eight million Hitler Youth members is cited in Koch, *The Hitler Youth*, chapter 11. For Hitler's successful annexations, see Koch, chapter 6, "Ideology", and for the refinement of the Nazi education system, see Detlev J. K. Peukert, *Inside Nazi Germany*, chapter 8, "Young People: Mobilisation and Refusal". For more on the German education system under Hitler, see Keeley, *Life in the Hitler Youth*, chapter 4, "The School Day of the Hitler Youth".

For the continuation of the Langemarck myth, see Koch, *The Hitler Youth*, chapter 1, "Traditions", and chapter 11. For the "I was only 17" quote, see Steinhoff, Pechel, and Showalter, *Voices from the Third Reich: An Oral History*, chapter 9, "The Reich Starts Shrinking", interview with Pater Basilius Heinrich Bartius Streithofen. For Melita Maschmann's revelation of selflessness, see *Account Rendered*, chapter 10. For Germany's victories in 1939 and 1940, see Steinhoff, Pechel, and Showalter, *Voices from the Third Reich: An Oral History*, chapter 3, "Blitzkrieg".

The immediate subsuming of the Hitler Youth within the demands of wartime is detailed in Koch, *The Hitler Youth*, chapter 8, "Education", and chapter 11. For the "on the back, a satchel" quote, see Koch, chapter 11. This chapter is also the source for the naming of 1940 as "The Year of the Trial". For the Hitler Youth and the administration of the rapidly expanding German empire, see Rempel, *Hitler's Children*, chapter 6, "Imperialists, Colonists, Exploiters".

For details of the French occupation, see Ian Ousby, *Occupation: The Ordeal of France, 1940–1944* (London: Pimlico, 1999), chapter 1, "Invasion and Exodus", and chapter 2, "Vichy and the New European Order". For the introduction of the yellow star in Holland, see Carol Ann Lee, *Roses from the Earth: The Biography of Anne Frank* (London: Penguin, 2000), part 2, "When the Sufferings of Us Jews Really Began", chapter 4. For the yellow star in France, see Ousby, *Occupation: The Ordeal of France, 1940–1944*, chapter 4, "Presence and Absence".

The activities of the *Einsatzkommandos* are vividly recalled in Solomon Perel, *Europa, Europa: A Memoir of World War II* (New York: John Wiley, 1997), chapter 1, "Flight to the East", and Andrea Warren, *Surviving Hitler: A Boy in the Nazi Death Camps* (New York: HarperCollins, 2001), chapter 2, "Occupation", and chapter 3, "A Growing Fear". For the Nazi policy in the Warthegau, see Rempel, *Hitler's Children*, chapter 5, "Peasants, Farmers, Warriors", and chapter 6; see also chapter 11.

For Melita Maschmann's account of serving in Posnan, see *Account Rendered*, chapters 6 and 7. For the quote "excessive demands", see chapter 9. For Solomon Perel on being caught in the Nazi advance, see *Europa, Europa*, chapter 1. For the increasing influence of the SS within the Hitler Youth, see Rempel, *Hitler's Children*, chapter 8, "Pied Pipers for an Elite". For the SS involvement in the occupied territories, see Rempel, chapter 5. This source includes the defence-peasants and "declaration of war on the liberal world".

For the naming of 1942 as the "Year of Service", see Koch, *The Hitler Youth*, chapter 11. For youth from occupied Europe pouring into the newly expanded Reich, see Rempel, *Hitler's Children*, chapter 5. For the increasing SS domination of the *Nationalpolitische Erziehungsanstalten* and the Adolf Hitler schools, see Koch, *The Hitler Youth*, chapter 9. For Solomon Perel's experiences in one of these elite schools, see *Europa, Europa*, chapter 3, "To Brunswick".

For the quote about the Waffen-SS having "outstanding equipment", see Steinhoff, Pechel, and Showalter, *Voices from the Third Reich: An Oral History*, chapter 15, "The Children's Crusade", interview with Theo Loch. The international September 1942 European Youth League Conference is cited in Koch, *The Hitler Youth*, chapter 11.

For Melita Maschmann's comments about higher party functionaries, see *Account Rendered*, chapter 8; for her bafflement at the attitude of her working-class charges, see chapter 12, and for her emotional reaction to seeing the Jewish ghetto at Kutno, see chapter 7. For the Nazi state reaching its zenith in late 1942, see Koch, *The Hitler Youth*, chapter 9.

23 RELUCTANT CONSCRIPTS AND SOCIALIST HEROES

The epigraph comes from *Children at War*, no. 3 in the Mass-Observation Teaching Booklet Series (University of Sussex, 1987), p. 27. For the Nazi threat becoming apparent, and Britain's mobilization, see Angus Calder, *The People's War: Britain 1939–1945* (London: Pimlico, 2002), chapter 1, "Prelude: Munich and the Thirties"; see also chapter 2, "This Strangest of Wars: September 1939–April 1940: Anticlimax".

For an assessment of the mood of British youth, see Mass-Observation Archive (M-O A), TC Conscientious Objectors, Report, July 1940. For Richard Hillary, see *The Last Enemy: The Memoir of a Spitfire*

Pilot (Jersey: Burford Books, 1997), chapter 1, "Under the Munich Umbrella". This chapter is also the source for his quotes about Nazi arrogance and his comments about his "Oxford Generation". For the quote from the grammar school headmaster in 1942, see *Children at War*, p. 5.

The "half-cynical boredom" of less privileged conscripts is cited in Calder, *The People's War: Britain 1939–1945*, chapter 2. The details about Mass-Observation's work with the Ministry of Information is contained in Tom Jeffery, *Mass-Observation: A Short History*, Occasional Paper No. 10, chapter 6, "War". For Mass-Observation on conscientious objectors, see M-O A, TC Conscientious Objectors, Box 1, July 1940.

For the William L. Shirer quote about British prisoners in Belgium, see *Berlin Diary: The Journal of a Foreign Correspondent, 1939–41* (New York: Knopf, 1941), part 2, "The War" diary entry for May 20, footnote. For Shirer's attitude to the Nazi regime, see, for example, his diary entry for September 19–20, 1939: "When Hitler brushed past me going down the aisle, he was followed by Himmler, Bruckner, Keitel and several others, all in dusty field grey. Most of them were unshaven, and I must say they looked like a pack of Chicago gangsters."

For the comparison between cannibal and Cockney adolescent raising, see Tom Harrisson, *The Hope of Youth: World Review*, M-O A, FR499, The Hope of Youth, November, 1940. The responses to the questionnaire, beginning with "a curious dead-end sort of position", come from M-O A, TC Youth 1937–43, 1/F, The Problems of the 18–20 Age-Group, October 1940. This is also the source for the quotes over the next couple of paragraphs. Harrisson's "there is always the possibility that after the war, Youth will blame Age" is from *The Hope of Youth*. This article is also the source for the quote about youth "largely left to its own devices".

For jitterbugs being thin on the ground, see M-O A, TC Music/Dancing, 1/A, Observations in Dance Halls, January 1941. For the quote "even to die", see the *Daily Mirror*, November 25, 1940, Call to Youth, M-O A, TC: Youth 1937–43, 1/D. For the figure of two million working boys and girls under eighteen, see A. P. Jephcott, *Girls Growing Up* (London: Faber and Faber, 1942), chapter 4, "Work". This chapter is also the source for the quote about youth "being a genuinely important part of the state".

Details of the long-planned evacuation scheme are contained in the Mass-Observation Teaching Booklet No. 2, *Evacuation* (University of Sussex, M-O A, 1987), pp. 1–2. For the quote "more akin to a cattle or slave market", see *Evacuation*, p. 5. The quote "they were delightfully oblivious" comes from *Evacuation*, p. 5; "if you say two words to them", p. 14; "the main problem between evacuees and hosts", p. 15. For the quote "aware of each other's existence", see M-O A, TC Evacuation, 1/1, Report from East Devon—Sidmouth. For the return to the inner cities, see *Evacuation*, p. 19.

For the blitz, see M-O Teaching Booklet No. 1, *The Blitz* (University of Sussex, M-O A, 1987), p. 5ff. For the figure of two million Londoners being made homeless, see Peter Lewis, *A People's War* (London: Methuen, 1986), chapter 4, "Bombs All Over". For looting and "a general slackening of moral sense among the young", see M-O A, TC Youth 1937–43, 2/K, Juveniles and the War, November 1940. This includes reports from social workers in Southwark, Rotherhithe, and Bermondsey. For the quotes on "rowdyism" and the youth problem and "practically no home life for youngsters", see M-O A, TC Youth 1937–43, 2/A, Youth Survey 1940–41, Paddington/Bermondsey, January 1941.

For schools being shut, damaged, and requisitioned, and other venues being closed, see Youth Survey 1940–41 as above. For the wartime increase of 33 per cent in under-seventeen delinquency, see Calder, *The People's War: Britain 1939–1945*, chapter 4, "Blitz: September 1940–May 1941". For the consensus that mischief accounted for a large part of the rise, see Anna W. M. Wolf, *Our Children Face War* (Massachusetts: Riverside Press, 1942), chapter 4, "Keeping Them Safe: What We Can Learn from Great Britain". For the phrase "youth is 'nowhere' in particular", see M-O A, TC Youth 1937–43, 2/A, Youth Survey 1940–41, as above.

For the quote "since the outbreak of war", see M-O A, TC Youth 1937–43, 1/D, "An Imperative Obligation", extract from newsletter vol. 4, no. 54, "Young Wage Earners" by N. Adler. For sensational press stories, see the *Daily Star*, January 1942, contained in M-O A, TC Youth 1937–43, 1/D. For the figures giving the lie to the press reports, see an article in the *Tribune* from January 1942, and from the *Times Educational Supplement* on January 31, 1942, photocopied in M-O A, TC Youth 1937–43, 2/C. The material in the next three paragraphs about youth leisure time and youth consumption comes from M-O A, TC Youth 1937–43, 2/E, Youth Survey, Paddington/Bermondsey, January 1941. The detailed quotes about clothes come from the same file.

The figure of 22 million employed is cited in Calder, *The People's War: Britain 1939–1945*, chapter 6, "The India-Rubber Island: Britain in 1943–44". For young women and jobs, including the quotes "the atmosphere is one of boredom" and "pleasant interlude", see M-O A, TC Youth 1937–43, 2/C, Attitudes to Jobs, November 1940. For fourteen- and fifteen-year-old girls being highly prized in factory work, see Jephcott, *Girls Growing Up*, chapter 4. For the quote "boys and girls are prepared", see chapter 5, "Leisure (2): Dancing and the Pictures".

Jephcott's description of a typical factory girl and her possessions is contained in *Girls Growing Up*, chapter 2, "Two Hundred and Forty Thousand Girls". This chapter is also the source for the girls' reading material: romance magazines and "erotic bloods". For Judy Garland, Mickey Rooney, and hot jazz, see Jephcott, chapter 5. This chapter is also the source for the quote "the hot rhythm and syncopated music".

The wartime increase in VD rates is detailed in John Costello, *Love Sex and War: Changing Values 1939–45* (London: Collins, 1985), chapter 6, "Plaster Saints". For the headline "Camp Followers; Girls 16–18 Running Wild", see M-O A, TC Youth 1937–43, 1/D, The People, January 1941. For girls "rushing rather than growing up", see Jephcott, *Girls Growing Up*, chapter 5. For parents being stuck "in the last generation", and the girl complaining that she had to lead an "Alice in Wonderland existence", see Jephcott, chapter 6, "Personal Relationships".

For women being drawn into the labour market and the Ernest Bevin quote, see Lewis, *A People's War*, chapter 5, "Daylight on Saturday". This chapter is also the source of the statistic of seven million women working and the quote "the cordite used to fly about". For the quote "girls were still inferior creatures in many homes", see Jephcott, *Girls Growing Up*, chapter 3, "Education (2): After School". For women working away from home and having a room of their own, see Lewis, *A People's War*, chapter 5.

For the report from the winter of 1941–42, quoting how many children had become "sullen and aggressive", see M-O A Teaching Booklet Series No. 3, *Children at War*, p. 16. This is a photocopy from an article in *The World's Children*, winter 1941–42, which was a magazine of the international Save the Children fund. The original article was titled "The London Child in War-time", written by Patricia Gilbert-Lodge. For the history of British youth service, see John R. Gillis, *Youth and History*, chapter 4, "Conformity and Delinquency: The Era of Adolescence, 1900–1950", part 5.

For the October 1940 circular "Youth Physical Recreation and Service", and details about youth service during the war, see M-O A, FR1353, The Service of Youth, August to September 1942, p. 2ff. This file report is also the source of the quote "I get fed up sitting around listening", and for the 1941 compulsory registration of all boys and girls from sixteen to eighteen years old, and reactions to this "Nazi-style state regimentation". Governmental involvement in almost every aspect of daily life is dealt with in Lewis, *A People's War*, chapter 6, "Women at War", and Calder, *The People's War: Britain 1939–1945*, chapter 5, "Through the Tunnel: October 1940–December 1942". The latter is the source for the CC41 Utility brand symbol.

For the drive to socialism, see Lewis, *A People's War*, chapter 10, "Leftward Look, the Land Is Bright". This chapter is also the source for the *Picture Post* material, 1941 *Plan for Britain*. The original is contained in *Picture Post*, vol. 10, issue 1, January 4, 1941. For army discussion groups, and soldiers' attitudes towards socialism, see Paul A. Thomas, *Post-War Hopes and Expectations, and Reaction to the Beveridge Report* (University of Sussex, M-O Teaching Booklet No. 9, 1988), pp. 5–7. The same pamphlet is the source for the quotes "schools such as Eton and Harrow should be abolished" (p. 8) and "the young people have their say".

For Richard Hillary's biography, see Sebastian Faulks, *The Fatal Englishmen: Three Short Lives* (London: Hutchinson, 1996), "Richard Hillary". See also Hillary, *The Last Enemy*, chapter 3, "Spitfires", and chapter 4, "The World of Peter Pease". For the Winston Churchill quote on the new Knights of the Round Table, see Stephen Bungay, *The Most Dangerous Enemy: A History of the Battle of Britain* (London: Aurum Press, 2000), chapter 1, "The Reason Why". See also Thomas, *Post-War Hopes and Expectations, and Reaction to the Beveridge Report*, p. 32ff. See also M-O A, FR1783, Social Security and Parliament, May 1943.

For the youth of fighter pilots, see Bungay, *The Most Dangerous Enemy*, chapter 13, "The Men". This chapter is also the source of the quote "it was just beer, women and Spitfires", and also for the powerful peer culture of "black humour and a sport-derived team spirit". The Churchill quote "never in the field of human conflict" is cited in Bungay, chapter 19, "Thinking Again". For Hillary refusing the role of national hero, and the quote "I got so sick of the stuff", see Faulks, *The Fatal Englishmen: Three Short Lives*, "Richard Hillary".

For the memorable quote from Hillary's mother, "You should be glad this has happened to you," see Hillary, *The Last Enemy*, chapter 5, "The Invaders". For the quote "it was impossible to look only to oneself", see chapter 9, "I See They Got You Too". For the remainder of Hillary's life after the publication, see Faulks, *The Fatal Englishmen: Three Short Lives*, "Richard Hillary".

24 SUB-DEBS AND GIs

The epigraph comes from Maureen Daly, *Seventeenth Summer* (New York: Scholastic, 1942). For the re-action of American adolescents to the war in Europe, see Richard Maring Ugland, *The Adolescent Experi-ence During World War II: Indianapolis as a Case Study* (Indianapolis: Department of History, Indiana University PhD, 1977; provided by UMI Dissertation Services from Proquest, Ann Arbor, Michigan), chapter 2, "Adjustment to War".

The "Yes, We Have Fifth Columnists" article was published in the *Reader's Digest*, October 1940 (Pleasantville, New York). The article was written by Edmond Taylor, and was reprinted from the maga-zine *America*, September 1940. For John Ray Carlson's exposé of the Bundist and KK groups working in America, see *Under Cover*. For the split in the American Youth Congress, see the Student Activism in the 1930s Web site, and go to "The Student Movement of the 1930s: Joseph P. Lash, interview", at http:// newdeal.feri.org/students/lash.htm.

For the passing of the Selective Service Bill, see Ugland, *The Adolescent Experience During World War II*, chapter 2, and Lee Kennett, *G.I.: The American Soldier in World War II* (New York: Warner Books, 1989), chapter 1, "The Draft". For rearmament beginning to take America out of the Depression, see Richard R. Lingeman, *Don't You Know There's a War On? The American Home Front, 1941–45* (New York: Putnam, 1970), chapter 1, "Prelude: Saturday". For the quote "today the word 'democratic' is on every-one's lips", see Ugland, *The Adolescent Experience During World War II*, chapter 2.

The details about the October 1940 Gallup poll are cited in George Gallup, *American Youth Speaks Up, Reader's Digest*, October 1940, pp. 51–55. For the American Youth Commission statement "we must face the realities of our situation" and "the hope and faith of our own young people are in danger", see Sidonie Matsner Gruenberg, ed., *The Family in a World at War* (New York: Harper and Bros, 1942), Howard Y. McCluskey, "The Outlook of Youth in a World at War".

The number of youth in American high schools during 1940 is tabulated from the figures given in Ugland, *The Adolescent Experience During World War II*, chapter 1, "Introduction", and James Gilbert, *A Cycle of Outrage* (New York: Oxford University Press, 1986), chapter 1, "A Problem of Behavior". The sta-tistic for the doubling of student numbers since 1930 comes from Ugland, *The Adolescent Experience During World War II*, chapter 3, "The High School at War". Ugland, chapter 8, "Conclusion", is also the source for the creation of the high school market.

For the unemployment figures among college-age adolescents, see Gruenberg, ed., *The Family in a World at War*, Howard Y. McCluskey, "The Outlook of Youth in a World at War". Geoffrey Gorer's ob-servations on the American high school come in *The Americans: A Study in National Character* (London: Cresset, 1948), chapter 3, "The All-American Child". For the quote "Middle Western Corn Belt commu-nity", see August B. Hollingshead, *Elmtown's Youth: The Impact of Social Classes on Adolescents* (New York: John Wiley, 1949), preface.

The importance of cliques is thoroughly discussed in Hollingshead, *Elmtown's Youth*, chapter 9, "Cliques and Dates". For the quote from Joyce Jensen, see the same chapter. For the broadcasting of clique styles back at youth, see Grace Palladino, *Teenagers*, chapter 4, "Swing Shift: Bobby Soxers Take the Stage"; this is also the source for the January 1941 *Life* magazine sub-debs article. For the early 1940s being "a propitious time to test specialized age merchandising", see Ugland, *The Adolescent Experience During World War II*, chapter 7, "The Emergence of the Teen-ager".

For temporary jobs, see Hollingshead, *Elmtown's Youth*, chapter 14, "Toil and Trouble". For the "Tricks for Teens" column, see Ugland, chapter 7. The first publication of *Calling All Girls* is described by Palladino in *Teenagers*, chapter 4; for extra details, see Lucy Rollin, *Twentieth-Century Teen Culture by the Decades: A Reference Guide*, chapter 4, "The 1940s." See also Michael Barson and Stephen Heller, *Teenage Confidential* (San Francisco: Chronicle Books, 1998), chapter 1, "Kleen Teens Never Die Young: The Dawn of Teen Culture".

Early 1940s youth movies are detailed in David M. Considine, *The Cinema of Adolescence*, chapter 2, "From Skid Row to Middletown 1930–1949". For the rise of Glenn Miller, see Lewis A. Erenberg, *Swin-gin' the Dream*, part 3, "Culture in the Wild 1942–1954", chapter 7, "Swing Goes to War: Glenn Miller and the Popular Music of World War II", and Gunter Schuller, *The Swing Era: The Development of Jazz, 1930–1945* (New York: Oxford University Press, 1989), chapter 7, "The White Bands, part 2: Glenn Miller".

For Maureen Daly on peer anxiety, see *Seventeenth Summer*, chapter 1, "June". For Hollingshead on "long before a young Middletowner is able to earn money", see *Elmtown's Youth*, chapter 7, "The Adolescent in the Community". For his hypothesis that "the social behavior of adolescents" betrayed their parents' social origins, see *Elmtown's Youth*, chapter 1, "The Research Problem", and chapter 7. Hollingshead's description of the five classes is contained in *Elmtown's Youth*, chapter 2, "Field Procedures", and chapter 5, "Cultural Characteristics of the Five Classes".

For the quote "a group of girls who think they are higher than us", see *Elmtown's Youth*, chapter 8, "The High School in Action". For the ostracism of Joan Meyers, see chapter 9, "Cliques and Dates". For the quote "almost like a secret police system", see Daly, *Seventeenth Summer*, chapter 1, "June". For the dress of Elmtown's young men, see *Elmtown's Youth*, chapter 15, "Leisure Hour Activities".

For the images of freedom in American popular culture see, *inter alia*, Rollin, *Twentieth-Century Teen Culture by the Decades: A Reference Guide*, chapter 4, and Palladino, *Teenagers*, chapter 4. For the "ill-defined no-man's-land" of adolescence, see Hollingshead, *Elmtown's Youth*, chapter 7.

For the conspiracy of silence between adults and adolescents, see *Elmtown's Youth*, chapter 12, "Recreation and Tabooed Pleasures", while the maturation of sexual capacities comes from chapter 16, "Sex and Marriage". The high school drop-out rates of Class IV and Class V adolescents are cited by Hollingshead in *Elmtown's Youth*, chapter 13, "Leaving School", and for the pursuit of adult sensations, see chapter 15. For the quote "cross-eyed, seventeen-year-old Class V girl", see chapter 14, "Toil and Trouble".

For the inevitability of America's involvement in the war, see Ugland, *The Adolescent Experience During World War II*, chapter 2. For the quote "students seemed to be waiting for something to force the issue", see Lingeman, *Don't You Know There's a War On?*, chapter I. For the shock of Pearl Harbor, see Ugland, chapter 2, and Lingeman, chapter 2, "In the Event of an Air Raid, Walk, Do Not Run". This chapter is also the source for the information about the swamping of the recruiting offices.

The stages of recruitment, training, and adaptation to army life are detailed in Kennett, *G.I.*, chapter 2, "Greetings . . . ", and chapter 4, "The View from the Barracks". For the quote "young people are still the prize resource of the nation", see Gruenberg, ed., *The Family in a World at War*, Howard Y. McCluskey, "The Outlook of Youth in a World at War". For the transition between a "fun-loving eighteen-year-old son" to a pilot "manipulating a bomber over Tokyo", see Anna W. M. Wolf, *Our Children Face War*, chapter 2, "Discipline for Danger".

For induction as "the knifing off of past experience", see Kennett, *G.I.*, chapter 3, "The World of the Training Camps". For bonding into another clique, see James Jones, *WWII* (New York: Ballantine, 1975), chapter 12, "Soldiers' Evolution". For profane and abusive sergeants, see Samuel A. Stouffer, Edward A. Suchman, Leland C. DeVinney, Shirley A. Star, and Robin M. Williams Jr, *The American Soldier: Adjustment During Army Life* (New York: Science Editions, 1965), vol. 1, chapter 5, "How Personal Adjustment Varied in the Army".

For the better education of high school recruits, see Stouffer et al., *The American Soldier*, chapter 2, "The Old Army and the New". This chapter is also the source of the quote "the Army tradition bigoted and medieval". The Arthur Miller quote about the GI being "a much more complicated character" comes in Kennett, *G.I.*, chapter 4. For war causing boys and girls to grow up overnight, see Gruenberg, ed., *The Family in a World at War*, Caroline B. Zachry, "The Adolescent and His Problems Today". This chapter is also the source of the quote "a lot of thinking has been going on".

The introduction of rationing within America is described by Lingeman in *Don't You Know There's a War On?*, chapter 7, "Shortages and Mr Black", and Palladino, *Teenagers*, chapter 4. The quote "nearly every student" comes from Ugland, *The Adolescent Experience During World War II*, chapter 2. The material about American high school readiness for war comes from Ugland, chapter 3.

This chapter is also the source for the material concerning the Office of Civilian Defense ten-point programme, the return of the ROTC, the acceleration of adolescent schooling, and the involvement of student publications. The quote about "sound discipline" being needed from American adolescents is from Wolf, *Our Children Face War*, chapter 2. For Bob Berger, see *Life* magazine, November 30, 1942, front cover and pp. 103–111.

For Ernie Pyle and the thumbnail sketches of some "boys", see *Here Is Your War: The Story of G.I. Joe* (New York: Forum Books, 1945), chapter 7, "Turns and Encounters". For the Bob Berger quote about why the war is being fought, see *Life*, November 30, 1942, p. 105. For the need for American youth to become "missionary-minded", see Gruenberg, ed., *The Family in a World at War*, Everett R. Clinchy, "Unity in Diversity". The Mark McCloskey quotes come from the same book, from the chapter "The Outlook of Youth in a World at War". The American Youth Congress quote also comes from this chapter.

For the agitation of Negroes for greater inclusion in American democracy, see John Morton Blum, *V Was for Victory* (New York: Harcourt Brace Jovanovich, 1976), part 6, "Black America: The Rising Wind", chapter 1, "Jim Crow"; for the Anna W. M. Wolf quote about America being "riddled with race prejudice and religious intolerance", see *Our Children Face War*, chapter 3, "What Can They Do to Help?" For the continuation of segregation in the army, see Blum, *V Was for Victory*, part 6, "Black America: The Rising Wind".

For Booker T. Washington and Joe Louis as role models, see E. Franklin Frazier, *Negro Youth at the Crossways* (Washington DC: American Council on Education, 1940), chapter 7, "Social Movements and Ideology." For the quote "I don't believe I or any other Negro", see chapter 3, "Neighbourhood Contacts". The quote "white people don't treat us fairly" comes from chapter 6, "Seeking Employment", as does the quote "Negroes don't get as good chances as white people".

For the release in sex, see *Negro Youth at the Crossways*, chapter 7: "Warren Wall". The quotes for the paragraph beginning "Others pursued the policy" come from chapter 2, "The Role of the Family". "I'd like to see all segregation wiped out" comes from chapter 6, "Seeking Employment". For the young man wishing to join the army, see Frazier, the introduction. The Negro march on Washington and the president's directive that "there shall be no discrimination" comes in Blum, *V Was for Victory*, part 6.

The Richard Wright quotes "even in times of peace" and "we watch strange moods fill our children" come from *Twelve Million Black Voices: A Folk History of the Negro in the United States of America* (London: Lindsay Drummond Ltd, 1947), part 3, "Death on the City Pavements". This part is also the source for the quotes "we play our guitars" and "our music makes the whole world dance". The snapshot of the young man stepping out of the Savoy Ballroom is on p. 129.

25 GERMAN SWING KIDS AND FRENCH *ZAZOUS*

The epigraph from Henry Sklow comes from Michael H. Kater, *Different Drummers: Jazz in the Culture of Nazi Germany*, chapter 3, "Jazz Goes to War: Compliance and Defiance, Demands of the Military". For swing in wartime Germany and the Nazi-occupied countries, see Kater, chapter 3, and Jean-Claude Loiseau, *Les Zazous* (Paris: Le Sagittaire, 1977), chapter 2ff.

For a general account, although not specifically referenced here, see Mike Zwerin, *La Tristesse de Saint-Louis: Jazz Under The Nazis* (New York: Beach Tree Books, 1985). This book contains an excellent account of meeting Heinz "Ganjo" Baldauf, the Gestapo agent who persecuted the Harlem clique of Frankfurt Swings—chapter 8, "Baldauf"—and a wonderful 1943 rant by a French schoolteacher named Henri Vermaine against the *Zazous* in chapter 17, "Zazou Hey!": "Swing plunges the subject into constant excitement. It causes nightmares, You get addicted to it. It's like drugs."

For juvenile delinquency in Nazi Germany after the outbreak of war, see Gerhard Rempel, *Hitler's Children*, chapter 4, "Police Boys, Informers and Rebels". For the figure of 95 per cent of German youth remaining in thrall to the regime, see Rempel, chapter 9, "The Final Sacrifice". The quote "be visited by terror" comes from Detlev J. K. Peukert, *Inside Nazi Germany*, chapter 11, "Order and Terror".

For the reappearance of the proletarian gangs, see Rempel, *Hitler's Children*, chapter 4. For the details of clothing, see Peukert, *Inside Nazi Germany*, chapter 8, "Young People: Mobilisation and Refusal", "Edelweiss Pirates". The quote "it's the Hitler Youth's own fault" comes from the same source. The details about the gang names come from Rempel, chapter 4, and Peukert, chapter 8. Peukert is the source for both the altered popular hits and the "every child knows who the Kittelsbach Pirates are" quote.

For Heinrich Himmler's June 1940 Police Order for the Protection of Youth and the expansion of the SRD, see Rempel, *Hitler's Children*, chapter 4. This chapter is also the source for the autumn 1940 Youth Service Arrest order. The statistics for offenders and arrests come from Rempel, chapter 4, and Peukert, *Inside Nazi Germany*, chapter 8. For the Nazis and gender segregation, see Rempel, chapter 4. The "sexual intercourse among minors" and following quotes come from Peukert, chapter 8, subsection "The Swing Movement".

For the continuation of swing clubs, see Peukert, *Inside Nazi Germany*, chapter 8, and Kater, *Different Drummers*, chapter 3, subsection "The War Inside the Great Germanic Reich". The Jutta Hipp quote comes from the latter source. The details of the Hamburg swing kids' clothes come from Kater, chapter 3, subsection "Hamburg's Different Drummers". For details of the Frankfurt clique and the authorities chasing swing fans with speedboats, see the same chapter. For the February 1940 Gestapo quote about a swing dance, see Peukert, chapter 8, subsection "The Swing Movement".

The story of Hamburg swings over the next few paragraphs is beautifully told by Kater, *Different*

Drummers, chapter 3, subsection "Hamburg's Different Drummers". The material about listening to the BBC comes from Kater, chapter 2, "Jazz Defiant: The Reassertion of a Culture, Jazz Within Politics". For the Reichsmusikkammer's banning of hot swing music, see Kater, chapter 3, subsection "The War Inside the Great Germanic Reich". For the movement underground of the Hamburg swings and the appeal to Reinhard Heydrich, see Kater, chapter 3, subsection "Hamburg's Different Drummers".

Himmler's response to the Hamburg swings is quoted in full in Peukert, *Inside Nazi Germany*, chapter 10, "Public Show and Private Perceptions". For the climactic Hamburg swing cabaret that featured impressions of Hitler and Goebbels, see Kater, *Different Drummers*, chapter 3; for the SS report on the summer 1942 Hamburg concert by the Willie Artelt band, see Peukert, *Inside Nazi Germany*, chapter 11, "Order and Terror".

The spring 1941 misbehaviour of the "petits Swings" is detailed in Loiseau, *Les Zazous*, chapter 2. For the symbiotic relationship of French swing to the occupation, see Ian Ousby, *Occupation: The Ordeal of France 1940–1944*, part 2, "The Shameful Peace", chapter 3, "Are You in Order?", and Herbert R. Lottman, *The Left Bank* (New York: Houghton Mifflin, 1982), part 3, "The German Years", chapter 23, "Topography of German Paris". For the quote "the excessive ecstasies", the material about swing as a pop fashion, and the quote "what could you do when you couldn't stand it?" see Loiseau, chapter 2.

The regimes of occupied France are covered in Ousby, *Occupation: The Ordeal of France 1940–1944*, part 1, "The Fall of France and the Path of Collaboration", chapter 2, "Vichy and the New European Order". For the *Blutfahne*, the blood banner, see Ousby, part 2, chapter 4, "Presence and Absence". The material about the Vichy regime comes from Ousby, part 1, chapter 2. For Pétain's quote "the spirit of youth", see Patrice Bollon, *Morale du masque: Merveilleux, Zazous, Dandies, Punks, etc.* (Editions du Seuil, 1990), chapter 7, "Zazou-zazou-zazouhé".

For the place of youth in this "agrarian utopia", see Julian Jackson, *France: The Dark Years, 1940–44* (Oxford: Oxford University Press, 2001), chapter 7, "The National Revolution". This chapter is also the source for the quote "the collective suicide of a nation". For the Vichy youth group Les Compagnons de France, see Ousby, part 1, chapter 2, and Loiseau, *Les Zazous*, chapter 1. For the pilgrimage to Le Puy, see Jackson, *France: The Dark Years, 1940–44*, chapter 11, "Propaganda, Policing and Administration".

The Simone de Beauvoir quote "the same violent prejudice" comes from *The Prime of Life* (Cleveland: World Publishing Company, 1962), chapter 7. For conditions in the Occupied Zone and the north of France, see Loiseau, *Les Zazous*, chapter 1; Ousby, *Occupation: The Ordeal of France 1940–1944*, chapter 3; and Jackson, *France: The Dark Years, 1940–44*, chapter 8, "Collaboration". For details about the collaborationist press, see Ousby, part 1, chapter 2.

For Robert Brasillach, see L. S. Kaplan, *The Collaborator: The Trial and Execution of Robert Brasillach* (Chicago: University of Chicago Press, 2000), chapter 1, "The Making of a Fascist Writer", and chapter 2, "Brasillach's War". For *Je Suis Partout* as the most popular *collabo* magazine, see Jackson, *France: The Dark Years, 1940–44*, chapter 9, "Collaborationism". For the column "Partout et ailleurs", see Herbert R. Lottman, *The Left Bank*, chapter 18, "The Structures of Collaboration", and Kaplan, *The Collaborator*, chapter 2, "Brasillach's War".

For Jean-Paul Sartre's "everything we did was equivocal", see ed. J. G. Weightman, *French Writing on English Soil* (London: Sylvan Press, 1945), postscript, "Paris Under the Occupation". For the Parisian schoolgirl's conflicted reaction about the Germans, see Jackson, *France: The Dark Years, 1940–44*, chapter 14, "Reconstructing Mankind". For execution as the instant result of resistance, see Ousby, *Occupation: The Ordeal of France 1940–1944*, chapter 5, "Living in Fear, Living in Hope". For the "petits Swings" beginning to dress up as a provocation, see Bollon, *Morale du masque*, chapter 7.

For the Albert Camus quote, see *The Rebel* (London: Hamish Hamilton, 1959), part 2, "Metaphysical Rebellion", subsection, "The Dandies' rebellion". For the change from the "petits Swings" to the "Ultra Swings", see Bollon, *Morale du masque*, chapter 7. For the censoring of jazz and swing after America's entering the war, see Loiseau, *Les Zazous*, chapter 2. For the closing of the cafés on the Boulevard St Michel, see Loiseau, chapter 4, and for the quote "danced on the edge of the volcano", see chapter 2.

For the *Zazous'* age and the J3 rebellion, see Ousby, *Occupation: The Ordeal of France 1940–1944*, part 2, chapter 3. The idea that the *Zazous* acted out a kind of Dadaism while preserving a blank, sarcastic façade is contained in Bollon, *Morale du masque*, chapter 8, "La mise en ironie du monde". For the quote "to bring us your twenty years", see Loiseau, *Les Zazous*, chapter 2. For the etymology of the word *Zazou*, see Loiseau, chapter 2, and Bollon, chapter 8.

The details of records by Slim Gaillard and Freddy Taylor are contained in Charles Delaunay's extremely thorough *New Hot Discography* (New York: Criterion, 1982), "Post 1930 Jazz". For the *Zazou* costume, see Bollon, *Morale du masque*, chapter 7, and Loiseau, *Les Zazous*, chapter 4. The quote "oiled like a salad" comes from the latter, and "large as ships" from the former source. For the quote "a generation of morons", see Loiseau, chapter 4, which is also the source for "the Zazou HQ". For the quote "spoiled little scumbags" see Loiseau, chapter 7.

For the Zazou surprise parties, see Loiseau, *Les Zazous*, chapter 5; for the mythology of America, see chapter 6. The quote "a question of attitude" comes from the same source. For the appreciation of Vichy kitsch, see chapter 5. This includes the quote "crystallised perfume of stupidity" and "with the spirit of contradiction". For Robert Brasillach criticizing the Zazous for not "having the fascist spirit", see Loiseau, chapter 8; for the "madness of jazz" quote, see chapter 6, and for the "they were not Frenchmen" quote, see chapter 8. The next *La Gerbe* quote, "These idiots are playing with fire", comes from the same chapter.

For the Zazous' clothes contravening rationing, see Loiseau, *Les Zazous*, chapter 4. For the quote "these young citizens of free France", see Loiseau, chapter 8; for the concept of *l'attentisme*, see Bollon, *Morale du Masque*, chapters 7 and 8, and for the Simone de Beauvoir quote, see *The Prime of Life*, chapter 7. For the Jacques Doriot quote, the Jeunes Populaires Français beating up Zazous, the *La Jeunesse* headline "RASEZ LE ZAZOU", and the Zazous being picked up in regular police sweeps, see Loiseau, chapter 9.

The detail about the yellow "swing" star comes from Loiseau, *Les Zazous*, chapter 10. For swing becoming a national fad during 1942, see the same chapter. For the forced-labour draft and youth arrests, and for the Zazous joining *les refractaires*, see Loiseau, chapter 11; the *"zazou triste"* is profiled in chapter 12. For the quote, "abstract, ambient horror", see J. G. Weightman, ed., *French Writing on English Soil*, postscript, "Paris Under the Occupation", by Jean-Paul Sartre.

Note: the translation of the French texts by Jean-Claude Loiseau and Patrice Bollon is the author's own.

26 ZOOT-SUITERS AND VICTORY GIRLS

The epigraph comes from Anna W. M. Wolf, *Our Children Face War*, foreword. For war hysteria after December 1941, see Richard R. Lingeman, *Don't You Know There's a War On?*, chapter 2, "In the Event of an Air Raid, Walk, Do Not Run". For Freud's view of the psychological forces unleashed by war, see "Thoughts for the Times on War and Death" (1915), collected in the *Standard Edition of the Complete Psychological Works of Sigmund Freud* (London: Hogarth Press and The Institute of Psychoanalysis, 1999), vol. 14, pp. 273–302.

For more on war hysteria, see Mauricio Mazon, *The Zoot Suit Riots: The Psychology of Symbolic Annihilation* (Austin, Texas: University of Texas Press, 2002), chapter 1, "Introduction", and chapter 6, "The Symbols, Imagery and Rhetoric of the Riots". The Chester Himes quote "It was the look on white people's faces", comes from *If He Hollers, Let Him Go* (New York: Thunder's Mouth Press, 1986), chapter 1. For the fate of the Nisei, see John Morton Blum, *V Was for Victory*, part 5, "Outsiders", chapter 2, "A Jap's a Jap". The other two quotes come from John Okada, *No-No Boy* (Seattle: University of Washington Press, 1979), preface.

For the disturbance in Detroit at the end of February 1942, see Blum, part 6, "Black America: The Rising Wind", chapter 3, "Race Riot". The quote "hundreds of whites" comes from Alfred McClung Lee, *Race Riot* (New York: Dryden Press, 1943), part 3, "Overcrowding in Dwellings, Recreation and Transportation", chapter 7, "What Really Caused the Detroit Riots?"

For details of the "Sleepy Lagoon" case, see Mazon, *The Zoot Suit Riots*, chapter 2, "The Sleepy Lagoon Case", and Manuel P. Servin, ed., *An Awakened Minority: The Mexican-Americans* (Beverly Hills: Glencoe Press, 1974), "The 1943 Zoot-Suit Riots: Brief Episode in a Long Conflict", by Patricia Rae Adler. For the lyrics of Harry James's hit, see Lingeman, *Don't You Know There's a War On?*, chapter 3, "The Changing Landscape: War Towns, War Brides and Washington".

For youngsters running amok in cinemas and the *Life* quote "suddenly the country is aware of what war is doing to children", see David M. Considine, *The Cinema of Adolescence*, part 4, "Juvenile Delinquency", chapter 8, "Dead Ends and Death Row, 1931–1949", and Abel Green and Joe Laurie Jr, *Show Biz from Vaude to Video*, chapter 49, "Soldiers in Grease Paint", subsection "zoot-suiters". For the difficulties of America's young in the first few years of the war in general, see Richard M. Ugland, *The Adolescent Experience During World War II*, chapter 5, "Stresses and Strains".

The quote "more affected by the war" comes from Sidonie Matsner Gruenberg, ed., *The Family in a World at War*, Caroline B. Zachry, "The Adolescent and His Problems Today". For the "avalanche" of youngsters into industry, see Lingeman, *Don't You Know There's a War On?*, chapter 5, "Give Us the Tools". For the statistics about youth employment, see Ugland, *The Adolescent Experience During World*

War II, chapter 4, "Youth Employment", and James Gilbert, *A Cycle of Outrage: America's Reaction to the Juvenile Delinquent in the 1950s* (New York: Oxford University Press, 1986), chapter 1, "A Problem of Behavior".

The quote "while the war lasts" comes from Ugland, *The Adolescent Experience During World War II*, chapter 4, as does "clamoring for outstanding boys and girls". The quote "the adolescent feels that the foundations of his universe have changed overnight" comes from Gruenberg, ed., *The Family in a World at War*, Caroline B. Zachry, "The Adolescent and His Problems Today". For patriotic movies, see Lingeman, *Don't You Know There's a War On?*, chapter 6, "Will This Picture Help Win the War?"

Flying Wildcats is a typical wartime book about "the flying exploits of the army, navy and marines": it was published in 1943 by the Hampton Publishing Company, New York, and was edited by Leo Margulies.

For the social definition of adolescence changing again, see Ugland, *The Adolescent Experience During World War II*, chapter 4. For this unprecedented visibility, see Ugland, chapter 8, "Conclusion", and for curfews, see Ugland, chapter 5. The two quotes "our whole way of life" and "I'll bet that when the ones of that council were fifteen" come from the same chapter. For America's industrial resurgence and exit from the Depression, see Blum, *V Was for Victory*, part 3, "Getting and Spending", chapter 1, "The Return of Prosperity", and chapter 2, "The Wartime Consumer".

The quote "frantic construction" comes from Lingeman, *Don't You Know There's a War On?*, chapter 3. For business demanding the end of socialist "nonsense", see Studs Terkel, *The Good War: An Oral History of World War II* (New York: Pantheon, 1984), book 3, "The Big Panjandrum: Interview with Thomas G. 'Tommy the Cork' Corcoran". For the Ford-run Willow Run plant and the lack of amenities, see Lingeman, chapter 3.

For the disadvantaged descending on Seneca, Illinois, see Terkel, *The Good War*, book 3, "Sudden Money", interview with Elsie Rossio. For the increase in marriages and the difficulties faced by young brides, see Lingeman, *Don't You Know There's a War On?*, chapter 3, and for 6.5 million entering the labour force, see Blum, *V Was for Victory*, part 3, chapter 2.

"Women are bursting out of the mold" comes from Max Lerner's fascinating collection of journalism, *Public Journal: Marginal Notes on Wartime America* (New York: Viking, 1945), "The New Amazons", originally published February 11, 1943. For life in the new defence towns, see Gruenberg, ed., *The Family in a World at War*, Mark A. McCloskey, "Educational Problems in Camp and Community". The Agnes Meyer quote "a social worker" comes from Lingeman, *Don't You Know There's a War On?*, chapter 3, as does the report from the cinema in Muncie, Indiana.

The moulding of young GIs is dealt with in Lingeman, *Don't You Know There's a War On?*, chapter 2; Mazon, *The Zoot Suit Riots*, chapter 1 and chapter 6; and James Jones, *WWII*, "I Didn't Raise My Boy . . . ", pp. 30–33. Jones also describes the carpe diem psychology of the GI in chapter 2, "Soldiers' Evolution", pp. 54–55, and the pin-ups in "First War Art", p. 57.

For the GI feeling free "to release his impulses", see Mazon, *The Zoot Suit Riots*, chapter 6. For off-duty servicemen, see chapter 4, "Servicemen and Zoot-Suiters". The Donald Vining quote comes from *A Gay Diary 1933–1946* (New York: Pepys Press, 1979), diary entry for Monday, May 4, 1942. The May 1943 discontent within America is described by Mazon in *The Zoot Suit Riots*, chapter 4. For the senior patrol officer report from June 8, see Mazon, appendix A.

The Carey McWilliams quote "marching through the streets of downtown Los Angeles" comes from Servin, ed., *An Awakened Minority: The Mexican-Americans*, "The 1943 Zoot-Suit Riots: Brief Episode in a Long Conflict", by Patricia Rae Adler. For the background to this conflict, see, in the same volume, "Wartime Labor Problems and Mexican-Americans in the War", by Robin Fitzgerald-Scott. For the quote "a boy of sixteen was ready", see Mazon, *The Zoot Suit Riots*, chapter 4.

For the zoot-suiters being "against not one but two cultures", see George J. Sanchez, *Becoming Mexican-American: Ethnicity, Culture and Identity in Chicano Los Angeles, 1900–1945* (New York: Oxford University Press, 1993), part 3, "Shifting Homelands", chapter 6, "Family Life and the Search for Stability". This chapter is also the source for the idea that the zoot suit became the standard for the *pachiquismo*. Malcolm X's famous quote about his first zoot suit comes from *The Autobiography of Malcolm X* (New York: Ballantine, 1984), chapter 3, "Home Boy".

For the origin of the zoot suit, see Mazon, *The Zoot Suit Riots*, chapter 1; Farid Chenoune, *A History of Men's Fashion* (Paris: Flammarion, 1993), part 4, "Pinstripes and Black Leather, 1940–1990", chapter 20, "Zazous and Zoot Suits: Funny Fashions for a Phoney War"; and Steve Chibnall, *Whistle and Zoot: The Changing Meaning of a Suit of Clothes* (London: History Workshop, issue #20, Autumn 1985). The detail about Clyde Duncan is contained on p. 9 of the full version of Chibnall's History Workshop paper

Style Politics: The Changing Meaning of a Suit of Clothes (Leicester Polytechnic: unpublished): thanks to the author.

The song "A Zoot Suit for My Sunday Gal" is cited in Chibnall, *Style Politics*, p. 3, and Lingeman, *Don't You Know There's a War On?*, chapter 9, "War Nerves". For the zoot suit being banned after the introduction of cloth rationing, see Sanchez, *Becoming Mexican-American*, part 4, "Ambivalent Americanism", chapter 12, "The Rise of the Second Generation", and Blum, *V Was for Victory*, part 3, chapter 1. For high school children flocking to Harlem to buy zoots, see Chibnall, *Style Politics*, p. 11.

For the linking of zoot suits to *pachucos* and the impact of the Sleepy Lagoon case, see Mazon, *The Zoot Suit Riots*, chapter 2, and Servin, ed., *An Awakened Minority: The Mexican-Americans*, "The 1943 Zoot-Suit Riots: Brief Episode in a Long Conflict", by Patricia Rae Adler. For the detail of thirty-five *pachuco* gangs, see Sanchez, *Becoming Mexican-American*, part 4, chapter 12.

The gang member quote "we were kids" comes from Servin, ed., *The Awakened Minority: The Mexican-Americans*, "The 1943 Zoot-Suit Riots: Brief Episode in a Long Conflict", by Patricia Rae Adler. The details of the Sleepy Lagoon case come from Mazon, *The Zoot Suit Riots*, chapter 2; Sanchez, *Becoming Mexican-American*, chapter 12; and Servin, ed., Patricia Rae Adler, as above. The last is the source of the quote "approximately six hundred persons".

For the description of the trial of the defendants in the Sleepy Lagoon case, including "ceremonial lynching" and "wild cats", see Mazon, *The Zoot Suit Riots*, chapter 2, and for the *Li'l Abner* zoot suit storyline, see Mazon, chapter 3, "The Zoot Suit Yokum Conspiracy". For the reasons behind the zoot suit riots, see Mazon, chapter 5, "The Zoot Suit Riots", and Servin, ed., Patricia Rae Adler, as above. For the Beatrice Griffiths quote and the police headlines, and the quote "mass lynching", see Mazon, chapter 5.

The military terminology used by the press is discussed by Mazon in *The Zoot Suit Riots*, chapter 6. For the whole of downtown Los Angeles being declared off-limits, see Servin, ed., Patricia Rae Adler, as above. For the vilification of zooters as "kids running together bent on devilment" and "mental abnormality" and being 4F, see Chibnall, *Style Politics*, pp. 15–16. For the *pachucos* claiming that "we're good Americans", see Chibnall, *Style Politics*, pp. 16–17.

For the Detroit race riot, see Lingeman, *Don't You Know There's a War On?* chapter 9, and Blum, *V Was For Victory*, part 6, chapter 3. The Alfred McClung Lee quote comes from *Race Riot*, part 1, "What Causes Race Riots?", chapter 1, "Why Do People Riot? An Opening Glimpse". For Detroit's population statistics, see Lingeman, chapter 9, and for the relationship between the races, see Blum, part 6, chapter 3.

The pitched battle in a city playground is cited in Lee, *Race Riot*, chapter 7, "What Really Caused the Detroit Riots?" The phrase "spontaneous combustion" comes from Blum, *V Was for Victory*, part 6, chapter 3, "Race Riot". For the mayor of Detroit saying that only the "Nazis and the Japs" would benefit, see Lee, part 2, "What Really Happened in Detroit?", chapter 3, "Did the Riot Really Start at Belle Isle? A Chronology". The vice-president's quote comes from Lee, chapter 4, "And Then What Happened? Chronology Concluded".

For the lack of facilities for adolescents in Detroit, see Lee, *Race Riot*, chapter 7; this chapter is also the source for the quote "the kids particularly get tired of the bars and the juke joints". For the activities of Fascist groups, see Lee, chapter 4. For the "19-year-old hoodlum" quote, see Lee, chapter 6, "Who Did the Rioting? Who Were the Casualties?"; for the white youths murdering a Negro "just for the Hell of it", see Lee, chapter 3.

President Roosevelt's letter criticizing the unrest is detailed in Blum, *V Was for Victory*, part 6, chapter 3. For the origins of the August 1943 Harlem riot, see Ted Fox, *Show-Time at the Apollo* (London: Quartet Books, 1985), chapter 4, "The Forties"; Malcolm X, *The Autobiography of Malcolm X*, chapter 7, "Hustler"; Lewis A. Erenberg, *Swingin' the Dream*, part 3, "Culture in the Wild, 1942–1954", chapter 7, "Swing Goes to War: Glenn Miller and the Popular Music of World War II".

For 1943 being the year when juvenile delinquency boiled over in the press, see Michael Barson and Stephen Heller, *Teenage Confidential*, chapter 2, "D Is for Delinquent: The Rise of Wayward Youth". This chapter is also the source for the quote "war unleashes" and for the story of the Massachusetts boy and girl killing a man for 48 cents. For middle-class children disrupting high school events and showing a lack of respect, see Ugland, *The Adolescent Experience During World War II*, chapter 5.

The case of a thirteen-year-old boy trying to dynamite a railway line is cited in Lingeman, *Don't You Know There's a War On?*, chapter 3. The description of the April 1943 Harry James show comes from Max Lerner, *Public Journal: Marginal Notes on Wartime America*, part 1, "This Favoured Land", "Dionysus and the Hepcats", originally published April 29, 1943. For the swing in popular taste back to a more romantic style, see Erenberg, *Swingin' the Dream*, chapter 7; this chapter is also the source for the Harry James quote "tomorrow he will have gone back to duty".

For more wartime American propaganda, see Lingeman, *Don't You Know There's a War On?*, chapter 6. For the quote concerning adolescent female "sex delinquency", see Gilbert, *A Cycle of Outrage*, chapter 2, "Rehearsal for a Crime Wave". For the quote "there is no dodging the fact that this is a nationwide problem", see Ugland, *The Adolescent Experience During World War II*, chapter 5. For "khaki-wacky" young women, see Grace Palladino, *Teenagers*, chapter 5, "Andy Hardy Goes to War: Soldiers, Defense Workers, 'V-Girls' and Zoot Suiters".

The description of the Victory Girls' MO comes from Ugland, *The Adolescent Experience During World War II*, chapter 5. Richard Lingeman's description of the Victory Girls comes from *Don't You Know There's a War On?*, chapter 3. For the V-Girls picking up servicemen for fun, see Ugland, chapter 5; for life being hard for females under conscription age, and the quote "being sixteen or seventeen", see Ugland, chapter 2, "Adjustment to War".

The quote about girls seeming "to mature overnight" comes from Ugland, *The Adolescent Experience During World War II*, chapter 5, as do the statistics concerning "sex delinquency". For the loss of innocence, see Terkel, *The Good War*, book 2, "Growing Up Here and There", interview with Jean Bartlett. The phrase "spurious maturity" comes from Ugland, chapter 5. The case of Josephine Tencza is described by Max Lerner in *Public Journal*, part 1, "This Favoured Land", "Seventeen", article originally published April 9, 1943.

For *Pic* magazine and the Josephine Tencza story, and the quotes "the average age of offenders" and "one of our most perplexing and ghastly social problems", see Barson and Heller, *Teenage Confidential*, chapter 2. This is also the source for the "exploitation" Hollywood movies like *Youth Runs Wild* and *Are These Our Parents?* The poster for *Where Are Your Children?* is illustrated on pp. 36–37. Adult condemnation is cited in Ugland, *The Adolescent Experience During World War II*, chapter 5; for the J. Edgar Hoover quote, see Barson and Heller, chapter 2.

The blaming of the youth media, as well as the quote "the style of boogie woogie", comes from Ugland, *The Adolescent Experience During World War II*, chapter 5. For the disparity between the increase in juvenile crime statistics and the reality, see Gilbert, *A Cycle of Outrage*, chapter 2. This is also the source for the Children's Bureau quote "we cannot say" and the details of the Pepper Committee hearings. For the quote "rather than discourage delinquent acts, sensational reporting glamorized and encouraged them", see Ugland, *The Adolescent Experience During World War II*, chapter 5.

For the word "psychopath", see Robert M. Lindner, *Rebel Without a Cause: The Hypno-analysis of a Criminal Psychopath* (New York: Grune and Stratton, 1944), introduction. For Lindner on his methodology, see *Rebel Without a Cause*, "The Method: Hypno-analysis". The contemporary impact of *Rebel Without a Cause* in 1944 is detailed by Gilbert, *A Cycle of Outrage*, chapter 2.

Lindner's definitions of the psychopath are all contained within *Rebel Without a Cause*, "The Problem: Criminal Psychopathy; part I: Psychological Aspects; part II: Physiological Aspects; part III: Sociological Aspects; and part IV: Political Aspects". The testimony of Harold, his subject, concerning guns is contained in "The Twenty-second Hour". The quote "perhaps that's the reason I committed all these crimes" is contained in "The Twenty-fifth Hour". The phrase "embryonic Storm-Troopers" is contained in "The Problem: Criminal Psychopathy; part IV: Political Aspects".

27 THE PEACEFUL INVADERS

The epigraph from a "fourteen-year-old son of a welder" comes from Angus Calder, *The People's War: Britain 1939–1945*, chapter 6, "The India-rubber Island: Britain in 1943–44, Stretched".

The Mass-Observation report on the Dead End Kids' Institute is to be found in M-O A, FR1353, The Service of Youth, July 1942, pp. 22–24. The quotes "the ideal school" and "where social activities would bring together people with differing tastes and interests" come from the same source, pictures, p. 1. The phrase "deserving of special study, care and treatment" comes from the same source, p. 24. For the quotes "co-operative living", "a permanent sense of well-being", and "transitory pleasure" see A. P. Jephcott, *Girls Growing Up*, chapter 8, "Girls, Boys and Clubs".

For the paragraph "self-determination was on the minds of Britain's youth", see "The Responses Come", from M-O A, FR1353, The Service of Youth, Youth QQ, July 1942, p. 125. For adolescents being "much more occupied" in January 1943, see M-O A, FR1780, Youth QQ, January 1943, p. 1ff. The attitudes of fourteen- to sixteen-year-old girls are reported in M-O A, FR1567, Report on Girls Between School Leaving and Registration Age, January 1943, p. 1ff.

The details of how Britain's adolescents were spending their money are contained in M-O A, FR1780, Youth QQ, January 1943. For the figure of 30 million cinema attendances a week, see John Costello,

Love, Sex and War, chapter 9, "Ammunition for the Heart". Pearl Jephcott meets a Carmen Miranda fan in *Girls Growing Up*, chapter 5, "Leisure (2): Dancing and the Pictures". The quotes about movies over the next couple of paragraphs come from the same chapter, including "there is much to be said for the Soviet Government's regulation of picturegoing".

For George Orwell's opinion on Yank mags, see *The Collected Essays, Journalism and Letters of George Orwell, Volume I: An Age Like This, 1920–1940*, item 163, "Boy's Weeklies", and Frank Richards's reply; the original article was published in *Horizon*, March 1940. Jephcott's critique of *No Orchids for Miss Blandish* is contained in *Girls Growing Up*, chapter 5, "Leisure (1): Reading". Orwell's essay on the same book is contained in *Decline of the English Murder and Other Essays* (London: Penguin, 1970), "Raffles and Miss Blandish".

Orwell's comments about the United States, including the quotes "up till about 1930", "the younger intellectuals", and "English working-class people", come from *The Collected Essays, Journalism and Letters of George Orwell, Volume II: My Country Right or Left, 1940–1943*, item 29, "London letter to *Partisan Review*": the original was published in March–April 1942. His quote "there are great numbers of English people who are partly Americanised" comes from *Decline of the English Murder and Other Essays*, "Raffles and Miss Blandish".

The "Americans are supposed to be boastful" quote comes from "London letter to *Partisan Review*", as above. Ed Murrow's opinion that Britain was "a relatively unimportant island" comes in Juliet Gardiner, *Over Here: The G.I.s in Wartime Britain* (London: Collins and Brown, 1992), chapter 3, "The Goddamn Yankee Army's Come". For Mass-Observation and British attitudes to the United States, see M-O A, FR1501, "What the British Think of the Americans", January 1943, p. 1ff.

For the phrase "peaceful invasion", see Gardiner *Over Here: The G.I.s in Wartime Britain,* chapter 1, "War on a Far Front". For the strains of colonization and the mobilization of the American army for D-Day, see Gardiner, chapter 2, "The Goddamn Yankee Army's Come", and Calder, *The People's War*, chapter 6. The *Instructions for American Servicemen in Britain 1942* pamphlet has been reprinted by the Bodleian Library (University of Oxford, 1994). The quote "at first you may not understand" comes from p. 13.

The British journalist's quote "when American soldiers landed in Great Britain" is cited in Gardiner, *Over Here: The G.I.s in Wartime Britain,* chapter 3. For the hosts meeting the invaders in public places, see Gardiner, chapter 5, "Getting to Know the Invaders". The warning against bragging and boasting comes in the *Instructions for American Servicemen in Britain*, p. 2, while the exchange of chewing gum etc. is described in Gardiner, chapter 12, "Nice Girls and Their Little Brothers", and Calder, *The People's War*, chapter 6.

The quote "Britain seemed so dull and corny" is cited in Gardiner, *Over Here: The G.I.s in Wartime Britain,* chapter 10, "Boy, Are We Going to Have Fun!" The *Picture Post* article about the "coloured" swing style comes from vol. 21, no. 12, December 18, 1943, *Highlights of the Lindy Hop*, by Leslie Blanch. For jitterbugging versus party dances and foxtrots, see M-O A, TC "Music Dancing and Jazz", Observations in Dance Halls, Box 1/4, "Will the War Change the English Style?", March 1940, and TC "Music, Dancing and Jazz", Dance Music Questionnaire, 1/8/D, September 1941.

For the quote "once you had learned how to do the jitterbug", see Peter Lewis, *A People's War*, chapter 8, "Time Off from War". The RAF serviceman's reminiscences about a concert in an aircraft hangar comes from Costello, *Love, Sex and War*, chapter 5, "Sentimental Bullets". For the story of the twelve-year-old girl bluffing her way in to see Glenn Miller, see Gardiner, *Over Here: The G.I.s in Wartime Britain,* chapter 10. For Glenn Miller at Rainbow Corner, see Gardiner, chapter 5.

For the "trips by special train to London" quote, see Gardiner, *Over Here: The G.I.s in Wartime Britain,* chapter 8, "Furloughs and Passes". Details about Rainbow Corner are contained in Gardiner, chapter 9, "Islands of Little America". The quote "time was slow" comes from Gardiner, chapter 7, "Warm Beer and Brussel Sprouts". For the seventeen-year-old Londoner remembering "these gorgeous men walking in", see Lewis, *A People's War*, chapter 9, "The Long, Hard Slog".

Odette Lesley's reminiscences, "a very big new world out there," are contained in Joanna Mack and Steve Humphries, *London at War: The Making of Modern London 1939–1945* (London: Sidgwick and Jackson, 1985), chapter 6, "A New Life". For GIs being "aggressive and undiscriminating in their pursuit of British girls", see Gardiner, *Over Here: The G.I.s in Wartime Britain,* chapter 10. This chapter is also the source for the quotes "brought with them colour" and the British serviceman's memory of GIs being "in general taller, bulkier and handsomer than we were".

For nineteen- to twenty-three-year-old women being hit hardest by pregnancies, see John Costello, chapter 15, "Oversexed, Overpaid and Over Here!" For the details about pregnancies, see Costello, chapter 13, "The Girls They Left Behind Them". The quote from the post exchange manager, "I did forty thousand dollars a month in beer", comes from Studs Terkel, *The Good War*, book 3, "Sudden Money", interview with Ray Wax.

The rise in crime figures is mentioned by David Hughes in his entertaining essay "The Spivs", collected in *Age of Austerity, 1945–1951*, eds Michael Sissons and Philip French (London: Penguin, 1964). John Wain's "everybody made hay" quote comes from *Strike the Father Dead* (New York: St Martin's, 1962), part 3, "Jeremy", p. 129ff. The quote "improvising, floating, free-wheeling population" comes from John Wain, *Strike the Father Dead*, part 4, "Jeremy", p. 203.

For the spiv as contact man, "a recognisible type," see Robert Murphy, *Smash and Grab: Gangsters in the London Underworld 1920–60*, chapter 7, "The Underworld at War". For more details on the spiv, see Murphy, chapter 7 as above, Steve Chibnall, *Whistle and Zoot: The Changing Meaning of a Suit of Clothes*, and *Style Politics: The Changing Meaning of a Suit of Clothes*. The "giant tongue poking vulgarly out at life" quote comes from David Hughes.

For *Picture Post* on "Negro troops", see vol. 17, issue 5, October 1942. For the continuation of segregation in the United Kingdom, see Gardiner, *Over Here: The G.I.s in Wartime Britain*, chapter 14, "Fighting a War on Two Fronts". This chapter is also the source for the details of the disturbances in Manchester and the battle in Newbury. For the quote about many British women finding "a peculiar fascination in associating with men of colour", see Costello, *Love, Sex and War*, chapter 15.

The Duke of Marlborough's comment about Negro troops is quoted in Gardiner, *Over Here: The G.I.s in Wartime Britain*, chapter 14. The 1943 Mass-Observation poll revealing that the British were "overwhelmingly opposed to racial discrimination" is quoted in Calder, *The People's War: Britain 1939–1945*, chapter 6. The original reference is M-O A, FR2021, February 1944, pp. 11–12. For the story of the Bristol girl and the black GIs in her father's pub, see Gardiner, chapter 14.

For the 1944 Education Act, see Lewis, *A People's War*, chapter 10, "Leftward, Look, the Land Is Bright".

For the importance of dance music to British youth, see, *inter alia*, Gardiner, *Over Here: The G.I.s in Wartime Britain*, chapter 10, and Jephcott, *Girls Growing Up*, chapter 5, "Leisure (2): Dancing and the Pictures". For the article about Rainbow Corner, see Elkan Allan, "Inside Rainbow Corner", *Picture Post*, vol. 26, issue 4, January 27, 1945, pp. 22–25. For the quote "I always talk to myself in an American accent", see Calder, *The People's War: Britain 1939–1945*, chapter 6.

28 HELMUTH HÜBENER, THE WHITE ROSE, AND ANNE FRANK

The epigraph comes from Inge Scholl, *The White Rose: Munich 1942–1943* (New Hampshire: Wesleyan University Press, 1983), part 2, "Leaflets of the White Rose", "The Last Leaflet". For details of Lucien Rebatet's book launch, see Julian Jackson, *France: The Dark Years, 1940–1944*, chapter 9, "Collaborationism", "Collaboration as Hatred and Fraternity: *Je suis partout*". The quotes "hate until death" and "joy at having seen in Germany the first Jews marked by their yellow star" come from Jean-Claude Loiseau, *Les Zazous*, chapter 8.

For Anne Frank's diary entry "many Jewish friends", see *The Diary of a Young Girl*, ed. Otto H. Frank and Mirjam Pressler (London: Penguin, 1997), diary entry for Friday, October 9, 1942. For summer 1942 being the high-water mark of the Third Reich, see H. W. Koch, *The Hitler Youth*, chapter 9, "Elites", and Gerhard Rempel, *Hitler's Children*, chapter 10, "Conclusion". See also Ronald Forster, *The World at War*, chapter 6, "The War in the Desert", and chapter 8, "Victory in the USSR".

For German cities being bombed with greater frequency and force, see Michael H. Kater, *Different Drummers*, chapter 3, "Jazz Goes to War: Demands of the Military". For the January 1942 Wannsee Conference, and the campaign to exterminate all the Jews, see Carol Ann Lee, *Roses From the Earth: the Biography of Anne Frank* (London: Penguin, 2000), part 2, "When the Sufferings of Us Jews Really Began, 1940–42", chapter 4.

Jack Mandelbaum's quote "We had no rights" is cited in Andrea Warren, *Surviving Hitler: A Boy in the Nazi Death Camps*, chapter 5, "The Right to Die". For the issuing of a striped uniform displaying a number, and the dehumanization, see Warren, chapter 5; for the quote "they wanted to terrorize us", see Warren, chapter 4, "Despair". For more details, see Warren, chapter 6, "Learning the Rules", and chapter 7, "The Game".

For the October 1942 enforcement of youth service duty, see Detlev J. K. Peukert, *Inside Nazi Germany*, notes to chapter 8, "Young People: Mobilisation and Refusal", note 16, p. 268. For the new SS-run camps, see Rempel, *Hitler's Children*, chapter 7, "Contestants, Boxers, Combatants". For the quote from the Cologne-area trainee, "These three weeks were for all of us a living hell", see Rempel, chapter 7. The other, more positive trainee testimonials come from the same source, as does the phrase "artists of death".

The details of Helmuth Hübener's execution are contained in the book compiled, translated, and edited by Blair R. Holmes and Alan F. Keele, *When Truth Was Treason: German Youth Against Hitler: The Story of the Helmuth Hübener Group* (Chicago: University of Illinois Press, 1995), document #62, from the Attorney-General of the People's Court, Berlin, October, 27, 1942, and document #60. Helmuth Hübener's last surviving letter is displayed as document #61.

For general information about explicit resistance within the Third Reich, including the figure of 800,000 German citizens imprisoned for resistance, see *When Truth Was Treason*, Klaus J. Hansen, "Foreword: History and Memory", and the introduction by Holmes and Keele.

The Karl-Heinz Schnibbe quotes in the first paragraph, "I did not like it any more", and "competing religious system", come from *When Truth Was Treason*, chapter 1, "Childhood in the Shadow of the Swastika". The description of the group's activities over the next eight paragraphs comes from chapter 2, "From Pogroms to War, from Radio to Resistance". All of Helmuth Hübener's leaflets from 1941 and 1942 are contained in documents #28 to #46.

The quote "do you want to tolerate having the happiness of your life taken from you" comes from the flyer titled "The Voice of Conscience". For the Hitler Youth as a "compulsory organization of the first order for the recruiting of Nazi-enslaved national comrades", see document #38, "Hitler Youth". For details of the Hübener group's arrest and imprisonment, see *When Truth Was Treason*, chapter 3, "Guests of the Gestapo".

For details of Hübener's arrest, see document #6, "Gestapo Report about the Arrest of Helmuth Hübener"; document #40 contains the full text of the final leaflet, called *Who Is Inciting Whom?* The quotes "absolute presumption of guilt" and "they never left us in peace" come from *When Truth Was Treason*, chapter 3, and the quote "to speak the truth" in those days was "a fatal luxury" comes from chapter 2.

The description of the Hübener group's trial comes from *When Truth Was Treason*, chapter 4, "Judgment and Destruction". This chapter is also the source for Hübener's remaining two months. His final letter is reproduced in document #65, Otto Berndt's reminiscences about Helmuth Hübener. The fact that his mother and grandparents died in the bombing of Hamburg comes in document #74, Hans Kunkel's reminiscences about Helmuth Hübener.

For general information about the White Rose, see Koch, *The Hitler Youth*, chapter 10, "Dissent". The quote "do you and your children want to suffer the same fate as that suffered by the Jews?" comes from the White Rose leaflet *A Call to All Germans*, January 1943, reproduced in Scholl, *The White Rose*, part 2, "Leaflets of the White Rose", "Leaflet of the Resistance". The background and foundation of the White Rose are well told in Scholl, *The White Rose*, part 1, "The White Rose".

For the quote from Hans Scholl's father, "the Pied Piper of Hamelin", see Scholl, *The White Rose*, part 1, p. 6; for Willi Graf belonging to one of the surviving Catholic youth organizations, see part 1, pp. 13–15. For the quote "Whoever today still doubts the reality, the existence of demonic powers," see *The White Rose*, part 2, "Leaflets of the White Rose", fourth leaflet. The quote "a sense of belonging" comes from *The White Rose*, part 1, pp. 6–7, the quote "what was really happening to our Fatherland?" from p. 11, and the quote "tear out our hearts" from p. 16.

Hans Scholl's father's quote that the regime had "lost every spark of respect for man" comes from *The White Rose*, part 1, p. 12; the background of the other members of the group is detailed on pp. 20–22. For the bishop of Münster's leaflets, see pp. 17–19, and for the quote "I can still see Hans standing there", see Johannes Steinhoff, Peter Pechel, and Denis Showalter, *Voices from the Third Reich*, part 3, "Defeat and Crimes", chapter 11, "Resistance", interview with Inge Aicher-Scholl.

The quote "on the present moment" comes from Scholl, *The White Rose*, part 1, p. 31. The impact of the leaflets comes on p. 31; the quote "offer passive resistance" comes from part 2, the first leaflet. The fact that the White Rose named themselves after a Spanish novel is given in document #1, "Indictment of Hans and Sophie Scholl and Christl Probst", part 3. The quote "We must gamble our 'No'" comes from Inge Scholl, *The White Rose*, document #1, p. 36.

For the details about Hans Scholl travelling to Berlin and his plan to "establish illegal student groups in every university", see Steinhoff, Pechel, and Showalter, *Voices from the Third Reich*, part 3, chapter 11, interview with Inge Aicher-Scholl. Sophie Scholl's back story is contained in *The White Rose*, part 1. For the Munich students humiliating the local *Gauleiter*, see Koch, chapter 10.

For the White Rose being responsible for the graffiti "Down with Hitler" and "Freedom", see Scholl,

The White Rose, part 1, pp. 48–50; for details of the leaflet *Fellow Fighters in the Resistance!*, see part 2, "The Last Leaflet". For details of their final action on February 18 and their arrest, see pp. 51–53. The letter from Else Gebel, relating the events and scenes of Sophie Scholl's days in prison, is cited as document #4.

The narrative for the next three paragraphs comes from *The White Rose*, part 1. This includes the quote "it was as if in these days their many unlived years"; the details of Sophie's final dream and their last testaments—Sophie scrawling the word "Freedom", and Hans writing the quotation from Goethe on his prison wall. The second wave of arrests are covered in part 1.

The quotes "days when every man" and "disgraced German youth" are contained in Scholl, *The White Rose*, document #3, transcript of the sentence of Alexander Schmorell, Kurt Huber, Wilhelm Graf, and others associated with the resistance of the White Rose, April 1943. Details of the mass meeting in New York are contained in document #10, extract from a letter from Kurt R. Grossmann to Inge Scholl, March 1969. The White Rose's critique of the Nazi youth policy comes in their leaflet *A Call to All Germans*, reprinted in part 2, "Leaflet of the Resistance".

For the White Rose being executed as "typical outsiders", see *The White Rose*, document #5, article in the *Münchner Neueste Nachrichten* for Monday, February 22, 1943. The details of the February 1942 "Factory Operation" are contained in Gad Beck, *An Underground Life: Memoirs of a Gay Jew in Nazi Berlin* (Madison: University of Wisconsin Press, 1999), chapter 4. For Anne Frank's diary entry about the episcopal letter, see *The Diary of a Young Girl*, entry for Saturday, February 27, 1943. (All the diary entries referred to subsequently come from the same edition.)

For the Frank family going underground, see Lee, *Roses from the Earth*, part 2, chapter 4. The quote "Let me out, where there's fresh air and laughter!" comes from the diary entry for Friday, October 29, 1943. Anne's self-description as the family's "mischief-maker" comes from the entry for Saturday, November 7, 1942. For the Eva Schloss quote, see Lee, *Roses from the Earth*, part 3, "A Deadly Sultry Silence Hangs Everywhere, 1942–44", chapter 5.

Anne Frank's quote "I never used to give it much thought" comes in her diary entry for Friday, November 20, 1942. For Anne calling her diary Kitty, see the entry for Saturday, June 20, 1942. For the origin of the name Kitty, see Lee, *Roses from the Earth*, part 3, chapter 5. For Anne wanting to be "different from what I am", see her diary entry for Saturday, November 28, 1942. For her ambition to "spend a year in Paris and London", see the diary entry for Monday, May 8, 1944.

For the fact that she was a fan of Deanna Durbin, see Lee, *Roses from the Earth*, part 2, chapter 3; for her fantasies of going shopping in Switzerland, see the diary entry for Wednesday, October 7, 1942. For her criticisms of her parents quoted in the next paragraph, see the diary entries for Thursday, March 16, and Friday, March 17, 1944. For the quotes "self-knowledge" and "I can watch myself as if I were a stranger", see the diary entry for Saturday, July 15, 1944.

Anne's key diary entry, looking back at her "unreal" former life and her life in the Annexe, is from Tuesday, March 7, 1944. Her conceptualization of her adolescence, "Girls my age feel very insecure", is from Thursday, January 6, 1944. For her attraction to Peter van Pels, see Tuesday, March 7, 1944. For her exploration of her vagina, see the diary entry for Friday, March 24, 1944; for the family crisis caused by Anne necking with Peter van Pels, see Friday, May 5, Saturday, May 6, and Sunday, May 7, 1944.

Her railing against "the destructive urge in people" comes from her diary entry for Wednesday, May 3, 1944. Her quote "I *know* I can write" comes in the entry for Wednesday, April 5, 1944; the quote "just imagine how interesting" comes from Wednesday, March 29, 1944; for details of her fifteenth birthday, see Wednesday, June 13, and for her discussion of the book *What Do You Think of the Modern Girl?* see Saturday, July 15, 1944.

For the "orgy of killing" at Auschwitz and "the furnaces in the crematoria", see Lee, *Roses from the Earth*, part 4, "Who Has Inflicted This Upon Us?", chapter 7. For the quote "prisoners died of disease", see Warren, *Surviving Hitler*, chapter 10, "Moniek". For the designation of 1943 as the "Year of War Service of the German Youth", see Koch, *The Hitler Youth*, chapter 11, "War". For the classes of 1926 and 1927 being packed off into the Waffen-SS, see Rempel, *Hitler's Children*, chapter 8, "Pied Pipers for an Elite".

The White Rose's prophecy, "finally all were imprisoned in a great dungeon", is cited in Scholl, *The White Rose*, part 1, p. 11. Details about the worsening situation in German cities and the authorities' systematic pull-out of half a million adolescents are contained in Koch, *The Hitler Youth*, chapter 11. For the *Wehrertüchtigungslager* as the prime unit of Nazi youth organization after 1943, see Rempel, *Hitler's Children*, chapter 7.

For 1944 being designated as the "Year of the War Volunteers", see Koch, chapter 11. For the underage mobilization of young Germans into the SS, see Rempel, chapter 8. For the American journalist observing that "many boys and girls of thirteen to fifteen years old work in war industries", see Jennifer Keeley, *Life in the Hitler Youth*, chapter 8, "The Hitler Youth at War". The original article was first published in *The Nation*, April 1944.

The details of the special 12th SS Panzer Division Hitlerjugend and their action in the D-Day landings over the next couple of paragraphs come from Koch, *The Hitler Youth*, chapter 11. The Melita Maschmann quote "They did not wish to spare themselves" comes from *Account Rendered*, chapter 13; this is also the source for the "no attempt to protect" quote, and for the Melita Maschmann quotes in the next paragraph.

For the increase in juvenile delinquency during 1943 and 1944 in Germany's blacked-out cities, see Koch, *The Hitler Youth*, chapter 10. For the Edelweiss Pirates and "these youngsters, aged between 12 and 17", see Peukert, *Inside Nazi Germany*, chapter 8, "Young People: Mobilisation and Refusal," "Edelweiss Pirates". This chapter is also the source for the quote "since this riff-raff" and for the graffiti "Down With Hitler".

The Nazis' 1943 criminal law for youth is detailed in Rempel, *Hitler's Children*, chapter 4, "Police Boys, Informers, Rebels". This chapter is also the source for Himmler's April 1944 order that all inmates of juvenile custody camps were to be classified by the Criminal Biological Institute, the quote "the constantly increasing number of cliques", and the definition of the three basic types of offender.

For the details of the fourth White Rose trial, see Scholl, *The White Rose*, part 1, pp. 70–72. For the White Rose link-up with the Hamburg swings and the quote "anything that starts with Ellington ends with an assassination attempt on the Führer!" see Kater, *Different Drummers*, chapter 4, "Near Defeat: Jazz Toward the 'Final Victory', September 1942–1945", "The Jazz Victims".

For Himmler's final youth directive of October 1944, and the public hanging of thirteen Edelweiss Pirates in Cologne's city centre, see Peukert, *Inside Nazi Germany*, chapter 8. For extra material on the Navajos and Bartel Schink, see the Wikipedia entry for "Edelweiss Pirates".

29 THE ARRIVAL OF THE TEENAGER

Weegee's hysterical account of Frank Sinatra's opening at the Paramount on Columbus Day 1944 is contained in *Naked City* (New York: Essential Books, 1945), "Frankie". More details come from Kitty Kelley, *His Way: The Unauthorised Biography of Frank Sinatra* (London: Bantam, 1987), chapter 8, and Arnold Shaw, *Sinatra: The Entertainer* (New York: Delilah Books, 1982), chapter 1, "I Sing the Songs: The Singer", "The Paramount Panics, 1943–44", pp. 21–22.

For the girls taking over Times Square, see Kelley, *His Way*, chapter 8, and Shaw, *Sinatra: The Entertainer*, "The Paramount Panics", as above. For Bruce Bliven's quote, see "The Voice and the Kids", *New Republic*, November 6, 1944, partially reproduced in *The Faber Book of Pop*, ed. Hanif Kureishi and Jon Savage (London: Faber and Faber, 1995). For Sinatra's December 1942 breakthrough, see Kelley, chapter 6; for Sinatra's quote "five thousand kids", see J. Randall Taraborrelli, *Sinatra: The Man Behind the Myth* (London: Mainstream, 1997), chapter 6.

Nic Sevano's memory of Sinatra's return to the Paramount in 1943, "This time, they threw more than roses", is cited in Kelley, *His Way*, chapter 6. For Sinatra's press agents "hiring girls to scream," see Shaw, *Sinatra: The Entertainer*, p. 21. For Sinatra's fame increasing, and the film *Higher and Higher*, see Kelley, chapter 7, and Shaw, section 2, "It's Only a Paper Moon: The Actor", p. 30.

For Sinatra's habit of singling out individuals in the crowd, see Taraborrelli, *Sinatra: The Man Behind the Myth*, chapter 6. For Sinatra's recordings from the period, see *The Voice, 1943–1952* (Sony/CBS Inc., 1986: 6 LP set) and Frank Sinatra, *The Best of the Columbia Years 1943–1952* (Sony Columbia Legacy, 4 CD box, 1995). For more on Sinatra's effect on the audience, see Kelley, *His Way*, chapters 7 and 8. Bruce Bliven's "when he sings sadly" is from "The Voice and the Kids".

Sinatra's background is well covered by Kelley, *His Way*, chapters 1 and 2; for his status and symbolism during the war, including his status as a Peter Pan figure, see Richard R. Lingeman, *Don't You Know There's a War On?*, chapter 8, "Pleasures, Pastimes, Fads and Follies", and Lewis A. Erenberg, *Swingin' the Dream*, part 3, "Culture Noir, 1942–1954", chapter 7, "Swing Goes to War: Glenn Miller and the Popular Music of World War II".

For the quote "it was the war years", see Taraborrelli, *Sinatra, the Man Behind the Myth*, chapter 6. For Bruce Bliven concerning how the bobby-soxers "found in him, for all his youthfulness", see Kelley, *His Way*, chapter 7; this chapter is also the source for the "he earns a million" quote. For the hostile reactions against Sinatra, including the quotes "artistic manifestation" and "control of their emotions", and for his 4F status, see Kelley, chapter 7; for the young men throwing eggs and tomatoes, see chapter 8.

For the fact that the GIs resented any man not in uniform, see Lee Kennett, *G.I.*, chapter 4, "The View from the Barracks". The quote "feather merchant" is also from this source. For Sinatra meeting President Roosevelt in September 1944, see Kelley, *His Way*, chapter 8.

The relative visibility of younger female adolescents during World War II is covered by Richard M. Ugland, *The Adolescent Experience During World War II*, chapter 8, "Conclusion". For youth employment, see Grace Palladino, *Teenagers*, part 2, "Bobby Soxers", chapter 5, "Andy Hardy Goes to War: Soldiers, Defense Workers, V-Girls and Zoot-Suiters". For the statistics of up to three million fourteen- to seventeen-year-olds working during 1944, see Lingeman, *Don't You Know There's a War On?*, chapter 5, "Give Us the Tools".

For this age group being the most affluent in American history, see Ugland, *The Adolescent Experience During World War II*, chapter 4, "Youth Employment." For the events of 1943 causing many parents to be fearful of their young, see Palladino, *Teenagers*, part 2, chapter 6, "Do You Know Where Your Children Are?: Juvenile Delinquency, Teen Canteens, and Democratic Solutions".

The 1944 film *Youth Runs Wild* is cited in Michael Barson and Stephen Heller, *Teenage Confidential*, chapter 2, "D Is for Delinquent", "The Rise of Wayward Youth", and David M. Considine, *The Cinema of Adolescence*, part 4, "Juvenile Delinquency", chapter 8, "Dead Ends and Death Row 1931–1949"; this latter chapter is also the source for the quote "we want to work". For the NYA ceasing operation, see Palladino, *Teenagers*, chapter 5. For the May 1944 *Look* feature about the Moline, Illinois, youth centre, see Barson and Heller, chapter 2.

For the Mark McCloskey quote "this world has been full of trying", see Palladino, *Teenagers*, chapter 6. For McCloskey canvassing America's young, see Ugland, *The Adolescent Experience During World War II*, chapter 6, "Planning Leisure Time". The McCloskey quote about Harry James comes from Palladino, chapter 6. His quote "your Boy Scouts, your Girls Scouts" and "a large group of tween-teens" are both from Ugland, chapter 6.

For details on the Teen Canteens, see Palladino, *Teenagers*, chapter 6, and Ugland, *The Adolescent Experience During World War II*, chapter 6. Ugland is the source for the quote "clean, wholesome recreational facilities", and Palladino the source for a Detroit bi-racial youth council. The quotes "hang-out recreation" and "the teenage movement" both come from Ugland, chapter 6.

The launch of *Seventeen* magazine is well covered in Barson and Heller, *Teenage Confidential*, chapter 1, "Kleen Teens Never Die Young: The Dawn of Teen Culture"; Palladino, *Teenagers*, chapter 6; and Ugland, *The Adolescent Experience During World War II*, chapter 7, "The Emergence of the Teen-ager". Ugland is also the source for the estimated teenage spending capacity of $750 million.

The quote "Young fashions & beauty" is contained in the cover slogan, *Seventeen*, issue no. 1, September 1944. For the information in the next three paragraphs, see *Seventeen*, issue no. 1; for the quotes "you're going to have to run this show", "SEVENTEEN is your magazine", and "write us", see Helen Valentine, "*Seventeen* Says Hello", p. 33. For "growing up and earning your living", see Alice Beaton, "For Seniors Only", pp. 60–61. The article "What Are You Doing About the War?" is from *Seventeen*, issue no. 1, pp. 54–56; the instruction to stay in high school comes from the article "Why Finish High School?", p. 76.

For the advertisements in the first issue, see Teen-Timer OHriginal, p. 21; The Blum Store "Teen Canteen", p. 22, Saks Fifth Avenue, p. 1. For the rise in *Seventeen*'s readership, see Ugland, *The Adolescent Experience During World War II*, chapter 7; for the quote "we are proud of SEVENTEEN", see *Seventeen*, issue no. 6, February 1945, letters, p. 147. For the quote "I felt that I must use Mom's stationery", see "Thank you for your letters", *Seventeen*, issue no. 6, p. 4.

The details of previous 1940s teen magazines, including *Calling All Girls*, are given by Barson and Heller, *Teenage Confidential*, chapter 1, and Ugland, *The Adolescent Experience During World War II*, chapter 7. For *Good Housekeeping* and the column "Teens of Our Times", see Palladino, *Teenagers*, part 2, chapter 4, "Bobby Soxers Take the Stage".

For newspapers publishing columns like "Sub-debs and Squires", for the two *Life* magazine articles about sub-debs, and for the *Life* article about high school fads, see Ugland, *The Adolescent Experience During World War II*, chapter 7. For the quote "you buy loafer moccasins", see *Seventeen*, issue no. 4, December 1944, p. 22. For details of *Parents* magazine's "Tricks for Teens" column, see Ugland, chapter 7; this is also the source for the material about Teen-Timers Inc. and the OHriginals line.

The quote "brought public attention down" comes from Ugland, *The Adolescent Experience During World War II*, chapter 7; for Helen Valentine commissioning Benson and Benson to conduct demographic research, and the details of *Life with Teena*, see Palladino, *Teenagers*, part 3, chapter 7, "The Advertising Age: *Seventeen*, Eugene Gilbert, and the Rise of the Teenage Market". The advertisements cited as being from a sample issue are all in *Seventeen*, issue no. 9, May 1945. For the feature "Ugly Duckling", see *Seventeen* issue no. 10, June 1945, pp. 20 and 22. For the quote "I love being seventeen", see *Seventeen*, issue no. 5, January 1945.

For the Talcott Parsons article, and the quotes over the next three paragraphs, see "Age and Sex in the Social Structure of the United States". This article was originally published in *American Sociological Review*, October 1942, pp. 604–616, and was reprinted in *Sociological Analysis: An Introductory Text and Case Book*, by Logan Wilson and William L. Kolb (New York: Harcourt, Brace and Co., 1949), part 5, "Institutional and Associational Structure of Community and Nation", chapter 17, "Family Organization".

For the coining of the words "teenage" and "teenager" during 1944, see Ugland, *The Adolescent Experience During World War II*, chapter 7. The etymology of the term is also discussed in this chapter, pp. 349–351. Extra data can also be found in Tom Dalzell, *Flappers 2 Rappers: American Youth Slang* (Springfield, MA: Merriam-Webster, 1996), chapter 4, "The 1940's: the Jive Generation", and Lucy Rollin, *Twentieth-Century Teen Culture by the Decades: A Reference Guide*, chapter 4, "The 1940s".

Note the early use of the word "teens", in quotation marks, in Stanley Hall's *Adolescence*, chapter 12, "Adolescent Feelings Toward Nature", vol. 2, p. 149. The term can be traced from Carl Ed's cartoon *Harold Teen* (1919) to its more general use from the mid-1930s on, such as in the magazine *American Speech* (1935) and the Home Institute's guidebook *Etiquette for the Teens* (1937). Its media incidence definitely increases during the early 1940s. For instance, see this December 1942 headline in the *New York Times*: "22,453 in 'Teen Age Added to Draft". A PhD thesis could be written on this topic alone.

30 YEAR ZERO

The epigraph is from Wolfgang Borchert, *The Man Outside* (New York: New Directions, 1971), "On the Move: A Generation Without Farewell". Elliot E. Cohen's "A Teen-Age Bill of Rights" was published in the *New York Times Magazine*, January 7, 1945, pp. 16–17. This is the source of the quotes over the next three paragraphs. For more contextual material on the Teen-Age Bill of Rights, see Lucy Rollin, *Twentieth-Century Teen Culture by the Decades*, chapter 4, "The 1940s", "Teens at Home".

For Barbara Gair's article, see "What Kind of World Do You Want?," *Seventeen*, issue no. 6, February 1945, p. 138. For Frank Sinatra's appearance in *The House I Live In*, as well as his reading Gunnar Myrdal's *An American Dilemma*, see Kitty Kelley, *His Way*, chapter 9, and Lewis A. Erenberg, *Swingin' the Dream*, part 3, chapter 7, "Swing Goes to War: Glenn Miller and the Popular Music of World War II". Gunnar Myrdal's *An American Dilemma: The Negro Problem and Modern Democracy* was published by Harper and Brothers, New York, 1944.

The Sinatra quote "I'll never forget how it hurt" is cited in J. Randall Taraborrelli, *Sinatra: The Man Behind the Myth*, chapter 8. For details of *It Happened in Springfield*, see *Seventeen*, issue no. 10, June 1945, p. 28, continued on p. 167. Ann Clark's "The Way the World Ends" was published in *Seventeen*, issue no. 7, July 1945, p. 69ff. For the letters responding to the story, see *Seventeen*, issue no. 13, September 1945, "Thank you for your letters", p. 4.

For the Anne Frank quote "I am afraid of prison cells", see Carol Ann Lee, *Roses from the Earth*, part 3, "A Deadly Sultry Silence Hangs Everywhere 1942–44", chapter 6. For Anne Frank in Bergen-Belsen, and the quote "the two were inseparable", see *Roses from the Earth*, part 4, "Who Has Inflicted This Upon Us? 1944–45", chapter 8. For details of Anne's arrest and their transport to Westerbork, including the Otto Frank quote, see *Roses from the Earth*, part 3, chapter 6. This chapter is also the source of the details of the journey to Auschwitz.

The quote "I did speak to Anne" comes from Carol Ann Lee, *The Hidden Life of Otto Frank* (London: Penguin, 2002), part 1, "A Thousand Old, Treasured Things, 1889–1945", chapter 4, "Unforgettable Marks On My Soul". For the arrival at Auschwitz and the quote "it was so insane", see Lee, *Roses from the Earth*, part 4, chapter 7. Apart from the material taken as below from *The Hidden Life of Otto Frank*, this chapter is the source of the details of Anne's imprisonment over the next three paragraphs.

For the quote "created and governed according to the principles of absolute evil" and "remember the look in Margot's eyes", see Lee, *The Hidden Life of Otto Frank*, part 1, chapter 4; this chapter is also the source for details of Otto Frank's liberation in January 1945. For Anne Frank being convinced that her parents were dead, and for her giving up hope after her sister died from dysentery, see Lee, *Roses from the Earth*, part 4, chapter 8.

Melita Maschmann's account of the failing Nazi regime, including the quote "this terrible mass death", is contained in *Account Rendered*, chapter 14. For the rapid Russian advance trapping half a million adolescents and the quote "vortex of disaster", see H. W. Koch, *The Hitler Youth*, chapter 11, "War".

For the "third wave" of seventeen-year-olds as an "iron reserve", see Gerhard Rempel, *Hitler's Children*, chapter 9, "The Final Sacrifice". The figure of 8.5 million Germans fleeing west from the Russian advance is cited by Antony Beevor in *Berlin, The Downfall, 1945* (London: Viking, 2002), chapter 3, "Fire and Sword and 'Noble Fury'".

Gottlob Berger's authorization to call up one-fifth of the seventeen-to-eighteen cohort is cited by Rempel, *Hitler's Children*, chapter 8, "Pied Pipers for an Elite". For details of the Volkssturm, see Koch, *The Hitler Youth*, chapter 11. For the quote "barbarization of warfare", see Rempel, chapter 9. This chapter is also the source for the details of the adolescent forces at Remagen. For the Artur Axmann quote "from the Hitler Youth", see Koch, chapter 11.

The Melita Maschmann quote "for them the call to the 'ultimate sacrifice' was no empty phrase" is from *Account Rendered*, chapter 14. For John P. Irwin on shooting dead a twelve-year-old, see *Another River, Another Town: A Teenage Tank Gunner Comes of Age in Combat—1945* (New York: Random House, 2002), chapter 3, "Closing the Rose Pocket". The doctor's story, "You dummy! Look at what this has gotten you!" is quoted in Johannes Steinhoff, Peter Pechel, and Denis Showalter, *Voices from the Third Reich: An Oral History*, part 4, "Catastrophe and Liberation", chapter 13, "Collapse", interview with Bernard Schmitt.

Irwin's description of the forced-labour camp at Nordhausen is contained in *Another River, Another Town*, chapter 6, "A Lesson in Depravity." The quote "World War II was in black and white with shades of gray" comes from the same chapter. For Artur Axmann authorizing 4,000 boys to act as tank-destroyer troops, see Rempel, *Hitler's Children*, chapter 9. For the details of the final Berlin Philharmonic performance, see Beevor, *Berlin, The Downfall, 1945*, chapter 12, "Waiting for the Onslaught".

The Melita Maschmann quote "while the distant thunder of battle" comes from *Account Rendered*, chapter 14. For Adolf Hitler's last public appearance, see Koch, *The Hitler Youth*, chapter 11. For Hitler's madness and his hypertrophied identification between himself and the German people, see Beevor, *Berlin, The Downfall, 1945*, chapter 10, "The *Kamarilla* and the General Staff", chapter 17, "The Führer's Last Birthday", and chapter 18, "The Flight of the Golden Pheasants".

The speech beginning "I am convinced that we shall be victorious" is cited in Jennifer Keeley, *Life in the Hitler Youth*, chapter 8, "The Hitler Youth at War". The Maschmann quote "they burned with the desire" is from *Account Rendered*, chapter 14. For Artur Axmann fleeing to the Alps on May 1, see Rempel, *Hitler's Children*, chapter 9. The Silesian Hitler Youth leader quote "died in atrocious agony" comes from the same source.

For the quote "we believed in Hitler", see Steinhoff, Pechel, and Showalter, *Voices from the Third Reich: An Oral History*, epilogue, "*Finis Germaniae?*", interview with Susanne Ritters. For the Hitler Youth's reaction to seeing the bodies at Dachau, see Koch, *The Hitler Youth*, chapter 11.

Details of the "Werewolves" guerrilla group can be found in Rempel, *Hitler's Children*, chapter 9, and Beevor, *Berlin, The Downfall, 1945*, chapter 12. Melita Maschmann's account of joining the Werewolves is contained in *Account Rendered*, chapter 15. This chapter is also the source for her reaction to Adolf Hitler's death, her wanderings throughout the Bavarian Alps, and for the quotes "I sought salvation" and "watching children at play".

For the euphoria in London on May 8, 1945, see Joanna Mack and Steve Humphries, *London at War*, chapter 6, "A New Life". There is an excellent eyewitness account in Humphrey Lyttelton, *I Play as I Please* (London: Pan Books, 1959), chapter 8, "After the Fireworks". For the UK casualty figures of half a million people, see John Costello, *Love, Sex and War*, chapter 17, "The Seeds of Sexual Revolution". For the popularity of GIs among European youth, see Lee Kennett, *G.I.*, chapter 6, "Aboard and Abroad."

The quote "humanism for millions" comes from Max Lerner, *Public Journal*, part 1, "This Favoured Land". "Reflections on a Seller's Market". The original article was published on December 23, 1943. For the "international appeal" of *Seventeen*, see Richard M. Ugland, *The Adolescent Experience During World War II*, chapter 7, "The Emergence of the Teen-ager". The original quote came from *Seventeen*, issue no. 8, April 1945. For the Tony Vaccaro pictures, see *Entering Germany: 1944–1949* (Cologne: Taschen, 2001).

The June 1945 *New York Times* article "Teen-Agers Are an American Invention" is cited in Ugland, *The Adolescent Experience During World War II*, chapter 7. The *Life* "Teen-Age Boys" issue was published on June 11, 1945; details about their diet, "eaten in huge amounts", are on p. 94. For Glenn Miller's AAF Orchestra playing at Nuremberg Stadium, and his interview with the Allied Expeditionary Forces network, see Erenberg, *Swingin' the Dream*, part 3, chapter 7.

For the results of the 1945 general election in Britain, see Peter Lewis, *A People's War*, chapter 10, "Leftward, Look, the Land Is Bright". The quote "among the servicemen" is given by Major Denis

Healey—later to become Chancellor of the Exchequer between 1974 and 1979 and one of Britain's most able post-war politicians. It comes from the same source. For the quotes "the Americans changed England more" and "it was so drab when they had gone", see Juliet Gardiner, *Over Here*, chapter 18, "Over There".

The copy for the US *Vogue* cover story on "Beauty and the Younger Generation" is contained in the issue of August 1945, p. 23ff. For the quote "an explosion of gigantic dimensions", see James Jones, *WWII*, "Mushroom". This chapter is also the source of the quote "suddenly a glaring whitish pinkish light". For the quote "once again, President Truman applied the psychological squeeze on Japan", see *Time*, vol. 46, no. 7, August 13, 1945, "The Nation: Birth of an Era", p. 17.

For the details of Eugene Gilbert's business, and the quotes over the next three paragraphs, see *Time* as above, vol. 46, no. 7, August 13, 1945, "Business & Finance" section, pp. 85–86. The article is called "Teen-age Gallup". For more on Eugene Gilbert, see Ugland, *The Adolescent Experience During World War II*, chapter 7, and Grace Palladino, *Teenagers*, part 3, chapter 7, "The Advertising Age: Eugene Gilbert and the Rise of the Teenage Market". For a detailed profile of Eugene Gilbert, see Dwight McDonald, "A Caste, A Culture, A Market, part one", *New Yorker*, November 22, 1958.

The exact details of the casualty rates in World War II vary from source to source. I have synthesized data from Mark Arnold-Forster, *The World at War*, chapter 13, "Death and Resistance in the Occupied Countries", Andrea Warren, *Surviving Hitler*, "Appendix: The Concentration Camps, the Human Cost of World War II", and the Wikipedia site on the Second World War. For the Lewis H. Lapham quote "passed into the American account", see Studs Terkel, *The Good War*, introduction.

For the full effect of the atom bomb, see the following: Robert Jungk, *Brighter Than 1,000 Suns: A Personal History of the Atomic Scientists* (London: Penguin, 1960); Donald Porter Geddes, ed., *The Atomic Age Opens* (New York: Pocket, 1945); and Jeff Nuttall, *Bomb Culture* (London: Paladin, 1970). For the Aristotle quote "their lives are lived principally in hope", see Norman Kiell, *The Universal Experience of Adolescence*, introduction. Stanley Hall's conception of adolescence as "a new birth" is contained in *Adolescence*, vol. 1, preface.

INDEX

Page numbers in *italics* refer to photo captions.

Page 3: (left) Photo Walery, Paris, from *Fountains of Youth: The Life of Marie Bashkirtseff*, by Dormer Creston (New York: Dutton, 1937); (right) from *Fiend: The Shocking True Story of America's Youngest Serial Killer*, by Harold Schechter (New York: Pocket Books, 2000)

Page 16: from *Youth, Empire and Society: British Youth Movements, 1883–1940*, by John Springhall (London: Croom Helm, 1977)

Page 24: Photo by Étienne Carjat, from *Somebody Else: Arthur Rimbaud in Africa, 1880–91*, by Charles Nicholl (London: Vintage, 1998)

Page 33: Museum of the City of New York/Jacob A. Riis Collection, #140

Page 43: from *Hooligan: A History of Respectable Fears*, by Geoffrey Pearson (London: Macmillan, 1983)

Page 49: Billy Rose Theater Division, New York Public Library for the Performing Arts, Astor, Lenox and Tilden Foundation

Page 63: Clark University Archives, Goddard Library

Page 77: Illustration by F. D. Bedford from *Peter Pan and Wendy*, by J. M. Barrie (London: Hodder and Stoughton, 1911)

Pages 91, 169, and 204: The Marshall Walker Collection

Page 101: from *Young Germany*, by Walter Z. Laqueur (London: Routledge and Kegan Paul, 1962)

Page 113: Lewis Hine Collection, National Child Labor Committee Papers, Library of Congress

Page 131: from *The New Pagans: Rupert Brooke and the Ordeal of Youth*, by Paul Delany (New York: Free Press, 1987)

Pages 140, 255, 422, and 469: The Granger Collection

Pages 157 and 335: © Hulton-Deutsch Collection/Corbis

Page 181: Kibbo Kift Foundation

Page 234: from *My First Life*, by Brenda Dean Paul (London: John Long, 1935)

Page 241: from *The Young Delinquent*, by Cyril Burt (London: University of London Press, 1925)

Page 276: from *Boy and Girl Tramps of America*, by Thomas Minehan (New York: Grosset and Dunlap, 1934)

Page 295: from *Wasted Lives*, by W. F. Lestrange (London: George Routledge and Sons, 1936)

Pages 315, 391, and 398: © Bettman/Corbis

Pages 345 and 434: © Hulton Archive/Getty Images

Page 360: Arthur Rothstein, Farm Security Agency, Library of Congress

Page 374: Louise Rosskam; courtesy of Anita Rosskam

Page 379: Courtesy of Grace Scheel

Page 411: Imperial War Museum

Page 425: Courtesy of Alan Keele

Page 454: Nina Leen/Time & Life Pictures/Getty Images

Pages xiv, 89, 174, 197, 217, 317, 375, 441, 444, 449, and 466: Author's collection